# Lecture Notes in Computer Science 7386

Commenced Publication in 1973
Founding and Former Series Editors:
Gerhard Goos, Juris Hartmanis, and Jan van Leeuwen

Martin Kutrib   Nelma Moreira
Rogério Reis (Eds.)

# Descriptional Complexity of Formal Systems

14th International Workshop, DCFS 2012
Braga, Portugal, July 23-25, 2012
Proceedings

 Springer

Volume Editors

Martin Kutrib
Universität Giessen, Institut für Informatik
Arndtstraße 2, 35392 Giessen, Germany
E-mail: kutrib@informatik.uni-giessen.de

Nelma Moreira
Universidade do Porto, Faculdade de Ciências
Departamento de Ciência de Computadores
Rua do Campo Alegre 1021/1055, 4169-007 Porto, Portugal
E-mail: nam@dcc.fc.up.pt

Rogério Reis
Universidade do Porto, Faculdade de Ciências
Departamento de Ciência de Computadores
Rua do Campo Alegre 1021/1055, 4169-007 Porto, Portugal
E-mail: rvr@dcc.fc.up.pt

ISSN 0302-9743               e-ISSN 1611-3349
ISBN 978-3-642-31622-7    e-ISBN 978-3-642-31623-4
DOI 10.1007/978-3-642-31623-4
Springer Heidelberg Dordrecht London New York

Library of Congress Control Number: 2012941230

CR Subject Classification (1998): F.1.1-3, F.4.2-3, F.3

LNCS Sublibrary: SL 1 – Theoretical Computer Science and General Issues

*Typesetting:* Camera-ready by author, data conversion by Scientific Publishing Services, Chennai, India

Printed on acid-free paper

Springer is part of Springer Science+Business Media (www.springer.com)

# Preface

The 14th International Workshop on Descriptional Complexity of Formal Systems (DCFS 2012) was held in Braga, Portugal, during July 23–25, 2012, and was jointly organized by Universidade do Porto, Universidade do Minho, and Universidade da Beira Interior. Braga is known as the "Portuguese Rome" for its concentration of religious architecture, roman remains, beautiful churches, and museums.

The DCFS workshop is the successor workshop and the merger of two related workshops, Descriptional Complexity of Automata, Grammars and Related Structures (DCAGRS) and Formal Descriptions and Software Reliability (FDSR). The DCAGRS workshop took place in Magdeburg, Germany (1999), London, Ontario, Canada (2000), and Vienna, Austria (2001), while the FDSR workshop took place in Paderborn, Germany (1998), Boca Raton, Florida, USA (1999), and San Jose, California, USA (2000). The DCFS workshop has previously been held in London, Ontario, Canada (2002), Budapest, Hungary (2003), London, Ontario, Canada (2004), Como, Italy (2005), Las Cruces, New Mexico, USA (2006), Nový Smokovec, Slovakia (2007), Charlottetown, Prince Edward Island, Canada (2008), Magdeburg, Germany (2009), Saskatoon, Saskatchewan, Canada (2010), and Giessen/Limburg, Germany (2011).

This volume of *Lecture Notes in Computer Science* contains the invited contributions and the accepted papers presented at DCFS 2012. Special thanks go to the invited speakers for accepting our invitation and presenting their recent results at DCFS 2012:

- Christos Kapoutsis (LIAFA, Paris)
- Dexter Kozen (Cornell University, USA)
- André Platzer (Carnegie Mellon University, USA)
- Pedro Silva (Universidade do Porto, Portugal)

There were 33 papers submitted to DCFS 2012 by a total of 65 authors from 17 different countries, from all over the world—Canada, Czech Republic, Estonia, Finland, Germany, India, Italy, Japan, Republic of Korea, Poland, Romania, Russian Federation, Slovakia, South Africa, Spain, UK, and USA. From these submissions, on the basis of three referee reports each, the Program Committee selected 20 papers—the submission and refereeing process was supported by the EasyChair conference management system. We warmly thank the members of the Program Committee for their excellent work in making this selection. Moreover, we also thank the additional external reviewers for their careful evaluation. All these efforts were the basis for the success of the workshop.

We are grateful to all the members of the Organizing Committee for their commitment in the preparation of the scientific sessions and social events. A special thanks goes to José Pedro Rodrigues for his help in the graphic design of all the conference materials. We express our gratitude to the staff of the

Department of Informatics of the University of Minho and of the D. Diogo de Sousa Museum of Archaeology, for their support during the conference. Thanks also go to Ivone Amorim, Rizó Israfov, Eva Maia, Davide Nabais, David Pereira, and Alexandra Silva.

We wish to thank the workshop sponsors: Universidade do Porto, Universidade do Minho, Universidade da Beira Interior, Centro de Matemática da Universidade do Porto, Município de Guimarães - Guimarães 2012, Multicert, and Critical Software.

We would also like to thank the staff of the Computer Science Editorial Department at Springer, for their efficient collaboration in making this volume available before the conference. Their timely instructions were very helpful for our preparation for this volume.

Finally, we would like to thank all the participants for attending the DCFS workshop. We hope that this year's workshop has stimulated new research and scientific co-operations in the field of descriptional complexity, as in previous years. Hope to see you at DCFS in 2013!


July 2012                                                          Martin Kutrib
                                                                   Nelma Moreira
                                                                   Rogério Reis

# Organization

DCFS 2012 was jointly organized by Universidade do Porto, Universidade do Minho, and Universidade da Beira Interior. The conference took place at the D. Diogo de Sousa Museum of Archaeology, Braga.

## Program Committee

| | |
|---|---|
| Cezar Câmpeanu | University of Prince Edward Island, Canada |
| Michael Domaratzki | University of Manitoba, Canada |
| Zoltan Ésik | University of Szeged, Hungary |
| Viliam Geffert | P. J. Safarik University, Košice, Slovakia |
| Markus Holzer | Universität Giessen, Germany |
| Galina Jirásková | Slovak Academy of Sciences, Slovakia |
| Jarkko Kari | University of Turku, Finland |
| Martin Kutrib | Universität Giessen, Germany (Co-chair) |
| Maurice Margenstern | University of Metz, France |
| Carlo Mereghetti | Università degli Studi di Milano, Italy |
| Nelma Moreira | Universidade do Porto, Portugal (Co-chair) |
| Giovanni Pighizzini | Università degli Studi di Milano, Italy |
| Rogério Reis | Universidade do Porto, Portugal (Co-chair) |
| Antonio Restivo | Università degli Studi di Palermo, Italy |
| Kai Salomaa | Queen's University, Kingston, Canada |
| Jeffrey O. Shallit | University of Waterloo, Canada |
| Bianca Truthe | Universität Magdeburg, Germany |
| György Vaszil | University of Debrecen, Hungary |

## External Referees

| | | |
|---|---|---|
| Nathalie Aubrun | Szabolcs Iván | Alexandros Palioudakis |
| Zuzana Bednárová | Sebastian Jakobi | Holger Petersen |
| Alberto Bertoni | Daniel Kirsten | Xiaoxue Piao |
| Maria Paola Bianchi | Peter Leupold | Narad Rampersad |
| Janusz Brzozowski | Baiyu Li | Panos Rondogiannis |
| Mark Burgin | Christof Löding | Jacques Sakarovitch |
| Alan Cain | Violetta Lonati | Ville Salo |
| Giusi Castiglione | Andreas Malcher | Marinella Sciortino |
| Jean-Marc Champarnaud | Florin Manea | Shinnosuke Seki |
| Christian Choffrut | Tomáš Masopust | Alexander Szabari |
| Jan Daciuk | Katja Meckel | Sergey Verlan |
| Dominik D. Freydenberger | Benedek Nagy | Claudio Zandron |
| Tero Harju | Tahl Nowik | Charalampos Zinoviadis |
| Géza Horváth | Friedrich Otto | |

## Organizing Committee

| | |
|---|---|
| Sabine Broda | Universidade do Porto, Portugal |
| Maria João Frade | Universidade do Minho, Portugal |
| Nelma Moreira | Universidade do Porto, Portugal |
| Rogério Reis | Universidade do Porto, Portugal |
| Simão Melo de Sousa | Universidade da Beira Interior, Portugal |

## Sponsoring Institutions

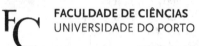

# Table of Contents

# Computing with Capsules

Jean-Baptiste Jeannin and Dexter Kozen

Department of Computer Science, Cornell University,
Ithaca, New York 14853–7501, USA
{jeannin,kozen}@cs.cornell.edu

**Abstract.** Capsules provide an algebraic representation of the state of a computation in higher-order functional and imperative languages. A capsule is essentially a finite coalgebraic representation of a regular closed $\lambda$-coterm. One can give an operational semantics based on capsules for a higher-order programming language with functional and imperative features, including mutable bindings. Static (lexical) scoping is captured purely algebraically without stacks, heaps, or closures. All operations of interest are typable with simple types, yet the language is Turing complete. Recursive functions are represented directly as capsules without the need for fixpoint combinators.

**Keywords:** capsules, semantics, functional programming, imperative programming.

## 1   Introduction

*Capsules* provide an algebraic representation of the state of a computation in higher-order functional and imperative programming languages. They conservatively extend the classical $\lambda$-calculus with mutable variables and assignment, enabling the construction of certain regular coterms (infinite terms) representing recursive functions without the need for fixpoint combinators. They have a well-defined statically-scoped evaluation semantics, are typable with simple types, and are Turing complete.

Representations of state have been studied in the past by many authors, e.g. [2–4, 8, 9, 18–20, 22, 23, 28, 29]. However, unlike previous approaches, capsules are purely algebraic. Perhaps their most important aspect is that their evaluation semantics captures static scoping without cumbersome combinatorial machinery needed to implement closures. Capsules replace heaps, stores, stacks, and pointers with the single mathematical concept of variable binding, yet are equally expressive and represent the same data dependencies and liveness structure. In a sense, capsules are to closures what graphs are to their adjacency list representations.

Formally, a capsule is a particular syntactic representation of a finite coalgebra of the same signature as the $\lambda$-calculus. A capsule represents a regular closed $\lambda$-coterm (infinite $\lambda$-term) under the unique morphism to the final coalgebra of this signature. This final coalgebra has been studied under the name *infinitary*

M. Kutrib, N. Moreira, and R. Reis (Eds.): DCFS 2012, LNCS 7386, pp. 1–19, 2012.

*λ-calculus*, focusing mostly on infinitary rewriting [7, 13]. It has been observed that the infinitary version does not share many of the desirable properties of its finitary cousin; for example, it is not confluent, and there exist coterms with no computational significance. However, all coterms represented by capsules are computationally meaningful.

One can give an operational semantics based on capsules for a higher-order programming language with functional and imperative features, including recursion and mutable variables. All operations of interest are typable with simple types. Recursive functions are constructed directly using *Landin's knot* without the need for fixpoint combinators, which involve self-application and are untypable with simple types. Moreover, the traditional $Y$ combinator forces a normal-order (lazy) evaluation strategy to ensure termination. Other more complicated fixpoint combinators can be used with applicative order by encapsulating the self-application in a thunk to delay evaluation, but this is even more unnatural. In contrast, the construction of recursive functions with Landin's knot is direct and simply typable, and corresponds more closely to implementations. Turing completeness is impossible with finite types and finite terms, as the simply-typed λ-calculus is strongly normalizing; so we must have either infinitary types or infinitary terms. Whereas the former is more conventional, we believe the latter is more natural.

*Dynamic scoping*, which was the scoping discipline in early versions of LISP and Python, and which still exists in many languages today, can be regarded as an implementation of lazy *β*-reduction that fails to observe the principle of safe substitution (*α*-conversion to avoid capture of free variables). We explain this view more fully with a detailed example in §3. In contrast, the λ-calculus with *β*-reduction and safe substitution is statically scoped. Both capsules and closures provide static scoping, but capsules do so without any extra combinatorial machinery. Moreover, capsules work correctly in the presence of mutable variables, whereas closures, naively implemented, do not (a counterexample is given in §4.4). To correctly handle mutable variables, closures require some form of indirection, and care must be taken to perform updates nondestructively. The connection between closures and capsules in the presence of mutable variables has been investigated recently by the first author [10].

Capsules provide a common framework for representing the global state of computation for both functional and imperative programs. Valuations of mutable variables used in the semantics of imperative programs are similar to closure structures used in the operational semantics of functional programs. We also get a clean definition of garbage collection: there is a natural notion of morphism, and the garbage-collected version of a capsule is the unique (up to isomorphism) initial object among its monomorphic preimages.

There is much previous work on reasoning about references and local state; see [8, 17–20, 24–27]. State is typically modeled by some form of heap from which storage locations can be allocated and deallocated [9, 18–20, 22, 28, 29]. Others have used game semantics to reason about local state [5, 6, 15]. Moggi [23] proposed monads, which can be used to model state and are implemented in Haskell. Our approach is most closely related to the work of Mason and Talcott [18–20] and

Felleisen and Hieb [8]. Objects can be modeled as collections of mutable bindings, as for example in the ς-calculus of Abadi and Cardelli [1]. Here we have avoided the introduction of mutable datatypes other than $\lambda$-terms in order to develop the theory in its simplest form and to emphasize that no auxiliary datatypes are needed to provide a basic operational semantics for a statically-scoped higher-order language with functional and imperative features.

This paper is organized as follows. In §2, we give formal definitions of capsules. In §3 we give a detailed motivating example illustrating how closures and capsules deal with scoping issues. In §4 we prove two theorems. The first (Theorem 1) establishes that capsule evaluation faithfully models $\beta$-reduction in the $\lambda$-calculus with safe substitution. The second (Theorem 2) defines closure conversion for capsules and proves soundness of the translation, provided there is no variable assignment. Taken together, these two theorems establish that closures also correctly model $\beta$-reduction in the $\lambda$-calculus with safe substitution. The same results hold in the presence of assignment, but the definition of closures must be extended; the definition of capsules remains the same [10]. The proof techniques in this section are purely algebraic and involve some interesting applications of coinduction. Finally, in §5, we describe a simply-typed functional/imperative language with mutable bindings and give an operational semantics in terms of capsules.

## 2  Definitions

### 2.1  Capsules

Consider the simply-typed $\lambda$-calculus with typed constants (e.g., 3 : int, true : bool, + : int $\rightarrow$ int $\rightarrow$ int, $\leq$ : int $\rightarrow$ int $\rightarrow$ bool). The set of $\lambda$-abstractions is denoted $\lambda$-Abs and the set of constants is denoted Const. A $\lambda$-term is *irreducible* if it is either a $\lambda$-abstraction $\lambda x.e$ or a constant $c$. The set of irreducible terms is Irred = $\lambda$-Abs + Const. Note that variables $x$ are not irreducible.

Let $\mathrm{FV}(e)$ denote the set of free variables of $e$. A *capsule* is a pair $\langle e, \sigma \rangle$, where $e$ is a $\lambda$-term and $\sigma : \mathrm{Var} \rightharpoonup \mathrm{Irred}$ is a partial function with finite domain dom $\sigma$, such that

(i) $\mathrm{FV}(e) \subseteq \mathrm{dom}\,\sigma$
(ii) if $x \in \mathrm{dom}\,\sigma$, then $\mathrm{FV}(\sigma(x)) \subseteq \mathrm{dom}\,\sigma$.

A capsule $\langle e, \sigma \rangle$ is *irreducible* if $e$ is.

Note that cycles are allowed; this is how recursive functions are represented. For example, we might have $\sigma(f) = \lambda n.\mathrm{if}\ n = 0\ \mathrm{then}\ 1\ \mathrm{else}\ n \cdot f(n-1)$.

### 2.2  Scope, Free and Bound Variables

Let $\langle e, \sigma \rangle$ be a capsule and let $d$ be either $e$ or $\sigma(y)$ for some $y \in \mathrm{dom}\,\sigma$. The *scope* of an occurrence of a binding operator $\lambda x$ in $d$ is its scope in the $\lambda$-term $d$ as normally defined.

Consider an occurrence of a variable $x$ in $d$. The closure conditions (i) and (ii) of §2.1 ensure that one of the following two conditions holds:

- that occurrence of $x$ falls in the scope of a binding operator $\lambda x$ in $d$, in which case it is bound to the innermost binding operator $\lambda x$ in $d$ in whose scope it lies; or
- it is free in $d$, but $x \in \mathsf{dom}\,\sigma$, in which case it is bound by $\sigma$ to the value $\sigma(x)$.

Thus every variable $x$ in a capsule is essentially bound. These conditions thus preclude catastrophic failure due to access of unbound variables.

It is important to note that scope does not extend through bindings in $\sigma$. For example, consider the capsule $\langle \lambda x.y,\ [y = \lambda z.x,\ x = 2]\rangle$. The free occurrence of $x$ in $\lambda z.x$ is not bound to the $\lambda x$ in $\lambda x.y$, but rather to the value 2. The coalgebra represented by the capsule has three states and represents the closed term $\lambda x.\lambda z.2$. For this reason, one cannot simply substitute $\sigma(y)$ for $y$ in $e$ without $\alpha$-conversion. This is also reflected in the evaluation rules to be given in §4.1. In a capsule $\langle e, \sigma \rangle$, all free variables in $e$ or $\sigma(y)$ are in $\mathsf{dom}\,\sigma$, therefore bound to a value; thus every capsule represents a closed coterm.

The term $\alpha$-conversion refers to the renaming of bound variables. With a capsule $\langle e, \sigma \rangle$, this can happen in two ways. The traditional form maps a subterm $\lambda x.d$ to $\lambda y.d[x/y]$, provided $y$ would not be captured in $d$. One can also rename a variable $x \in \mathsf{dom}\,\sigma$ and all free occurrences of $x$ in $e$ and $\sigma(z)$ for $z \in \mathsf{dom}\,\sigma$ to $y$, provided $y \notin \mathsf{dom}\,\sigma$ already and $y$ would not be captured.

## 3    Scoping Issues

We motivate the results of §4 with an example illustrating how dynamic scoping arises from a naive implementation of lazy substitution and how capsules and closures remedy the situation.

### 3.1    The λ-Calculus

The oldest and simplest of all functional languages is the $\lambda$-calculus. In this system, a *state* is a closed $\lambda$-term, and *computation* consists of a sequence of $\beta$-reductions

$$(\lambda x.d)\ e\ \to\ d[x/e],$$

where $d[x/e]$ denotes the safe substitution of $e$ for all free occurrences of $x$ in $d$. *Safe substitution* means that bound variables in $d$ may have to be renamed ($\alpha$-converted) to avoid capturing free variables of the substituted term $e$.

For example, consider the closed $\lambda$-term $(\lambda y.(\lambda z.\lambda y.z\ 4)\ \lambda x.y)\,3\,2$. Evaluating this term in (shallow) applicative order[1], we get the following sequence of terms leading to the value 3:

$$(\lambda y.(\lambda z.\lambda y.z\ 4)\ \lambda x.y)\ 3\ 2 \to (\lambda z.\lambda y.z\ 4)\ (\lambda x.3)\ 2$$
$$\to (\lambda y.(\lambda x.3)\ 4)\ 2 \to (\lambda x.3)\ 4 \to 3 \qquad (1)$$

---

[1] Also known as *left-to-right call-by-value order*, the order of evaluation in which the leftmost innermost redex is reduced first, except that redexes in the scope of binding operators $\lambda x$ are ineligible for reduction.

No $\alpha$-conversion was necessary. In fact, no $\alpha$-conversion is *ever* necessary with applicative-order evaluation of closed terms, because the argument substituted for a parameter in a $\beta$-reduction is closed, thus has no free variables to be captured.

However, the $\lambda$-calculus is confluent, and we may choose a different order of evaluation; but an alternative order may require $\alpha$-conversion. For example, the following reduction sequence is also valid:

$$(\lambda y.(\lambda z.\lambda y.z \; 4) \; \lambda x.y) \; 3 \; 2 \to (\lambda y.\lambda w.(\lambda x.y) \; 4) \; 3 \; 2$$
$$\to (\lambda w.(\lambda x.3) \; 4) \; 2 \to (\lambda x.3) \; 4 \to 3 \qquad (2)$$

A change of bound variable was required in the first step to avoid capturing the free occurrence of $y$ in $\lambda x.y$ substituted for $z$. Failure to do so results in the erroneous value 2:

$$(\lambda y.(\lambda z.\lambda y.z \; 4) \; \lambda x.y) \; 3 \; 2 \to (\lambda y.\lambda y.(\lambda x.y) \; 4) \; 3 \; 2$$
$$\to (\lambda y.(\lambda x.y) \; 4) \; 2 \to (\lambda x.2) \; 4 \to 2 \qquad (3)$$

## 3.2 Dynamic Scoping

In the early development of functional programming, specifically with the language LISP, it was quickly determined that physical substitution is too inefficient because it requires copying. This led to the introduction of *environments*, used to effect lazy substitution. Instead of doing the actual substitution when performing a $\beta$-reduction, one can defer the substitution by saving it in an environment, then look up the value when needed.

An *environment* is a partial function $\sigma : \mathsf{Var} \rightharpoonup \mathsf{Irred}$ with finite domain. A *state* is a pair $\langle e, \sigma \rangle$, where $e$ is the term to be evaluated and $\sigma$ is an environment with bindings for the free variables in $e$. Environments need to be updated, which requires a *rebinding operator*

$$\sigma[x/e](y) = \begin{cases} e, & \text{if } x = y, \\ \sigma(y), & \text{if } x \neq y \end{cases}$$

Naively implemented, the rules are

$$\langle (\lambda x.d) \; e, \sigma \rangle \to \langle d, \sigma[x/e] \rangle \qquad \langle y, \sigma \rangle \to \langle \sigma(y), \sigma \rangle$$

where the first rule saves the deferred substitution in the environment and the second looks up the value. This is quite easy to implement. Moreover, it stands to reason that if $\beta$-reduction in applicative order does not require any $\alpha$-conversions, then the lazy approach should not either. After all, the same terms are being substituted, just at a later time.

However, this is not the case. In the example above, we obtain the following sequence of states leading to the value 2:

$$\langle (\lambda y.(\lambda z.\lambda y.z\ 4)\ \lambda x.y)\ 3\ 2,\ [\ ]\rangle,\ \langle (\lambda z.\lambda y.z\ 4)\ (\lambda x.y)\ 2,\ [y = 3]\rangle,$$
$$\langle (\lambda y.z\ 4)\ 2,\ [y = 3,\ z = \lambda x.y]\rangle,\ \langle z\ 4,\ [y = 2,\ z = \lambda x.y]\rangle,$$
$$\langle (\lambda x.y)\ 4,\ [y = 2,\ z = \lambda x.y]\rangle,\ \langle y,\ [y = 2,\ z = \lambda x.y,\ x = 4]\rangle,$$
$$\langle 2,\ [y = 2,\ z = \lambda x.y,\ x = 4]\rangle.$$

The issue is that the lazy approach fails to observe safe substitution. This example effectively performs the deferred substitutions in the order (3) without the change of bound variable. Nevertheless, this was the strategy adopted by early versions of LISP [21]. It was not considered a bug but a feature and was called *dynamic scoping*.

### 3.3   Static Scoping with Closures

The semantics of evaluation was brought more in line with the $\lambda$-calculus with the introduction of *closures* [16, 21]. Formally, a *closure* is defined as a pair $\{\lambda x.e, \sigma\}$, where the $\lambda x.e$ is a $\lambda$-abstraction and $\sigma$ is a partial function from variables to values that is used to interpret the free variables of $\lambda x.e$. When a $\lambda$-abstraction is evaluated, it is paired with the environment $\sigma$ at the point of the evaluation, and the value is the closure $\{\lambda x.e, \sigma\}$. Thus we have

$$\sigma : \mathsf{Var} \rightharpoonup \mathsf{Val} \qquad\qquad \mathsf{Val} = \mathsf{Const} + \mathsf{Cl}$$

where $\mathsf{Cl}$ denotes the set of closures. We require that for a closure $\{\lambda x.e, \sigma\}$, $\mathsf{FV}(\lambda x.e) \subseteq \mathrm{dom}\,\sigma$. Note that the definitions of values and closures are mutually dependent.

The new reduction rules are

$$\langle \lambda x.d, \sigma \rangle \;\rightarrow\; \{\lambda x.d, \sigma\} \quad \langle \{\lambda x.d, \sigma\}\ e, \tau\rangle \;\rightarrow\; \langle d, \sigma[x/e]\rangle \quad \langle y, \sigma\rangle \;\rightarrow\; \sigma(y).$$

The second rule says that an application uses the context $\sigma$ that was in effect when the closure was created, not the context $\tau$ of the call. Turning to our running example,

$$\langle (\lambda y.(\lambda z.\lambda y.z\ 4)\ \lambda x.y)\ 3\ 2,\ [\ ]\rangle,\ \langle (\lambda z.\lambda y.z\ 4)\ (\lambda x.y)\ 2,\ [y = 3]\rangle,$$
$$\langle (\lambda y.z\ 4)\ 2,\ [y = 3,\ z = \{\lambda x.y,\ [y = 3]\}]\rangle,\ \langle z\ 4,\ [y = 2,\ z = \{\lambda x.y,\ [y=3]\}]\rangle,$$
$$\langle \{\lambda x.y,\ [y = 3]\}\ 4,\ [y = 2,\ z = \{\lambda x.y,\ [y = 3]\}]\rangle,\ \langle (\lambda x.y)\ 4,\ [y = 3]\rangle,$$
$$\langle y,\ [y = 3,\ x = 4]\rangle,\ \langle 3,\ [y = 3,\ x = 4]\rangle.$$

### 3.4   Static Scoping with Capsules

Closures correctly capture the semantics of $\beta$-reduction with safe substitution, but at the expense of introducing extra combinatorial machinery to represent and manipulate pairs $\{\lambda x.e, \sigma\}$. Capsules allow us to revert to a purely $\lambda$-theoretic framework without losing the benefits of closures.

Capsules were defined formally in §2.1. The small-step reduction rules for capsules are

$$\langle (\lambda x.e)\ v,\ \sigma \rangle \to \langle e[x/y],\ \sigma[y/v] \rangle \quad (y\ \text{fresh}) \qquad \langle y,\ \sigma \rangle \to \langle \sigma(y),\ \sigma \rangle$$

The key difference is the introduction of the fresh variable $y$ in the application rule. This is tantamount to performing an $\alpha$-conversion on the parameter of a function just before applying it. Turning to our running example, we see that this approach gives the correct result.

$$\langle (\lambda y.(\lambda z.\lambda y.z\ 4)\ \lambda x.y)\ 3\ 2,\ [\ ] \rangle,\ \langle (\lambda z.\lambda y.z\ 4)\ (\lambda x.y')\ 2,\ [y'=3] \rangle,$$
$$\langle (\lambda y.z'\ 4)\ 2,\ [y'=3,\ z'=\lambda x.y'] \rangle,\ \langle z'\ 4,\ [y'=3,\ z'=\lambda x.y',\ y''=2] \rangle,$$
$$\langle (\lambda x.y')\ 4,\ [y'=3,\ z'=\lambda x.y',\ y''=2] \rangle,$$
$$\langle y',\ [y'=3,\ z'=\lambda x.y',\ y''=2,\ x'=4] \rangle,$$
$$\langle 3,\ [y'=3,\ z'=\lambda x.y',\ y''=2,\ x'=4] \rangle.$$

We prove soundness formally in §4.

## 4  Soundness

In this section we show that capsule evaluation is statically scoped under applicative-order evaluation and correctly models $\beta$-reduction in the $\lambda$-calculus with safe substitution.

### 4.1  Evaluation Rules for Capsules

Let $d, e, \ldots$ denote $\lambda$-terms and $u, v, \ldots$ irreducible $\lambda$-terms ($\lambda$-abstractions and constants). Variables are denoted $x, y, \ldots$ and constants $c, f$.

The small-step evaluation rules for capsules consist of reduction rules

$$\langle (\lambda x.e)\ v,\ \sigma \rangle \to \langle e[x/y],\ \sigma[y/v] \rangle\ (y\ \text{fresh}) \tag{4}$$
$$\langle f\ c,\ \sigma \rangle \to \langle f(c),\ \sigma \rangle \tag{5}$$
$$\langle y,\ \sigma \rangle \to \langle \sigma(y),\ \sigma \rangle \tag{6}$$

and context rules

$$\frac{\langle d,\ \sigma \rangle \xrightarrow{*} \langle d',\ \tau \rangle}{\langle d\ e,\ \sigma \rangle \xrightarrow{*} \langle d'\ e,\ \tau \rangle} \qquad \frac{\langle e,\ \sigma \rangle \xrightarrow{*} \langle e',\ \tau \rangle}{\langle v\ e,\ \sigma \rangle \xrightarrow{*} \langle v\ e',\ \tau \rangle} \tag{7}$$

The reduction rules (4)–(6) identify three forms of redex: an application $(\lambda x.e)\ v$, an application $f\ c$ where $f$ and $c$ are constants, or a variable $y \in \operatorname{dom} \sigma$. The context rules (7) uniquely identify a redex in a well-typed non-irreducible capsule according to an applicative-order reduction strategy.

The corresponding large-step rules are

$$\langle y, \sigma \rangle \rightarrow \langle \sigma(y), \sigma \rangle \tag{8}$$

$$\frac{\langle d, \sigma \rangle \xrightarrow{*} \langle f, \tau \rangle \qquad \langle e, \tau \rangle \xrightarrow{*} \langle c, \rho \rangle}{\langle d\ e, \sigma \rangle \xrightarrow{*} \langle f(c), \rho \rangle} \tag{9}$$

$$\frac{\langle d, \sigma \rangle \xrightarrow{*} \langle \lambda x.a, \tau \rangle \qquad \langle e, \tau \rangle \xrightarrow{*} \langle v, \rho \rangle \qquad \langle a[x/y], \rho[y/v] \rangle \xrightarrow{*} \langle u, \pi \rangle}{\langle d\ e, \sigma \rangle \xrightarrow{*} \langle u, \pi \rangle} \ (y \text{ fresh}) \tag{10}$$

These rules are best understood in terms of the interpreter they generate:

$$\begin{aligned}
\mathsf{Eval}(c, \sigma) &= \langle c, \sigma \rangle \\
\mathsf{Eval}(\lambda x.e, \sigma) &= \langle \lambda x.e, \sigma \rangle \\
\mathsf{Eval}(y, \sigma) &= \langle \sigma(y), \sigma \rangle \\
\mathsf{Eval}(d\ e, \sigma) &= \mathsf{let}\ \langle u, \tau \rangle = \mathsf{Eval}(d, \sigma)\ \mathsf{in} \\
&\quad\ \mathsf{let}\ \langle v, \rho \rangle = \mathsf{Eval}(e, \tau)\ \mathsf{in} \\
&\quad\ \mathsf{Apply}(u, v, \rho)
\end{aligned} \tag{11}$$

$$\begin{aligned}
\mathsf{Apply}(f, c, \sigma) &= \langle f(c), \sigma \rangle \\
\mathsf{Apply}(\lambda x.e, v, \sigma) &= \mathsf{Eval}(e[x/y], \sigma[y/v]) \quad (y \text{ fresh})
\end{aligned} \tag{12}$$

## 4.2   $\beta$-Reduction

The small-step evaluation rules for $\beta$-reduction in applicative order are the same as for capsules, except we replace (4) with

$$\langle (\lambda x.e)\ v, \sigma \rangle \rightarrow \langle e[x/v], \sigma \rangle \tag{13}$$

(substitution instead of rebinding). The other rules (5)–(7) are the same. This makes sense even in the presence of cycles (recursive functions).

Note that the initial valuation $\sigma$ persists unchanged throughout the computation. We might suppress it to simplify notation, giving

$$(\lambda x.e)\ v \rightarrow e[x/v] \qquad\qquad f\ c \rightarrow f(c) \qquad\qquad y \rightarrow \sigma(y)$$

$$\frac{d \xrightarrow{*} d'}{(d\ e) \xrightarrow{*} (d'\ e)} \qquad\qquad \frac{e \xrightarrow{*} e'}{(v\ e) \xrightarrow{*} (v\ e')}$$

However, it is still implicitly present, as it is needed to evaluate variables $y$.

The corresponding interpreter $\mathsf{Eval}_\beta$ is defined exactly like $\mathsf{Eval}$ except for rule (12), which we replace with

$$\mathsf{Apply}_\beta(\lambda x.e, v, \sigma) = \mathsf{Eval}_\beta(e[x/v], \sigma).$$

## 4.3   Soundness

Let $S$ denote a sequential composition of rebinding operators $[y_1/v_1]\cdots[y_k/v_k]$, applied from left to right. Applied to a partial valuation $\sigma : \mathsf{Var} \rightharpoonup \mathsf{Irred}$, the operator $S$ sequentially rebinds $y_1$ to $v_1$, then $y_2$ to $v_2$, and so on. The result is denoted $\sigma S$. Formally, $\sigma(S[y/v]) = (\sigma S)[y/v]$.

To every rebinding operator $S = [y_1/v_1]\cdots[y_k/v_k]$ there corresponds a safe substitution operator $S^- = [y_k/v_k]\cdots[y_1/v_1]$, also applied from left to right. Applied to a $\lambda$-term $e$, $S^-$ safely substitutes $v_k$ for all free occurrences of $y_k$ in $e$, then $v_{k-1}$ for all free occurrences of $y_{k-1}$ in $e[y_k/v_k]$, and so on. The result is denoted $eS^-$. Formally, $e(S^-[y/v]) = (eS^-)[y/v]$. Note that $(ST)^- = T^-S^-$.

If $S = [y_1/v_1]\cdots[y_k/v_k]$, we assume that $y_i$ does not occur in $v_j$ for $i \geq j$; however, $y_i$ may occur in $v_j$ if $i < j$. This means that if $\mathsf{FV}(e) \subseteq \{y_1,\ldots,y_k\}$ and $\mathsf{FV}(v_j) \subseteq \{y_1,\ldots,y_{j-1}\}$, $1 \leq j \leq k$, then $eS^-$ is closed.

The following theorem establishes soundness of capsule evaluation with respect to $\beta$-reduction in the $\lambda$-calculus.

**Theorem 1.** $\mathsf{Eval}_\beta(e,\sigma) = \langle v, \sigma \rangle$ *if and only if there exist irreducible terms* $v_1,\ldots,v_k,u$ *and a rebinding operator* $S = [y_1/v_1]\cdots[y_k/v_k]$, *where* $y_1,\ldots,y_k$ *do not occur in* $e$, $v$, *or* $\sigma$, *such that* $\mathsf{Eval}(e,\sigma) = \langle u, \sigma S \rangle$ *and* $v = uS^-$.

*Proof.* We show the implication in both directions by induction on the number of steps in the evaluation. The result is trivially true for inputs of the form $\langle c, \sigma \rangle$, $\langle \lambda x.e, \sigma \rangle$, and $\langle \sigma(y), \sigma \rangle$, and this gives the basis of the induction.

For an input of the form $\langle d\ e, \sigma \rangle$, we show the implication in both directions. We first show that if $\mathsf{Eval}(d\ e, \sigma)$ is defined, then so is $\mathsf{Eval}_\beta(d\ e, \sigma)$, and the relationship between the two values is as described in the statement of the theorem. By definition of $\mathsf{Eval}$, we have

$$\mathsf{Eval}(d,\sigma) = (u, \sigma S) \qquad\qquad \mathsf{Eval}(e, \sigma S) = (v, \sigma ST)$$

for some $S = [y_1/v_1]\cdots[y_m/v_m]$ and $T = [y_{m+1}/v_{m+1}]\cdots[y_n/v_n]$, and where $y_1,\ldots,y_n$ are the fresh variables and $v_1,\ldots,v_n$ the irreducible terms bound to them in applications of the rule (12) during the evaluation of $d$ and $e$. By the induction hypothesis, we have

$$\mathsf{Eval}_\beta(d,\sigma) = \langle uS^-, \sigma \rangle \qquad\qquad \mathsf{Eval}_\beta(e, \sigma S) = \langle vT^-, \sigma S \rangle.$$

Since the variables $y_1,\ldots,y_m$ do not occur in $e$, they are not accessed in its evaluation, thus $\mathsf{Eval}_\beta(e,\sigma) = \langle vT^-, \sigma \rangle$. Also, since $y_{m+1},\ldots,y_n$ do not occur in $u$ and $y_1,\ldots,y_m$ do not occur in $v$, we have $uS^- = u(ST)^-$ and $vT^- = v(ST)^-$, thus

$$\mathsf{Eval}_\beta(d,\sigma) = \langle u(ST)^-, \sigma \rangle \qquad\qquad \mathsf{Eval}_\beta(e,\sigma) = \langle v(ST)^-, \sigma \rangle.$$

We thus have

$$\mathsf{Eval}(d\ e, \sigma) = \mathsf{Apply}(u, v, \sigma ST) \quad \mathsf{Eval}_\beta(d\ e, \sigma) = \mathsf{Apply}_\beta(u(ST)^-, v(ST)^-, \sigma)$$

If $u$ and $v$ are constants, say $u = f$ and $v = c$, then

$$\mathsf{Eval}(d\ e, \sigma) = \mathsf{Apply}(f, c, \sigma ST) = \langle f(c),\ \sigma ST \rangle$$
$$\mathsf{Eval}_\beta(d\ e, \sigma) = \mathsf{Apply}_\beta(f, c, \sigma) = \langle f(c),\ \sigma \rangle,$$

and the implication holds. If $u$ is a $\lambda$-abstraction, say $u = \lambda x.a$, then $u(ST)^- = \lambda x.a(ST)^-$. Then

$$a(ST)^-[x/v(ST)^-] = a[x/v](ST)^- = a[x/y_{n+1}][y_{n+1}/v](ST)^-$$
$$= a[x/y_{n+1}](ST[y_{n+1}/v])^-,$$

therefore

$$\mathsf{Eval}(d\ e, \sigma) = \mathsf{Apply}(\lambda x.a, v, \sigma ST) = \mathsf{Eval}(a[x/y_{n+1}], \sigma ST[y_{n+1}/v])$$
$$\mathsf{Eval}_\beta(d\ e, \sigma) = \mathsf{Apply}_\beta(\lambda x.a(ST)^-, v(ST)^-, \sigma) = \mathsf{Eval}_\beta(a(ST)^-[x/v(ST)^-], \sigma)$$
$$= \mathsf{Eval}_\beta(a[x/y_{n+1}](ST[y_{n+1}/v])^-, \sigma),$$

and the implication holds in this case as well.

For the reverse implication, assume that $\mathsf{Eval}_\beta(d\ e, \sigma)$ is defined. Let $\langle u, \sigma \rangle = \mathsf{Eval}_\beta(d, \sigma)$ and $\langle v, \sigma \rangle = \mathsf{Eval}_\beta(e, \sigma)$. By the induction hypothesis, there exist variables $y_1, \ldots, y_m$ and irreducible terms $v_1, \ldots, v_m$ and $r$ such that

$$u = rS^- \qquad\qquad \mathsf{Eval}(d, \sigma) = \langle r, \sigma S \rangle,$$

where $S = [y_1/v_1] \cdots [y_m/v_m]$. We also have $\langle v, \sigma S \rangle = \mathsf{Eval}_\beta(e, \sigma S)$, since the evaluation of $e$ does not depend on the variables $y_1, \ldots, y_m$. Again by the induction hypothesis, there exist variables $y_{m+1}, \ldots, y_n$ and irreducible terms $v_{m+1}, \ldots, v_n$ and $s$ such that

$$v = sT^- = sT^-S^- = s(ST)^- \qquad\qquad \mathsf{Eval}(e, \sigma S) = \langle s, \sigma ST \rangle,$$

where $T = [y_{m+1}/v_{m+1}] \cdots [y_n/v_n]$. Then $ST = [y_1/v_1] \cdots [y_n/v_n]$ and

$$\mathsf{Eval}_\beta(d\ e, \sigma) = \mathsf{Apply}_\beta(u, v, \sigma) \qquad \mathsf{Eval}(d\ e, \sigma) = \mathsf{Apply}(r, s, \sigma ST).$$

If $u$ and $v$ are constants, say $u = f$ and $v = c$, then $r = f$ and $s = c$. In this case we have

$$\mathsf{Eval}_\beta(d\ e, \sigma) = \mathsf{Apply}_\beta(f, c, \sigma) = \langle f(c),\ \sigma \rangle$$
$$\mathsf{Eval}(d\ e, \sigma) = \mathsf{Apply}(f, c, \sigma ST) = \langle f(c),\ \sigma ST \rangle,$$

and the implication holds. If $u$ is a $\lambda$-abstraction, then $r = \lambda x.a$ and $u = \lambda x.aS^- = \lambda x.a(^sST)^-$. In this case

$$a(ST)^-[x/s(ST)^-] = a[x/s](ST)^- = a[x/y_{n+1}][y_{n+1}/s](ST)^-$$
$$= a[x/y_{n+1}](ST[y_{n+1}/s])^-,$$

thus

$$\mathsf{Eval}_\beta(d\ e, \sigma) = \mathsf{Apply}_\beta(\lambda x.a(ST)^-, v, \sigma) = \mathsf{Eval}_\beta(a(ST)^-[x/s(ST)^-], \sigma)$$
$$= \mathsf{Eval}_\beta(a[x/y_{n+1}](ST[y_{n+1}/s])^-, \sigma),$$
$$\mathsf{Eval}(d\ e, \sigma) = \mathsf{Apply}(\lambda x.a, s, \sigma ST) = \mathsf{Eval}(a[x/y_{n+1}], \sigma ST[y_{n+1}/s]),$$

so the implication holds in this case as well.

## 4.4   Closure Conversion

In this section we demonstrate how to closure-convert a capsule and show that the transformation is sound with respect to the evaluation semantics of closures and capsules in applicative-order evaluation, provided variables are not mutable.

Closures do not work in the presence of mutable variables without introducing the further complication of references and indirection. This is because closures fix the environment once and for all when the closure is formed, whereas mutable variables allow the environment to be subsequently changed. An example is given by $(\lambda y.(\lambda x.y)\ (y := 4; y))\ 3$, for which capsules give 4 and closures 3; in the latter, the assignment has no effect.

Care must also be taken to implement updates nondestructively so as not to overwrite parameters and local variables of recursive procedures, an issue that is usually addressed at the implementation level. Again, the issue does not arise with capsules.

Even without indirection, the types of closures and closure environments are more involved than those of capsules. The definitions are mutually dependent and require a recursive type definition. The types are

$$\begin{array}{lll} \mathsf{Env} = \mathsf{Var} \rightharpoonup \mathsf{Val} & & \text{closure environments} \\ \mathsf{Val} = \mathsf{Const} + \mathsf{Cl} & & \text{values} \\ \mathsf{Cl} = \lambda\text{-}\mathsf{Abs} \times \mathsf{Env} & & \text{closures} \end{array}$$

We use boldface for closure environments $\boldsymbol{\sigma} : \mathsf{Env}$ to distinguish them from the simpler capsule environments. Closures $\{\lambda x.e, \boldsymbol{\sigma}\}$ must satisfy the additional requirement that $\mathsf{FV}(\lambda x.e) \subseteq \mathrm{dom}\,\boldsymbol{\sigma}$.

A *state* is now a pair $\langle e, \sigma \rangle$, where $\mathsf{FV}(e) \subseteq \mathrm{dom}\,\sigma$, but the result of an evaluation is a Val. The evaluation semantics for closures, expressed as an interpreter $\mathsf{Eval_c}$, is

$$
\begin{aligned}
\mathsf{Eval_c}(c, \sigma) &= c \\
\mathsf{Eval_c}(\lambda x.e, \sigma) &= \{\lambda x.e,\, \sigma\} \\
\mathsf{Eval_c}(y, \sigma) &= \sigma(y) \\
\mathsf{Eval_c}(d\ e, \sigma) &= \mathsf{let}\ u = \mathsf{Eval_c}(d, \sigma)\ \mathsf{in} \\
&\qquad \mathsf{let}\ v = \mathsf{Eval_c}(e, \sigma)\ \mathsf{in} \\
&\qquad \mathsf{Apply_c}(u, v)
\end{aligned}
$$

$$
\begin{aligned}
\mathsf{Apply_c}(f, c) &= f(c) \\
\mathsf{Apply_c}(\{\lambda x.a,\, \rho\}, v) &= \mathsf{Eval_c}(a, \rho[x/v])
\end{aligned}
\tag{14}
$$

The types are

$$
\mathsf{Eval_c} : T_\lambda \times \mathsf{Env}\ \rightharpoonup\ \mathsf{Val} \qquad\qquad \mathsf{Apply_c} : \mathsf{Val} \times \mathsf{Val}\ \rightharpoonup\ \mathsf{Val}.
$$

The correspondence with capsules becomes simpler to state if we modify the interpreter to $\alpha$-convert the term $\lambda x.a$ to $\lambda y.a[x/y]$ just before applying it, where $y$ is the fresh variable that would be chosen by the capsule interpreter. Accordingly, we replace (14) with

$$
\mathsf{Apply_c}(\{\lambda x.a,\, \rho\}, v) = \mathsf{Eval_c}(a[x/y], \rho[y/v]) \quad (y\ \mathrm{fresh})
$$

The corresponding large-step rules are

$$
\langle c, \sigma \rangle \xrightarrow[c]{} c \qquad\qquad \langle \lambda x.e, \sigma \rangle \xrightarrow[c]{} \{\lambda x.e,\, \sigma\} \qquad\qquad \langle y, \sigma \rangle \xrightarrow[c]{} \sigma(y)
\tag{15}
$$

$$
\frac{\langle d, \sigma \rangle \xrightarrow[c]{*} f \qquad \langle e, \sigma \rangle \xrightarrow[c]{*} c}{\langle d\ e, \sigma \rangle \xrightarrow[c]{*} f(c)}
\tag{16}
$$

$$
\frac{\langle d, \sigma \rangle \xrightarrow[c]{*} \{\lambda x.a,\, \rho\} \qquad \langle e, \sigma \rangle \xrightarrow[c]{*} v \qquad \langle a[x/y],\, \rho[y/v] \rangle \xrightarrow[c]{*} u}{\langle d\ e, \sigma \rangle \xrightarrow[c]{*} u} \quad (y\ \mathrm{fresh})
\tag{17}
$$

The closure-converted form of a capsule $\langle e, \sigma \rangle$ is $\langle e, \bar{\sigma} \rangle$, where

$$
\bar{\sigma}(y) = \begin{cases} \{\sigma(y),\, \bar{\sigma}\}, & \text{if } \sigma(y) : \lambda\text{-Abs}, \\ \sigma(y), & \text{if } \sigma(y) : \text{Const}. \end{cases}
$$

This definition is not circular, it is coinductive! In an OCaml-like language, the definition might look like

```
let rec σ̄ = λy . match σ(y) with
  | Const(c) → c
  | λ-Abs(λx.e) → {λx.e, σ̄}
```

To state the relationship between capsules and closures, we define a binary relation $\sqsubseteq$ on capsule environments, closure environments, and values. For capsule environments, define $\sigma \sqsubseteq \tau$ if $\operatorname{dom} \sigma \subseteq \operatorname{dom} \tau$ and for all $y \in \operatorname{dom} \sigma$, $\sigma(y) = \tau(y)$. The definition for values and closure environments is by mutual coinduction: $\sqsubseteq$ is defined to be the largest relation such that

- on closure environments, $\boldsymbol{\sigma} \sqsubseteq \boldsymbol{\tau}$ if
  - $\operatorname{dom} \boldsymbol{\sigma} \subseteq \operatorname{dom} \boldsymbol{\tau}$, and
  - for all $y \in \operatorname{dom} \boldsymbol{\sigma}$, $\boldsymbol{\sigma}(y) \sqsubseteq \boldsymbol{\tau}(y)$; and
- on values, $u \sqsubseteq v$ if either
  - $u$ and $v$ are constants and $u = v$; or
  - $u = \{\lambda x.e, \boldsymbol{\rho}\}$, $v = \{\lambda x.e, \boldsymbol{\pi}\}$, and $\boldsymbol{\rho} \sqsubseteq \boldsymbol{\pi}$.

**Lemma 1.** *The relation $\sqsubseteq$ is transitive.*

*Proof.* This is obvious for capsule environments.

For closure environments and values, we proceed by coinduction. Suppose $\boldsymbol{\sigma} \sqsubseteq \boldsymbol{\tau} \sqsubseteq \boldsymbol{\rho}$. Then $\operatorname{dom} \boldsymbol{\sigma} \subseteq \operatorname{dom} \boldsymbol{\tau} \subseteq \operatorname{dom} \boldsymbol{\rho}$, so $\operatorname{dom} \boldsymbol{\sigma} \subseteq \operatorname{dom} \boldsymbol{\rho}$, and for all $y \in \operatorname{dom} \boldsymbol{\sigma}$, $\boldsymbol{\sigma}(y) \sqsubseteq \boldsymbol{\tau}(y) \sqsubseteq \boldsymbol{\rho}(y)$, therefore $\boldsymbol{\sigma}(y) \sqsubseteq \boldsymbol{\rho}(y)$ by the transitivity of $\sqsubseteq$ on values.

For values, suppose $u \sqsubseteq v \sqsubseteq w$. If $u = c$, then $v = c$ and $w = c$. If $u = \{\lambda x.e, \boldsymbol{\sigma}\}$, then $v = \{\lambda x.e, \boldsymbol{\tau}\}$ and $w = \{\lambda x.e, \boldsymbol{\rho}\}$ and $\boldsymbol{\sigma} \sqsubseteq \boldsymbol{\tau} \sqsubseteq \boldsymbol{\rho}$, therefore $\boldsymbol{\sigma} \sqsubseteq \boldsymbol{\rho}$ by the transitivity of $\sqsubseteq$ on closure environments.

**Lemma 2.** *Closure conversion is monotone with respect to $\sqsubseteq$. That is, if $\sigma \sqsubseteq \tau$, then $\bar{\sigma} \sqsubseteq \bar{\tau}$.*

*Proof.* We have $\operatorname{dom} \bar{\sigma} = \operatorname{dom} \sigma \subseteq \operatorname{dom} \tau = \operatorname{dom} \bar{\tau}$. Moreover, for $y \in \operatorname{dom} \sigma$,

$$
\bar{\sigma}(y) = \begin{cases} \{\lambda x.e, \bar{\sigma}\}, & \text{if } \sigma(y) = \lambda x.e, \\ c, & \text{if } \sigma(y) = c \end{cases} = \begin{cases} \{\lambda x.e, \bar{\sigma}\}, & \text{if } \tau(y) = \lambda x.e, \\ c, & \text{if } \tau(y) = c \end{cases}
$$

$$
\sqsubseteq \begin{cases} \{\lambda x.e, \bar{\tau}\}, & \text{if } \tau(y) = \lambda x.e, \\ c, & \text{if } \tau(y) = c \end{cases} = \bar{\tau}(y).
$$

The $\sqsubseteq$ step in the above reasoning is by the coinduction hypothesis.

Define a map $V : \mathsf{Cap} \to \mathsf{Val}$ on irreducible capsules as follows:

$$
V(\lambda x.a, \sigma) = \{\lambda x.a, \bar{\sigma}\} \qquad\qquad V(c, \sigma) = c. \tag{18}
$$

**Lemma 3.** $\bar{\sigma}(y) = V(\sigma(y), \sigma)$.

*Proof.*

$$
\bar{\sigma}(y) = \begin{cases} \{\lambda x.e, \bar{\sigma}\}, & \text{if } \sigma(y) = \lambda x.e, \\ c & \text{if } \sigma(y) = c \end{cases} = \begin{cases} V(\lambda x.e, \sigma), & \text{if } \sigma(y) = \lambda x.e, \\ V(c, \sigma) & \text{if } \sigma(y) = c \end{cases}
$$

$$
= V(\sigma(y), \sigma).
$$

**Lemma 4.** *If $y \notin \operatorname{dom} \sigma$, then $\bar{\sigma}[y/V(v,\sigma)] \sqsubseteq \sigma[\bar{y}/v]$.*

*Proof.* By Lemma 3,

$$\sigma[\bar{y}/v](y) = V(\sigma[\bar{y}/v](y), \sigma[\bar{y}/v]) = V(v, \sigma[\bar{y}/v]). \tag{19}$$

If $y \notin \operatorname{dom} \sigma$, then

$$\bar{\sigma}[y/V(v,\sigma)] \sqsubseteq \sigma[\bar{y}/v][y/V(v,\sigma)] \sqsubseteq \sigma[\bar{y}/v][y/V(v,\sigma[y/v])] = \sigma[\bar{y}/v],$$

the first two inequalities by Lemma 2 and the last equation by (19).

**Lemma 5.** *If $\sigma \sqsubseteq \tau$, then $\mathsf{Eval}_c(e,\sigma)$ exists if and only if $\mathsf{Eval}_c(e,\tau)$ does, and $\mathsf{Eval}_c(e,\sigma) \sqsubseteq \mathsf{Eval}_c(e,\tau)$. Moreover, they are derivable by the same large-step proofs.*

*Proof.* We proceed by induction on the proof tree under the large-step rules (15)–(17). For the single-step rules (15), we have

$$\mathsf{Eval}_c(c,\sigma) = c = \mathsf{Eval}_c(c,\tau)$$
$$\mathsf{Eval}_c(\lambda x.a,\sigma) = \{\lambda x.a, \ \sigma\} \sqsubseteq \{\lambda x.a, \ \tau\} = \mathsf{Eval}_c(\lambda x.a,\tau)$$
$$\mathsf{Eval}_c(y,\sigma) = \sigma(y) \sqsubseteq \tau(y) = \mathsf{Eval}_c(y,\tau).$$

For the rule (16), $\langle d\ e, \sigma \rangle \xrightarrow[c]{*} f(c)$ is derivable by an application of (16) iff $\langle d, \sigma \rangle \xrightarrow[c]{*} f$ and $\langle e, \sigma \rangle \xrightarrow[c]{*} c$ are derivable by smaller proofs. Similarly, $\langle d\ e, \tau \rangle \xrightarrow[c]{*} f(c)$ is derivable by an application of (16) iff $\langle d, \tau \rangle \xrightarrow[c]{*} f$ and $\langle e, \tau \rangle \xrightarrow[c]{*} c$ are derivable by smaller proofs. By the induction hypothesis, $\langle d, \sigma \rangle \xrightarrow[c]{*} f$ and $\langle d, \tau \rangle \xrightarrow[c]{*} f$ are derivable by the same proof, and similarly $\langle e, \sigma \rangle \xrightarrow[c]{*} c$ and $\langle e, \tau \rangle \xrightarrow[c]{*} c$ are derivable by the same proof.

Finally, for the rule (17), $\langle d\ e, \sigma \rangle \xrightarrow[c]{*} u_1$ is derivable by an application of (17) iff $\langle d, \sigma \rangle \xrightarrow[c]{*} \{\lambda x.a, \rho_1\}$, $\langle e, \sigma \rangle \xrightarrow[c]{*} v_1$, and $\langle a[x/y], \rho_1[y/v_1] \rangle \xrightarrow[c]{*} u_1$ are derivable by smaller proofs. Similarly, $\langle d\ e, \tau \rangle \xrightarrow[c]{*} u_2$ is derivable by an application of (17) iff $\langle d, \tau \rangle \xrightarrow[c]{*} \{\lambda x.a, \rho_2\}$, $\langle e, \tau \rangle \xrightarrow[c]{*} v_2$, and $\langle a[x/y], \rho_2[y/v_2] \rangle \xrightarrow[c]{*} u_2$ are derivable by smaller proofs. By the induction hypothesis, $\langle d, \sigma \rangle \xrightarrow[c]{*} \{\lambda x.a, \rho_1\}$ and $\langle d, \tau \rangle \xrightarrow[c]{*} \{\lambda x.a, \rho_2\}$ are derivable by the same proof, and $\rho_1 \sqsubseteq \rho_2$. Similarly, $\langle e, \sigma \rangle \xrightarrow[c]{*} v_1$ and $\langle e, \tau \rangle \xrightarrow[c]{*} v_2$ are derivable by the same proof, and $v_1 \sqsubseteq v_2$. It follows that $\rho_1[y/v_1] \sqsubseteq \rho_2[y/v_2]$. Again by the induction hypothesis, $\langle a[x/y], \rho_1[y/v_1] \rangle \xrightarrow[c]{*} u_1$ and $\langle a[x/y], \rho_2[y/v_2] \rangle \xrightarrow[c]{*} u_2$ are derivable by the same proof, and $u_1 \sqsubseteq u_2$.

The following theorem establishes the soundness of closure conversion for capsules.

**Theorem 2.** $\mathsf{Eval}(e,\sigma)$ *exists if and only if $\mathsf{Eval}_c(e,\bar{\sigma})$ does, and $\mathsf{Eval}_c(e,\bar{\sigma}) \sqsubseteq V(\mathsf{Eval}(e,\sigma))$. Moreover, they are derivable by isomorphic large-step proofs under the obvious correspondence between the large-step rules of both systems.*[2]

---

[2] For this purpose, the definition of $V$ in (18) can be viewed as a pair of proof rules corresponding to the first two rules of (15).

*Proof.* We proceed by induction on the proof tree under the large-step rules. The proof is similar to the proof of Lemma 5. We write $\xrightarrow[c]{*}$ for the derivability relation under the large-step rules (15)–(17) for closures to distinguish them from the corresponding large-step rules (8)–(10) for capsules, which we continue to denote by $\xrightarrow{*}$.

For the single-step rules (15), we have

$$\mathsf{Eval}_c(c, \bar{\sigma}) = c = V(\mathsf{Eval}(c, \sigma))$$
$$\mathsf{Eval}_c(\lambda x.a, \bar{\sigma}) = \{\lambda x.a, \ \bar{\sigma}\} = V(\lambda x.a, \sigma) = V(\mathsf{Eval}(\lambda x.a, \sigma))$$
$$\mathsf{Eval}_c(y, \bar{\sigma}) = \bar{\sigma}(y) = V(\sigma(y), \sigma) = V(\mathsf{Eval}(y, \sigma)).$$

The last line uses Lemma 3.

Consider the corresponding rules (9) and (16). A conclusion $\langle d\ e,\ \bar{\sigma}\rangle \xrightarrow[c]{*} f(c)$ is derivable by an application of (16) iff $\langle d,\ \bar{\sigma}\rangle \xrightarrow[c]{*} f$ and $\langle e,\ \bar{\sigma}\rangle \xrightarrow[c]{*} c$ are derivable by smaller proofs. Similarly, $\langle d\ e,\ \sigma\rangle \xrightarrow{*} \langle f(c), \rho\rangle$ is derivable by an application of (9) iff $\langle d, \sigma\rangle \xrightarrow{*} \langle f, \sigma S\rangle$ and $\langle e, \sigma S\rangle \xrightarrow{*} \langle c, \sigma ST\rangle$ are derivable by smaller proofs.

By the induction hypothesis, $\langle d, \bar{\sigma}\rangle \xrightarrow[c]{*} f = V(f, \sigma S)$ and $\langle d, \sigma\rangle \xrightarrow{*} \langle f, \sigma S\rangle$ are derivable by isomorphic proofs. By Lemma 5, $\langle e, \bar{\sigma}\rangle \xrightarrow[c]{*} c$ and $\langle e, \sigma \bar{S}\rangle \xrightarrow[c]{*} c$ are derivable by the same proof. Again by the induction hypothesis, $\langle e, \sigma S\rangle \xrightarrow[c]{*} c$ and $\langle e, \sigma S\rangle \xrightarrow{*} \langle c, \sigma ST\rangle$ are derivable by isomorphic proofs, therefore so are $\langle e, \bar{\sigma}\rangle \xrightarrow[c]{*} c = V(c, \sigma ST)$ and $\langle e, \sigma S\rangle \xrightarrow{*} \langle c, \sigma ST\rangle$.

Finally, consider the corresponding rules (10) and (17). A conclusion $\langle d\ e, \bar{\sigma}\rangle \xrightarrow[c]{*} u$ is derivable by an application of (17) iff for some $\lambda x.a$, $\rho$, and $v$,

$$\langle d, \bar{\sigma}\rangle \xrightarrow[c]{*} \{\lambda x.a, \rho\} \qquad \langle e, \bar{\sigma}\rangle \xrightarrow[c]{*} v \qquad \langle a[x/y], \rho[y/v]\rangle \xrightarrow[c]{*} u$$

are derivable by smaller proofs. Similarly, $\langle d\ e, \sigma\rangle \xrightarrow{*} \langle t, \tau\rangle$ is derivable by an application of (10) iff for some $\lambda z.b$, $S$, $T$, and $w$,

$$\langle d, \sigma\rangle \xrightarrow{*} \langle \lambda z.b, \sigma S\rangle \quad \langle e, \sigma S\rangle \xrightarrow{*} \langle w, \sigma ST\rangle \quad \langle b[z/y], \sigma ST[y/w]\rangle \xrightarrow{*} \langle t, \tau\rangle$$

are derivable by smaller proofs.

By the induction hypothesis, $\langle d, \bar{\sigma}\rangle \xrightarrow[c]{*} \{\lambda x.a, \rho\}$ and $\langle d, \sigma\rangle \xrightarrow{*} \langle \lambda z.b, \sigma S\rangle$ are derivable by isomorphic proofs, and $\{\lambda x.a, \rho\} \sqsubseteq V(\lambda z.b, \sigma S) = \{\lambda z.b, \bar{\sigma}S\}$, therefore $\lambda x.a = \lambda z.b$ and $\rho \sqsubseteq \bar{\sigma}S \sqsubseteq \sigma \bar{S}T$.

By Lemmas 2 and 5, for some $v'$, $\langle e, \bar{\sigma}\rangle \xrightarrow[c]{*} v$ and $\langle e, \sigma \bar{S}\rangle \xrightarrow[c]{*} v'$ are derivable by the same proof, and $v \sqsubseteq v'$. Again by the induction hypothesis, $\langle e, \sigma \bar{S}\rangle \xrightarrow[c]{*} v'$ and $\langle e, \sigma S\rangle \xrightarrow{*} \langle w, \sigma ST\rangle$ are derivable by isomorphic proofs, and $v' \sqsubseteq V(w, \sigma ST)$. By transitivity, $\langle e, \bar{\sigma}\rangle \xrightarrow[c]{*} v$ and $\langle e, \sigma S\rangle \xrightarrow{*} \langle w, \sigma ST\rangle$ are derivable by isomorphic proofs, and $v \sqsubseteq V(w, \sigma ST)$. By Lemma 4,

$$\rho[y/v] \sqsubseteq \sigma \bar{S}T[y/V(w, \sigma ST)] \sqsubseteq \sigma ST[y/w].$$

Again by Lemma 5, for some $u'$, $\langle a[x/y], \rho[y/v]\rangle \xrightarrow[c]{*} u$ and $\langle a[x/y], \sigma ST[y/w]\rangle \xrightarrow[c]{*} u'$ are derivable by the same proof, and $u \sqsubseteq u'$; and again by the induction hypothesis, $\langle a[x/y], \sigma ST[y/w]\rangle \xrightarrow[c]{*} u'$ and $\langle a[x/y], \sigma ST[y/w]\rangle \xrightarrow{*} \langle t, \tau\rangle$ are derivable by isomorphic proofs, and $u' \sqsubseteq V(t, \tau)$. By transitivity, $\langle a[x/y], \rho[y/v]\rangle \xrightarrow[c]{*} u$ and $\langle a[x/y], \sigma ST[y/w]\rangle \xrightarrow[c]{*} \langle t, \tau\rangle$ are derivable by isomorphic proofs, and $u \sqsubseteq V(t, \tau)$.

## 5    A Functional/Imperative Language

In this section we give an operational semantics for a simply-typed higher-order functional and imperative language with mutable bindings.

### 5.1    Expressions

Expressions $\mathsf{Exp} = \{d, e, \ldots\}$ contain both functional and imperative features. There is an unlimited supply of *variables* $x, y, \ldots$ of all (simple) types, as well as constants $f, c, \ldots$ for primitive values. In addition, there are functional features

- $\lambda$-abstraction      $\lambda x.e$
- application          $(d\ e)$,

imperative features

- assignment       $x := e$
- composition      $d; e$
- conditional       if $b$ then $d$ else $e$
- repeat loop      repeat $e$ until $b$,

and syntactic sugar

- let $x = d$ in $e$      $(\lambda x.e)\ d$
- let rec $f = g$ in $e$      let $f = h$ in $f := g; e$

where $h$ is any term of the appropriate type.

### 5.2    Types

Types are just simple types built inductively from the base types and a type constructor $\to$ representing *partial* functions. The typing rules are:

$$\frac{x : \alpha \quad e : \beta}{\lambda x.e : \alpha \to \beta} \qquad \frac{d : \alpha \to \beta \quad e : \alpha}{(d\ e) : \beta} \qquad \frac{d : \alpha \quad e : \beta}{d; e : \beta}$$

$$\frac{b : \mathsf{bool} \quad d : \alpha \quad e : \alpha}{\text{if } b \text{ then } d \text{ else } e : \alpha} \qquad \frac{b : \mathsf{bool} \quad e : \alpha}{\text{repeat } e \text{ until } b : \alpha} \qquad \frac{x : \alpha \quad e : \alpha}{x := e : \alpha}$$

### 5.3    Evaluation

A *value* is the equivalence class of an irreducible capsule modulo bisimilarity and $\alpha$-conversion; equivalently, the $\lambda$-coterm represented by the capsule modulo $\alpha$-conversion.

A program determines a binary relation on capsules. The functional features are interpreted by the rules of §4.1. Assignment is interpreted by the following large-step and small-step rules, respectively:

$$\frac{\langle e, \sigma \rangle \xrightarrow{*} \langle v, \tau \rangle}{\langle x := e, \sigma \rangle \xrightarrow{*} \langle v, \tau[x/v] \rangle} \ (x \in \mathrm{dom}\,\sigma) \quad \langle x := v, \tau \rangle \to \langle v, \tau[x/v] \rangle \ (x \in \mathrm{dom}\,\tau)$$

The remaining imperative constructs are defined by the following large-step rules.

$$\frac{\langle d, \sigma \rangle \xrightarrow{*} \langle u, \rho \rangle \qquad \langle e, \rho \rangle \xrightarrow{*} \langle v, \tau \rangle}{\langle d; e, \sigma \rangle \xrightarrow{*} \langle v, \tau \rangle}$$

$$\frac{\langle b, \sigma \rangle \xrightarrow{*} \langle \mathsf{true}, \rho \rangle \qquad \langle d, \rho \rangle \xrightarrow{*} \langle v, \tau \rangle}{\langle \mathsf{if}\ b\ \mathsf{then}\ d\ \mathsf{else}\ e, \sigma \rangle \xrightarrow{*} \langle v, \tau \rangle} \qquad \frac{\langle b, \sigma \rangle \xrightarrow{*} \langle \mathsf{false}, \rho \rangle \qquad \langle e, \rho \rangle \xrightarrow{*} \langle v, \tau \rangle}{\langle \mathsf{if}\ b\ \mathsf{then}\ d\ \mathsf{else}\ e, \sigma \rangle \xrightarrow{*} \langle v, \tau \rangle}$$

$$\frac{\langle e, \sigma \rangle \xrightarrow{*} \langle v, \rho \rangle \qquad \langle b, \rho \rangle \xrightarrow{*} \langle \mathsf{true}, \tau \rangle}{\langle \mathsf{repeat}\ e\ \mathsf{until}\ b, \sigma \rangle \xrightarrow{*} \langle v, \tau \rangle}$$

$$\frac{\langle e; b, \sigma \rangle \xrightarrow{*} \langle \mathsf{false}, \rho \rangle \qquad \langle \mathsf{repeat}\ e\ \mathsf{until}\ b, \rho \rangle \xrightarrow{*} \langle v, \tau \rangle}{\langle \mathsf{repeat}\ e\ \mathsf{until}\ b, \sigma \rangle \xrightarrow{*} \langle v, \tau \rangle}$$

## 5.4  Garbage Collection

A *monomorphism* $h : \langle d, \sigma \rangle \to \langle e, \tau \rangle$ is an injective map $h : \mathsf{dom}\,\sigma \to \mathsf{dom}\,\tau$ such that

- $\tau(h(x)) = h(\sigma(x))$ for all $x \in \mathsf{dom}\,\sigma$, where $h(e) = e[x/h(x)]$ (safe substitution); and
- $h(d) = e$.

The collection of monomorphic preimages of a given capsule contains an initial object that is unique up to $\alpha$-conversion. This is the *garbage collected* version of the capsule.

# 6   Conclusion

Capsules provide an algebraic representation of state for higher-order functional and imperative programs. They are mathematically simpler than closures and correctly model static scope without auxiliary data constructs, even in the presence of recursion and mutable variables. Capsules form a natural coalgebraic extension of the $\lambda$-calculus, and we have shown how coalgebraic techniques can be brought to bear on arguments involving state. We have shown that capsule evaluation is faithful to $\beta$-reduction with safe substitution in the $\lambda$-calculus. We have shown how to closure-convert capsules, and we have proved soundness of the transformation in the absence of assignments. Finally, we have shown how capsules can be used to give a natural operational semantics to a higher-order functional and imperative language with mutable bindings.

Subsequent to this work, the relationship between capsules and closures established in Theorem 2 has been strengthened to small-step bisimulation [11]. Also, with appropriate extensions to the definition of closure to allow indirection, the same relationship has been shown to hold in the presence of assignment [10]. Capsules have also been used to model objects [14] and to provide a semantics for separation logic [12].

**Acknowledgments.** Thanks to Robert Constable, Nate Foster, Konstantinos Mamouras, Andrew Myers, Mark Reitblatt, Fred Schneider, Alexandra Silva, and all the members of the PLDG seminar at Cornell for valuable discussions.

# References

1. Abadi, M., Cardelli, L.: A Theory of Objects. Springer (1996)
2. Aboul-Hosn, K.: Programming with Private State. Honors Thesis, The Pennsylvania State University (December 2001),
   http://www.cs.cornell.edu/%7Ekamal/thesis.pdf
3. Aboul-Hosn, K., Kozen, D.: Relational Semantics for Higher-Order Programs. In: Yu, H.-J. (ed.) MPC 2006. LNCS, vol. 4014, pp. 29–48. Springer, Heidelberg (2006)
4. Aboul-Hosn, K., Kozen, D.: Local variable scoping and Kleene algebra with tests. J. Log. Algebr. Program. (2007), doi:10.1016/j.jlap.2007.10.007
5. Abramsky, S., Honda, K., McCusker, G.: A fully abstract game semantics for general references. In: LICS 1998: Proceedings of the 13th Annual IEEE Symposium on Logic in Computer Science, pp. 334–344. IEEE Computer Society, Washington, DC, USA (1998)
6. Abramsky, S., McCusker, G.: Linearity, sharing and state: a fully abstract game semantics for idealized ALGOL with active expressions. Electr. Notes Theor. Comput. Sci. 3 (1996)
7. Barendregt, H.P., Klop, J.W.: Applications of infinitary lambda calculus. Inf. and Comput. 207(5), 559–582 (2009)
8. Felleisen, M., Hieb, R.: The revised report on the syntactic theories of sequential control and state. Theoretical Computer Science 103, 235–271 (1992)
9. Halpern, J.Y., Meyer, A.R., Trakhtenbrot, B.A.: The semantics of local storage, or what makes the free-list free? In: Proc. 11th ACM Symp. Principles of Programming Languages (POPL 1984), New York, NY, USA, pp. 245–257 (1984)
10. Jeannin, J.B.: Capsules and closures. In: Mislove, M., Ouaknine, J. (eds.) Proc. 27th Conf. Math. Found. Programming Semantics (MFPS XXVII), Pittsburgh, PA. Elsevier Electronic Notes in Theoretical Computer Science (May 2011)
11. Jeannin, J.B.: Capsules and Closures: A Small-Step Approach. In: Constable, R.L., Silva, A. (eds.) Kozen Festschrift. LNCS, vol. 7230, pp. 106–123. Springer, Heidelberg (2012)
12. Jeannin, J.B., Kozen, D.: Capsules and separation. Tech. Rep., Computing and Information Science, Cornell University (January 2012),
    http://hdl.handle.net/1813/28284; Conf. Logic in Computer Science (LICS 2012), Dubrovnik, Croatia (to appear, June 2012)
13. Klop, J.W., de Vrijer, R.C.: Infinitary normalization. In: Artemov, S., Barringer, H., d'Avila Garcez, A.S., Lamb, L.C., Woods, J. (eds.) We Will Show Them: Essays in Honour of Dov Gabbay, vol. 2, pp. 169–192. College Publications (2005)
14. Kozen, D.: New. Tech. Rep., Computing and Information Science, Cornell University (March 2012), http://hdl.handle.net/1813/28632; Conf. Mathematical Foundations of Programming Semantics (MFPS XXVIII), Bath, UK (to appear, June 2012)
15. Laird, J.: A Game Semantics of Local Names and Good Variables. In: Walukiewicz, I. (ed.) FOSSACS 2004. LNCS, vol. 2987, pp. 289–303. Springer, Heidelberg (2004)
16. Landin, P.J.: The mechanical evaluation of expressions. Computer Journal 6(4), 308–320 (1964)

17. Mason, I.A., Talcott, C.L.: References, local variables and operational reasoning. In: Seventh Annual Symposium on Logic in Computer Science, pp. 186–197. IEEE (1992), http://www-formal.stanford.edu/MT/92lics.ps.Z

18. Mason, I., Talcott, C.: Programming, transforming, and proving with function abstractions and memories

19. Mason, I., Talcott, C.: Axiomatizing operational equivalence in the presence of side effects. In: IEEE Fourth Annual Symposium on Logic in Computer Science, pp. 284–293. IEEE Computer Society Press (1989)

20. Mason, I., Talcott, C.: Equivalence in functional languages with effects (1991)

21. McCarthy, J.: History of LISP. In: Wexelblat, R.L. (ed.) History of Programming Languages I, pp. 173–185. ACM (1981)

22. Milne, R., Strachey, C.: A Theory of Programming Language Semantics. Halsted Press, New York (1977)

23. Moggi, E.: Notions of computation and monads. Information and Computation 93(1) (1991)

24. Pitts, A.M.: Operationally-based theories of program equivalence. In: Dybjer, P., Pitts, A.M. (eds.) Semantics and Logics of Computation, pp. 241–298. Publications of the Newton Institute, Cambridge University Press (1997), http://www.cs.tau.ac.il/~nachumd/formal/exam/pitts.pdf

25. Pitts, A.M.: Operational semantics and program equivalence. Tech. rep., INRIA Sophia Antipolis (2000), http://www.springerlink.com/media/1f99vvygyh3ygrykklby/contributions/l/w/f/6/lwf6r3jxn7a2lkq0.pdf; lectures at the International Summer School On Applied Semantics, APPSEM 2000, Caminha, Minho, Portugal (September 2000)

26. Pitts, A.M., Stark, I.D.B.: Operational reasoning in functions with local state. In: Gordon, A.D., Pitts, A.M. (eds.) Higher Order Operational Techniques in Semantics, pp. 227–273. Cambridge University Press (1998), http://homepages.inf.ed.ac.uk/stark/operfl.pdf

27. Pitts, A.M., Stark, I.D.B.: Observable Properties of Higher Order Functions that Dynamically Create Local Names, or What's New? In: Borzyszkowski, A.M., Sokolowski, S. (eds.) MFCS 1993. LNCS, vol. 711, pp. 122–141. Springer, Heidelberg (1993)

28. Scott, D.: Mathematical concepts in programmng language semantics. In: Proc. 1972 Spring Joint Computer Conferences, pp. 225–234. AFIPS Press, Montvale (1972)

29. Stoy, J.E.: Denotational Semantics: The Scott-Strachey Approach to Programming Language Theory. MIT Press, Cambridge (1981)

# Minicomplexity

Christos A. Kapoutsis*

LIAFA, Université Paris VII, France

**Abstract.** This is a talk on *minicomplexity*, namely on the *complexity of two-way finite automata*. We start with a smooth introduction to its basic concepts, which also brings together several seemingly detached, old theorems. We then record recent advances, both in the theory itself and in its relation to Turing machine complexity. Finally, we illustrate a proof technique, which we call *hardness propagation by certificates*. The entire talk follows, extends, and advocates the Sakoda-Sipser framework.

## 1 Introduction

In Theory of Computation, the distinction between *computability* and *complexity* is clear. In computability, we ask whether a problem can be solved by a Turing machine (TM), namely whether the problem is *decidable*. In complexity, we focus exclusively on problems that indeed can be solved, and we ask how much of the TM's resources they require, the main resource of interest being *time* or *space*.

This distinction is also valid in finite automata (FAs). In FA-*computability*, we ask whether a problem can be solved by a FA; often, but not always, this is the same as asking whether the problem is *regular*. In FA-*complexity*, we focus exclusively on problems that indeed can be solved, and we ask how much of the FA's resources they require; often, but not always, the resource of interest is *size* (as expressed, e.g., by the number of states). Hence, much like the theory of TMs, the theory of FAs also consists of a computability and a complexity component.

This distinction is not widely realized. Specifically, the complexity component is often overlooked. Standard textbooks essentially identify the entire theory of FAs with FA-computability (see, e.g., [30, Chap. 1]), barely addressing any FA-complexity issues (as, e.g., in [30, Probs. 1.60-1, 1.65]). Perhaps one might try to justify this systematic neglect by claiming that these issues are not really a theory; they are just a list of detached observations on the relative succinctness of FAs. We disagree. Before explaining, let us discuss another systematic neglect.

This is the systematic neglect of *two-way* FAs (2FAs, whose input head can move in either direction) in favor of *one-way* FAs (1FAs, whose input head can move only forward). Standard textbooks essentially identify FAs with 1FAs (see, e.g., [20, Chaps. 3–16]), only briefly addressing 2FAs, if at all, as a natural generalization (as, e.g., in [20, Chaps. 17–18]). As before, one might perhaps try to

---

* Supported by a Marie Curie Intra-European Fellowship (PIEF-GA-2009-253368) within the European Union Seventh Framework Programme (FP7/2007-2013).

M. Kutrib, N. Moreira, and R. Reis (Eds.): DCFS 2012, LNCS 7386, pp. 20–42, 2012.

justify this systematic neglect by pointing out that 2FAs are no more powerful than 1FAs [27], and are thus worthy of no special attention. We again disagree.

Once we realize that the theory of FAs is neither only about computability nor only about one-way automata, we are rewarded with the meaningful, elegant, and rich *complexity theory of two-way finite automata*: a mathematical theory with all standard features of a complexity theory, including computational problems, complexity classes, reductions, and completeness; with challenging, decades-old open questions; and with strong links to TM-complexity and logic. Unfortunately, this theory has eluded the systematic attention of researchers for a long time now. Our goal in this talk is to help repair this ... public-relations disaster.

In the title, we already make a solid first step. We suggest for this theory a (hopefully catchy) new name. We call it *minicomplexity*, because we view it as a 'miniature version' of the standard complexity theory for TMs.

In Sect. 2, we present the fragment of minicomplexity which concerns 1FAs. We focus on determinism, nondeterminism, and alternation. By a series of examples of computational problems of increasing difficulty, we introduce complexity classes, reductions, and completeness, also discussing the differences from the respective concepts of TM-complexity. All problems and proofs are elementary. The goal is to show how a list of old, seemingly detached facts about the relative succinctness of 1FAs are really part of one coherent complexity theory.

In Sect. 3, we continue to 2FAs. We focus on the Sakoda-Sipser conjecture and two stronger variants of it, recording their history and some recent advances. We then discuss alternation and the relationship to TM-complexity.

In Sect. 4, we present a technique for separating micomplexity classes, using closure properties (for upper bounds) together with *hardness propagation by certificates* (for lower bounds). To illustrate it, we outline a modular proof which implies an improvement on the main theorem of [9].

For $h \geq 0$, we let $[h]$ and $[\![h]\!]$ be $\{0, \ldots, h-1\}$ and its powerset. Our 2FAs are tuples $(S, \Sigma, \delta, q_s, q_a)$ of a state set, an alphabet, a transition function, a start, and an accept state. Our *parallel automata* ($\mathrm{P_{2}1DFAs}$, $\cup_{l1}\mathrm{DFAs}$, $\cup_{R1}\mathrm{DFAs}$, $\cap_{l1}\mathrm{DFAs}$) are as in [16]. Our *finite transducers* (2DFTs, 1DFTs) are as in [19].

A (*promise*) *problem* over $\Sigma$ is a pair $\mathfrak{L} = (L, \tilde{L})$ of disjoint subsets of $\Sigma^*$. Every $w \in L \cup \tilde{L}$ is an *instance* of $\mathfrak{L}$: *positive*, if $w \in L$; or *negative*, if $w \in \tilde{L}$. To solve $\mathfrak{L}$ is to accept all $w \in L$ but no $w \in \tilde{L}$. The *reverse, complement, conjunctive star*, and *disjunctive star* of $\mathfrak{L}$ are the problems $\mathfrak{L}^R := (L^R, \tilde{L}^R)$, $\neg \mathfrak{L} := (\tilde{L}, L)$,

$$\bigwedge \mathfrak{L} := \left( \ \{\#x_1\# \cdots \#x_l\# \mid (\forall i)(x_i \in L)\}, \ \{\#x_1\# \cdots \#x_l\# \mid (\exists i)(x_i \in \tilde{L})\} \ \right), \text{ and}$$

$$\bigvee \mathfrak{L} := \left( \ \{\#x_1\# \cdots \#x_l\# \mid (\exists i)(x_i \in L)\}, \ \{\#x_1\# \cdots \#x_l\# \mid (\forall i)(x_i \in \tilde{L})\} \ \right),$$

where $\#x_1\# \cdots \#x_l\#$ means $l \geq 0$, each $x_i \in L \cup \tilde{L}$, and $\#$ is a fresh symbol. Easily,

$$\neg(\mathfrak{L}^R) = (\neg\mathfrak{L})^R \quad \neg(\bigwedge\mathfrak{L}) = \bigvee\neg\mathfrak{L} \quad \neg(\bigvee\mathfrak{L}) = \bigwedge\neg\mathfrak{L} \quad (\bigwedge\mathfrak{L})^R = \bigwedge\mathfrak{L}^R \quad (\bigvee\mathfrak{L})^R = \bigvee\mathfrak{L}^R$$

by the definitions. The *conjunctive concatenation* $\mathfrak{L} \wedge \mathfrak{L}'$ and *ordered star* $\mathfrak{L} < \mathfrak{L}'$ of two problems $\mathfrak{L}, \mathfrak{L}'$ are defined in [16] and [9]. Families of promise problems admit analogous operations. For more careful definitions, see [16,9].

# 2   One-Way Automata

## 2.1   Size Complexity Basics

Let $h \geq 1$, and consider the following elementary computational problem:

$$\vdash \boxed{i \mid \alpha} \dashv \qquad \textit{Given a number } i \in [h] \textit{ and a set } \alpha \subseteq [h], \textit{ check that } i \in \alpha.$$

The input tape is shown on the left. Every instance fits in just two tape cells, because we use the large alphabet $\Sigma := [h] \cup [\![h]\!]$. The instance is surrounded by the end-markers $\vdash$ and $\dashv$, a feature unimportant for 1FAs but essential for 2FAs. Moreover, every instance is promised to be of this form, i.e., a number followed by a set; all other strings over $\Sigma$ are irrelevant to this computational problem.

Solving this problem is trivial. We easily design a 1DFA $M = ([h], \Sigma, \,.\,, 0, 0)$ whose transition function implements the following obvious algorithm:

$$\vdash \boxed{3 \mid {}_4^0 1} \dashv \qquad \vdash \boxed{3 \mid {}_4^0 3} \dashv$$
$$0 \to 0 \to 3 \qquad\quad 0 \to 0 \to 3 \to 0 \to 0$$

From state 0 on $\vdash$, move to 0 on the 1st cell. Reading $i$, move to state $i$ on the 2nd cell. Reading $\alpha$ in state $i$, check whether $i \in \alpha$. If not, then hang. Otherwise, move to state 0 on $\dashv$. Then fall off $\dashv$, again in state 0.

Two computations, on a negative and a positive instance (for $h = 5$), are shown on the left. Note how $M$ is designed only for instances of the promised form.

Now consider the reverse of this problem, where the set precedes the number:

$$\vdash \boxed{\alpha \mid i} \dashv \qquad \textit{Given a set } \alpha \subseteq [h] \textit{ and a number } i \in [h], \textit{ check that } i \in \alpha.$$

This problem is again trivial. We easily design a 1DFA $M^{\text{R}} = ([\![h]\!], \Sigma, \,.\,, \emptyset, \emptyset)$:

$$\vdash \boxed{{}_4^0 1 \mid 3} \dashv \qquad \vdash \boxed{{}_4^0 3 \mid 3} \dashv$$
$$\emptyset \to \emptyset \to {}_4^0 1 \qquad\quad \emptyset \to \emptyset \to {}_4^0 3 \to \emptyset \to \emptyset$$

From state $\emptyset$ on $\vdash$, move to $\emptyset$ on the 1st cell. Reading $\alpha$, move to state $\alpha$ on the 2nd cell. Reading $i$ in state $\alpha$, check whether $i \in \alpha$. If not, then hang. Otherwise, move to state $\emptyset$ on $\dashv$. Then fall off $\dashv$, again in state $\emptyset$.

However, $M^{\text{R}}$ uses $2^h$ states, whereas $M$ uses only $h$. Moreover, this is not due to poor design; we easily see that $M^{\text{R}}$ could not have done significantly better:

> *Proof.* Assume a 1DFA solver $X$ with $< 2^h - 1$ states. For each $\emptyset \neq \alpha \subseteq [h]$, the prefix $\vdash \alpha$ forces $X$ to cross its right boundary (or else $X$ hangs earlier, and fails to accept $\vdash \alpha i \dashv$ for $i \in \alpha$); let $q_\alpha$ be the state after this crossing. Since the states of $X$ are fewer than the non-empty subsets of $[h]$, there exist distinct $\emptyset \neq \alpha, \beta \subseteq [h]$ with $q_\alpha = q_\beta$. If $i \in (\alpha \setminus \beta) \cup (\beta \setminus \alpha)$, then $X$ treats $\alpha i$ and $\beta i$ the same, a contradiction.

Therefore, the reverse problem is indeed substantially different from the original.

To capture this difference formally, we first introduce a meaningful name for the original problem: we call it MEMBERSHIP. We then note that this "problem" is in fact a *family of problems*, with a different member for every $h \geq 1$:

$$\text{MEMBERSHIP} := (\text{MEMBERSHIP}_h)_{h \geq 1} \,.$$

In turn, each member is a *promise problem* over the alphabet $\Sigma_h := [h] \cup [\![h]\!]$:

$$\text{MEMBERSHIP}_h := (\, \{i\alpha \mid \alpha \subseteq [h] \ \& \ i \in \alpha\}, \{i\alpha \mid \alpha \subseteq [h] \ \& \ i \in \overline{\alpha}\} \,) . \quad (1)$$

At the same time, our "algorithm" for MEMBERSHIP has been a *family of* 1DFAs:

$$\mathcal{M} := (M_h)_{h \geq 1} \quad \text{with } M_h := ([h], \Sigma_h, ., 0, 0).$$

Likewise, the reverse "problem" is a family MEMBERSHIP$^R$ := (MEMBERSHIP$^R_h$)$_{h \geq 1}$ with its $h$-th member as in (1) but with the order of $i$ and $\alpha$ reversed; and the "algorithm" for it is a family $\mathcal{M}^R := (M^R_h)_{h \geq 1}$ with $M^R_h := (\llbracket h \rrbracket, \Sigma_h, ., \emptyset, \emptyset)$.

(Hence, all this time we used the terms "problem"/"algorithm" and a single description in terms of $h$ to informally refer to and describe an entire family of promise problems/FAs. This is standard practice, which we will repeat. Also, instead of the traditional $n$, which is reserved for denoting input length, the name for the important parameter is $h$, for "height" and because $h$ looks like $n$.)

In our new formal terms, the substantial difference between MEMBERSHIP and MEMBERSHIP$^R$ is that the former can be solved by a family of 1DFAs which grow linearly with $h$ (each $M_h$ has $h$ states), whereas the latter can be solved by some family of exponential growth (each $M^R_h$ has $2^h$ states) and by no family of sub-exponential growth. To state this more succinctly, we introduce the complexity classes 1D and $2^{1D}$ of all problems which admit 1DFA algorithms with at most polynomially or at most exponentially many states, respectively. More carefully,

$$1D := \left\{ (\mathfrak{L}_h)_{h \geq 1} \;\middle|\; \begin{array}{l} \text{for some polynomial } p \text{ and 1DFA family } (M_h)_{h \geq 1}, \\ \text{every } M_h \text{ solves } \mathfrak{L}_h \text{ with } \leq p(h) \text{ states} \end{array} \right\}, \quad (2)$$

and similarly for $2^{1D}$, with $2^{p(h)}$ instead of $p(h)$. Then our observations so far are summarized by the two statements

MEMBERSHIP $\in 1D$  and  MEMBERSHIP$^R \in 2^{1D} \setminus 1D$,

and by the map on the side, including the obvious fact $1D \subseteq 2^{1D}$.

From now on, we will informally say that an algorithm or automaton that is described in terms of $h$ is "small" if in the implicit family of finite automata the $h$-th member has $\leq p(h)$ states, for some polynomial $p$ and all $h$.

## 2.2   More Problems

The profile of MEMBERSHIP is shared by several other elementary problems that have appeared sporadically in the literature.[1] We list some of them below. When appropriate, the endnotes explain who introduced them and why.

We start with a variant of MEMBERSHIP, where the set is replaced by a list. We call it ∃EQUALITY. The alphabet consists of $[h]$ and $\{\breve{\imath} \mid i \in [h]\}$, a tagged copy of $[h]$ which is used for distinguishing the query number:

$\vdash \boxed{\breve{\imath} \mid i_1 \mid i_2 \mid \cdots} \dashv$   *Given a tagged $i \in [h]$ and a list $i_1, i_2, \ldots, i_l \in [h]$, check that $i = i_j$ for some $j$.*

Easily, ∃EQUALITY $\in 1D$ but ∃EQUALITY$^R \in 2^{1D} \setminus 1D$. The same holds for a variant problem, which we call SORTED ∃EQUALITY, where the numbers in the list are promised to be strictly increasing: $i_1 < i_2 < \cdots < i_l$.[2]

The next two problems are called PROJECTION and COMPOSITION.[3] [4] The first one uses the alphabet $[h] \cup [h]^h$ of all numbers in $[h]$ and $h$-tuples over $[h]$:

$\vdash \boxed{\;i\;|\;j\;|\;u\;} \dashv$  *Given a number $i \in [h]$, an index $j \in [h]$, and a tuple $u \in [h]^h$,*
*check that $i = u(j)$.*

The second problem uses the alphabet $([h] \rightharpoonup [h])$ of all partial functions on $[h]$:

$\vdash \boxed{\;f\;|\;g\;} \dashv$     *Given two functions $f, g : [h] \rightharpoonup [h]$, check that $f(g(0)) = 0$.*

Easily, PROJECTION, COMPOSITION$^R \in$ 1D but their reverses are in $2^{1D} \setminus$ 1D.

Finally, a classic. We call it RETROCOUNT, for the obvious reason: [5]

$\vdash \boxed{\;\cdots\;|\;1\;|\;\cdots\;} \dashv$ *Given a binary string, check that its $h$-th rightmost bit is $1$.*

Easily, RETROCOUNT$^R \in$ 1D but RETROCOUNT $\in 2^{1D} \setminus$ 1D. The same holds for two variant problems: ∃RETROCOUNT, where we must check that a 1 exists at some distance from the end which is a multiple of $h$; and SHORT RETROCOUNT, where the input is promised to be of length $< 2h$.[6]

The map on the right summarizes our observations so far. All problems shown in it are in $2^{1D} \setminus$ 1D, whereas their reverses are in 1D. Perhaps this looks like an unstructured list of detached observations on how reversal affects the size of 1DFAs. We will soon see that this map does contain some structure. Even at this early level, we can still classify problems in terms of hardness, and use the resulting lattice to deduce algorithms and lower bounds.

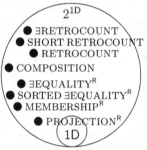

### 2.3  Reductions

Roughly speaking, a problem reduces to another 'in one-way polynomial size' if a *small* 1DFT can convert its positive/negative instances to positive/negative instances of the other problem, respectively, with only a *small* increase in height.

For example, consider the following simple algorithm for converting instances of MEMBERSHIP$_h^R$ to instances of PROJECTION$_h^R$:

Reading $\alpha \subseteq [h]$, print the characteristic vector of $\alpha$, namely $u \in [2]^h$ such that $u(x) = 1$ iff $x \in \alpha$, for all $x$. Reading $i \in [h]$, print the two-symbol string $i1$. $\vdash \boxed{\;\alpha\;|\;i\;} \dashv \quad \vdash \boxed{\;u\;|\;i\;|\;1\;} \dashv$

Clearly, every instance $\alpha i$ of MEMBERSHIP$_h^R$ is mapped into a string $ui1$ which is indeed an instance of PROJECTION$_h^R$; and $\alpha i$ is positive iff $i \in \alpha$, namely iff $u(i) = 1$, namely iff $ui1$ is also positive. Moreover, this conversion can be easily implemented by a 1-state 1DFT and does not increase $h$ across the two problems.

For another example, consider converting PROJECTION$_h^R$ to COMPOSITION$_{h^2}$ by the following algorithm, which can be implemented by an $(h+1)$-state 1DFT:

Reading $u \in [h]^h$, print a characteristic function of $u$, $f : [h^2] \to [2]$ such that $f(y \cdot h + x) = 0$ iff $u(y) = x$, for all $x, y$. Reading $j \in [h]$, store $j$. Reading $i$, print any function $g : [h^2] \rightharpoonup [h^2]$ such that $g(0) = j \cdot h + i$. $\vdash \boxed{\;u\;|\;j\;|\;i\;} \dashv \quad \vdash \boxed{\;f\;|\;g\;} \dashv$

Easily, every instance $uji$ maps to an instance $fg$ which satisfies $f(g(0)) = 0$ iff $u(j) = i$. Also, the increase in height, from $h$ to $h^2$, is small.

Formally, for two families of promise problems $\mathcal{L} = (\mathfrak{L}_h)_{h \geq 1}$ and $\mathcal{L}' = (\mathfrak{L}'_h)_{h \geq 1}$, we write $\mathcal{L} \leq_{1D} \mathcal{L}'$ and say $\mathcal{L}$ *reduces to* $\mathcal{L}'$ *in one-way polynomial size*, if there is a family of 1DFTs $(T_h)_{h \geq 1}$ and two polynomial functions $s, e$ such that every $T_h$ has $s(h)$ states and maps instances of $\mathfrak{L}_h$ to instances of $\mathfrak{L}'_{e(h)}$ so that, for all $x$:

$$x \in L_h \implies T_h(x) \in L'_{e(h)} \quad \text{and} \quad x \in \tilde{L}_h \implies T_h(x) \in \tilde{L}'_{e(h)}.$$

In the special case where $s(h) = 1$ for all $h$, every $T_h$ is nothing more that just a mapping from symbols to strings. We then say $\mathcal{L}$ *homomorphically reduces to* $\mathcal{L}'$ and write $\mathcal{L} \leq_h \mathcal{L}'$. Hence, by our two algorithms above, we have already shown:

$$\text{MEMBERSHIP}^R \leq_h \text{PROJECTION}^R \leq_{1D} \text{COMPOSITION},$$

with $s(h) = 1$, $e(h) = h$ and with $s(h) = h+1$, $e(h) = h^2$, respectively.

A final, more interesting example, which involves problems of arbitrarily long instances, is the reduction of $\exists\text{RETROCOUNT}_h$ to $\exists\text{EQUALITY}^R_h$:

Scan the input bits $b_1 b_2 \cdots b_n$; whenever $b_j = 0$, print nothing; whenever $b_j = 1$, print $j \bmod h$ untagged. On reaching $\dashv$, print $(n+1) \bmod h$ tagged.

To see why this works, note that the input instance is positive iff it has a 1 among all $b_j$ which satisfy $j = n - \lambda h + 1$ for some $\lambda \geq 1$, namely $j = (n+1) \bmod h$. Equivalently, the instance is positive iff the critical value $(n+1) \bmod h$ appears in the list of the modulo-$h$ values of all positions of 1s. So, the algorithm outputs this list, followed by the critical value. Easily, this can be implemented by an $h$-state 1DFT which simply keeps track of the index of the current position modulo $h$. Therefore $\exists\text{RETROCOUNT} \leq_{1D} \exists\text{EQUALITY}^R$, with $s(h) = e(h) = h$.

One-way polynomial-size reductions do have the two nice properties we would expect from them. The first one is, of course, transitivity:

$$\mathcal{L} \leq_{1D} \mathcal{L}' \quad \& \quad \mathcal{L}' \leq_{1D} \mathcal{L}'' \implies \mathcal{L} \leq_{1D} \mathcal{L}''. \tag{3}$$

This holds because we can combine an $s_1$-state 1DFT $T_1$ with an $s_2$-state 1DFT $T_2$ in standard cartesian-product style to build an $s_1 \cdot s_2$-state 1DFT which outputs $T_2(T_1(x))$ for all $x$. Note that, if $s_1, e_1$ and $s_2, e_2$ are the polynomial functions associated with the assumption of (3), then the corresponding functions for the conclusion are $s_1(h) \cdot s_2(e_1(h))$ and $e_2(e_1(h))$; hence, homomorphic reductions are also transitive. The second nice property of one-way polynomial-size reductions is that our complexity classes are closed under them. For example,

$$\mathcal{L} \leq_{1D} \mathcal{L}' \quad \& \quad \mathcal{L}' \in 1D \implies \mathcal{L} \in 1D, \tag{4}$$

and similarly for $2^{1D}$. This time, from an $s_1$-state 1DFT $T$ and an $s_2$-state 1DFA $M$ we get an $s_1 \cdot s_2$-state 1DFA which accepts $x$ iff $M$ accepts $T(x)$, for all $x$. If the polynomial functions associated with the assumption of (4) are $s_1, e_1$ and $s_2$, then the respective function for the conlusion is $s_1(h) \cdot s_2(e_1(h))$.

By transitivity and a few more reductions, we arrive at the lattice on the right, where arrows and lines denote $\leq_{1D}$ in one and both directions, respectively. So, by the closures and this lattice, all observations of Sect. 2.2 now follow from the three facts MEMBERSHIP$^R \notin$ 1D and $(\exists)$ RETROCOUNT $\in 2^{1D}$.

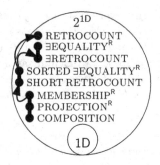

An analogy is now clear, between 1D, $2^{1D}$, and $\leq_{1D}$ on one hand, and settings of TM-complexity on the other: P, EXP, and polynomial-time reductions; or L, PSPACE, and logarithmic-space reductions. So, a natural next question is whether this map also contains an analog of NP and NL.

## 2.4　Nondeterminism

The class 1N is defined as in (2), but for 1NFAs. To place it on our map, we note that $1D \subseteq 1N \subseteq 2^{1D}$ (by the definitions and the subset construction [23]), that RETROCOUNT, $\exists$EQUALITY$^R \in$ 1N (easily [21]), and that 1N is closed under $\leq_{1D}$ (by adapting the argument for (4)). The result is shown on the side.

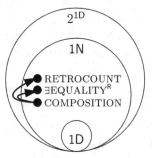

Naturally, the next step is to look for problems in $2^{1D} \setminus$ 1N. We consider the following problem, defined over $[\![h]\!]$, which we call INCLUSION:

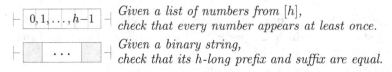　　　*Given two sets $\alpha, \beta \subseteq [h]$, check that $\alpha \subseteq \beta$.*

We also consider two related problems: SET EQUALITY, which asks whether $\alpha = \beta$; and DISJOINTNESS, which asks whether $\alpha \cap \beta = \emptyset$.[(7)] Clearly, all three problems are in $2^{1D}$. However, none is in 1N. The argument for INCLUSION is a classic:

> *Proof.* Assume a 1NFA solver $X$ with $< 2^h$ states. Let $\alpha_0, \ldots, \alpha_{2^h-1}$ list all subsets of $[h]$ so that the characteristic vector of each $\alpha_i$ is the binary representation of $i$. Consider the $2^h \times 2^h$ matrix with $(i,j)$-th entry the instance $\alpha_i \alpha_j$. Clearly, every $\alpha_i \alpha_i$ on the diagonal is positive, so $X$ accepts it; pick an accepting branch, and let $q_i$ be its state right after crossing into the second set. Since the states $q_0, \ldots, q_{2^h-1}$ outnumber those of $X$, we have $q_i = q_j$ for some $i > j$. By a standard cut-and-paste argument, this implies that $X$ accepts $\alpha_i \alpha_j$. By $i > j$, some 1 in the representation of $i$ is a 0 for $j$, so $\alpha_i \nsubseteq \alpha_j$. So, $X$ accepts a negative instance, a contradiction.

The argument for SET EQUALITY is identical. As for DISJOINTNESS, the simple 1DFT which replaces $\beta$ with $\overline{\beta}$ proves INCLUSION $\leq_{1D}$ DISJOINTNESS (easily); so, by the closure of 1N under $\leq_{1D}$, this problem is also not in 1N.

Two more problems in this category are ROLL CALL and EQUAL ENDS:[(8)][(9)]

$\vdash \boxed{0,1,\ldots,h-1} \dashv$　　*Given a list of numbers from $[h]$, check that every number appears at least once.*

$\vdash \boxed{\phantom{xx} \cdots \phantom{xx}} \dashv$　　*Given a binary string, check that its $h$-long prefix and suffix are equal.*

We also consider their restrictions SHORT ROLL CALL and SHORT EQUAL ENDS, where every instance is promised to be of length $\leq 2h$.[10] Easily, all four problems are in $2^{1D}$. But none of them is in 1N, as DISJOINTNESS $\leq_h$ SHORT ROLL CALL and SET EQUALITY $\leq_h$ SHORT EQUAL ENDS, by straightforward reductions.

Before we update our map with the new problems, we note one more feature that they have in common: although they do not admit small 1NFAs, their complements do. E.g., $\neg$INCLUSION$_h$ is solved by an $(h+1)$-state 1NFA which 'guesses' an $i \in \alpha \setminus \beta$. This leads us to the class co1N, which is defined as in (2) but with "$M_h$ solves $\neg \mathfrak{L}_h$". So, all seven of our new problems are actually in co1N $\setminus$ 1N.

The new map is on the right. We have used a few additional easy reductions, together with the chain 1D $\subseteq$ co1N $\subseteq 2^{1D}$ (since 1D $\subseteq$ 1N $\subseteq 2^{1D}$ and because 1D and $2^{1D}$ are closed under complement). Of course, all problems shown here have their complements in 1N $\setminus$ co1N. Also, all problems from Sect. 2.2 are in 1N $\cap$ co1N: this follows, e.g., because (3) RETROCOUNT and its complement homomorphically reduce to each other (by flipping the bits) and co1N is closed under $\leq_{1D}$ (since 1N is).

At this point, two natural questions are whether 1N also contains complete problems, by analogy to NP and NL; and whether we can also find problems in $2^{1D} \setminus (1N \cup co1N)$. We postpone the answers for Sect. 2.6 and Sect. 2.7. In the meantime, the next section examines 1N $\cap$ co1N a bit more carefully.

## 2.5   Complement and Reversal

In Sect. 2.1 we showed that 1D is not closed under reversal, and in Sect. 2.4 we showed that 1N is not closed under complement. In contrast, 1D is closed under complement (as every 1DFA can be 'complemented' just by swapping accepting and rejecting states, after adding a new one as sink [23]) and 1N is closed under reversal (as every 1NFA can be 'reversed' just by reversing all transitions, before adding a fresh start state [23]). We thus have

$$\text{co1D} = \text{1D} \neq \text{re1D} \qquad \text{and} \qquad \text{co1N} \neq \text{1N} = \text{re1N} \,,$$

where co1D is defined as co1N but for 1DFAs, and the classes re1D and re1N are defined as in (2) but with "$M_h$ solves $\mathfrak{L}_h^R$".

To place the new class re1D on our map, we note that it is in 1N $\cap$ co1N (by 1D $\subseteq$ 1N and the two closures we just mentioned), and that both the difference (1N $\cap$ co1N) $\setminus$ (1D $\cup$ re1D) and the intersection 1D $\cap$ re1D are non-empty. For the difference, consider the conjunctive concatenation (cf. Sect. 1) of any two problems that witness the two sides of the symmetric difference of 1D and re1D, e.g., MEMBERSHIP$^R$ and MEMBERSHIP:

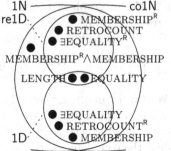

this defies small 1DFAs in either direction (as each of the original problems $\leq_h$-reduces to it), but small 1NFAs can solve both it and its complement (easily). As for 1D ∩ re1D, consider any elementary problem which is the reverse of itself:

⊢ $i$ $j$ ⊣    *Given two numbers $i, j \in [h]$, check that $i = j$.*

⊢ 0 0 ⋯ 0 0 ⊣   *Given a string $w \in \{0\}^*$, check that $|w| = h$.*

We call these two problems EQUALITY and LENGTH, respectively.[11]

## 2.6  Completeness

A problem is 1N-*complete* if it is in 1N and every problem in 1N reduces to it. This notion was introduced by Sakoda and Sipser [24] together with the first proof of 1N-completeness, for a problem which we call ONE-WAY LIVENESS (or just OWL).[12] A few years earlier, Seiferas [26] had introduced two problems which would also turn out to be 1N-complete, and which we call SEPARABILITY (or just SEP) and ZERO-SAFE PROGRAMS (or just ZSP).[13] [14]

For SEPARABILITY, the alphabet is $[\![h]\!]$. To define it, we use the notion of a 'block': a string of sets $\alpha_0 \alpha_1 \cdots \alpha_l$ in which the first one contains the number of those that follow, i.e., $\alpha_0 \ni l$. E.g., $\{0,2,4\}\emptyset\{1,4\}$ and $\{0,2\}$ are blocks, but $\emptyset$ and $\{0,2,4\}\{1,4\}$ are not. A list of sets is 'separable' if it can be split into blocks.

⊢ $\alpha_1$ $\alpha_2$ ⋯ $\alpha_n$ ⊣   *Given a list of sets $\alpha_1, \alpha_2, \ldots, \alpha_n \subseteq [h]$, check that it is separable.*

For ZERO-SAFE PROGRAMS, the alphabet is $[h] \cup [h]^2$. A symbol $\iota$ is seen as an instruction, applied to a variable $\alpha \subseteq [h]$: an $i \in [h]$ means "remove $i$ from $\alpha$"; a $(j, i) \in [h]^2$ means "if $j \in \alpha$, then add $i$ to $\alpha$". A string $\iota_1 \iota_2 \cdots \iota_n$ is seen as a program. We call it '0-safe' if it satisfies: $0 \in \alpha$ at start $\Longrightarrow 0 \in \alpha$ in the end.

⊢ $\iota_1$ $\iota_2$ ⋯ $\iota_n$ ⊣   *Given a program $\iota_1, \iota_2, \ldots, \iota_n \in [h] \cup [h]^2$, check that it is 0-safe.*

For ONE-WAY LIVENESS, the alphabet is $\mathbb{P}([h]^2)$. A symbol $\gamma$ is seen as a 2-column graph of height $h$, with its pairs $(i, j) \in \gamma$ as rightward arrows. A string $\gamma_1 \gamma_2 \cdots \gamma_n$ is seen as an $h$-tall, $(n+1)$-column graph. We call this graph 'live' if column $n+1$ is reachable from column 1.

⊢ ⋯ ⊣   *Given a $h$-tall, one-way, multi-column graph, check that it is live.*

We also call COMPACT OWL the restriction where all instances have length $n = 2$.

The completeness of OWL (under $\leq_h$) was proved in [24]. The completeness of SEP was announced there, too (see [14], for an outline of OWL $\leq_h$ SEP). Here, we show the completeness of ZSP, which seems not to have been announced before.

*Proof.* We copy the intuition of [26, p. 3] to homomorphically reduce SEP$_h$ to ZSP$_{2h}$.

Before we start, we need to consider how a $2^h$-state 1DFA solves SEP$_h$. The strategy is to keep track of the 'overhang set' of the input so far. This is the set $\tilde{\alpha}$ of all $i \in [h]$ such that the input will be separable if it has exactly $i$ more symbols. At start, $\tilde{\alpha} = \{0\}$, because the empty string is separable. Then, on reading an $\alpha \subseteq [h]$, we update $\tilde{\alpha}$ as follows: (1) every $0 \neq i \in \tilde{\alpha}$ is replaced by $i-1$, because we just read 1 symbol, and (2) if $0 \in \tilde{\alpha}$, then 0 is replaced by all $i \in \alpha$, because in the 'thread' encoded by 0 this $\alpha$ starts a new block. In the end, the input is accepted if $0 \in \tilde{\alpha}$.

Our 1-state 1DFT maps an instance $\alpha_1 \alpha_2 \cdots \alpha_n$ of SEP$_h$ to an instance $p_1 p_2 \cdots p_n$ of ZSP$_{2h}$ which uses the set variable to keep track of the overhang set $\tilde{\alpha}$. Each $p_k$ is a sub-program $f(\alpha_k)$ which applies to $\tilde{\alpha}$ the updates (1)-(2) caused by $\alpha_k$. For (1), we use instruction pairs $(i, i-1)i$, which replace $i$ by $i-1$ if $i \in \tilde{\alpha}$, listing them by increasing $i$ so that newly-added values do not interfere with pre-existing ones:

$$(1,0)1 \quad (2,1)2 \quad \cdots \quad (h-1, h-2)h-1. \tag{$*$}$$

For (2), we can use one instruction $(0, i)$ for each $i \in \alpha_k$, and a final instruction 0 to remove 0. But there is a problem. These instructions must precede $(*)$, because all tests for $0 \in \tilde{\alpha}$ must precede $(1,0)$, which may add 0 to $\tilde{\alpha}$; but then, placing the instructions before $(*)$, causes interference between the values added by them and the values tested for by $(*)$.

This is why we reduce to ZSP$_{2h}$, and not just ZSP$_h$: to use a set variable with both a 'lower half' in $[h]$ and an 'upper half' in $[2h] \setminus [h]$. This way, we can implement (2) in two stages, one before $(*)$ and one after. The first stage uses one instruction $(0, h+i)$ for every $i \in \alpha_k$ to copy $\alpha_k$ into the upper half of $\tilde{\alpha}$, 'above' all pre-existing values, followed by the instruction 0 to remove 0. Then, after $(*)$ has correctly updated the lower half, the second stage uses one instruction pair $(h+i, i)h+i$ for every $i \in \alpha_k$ to transpose the copy of $\alpha_k$ into the lower half, leaving the upper half empty again.

Overall, our 1DFT replaces every $\alpha \subseteq [h]$ in its input $x$ with the sub-program

$$f(\alpha) := \quad \big((0, h+i)\big)_{i \in \alpha} 0 \quad (1,0)1 \ (2,1)2 \ \cdots \ (h-1, h-2)h-1 \quad \big((h+i, i)h+i\big)_{i \in \alpha}$$

to produce a program $f(x)$. By our discussion above, $x$ is separable iff its overhang set contains 0 in the end, which holds iff $f(x)$ transforms $\{0\}$ into a superset of $\{0\}$. In turn, this holds iff $f(x)$ is 0-safe (for the 'only if' direction, note that starting with a superset of $\{0\}$ cannot shrink any of the intermediate sets). $\square$

Finally, it is interesting (and easy) to note that COMPACT OWL is $\leq_{1D}$-equivalent to the complement of DISJOINTNESS, and thus also of INCLUSION.

## 2.7  Harder Problems

For a problem in $2^{1D} \setminus (1N \cup co1N)$, we may consider the conjunctive concatenation of any two problems from the two sides of the symmetric difference of 1N and co1N, e.g., INCLUSION $\wedge \neg$INCLUSION: this is $\leq_h$-harder than both INCLUSION and $\neg$INCLUSION, but still in $2^{1D}$. Two more interesting examples are RELATIONAL MATCH and RELATIONAL PATH.[15] [16]

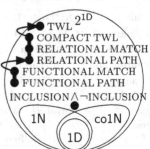

For RELATIONAL MATCH, the alphabet is two copies of $\mathbb{P}([h]^2)$, one of them tagged. Every symbol $A \subseteq [h]^2$ is seen as an $h$-tall, 2-column graph with rightward arrows (as in OWL), if it is untagged, or with leftward arrows, if it is tagged. A pair $A\check{B}$ is seen as the overlay (union) of the corresponding two graphs. If this overlay contains a cycle, we say that the binary relations $A$ and $B$ 'match'.

$\vdash \boxed{A \;\; \check{B}} \dashv$    Given a relation $A \subseteq [h]^2$ and a tagged $B \subseteq [h]^2$, check that $A$ and $B$ match.

For RELATIONAL PATH, the alphabet includes in addition two copies of $[h]$, one tagged. A string $iA\check{B}j$ is seen again as the overlay for $A\check{B}$, but now with the $i$-th left-column node and the $j$-th right-column node marked respectively as 'entry' and 'exit'.

$\vdash \boxed{i \;\; A \;\; \check{B} \;\; \check{j}} \dashv$    Given $i \in [h]$ and $A \subseteq [h]^2$, and tagged $B \subseteq [h]^2$ and $j \in [h]$, check that the resulting overlay has a entry-to-exit path.

By FUNCTIONAL MATCH and FUNCTIONAL PATH we mean the restrictions where both relations are promised to be partial functions, i.e., in $([h] \rightharpoonup [h])$.[17] [18]

To place these problems on the map, note that FUNCTIONAL MATCH $\not\subseteq$ co1N (because ¬DISJOINTNESS $\leq_{1D}$-reduces to it, by a 1DFT which maps $\alpha\beta$ to $A\check{B}$ for $A := \{(i,i) \mid i \in \alpha\}$, $B := \{(i,i) \mid i \in \beta\}$) and that FUNCTIONAL PATH $\not\subseteq$ 1N [10]. Hence, both problems are outside 1N $\cup$ co1N, provided that they reduce to each other. Indeed they do, but to prove so we need two new, variant concepts.

First, the variant problem FUNCTIONAL ZERO-MATCH. This asks only that $A$ and $B$ '0-*match*', i.e., that their overlay contains a cycle through the 0-th left-column node.[19] This is known to be $\leq_h$-equivalent to FUNCTIONAL MATCH [19].

Second, a variant '*nondeterministic* one-way polynomial-size reduction', $\leq_{1N}$. This differs from $\leq_{1D}$ in that the underlying transducer $T$ is nondeterministic (a 1NFT), and such that every input $x$ causes all accepting branches to produce the same output $T(x)$. Easily, $\leq_{1N}$ is also transitive and 1N is closed under it.

We now prove FUNCTIONAL MATCH and FUNCTIONAL PATH $\leq_{1N}$-equivalent. First, we replace the first problem by its equivalent FUNCTIONAL ZERO-MATCH. Then, FUNCTIONAL ZERO-MATCH$_h$ reduces to FUNCTIONAL PATH$_{h+1}$ by a 1-state 1DFT which adds a fresh node $h$ which is both entry and exit, directs the entry $h$ into the path out of 0, and redirects 0 to the exit $h$:

Reading $A$, print $hA'$, where $A'(t) := A(t)$ for $t \neq 0, h$, whereas $A'(h) := A(0)$ and $A'(0) := h$. Reading $\check{B}$, print $\check{B}'\check{h}$, where $B'(t) := B(t)$ for $t \neq h$, whereas $B'(h)$ is undefined.

$\vdash \boxed{A \;\; \check{B}} \dashv$

$\vdash \boxed{h \;\; A' \;\; \check{B}' \;\; \check{h}} \dashv$

Conversely, FUNCTIONAL PATH$_h$ reduces to FUNCTIONAL ZERO-MATCH$_{h+1}$ by the simple $h$-state 1NFT which first transposes $A, \check{B}$ from $[h]$ to $[h+1] \setminus \{0\}$, then connects the 0-th left-column node to the transposed entry (via the 0-th right-column node), and the transposed exit back to the 0-th left-column node:

Reading $i$, store $i$. Reading $A$, print $A'$, where $A'(0) := 0$ and $A'(t) := A(t-1)+1$ for $t \neq 0$. Reading $\check{B}$ and recalling $i$, guess $j' \in [h]$; print $\check{B}'$, where $B'(0) := i+1$, $B'(j'+1) := 0$, and $B'(t) := B(t-1)+1$ for $t \neq 0, j'+1$; and store $j'$ in place of $i$. Reading $j$ and recalling $j'$, accept iff $j = j'$.

$\vdash \boxed{i \;\; A \;\; \check{B} \;\; \check{j}} \dashv$

$\vdash \boxed{A' \;\; \check{B}'} \dashv$

Note how nondeterminism allows the machine to use the exit $j$ before reading it.

Appropriately adjusted, both of the above reductions work even when $A$ and $B$ are relations. Hence, RELATIONAL MATCH and RELATIONAL PATH are also $\leq_{1N}$-equivalent, through the variant RELATIONAL ZERO-MATCH of the first problem, which is again known to be $\leq_h$-equivalent to it [19].[20]

Finally, we also introduce TWO-WAY LIVENESS (or just TWL).[21] This generalizes OWL to the alphabet $\mathbb{P}([2h]^2)$ of all $h$-tall, 2-column graphs with arbitrary arrows. The restriction to instances of length 2 is called COMPACT TWL, and is $\leq_{1D}$-equivalent to RELATIONAL MATCH (by a modification of [19, Lemma 8.1]).[22] Hence, COMPACT TWL and TWL are also outside $1N \cup co1N$ —as well as (easily) inside $2^{1D}$.

## 2.8 Alternation

The classes $1N$ and $co1N$ are on the first level of a *one-way polynomial-size hierarchy* which is defined by analogy to the polynomial-time hierarchy and the space alternating hierarchies of TM-complexity.

For each $k \geq 1$, we define the class $1\Sigma_k$ (resp., $1\Pi_k$) as in (2) but for $1\Sigma_k FAS$ ($1\Pi_k FAS$), namely for alternating 1FAs which perfrom $< k$ alternations between existential and universal states, starting with an existential (universal) one. We also let $1\Sigma_0, 1\Pi_0 := 1D$ and $1H := \bigcup_{k\geq0}(1\Sigma_k \cup 1\Pi_k)$. Then

$$1D \subseteq 1\Sigma_k, 1\Pi_k \subseteq 1\Sigma_{k+1}, 1\Pi_{k+1} \subseteq 1H$$

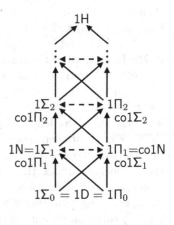

(by the definitions) and $co1\Sigma_k = 1\Pi_k$ and $1\Sigma_k = co1\Pi_k$ (easily), for all $k \geq 0$, causing $co1H = 1H$.

The natural question is whether this hierarchy of classes is strict. For the first level, we already know (Sect. 2.4) that, e.g., $\neg$INCLUSION $\in 1\Sigma_1 \setminus 1\Pi_1$ and INCLUSION $\in 1\Pi_1 \setminus 1\Sigma_1$. For the higher levels, we use the (much more powerful) theorems of [4]. We start with a 'core' problem, which we call $\exists$INCLUSION: [23]

$$\vdash \boxed{\check{\alpha} \mid \alpha_1 \mid \alpha_2 \mid \cdots} \dashv \qquad \begin{array}{l} \text{Given a tagged } \alpha \subseteq [h] \text{ and a list } \alpha_1, \alpha_2, \ldots, \alpha_l \subseteq [h], \\ \text{check that } \alpha \subseteq \alpha_j \text{ for some } j. \end{array}$$

Then, by alternate applications of conjunctive and disjunctive star (cf. Sect. 1), we build the following table of witnesses for all levels, where 'INCL' abbreviates 'INCLUSION' (for $k = 1$, reversal is redundant; we use it only for symmetry):

| $1\Sigma_1\backslash1\Pi_1$ | $1\Sigma_2\backslash1\Pi_2$ | $1\Sigma_3\backslash1\Pi_3$ | $1\Sigma_4\backslash1\Pi_4$ | $1\Sigma_5\backslash1\Pi_5$ | $\cdots$ |
|---|---|---|---|---|---|
| $\neg$INCL$^R$ | $\exists$INCL$^R$ | $\bigvee\neg\exists$INCL$^R$ | $\bigvee\bigwedge \exists$INCL$^R$ | $\bigvee\bigwedge\bigvee\neg\exists$INCL$^R$ | $\cdots$ |
| INCL$^R$ | $\neg\exists$INCL$^R$ | $\bigwedge \exists$INCL$^R$ | $\bigwedge\bigvee\neg\exists$INCL$^R$ | $\bigwedge\bigvee\bigwedge \exists$INCL$^R$ | $\cdots$ |
| $1\Pi_1\backslash1\Sigma_1$ | $1\Pi_2\backslash1\Sigma_2$ | $1\Pi_3\backslash1\Sigma_3$ | $1\Pi_4\backslash1\Sigma_4$ | $1\Pi_5\backslash1\Sigma_5$ | $\cdots$ |

(5)

In fact, [4] shows that all lower bounds in this table for $k \geq 2$ are valid even for 2FAs (see also the discussion in Sect. 3.4).

# 3  Two-Way Automata

## 3.1  The Sakoda-Sipser Conjecture

For 2FAs, the main complexity classes, analogous
to 1D and 1N, are 2D and 2N. To place them on
the map, we note that $1D \subseteq 2D \subseteq 2N \subseteq 2^{1D}$ (by the
definitions and [27]), that $2D = re2D$ and $2N = re2N$
(easily), and that $2D = co2D$ (by [28]). So, the chain

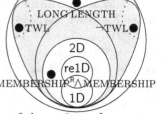

$$1D, re1D \ \subsetneq \ 2D \ \subseteq \ 2N, co2N \ \subsetneq \ 2^{1D}$$

mentions all interesting classes. The first inclusion is
strict, because of, e.g., MEMBERSHIP$^R$∧MEMBERSHIP
(cf. Sect. 2.5). The last inclusion is also strict, because of the variant of LENGTH
(cf. Sect. 2.5) for length $2^h$, which we call LONG LENGTH (by [3, Fact 5.2], and
then by [7, Cor. 4.3]). The *Sakoda-Sipser conjecture* [24] says that the middle
inclusion is also strict: $2D \neq 2N$. In fact, it is believed that even $2N \neq co2N$ [7].

A two-way head is very powerful. All problems mentioned in Sect. 2.1–2.7 are
in 2N. In fact, all of them are known to be already in 2D, except for:

- ONE-WAY LIVENESS, SEPARABILITY, and ZERO-SAFE PROGRAMS;
- COMPACT TWL, RELATIONAL MATCH, and RELATIONAL PATH; and
- TWO-WAY LIVENESS.

The first three problems are $\leq_h$-equivalent (Sect. 2.6). So, 2D contains either all
three or none of them (because it is closed under $\leq_h$ [24,15]). The next three
problems reduce to each other under $\leq_{1D}$ or $\leq_{1N}$ (Sect. 2.7). However, all six of
the reductions among them can be easily replaced by $\leq_{2D}^{lac}$-reductions, namely
'*(two-way) polynomial-size/print reductions*' [19]. These differ from $\leq_{1D}$ in that
the underlying transducer is two-way (a 2DFT), and restricted to print only
poly($h$) times on its output tape. So, 2D again contains either all three or none
of the problems in the second group (because 2D is also closed under $\leq_{2D}^{lac}$ [19]).

Overall, we are essentially left with only three problems that could potentially
witness the Sakoda-Sipser conjecture: TWL and its severe restrictions to one-way
graphs and to two-symbol graphs, respectively OWL and COMPACT TWL.

The full problem is actually 2N-complete under $\leq_h$ [24]. Hence, by the closure
of 2D and 2N under $\leq_h$ [24], we get the following equivalences:

$$2D = 2N \Longleftrightarrow \text{TWL} \in 2D \qquad \text{and} \qquad 2N = co2N \Longleftrightarrow \neg\text{TWL} \in 2N \,.$$

So, the Sakoda-Sipser conjecture is concretely reformulated as TWL $\notin$ 2D, i.e.:

> *no poly($h$)-state* 2DFA *can check that an $h$-tall, two-way, multi-column
> graph contains a path from its leftmost to its rightmost column.* (6)

Similarly, the conjecture that $2N \neq co2N$ has the concrete reformulation that
$\neg$TWL $\notin$ 2N, namely that:

> *no poly($h$)-state* 2NFA *can check that an $h$-tall, two-way, multi-column
> graph contains no path from its leftmost to its rightmost column.* (7)

In the next two sections we discuss stronger versions of these two conjectures.

## 3.2   A Stronger Conjecture I

The restriction of TWL to OWL leads to a stronger
conjecture, also from [24], that even OWL $\not\subseteq$ 2D, i.e.,
that (6) holds even if the graph is one-way. Since
OWL is 1N-complete, this is equivalent to 1N $\not\subseteq$ 2D,
which was conjectured already in [26]. This stronger
claim has been the focus of most attacks against the
Sakoda-Sipser conjecture over the past four decades.
The typical strategy has been to confirm it for some
subclass of 2DFAs of restricted bidirectionality or
restricted information. A chronological list follows.

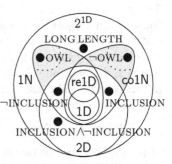

- In [26], a fairly simple argument confirmed the claim for *single-pass* 2DFAs,
  that is, 2DFAs which halt upon reaching an end-marker (cf. Note 13). However, this provably avoided the full claim, because, as noted also in [26],
  unrestricted small 2DFAs are strictly more powerful (cf. Note 9).
- In [29], a breakthrough argument confirmed the claim for *sweeping* 2DFAs,
  that is, 2DFAs which reverse their head only on end-markers. The structure
  and tools of that proof have since been copied and reused several times (see,
  e.g., [13,16,9]). Again, the result provably avoided the full claim, because
  unrestricted small 2DFAs are strictly more powerful [29, by J. Seiferas].
- In [8], a reduction argument confirmed the claim for *almost oblivious* 2DFAs,
  that is, 2DFAs whose number of distinct trajectories over $n$-long inputs is
  only $o(n)$ (instead of the $2^{O(n \log n)}$ maximum). The proof first showed that
  small 2DFAs of this kind are as powerful as sweeping ones, then made black-
  box use of [29]. As a result, the full claim was once again provably avoided.
- In [13], a computability argument confirmed the claim for 2DFA *moles*, that
  is, 2DFAs which explore the multi-column graph of an instance of OWL as a
  'system of tunnels'. In fact, the proof showed that $\text{OWL}_5$ is already unsolvable
  by 2DFA moles of any size. Hence, it also completely avoided the full claim.
- In [9], a recent argument confirmed the claim for 2DFAs *with few reversals*,
  that is, 2DFAs whose number of head reversals is only $o(n)$ (instead of the
  $O(n)$ maximum). This again avoided the full claim, because, as shown also
  in [9], unrestricted small 2DFAs are strictly more powerful. In fact, more
  recent arguments show that few-reversal 2DFAs necessarily perform only
  $O(1)$ reversals [18, Thm. 1], and that an infinite hierarchy of computational
  power exists below them [18, Thm. 2]. In Sect. 4 we use these arguments to
  give a simpler, modular argument for improving the main theorem of [9].

In conclusion, if the full claim OWL $\not\subseteq$ 2D is false, then this can only be by a
multi-pass 2DFA algorithm which uses the full information of every symbol and,
infinitely often, performs $\Theta(n)$ reversals and exhibits $\Omega(n)$ trajectories.

A similar strengthening is also possible for the second conjecture of Sect. 3.1:
we believe that even $\neg$OWL $\not\subseteq$ 2N, i.e., that (7) holds even if the graph is one-way.
One advance in this direction concerns 2NFAs of restricted bidirectionality:

- In [12], it was confirmed that $\neg$OWL admits no small *sweeping* 2NFAs.

A tractable next goal could be to confirm the same for 2NFAs with few reversals.

### 3.3   A Stronger Conjecture II

The restriction of TWL to COMPACT TWL leads to
the stronger conjecture, suggested in [19], that even
COMPACT TWL $\not\subseteq$ 2D, i.e., that (6) holds even for
three-column graphs. This is part of an approach
in which we focus on subclasses of 2N for restricted
instance length, and ask whether 2D contains any
of them. Specifically, we introduce the subclasses

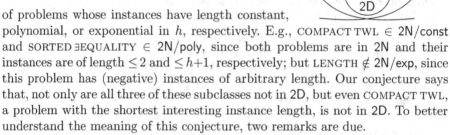

$$2\mathsf{N}/\mathsf{const} \subsetneq 2\mathsf{N}/\mathsf{poly} \subsetneq 2\mathsf{N}/\mathsf{exp} \subsetneq 2\mathsf{N}$$

of problems whose instances have length constant,
polynomial, or exponential in $h$, respectively. E.g., COMPACT TWL $\in$ 2N/const
and SORTED ∃EQUALITY $\in$ 2N/poly, since both problems are in 2N and their
instances are of length $\leq 2$ and $\leq h+1$, respectively; but LENGTH $\not\in$ 2N/exp, since
this problem has (negative) instances of arbitrary length. Our conjecture says
that, not only are all three of these subclasses not in 2D, but even COMPACT TWL,
a problem with the shortest interesting instance length, is not in 2D. To better
understand the meaning of this conjecture, two remarks are due.

First, COMPACT TWL does admit sub-exponential 2DFAs. This can be shown
directly, by applying Savitch's algorithm [25]. However, it also follows from a
more general phenomenon, involving *outer-nondeterministic* 2FAs (2OFAs, i.e.,
2NFAs which perform nondeterminstic choices only on the end-markers), and the
respective class 2O. We know that 2N/poly $\subseteq$ 2O (a simple argument [19]) and
2O $\subseteq$ 2DSIZE($2^{\mathrm{poly}(\log h)}$) (a theorem of [5], which uses [25]). So, COMPACT TWL
admits quasi-polynomially large 2DFAs because all problems in 2O do.

We note that, like 2N/poly, the class 2N/unary of all unary problems of 2N is
also in 2O (by [6]), and 2D contains either subclass iff it contains the entire 2O:

$$2\mathsf{N}/\mathsf{poly} \subseteq 2\mathsf{D} \quad \Longleftrightarrow \quad 2\mathsf{O} \subseteq 2\mathsf{D} \quad \Longleftrightarrow \quad 2\mathsf{N}/\mathsf{unary} \subseteq 2\mathsf{D} \qquad (8)$$

(because each subclass shares with 2O a common complete problem, for appropriate reductions under which 2D is closed [19]). Moreover, 2O = co2O (another
theorem of [5]), so that this entire discussion takes place inside 2N ∩ co2N.

The second remark about our stronger conjecture is the equivalence [19]:

$$\text{COMPACT TWL} \not\in 2\mathsf{D} \quad \Longleftrightarrow \quad \text{RELATIONAL MATCH} \not\leq_h \text{FUNCTIONAL MATCH}. \qquad (9)$$

This connects our conjecture on the left-hand side, which is clearly an *algorithmic*
statement, to the purely *combinatorial* statement on the right-hand side:

> *no pair of systematic ways of replacing h-tall relations
> by* poly($h$)*-tall functions respects the existence of cycles.*   (10)

So, in regard to the well-known dichotomy of intuition betweeen algorithms and
combinatorics for upper and lower bounds respectively, we see that both sides
are supported: *to disprove the conjecture*, one may focus on the left-hand side
of (9) and search for a small algorithm for liveness on $h$-tall, two-way, two-symbol
graphs; *to prove the conjecture*, one may focus on the right-hand side and search
for a proof of (10). We continue this discussion in Sect. 3.5.

## 3.4    Alternation Again

The *two-way polynomial-size hierarchy* is defined as
in Sect. 2.8 but for 2FAs. With the same witnesses
as for 1FAs, we know this hierarchy does not collapse
either [4]. However, there are two important differences. First, the witnesses of (5) work only for $k \geq 2$;
for $k = 1$, we still do not know:

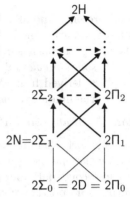

- whether the inclusion $2\Sigma_0 \subseteq 2\Sigma_1$ is strict,
- whether the inclusion $2\Pi_0 \subseteq 2\Pi_1$ is strict, and
- whether $2\Sigma_1$ and $2\Pi_1$ are incomparable.

Second, although the first of these questions is indeed the Sakoda-Sipser conjecture, the last two are
*not* about 2D vs. co2N and 2N vs. co2N: for $k \geq 1$, it
is open whether $\mathrm{co}2\Sigma_k = 2\Pi_k$ (and thus also whether $2\Sigma_k = \mathrm{co}2\Pi_k$). In fact,
Geffert [4, §7] conjectures that $\mathrm{co}2\Pi_1$ is not even in 2H, and thus $\mathrm{co}2\mathrm{H} \neq 2\mathrm{H}$.

## 3.5    Relation to Turing Machine Complexity

Minicomplexity is related to log-space TM-complexity as shown below. The main
link is that log-space deterministic TMs with short advice can simulate log-space
nondeterministic TMs ($\mathsf{L/poly} \supseteq \mathsf{NL}$) iff small 2DFAs can simulate small 2NFAs on
short inputs ($\mathsf{2D} \supseteq \mathsf{2N/poly}$). This remains true if we reduce space to $\log\log n$
and advice to $\mathrm{poly}(\log n)$ ($\mathsf{LL/polylog} \supseteq \mathsf{NLL}$) and lengthen the inputs to $2^{\mathrm{poly}(h)}$
($\mathsf{2D} \supseteq \mathsf{2N/exp}$). The problems SHORT TWL and LONG TWL are the restrictions of
TWL to inputs of promised length $\leq h$ and $\leq 2^h$, respectively.[24]

$$
\begin{array}{ccccccc}
& & & & \mathsf{2D} \supseteq \mathsf{2N/const} & \Longrightarrow & \mathsf{2D} \ni \text{COMPACT TWL} \\
& & & & \Uparrow & & \Uparrow \\
\mathsf{L} \supseteq \mathsf{NL} & \Longrightarrow & \mathsf{L/poly} \supseteq \mathsf{NL} & \overset{[2,15]}{\Longleftrightarrow} & \mathsf{2D} \supseteq \mathsf{2N/poly} & \overset{[15,19]}{\Longleftrightarrow} & \mathsf{2D} \ni \text{SHORT TWL} \\
\Uparrow {\scriptstyle [31]} & & & & \Uparrow & & \Uparrow \\
\mathsf{LL} \supseteq \mathsf{NLL} & \Longrightarrow & \mathsf{LL/polylog} \supseteq \mathsf{NLL} & \overset{[15]}{\Longleftrightarrow} & \mathsf{2D} \supseteq \mathsf{2N/exp} & \overset{[15]}{\Longleftrightarrow} & \mathsf{2D} \ni \text{LONG TWL} \\
& & & & \Uparrow & & \Uparrow \\
& & & & \mathsf{2D} \supseteq \mathsf{2N} & \overset{[24]}{\Longleftrightarrow} & \mathsf{2D} \ni \text{TWL}
\end{array}
$$

Note that, by (8), $\mathsf{2D} \supseteq \mathsf{2N/unary}$ is yet another reformulation of $\mathsf{L/poly} \supseteq \mathsf{NL}$.
Also, all inclusions and memberships in this diagram are conjectured to be false.

The diagram can be interpreted in two ways. On one hand, people interested in
space-bounded TMs can see that 2D vs. 2N offers a unifying setting for studying
L vs. NL. Confirming $\mathsf{2D} \not\supseteq \mathsf{2N}$ could be a first step in a gradual attack towards
$\mathsf{2D} \not\supseteq \mathsf{2N/exp}$ and $\mathsf{2D} \not\supseteq \mathsf{2N/poly}$, hence $\mathsf{LL} \neq \mathsf{NLL}$ and $\mathsf{L} \neq \mathsf{NL}$. Or, confirming
$\mathsf{2D} \not\ni \text{COMPACT TWL}$ (or its combinatorial version (10)) could be a single step to
$\mathsf{L} \neq \mathsf{NL}$. On the other hand, people stydying 2D vs. 2N can use this diagram to
appreciate the difficulty of proving a separation on bounded-length inputs.

Analogous diagrams can be drawn for other modes. E.g., replacing 2N by its
counterpart 2A for alternating 2FAs, we get $\mathsf{L/poly} \supseteq \mathsf{P} \Longleftrightarrow \mathsf{2D} \supseteq \mathsf{2A/poly}$ [15],
since alternating log-space coincides with deterministic polynomial time.

# 4   Hardness Propagation by Certificates

We now present a modular method of separating minicomplexity classes [16,18]. This has two parts, one for upper bounds and one for lower bounds.

The first part consists in proving 'closure lemmas' of the form: *if an s-state* FA *of type X solves problem* $\mathfrak{L}$, *then a* poly($s$)-*state* FA *of type X solves problem* $\mathfrak{L}'$, where $\mathfrak{L}'$ is derived from $\mathfrak{L}$ by via some problem operator (cf. Sect. 1). E.g., if 1UFAs are the unambiguous 1NFAs, then a straightforward closure lemma is:

**Lemma 1.** *If an s-state* 1UFA *solves* $\mathfrak{L}$, *then a* $O(s)$-*state* 1UFA *solves* $\bigwedge\mathfrak{L}$.

Intuitively, such a lemma says that type $X$ can absorb the 'increase in hardness' caused by the operator which derives $\mathfrak{L}'$ from $\mathfrak{L}$.

In the second part, our approach proves 'hardness-propagation lemmas', of the form: *if no* poly($s$)-*state* FA *of type X solves problem* $\mathfrak{L}$, *then no s-state* FA *of type X' solves problem* $\mathfrak{L}'$, where type $X'$ is more powerful than $X$. E.g., a straightforward lemma involving parallel automata (cf. Sect. 1) is [9, Fact 12]:

**Lemma 2.** (a) *If no* $\cup_{|1}$DFA *with s-state components solves* $\mathfrak{L}$, *then no* $\cup_{\mathsf{R}|1}$DFA *with s-state components solves* $\mathfrak{L}^{\mathsf{R}}$. (b) *If no* $\cap_{|1}$DFA *with* $(s+1)$-*state components solves* $\mathfrak{L}$, *then no* $\cup_{|1}$DFA *with s-state components solves* $\neg\mathfrak{L}$.

Intuitively, every such lemma describes a 'propagation of hardness' from $X$ vs. $\mathfrak{L}$ to $X'$ vs. $\mathfrak{L}'$. Typically, we prove the contrapositive. Assuming an $s$-state FA $M'$ of type $X'$ for $\mathfrak{L}'$, we find in $M'$ a class of objects (e.g., tuples of states, crossing sequences) which can serve as 'certificates' for the positive instances of $\mathfrak{L}$, in the sense that an instance of $\mathfrak{L}$ is positive iff it has such a certificate; then, we build a poly($s$)-state FA of type $X$ which solves $\mathfrak{L}$ by simply searching for certificates.

As an example, we prove that 2D[$O(1)$] $\not\supseteq$ 1U, where 1U is the restriction of 1N to problems solvable by small 1UFAs, and 2D[$O(1)$] is the restriction of 2D to problems solvable by small 2DFAs *with* $O(1)$ *reversals* [18]. (By [18, Thm. 1], this strengthens the recent [9, Thm. 1].) As witness, we use the problem:

$$\mathcal{R} = (\mathfrak{R}_h)_{h\geq 1} := \bigwedge\left[\left(\bigwedge\text{MEMBERSHIP}^{\mathsf{R}}\right) < \left(\bigwedge\text{MEMBERSHIP}\right)\right].$$

More concretely, an instance of $\mathfrak{R}_h$ is a list of the form \$$y_1$\$$\cdots$\$$y_l$\$; each $y_j$ is a list of the form $*x_1*\cdots*x_l*$; and each $x_j$ is a list of the form $\#\alpha_1 i_1\#\cdots\#\alpha_l i_l\#$ or $\#i_1\alpha_1\#\cdots\#i_l\alpha_l\#$. The task is to check that, in every $y_j$: either every $x_j$ has some $i_j$ not in the adjacent $\alpha_j$; or $x_j$ of both forms exist with all their $i_j$ in the adjacent $\alpha_j$, and those in set-number form precede those in number-set form.

The upper bound of this theorem, $\mathcal{R} \in$ 1U, follows by the easy facts that MEMBERSHIP, MEMBERSHIP$^{\mathsf{R}} \in$ 1U $\cap$ co1U, and by Lemmas 1 and 3:

**Lemma 3.** (a) *If s-state* 1UFAs *solve* $\mathfrak{L}, \neg\mathfrak{L}$, *then a* $O(s)$-*state* 1UFA *solves* $\bigvee\mathfrak{L}$. (b) *If s-state* 1UFAs *solve* $\mathfrak{L}_{\mathsf{L}}, \neg\mathfrak{L}_{\mathsf{L}}, \mathfrak{L}_{\mathsf{R}}, \neg\mathfrak{L}_{\mathsf{R}}$, *then a* $O(s)$-*state* 1UFA *solves* $\mathfrak{L}_{\mathsf{L}} < \mathfrak{L}_{\mathsf{R}}$.

The lower bound, $\mathcal{R} \notin$ 2D[$O(1)$], uses Lemma 2 and the additional hardness-propagation Lemmas 4–6 below, which are [16, Lemma 5], [18, Lemma 4*], and (an extension of) [18, Lemma 6*]. For each of them, we outline a proof, describing only the certificates and their usage. For the full arguments, definitions, and notation, see [16,18]. The lower bound itself is proved in the end.

**Lemma 4.** *If no $s$-state 1DFA solves $\mathfrak{L}$, then no $\cap_{\mathrm{l}}$1DFA with $s$-state components solves $\bigvee \mathfrak{L}$.*

*Proof.* Suppose some $\cap_{\mathrm{l}}$1DFA $M = (\mathcal{A}, \emptyset)$ solves $\bigvee \mathfrak{L}$ with $k$ $s$-state components, where $k$ is minimum possible. Pick any $D_* \in \mathcal{A}$. Let $M' = (\mathcal{A}', \emptyset) := (\mathcal{A} \backslash \{D_*\}, \emptyset)$. Since $k$ is minimum, $M'$ does not solve $\bigvee \mathfrak{L}$, neither does any $\cap_{\mathrm{l}}$1DFA that differs from $M'$ only in the selection of final states. By [16, Lemma 2], some string $y = \#x_1\# \cdots \#x_l\#$ is *confusing* for $M'$ on $\bigvee \mathfrak{L} = (K, \tilde{K})$, namely:

$$\text{or} \quad \begin{array}{ll} y \in K & \& \quad (\exists D \in \mathcal{A}')(D(y) = \bot) \\ y \in \tilde{K} & \& \quad (\forall D \in \mathcal{A}')(\exists \tilde{y} \in K)(D(y) = D(\tilde{y})) \,. \end{array}$$

We know $y \in \tilde{K}$. [Otherwise, $y \in K$ and some $D \in \mathcal{A}'$ hangs on it, so $M$ does not accept $y$, so it does not solve $(K, \tilde{K})$, contradiction.] We also know $D_*(y) \neq \bot$. [Otherwise, $D_*(yx\#) = \bot$ for any positive $x$, as well, hence $M$ does not accept $yx\# \in K$, so it does not solve $(K, \tilde{K})$, contradiction.] Let $p_* := D_*(y)$.

*Definition.* A state $q$ of $D_*$ is a *certificate* for an instance $x$ of $\mathfrak{L}$ if it satisfies: (i) $\mathrm{LCOMP}_{D_*, p_*}(x)$ hits right into $q$ and (ii) $D_*$ from $q$ on $\#$ moves to a final state.

*Claim.* An instance of $\mathfrak{L}$ is positive iff it has a certificate.

Hence, to solve $\mathfrak{L}$, an $s$-state 1DFA simulates $D_*$ from $p_*$ and checks that $\dashv$ is reached in a state $q$ from which $D_*$ would move to a final state if it read $\#$. $\quad\square$

**Lemma 5.** *If no $\cup_{\mathrm{l}}$1DFA with $1 + \binom{s}{2}$-state components solves $\mathfrak{L}_\mathrm{L}$ and no $\cup_\mathrm{R}$1DFA with $1 + \binom{s}{2}$-state components solves $\mathfrak{L}_\mathrm{R}$, then no $\mathrm{P}_{21}$DFA with $s$-state components solves $\mathfrak{L}_\mathrm{L} < \mathfrak{L}_\mathrm{R}$.*

*Proof.* Let $\mathfrak{L}_\mathrm{L} = (L_\mathrm{L}, \tilde{L}_\mathrm{L})$, $\mathfrak{L}_\mathrm{R} = (L_\mathrm{R}, \tilde{L}_\mathrm{R})$. Suppose some $\mathrm{P}_{21}$DFA $M = (\mathcal{A}, \mathcal{B}, F)$ solves $\mathfrak{L}_\mathrm{L} < \mathfrak{L}_\mathrm{R}$ with $s$-state components. Let $\vartheta$ be a *generic* string for $M$ over the strings $L := \{\#x_1\# \cdots \#x_l\# \mid l \geq 0 \ \& \ (\forall i)(x_i \in \tilde{L}_\mathrm{L} \cup \tilde{L}_\mathrm{R})\}$ of negatives of $\mathfrak{L}_\mathrm{L}, \mathfrak{L}_\mathrm{R}$.

*Definition.* A pair $\{p, q\}$ of distinct states in $M$ is a *forward certificate* for an instance $x$ of $\mathfrak{L}_\mathrm{L}$ or $\mathfrak{L}_\mathrm{R}$ if there exists $D \in \mathcal{A}$ such that

$$p, q \in Q_{\mathrm{LR}}^D(\vartheta) \quad \text{and} \quad \begin{array}{l} \text{if both } \mathrm{LCOMP}_{D,p}(x\vartheta) \text{ and } \mathrm{LCOMP}_{D,q}(x\vartheta) \text{ hit right,} \\ \text{then they do so into the same state.} \end{array}$$

A *backward certificate* is defined symmetrically, with $\mathcal{A}$, $Q_{\mathrm{LR}}^D$, $\mathrm{LCOMP}_{D,.}(x\vartheta)$, and "hit right" replaced respectively by $\mathcal{B}$, $Q_{\mathrm{RL}}^D$, $\mathrm{RCOMP}_{D,.}(\vartheta x)$, and "hit left".

*Claim.* At least one is true: (i) an instance of $\mathfrak{L}_\mathrm{L}$ is positive iff it has a forward certificate, or (ii) an instance of $\mathfrak{L}_\mathrm{R}$ is positive iff it has a backward certificate.

If (i) is true, then an instance $x$ of $\mathfrak{L}_L$ is positive iff there is $D \in \mathcal{A}$ and distinct $p, q \in Q_{LR}^D(\vartheta)$ such that *either* one of $\hat{c}_p := \mathrm{LCOMP}_{D,p}(x\vartheta)$ or $\hat{c}_q := \mathrm{LCOMP}_{D,q}(x\vartheta)$ hangs *or* both hit right into the same state. Hence, to solve $\mathfrak{L}_L$, a $\cup_{l1}\mathrm{DFA}$ checks this condition using one $1 + \binom{s}{2}$-state component $D_{p,q}$ for every such combination of $D$ and $p, q$. On input $x$, $D_{p,q}$ runs a synchronized simulation of the prefixes $c_p := \mathrm{LCOMP}_{D,p}(x)$ and $c_q := \mathrm{LCOMP}_{D,q}(x)$ of $\hat{c}_p$ and $\hat{c}_q$. If at any point $c_p, c_q$ are about to enter the same state or one of them is about to hang, then $D_{p,q}$ enters a special state $\top$ which consumes the rest of $x$ and accepts. Otherwise, $c_p, c_q$ hit right into distinct states $p', q'$; then $D_{p,q}$ accepts iff one of $\mathrm{LCOMP}_{D,p'}(\vartheta)$ or $\mathrm{LCOMP}_{D,q'}(\vartheta)$ hangs or they both hit right into the same state.

If (ii) is true, we work symmetrically with $\mathfrak{L}_R$ and backward certificates.    $\square$

**Lemma 6.** *If no* $\mathrm{P_{21}DFA}$ *with $s$-state components solves* $\mathfrak{L}$, *then no $s$-state* $2\mathrm{DFA}$ *with $O(1)$ reversals solves* $\bigwedge\mathfrak{L}$.

*Proof.* Let $\mathfrak{L} = (L, \tilde{L})$. Let $M$ be an $s$-state $2\mathrm{DFA}$ with $O(1)$ reversals for $\bigwedge\mathfrak{L}$. Then $M$ performs $< r_*$ reversals on every input of length $> n_*$, for some $r_*, n_*$. Let $Q = \{0, \ldots, s-1\}$ be the state set of $M$, and let $m_* := \max(r_*, n_*)$.

Pick any $x \in L$. Then $w := \#(x\#)^{m_*}$ is a positive of $\bigwedge\mathfrak{L}$. So, $c := \mathrm{COMP}_M(w)$ is accepting. Since $|w| \geq m_* + 1 > n_*$, the reversals in $c$ are $< r_* \leq m_*$, hence fewer than the copies of $x$ in $w$. So, on some of these copies, $c$ performs $0$ reversals.

Fix any of the copies with $0$ reversals. On it, $c$ consists of $t \leq 2s$ one-way traversals (one-way, since there
are $0$ reversals; and $\leq 2s$, or else $c$ would repeat a state
on the first cell of $x$, and loop). Let $\bar{p}_x := (p_1, \ldots, p_t)$
and $\bar{q}_x := (q_1, \ldots, q_t)$ be the crossing sequences of $c$ on
the outer boundaries of the particular copy of $x$.

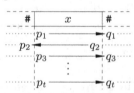

Let $\mathcal{C} := \{(\bar{p}_x, \bar{q}_x) \mid x \in L\}$ be all crossing-sequence pairs created like this.

*Definition.* A pair $(\bar{p}, \bar{q})$ of $t$-long sequences of states of $M$ is a *certificate* for an instance $x$ of $\mathfrak{L}$ if (i) it is in $\mathcal{C}$, and
(ii) For every odd $i = 1, \ldots, t$: $\mathrm{LCOMP}_{M,p_i}(x)$ is one-way and hits right into $q_i$.
(iii) For every even $i = 1, \ldots, t$: $\mathrm{RCOMP}_{M,q_i}(x)$ is one-way and hits left into $p_i$.

*Claim.* An instance of $\mathfrak{L}$ is positive iff it has a certificate.

Hence, to solve $\mathfrak{L}$, a $\mathrm{P_{21}DFA}$ $P := (\{A_p \mid p \in Q\}, \{B_p \mid p \in Q\}, F)$ searches for a certificate. Each component $A_p$ (resp., $B_p$) simulates $M$ from $p$ for as long as it moves right (left); if $M$ ever attempts to reverse, the component hangs. Thus, on input $x$, $P$ simulates $M$ from every state and in either fixed direction, covering all possible one-way traversals of $x$. In the end, $P$ checks whether $x$ has a certificate by comparing the results of these $2s$ computations against every $(\bar{p}, \bar{q}) \in \mathcal{C}$. Formally, for each $\bar{p} = (p_1, \ldots, p_t)$ and $\bar{q} = (q_1, \ldots, q_t)$ we let $F_{(\bar{p}, \bar{q})}$ be the set of all $2s$-tuples that we can build from two copies of $Q$

$$( \ 0, 1, \ldots, s-1, \ \ 0, 1, \ldots, s-1 \ ),$$

by replacing (i) every odd-indexed $p_i$ in the left copy with the respective $q_i$ (so that $A_{p_i}$ hits right into $q_i$); (ii) every even-indexed $q_i$ in the right copy with the respective $p_i$ (so that $B_{q_i}$ hits left into $p_i$) and (iii) all other states in either copy with any result in $Q \cup \{\bot\}$ (to let all other 1DFAs free). Thus, $F_{(\overline{p}, \overline{q})}$ is all tuples which prove that $(\overline{p}, \overline{q})$ is a certificate. Finally, we let $F := \bigcup_{(\overline{p}, \overline{q}) \in \mathcal{C}} F_{(\overline{p}, \overline{q})}$. $\square$

We now prove that $\mathcal{R} \notin 2D[O(1)]$. This follows by applying Lemmas 2, 4–6 to the fact that $\neg\mathrm{MEMBERSHIP}^R \notin 1D$. For brevity, we let $\mathfrak{M}_h := \mathrm{MEMBERSHIP}_h$.

1. No $(2^h - 2)$-state 1DFA solves $\neg\mathfrak{M}_h^R$, by a proof similar to that of Sect. 2.1.
2. No $\cap_{l1}$DFA with $(2^h - 2)$-state components solves $\bigvee \neg\mathfrak{M}_h^R$, by 1 and Lemma 4.
3. No $\cup_{l1}$DFA with $(2^h - 3)$-state components solves $\bigwedge \mathfrak{M}_h^R$, by 2 and Lemma 2b.
4. No $\cup_{R1}$DFA with $(2^h - 3)$-state components solves $\bigwedge \mathfrak{M}_h$, by 3 and Lemma 2a.
5. Every $\mathrm{P}_{21}$DFA for $\bigwedge \mathfrak{M}_h^R < \bigwedge \mathfrak{M}_h$ has at least one $\Omega(2^{h/2})$-state component, by 3, 4, and Lemma 5.
6. Every $O(1)$-reversal 2DFA for $\mathfrak{R}_h$ has $\Omega(2^{h/2})$ states, by 5 and Lemma 6.

This proves the lower bound for $\mathcal{R}$, completing the proof that $2D[O(1)] \not\supseteq 1U$.

## 5 Conclusion

This was an introduction to the *complexity of two-way finite automata*, or *minicomplexity*. We presented it within the Sakoda-Sipser framework, to emphasize the tight analogy with standard TM-complexity. We believe that this view helps reveal important structure, which otherwise passes unnoticed. This is, of course, a coarse view, which is unable to distinguish beyond polynomial differences. For finer views, at the level of asymptotic or exact values, one should resort to the more standard vocabulary in terms of 'trade-offs'.

We focused on one-way and two-way heads and on deterministic, nondeterministic, and alternating modes. However, minicomplexity also includes other heads (rotating, sweeping) and other standard modes from TM-complexity (probabilistic, quantum, interactive); see [14] for a broader view. It can also mimic TM-complexity in other ways. E.g., see [17] for a first step towards *descriptive minicomplexity*, where minicomplexity classes receive logical characterizations.

The selection of the presented material reflects this author's immediate interests and space restrictions. The effort to systematically record, organize, and present material of this kind continues online, at www.minicomplexity.org.

**Acknowledgment.** Many thanks to Viliam Geffert for his kind help with some of his theorems from [4] concerning alternating 2FAs.

## References

1. Barnes, B.H.: A two-way automaton with fewer states than any equivalent one-way automaton. IEEE Transactions on Computers C-20(4), 474–475 (1971)
2. Berman, P., Lingas, A.: On complexity of regular languages in terms of finite automata. Report 304, Institute of Computer Science, Polish Academy of Sciences, Warsaw (1977)

3. Birget, J.C.: Two-way automata and length-preserving homomorphisms. Mathematical Systems Theory 29, 191–226 (1996)
4. Geffert, V.: An alternating hierarchy for finite automata. Theoretical Computer Science (to appear)
5. Geffert, V., Guillon, B., Pighizzini, G.: Two-Way Automata Making Choices Only at the Endmarkers. In: Dediu, A.-H., Martín-Vide, C. (eds.) LATA 2012. LNCS, vol. 7183, pp. 264–276. Springer, Heidelberg (2012)
6. Geffert, V., Mereghetti, C., Pighizzini, G.: Converting two-way nondeterministic unary automata into simpler automata. Theoretical Computer Science 295, 189–203 (2003)
7. Geffert, V., Mereghetti, C., Pighizzini, G.: Complementing two-way finite automata. Information and Computation 205(8), 1173–1187 (2007)
8. Hromkovič, J., Schnitger, G.: Nondeterminism Versus Determinism for Two-Way Finite Automata: Generalizations of Sipser's Separation. In: Baeten, J.C.M., Lenstra, J.K., Parrow, J., Woeginger, G.J. (eds.) ICALP 2003. LNCS, vol. 2719, pp. 439–451. Springer, Heidelberg (2003)
9. Kapoutsis, C.A.: Nondeterminism is essential in small two-way finite automata with few reversals. Information and Computation (to appear)
10. Kapoutsis, C.A.: Removing Bidirectionality from Nondeterministic Finite Automata. In: Jedrzejowicz, J., Szepietowski, A. (eds.) MFCS 2005. LNCS, vol. 3618, pp. 544–555. Springer, Heidelberg (2005)
11. Kapoutsis, C.A.: Algorithms and lower bounds in finite automata size complexity. Phd thesis, Massachusetts Institute of Technology (June 2006)
12. Kapoutsis, C.A.: Small Sweeping 2NFAs Are Not Closed Under Complement. In: Bugliesi, M., Preneel, B., Sassone, V., Wegener, I. (eds.) ICALP 2006. LNCS, vol. 4051, pp. 144–156. Springer, Heidelberg (2006)
13. Kapoutsis, C.A.: Deterministic moles cannot solve liveness. Journal of Automata, Languages and Combinatorics 12(1-2), 215–235 (2007)
14. Kapoutsis, C.A.: Size Complexity of Two-Way Finite Automata. In: Diekert, V., Nowotka, D. (eds.) DLT 2009. LNCS, vol. 5583, pp. 47–66. Springer, Heidelberg (2009)
15. Kapoutsis, C.A.: Two-Way Automata versus Logarithmic Space. In: Kulikov, A., Vereshchagin, N. (eds.) CSR 2011. LNCS, vol. 6651, pp. 359–372. Springer, Heidelberg (2011)
16. Kapoutsis, C.A., Královič, R., Mömke, T.: On the Size Complexity of Rotating and Sweeping Automata. In: Ito, M., Toyama, M. (eds.) DLT 2008. LNCS, vol. 5257, pp. 455–466. Springer, Heidelberg (2008)
17. Kapoutsis, C.A., Lefebvre, N.: Analogs of Fagin's Theorem for small nondeterministic finite automata. In: Proceedings of DLT (to appear, 2012)
18. Kapoutsis, C.A., Pighizzini, G.: Reversal hierarchies for small 2DFAs (submitted)
19. Kapoutsis, C.A., Pighizzini, G.: Two-way automata characterizations of L/poly versus NL. In: Proceedings of CSR, pp. 222–233 (2012)
20. Kozen, D.C.: Automata and computability. Springer (1997)
21. Meyer, A.R., Fischer, M.J.: Economy of description by automata, grammars, and formal systems. In: Proceedings of FOCS, pp. 188–191 (1971)
22. Moore, F.R.: On the bounds for state-set size in the proofs of equivalence between deterministic, nondeterministic, and two-way finite automata. IEEE Transactions on Computers 20(10), 1211–1214 (1971)

23. Rabin, M.O., Scott, D.: Finite automata and their decision problems. IBM Journal of Research and Development 3, 114–125 (1959)

24. Sakoda, W.J., Sipser, M.: Nondeterminism and the size of two-way finite automata. In: Proceedings of STOC, pp. 275–286 (1978)

25. Savitch, W.J.: Relationships between nondeterministic and deterministic tape complexities. Journal of Computer and System Sciences 4, 177–192 (1970)

26. Seiferas, J.I.: Untitled (October 1973), manuscript

27. Shepherdson, J.C.: The reduction of two-way automata to one-way automata. IBM Journal of Research and Development 3, 198–200 (1959)

28. Sipser, M.: Halting space-bounded computations. Theoretical Computer Science 10, 335–338 (1980)

29. Sipser, M.: Lower bounds on the size of sweeping automata. Journal of Computer and System Sciences 21(2), 195–202 (1980)

30. Sipser, M.: Introduction to the theory of computation. Thomson Course Technology, 2nd edn. (2006)

31. Szepietowski, A.: If deterministic and nondeterministic space complexities are equal for $\log \log n$ then they are also equal for $\log n$. In: Proceedings of STACS, pp. 251–255 (1989)

# Notes

$^{(1)}$MEMBERSHIP: Introduced in [16, p. 459], as a problem whose reverse can be used as 'core' for building witnesses of separations of complexity classes. See also [9, Eq. (7)].

$^{(2)}$SORTED ∃EQUALITY: Introduced in [21, Prop. 3] (essentially), as a problem whose reverse has logarithmically-small 1-pebble 2DFAs, but admits no small 1DFAs.

$^{(3)}$PROJECTION: Introduced in [21, Prop. 2] (essentially), as a problem whose reverse witnesses the asymptotic value of the trade-off in converting 2DFAs to 1DFAs.

$^{(4)}$COMPOSITION: Introduced in [22, p. 1213] (essentially), as a problem which witnesses the asymptotic value of the trade-off in converting 2DFAs to 1DFAs.

$^{(5)}$RETROCOUNT: Introduced in [21] (attributed to M. Paterson), as a simple problem which witnesses the asymptotic value of the trade-off in converting 1NFAs to 1DFAs.

$^{(6)}$SHORT RETROCOUNT: Introduced in [21] (essentially), for restricting RETROCOUNT to finitely many instances which still admit no small 1DFAs.

$^{(7)}$DISJOINTNESS: A classic, from Communication Complexity.

$^{(8)}$ROLL CALL: Introduced in [1] (essentially), as a witnesss of 2D \ 1D.

$^{(9)}$EQUAL ENDS: Introduced in [26, Prop. 2], as a problem which has small general 2DFAs but no small single-pass 2DFAs.

$^{(10)}$SHORT EQUAL ENDS: Introduced in [26, Prop. 1] (essentially), as a problem which has small single-pass 2DFAs but no small 1NFAs.

$^{(11)}$LENGTH: Introduced in [21, Prop. 4], as a problem against which 1NFAs are forced to stay essentially as large as 1DFAs.

$^{(12)}$ONE-WAY LIVENESS: Introduced in [24, §2.1], as the first 1N-complete problem.

$^{(13)}$SEPARABILITY: Introduced in [26, p. 1], as a problem that has small 1NFAs but no small single-pass 2DFAs, and is also conjectured to have no small general 2DFAs.

$^{(14)}$ZERO-SAFE PROGRAMS: Introduced in [26, p. 2] (essentially), as a problem which appears to be "easier" than SEPARABILITY but still hard enough to have no small 2DFAs.

$^{(15)}$RELATIONAL MATCH: Introduced in [19], for describing a conjecture which is equivalent to COMPACT TWL $\not\subseteq$ 2D.

$^{(16)}$RELATIONAL PATH: Introduced in [11] (essentially), as a problem which witnesses the exact value of the trade-off in converting 2NFAs to 1DFAs.

[17] FUNCTIONAL MATCH: Introduced in [19], as a restriction of RELATIONAL MATCH, useful for describing a conjecture equivalent to COMPACT TWL $\not\subseteq$ 2D.

[18] FUNCTIONAL PATH: Introduced in [10,11], as a problem which witnesses the exact value of the trade-off in converting 2NFAs or 2DFAs to 1NFAs, and 2DFAs to 1DFAs.

[19] FUNCTIONAL ZERO-MATCH: Introduced in [19], for facilitating reductions.

[20] RELATIONAL ZERO-MATCH: Introduced in [19], for facilitating reductions.

[21] TWO-WAY LIVENESS: Introduced in [24, §2.1], as the first 2N-complete problem.

[22] COMPACT TWL: Introduced in [19], for stating a conjecture that implies $\mathsf{L/poly} \not\supseteq \mathsf{NL}$.

[23] ∃INCLUSION: Introduced in [4] (essentially), as a problem whose reverse can be used as 'core' for building witnesses for all $1\Sigma_k \setminus 2\Pi_k$ and $1\Pi_k \setminus 2\Sigma_k$, where $k \geq 2$.

[24] SHORT TWL: Introduced in [19], as a problem complete for 2N/poly under $\leq_h$.

# Logical Analysis of Hybrid Systems*
## A Complete Answer to a Complexity Challenge

André Platzer

Computer Science Department, Carnegie Mellon University,
Pittsburgh, USA
aplatzer@cs.cmu.edu

**Abstract.** Hybrid systems have a complete axiomatization in differential dynamic logic relative to continuous systems. They also have a complete axiomatization relative to discrete systems. Moreover, there is a constructive reduction of properties of hybrid systems to corresponding properties of continuous systems or to corresponding properties of discrete systems. We briefly summarize and discuss some of the implications of these results.

## 1 Overview

Hybrid systems [2,6,11] are dynamical systems that combine discrete and continuous dynamics. They are important for modeling embedded systems and cyber-physical systems. Hybrid systems are very natural models for many application scenarios, especially because each part of the system can be modeled in the most natural way. Discrete aspects of the system, e.g., discrete switching, computing, and control decisions can be modeled by discrete dynamics. Continuous aspects of the system, e.g., motion or continuous physical processes can be modeled by continuous dynamics. And hybrid systems simply combine either kind of dynamics with each other as one hybrid system in very flexible ways.

This flexibility makes hybrid systems very natural for system modeling. Even very complicated systems can be modeled as hybrid systems. Yet, reachability in hybrid systems is undecidable [11]. Even purely discrete systems are already undecidable, as witnessed by the halting problem. And even purely continuous systems are already undecidable [23, Theorem 2]. Are hybrid systems fundamentally more difficult than purely discrete or purely continuous systems? Or do they only add natural ways of expressing system models without causing additional complexities that are fundamentally more difficult to solve? Are hybrid systems more complex than discrete systems? Are they more complex than

---

* This material is based upon work supported by the National Science Foundation under NSF CAREER Award CNS-1054246, NSF EXPEDITION CNS-0926181, and under Grant Nos. CNS-1035800 and CNS-0931985, by the ONR award N00014-10-1-0188, by the Army Research Office under Award No. W911NF-09-1-0273, and by the German Research Council (DFG) as part of the Transregional Collaborative Research Center "Automatic Verification and Analysis of Complex Systems" (SFB/TR 14 AVACS).

M. Kutrib, N. Moreira, and R. Reis (Eds.): DCFS 2012, LNCS 7386, pp. 43–49, 2012.

continuous systems? And: are continuous systems more complex or are discrete systems more complex?

Since hybrid systems combine two independent sources of undecidability, discrete and continuous dynamics, the first intuition may be that hybrid systems should be fundamentally more difficult than either of the fragments. That turns out not to be the case, because there are complete proof-theoretical alignments of the discrete dynamics, continuous dynamics, and hybrid dynamics [23, 30]. In this paper, we explain a few of the consequences of these results.

For background on logic for hybrid systems, we refer to the literature [23, 26, 31]. Dynamic logic [39] has been developed and used very successfully for conventional discrete programs, both for theoretical [7–10,12,14,15,18,20,21,42] and practical purposes [4,9,40]. We refer to other sources for more detail on dynamic logic for hybrid systems [22–26, 30]. Logic of hybrid systems has been used to obtain interesting theoretical results [22–30, 32], while, at the same time, enabling the practical verification of complex applications across different fields [3, 16, 17, 19, 24, 26, 35, 37, 41] and inspiring algorithmic logic-based verification approaches [24, 26, 33, 34, 36, 38, 41]. Extensions to logic for distributed hybrid systems [27, 29] and logic for stochastic hybrid systems [28] can be found elsewhere.

## 2    Differential Dynamic Logic

Differential dynamic logic d$\mathcal{L}$ [22, 23, 30, 31] is a dynamic logic [39] for hybrid systems [6, 11]. To set the stage, we give a brief introduction to d$\mathcal{L}$. We refer to previous work [23, 26, 30, 31] for more details.

**Regular Hybrid Programs.** We use (regular) *hybrid programs* (HP) [23] as hybrid system models. HPs form a Kleene algebra with tests [13]. The *atomic HPs* are instantaneous discrete jump *assignments* $x := \theta$, *tests* $?H$ of a first-order formula[1] $H$ of real arithmetic, and *differential equation (systems)* $x' = \theta \,\&\, H$ for a continuous evolution restricted to the domain of evolution described by a first-order formula $H$. Compound HPs are generated from these atomic HPs by nondeterministic choice ($\cup$), sequential composition (;), and Kleene's nondeterministic repetition (*). We use polynomials with rational coefficients as terms. HPs are defined by the following grammar ($\alpha, \beta$ are HPs, $x$ a variable, $\theta$ a term possibly containing $x$, and $H$ a formula of first-order logic of real arithmetic):

$$\alpha, \beta \ ::= \ x := \theta \ | \ ?H \ | \ x' = \theta \,\&\, H \ | \ \alpha \cup \beta \ | \ \alpha; \beta \ | \ \alpha^*$$

The first three cases are called atomic HPs, the last three compound HPs. These operations can define all hybrid systems [26]. We, e.g., write $x' = \theta$ for the unrestricted differential equation $x' = \theta \,\&\, true$. We allow differential equation systems and use vectorial notation. Vectorial assignments are definable from scalar assignments (and ;).

---

[1] The test $?H$ means "if $H$ then *skip* else *abort*".

A *state* $\nu$ is a mapping from variables to $\mathbb{R}$. Hence $\nu(x) \in \mathbb{R}$ is the value of variable $x$ in state $\nu$. The set of states is denoted $\mathcal{S}$. We denote the value of term $\theta$ in $\nu$ by $\nu[\![\theta]\!]$. Each HP $\alpha$ is interpreted semantically as a binary reachability relation $\rho(\alpha)$ over states, defined inductively by:

- $\rho(x := \theta) = \{(\nu, \omega) : \omega = \nu$ except that $\omega[\![x]\!] = \nu[\![\theta]\!]\}$
- $\rho(?H) = \{(\nu, \nu) : \nu \models H\}$
- $\rho(x' = \theta \,\&\, H) = \{(\varphi(0), \varphi(r)) : \varphi(t) \models x' = \theta$ and $\varphi(t) \models H$ for all $0 \le t \le r$ for a solution $\varphi : [0, r] \to \mathcal{S}$ of any duration $r\}$;
  i.e., with $\varphi(t)(x') \overset{\text{def}}{=} \frac{d\varphi(\zeta)(x)}{d\zeta}(t)$, $\varphi$ solves the differential equation and satisfies $H$ at all times [23]
- $\rho(\alpha \cup \beta) = \rho(\alpha) \cup \rho(\beta)$
- $\rho(\alpha; \beta) = \rho(\beta) \circ \rho(\alpha)$
- $\rho(\alpha^*) = \bigcup_{n \in \mathbb{N}} \rho(\alpha^n)$ with $\alpha^{n+1} \equiv \alpha^n; \alpha$ and $\alpha^0 \equiv ?true$.

We refer to our book [26] for a comprehensive background. We also refer to [23,26] for an elaboration how the case $r = 0$ (in which the only condition is $\varphi(0) \models H$) is captured by the above definition.

**d$\mathcal{L}$ Formulas.** The *formulas of differential dynamic logic* (d$\mathcal{L}$) are defined by the grammar (where $\phi, \psi$ are d$\mathcal{L}$ formulas, $\theta_1, \theta_2$ terms, $x$ a variable, $\alpha$ a HP):

$$\phi, \psi ::= \theta_1 \ge \theta_2 \mid \neg\phi \mid \phi \wedge \psi \mid \forall x\, \phi \mid [\alpha]\phi$$

The *satisfaction relation* $\nu \models \phi$ is as usual in first-order logic (of real arithmetic) with the addition that $\nu \models [\alpha]\phi$ iff $\omega \models \phi$ for all $\omega$ with $(\nu, \omega) \in \rho(\alpha)$. The operator $\langle \alpha \rangle$ dual to $[\alpha]$ is defined by $\langle \alpha \rangle \phi \equiv \neg[\alpha]\neg\phi$. Consequently, $\nu \models \langle \alpha \rangle \phi$ iff $\omega \models \phi$ for some $\omega$ with $(\nu, \omega) \in \rho(\alpha)$. Operators $=, >, \le, <, \vee, \to, \leftrightarrow, \exists x$ can be defined as usual in first-order logic. A d$\mathcal{L}$ formula $\phi$ is *valid*, written $\models \phi$, iff $\nu \models \phi$ for all states $\nu$.

## 3  Complete Relations

Even though hybrid systems are very expressive, they nevertheless have a complete axiomatization in differential dynamic logic d$\mathcal{L}$ [23,30] relative to elementary properties of differential equations. The completeness notions are inspired by those of Cook [5] and Harel et al. [10], yet different, because the data logic of hybrid systems is perfectly decidable (first-order real arithmetic). Using the proof calculus of d$\mathcal{L}$, the problem of proving properties of hybrid systems reduces to proving properties of continuous systems [23]. Furthermore, the proof calculus of d$\mathcal{L}$ reduces the problem of proving properties of hybrid systems to proving properties of discrete systems [30].

FOD is the *first-order logic of differential equations*, i.e., first-order real arithmetic augmented with formulas expressing properties of differential equations, that is, d$\mathcal{L}$ formulas of the form $[x' = \theta]F$ with a first-order formula $F$. We have shown that the d$\mathcal{L}$ calculus is a sound and complete axiomatization relative to FOD.

**Theorem 1 (Continuous relative completeness of d$\mathcal{L}$ [23, 30]).** *The* d$\mathcal{L}$ *calculus is a* sound and complete axiomatization *of hybrid systems relative to its continuous fragment FOD, i.e., every valid* d$\mathcal{L}$ *formula can be derived from FOD tautologies:*

$$\vDash \phi \ \textit{iff} \ \text{Taut}_{FOD} \vdash \phi$$

In particular, if we want to prove properties of hybrid systems, all we need to do is to, instead, prove properties of continuous systems, because the d$\mathcal{L}$ calculus completely handles all other steps in the proofs that deal with discrete or hybrid systems. Since the proof of Theorem 1 is constructive, there even is a complete constructive reduction of properties of hybrid systems to corresponding properties of continuous systems. The d$\mathcal{L}$ calculus can prove hybrid systems properties exactly as good as properties of the corresponding continuous systems can be verified. One important step in the proof of Theorem 1 shows that all required invariants and variants for repetitions can be expressed in the logic d$\mathcal{L}$. Furthermore, the d$\mathcal{L}$ calculus defines a decision procedure for d$\mathcal{L}$ sentences (closed formulas) relative to an oracle for FOD.

This result implies that the continuous dynamics dominates the discrete dynamics for once the continuous dynamics is handled, all discrete and hybrid dynamics can be handled as well. This is reassuring, because we get the challenges of discrete dynamics solved for free (i.e., by the d$\mathcal{L}$ calculus) once we address continuous dynamics.

However, in a certain sense, continuous dynamics may appear to be more complicated to handle by discrete proof systems than continuous dynamics. After all, computers are discrete, so mechanized proofs on computers will ultimately need to understand continuous effects from a purely discrete perspective. If the continuous dynamics are not just subsuming discrete dynamics but were inherently more, then that could be understood as an indicator that hybrid systems verification is fundamentally impossible with discrete means. Of course, if this were the case, the argument would not even be quite so simple, because meta-proofs may still enable discrete finitary proof objects to entail infinite continuous object-properties. In fact, they do, because finite d$\mathcal{L}$ proof objects entail properties in uncountable continuous spaces.

Fortunately, we can settle worries about the insufficiency of discrete ways of understanding continuous phenomena once and for all by studying the proof-theoretical relationship between discrete and continuous dynamics. We have shown not only that the axiomatization of d$\mathcal{L}$ is complete relative to the continuous fragment, but that it is also complete relative to the discrete fragment [30]. The *discrete fragment* of d$\mathcal{L}$ is denoted by DL, i.e., the fragment without differential equations. It is, in fact, sufficient to restrict DL to the operators $:=, ^*$ and allow either ; or vector assignments.

**Theorem 2 (Discrete relative completeness of d$\mathcal{L}$ [30]).** *The* d$\mathcal{L}$ *calculus is a* sound and complete axiomatization *of hybrid systems relative to its discrete fragment DL, i.e., every valid* d$\mathcal{L}$ *formula can be derived from DL tautologies.*

$$\vDash \phi \ \textit{iff} \ \text{Taut}_{DL} \vdash \phi$$

Thus, the d$\mathcal{L}$ calculus can prove properties of hybrid systems exactly as good as properties of discrete systems can be proved. Again, the proof of Theorem 2 is constructive, entailing that there is a constructive way of reducing properties of hybrid systems to properties of discrete systems using the d$\mathcal{L}$ calculus. Furthermore, the d$\mathcal{L}$ calculus defines a decision procedure for d$\mathcal{L}$ sentences relative to an oracle for DL.

As a corollary to Theorems 1 and 2, we can proof-theoretically and constructively equate

$$\text{hybrid} = \text{continuous} = \text{discrete}$$

Even though each kind of dynamics comes from fundamentally different principles, they all meet in terms of their proof problems being interreducible, even constructively. The complexity of the proof problem of hybrid systems, the complexity of the proof problem of continuous systems, and the complexity of the proof problem of discrete systems are, thus, equivalent.

Since the proof problems interreduce constructively, every technique that is successful for one kind of dynamics perfectly lifts to the other kind of dynamics through the d$\mathcal{L}$ calculus. Induction is the primary technique for proving properties of discrete systems. Hence, by Theorem 2, there is a corresponding induction technique for continuous systems and for hybrid systems. And, indeed, *differential invariants* [25] are such an induction technique for differential equations that has been used very successfully for hybrid systems with more advanced differential equations [26, 33–35, 37]. Differential invariants had already been introduced in 2008 [25] before Theorem 2 was proved [30], but Theorem 2 implies that a differential invariant induction technique has to exist.

## 4    Conclusions and Future Work

We have summarized recent results about complete axiomatizations of hybrid systems relative to continuous systems and relative to discrete systems. These axiomatizations equate the proof problems for all three classes of systems and align the complexity of the their proof problems. Practical consequences of this result include differential invariants and the utility of discretization schemes, but many other consequences are just waiting to be discovered.

## References

1. Proceedings of the 27th Annual ACM/IEEE Symposium on Logic in Computer Science, LICS 2012, Dubrovnik, Croatia, June 25-28. IEEE Computer Society (2012)
2. Alur, R., Courcoubetis, C., Halbwachs, N., Henzinger, T.A., Ho, P.H., Nicollin, X., Olivero, A., Sifakis, J., Yovine, S.: The algorithmic analysis of hybrid systems. Theor. Comput. Sci. 138(1), 3–34 (1995)
3. Aréchiga, N., Loos, S.M., Platzer, A., Krogh, B.H.: Using theorem provers to guarantee closed-loop system properties. In: Tilbury, D. (ed.) ACC (2012)
4. Beckert, B., Hähnle, R., Schmitt, P.H. (eds.): Verification of Object-Oriented Software. LNCS (LNAI), vol. 4334. Springer, Heidelberg (2007)

5. Cook, S.A.: Soundness and completeness of an axiom system for program verification. SIAM J. Comput. 7(1), 70–90 (1978)
6. Davoren, J.M., Nerode, A.: Logics for hybrid systems. IEEE 88(7), 985–1010 (2000)
7. Fischer, M.J., Ladner, R.E.: Propositional dynamic logic of regular programs. J. Comput. Syst. Sci. 18(2), 194–211 (1979)
8. Harel, D.: First-Order Dynamic Logic. Springer, New York (1979)
9. Harel, D., Kozen, D., Tiuryn, J.: Dynamic logic. MIT Press, Cambridge (2000)
10. Harel, D., Meyer, A.R., Pratt, V.R.: Computability and completeness in logics of programs (preliminary report). In: STOC, pp. 261–268. ACM (1977)
11. Henzinger, T.A.: The theory of hybrid automata. In: LICS, pp. 278–292. IEEE Computer Society, Los Alamitos (1996)
12. Istrail, S.: An arithmetical hierarchy in propositional dynamic logic. Inf. Comput. 81(3), 280–289 (1989)
13. Kozen, D.: Kleene algebra with tests. ACM Trans. Program. Lang. Syst. 19(3), 427–443 (1997)
14. Kozen, D., Parikh, R.: An elementary proof of the completeness of PDL. Theor. Comp. Sci. 14, 113–118 (1981)
15. Leivant, D.: Matching explicit and modal reasoning about programs: A proof theoretic delineation of dynamic logic. In: LICS, pp. 157–168. IEEE Computer Society (2006)
16. Loos, S.M., Platzer, A.: Safe intersections: At the crossing of hybrid systems and verification. In: Yi, K. (ed.) ITSC, pp. 1181–1186. Springer (2011)
17. Loos, S.M., Platzer, A., Nistor, L.: Adaptive Cruise Control: Hybrid, Distributed, and Now Formally Verified. In: Butler, M., Schulte, W. (eds.) FM 2011. LNCS, vol. 6664, pp. 42–56. Springer, Heidelberg (2011)
18. Meyer, A.R., Parikh, R.: Definability in dynamic logic. J. Comput. Syst. Sci. 23(2), 279–298 (1981)
19. Mitsch, S., Loos, S.M., Platzer, A.: Towards formal verification of freeway traffic control. In: Lu, C. (ed.) ICCPS, pp. 171–180. IEEE (2012)
20. Parikh, R.: The Completeness of Propositional Dynamic Logic. In: Winkowski, J. (ed.) MFCS 1978. LNCS, vol. 64, pp. 403–415. Springer, Heidelberg (1978)
21. Peleg, D.: Concurrent dynamic logic. J. ACM 34(2), 450–479 (1987)
22. Platzer, A.: Differential Dynamic Logic for Verifying Parametric Hybrid Systems. In: Olivetti, N. (ed.) TABLEAUX 2007. LNCS (LNAI), vol. 4548, pp. 216–232. Springer, Heidelberg (2007)
23. Platzer, A.: Differential dynamic logic for hybrid systems. J. Autom. Reas. 41(2), 143–189 (2008)
24. Platzer, A.: Differential Dynamic Logics: Automated Theorem Proving for Hybrid Systems. Ph.D. thesis, Department of Computing Science, University of Oldenburg (December 2008) (appeared with Springer)
25. Platzer, A.: Differential-algebraic dynamic logic for differential-algebraic programs. J. Log. Comput. 20(1), 309–352 (2010)
26. Platzer, A.: Logical Analysis of Hybrid Systems: Proving Theorems for Complex Dynamics. Springer, Heidelberg (2010)
27. Platzer, A.: Quantified Differential Dynamic Logic for Distributed Hybrid Systems. In: Dawar, A., Veith, H. (eds.) CSL 2010. LNCS, vol. 6247, pp. 469–483. Springer, Heidelberg (2010)
28. Platzer, A.: Stochastic Differential Dynamic Logic for Stochastic Hybrid Programs. In: Bjørner, N., Sofronie-Stokkermans, V. (eds.) CADE 2011. LNCS, vol. 6803, pp. 446–460. Springer, Heidelberg (2011)

29. Platzer, A.: A complete axiomatization of quantified differential dynamic logic for distributed hybrid systems. In: Logical Methods in Computer Science (2012); special issue for selected papers from CSL 2010
30. Platzer, A.: The complete proof theory of hybrid systems. In: LICS [1]
31. Platzer, A.: Logics of dynamical systems (invited tutorial). In: LICS [1]
32. Platzer, A.: The structure of differential invariants and differential cut elimination. In: Logical Methods in Computer Science (to appear, 2012)
33. Platzer, A., Clarke, E.M.: Computing Differential Invariants of Hybrid Systems as Fixedpoints. In: Gupta, A., Malik, S. (eds.) CAV 2008. LNCS, vol. 5123, pp. 176–189. Springer, Heidelberg (2008)
34. Platzer, A., Clarke, E.M.: Computing differential invariants of hybrid systems as fixedpoints. Form. Methods Syst. Des. 35(1), 98–120 (2009); special issue for selected papers from CAV 2008
35. Platzer, A., Clarke, E.M.: Formal Verification of Curved Flight Collision Avoidance Maneuvers: A Case Study. In: Cavalcanti, A., Dams, D.R. (eds.) FM 2009. LNCS, vol. 5850, pp. 547–562. Springer, Heidelberg (2009)
36. Platzer, A., Quesel, J.-D.: KeYmaera: A Hybrid Theorem Prover for Hybrid Systems (System Description). In: Armando, A., Baumgartner, P., Dowek, G. (eds.) IJCAR 2008. LNCS (LNAI), vol. 5195, pp. 171–178. Springer, Heidelberg (2008)
37. Platzer, A., Quesel, J.-D.: European Train Control System: A Case Study in Formal Verification. In: Breitman, K., Cavalcanti, A. (eds.) ICFEM 2009. LNCS, vol. 5885, pp. 246–265. Springer, Heidelberg (2009)
38. Platzer, A., Quesel, J.-D., Rümmer, P.: Real World Verification. In: Schmidt, R.A. (ed.) CADE 2009. LNCS, vol. 5663, pp. 485–501. Springer, Heidelberg (2009)
39. Pratt, V.R.: Semantical considerations on Floyd-Hoare logic. In: FOCS, pp. 109–121. IEEE (1976)
40. Reif, W., Schellhorn, G., Stenzel, K.: Proving System Correctness with KIV 3.0. In: McCune, W. (ed.) CADE 1997. LNCS, vol. 1249, pp. 69–72. Springer, Heidelberg (1997)
41. Renshaw, D.W., Loos, S.M., Platzer, A.: Distributed Theorem Proving for Distributed Hybrid Systems. In: Qin, S., Qiu, Z. (eds.) ICFEM 2011. LNCS, vol. 6991, pp. 356–371. Springer, Heidelberg (2011)
42. Segerberg, K.: A completeness theorem in the modal logic of programs. Notices AMS 24, 522 (1977)

# Groups and Automata: A Perfect Match

Pedro V. Silva

Centro de Matemática, Faculdade de Ciências, Universidade do Porto,
R. Campo Alegre 687, 4169-007 Porto, Portugal
pvsilva@fc.up.pt

**Abstract.** We present a personal perspective, inspired by our own research experience, of the interaction between group theory and automata
theory: from Benois' Theorem to Stallings' automata, from hyperbolic
to automatic groups, not forgetting the exotic automaton groups.

## 1 Introduction

Among abstract structures, it is groups which model the idea of symmetry in
Mathematics. Moreover, the existence of inverses makes them a natural model
for reversibility in theoretical computer science (see [37] for a model for *partial
reversibility*). At the present time, when quantum computation gives its first
steps (note than in quantum mechanics transformations are always assumed reversible), it is appropriate to make the history of the interaction between group
theory and automata theory, undoubtedly the branch of theoretical computer
science which has been playing the major role in the development of combinatorial and geometric group theory.

We intend this text to be a brief and light account of these interactions, under
a personal perspective which emerged from our own work on the subject, and
relating to our talk at DCFS 2012. We therefore chose to leave out finite groups
(and the connections with group languages), being out of our own experience.
Anyway, such connections are well known in theoretical computer science and
can be easily found in the literature on finite automata [8,32].

A deeper and more extended survey on the interactions groups/automata can
be found out in two Handbook chapters written by Bartholdi and the author [5,4].

We shall pay special attention to free groups: we introduce them in Section 2,
discuss language-theoretic concepts in Section 3 and the representation of finitely
generated subgroups by automata in Section 4. We shall also explain the role
played by automata in the study of three important classes of groups: hyperbolic
groups in Section 5, automatic groups in Section 6 and automaton groups (also
known as self-similar groups) in Section 7. In Section 8, we present an example of
our recent research combining automata-theoretic and group-theoretic results.

We assume the reader to be familiar with the basic concepts of language
theory and automata theory, and to know the most basic definitions of group
theory. Throughout the whole paper, we assume alphabets to be *finite*.

M. Kutrib, N. Moreira, and R. Reis (Eds.): DCFS 2012, LNCS 7386, pp. 50–63, 2012.

## 2  Free Groups

We start by introducing free groups. Informally, the free group on $A$ is supposed to be the most general group $F_A$ we can generate from a given set $A$, in the sense that every other group generated by $A$ turns out to be a quotient of $F_A$. Hence free groups play pretty much in the context of groups the same role that free monoids play in the context of monoids.

We present now the formal definition. Given an alphabet $A$, we denote by $A^{-1}$ a set of *formal inverses* of $A$. We write $\widetilde{A} = A \cup A^{-1}$ and $(a^{-1})^{-1} = a$ for every $a \in A$. The *free group on* $A$, denoted by $F_A$, is the quotient of $\widetilde{A}^*$ by the congruence generated by the relation

$$\mathcal{R}_A = \{(aa^{-1}, 1) \mid a \in \widetilde{A}\}.$$

Thus two words $u, v \in \widetilde{A}^*$ are equivalent in $F_A$ if and only if one can be transformed into the other by successively inserting/deleting factors of the form $aa^{-1}$ ($a \in \widetilde{A}$). We denote by $\theta : \widetilde{A}^* \to F_A$ the canonical morphism.

We recall that a (finite) *rewriting system* on $A$ is a (finite) subset $\mathcal{R}$ of $A^* \times A^*$. Given $u, v \in A^*$, we write $u \longrightarrow_{\mathcal{R}} v$ if there exist $(r, s) \in \mathcal{R}$ and $x, y \in A^*$ such that $u = xry$ and $v = xsy$. The reflexive and transitive closure of $\longrightarrow_{\mathcal{R}}$ is denoted by $\longrightarrow_{\mathcal{R}}^*$.

We say that $\mathcal{R}$ is:

- *length-reducing* if $|r| > |s|$ for every $(r, s) \in \mathcal{R}$;
- *confluent* if, whenever $u \longrightarrow_{\mathcal{R}}^* v$ and $u \longrightarrow_{\mathcal{R}}^* w$, there exists some $z \in A^*$ such that $v \longrightarrow_{\mathcal{R}}^* z$ and $w \longrightarrow_{\mathcal{R}}^* z$.

A word $u \in A^*$ is an *irreducible* if no $v \in A^*$ satisfies $u \longrightarrow_{\mathcal{R}} v$. We denote by Irr $\mathcal{R}$ the set of all irreducible words in $A^*$ with respect to $\mathcal{R}$.

If $\mathcal{R}$ is symmetric, then $\tau = \longrightarrow_{\mathcal{R}}^*$ is a congruence on $A^*$ and we can say that the pair $\langle A \mid \mathcal{R} \rangle$ constitutes a (monoid) *presentation*, defining the monoid $A^*/\tau$.

If we view $\mathcal{R}_A$ as a rewriting system on $\widetilde{A}$, then it turns out to be both length-reducing and confluent, and so, for every $g \in F_A$, $g\theta^{-1}$ contains a unique irreducible word, denoted by $\bar{g}$ (see [9]). We write also $\bar{u} = \overline{u\theta}$ for every $u \in \widetilde{A}^*$. Note that the equivalence $u\theta = v\theta \Leftrightarrow \bar{u} = \bar{v}$ holds for all $u, v \in \widetilde{A}^*$, providing the usual solution for the word problem of a free group (deciding whether two words on the generators represent the same element of the group). Thus the elements of a free group can be efficiently described as irreducible words. We denote by

$$R_A = \widetilde{A}^* \setminus (\cup_{a \in \widetilde{A}} \widetilde{A}^* aa^{-1} \widetilde{A}^*)$$

the set of all *irreducible words* in $\widetilde{A}^*$ for the rewriting system $\mathcal{R}_A$. Clearly, $R_A$ is a rational language.

## 3  Language Theory for Groups

If we follow Berstel's general approach to language theory [8], *rational* and *recognizable* emerge as two of the most important basic concepts. In this context, recognizable refers to finite syntactic monoids or recognizability by finite monoids.

Of course, both concepts coincide for free monoids (Kleene's Thorem [8, Theorem I.4.1]) but nor for arbitrary monoids. Given a monoid $M$, we denote by $\operatorname{Rat} M$ (respectively $\operatorname{Rec} M$) the set of all rational (respectively recognizable) subsets of $M$.

To understand the situation in the context of groups, we need the following classical result of Anisimov and Seifert:

**Proposition 31.** [8, Theorem III.2.7] *Let $H$ be a subgroup of a group $G$. Then $H \in \operatorname{Rat} G$ if and only if $H$ is finitely generated.*

The analogous result for recognizable is part of the folklore of the theory. We recall that a subgroup $H$ of $G$ has *finite index* if $G$ is a finite union of cosets $Hg$ $(g \in G)$.

**Proposition 32.** *Let $H$ be a subgroup of a group $G$. Then $H \in \operatorname{Rec} G$ if and only if $H$ has finite index in $G$.*

Since the trivial subgroup has finite index in $G$ if and only if $G$ is finite, it follows that $\operatorname{Rat} G = \operatorname{Rec} G$ if and only if $G$ is finite. In general, these two classes fail most nontrivial closure properties. However, free groups present a much better case, due to the seminal *Benois' Theorem*:

**Theorem 33.** [7]

   (i) *If $L \in \operatorname{Rat} \widetilde{A}^*$, then $\overline{L} \in \operatorname{Rat} \widetilde{A}^*$ and can be effectively constructed from $L$.*
   (ii) *If $X \subseteq F_A$, then $X \in \operatorname{Rat} G$ if and only if $\overline{X} \in \operatorname{Rat} \widetilde{A}^*$.*

The proof consists essentially on successively adding edges labelled by the empty word to an automaton recognizing $L$ (whenever a path is labelled by $aa^{-1}$ ($a \in \widetilde{A}$)) and intersecting in the end the corresponding language with the rational language $R_A$.

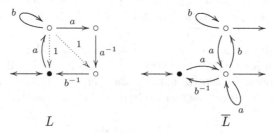

$$L \qquad\qquad\qquad \overline{L}$$

The following result summarizes some of the most direct consequences of Benois' Theorem:

**Corollary 34.** *(i) Every $X \in \operatorname{Rat} F_A$ is recursive.*
*(ii) $\operatorname{Rat} F_A$ is closed under the boolean operations.*

We remark that Theorem 33 has been successively adapted to groups/ monoids defined by more general classes of rewriting systems, the most general versions being due to Sénizergues [33,34].

Since $F_A$ is a finitely generated monoid, it follows that every recognizable subset of $F_A$ is rational [8, Proposition III.2.4]. The problem of deciding which rational subsets of $F_A$ are recognizable was first solved by Sénizergues [34]. A shorter alternative proof was presented by the author in [36], where a third alternative proof, of a more combinatorial nature, was also given.

These results are also related to the Sakarovitch conjecture [32], solved in [34] (see also [36]), which states that every rational subset of $F_A$ must be either recognizable or *disjunctive* (it has trivial syntactic congruence).

The quest for groups $G$ such that $\text{Rat}\,G$ enjoys good properties has spread over the years to wider classes of groups. An important case is given by *virtually free groups*, i.e. groups having a free subgroup of finite index, as remarked by Grunschlag [21]. In fact, in view of Nielsen's Theorem, this free subgroup can be assumed to be *normal* [27]. Virtually free groups will keep making unexpected appearances throughout this paper.

Another important case is given by free partially abelian groups (the group-theoretic version of trace monoids). Lohrey and Steinberg proved in [26] that the recursiveness of the rational subsets depends on the independence graph being a *transitive forest*.

A different idea of relating groups and language theory involves the classification of the set $1\pi^{-1} \subseteq \widetilde{A}^*$ which collects all the words representing the identity for a given matched surjective homomorphism $\pi : \widetilde{A}^* \to G$ (matched in the sense that $a^{-1}\pi = (a\pi)^{-1}$ for every $a \in A$). Clearly, $1\pi^{-1}$ determines the structure of $G$, and it is a simple exercise to show that $1\pi^{-1}$ is rational if and only if $G$ is finite. What about higher classes in the Chomsky's hierarchy? The celebrated theorem proved by Muller and Schupp (with a contribution from Dunwoody) states the following:

**Theorem 35.** [30,10] *Let* $\pi : \widetilde{A}^* \to G$ *be a matched homomorphism onto a group* $G$. *Then* $1\pi^{-1}$ *is a context-free language if and only if* $G$ *is virtually free.*

## 4   Stallings Automata

Finite automata became over the years the standard representation of finitely generated subgroups $H$ of a free group $F_A$. The *Stallings construction* constitutes a simple and efficient algorithm for building an automaton $\mathcal{S}(H)$ which can be used for solving the membership problem for $H$ in $F_A$ and many other applications. Many features of $\mathcal{S}(H)$, which has a geometric interpretation (the core of the Schreier graph of $H$) were (re)discovered over the years and were known to Reidemeister, Schreier, and particularly Serre [35]. One of the greatest contributions of Stallings [41] is certainly the algorithm to construct $\mathcal{S}(H)$: taking a finite set of generators $h_1, \ldots, h_m$ of $H$ in reduced form, we start with the so-called flower automaton $\mathcal{F}(H)$, where *petals* labelled by the words $h_i$ (and their inverse edges) are glued to a basepoint $q_0$ (both initial and terminal vertex):

Then we proceed by successively folding pairs of edges of the form $q \xleftarrow{a} p \xrightarrow{a} r$ until reaching a deterministic automaton. And we will have just built $\mathcal{S}(H)$. For details and applications of the Stallings construction, see [5,24,29].

The geometric interpretation of $\mathcal{S}(H)$ shows that its construction is independent of the finite set of generators of $H$ chosen at the beginning, and of the particular sequence of foldings followed. And the membership problem is a consequence of the following result:

**Theorem 41.** [41] *Let $H$ be a finitely generated subgroup of $F_A$ and let $u \in R_A$. Then $u$ represents an element of $H$ if and only if $u \in L(\mathcal{S}(H))$.*

The main reason for this is that any irreducible word representing an element of $H$ can be obtained by successively cancelling factors $aa^{-1}$ in a word accepted by the flower automaton of $H$, and folding edges is a geometric realization of such cancellations.

For instance, taking $H = \langle aba^{-1}, aba^2 \rangle$, we get

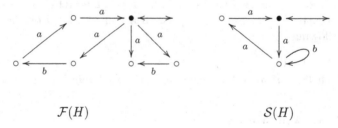

$$\mathcal{F}(H) \qquad\qquad\qquad \mathcal{S}(H)$$

We can then deduce that $a^3$ represents an element of $H$ but $a^4$ does not.

The applications of Stallings automata to the algorithmics of finitely generated subgroups of a free group are immense. One of the most important is the construction of a *basis* for $H$ (a free group itself by Nielsen's Theorem) using a *spanning tree* of $\mathcal{S}(H)$.

The following result illustrates how automata-theoretic properties of $\mathcal{S}(H)$ can determine group-theoretic properties of $H$:

**Proposition 42.** [41] *Let $H$ be a finitely generated subgroup of $F_A$. Then $H$ is a finite index subgroup of $F_A$ if and only if $\mathcal{S}(H)$ is a complete automaton.*

Note that Stallings automata constitute examples of *inverse* automata: they are deterministic, trim and $(p, a, q)$ is an edge if and only if $(q, a^{-1}, p)$ is an edge. Inverse automata play a major role in the geometric theories of groups and, more generally, inverse monoids [42].

The Stallings construction invites naturally generalizations for further classes of groups. For instance, an elegant geometric construction of Stallings type automata was achieved for amalgams of finite groups by Markus-Epstein [28]. On the other hand, the most general results were obtained by Kapovich, Weidmann and Miasnikov [25], but the complex algorithms were designed essentially to solve the generalized word problem, and it seems very hard to extend other features of the free group case, either geometric or algorithmic. In joint work with Soler-Escrivà and Ventura [39], the author developed a new idea: restricting the type of irreducible words used to represent elements (leading to the concept of *Stallings section*), find out which groups admit a representation of finitely generated subgroups by finite automata obtained through edge folding from some sort of flower automaton. It turned out that the groups admitting a Stallings section are precisely the virtually free groups! And many of the geometric/algorithmic features of the classical free group case can then be generalized to the virtually free case.

## 5   Hyperbolic Groups

Automata also play an important role in the beautiful geometric theory of hyperbolic groups, introduced by Gromov in the eighties [20]. For details on this class of groups, the reader is referred to [12].

Let $\pi : \widetilde{A}^* \to G$ be a matched epimorphism onto a group $G$. The *Cayley graph* $\Gamma_A(G)$ of $G$ with respect to $\pi$ has vertex set $G$ and edges $g \xrightarrow{a} g(a\pi)$ for all $g \in G$ and $a \in \widetilde{A}$. If we fix the identity as basepoint, we get an inverse automaton (which is precisely the minimal automaton of the language $1\pi^{-1}$).

If $G = F_A$ and $\pi$ is canonical, then $\Gamma_A(F_A)$ is an infinite tree. In particular, the local structure of $\Gamma_A(F_A)$ determines the global structure... and if we understand the global structure of the Cayley graph, then we understand the group.

So the aim is to consider geometric conditions on the structure of $\Gamma_A(G)$ that can lead to a global understanding of the Cayley graph through the local structure (taking finitely many finite subgraphs of $\Gamma_A(G)$ as local charts, actually). But which conditions? The answer came in the form of *hyperbolic geometry*. What does this mean and how does it relate to automata or theoretical computer science in general?

We say that a path $p \xrightarrow{u} q$ in $\Gamma_A(G)$ is a *geodesic* if it has shortest length among all the paths connecting $p$ to $q$ in $\Gamma_A(G)$. We denote by $\mathrm{Geo}_A(G)$ the set of labels of all geodesics in $\Gamma_A(G)$. Note that, since $\Gamma_A(G)$ is vertex-transitive (the left action of $G$ on itself produces enough automorphisms of $\Gamma_A(G)$ to make it completely symmetric), it is irrelevant whether or not we fix a basepoint for this purpose.

The *geodesic distance* $d$ on $G$ is defined by taking $d(g, h)$ to be the length of a geodesic from $g$ to $h$. Given $X \subseteq G$ nonempty and $g \in G$, we define

$$d(g, X) = \min\{d(g, x) \mid x \in X\}.$$

A *geodesic triangle* in $\Gamma_A(G)$ is a collection of three geodesics

$$P_1 : g_1 \longrightarrow g_2, \quad P_2 : g_2 \longrightarrow g_3, \quad P_3 : g_3 \longrightarrow g_1$$

connecting three vertices $g_1, g_2, g_3 \in G$. Let $V(P_i)$ denote the set of vertices occurring in the path $P_i$. We say that $\Gamma_A(G)$ is $\delta$-*hyperbolic* for some $\delta \geq 0$ if

$$\forall g \in V(P_1) \qquad d(g, V(P_2) \cup V(P_3)) < \delta$$

holds for every geodesic triangle $\{P_1, P_2, P_3\}$ in $\Gamma_A(G)$. If this happens for some $\delta$, we say that $G$ is *hyperbolic*. It is well known that the concept is independent from both alphabet and matched epimorphism, but the hyperbolicity constant $\delta$ may change. Virtually free groups are among the most important examples of hyperbolic groups (in fact, they can be characterized by strengthening the geometric condition in the definition of hyperbolicity, replacing geodesic triangles by geodesic polygons). However, the free Abelian group $\mathbb{Z} \times \mathbb{Z}$, whose Cayley graph (for the canonical generators) is the infinite grid is not hyperbolic. However, there exist plenty of hyperbolic groups: Gromov remarked that, under some reasonable assumptions, the probability of a finitely presented group being hyperbolic is 1.

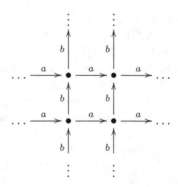

One of the extraordinary geometric properties of hyperbolic groups is closure under quasi-isometry, being thus one of the few examples where algebra deals well with the concept of *deformation*.

From an algorithmic viewpoint, hyperbolic groups enjoy excellent properties: they have solvable word problem, solvable conjugacy problem and many other positive features. We shall enhance three, which relate to theoretic computer science.

The first result states that geodesics constitute a rational language.

**Theorem 51.** [11, Theorem 3.4.5] *Let* $\pi : \widetilde{A}^* \to G$ *be a matched homomorphism onto a hyperbolic group* $G$. *Then the set of geodesics* $\text{Geo}_A(G)$ *is a rational language.*

The second one shows how $1\pi^{-1}$ can be described by means of a suitable rewriting system:

**Theorem 52.** [2] *Let* $\pi : \widetilde{A}^* \to G$ *be a matched homomorphism onto a group* $G$. *Then the following conditions are equivalent:*

*(i)* $G$ *is hyperbolic;*
*(ii)* *there exists a finite length-reducing rewriting system* $\mathcal{R}$ *such that*

$$\forall u \in \widetilde{A}^* \qquad u \in 1\pi^{-1} \Leftrightarrow u \longrightarrow_{\mathcal{R}}^* 1.$$

It follows easily that $1\pi^{-1}$ is a context-sensitive language if $G$ is hyperbolic. However, the converse fails, $\mathbb{Z} \times \mathbb{Z}$ being a counter-example.

In connection with the preceding theorem, it is interesting to recall a result by Gilman, Hermiller, Holt and Rees [14, Theorem 1], which states that a group $G$ is virtually free if and only if there exists a matched homomorphism $\pi : \widetilde{A}^* \to G$ and a finite length-reducing rewriting system $\mathcal{R} \subseteq \operatorname{Ker} \pi$ such that $\operatorname{Irr} \mathcal{R} = \operatorname{Geo}_A(G)$.

The third property is possibly the most intriguing. To present it, we need to introduce the concept of isoperimetric function.

Suppose that $G$ is a group defined by a finite presentation $\mathcal{P} = \langle \widetilde{A} \mid \mathcal{R} \rangle$, and let $\pi : \widetilde{A}^* \to G$ be the respective matched homomorphism. We say that $\delta : \mathbb{N} \to \mathbb{N}$ is an *isoperimetric function* for $\mathcal{P}$ if, whenever $u \in 1\pi^{-1}$, we need at most $\delta(|u|)$ transitions $\longrightarrow_{\mathcal{R}}$ to transform $u$ into the empty word 1. In other words, an isoperimetric function bounds the number of elementary transitions we need to transform a word of a certain length into the empty word.

It is easy to see that the existence of an isoperimetric function belonging to a certain complexity class depends only on the group and not on the finite presentation considered. We note also that every hyperbolic group is finitely presented.

**Theorem 53.** [20] *Let* $G$ *be a finitely presented group. Then the following conditions are equivalent:*

*(i)* $G$ *is hyperbolic;*
*(ii)* $G$ *admits a linear isoperimetric function;*
*(iii)* $G$ *admits a subquadratic isoperimetric function.*

In this extraordinary result, geometry unexpectedly meets complexity theory.

## 6   Automatic Groups

Also in the eighties, another very interesting idea germinated in geometric group theory, and automata were to play the leading role. The new concept was due to Cannon, Epstein, Holt, Levy, Paterson and Thurston [11] (see also [6]).

In view of Theorem 51, it is easy to see that every hyperbolic group admits a rational set of normal forms. But this is by no means an exclusive of hyperbolic groups, and rational normal forms are not enough to understand the structure of a group. We need to understand the product, or at least the action of generators on the set of normal forms. Can automata help?

There are different ways of encoding mappings as languages, synchronously or asynchronously. We shall mention only the most popular way of doing it, through *convolution*.

Given an alphabet $A$, we assume that $ is a new symbol (called the *padding symbol*) and define a new alphabet

$$A_\$ = (A \times A) \cup (A \times \{\$\}) \cup (\{\$\} \times A).$$

For all $u, v \in A^*$, $u \diamond v$ is the unique word in $A_\$^*$ whose projection to the first (respectively second) components yields a word in $u\$^*$ (respectively $v\$^*$). For instance, $a \diamond ba = (a, b)(\$, a)$.

Let $\pi : A^* \to G$ be a homomorphism onto a group $G$. We say that $L \in \operatorname{Rat} A^*$ is a *section* for $\pi$ if $L\pi = G$. For every $u \in A^*$, write

$$L_u = \{v \diamond w \mid v, w \in L, \ (vu)\pi = w\pi\}.$$

We say that $L \in \operatorname{Rat} A^*$ is an *automatic structure* for $\pi$ if:

- $L$ is a section for $\pi$;
- $L_a \in \operatorname{Rat} A_\$^*$ for every $a \in A \cup \{1\}$.

It can be shown that the existence of an automatic structure is independent from the alphabet $A$ or the homomorphism $\pi$, and implies the existence of an *automatic structure with uniqueness* (where $\pi|_L$ is injective). A group is said to be *automatic* if it admits an automatic structure.

The class of automatic groups contains all hyperbolic groups (in fact, $\operatorname{Geo}_A(G)$ is then an automatic structure!) and is closed under such operators as free products, finite extensions or direct products. As a consequence, it contains all free abelian groups of finite rank and so automatic groups need not be hyperbolic. By the following result of Gilman, hyperbolic groups can be characterized within automatic groups by a language-theoretic criterion:

**Theorem 61.** [13] *Let $G$ be a group. Then the following conditions are equivalent:*

*(i) $G$ is hyperbolic;*
*(ii) $G$ admits an automatic structure with uniqueness $L$ such that the language $\{u\$v\$w \mid u, v, w \in L, \ uvw =_G 1\}$ is context-free.*

Among many other good algorithmic properties, automatic groups are finitely presented, have decidable word problem (in quadratic time) and admit a quadratic isoperimetric function (but the converse is false, unlike Theorem 53). The reader is referred to [6,11] for details.

Geometry also plays an important part in the theory of automatic groups, through the *fellow traveller property*. Given a word $u \in A^*$, let $u^{[n]}$ denote the prefix of $u$ of length $n$ (or $u$ itself if $n > |u|$). Let $\pi : \widetilde{A}^* \to G$ be a matched homomorphism and recall the geodesic distance $d$ on $G$ introduced in Section 5 in connection with the Cayley graph $\Gamma_A(G)$. We say that a section $L$ for $\pi$

satisfies the fellow traveller property if there exists some constant $K > 0$ such that

$$\forall u, v \in L \ (d(u\pi, v\pi) \leq 1 \Rightarrow \forall n \in \mathbb{N} \ d(u^{[n]}\pi, v^{[n]}\pi) \leq K).$$

Intuitively, this expresses the fact that two paths in $\Gamma_A(G)$ labelled by words $u, v \in L$ which start at the same vertex and end up in neighbouring (or equal) vertices *stay close all the way through*.

This geometric property provides an alternative characterization of automatic groups which avoids convolution:

**Theorem 62.** [11, Theorem 2.3.5] *Let* $\pi : \widetilde{A}^* \to G$ *be a matched homomorphism onto a group* $G$ *and let* $L$ *be a rational section for* $\pi$. *Then the following conditions are equivalent:*

(i) $L$ *is an automatic structure for* $\pi$;
(ii) $L$ *satisfies the fellow traveller property.*

The combination of automata-theoretic and geometric techniques is typical of the theory of automatic groups.

# 7  Automaton Groups

Automaton groups, also known as self-similar groups, were introduced in the sixties by Glushkov [15] (see also [1]) but it was through the leading work of Grigorchuk in the eighties [18] that they became a main research subject in geometric group theory. Here automata play a very different role compared with previous sections.

We can view a free monoid $A^*$ as a rooted tree $T$ with edges $u$ — $ua$ for all $u \in A^*$, $a \in A$ and root 1. The automorphism group of $T$, which is uncountable if $|A| > 1$, is self-similar in the following sense: if we restrict an automorphism $\varphi$ of $T$ to a cone $uA^*$, we get a mapping of the form $uA^* \to (u\varphi)A^* : uv \mapsto (u\varphi)(v\psi)$ for some automorphism $\psi$ of $T$. This leads to wreath product decompositions (see [31]) and the possibility of recursion.

But Aut$T$ is huge and non finitely generated except in trivial cases, hence it is a natural idea to study subgroups $G$ of $T$ generated by a finite set of self-similar generators (in the above sense) to keep all the chances of effective recursion methods within a finitely generated context. It turns out that this is equivalent to define $G$ through a finite invertible *Mealy automaton*.

A Mealy automaton on the alphabet $A$ is a finite complete deterministic transducer where edges are labelled by pairs of letters of $A$. No initial/terminal vertices are assigned. It is said to be invertible if the local transformations of $A$ (induced by the labels of the edges leaving a given vertex) are permutations. Here is a famous example of an invertible Mealy automaton:

The transformations of $A = \{0,1\}$ induced by the vertices $a$ and $b$ are the identity mapping and the transposition $(01)$, respectively.

Each vertex $q$ of a Mealy automaton $\mathcal{A}$ defines an endomorphism $\varphi_q$ of the tree $T$ through the paths $q \xrightarrow{u|u\varphi_q} \ldots$ ($u \in A^*$). If the automaton is invertible, each $\varphi_q$ is indeed an automorphism and the set of all $\varphi_q$, for all vertices $q$ of $\mathcal{A}$, satisfies the desired self-similarity condition. The (finitely generated) subgroup of $\text{Aut} T$ generated by the $\varphi_q$ is the automaton group $\mathcal{G}(\mathcal{A})$ generated by $\mathcal{A}$.

For instance, the automaton group generated by the Mealy automaton in the above example is the famous *lamplighter group* [17].

Automaton groups have decidable word problem. Moreover, the recursion potential offered by their wreath product decompositions allowed successful computations which were hard to foresee with more traditional techniques and turned automaton groups into the most rich source of counterexamples in infinite group theory ever. The Grigorchuk group [18] is the most famous of the lot, but their exist many others exhibiting fascinating exotic properties [22,19].

An interesting infinite family of Mealy automata was studied by the author in collaboration with Steinberg [40] and Kambites and Steinberg [23]: Cayley machines of finite groups $G$ (the Cayley graph is adapted by taking edges $g \xrightarrow{a|g(a\pi)} g(a\pi)$, and all the elements of the group as generators). If $G$ is abelian, these Cayley machines generate the wreath product $G \text{ wr } \mathbb{Z}$, and the lamplighter group corresponds to the case $G = \mathbb{Z}_2$.

Surprising connections with fractals were established in recent years. We shall briefly describe one instance. Given a matched homomorphism $\pi : \widetilde{A}^* \to G$ and a subgroup $P$ of $G$, the *Schreier graph* $\Gamma_A(G, P)$ has the cosets $Pg$ as vertices and edges $Pg \xrightarrow{a} Pg(a\pi)$ for all $g \in G$ and $a \in \widetilde{A}$. Note that $P = \{1\}$ yields the familiar Cayley graph $\Gamma_A(G)$. It turns out that classical fractals can be obtained as limits of the sequence of graphs $(\Gamma_A(G, P_n))_n$ for some adequate automaton group $G$, where $P_n$ denotes the stabilizer of the $n$th level of the three $T$ [3,31]. Note that $P_n$ has finite index and so the Schreier graphs $\Gamma_A(G, P_n)$ are finite.

## 8  Automata and Dynamics

Automata appear also as a major tool in the study of the dynamics of many families of group endomorphisms. We shall present an example taken from our own recent research work [38].

We shall call $\mathcal{T} = (Q, q_0, \delta, \lambda)$ an $A$-*transducer* if:

- $Q$ is a (finite) set;
- $q_0 \in Q$;
- $\delta : Q \times A \to Q$ and $\lambda : Q \times A \to A^*$ are mappings.

We can view $\mathcal{T}$ as a directed graph with edges labelled by elements of $A \times A^*$ (represented in the form $a|w$) by identifying $(p, a)\delta = q$, $(p, a)\lambda = w$ with the edge $p \xrightarrow{a|w} q$.

We may extend $\delta$ and $\lambda$ to $Q \times A^*$ by considering the paths $q \xrightarrow{u|(q,u)\lambda} (q, u)\delta$ for all $u \in A^*$. When the transducer is clear from the context, we write $qa = (q, a)\delta$. The transformation $\widehat{\mathcal{T}} : A^* \to A^*$ is defined by $u\widehat{\mathcal{T}} = (q_0, u)\lambda$.

If $\mathcal{T} = (Q, q_0, T, \delta, \lambda)$ is an $\widetilde{A}$-transducer such that

$$p \xrightarrow{a|u} q \text{ is an edge of } \mathcal{T} \text{ if and only if } q \xrightarrow{a^{-1}|u^{-1}} p \text{ is an edge of } \mathcal{T},$$

then $\mathcal{T}$ is said to be *inverse*.

As an easy consequence of this definition, we get:

**Proposition 81.** [38, Proposition 3.1] *Let* $\mathcal{T} = (Q, q_0, \delta, \lambda)$ *be an inverse* $\widetilde{A}$-*transducer. Then:*

*(i)* $\delta : Q \times \widetilde{A}^* \to Q$ *induces a mapping* $\widetilde{\delta} : Q \times F_A \to Q$ *by* $(q, u\theta)\widetilde{\delta} = (q, u)\delta$;
*(ii)* $\widehat{\mathcal{T}} : \widetilde{A}^* \to \widetilde{A}^*$ *induces a partial mapping* $\widetilde{\mathcal{T}} : F_A \to F_A$ *by* $u\theta\widetilde{\mathcal{T}} = u\widehat{\mathcal{T}}\theta$.

We can prove the following result:

**Theorem 82.** [38, Theorem 3.2] *Let* $\mathcal{T}$ *be a finite inverse* $\widetilde{A}$-*transducer and let* $z \in F_A$. *Then*

$$L = \{g \in F_A \mid g\widetilde{\mathcal{T}} = gz\}$$

*is rational.*

The proof is inspired in Goldstein and Turner's proof [16] for endomorphisms of the free group. We give a brief sketch.

Write $\mathcal{T} = (Q, q_0, \delta, \lambda)$. For every $g \in F_A$, let $P_1(g) = g^{-1}(g\widetilde{\mathcal{T}}) \in F_A$ and write $q_0 g = (q_0, g)\widetilde{\delta}$, $P(g) = (P_1(g), q_0 g)$. Note that $g \in L$ if and only if $P_1(g) = z$. We define a deterministic $\widetilde{A}$-automaton $\mathcal{A}_\varphi = (P, (1, q_0), S, E)$ by

$$P = \{P(g) \mid g \in F_A\};$$
$$S = P \cap (\{z\} \times Q);$$
$$E = \{(P(g), a, P(ga)) \mid g \in F_A, \ a \in \widetilde{A}\}.$$

Clearly, $\mathcal{A}_\varphi$ is a possibly infinite automaton. Note that, since $\mathcal{T}$ is inverse, we have $qaa^{-1} = q$ for all $q \in Q$ and $a \in \widetilde{A}$. It follows that, whenever $(p, a, p') \in E$, then also $(p', a^{-1}, p) \in E$. We say that such edges are the *inverse* of each other.

Since every $w \in \widetilde{A}^*$ labels a unique path $P(1) \xrightarrow{w} P(w\theta)$, it follows that

$$L(\mathcal{A}_\varphi) = L\theta^{-1}.$$

To prove that $L$ is rational, we show that only finitely many edges can occur in the successful paths of $\mathcal{A}_\varphi$ labelled by reduced words.

This is achieved by defining an appropriate subset $E' \subseteq E$ satisfying $E = E' \cup (E')^{-1}$ and showing that there are only finitely many vertices in $\mathcal{A}_\varphi$ which are starting points for more than one edge in $E'$.

Theorem 82 can be used to produce an alternative proof [38, Theorem 4.1] of the following Sykiotis' theorem:

**Theorem 83.** [43, Proposition 3.4] *Let* $\varphi$ *be an endomorphism of a finitely generated virtually free group. Then* $\mathrm{Fix}\,\varphi$ *is finitely generated.*

Automata are also at the heart of other results in [38], concerning the *infinite fixed points* of endomorphism extensions to the boundary of virtually free groups. The boundary is a very important topological concept defined for hyperbolic groups [12], but out of the scope of this paper.

**Acknowledgements.** The author acknowledges support from the European Regional Development Fund through the programme COMPETE and from the Portuguese Government through FCT – Fundação para a Ciência e a Tecnologia, under the project PEst-C/MAT/UI0144/2011.

# References

1. Aleshin, S.V.: Finite automata and the burnside problem for periodic groups. Mat. Zametki 11, 319–328 (1972) (Russian)
2. Alonso, J., Brady, T., Cooper, D., Ferlini, V., Lustig, M.M., Shapiro, M., Short, H.: Notes on word-hyperbolic groups. In: Ghys, E., Haefliger, A., Verjovsky, A. (eds.) Proc. Conf. Group Theory from a Geometrical Viewpoint. World Scientific, Singapore (1991)
3. Bartholdi, L., Grigorchuk, R.I., Nekrashevych, V.V.: From fractal groups to fractal sets. In: Fractals in Graz 2001, trends math. edn., pp. 25–118. Birkhauser, Basel (2003)
4. Bartholdi, L., Silva, P.V.: Groups defined by automata. In: Handbook AutoMathA, ch. 24 (2010) (to appear)
5. Bartholdi, L., Silva, P.V.: Rational subsets of groups. In: Handbook AutoMathA, ch. 23 (2010) (to appear)
6. Baumslag, G.B., Gersten, S.M., Shapiro, M., Short, H.: Automatic groups and amalgams. J. Pure Appl. Algebra 76, 229–316 (1991)
7. Benois, M.: Parties rationnelles du groupe libre. C. R. Acad. Sci. Paris 269, 1188–1190 (1969)
8. Berstel, J.: Transductions and Context-free Languages. Teubner, Stuttgart (1979)
9. Book, R.V., Otto, F.: String-Rewriting Systems. Springer, New York (1993)
10. Dunwoody, M.J.: The accessibility of finitely presented groups. Invent. Math. 81.3, 449–457 (1985)
11. Epstein, D.B.A., Cannon, J.W., Holt, D.F., Levy, S.V.F., Paterson, M.S., Thurston, W.P.: Word processing in groups. Jones and Bartlett Publishers, Boston (1992)
12. Ghys, E., de la Harpe, P. (eds.): Sur les Groupes Hyperboliques d'après Mikhael Gromov. Birkhauser, Boston (1990)
13. Gilman, R.H.: On the definition of word hyperbolic groups. Math. Z. 242(3), 529–541 (2002)
14. Gilman, R.H., Hermiller, S., Holt, D.F., Rees, S.: A characterization of virtually free groups. Arch. Math. 89, 289–295 (2007)
15. Glushkov, V.M.: Abstract theory of automata. Uspehi Mat. Nauk. 16(5), 3–62 (1961) (Russian)
16. Goldstein, R.Z., Turner, E.C.: Fixed subgroups of homomorphisms of free groups. Bull. London Math. Soc. 18, 468–470 (1986)
17. Grigorchuk, R., Zuk, A.: The lamplighter group as a group generated by a 2-state automaton. Geom. Dedicata 87(1-3), 209–244 (2001)
18. Grigorchuk, R.I.: On burnside's problem on periodic groups. Funktsional. Anal. i Prilozhen 14(1), 53–54 (1980) (Russian)
19. Grigorchuk, R.I., Zuk, A.: On a torsion-free weakly branch group defined by a three state automaton. Internat. J. Algebra Comput. 12(1&2), 223–246 (2002)
20. Gromov, M.L.: Hyperbolic groups. In: Essays in Group Theory. Math. Sci. Res. Inst. Publ., vol. 8, pp. 75–263. Springer, New York (1987)

21. Grünschlag, Z.: Algorithms in geometric group theory. Ph.d. thesis, University of California at Berkeley (1999)
22. Gupta, N.D., Sidki, S.N.: Some infinite p-groups. Algebra i Logika 22(5), 584–589 (1983) (English, with Russian summary)
23. Kambites, M., Silva, P.V., Steinberg, B.: The spectra of lamplighter groups and cayley machines. Geometriae Dedicata 120(1), 193–227 (2006)
24. Kapovich, I., Miasnikov, A.: Stallings foldings and subgroups of free groups. J. Algebra 248, 608–668 (2002)
25. Kapovich, I., Weidmann, R., Miasnikov, A.: Foldings, graphs of groups and the membership problem. Internat. J. Algebra Comput. (2005)
26. Lohrey, M., Steinberg, B.: The submonoid and rational subset membership problems for graph groups. J. Algebra 320(2), 728–755 (2008)
27. Lyndon, R.C., Schupp, P.E.: Combinatorial Group Theory. Springer (1977)
28. Markus-Epstein, L.: Stallings foldings and subgroups of amalgams of finite groups. Internat. J. Algebra Comput. 17(8), 1493–1535 (2007)
29. Miasnikov, A., Ventura, E., Weil, P.: Algebraic extensions in free groups. In: Geometric Group Theory. Trends Math., pp. 225–253. Birkhäuser, Basel (2007)
30. Muller, D.E., Schupp, P.E.: Groups, the theory of ends, and context-free languages. J. Comput. System Sci. 26(3), 295–310 (1983)
31. Nekrashevych, V.: Self-similar groups. In: Mathematical Surveys and Monographs, vol. 117. Amer. Math. Soc., Providence (2005)
32. Sakarovitch, J.: A problem on rational subsets of the free group. Amer. Math. Monthly 91, 499–501 (1984)
33. Sénizergues, G.: Some decision problems about controlled rewriting systems. Theoret. Comput. Sci. 71(3), 281–346 (1990)
34. Sénizergues, G.: On the rational subsets of the free group. Acta Informatica 33(3), 281–296 (1996)
35. Serre, J.P.: Arbres, amalgames, $sl_2$. In: Astérisque 46. Soc. Math., France (1977); english translation: Trees. Springer Monographs in Mathematics. Springer (2003)
36. Silva, P.V.: Free group languages: rational versus recognizable. Theoret. Informatics and Appl. 38, 49–67 (2004)
37. Silva, P.V.: Rational subsets of partially reversible monoids. Theor. Comp. Science 409(3), 537–548 (2008)
38. Silva, P.V.: Fixed points of endomorphisms of virtually free groups. Tech. Rep. preprint 2012-10, CMUP (2012), arXiv:1203.1355
39. Silva, P.V., Soler-Escrivà, X., Ventura, E.: Finite automata for schreier graphs of virtually free groups. Tech. Rep. preprint 2012-2, CMUP (2012), arXiv:1112.5709
40. Silva, P.V., Steinberg, B.: On a class of automata groups generalizing lamplighter groups. Int. J. Alg. Comput. 15(5/6), 1213–1234 (2005)
41. Stallings, J.: Topology of finite graphs. Invent. Math. 71, 551–565 (1983)
42. Stephen, J.B.: Presentations of inverse monoids. J. Pure Appl. Algebra 63, 81–112 (1990)
43. Sykiotis, M.: Fixed points of symmetric endomorphisms of groups. Internat. J. Algebra Comput. 12(5), 737–745 (2002)

# Uniform Distributed Pushdown Automata Systems

Fernando Arroyo[1], Juan Castellanos[2], and Victor Mitrana[3,*]

[1] Department of Languages, Projects and Computer Information Systems,
University School of Informatics, Polytechnic University of Madrid,
Crta. de Valencia km. 7, 28031 Madrid, Spain
farroyo@eui.upm.es
[2] Department of Artificial Intelligence,
Faculty of Informatics, Polytechnic University of Madrid,
28660 Boadilla del Monte, Madrid, Spain
jcastellanos@fi.upm.es
[3] Department of Organization and Structure of Information,
University School of Informatics, Polytechnic University of Madrid,
Crta. de Valencia km. 7, 28031 Madrid, Spain
victor.mitrana@upm.es

**Abstract.** A distributed pushdown automata system consists of several pushdown automata which work in turn on the input word placed on a common one-way input tape under protocols and strategies similar to those in which cooperating distributed (CD) grammar systems work. Unlike the CD grammar systems case, where one may add or remove duplicate components without modifying the generated language, the identical components play an important role in distributed pushdown automata systems. We consider here uniform distributed pushdown automata systems (UDPAS), namely distributed pushdown automata systems having all components identical pushdown automata.

We consider here just a single protocol for activating/deactivating components, namely a component stays active as long as it can perform moves, as well as two ways of accepting the input word: by empty stacks (all components have empty stacks) or by final states (all components are in final states), when the input word is completely read. We mainly investigate the computational power of UDPAS accepting by empty stacks and a few decidability and closure properties of the families of languages they define. Some directions for further work and open problems are also discussed.

## 1 Introduction

In the last decades, researchers and practitioners have shown an increasing interest in distributed systems. Among various models a formal language theoretic paradigm called *grammar system* has been proposed [5]. Two main architectures

* Work supported by the Project TIN2011-28260-C03-03.

M. Kutrib, N. Moreira, and R. Reis (Eds.): DCFS 2012, LNCS 7386, pp. 64–75, 2012.

have been distinguished in the area, cooperating distributed (CD) grammar systems [4] and parallel communicating (PC) grammar systems [15]. Several motivations have been involved in introducing the CD grammar system concept:

– A generalization of the two-level substitution grammars. This was the main purpose of the paper [14] where the syntagma *cooperating grammar system* was proposed.
– In the architecture of a CD grammar system one can recognize the structure of a blackboard model, as used in problem-solving area: the common sentential form is the "blackboard" (the common data structure containing the current state of the problem which is to be solved), the component grammars are the knowledge sources contributing to solving the problem, the protocol of cooperation encodes the control on the work of the knowledge sources [10]. This was the explicit motivation of [4], the paper where CD grammar systems were introduced in the form we consider here.
– The increase of the computational power of components by cooperation and communication and the decrease of the complexity of different tasks by distribution and parallelism.

An entire theory has been developed for both types of grammar systems, see the monograph [5] and more recently the chapter [8] in [16]. The obtained results showed that cooperation and communication increases the power of individual components: large language classes were described by systems of very simple grammars belonging to grammar classes with weak computational power. In spite of this notable development, very little has been done with respect to automata systems working under similar strategies. These investigations might be of particular interest from several points of view: they might lead to a comparison between the power of distributed generative and accepting devices, and might give information on the boundaries of describing language classes in terms of automata systems. A series of papers [6,12,13,3,2] was devoted to PC automata systems whose components are finite or pushdown automata. We briefly recall the previous works dealing with distributed systems formed by automata done in this respect.

In [9] some special types of multi-stack pushdown automata were introduced. These mechanisms are usual multi-stack pushdown automata whose stacks cooperate in the accepting process under some strategies borrowed from CD grammar systems. However, they cannot be seen as the automata counterpart of CD grammar systems. A similar approach has been reported in [11].

The first (and unique so far) work considering systems of pushdown automata whose working mode is very close to that of CD grammar systems is [7]. A distributed pushdown automata system (DPAS) has a common one-way input tape, one reading head, and several central units. Each central unit is in a state from its own finite sets of states and accesses the topmost of its own pushdown memory. At any moment only one central unit is active, the others are "frozen". When active, the central unit can also read the current input symbol by means of the common reading head. Activation of some component means that the central unit of that component takes control over the reading head. We defined several protocols for activating components. Two ways of accepting were defined: by empty stacks or by final states meaning that all components have empty stacks or are in final states, respectively, when the input word is completely read.

This note considers a problem of interest in our view which is represented by the DPAS with identical components, that is all components are identical pushdown automata. Such DPAS are called here *uniform DPAS (UDPAS)*. This aspect makes no difference for CD grammar systems; in other words, one can add or remove identical components in a CD grammar system without modifying the generated language. Unlike the CD grammar systems case, the identical components play an important role in DPAS as we shall see in the sequel. Returning to the original motivation mentioned in the beginning of this paper (blackboard model of problem solving), it is not artificial to assume that all agents which participate in the problem solving process have the same knowledge. This approach suggests a close connection with *amorphous systems*: (i) each component has rather modest computing power, (ii) each component is programmed identically though each has means for storing local state and memory, (iii) each component has no a priori knowledge of its position within the system.

We first prove that UDPAS accepting by final states are strictly more powerful than UDPAS accepting by empty stacks. Then we mainly consider UDPAS accepting by empty stacks and investigate their computational power and a few decidability and closure properties of the families of languages they define. Some directions for further work and open problems are also discussed.

## 2    Basic Definitions

We assume the reader to be familiar with the basic concepts in automata and formal language theory; for further details, we refer to [16].

An alphabet is a finite and nonempty set of symbols. Any sequence of symbols from an alphabet $V$ is called word over $V$. For an alphabet $V$, we denote by $V^*$ the free monoid generated by $V$ under the operation of concatenation; the empty word is denoted by $\varepsilon$ and the semigroup $V^* - \{\varepsilon\}$ is denoted by $V^+$. The length of $x \in V^*$ is denoted by $|x|$ while $|x|_a$ denotes the number of occurrences of the symbol $a$ in $x$. A subset of $V^*$ is called language over $V$. The Parikh mapping over an alphabet $V = \{a_1, a_2, \ldots, a_k\}$ denoted by $\psi_V$ is a morphism from $V^*$ to $\mathbb{N}^k$, where $\psi_V(a_i)$ is the vector having all its entries equal to 0 except the $i$-th entry which is 1. If $L \subseteq V^*$, then the Parikh image of $L$ is $\psi(L) = \{\psi_V(x) \mid x \in L\}$. We omit the subscript $V$ whenever the alphabet is understood from the context.

We shall also denote by $Rec_X(A)$ the language accepted by a pushdown automaton $A$ with final state if $X = f$, or with empty stack if $X = \varepsilon$. We note that pushdown automata characterize the class of context-free languages in both modes of acceptance. The family of context-free languages is denoted by $CF$. Remember that the Parikh image of any context-free language is a semilinear set.

We now give the definition of the main concept of the paper following [7]. A *distributed pushdown automata system* (DPAS for short) of degree $n$ is a construct

$$\mathcal{A} = (V, A_1, A_2, \ldots, A_n),$$

where $V$ is an alphabet and for each $1 \leq i \leq n$, $A_i = (Q_i, V, \Gamma_i, f_i, q_i, Z_i, F_i)$ is a nondeterministic pushdown automaton with the set of states $Q_i$, the initial state $q_i \in Q_i$, the alphabet of input symbols $V$, the alphabet of pushdown symbols $\Gamma_i$, the initial contents of the pushdown memory $Z_i \in \Gamma_i$, the set of final states $F_i \subseteq Q_i$, and the transition mapping $f_i$ from $Q_i \times V \cup \{\varepsilon\} \times \Gamma_i$ into the finite subsets of $Q_i \times \Gamma_i^*$. We refer to the automaton $A_i$, $1 \leq i \leq n$, as the $i^{\text{th}}$ component of $\mathcal{A}$.

An *instantaneous description* (ID) of a DPAS as above is $2n + 1$-tuple

$$(x, s_1, \alpha_1, s_2, \alpha_2, \ldots, s_n, \alpha_n),$$

where $x \in V^*$ is the part of the input word to be read, and for each $1 \leq i \leq n$, $s_i$ is the current state of the automaton $A_i$ and $\alpha_i \in \Gamma_i^*$ is the pushdown memory content of the same automaton.

A one step move of $\mathcal{A}$ done by the component $i$, $1 \leq i \leq n$, is represented by a binary relation $\vdash_i$ on all IDs defined in the following way:

$$(ax, s_1, \alpha_1, s_2, \alpha_2, \ldots, s_i, \alpha_i, \ldots, s_n, \alpha_n) \vdash_i (x, s_1, \alpha_1, s_2, \alpha_2, \ldots, r_i, \beta, \ldots, s_n, \alpha_n)$$

if and only if $(r_i, \delta) \in f_i(s_i, a, A)$, where $a \in V \cup \{\varepsilon\}$, $\alpha_i = A\gamma$, and $\beta = \delta\gamma$.

As usual, $\vdash_i^*$ denotes the reflexive and transitive closure of $\vdash_i$. Let now $C_1, C_2$ be two IDs of a DPAS. We say that $C_1$ directly derives $C_2$ by a move representing a sequence of steps done by the component $i$ that cannot be continued, denoted by $C_1 \vdash_{\mathcal{A}}^t C_2$, if and only if $C_1 \vdash_i^* C_2$ for some $1 \leq i \leq n$, and there is no $C'$ with $C_2 \vdash_i C'$. In other words, as soon as a component is activated, it remains active as long as it is possible.

The language accepted by a DPAS $\mathcal{A}$ as above by final states is defined by

$$Rec_f(\mathcal{A}) = \{w \mid w \in V^*, \ (w, q_1, Z_1, q_2, Z_2, \ldots, q_n, Z_n)(\vdash_{\mathcal{A}}^t)^*$$
$$(\varepsilon, s_1, \alpha_1, s_2, \alpha_2, \ldots, s_n, \alpha_n) \text{ with } \alpha_i \in \Gamma_i^*, \ s_i \in F_i, \text{ for all } 1 \leq i \leq n\}$$

Similarly, the language accepted by DPAS $\mathcal{A}$ as above by empty stacks is defined by

$$Rec_\varepsilon(\mathcal{A}) = \{w \mid w \in V^*, \ (w, q_1, Z_1, q_2, Z_2, \ldots, q_n, Z_n)(\vdash_{\mathcal{A}}^t)^*$$
$$(\varepsilon, s_1, \varepsilon, s_2, \varepsilon, \ldots, s_n, \varepsilon) \text{ for some } s_i \in Q_i, 1 \leq i \leq n\}$$

For the rest of this paper we consider *uniform DPAS* (UDPAS) only. A DPAS $\mathcal{A} = (V, A_1, A_2, \ldots, A_n)$ with $A_1 = A_2 = \cdots = A_n = A$, which is simply denoted by $\mathcal{A} = (n, V, A)$, is said to be uniform. Therefore, for each UDPAS it suffices to give its degree (number of components) and the pushdown automaton. We illustrate the above notions through an example which will also be useful in the sequel.

**Example 1.** *Let $\mathcal{A}$ be the UDPAS of degree 2 with the pushdown automaton defined by the following transition mapping:*

$f(q_0, X, Z_0) = \{(s_X, XZ_0)\}, X \in \{a, b\}$    $f(s_X, X, X) = \{(s_X, XX)\}, X \in \{a, b\},$
$f(s_a, c, a) = \{(s_a, \varepsilon)\}$    $f(s_b, d, b) = \{(s_b, \varepsilon)\},$
$f(s_X, X, Z_0) = \{(s_X, XZ_0)\}, X \in \{a, b\}$    $f(s_X, \varepsilon, Z_0) = \{(s, \varepsilon)\}, X \in \{a, b\}$

*The set $\{s\}$ is the set of final states. We first note that the language accepted by the pushdown automaton by final states/empty stack is $L_0 = D_{a,c} \cup D_{b,d}$. Here $D_{x,y}$ is the Dyck language over the alphabet $\{x, y\}$. Second, the language recognized by $\mathcal{A}$ by final states/empty stacks is the language $L_1$ that includes $D_{a,c}^2 \cup D_{b,d}^2$ and all words formed by interleaving words from $D_{a,c}$ and $D_{b,d}$.*

The families of languages accepted by UDPAS of degree $n$ by final states or empty stacks are denoted by $\mathcal{L}_f(UDPAS, n)$ or $\mathcal{L}_\varepsilon(UDPAS, n)$, respectively.

Example 1 shows a strong connection between the languages recognized by (U)DPAS and languages obtained by means of the following operation intensively investigated in the formal language and concurrency theory. The *shuffle* operation applied to two words leads to the set of all words obtained from the original two words by interleaving their letters but keeping their order in the two words like interleaving two decks of cards. Formally, this operation is defined recursively on words over an alphabet $V$ as follows:

$$\amalg(\varepsilon, x) = \amalg(x, \varepsilon) = \{x\}, \text{ for any } x \in V^*$$
$$\amalg(ax, by) = \{a\} \amalg(x, by) \cup \{b\} \amalg(ax, y), \text{ for all } a, b \in V, \ x, y \in V^*.$$

This operation may naturally be extended to languages and to have $k$ arguments as

$$\amalg(L_1, L_2) = \bigcup_{x \in L_1, y \in L_2} \amalg(x, y),$$

and $\amalg_k(x_1, x_2, \ldots, x_k) = \amalg(\amalg_{k-1}(x_1, x_2, \ldots, x_{k-1}), \{x_k\})$, respectively. Also, $\amalg_k$ is extended to languages as

$$\amalg_k(L_1, L_2, \ldots, L_k) = \bigcup_{x_i \in L_i, 1 \le i \le k} \amalg_k(x_1, x_2, \ldots, x_k).$$

If each language $L_1, L_2, \ldots, L_k$ equals $L$, we denote

$$\amalg^0(L) = \{\varepsilon\},$$
$$\amalg^{k+1}(L) = \amalg(\amalg^k(L), L)), \text{ for all } k \ge 0,$$
$$\amalg^*(L) = \bigcup_{k \ge 0} \amalg^k(L).$$

## 3   Computational Power

It is worth mentioning in the beginning of this section that any context-free language can be accepted by a DPAS of degree $n$ for all $n \ge 1$. This is not true anymore for UDPAS as we shall see in the sequel. We start with a result that will be useful in what follows.

**Lemma 1.** *For any UDPAS $\mathcal{A}$ of degree $n$ there exists a context-free language $L$ such that $L^n \subseteq Rec_\varepsilon(\mathcal{A}) \subseteq \amalg{}^n(L)$.*

*Proof.* Let $\mathcal{A}$ be a UDPAS formed by $n$ copies of a pushdown automaton $A$. The statement follows immediately as soon as we take the context-free language as the language accepted with empty stack by $A$.    □

It is known that pushdown automata accepting by empty stack or final state define the same class of languages. The situation is different for UDPAS.

**Theorem 1.** $\mathcal{L}_\varepsilon(UDPAS,p) \subset \mathcal{L}_f(UDPAS,p)$, *for all $p \geq 2$.*

*Proof.* The inclusion is proved by the standard construction that transforms a pushdown automaton accepting with empty stack into a pushdown automaton accepting with final states. For proving the properness of this inclusion we construct the UDPAS with $p \geq 2$ identical copies of the pushdown automaton $A$ defined as follows:

$$f(q_0, a, Z_0) = \{(s_1, aZ_0)\}, \qquad f(q_0, b, Z_0) = \{(s_2, bZ_0)\},$$
$$f(s_1, a, a) = \{(s_1, aa)\} \qquad\qquad f(s_2, b, b) = \{(s_2, bb)\},$$
$$f(s_1, X, a) = \{(s_e, a)\}, X \in \{b, c, d\} \quad f(s_2, X, b) = \{(s_e, b)\}, X \in \{a, c, d\},$$
$$f(s_1, \varepsilon, a) = \{(p_1, a)\} \qquad\qquad f(s_2, \varepsilon, b) = \{(p_2, b)\},$$
$$f(p_1, c, a) = \{(p_1, \varepsilon)\} \qquad\qquad f(p_2, d, b) = \{(p_2, \varepsilon)\},$$
$$f(p_1, X, a) = \{(s_e, a)\}, X \in \{a, b, d\} \quad f(p_2, X, b) = \{(s_e, b)\}, X \in \{a, b, c\},$$
$$f(p_1, \varepsilon, Z_0) = \{(s_f^1, Z_0)\} \qquad\qquad f(p_2, \varepsilon, Z_0) = \{(s_f^2, Z_0)\},$$
$$f(s_f^1, X, Z_0) = \{(s_e, Z_0)\}, X \in \{a, b, c\} \quad f(s_f^2, X, Z_0) = \{(s_e, Z_0)\}, X \in \{a, b, c, d\},$$
$$f(q_0, \varepsilon, Z_0) = \{(s_f^3, Z_0)\}.$$

It is easy to note that $Rec_f(A) = \{a^n c^n \mid n \geq 0\} \cup \{b^n d^n \mid n \geq 0\}$, where the set of final states of $A$ is $\{s_f^1, s_f^2, s_f^3\}$. We now make a discussion about the language accepted by $\mathcal{A}$ with final states. First, any non-empty input word must start with either $a$ or $b$. If the prefix of the input word composed by $a$ is followed by a $d$, it is plain that the input word cannot be accepted. We now consider the case when the prefix of the input word composed by $a$ is followed by $c$. Two situations may appear:

- The whole prefix of $a$'s is processed continuously by the same component. In this case this component may either reach the final state $s_f^1$, if the input word is of the form $a^n c^n$ for some $n \geq 1$, or get stuck.
- Only a part of the prefix of $a$'s is read by the first activated component; it follows that other components have to read the remaining part of this prefix. Now the next segment formed by $c$'s of the input word will block at least one of all these two components.

Therefore, an input word of the form $a^+ c^+ (a+b+c+d)^*$ is accepted by $\mathcal{A}$ if and only if it is of the form $a^n c^n$ for some $n \geq 1$. Note that all the other components different than that which starts the computation can reach the final state $s_f^3$ by reading the empty word.

We analyze now the computation on an input word of the form $a^+b^+(a+b+c+d)^*$. Such a word might lead to acceptance if one component reads completely the prefix of $a$'s while another reads completely the next factor formed by $b$ only. Furthermore, neither $a$ nor $d$ can be the next symbol after the segment of $b$'s. Indeed, an $a$ blocks both these components while a $d$ blocks at least one of them. The analysis may continue in the same way until we conclude that the input word is of the form $a^+b^+c^+d^+$. More precisely, it has to be of the form $a^nb^mc^nd^m$ for some $n, m \geq 1$. Analogously, any input word starting with $b$ that is eventually accepted is either of the form $b^md^m$ or of the form $b^ma^nc^nd^m$ for some $n, m \geq 1$. Consequently,

$$Rec_f(\mathcal{A}) = \{a^nb^mc^nd^m \mid n, m \geq 0\} \cup \{b^ma^nc^nd^m \mid n, m \geq 0\}.$$

Note that every correct input word is actually accepted by means of only two components of $\mathcal{A}$. All the other components reach their final states by just one move when nothing from the input tape is effectively read.

By Lemma 1, since there is no context-free language $L$ and $k \geq 2$ such that $L^k \subseteq Rec_f(\mathcal{A})$, therefore $Rec_f(\mathcal{A})$ cannot lie in $\mathcal{L}_\varepsilon(UDPAS, k)$ for any $k \geq 2$. □

For the rest of this note we shall consider mainly UDPAS accepting by empty stacks. As one can see in Lemma 1, every language accepted by a UPDAS of degree $p$ with empty stacks is a subset of $\sqcup\!\sqcup^P(L)$ for some context-free language $L$. The following problem naturally arises: When do we have equality? What conditions should $L$ satisfy such that $\sqcup\!\sqcup^P(L)$ is accepted by a UPDAS with empty stacks? It is worth mentioning that for every context-free language $L$, the language $\sqcup\!\sqcup^P(L)$ is accepted by a UDPAS of degree $p$ with empty stacks if we change the protocol of activating/deactivating the components. More precisely, if we define the language accepted by a UDPAS $\mathcal{A}$ with empty stacks as follows

$$Rec_\varepsilon(\mathcal{A}, *) = \{w \mid w \in V^*, \ (w, q_1, Z_1, q_2, Z_2, \ldots, q_n, Z_n) \vdash^*_{i_1}$$
$$(w_1, s_1^{(1)}, \alpha_1^{(1)}, s_2^{(1)}, \alpha_2^{(1)}, \ldots, s_n^{(1)}, \alpha_n^{(1)}) \vdash^*_{i_2}$$
$$(w_2, s_1^{(2)}, \alpha_1^{(2)}, s_2^{(2)}, \alpha_2^{(2)}, \ldots, s_n^{(2)}, \alpha_n^{(2)}) \vdash^*_{i_3} \cdots \vdash^*_{i_m}$$
$$(\varepsilon, s_1^{(m)}, \varepsilon, s_2^{(m)}, \varepsilon, \ldots, s_n^{(m)}, \varepsilon) \text{ with } m \geq 1, 1 \leq i_1, i_2, \ldots, i_m \leq n$$
$$\text{and } s_i^{(m)} \in Q_i, 1 \leq i \leq n\},$$

then we can state that $Rec_\varepsilon(\mathcal{A}, *) = \sqcup\!\sqcup^P(L)$, where $\mathcal{A}$ is a UDPAS formed by $p$ copies of the pushdown automaton recognizing $L$. Therefore, the problem can be reformulated as follows: Can our protocol of activating/deactivating the components lead to more computational power than the protocol just defined above?

We do not have an answer to this problem. However, along the same lines we can show:

**Proposition 1.** *There are finite languages $L$ such that $\sqcup\!\sqcup^*(L)$ do not belong to $\mathcal{L}_\varepsilon(UDPAS, n)$, for any $n \geq 1$.*

*Proof.* We take the finite language $\{abc\}$ and prove that

$$⫰^*(abc) = \{w \in \{a,b,c\}^+ \mid |w|_a = |w|_b = |w|_c \ \& \ |x|_a \geq |x|_b \geq |x|_c$$
$$\text{for any prefix } x \text{ of } w\},$$

none of the families $\mathcal{L}_\varepsilon(UDPAS, n)$, $n \geq 1$, contains this language.

Assume the contrary, by Lemma 1, there must be a context-free language $L$ such that

$$L^n \subseteq ⫰^*(abc) \subseteq ⫰^n(L).$$

Let $a^m b^m c^m$, for some $m \geq 1$, be a word in $⫰^*(abc)$; there must exist the words $w_i \in L$, $1 \leq i \leq n$, such that $a^m b^m c^m \in ⫰_n(w_1, w_2, \ldots, w_n)$. On the other hand, for any permutation $\sigma$ of $\{1, 2, \ldots, n\}$ the word $w_{\sigma(1)} w_{\sigma(2)} \cdots w_{\sigma(n)}$ belongs to $⫰^*(abc)$, which means that $w_i \in a^+ b^+ c^+$ for all $i$. Furthermore, if $w_i = a^p b^q c^r$, for some $p, q, r \geq 1$, we have $p \geq q \geq r$. We further note that for each $1 \leq i \neq j \leq n \mid \psi(w_i) - \psi(w_j) \mid = (k, k, k)$ holds for some $k \geq 0$. By these considerations and the fact that all words $a^m b^m c^m$, $m \geq 1$, are in $⫰^*(abc)$, we infer that $L \cap a^+ b^+ c^+$ is an infinite language of the form

$$L \cap a^+ b^+ c^+ = \{a^{s+k} b^{p+k} c^{q+k} \mid k \in H\},$$

where $H$ is an infinite set of natural numbers. As $L \cap a^+ b^+ c^+$ is not context-free, it follows that $L$ is not context-free either, which is a contradiction.    □

**Proposition 2.**
1. *The family $\mathcal{L}_\varepsilon(UDPAS, n)$, $n \geq 1$, contains semilinear languages only.*
2. *There are semilinear languages that do not belong to any of these families.*

*Proof.* 1. By Lemma 1, for every UDPAS $\mathcal{A}$ of degree $n$, $\psi(Rec_\varepsilon(\mathcal{A})) = \psi(L^n)$ holds for some context-free language $L$, hence $Rec_\varepsilon(\mathcal{A})$ is semilinear.

2. The language considered in Theorem 1 proves the second statement.    □

## 4   Decidability and Closure Properties

**Proposition 3.** *The emptiness and finiteness problems are decidable for all families $\mathcal{L}_X(UDPAS, n)$, $X \in \{f, \varepsilon\}$, $n \geq 1$.*

*Proof.* Obviously, the language accepted by a UDPAS is empty/finite if and only if the language accepted by its components is empty/finite. Therefore, the assertion follows from the decidability properties of context-free languages class.

**Theorem 2.** *None of the families $\mathcal{L}_\varepsilon(UDPAS, n)$ is closed under union and concatenation with singleton languages, union, concatenation, intersection with regular sets, non-erasing morphisms.*

*Proof.* As we shall see, it suffices to give the reasoning for $n = 2$ only. Let us take the language

$$L = L_1^2 \cup L_2^2 \cup (⫰(L_1, L_2)),$$

where

$$L_1 = \{a^n b^n \mid n \geq 1\}, \qquad L_2 = \{c^m d^m \mid m \geq 1\}.$$

The language $L$ can be accepted by a UDPAS of degree 2. A construction for this system can be easily derived from the definition of the UDPAS in Example 1. We show that $L \cdot \{dcba\}$ cannot be accepted by any UDPAS (no matter its degree) with empty stacks. Assume the contrary, by Lemma 1 there exist a context-free languages $E$ and $k \geq 2$ such that $E^k \subseteq L\{dcba\}$. Therefore, each word in $E$ has to be of the form $xdcba$. We take $k$ words in $E$, $x_1 dcba, x_2 dcba, \ldots, x_k dcba$ such that $x_1 dcba x_2 dcba \ldots x_k dcba \in L\{dcba\}$, hence $x_1 dcba x_2 dcba \ldots x_k \in L$ which is a contradiction.

In similar way one can argue that $L \cup \{dcba\}$ does not belong to any family $\mathcal{L}_\varepsilon(UDPAS, n)$.

On the other hand, each regular language $R_k = \{dcba^n \mid n \geq k\}$, $k \geq 2$, belongs to $\mathcal{L}_\varepsilon(UDPAS, k)$. It follows that $\mathcal{L}_\varepsilon(UDPAS, n)$ is not closed under concatenation and union either.

In order to prove the non-closure under intersection with regular sets we return to Example 1. The language accepted by the UPDAS from Example is $L_1$. But

$$L_1 \cap a^+ b^+ c^+ d^+ = \{a^p b^q c^p d^q \mid p, q \geq 1\},$$

which, by the proof of Theorem 1, does not belong to any family $\mathcal{L}_\varepsilon(DPAS, n)$, $n \geq 2$.

The proof for the non-closure under morphisms is a bit more involved. We consider the language

$$L = \{xxyy, xyxy, xyyx, yyxx, yxyx, yxxy \mid x \in \{a^n \# \mid n \geq 1\},$$
$$y \in \{b^n \# \mid n \geq 1\}\}$$

which lies in $\mathcal{L}_\varepsilon(UDPAS, 2)$. The construction of a UDPAS of degree 2 which accepts $L$ by empty stacks is left to the reader. We prove that the language $h(L)$, where $h(a) = h(b) = a$ and $h(\#) = c$, cannot be accepted by any DPAS (not only UDPAS) by empty stacks.

Suppose that $h(L) = Rec_\varepsilon(\mathcal{A})$ with $\mathcal{A} = (\{a, c\}, A_1, A_2, \ldots, A_p)$ for some $p \geq 2$. We may assume that we need at least two components as $h(L)$ is not context-free. There exists a word $z \in Rec_\varepsilon(\mathcal{A})$ such that the following conditions are satisfied with respect to the accepting process of $z$:

(i) $z = x_1 x_2 \ldots x_s$ for some $s > p$, $x_j \in (a + c)^+$.
(ii) For each $1 \leq j \leq s$, the component $i_j$, $1 \leq i_j \leq p$, is activated when the system starts to read $x_j$.
(iii) There exist $1 \leq j < t \leq s$ such that $i_j = i_t$ and all numbers $i_{j+1}, \ldots, i_s$ are distinct. That is, for the suffix $x_{j+1} \ldots x_s$ of $z$ each component of $\mathcal{A}$ is activated at most once.

Under these circumstances, the word

$$w = x_1 x_2 \ldots x_{j-1} x_j x_t x_{j+1} \ldots x_{t-1} x_{t+1} \ldots x_s$$

is in $Rec_\varepsilon(\mathcal{A})$ as well. If $t \neq s$, then also the word

$$y = x_1 x_2 \ldots x_{j-1} x_j x_{j+1} \ldots x_{t-1} x_{t+1} \ldots x_s x_t$$

is in $Rec_\varepsilon(\mathcal{A})$. Furthermore, the first letter of $x_{j+1}$ is different from the first letter of $x_t$. There are two possibilities:

(I) $x_{j+1} \in a(a+c)^*, x_t \in c(a+c)^*$.
First, let us note that if $x_t$ ends with $a$, then $t \neq s$ holds, hence $y$ must be in $h(L)$, But, $y$ ends with $a$, a contradiction. Therefore, $x_t$ must start and end with $c$. We note also that $t$ cannot equals $s$ because, if this were the case, then $w$ would ends with $a$. Then, it follows that $y$ contains two adjacent occurrences of $c$ which is contradictory. Hence, the first case leads to a contradiction.

(II) $x_{j+1} \in c(a+c)^*, x_t \in a(a+c)^*$.
First we note that $x_t$ cannot start and end with $a$. Indeed, if $x_t$ starts and ends with $a$, then $t \neq s$ and $y$ ends with $a$, a contradiction. But if $x_t$ starts with $a$ and ends with $c$, then $w$ contains two adjacent occurrences of $c$ since the segment $x_j x_t x_{j+1}$ has this property.

Therefore, $h(L) \notin \mathcal{L}_\varepsilon(DPAS, n)$ for any $n \geq 2$, which proves the closure of none of the families $\mathcal{L}_\varepsilon(DPAS, n)$, $n \geq 2$, under morphisms.     $\square$

## 5   Final Remarks

We briefly discuss here a few open problems and possible directions for further developments. We start with the problem formulated in Section 3.

**Open Problem 1.** *What conditions should a context-free language $L$ satisfy such that $⧢^P(L)$ is accepted by a UPDAS with empty stacks?*
It is worth mentioning that one can increase the degree of the UPDAS from the proof of Theorem 1 without modifying the accepted language. This is especially due to the fact that the pushdown automaton $A$ recognizes the empty word. Does this hold for any UDPAS accepting the empty word? Which is the situation for acceptance with empty stacks? More generally,

**Open Problem 2.** *Is there any hierarchy depending on the number of components?*
However, if the classes of languages accepted by UPDAS with empty stacks form a hierarchy depending on the number of components, then this hierarchy is necessarily infinite.

**Theorem 3.** *There exist arbitrarily many natural numbers $n$ such that*

$$\mathcal{L}_\varepsilon(UPDAS, n) \setminus \mathcal{L}_\varepsilon(UPDAS, k) \neq \emptyset.$$

*Proof.* Let $A$ be the pushdown automaton accepting the language

$$L = \{\#a^m b^m \$ \mid m \geq 1\} \cup \{\#c^m d^m \$ \mid m \geq 1\},$$

and $\mathcal{A}$ be the UPDAS formed by $n$ copies of $A$, where $n$ is a prime number. We first note that $Rec_\varepsilon(\mathcal{A})$ is not a context-free language. Indeed,

$$Rec_\varepsilon(\mathcal{A}) \cap \#^n a^+ c^+ b^+ d^+ \$^n = \{\#^n a^p c^q b^p d^q \$^n \mid p, q \geq 1, p + q \geq n\},$$

hence $Rec_\varepsilon(\mathcal{A})$ cannot be context-free. We now claim that $Rec_\varepsilon(\mathcal{A})$ cannot be accepted by any UPDAS of a degree inferior to $n$. Assume the contrary and let $\mathcal{A}'$ be a UPDAS of degree $k < n$ such that $Rec_\varepsilon(\mathcal{A}) = Rec_\varepsilon(\mathcal{A}')$. By Lemma 1, there exists a context-free language $R$ such that

$$R^k \subseteq Rec_\varepsilon(\mathcal{A}) = Rec_\varepsilon(\mathcal{A}') \subseteq \text{Ш}^k(R).$$

Clearly, for every word $w \in Rec_\varepsilon(\mathcal{A})$, $|w|_\# = |w|_\$ = n$ holds. Therefore, for any word $x \in R$, $|x|_\# = |x|_\$ = p$, with $kp = n$ must hold. This implies that $k = 1$, hence $R = Rec_\varepsilon(\mathcal{A})$ which is a contradiction. $\qquad\square$

As we have seen the emptiness and finiteness problems are decidable for UDPAS accepting by empty stacks and the complexity of these problems is directly derived from the complexity of the same problems for usual pushdown automata. The situation seems to be different for the membership problem. We recall that for the shuffling of two context-free languages, the non-uniform version of the membership problem is already NP-hard [1]. However, we ask:

**Open Problem 3.** *Which is the complexity of the membership problem for UPDAS accepting with empty stacks?*

We have proved that UDPAS accepting by final states are strictly more powerful than UDPAS accepting by empty stacks. In our view, the classes $\mathcal{L}_f(DPAS, n)$, $n \geq 1$, deserve to be further investigated.

Last but not least, the deterministic variants of the automata systems considered here appear to be attractive.

# References

1. Berglund, M., Björklund, H., Högberg, J.: Recognizing Shuffled Languages. In: Dediu, A.-H., Inenaga, S., Martín-Vide, C. (eds.) LATA 2011. LNCS, vol. 6638, pp. 142–154. Springer, Heidelberg (2011)
2. Bordihn, H., Kutrib, M., Malcher, A.: Undecidability and hierarchy results for parallel communicating finite automata. Int. J. Found. Comput. Sci. 22, 1577–1592 (2011)
3. Choudhary, A., Krithivasan, K., Mitrana, V.: Returning and non-returning parallel communicating finite automata are equivalent. Information Processing Letters 41, 137–145 (2007)
4. Csuhaj-Varju, E., Dassow, J.: On cooperating distributed grammar systems. J. Inform. Process. Cybern., EIK 26, 49–63 (1990)
5. Csuhaj-Varju, E., Dassow, J., Kelemen, J., Păun, G.: Grammar Systems. A grammatical approach to distribution and cooperation. Gordon and Breach (1994)
6. Csuhaj-Varju, E., Martín-Vide, C., Mitrana, V., Vaszil, G.: Parallel communicating pushdown automata systems. Int. J. Found. Comput. Sci. 11, 633–650 (2000)

7. Csuhaj-Varju, E., Mitrana, V., Vaszil, G.: Distributed Pushdown Automata Systems: Computational Power. In: Ésik, Z., Fülöp, Z. (eds.) DLT 2003. LNCS, vol. 2710, pp. 218–229. Springer, Heidelberg (2003)
8. Dassow, J., Păun, G., Rozenberg, G.: Grammar systems. In: [16], vol. 2
9. Dassow, J., Mitrana, V.: Stack cooperation in multi-stack pushdown automata. J. Comput. System Sci. 58, 611–621 (1999)
10. Durfee, E.H., et al.: Cooperative distributed problem solving. In: Barr, A., Cohen, P.R., Feigenbaum, E.A. (eds.) The Handbook of AI, vol. 4. Addison-Wesley, Reading (1989)
11. Krithivasan, K., Sakthi Balan, M., Harsha, P.: Distributed processing in automata. Int. J. Found. Comput. Sci. 10, 443–464 (1999)
12. Martín-Vide, C., Mitrana, V.: Some undecidable problems for parallel communicating finite automata systems. Information Processing Letters 77, 239–245 (2001)
13. Martín-Vide, C., Mateescu, A., Mitrana, V.: Parallel finite automata systems communicating by states. Int. J. Found. Comput. Sci. 13, 733–749 (2002)
14. Meersman, R., Rozenberg, G.: Cooperating Grammar Systems. In: Winkowski, J. (ed.) MFCS 1978. LNCS, vol. 64, pp. 364–374. Springer, Heidelberg (1978)
15. Păun, G., Sântean, L.: Parallel communicating grammar systems: the regular case. Ann. Univ. Bucharest, Ser. Matem.-Inform. 38, 55–63 (1989)
16. Rozenberg, G., Salomaa, A.: Handbook of Formal Languages, vol. 1-3. Springer, Berlin (1997)

# Removing Nondeterminism
# in Constant Height Pushdown Automata[*]

Zuzana Bednárová[1,**], Viliam Geffert[1,**], Carlo Mereghetti[2],
and Beatrice Palano[2]

[1] Department of Computer Science, P. J. Šafárik University,
Jesenná 5, 04154 Košice, Slovakia
ivazuzu@eriv.sk, viliam.geffert@upjs.sk
[2] Dipartimento di Informatica, Università degli Studi di Milano,
via Comelico 39, 20135 Milano, Italy
{carlo.mereghetti,beatrice.palano}@unimi.it

**Abstract.** We study the descriptional cost of converting *constant height nondeterministic pushdown automata* into equivalent deterministic devices. We show a double-exponential upper bound for this conversion, together with a super-exponential lower bound.

**Keywords:** descriptional complexity, finite state automata, regular languages, deterministic and nondeterministic pushdown automata.

## 1 Introduction

The first and most relevant generalization to computational devices is certainly the introduction of *nondeterminism*. Among others, nondeterminism represents an elegant tool to capture certain classes of problems and languages. Although not existing in nature, a nondeterministic dynamic may in principle be "simulated" by actual paradigms, such as probabilistic or quantum frameworks (see, e.g., [8,12,16]). Nondeterministic variants of Turing machines, finite state automata, pushdown automata, and many other devices, have been studied from the very beginning.

The investigation on nondeterminism may be pursued along several lines. First, we may want to know whether nondeterminism really increases *computational power* of the underlying computational model. For example (see, e.g., [4,11]), it is well-known that nondeterminism does not increase the computational power of Turing machines or finite state automata. On the other hand, it is well-known that nondeterministic pushdown automata (NPDAs) are strictly more powerful than their deterministic counterpart (DPDAs), corresponding to

---

[*] Supported by the Slovak Grant Agency for Science under contract VEGA 1/0479/12 "Combinatorial Structures and Complexity of Algorithms" and by the Slovak Research and Development Agency under contract APVV-0035-10 "Algorithms, Automata, and Discrete Data Structures".

[**] Corresponding author.

M. Kutrib, N. Moreira, and R. Reis (Eds.): DCFS 2012, LNCS 7386, pp. 76–88, 2012.

the respective classes of context-free and deterministic context-free languages. Finally, for certain devices, the problem is not yet solved, e.g., it is still not known whether the computational power of two-way DPDAs and NPDAs coincide.

Another interesting line of research is the study of how nondeterminism helps in presence of limited computational resources. Questions of this type, like P vs NP or L vs NL, go to the very heart of theoretical computer science (see, e.g., [4,11]).

In the realm of finite memory machines, the impact of nondeterminism on device efficiency is usually evaluated by considering its *size* [7,10]. A classical result of this kind [15,17] establishes an optimal exponential gap between the number of finite control states in deterministic and nondeterministic finite state automata (DFAs and NFAs, respectively).

In this paper, we tackle the impact of nondeterminism on descriptional complexity of *constant height pushdown automata* [1,5]. Roughly speaking, these devices are traditional pushdown automata (see, e.g., [11]) with a built-in constant limit, not depending on the input length, on the height of the pushdown. It is a routine exercise to show that their deterministic and nondeterministic versions accept exactly regular languages, and hence they share the same computational power. Nevertheless, a representation of regular languages by constant height pushdown automata can potentially be more succinct than by standard devices. In fact, in [5], optimal exponential and double-exponential gaps are proved between the size of constant height DPDAs/NPDAs, and DFAs and NFAs. The diagram in Fig. 1 quickly resumes such gaps.

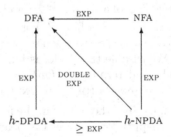

**Fig. 1.** Costs of conversion among different types of automata. Here $h$-NPDA ($h$-DPDA) denote constant height NPDAs (DPDAs). An arrow labeled by EXP (DOUBLE EXP) from $A$ to $B$ means that an automaton of type $A$ can be converted to an equivalent automaton of type $B$, paying by an exponential (double-exponential) increase in size. All costs were known to be *optimal*, except for the cost of $h$-DPDA$\longleftarrow$ $h$-NPDA conversion, which we study in this paper.

The problem of optimal size cost of converting constant height NPDAs into their deterministic counterparts was left open in [5], and will be the subject of this contribution. What can be easily derived from Fig. 1 is that such a cost cannot be smaller than exponential. In fact, a sub-exponential cost combined with the optimal exponential cost for $h$-DPDA $\rightarrow$ DFA would lead to a sub-double-exponential cost of $h$-NPDA $\rightarrow$ DFA, thus contradicting the optimality of the double-exponential cost. *We are going to show that elimination of nondeterminism in constant height pushdown automata is at least super-exponential, i.e., it cannot be bounded by* $2^{p(h)}$, *for no polynomial* $p(h)$.

We start from the fact that any constant height NPDA, working with a finite state set $Q$, pushdown alphabet $\Gamma$, and constant pushdown height $h$, can be converted into an equivalent DFA with $2^{\|Q\| \cdot \|\Gamma^{\leq h}\|}$ states, which is of course a constant height DPDA that does not actually use the power of pushdown storage.

One may think that a more sophisticated technique could lead to a smaller constant height DPDA, utilizing the capabilities of its pushdown store in a smarter way. However, we shall show that this is not the case. In fact, we design $\{L_h\}_{h\geq 1}$, a family of languages, such that *(i)* $L_h$ can be accepted by a constant height NPDA using $O(h)$ many states and pushdown height $h$ with binary pushdown alphabet, but *(ii)* any constant height DPDA for $L_h$ (with no restrictions on the size of pushdown alphabet) cannot have both the number of states and the pushdown height below $2^{p(h)}$, for any polynomial $p$.

Note that a super-exponential lower bound cannot be obtained by standard pigeonhole arguments directly, since already a machine with a single-exponential pushdown height can reach a double-exponential number of different pushdown configurations, so we need a more sophisticated counting argument.

## 2   Preliminaries

The set of words on an alphabet $\Sigma$, including the empty word $\varepsilon$, is denoted here by $\Sigma^*$. By $|\varphi|$, we denote the length of a word $\varphi \in \Sigma^*$ and by $\Sigma^i$ the set of words of length $i$, with $\Sigma^0 = \{\varepsilon\}$ and $\Sigma^{\leq h} = \bigcup_{i=0}^{h} \Sigma^i$. For a word $\varphi = a_1 \cdots a_\ell$, let $\varphi^R = a_\ell \cdots a_1$ denote its reversal. By $\|S\|$, we denote the cardinality of a set $S$, and by $S^c$ its complement. We assume the reader is familiar with the standard models of deterministic and nondeterministic *finite state automata* (DFA and NFA, for short) and *pushdown automata* (DPDA and NPDA, see, e.g., [11]).

For technical reasons, we introduce the NPDAs in the following form [5], where instructions manipulating the pushdown store are clearly distinguished from those reading the input tape: an NPDA is a sextuplet $A = \langle Q, \Sigma, \Gamma, H, q_1, F \rangle$, where $Q$ is the finite set of states, $\Sigma$ the input alphabet, $\Gamma$ the pushdown alphabet, $q_1 \in Q$ the initial state, $F \subseteq Q$ and $Q \setminus F$ the sets of accepting and rejecting states, respectively, and $H \subseteq Q \times (\{\varepsilon\} \cup \Sigma \cup \{+, -\} \cdot \Gamma) \times Q$ the *transition relation*, establishing machine instructions with the following meaning:

(i) $(p, \varepsilon, q) \in H$: $A$ gets from $p$ to $q$ without using the input tape or the pushdown store.

(ii) $(p, a, q) \in H$: if the next input symbol is $a$, $A$ gets from $p$ to $q$ by reading the symbol $a$, not using the pushdown store.

(iii) $(p, -X, q) \in H$: if the symbol on top of the pushdown is $X$, $A$ gets from $p$ to $q$ by popping $X$, not using the input tape.

(iv) $(p, +X, q) \in H$: $A$ gets from $p$ to $q$ by pushing the symbol $X$ onto the pushdown, not using the input tape.

Such a machine does not need any initial pushdown symbol. An *accepting computation* begins in the state $q_\mathrm{I}$ with the empty pushdown store, and ends in an accepting state $p \in F$ after reading the entire input. As usual, $L(A)$ denotes the language accepted by the NPDA $A$.

A *deterministic pushdown automaton* (DPDA) is obtained from NPDA by claiming that the transition relation does not allow to execute more than one possible instruction at a time. (As an example, a DPDA cannot have a pair of instructions of the form $(p, \varepsilon, q_1)$ and $(p, a, q_2)$, starting from the same state $p$.)

Traditionally (see, e.g., [11]), the dynamics of NPDAs is defined by a function $\delta : Q \times (\Sigma \cup \{\varepsilon\}) \times \Gamma \to 2^{Q \times \Gamma^*}$, combining input and pushdown operations into a single step. However, a NPDA in this classical form can be easily turned into our form and vice versa, preserving determinism in the case of DPDAs.[1]

Given a constant $h \geq 0$, we say that the NPDA $A$ is of pushdown height $h$ if, for any $\varphi \in L(A)$, there exists an accepting computation along which the pushdown store never contains more than $h$ symbols. Such a machine will be denoted by a septuplet $A = \langle Q, \Sigma, \Gamma, H, q_\mathrm{I}, F, h \rangle$, where $h \geq 0$ is a constant denoting the pushdown height, and all other elements are defined as above. By definition, the meaning of the transitions in the form (iv) is modified as follows:

(iv) $(p, +X, q) \in H$: *if the current pushdown store height is smaller than $h$, then $A$ gets from the state $p$ to the state $q$ by pushing the symbol $X$ onto the pushdown, not using the input tape; otherwise $A$ aborts and rejects.*

For $h = 0$, the definition of constant height NPDA (DPDA) coincides with that of an NFA (DFA). For constant height NPDAs, a fair descriptional complexity measure takes into account all the components the device consists of, i.e., *(i)* the number of finite control states, *(ii)* the height of the pushdown store, and *(iii)* the size of the pushdown alphabet [5].

In [1], the cost of implementing Boolean language operations on constant height DPDAs is investigated. In this paper, we shall need the following results:

**Theorem 1 ([1, Thms. 3.1 and 3.2]).** *Each constant height DPDA $A = \langle Q, \Sigma,$ $\Gamma, H, q_\mathrm{I}, F, h \rangle$ can be replaced by*
   (i) *an equivalent constant height DPDA $A'$ such that, on any input string, the computation halts after reading the entire input (i.e., its computations are never blocked in the middle of the input),*
   (ii) *a constant height DPDA $A''$ accepting the complement of $L(A)$.*
*Both $A'$ and $A''$ use the same pushdown alphabet and pushdown height as does $A$, with at most $\|Q\|(h+1)+1$ states.*

---

[1] A classical transition $\delta(p, a, X) \ni (q, X_1 \ldots X_k)$ can be simulated by $(p, -X, p_X)$, $(p_X, a, q_0)$, $(q_0, +X_1, q_1)$, $\ldots$, $(q_{k-2}, +X_{k-1}, q_{k-1})$, $(q_{k-1}, +X_k, q)$, where $p_X$ and $q_0, \ldots, q_{k-1}$ are new states, with obvious modifications for $k < 2$. This also requires to store an initial pushdown symbol $X_\mathrm{I}$ at the very beginning, using $(q'_\mathrm{I}, +X_\mathrm{I}, q_\mathrm{I})$, where $q'_\mathrm{I}$ is a new initial state. The converse transformation is also straightforward.

## 3    A Double-Exponential Upper Bound

Here we show that a double-exponential increase in size is *sufficient* for simulating a constant height NPDA by an equivalent constant height DPDA. Our approach goes through the following steps: First, "remove the pushdown store" by keeping all data in the finite state control, i.e., simulate an NPDA working with a state set $Q$, a constant height $h$, and a pushdown alphabet $\Gamma$ by an equivalent NFA with at most $\|Q\| \cdot \|\Gamma^{\leq h}\|$ states. Second, make this NFA deterministic, i.e., transform it into a DFA with at most $2^{\|Q\| \cdot \|\Gamma^{\leq h}\|}$ states, by the standard power set construction. Let us begin with the first step (see also [5, Prop. 3]):

**Lemma 2.** *For each constant height* NPDA $A = \langle Q, \Sigma, \Gamma, H, q_1, F, h \rangle$, *there exists an equivalent* NFA $A' = \langle Q', \Sigma, H', q_1', F' \rangle$ *with* $\|Q'\| \leq \|Q\| \cdot \|\Gamma^{\leq h}\|$.

*Proof.* The key idea is to keep the pushdown content of $A$, represented here by a string $\gamma \in \Gamma^{\leq h}$ (growing to the right), in the finite control state. The transitions of $A'$ reflect step-by-step the evolution of both state and pushdown content.

Thus, we set $Q' = Q \times \Gamma^{\leq h}$, $q_1' = [q_1, \varepsilon]$, $F' = F \times \Gamma^{\leq h}$, and define $H'$ as follows, for any $p, q \in Q$, $\gamma \in \Gamma^{\leq h}$, $a \in \Sigma$, and $X \in \Gamma$:

- If $(p, \varepsilon, q) \in H$, then $([p, \gamma], \varepsilon, [q, \gamma]) \in H'$.
- If $(p, a, q) \in H$, then $([p, \gamma], a, [q, \gamma]) \in H'$.
- If $(p, +X, q) \in H$ and $|\gamma| < h$, then $([p, \gamma], \varepsilon, [q, \gamma X]) \in H'$.
- If $(p, -X, q) \in H$ and $|\gamma| < h$, then $([p, \gamma X], \varepsilon, [q, \gamma]) \in H'$.

The reader may easily verify that $L(A') = L(A)$.                                  □

**Corollary 3.** *For each constant height* NPDA $A = \langle Q, \Sigma, \Gamma, H, q_1, F, h \rangle$, *there exists an equivalent constant height* DPDA $A'' = \langle Q'', \Sigma, \Gamma'', H'', q_1'', F'', h'' \rangle$ *with* $\|Q''\| \leq 2^{\|Q\|\|\Gamma^{\leq h}\|}$, $\Gamma'' = \emptyset$, *and* $h' = 0$.

*Proof.* The double-exponential upper bound is obtained by applying the standard power set construction, making the NFA $A'$ of Lem. 2 deterministic. The resulting DFA $A''$ can obviously be viewed as a restricted constant-height DPDA, not using its pushdown store, with the claimed size.                                  □

Since the machine obtained in the above corollary does not, in fact, use the pushdown storage at all, one may suspect that a more sophisticated technique — using a full-featured constant height pushdown — could dramatically decrease such a huge number of states. Surprisingly enough, we will show that our two-step conversion is asymptotically optimal.

## 4    A Super-Exponential Lower Bound

Let us define the family of witness languages $\{L_h\}_{h \geq 1}$ we shall be dealing with. First, we fix the input alphabet to $\Sigma = \{0, 1, \$\}$ and let $\mathcal{X} = \{0, 1\}^h$. In what follows, the elements of $\mathcal{X}$ will be called *blocks*. Clearly, we have $\|\mathcal{X}\| = 2^h$ many different blocks. We say that a string $\varphi$ is *well formed*, if it has the following block structure:

$$\varphi = x_1 x_2 \cdots x_s \$ y_1 y_2 \cdots y_r,$$

where $s, r \geq 0$ and $x_i, y_j \in \mathcal{X}$, for $i \in \{1, \ldots, s\}$ and $j \in \{1, \ldots, r\}$.

**Definition 4.** *For each $h \geq 1$, let $L_h$ be the language consisting of*

- *all strings $\varphi \in \{0, 1, \$\}^*$ which are not well formed,*
- *plus all well formed strings for which $\cup_{i=1}^{s} \{x_i\} \cap \cup_{j=1}^{r} \{y_j^{\mathrm{R}}\} \neq \emptyset$, that is, $x_i = y_j^{\mathrm{R}}$ for some $i, j$.*

We need also an additional notation. We say that a string $x = x_1 \cdots x_s \in \mathcal{X}^*$ *contains* a block $y_j^{\mathrm{R}} \in \mathcal{X}$, if $y_j^{\mathrm{R}} \in \cup_{i=1}^{s} \{x_i\}$. This can also be denoted by "$y_j^{\mathrm{R}} \in x$". In other words, $|y_j^{\mathrm{R}}| = h$, and $y_j^{\mathrm{R}}$ is a substring of $x$ that begins at a block boundary.

We are going to prove that the languages $\{L_h\}_{h \geq 1}$ can be accepted by constant height NPDAS $\{A_h\}_{h \geq 1}$ with $O(h)$ states, pushdown height $h$, and the binary pushdown alphabet but, in any constant height DPDAS for these languages, either the number of states or the pushdown height must be super-exponential (growing faster than any exponential in $h$), no matter how large is the pushdown alphabet. It is not hard to give a constant height NPDA for $L_h$:

**Lemma 5.** *The language $L_h$ can be recognized by a constant height NPDA $A$ using $O(h)$ states, pushdown height $h$, and binary pushdown alphabet.*

*Proof.* Let us informally describe the dynamics of $A$. In the first phase, it counts the length of the initial part of the input (up to the symbol $\$$) modulo $h$. If this length is not an integer multiple of $h$, the input is not well formed an hence $A$ accepts immediately. While doing this, at each block boundary, $A$ nondeterministically chooses either to load the current input block in the pushdown or to postpone the loading operation on some later block. If $A$ never encounters $\$$, it accepts, since the input is not well formed.

In the second phase, after reading the symbol $\$$, $A$ similarly counts the length of the second part of the input (the suffix from $\$$) modulo $h$, but now, at each block boundary, it nondeterministically chooses either to match the current input block against the block loaded in the pushdown or to postpone the check on a future block. $A$ accepts if one of these block matchings is successful, if a second $\$$ is read, or if the second part is not an integer multiple of $h$.

Clearly, since $A$ counts modulo $h$, the number of states in $A$ is bounded by $O(h)$. Moreover, since $A$ stores a single block from $\mathcal{X} = \{0, 1\}^h$ in the pushdown, we use the pushdown alphabet $\Gamma = \{0, 1\}$ and the pushdown height $h$. $\square$

Consider now membership in $L_h^c$. By negating the membership condition in $L_h$, we get that a string $\varphi$ belongs to $L_h^c$ if and only if:

- $\varphi$ is well formed, i.e., $\varphi = x_1 x_2 \cdots x_s \$ y_1 y_2 \cdots y_r$ for some $x_i, y_j \in \mathcal{X}$, and
- $\cup_{i=1}^{s} \{x_i\} \cap \cup_{j=1}^{r} \{y_j^{\mathrm{R}}\} = \emptyset$, that is, $x_i \neq y_j^{\mathrm{R}}$ for each $i, j$.

**Theorem 6.** *Let $\{A_h\}_{h\geq 1}$ be any constant height DPDAs accepting the languages $\{L_h^c\}_{h\geq 1}$, with no restrictions on the size of pushdown alphabets. Then, for any polynomial $p(h)$ and each sufficiently large $h$, the number of states and the pushdown height of $A_h$ cannot be both smaller than $2^{p(h)}$.*

*Proof.* From now on, for the sake of readability, we shall often write $A$ instead of $A_h$, and $p$ instead of $p(h)$.

Assume now, for contradiction, the existence of a constant height DPDA $A = \langle Q, \Sigma, \Gamma, H, q_1, F, t \rangle$ accepting $L_h^c$, in which both $\|Q\|$ and $t$, the number of states and the pushdown height, are smaller than $2^p$, for some polynomial $p$, using an arbitrary pushdown alphabet $\Gamma$. By Thm. 1, we can assume without loss of generality that, for any input string, $A$ completely scans the entire input until the end. (This only increases the number of states from $2^p$ to $\|Q\|(t+1)+1 \leq 2^{2p+2}$, keeping the same pushdown store.) We can also assume that $p = p(h) \geq h$. Now we are going to fool $A$, i.e., to show the existence of (at least) two strings $\varphi_1, \varphi_2$ such that $\varphi_1 \in L_h^c$ and $\varphi_2 \notin L_h^c$, but $A$ accepts $\varphi_1$ if and only if it accepts $\varphi_2$.

First, we partition the blocks in $\mathcal{X} = \{0,1\}^h$, upon which $L_h$ is defined, into two disjoint sets

$$\mathcal{U} = \{x_i \in \mathcal{X} : \operatorname{num}(x_i) < \tfrac{1}{8}2^h\} \quad \text{and} \quad \mathcal{W} = \{x_i \in \mathcal{X} : \operatorname{num}(x_i) \geq \tfrac{1}{8}2^h\},$$

where $\operatorname{num}(x_i)$ denotes the integer represented by the binary string $x_i$. Clearly, we have $\|\mathcal{U}\| = \tfrac{1}{8}2^h$ and $\|\mathcal{W}\| = \|\mathcal{X}\| - \|\mathcal{U}\| = \tfrac{7}{8}2^h$. Define now the following sets of strings composed of these blocks:

$$X_0 = \{x_1 \cdots x_s : \operatorname{num}(x_1) < \ldots < \operatorname{num}(x_s), \ x_1, \ldots, x_s \in \mathcal{X}\},$$
$$U_0 = \{u_1 \cdots u_s : \operatorname{num}(u_1) < \ldots < \operatorname{num}(u_s), \ u_1, \ldots, u_s \in \mathcal{U}\},$$
$$W_0 = \{w_1 \cdots w_s : \operatorname{num}(w_1) < \ldots < \operatorname{num}(w_s), \ w_1, \ldots, w_s \in \mathcal{W}\}.$$

Clearly, $X_0 = U_0 \cdot W_0$. This follows from the fact that the blocks in each $x \in X_0$ are sorted. Thus, $x$ can be partitioned into $x = uw$, for some $u \in U_0$ and $w \in W_0$, with boundary between $u$ and $w$ unambiguously given by the position of the first block $x_i$ for which we have $\operatorname{num}(x_i) \geq \tfrac{1}{8}2^h$. It is obvious that $|u|$ and $|w|$ are integer multiples of $h$, that $|u| \leq h \cdot \tfrac{1}{8}2^h$, and that $|w| \leq h \cdot \tfrac{7}{8}2^h$, not excluding the possibility of $u = \varepsilon$ or $w = \varepsilon$.

This established a one-to-one correspondence between the subsets of $\mathcal{X}$ and strings in $X_0$: each $B = \{x_1, x_2, \ldots, x_s\} \subseteq \mathcal{X}$ corresponds to a binary string $x_B \in X_0$, in which we list all blocks in sorted order. The same correspondence holds between the subsets of $\mathcal{U}, \mathcal{W}$ and strings in $U_0, W_0$, respectively. Thus,

$$\|X_0\| = 2^{\|\mathcal{X}\|} = 2^{2^h}, \quad \|U_0\| = 2^{\|\mathcal{U}\|} = 2^{1/8 \cdot 2^h}, \quad \|W_0\| = 2^{\|\mathcal{W}\|} = 2^{7/8 \cdot 2^h}. \tag{1}$$

Consider now a computation of $A$ on a string $x\$ = uw\$$, where $u \in U_0$, $w \in W_0$, and hence $x \in X_0$. For this computation, we define the following parameters (see also Fig. 2):

- $\ell_y \in \{0, \ldots, t\}$, the lowest height of pushdown store in the course of reading the string $w\$$,

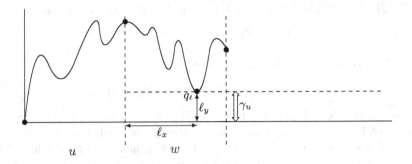

**Fig. 2.** Parameters along the first phase of the computation

- $q_\ell \in Q$, the state in which the height $\ell_y$ is attained for the last time, along $w\$$,
- $\ell_x \in \{0, \ldots, |w\$|\}$, the distance from the beginning of $w\$$ to the input position in which $q_\ell$ is entered,
- $\gamma_u$ be the pushdown content at the moment when $q_\ell$ is entered. Clearly, since $|\gamma_u| = \ell_y$, all symbols of $\gamma_u$ had to be loaded in the pushdown in the course of reading $u$, not modified in the course of reading $w\$$, and hence $\gamma_u$ does not depend on $w$.

Since the machine uses $\|Q\| \leq 2^p$ states, $\ell_x \leq |w|+1 \leq h \cdot \frac{7}{8}2^h +1$, and the pushdown height is $t \leq 2^p$, the number of different triples $[q_\ell, \ell_x, \ell_y]$ can be bounded by $\|Q\| \cdot (h \cdot \frac{7}{8}2^h + 1) \cdot t \leq 2^{4p}$, for each sufficiently large $h$. Now, by considering (1) and a pigeonhole argument, we get the existence of a set $X_1 \subseteq X_0$, with

$$\|X_1\| \geq \frac{\|X_0\|}{2^{4p}} = 2^{2^h - 4p}, \tag{2}$$

such that all strings in $X_1$ share the same triple $[q_\ell, \ell_x, \ell_y]$. Let us now build the following "projection" sets from $X_1$:

$$U_1 = \{u \in U_0 : \exists w, \text{ such that } uw \in X_1\},$$
$$W_1 = \{w \in W_0 : \exists u, \text{ such that } uw \in X_1\}.$$

Clearly, $\|U_1\| \leq \|U_0\| = 2^{1/8 \cdot 2^h}$ and $\|W_1\| \leq \|W_0\| = 2^{7/8 \cdot 2^h}$, using (1). Note also that $X_1 \subseteq U_1 \cdot W_1$, with $\|X_1\| > 0$, and hence also with $\|U_1\| > 0$ and $\|W_1\| > 0$. Thus, we have $\|X_1\| \leq \|U_1\| \cdot \|W_1\|$, whence

$$\|W_1\| \geq \frac{\|X_1\|}{\|U_1\|} \geq \frac{2^{2^h - 4p}}{2^{1/8 \cdot 2^h}} = 2^{7/8 \cdot 2^h - 4p}.$$

Now, let us split $W_1$ into the following two disjoint sets:

$$W_2 = \{w \in W_1 : \text{there exist more than one } u \in U_1 \text{ such that } uw \in X_1\},$$
$$W_2^c = \{w \in W_1 : \text{there exists exactly one } u \in U_1 \text{ such that } uw \in X_1\}.$$

Let $\xi = \|W_2\|$. First, using $\|W_1\| \leq \|W_0\|$ and (1), it is easy to see that

$$\|W_2^c\| = \|W_1\| - \xi \leq 2^{7/8 \cdot 2^h} - \xi\,.$$

To evaluate a lower bound for $\xi = \|W_2\|$, observe that

$$X_1 \subseteq U_1 \cdot W_1 = (U_1 \cdot W_2^c) \cup (U_1 \cdot W_2)\,,$$

but the contribution of elements from $U_1 \cdot W_2^c$ to the total number of elements in $X_1$ must be very "small". Consequently, the contribution from $U_1 \cdot W_2$ must be "large". More precisely, observe that if $w \in W_2^c$, then it is impossible to have $\dot{u}w \in X_1$ and $\ddot{u}w \in X_1$ for two different strings $\dot{u}, \ddot{u} \in U_1$. On the other hand, if $w \in W_2$, the number of strings $uw \in X_1$ sharing this $w$ is bounded only by $\|U_1\| \leq \|U_0\| = 2^{1/8 \cdot 2^h}$, by (1). This gives us that

$$\|X_1\| \leq 1 \cdot \|W_2^c\| + \|U_1\| \cdot \|W_2\| \leq (2^{7/8 \cdot 2^h} - \xi) + 2^{1/8 \cdot 2^h} \cdot \xi\,.$$

By considering (2), one gets, for each sufficiently large $h$,

$$\|W_2\| = \xi \geq \frac{\|X_1\| - 2^{7/8 \cdot 2^h}}{2^{1/8 \cdot 2^h} - 1} \geq \frac{2^{2^h - 4p} - 2^{7/8 \cdot 2^h}}{2^{1/8 \cdot 2^h}} \tag{3}$$
$$= 2^{7/8 \cdot 2^h - 4p} - 2^{6/8 \cdot 2^h} \geq 2^{7/8 \cdot 2^h - 4p - 1}\,.$$

Let us now take, for each $w \in W_2$, the first two different strings $\dot{u}, \ddot{u} \in U_1$ such that $\dot{u}w \in X_1$ and $\ddot{u}w \in X_1$. (By definition of $W_2$, such strings must exist.) Since the number of pairs $\dot{u} \neq \ddot{u}$ is clearly bounded by $\|U_1\| \cdot \|U_1\| \leq 2^{1/8 \cdot 2^h} \cdot 2^{1/8 \cdot 2^h} = 2^{1/4 \cdot 2^h}$, again a simple pigeonhole argument yields a nonempty set $W_3 \subseteq W_2$, in which all strings $w$ share the same pair $\dot{u} \neq \ddot{u}$ satisfying $\dot{u}w \in X_1$ and $\ddot{u}w \in X_1$. More precisely, using (3), we have

$$\|W_3\| \geq \frac{\|W_2\|}{\|U_1\| \cdot \|U_1\|} \geq \frac{2^{7/8 \cdot 2^h - 4p - 1}}{2^{1/4 \cdot 2^h}} = 2^{5/8 \cdot 2^h - 4p - 1}\,. \tag{4}$$

To sum up, we have found a set $W_3$ such that all strings $w \in W_3$ share the same common pair $\dot{u} \neq \ddot{u}$ and also the same triplet $[q_\ell, \ell_x, \ell_y]$ along the computations on the inputs $\dot{u}w\$$ and $\ddot{u}w\$$. Since $\dot{u} \neq \ddot{u}$, there must exist a block $y_1^R \in \mathcal{U}$ such that $y_1^R \in \ddot{u}$ but $y_1^R \notin \dot{u}$. (The argument for $y_1^R \notin \ddot{u}$ with $y_1^R \in \dot{u}$ is symmetrical, by swapping the roles of $\ddot{u}$ and $\dot{u}$.)

Now, for all $w \in W_3$, let us consider the computations of $A$ on the strings $\dot{u}w\$y_1$. All these computations reach the same state $q_\ell$ after consuming $\dot{u}$ and the first $\ell_x$ symbols of $w$, with the same pushdown height at this moment, equal to $\ell_y$. Recall that $\ell_y$ is the lowest height of pushdown store in the course of reading the string $w\$$. Thus, also the pushdown content must be the same, some $\gamma_{\dot{u}}$ of length $\ell_y$, loaded in the course of reading $\dot{u}$. Moreover, these deepest $\ell_y$ symbols in the pushdown will not be modified until the machine scans the symbol $\$$.

At this point, we distinguish between the following two cases, depending on whether, along the block $y_1$, these computations will use the deepest $\ell_y$ symbols in the pushdown store. More precisely, we have:

CASE I: *There exists at least one $w \in W_3$ such that the computation on $\dot{u}w\$y_1$ never visits the deepest $\ell_y$ symbols in the pushdown store while processing $y_1$.*
First, let us *fix one* such string $\hat{w}$. Since $\hat{w} \in W_3 \subseteq W_0 \subseteq \mathcal{W}^*$, the string $\hat{w}$ is composed only of blocks $w_i$ satisfying $\text{num}(w_i) \geq \frac{1}{8}2^h$. On the other hand, recall that the block $y_1^{\text{R}} \in \mathcal{U}$, and hence $\text{num}(y_1^{\text{R}}) < \frac{1}{8}2^h$. This gives $y_1^{\text{R}} \notin \hat{w}$. Recall also that $y_1^{\text{R}} \in \ddot{u}$ but $y_1^{\text{R}} \notin \dot{u}$. Therefore, $\dot{u}\hat{w}\$y_1 \in L_h^c$ but $\ddot{u}\hat{w}\$y_1 \notin L_h^c$.

Compare now the computations on the inputs $\dot{u}\hat{w}\$y_1$ and $\ddot{u}\hat{w}\$y_1$. These two computations are generally different. (See also Fig. 3.) However, after reading the

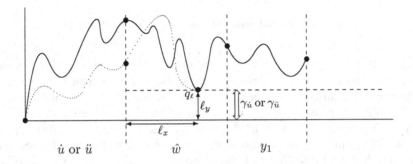

**Fig. 3.** The second phase of the computation—CASE I

first $\ell_x$ symbols of the string $\hat{w}\$$, they both pass through the same state $q_\ell$ and the respective pushdown contents at this moment are $\gamma_{\dot{u}}$ and $\gamma_{\ddot{u}}$, with $|\gamma_{\dot{u}}| = |\gamma_{\ddot{u}}| = \ell_y$. From the state $q_\ell$ forward, up to the end of the input, both computations are identical, since they: *(i)* start from the same state $q_\ell$, *(ii)* read the same input symbols (namely, the last $|\hat{w}\$|-\ell_x$ symbols of the string $\hat{w}\$$ plus the entire string $y_1$), and *(iii)* never visit the deepest $\ell_y$ symbols in the pushdown ($\gamma_{\dot{u}}$ or $\gamma_{\ddot{u}}$, respectively). Hence, $\dot{u}\hat{w}\$y_1$ is accepted if and only if $\ddot{u}\hat{w}\$y_1$ is accepted, which contradicts the fact that $\dot{u}\hat{w}\$y_1 \in L_h^c$ but $\ddot{u}\hat{w}\$y_1 \notin L_h^c$.

CASE II: *For all $w \in W_3$, the computations on $\dot{u}w\$y_1$ do visit the deepest $\ell_y$ symbols in the pushdown store while processing $y_1$.* Hence, we can fix additional parameters *for each* string $w \in W_3$, namely:

- $q_k \in Q$, the state in which the height $\ell_y$ is decreased to $\ell_y-1$ for the first time, in the course of reading $y_1$,
- $k_x \in \{1, \ldots, |y_1|\}$, the distance from the beginning of $y_1$ to the input position in which $q_k$ is entered. (See also Fig. 4.)

Since $\|Q\| \leq 2^p$ and $|y_1| = h$, the number of different pairs $[q_k, k_x]$ is bounded by $\|Q\| \cdot h \leq 2^{2p}$. This, together with (4) and a pigeonhole argument, requires the existence of a set $W_4 \subseteq W_3$, such that all $w \in W_4$ share the same pair $[q_k, k_x]$ and hence, for each sufficiently large $h$,

$$\|W_4\| \geq \frac{\|W_3\|}{2^{2p}} \geq \frac{2^{5/8 \cdot 2^h - 4p - 1}}{2^{2p}} = 2^{5/8 \cdot 2^h - 6p - 1} \geq 2.$$

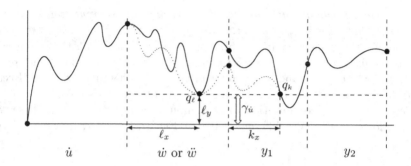

**Fig. 4.** The second phase of the computation — CASE II

Thus, $\|W_4\| \geq 2$, and we can choose two different strings $\dot{w}, \ddot{w} \in W_4$. It means that $\dot{w} \neq \ddot{w}$ share the same $\dot{u}$ (we now forget about $\ddot{u}$, no longer required) and, on the respective inputs $\dot{u}\dot{w}\$y_1$ and $\dot{u}\ddot{w}\$y_1$, the same $[q_\ell, \ell_x, \ell_y]$ and also the same $[q_k, k_x]$. Again, because $\dot{w} \neq \ddot{w}$, we can find a block $y_2^{\mathrm{R}} \in W$ such that $y_2^{\mathrm{R}} \in \ddot{w}$ but $y_2^{\mathrm{R}} \notin \dot{w}$. (The argument for $y_2^{\mathrm{R}} \notin \ddot{w}$ with $y_2^{\mathrm{R}} \in \dot{w}$ is symmetrical, by swapping the roles of $\ddot{w}$ and $\dot{w}$.) Recall also that $y_1$ was chosen so that $y_1^{\mathrm{R}} \notin \dot{u}$. Second, by a reasoning similar to that in CASE I, we also get $y_1^{\mathrm{R}} \notin \dot{w}$ and $y_2^{\mathrm{R}} \notin \dot{u}$, taking into account that $\mathrm{num}(y_1^{\mathrm{R}}) < \frac{1}{8}2^h$, but all blocks in $\dot{w}$ satisfy $\mathrm{num}(w_i) \geq \frac{1}{8}2^h$, and that $\mathrm{num}(y_2^{\mathrm{R}}) \geq \frac{1}{8}2^h$ but, for blocks in $\dot{u}$, we have $\mathrm{num}(u_i) < \frac{1}{8}2^h$. Putting these facts together, we have that $\dot{u}\dot{w}\$y_1y_2 \in L_h^{\mathrm{c}}$ but $\dot{u}\ddot{w}\$y_1y_2 \notin L_h^{\mathrm{c}}$.

The computations of $A$ on these two inputs are clearly identical while processing $\dot{u}$, and they generally differ in the subsequent segments $\dot{w}\$$ and $\ddot{w}\$$, respectively. However, after reading the first $\ell_x$ symbols of these segments, both computations pass through the same state $q_\ell$ and the pushdown content is also the same at this moment, namely, $\gamma_{\dot{u}}$ of length $\ell_y$, loaded in the course of processing $\dot{u}$. After passing through the state $q_\ell$, up to reaching $q_k$, the computations may differ again. However, the lower $\ell_y$ symbols in the pushdown will stay unchanged. Thus, both computations reach the state $q_k$ with the pushdown content equal to $\gamma_{\dot{u}}$. By considering this latter fact, and due to the common suffix on the input, namely, the last $|y_1y_2| - k_x$ symbols of the string $y_1y_2$, we get that, from $q_k$ on, both computations turn out to proceed identically again, and hence $\dot{u}\dot{w}\$y_1y_2$ is accepted if and only if $\dot{u}\ddot{w}\$y_1y_2$ is accepted. This contradicts the fact that $\dot{u}\dot{w}\$y_1y_2 \in L_h^{\mathrm{c}}$ but $\dot{u}\ddot{w}\$y_1y_2 \notin L_h^{\mathrm{c}}$.

In conclusion, for each polynomial $p = p(h)$ and each sufficiently large $h$, each DPDA $A = A_h$ accepting $L_h^{\mathrm{c}}$ must use either more than $2^{p(h)}$ states or a pushdown height larger than $2^{p(h)}$. □

We are now ready to present the main super-exponential blow up:

**Theorem 7.** *There exists* $\{L_h\}_{h\geq 1}$, *a family of regular languages, such that*

*(i) there exists* $\{N_h\}_{h\geq 1}$, *a sequence of constant height* NPDAs *accepting these languages with binary pushdown alphabet,* $O(h)$ *many states, and pushdown height* $h$, *but*

*(ii) for any constant height* DPDAs $\{D_h\}_{h\geq 1}$ *accepting these languages (with no restrictions on the size of pushdown alphabets), for any polynomial $p(h)$, and for any sufficiently large $h$, either the number of states in $D_h$ or its pushdown height is above $2^{p(h)}$.*

*Proof.* The constant height NPDA for $L_h$ (introduced in Def. 4) was given by Lem. 5, which completes the argument for (i).

Now, suppose that $L_h$ can be accepted by a constant height DPDA having both the number of states and the pushdown height bounded by $2^{p(h)}$, for some polynomial $p(h)$. But then, by Thm. 1, the *complement of $L_h$* could be accepted by a constant height DPDA using $2^{p(h)} \cdot (2^{p(h)}+1)+1 \leq 2^{2p(h)+2}$ states and the pushdown height bounded by $2^{p(h)} \leq 2^{2p(h)+2}$, which contradicts Thm. 6. □

## 5   Conclusions and Open Problems

We tackled the problem of converting nondeterministic constant height pushdown automata, NPDAs, into their deterministic version, DPDAs, proving *super-exponential blow up* in the size, by exhibiting a family of witness regular languages. It may be interesting to remark that in the realm of finite memory devices, with the exception of converting alternating machines into simpler ones [2], to the best of our knowledge this is the only case where elimination of a single added feature is paid by a super-exponential blow up. Several interesting questions may represent future research topics.

First, an interesting open problem is the complexity of converting an $h$-DPDA into NFA, i.e., giving up the pushdown store, but allowing nondeterminism, or the other way around. For both conversions, exponential upper bounds follow easily, but it is not known whether one or both conversions could not be done better.

Second, it may be worth investigating the cost of eliminating nondeterminism for *restricted* versions of NPDAs. For instance, one could study the cost for NPDAs accepting *unary* languages, built over a single-letter alphabet. The same investigation on NFAs shows interesting asymmetries: the conversion of an $n$-state unary NFA into an equivalent DFA has a tight bound $e^{(1+o(1))\cdot\sqrt{n\cdot\ln n}}$ states while, in the general case, the corresponding blow up is $2^n$ [3]. By using this result in the proof of Cor. 3, we can immediately improve our simulation and obtain that *any unary constant height* NPDA *can be simulated by a constant height* DPDA *(actually a DFA) with* $e^{(1+o(1))\cdot\sqrt{\|Q\|\cdot\|\Gamma^{\leq h}\|\cdot(\ln\|Q\|+h\cdot\ln\|\Gamma\|)}}$ *many states.* Clearly, it remains to show the optimality of this cost or to design a more sophisticated simulation for unary constant height NPDAs.

One could also investigate the corresponding cost for *counter machines* (see, e.g., [9,11]) of constant height, which are constant height NPDAs with a unary pushdown alphabet. From Cor. 3, we directly get an equivalent deterministic counter machine with only a *single-exponential* upper bound, namely $2^{\|Q\|\cdot h}$ states. Again, the optimality of this trade-off should be certified.

Finally, in analogy to what has been done for finite state automata (see, e.g., [6,13,14,18]), we would like to emphasize the interest in *two-way* devices.

**Acknowledgements.** The authors wish to thank the anonymous referees for useful comments and remarks.

# References

1. Bednárová, Z., Geffert, V., Mereghetti, C., Palano, B.: The Size-Cost of Boolean Operations on Constant Height Deterministic Pushdown Automata. In: Holzer, M. (ed.) DCFS 2011. LNCS, vol. 6808, pp. 80–92. Springer, Heidelberg (2011)
2. Chandra, A., Kozen, D., Stockmeyer, L.: Alternation. J. ACM 28, 114–133 (1981)
3. Chrobak, M.: Finite automata and unary languages. Theoret. Comput. Sci. 302, 497–498 (2003); Corrigendum, ibid. 302, 497–498 (2003)
4. Garey, M.R., Johnson, D.S.: Computers and Intractability: A Guide to the Theory of NP-Completeness. W.H. Freeman and Co., New York (1979)
5. Geffert, V., Mereghetti, C., Palano, B.: More concise representation of regular languages by automata and regular expressions. Inf. and Comput. 208, 385–394 (2010); A preliminary version appears. In: Jto, M., Toyama, M. (eds.) DLT 2008. LNCS, vol. 5257, pp. 359–370. Springer, Heidelberg (2008)
6. Geffert, V., Mereghetti, C., Pighizzini, G.: Converting two-way nondeterministic unary automata into simpler automata. Theoret. Comput. Sci. 295, 189–203 (2003)
7. Goldstine, J., Kappes, M., Kintala, C.M.R., Leung, H., Malcher, A., Wotschke, D.: Descriptional complexity of machines with limited resources. J. Univ. Comput. Sci. 8, 193–234 (2002)
8. Gruska, J.: Quantum Computing. McGraw-Hill (1999)
9. Gurari, E.M., Ibarra, O.H.: Simple counter machines and number-theoretic problems. J. Comput. Syst. Sci. 19, 145–162 (1979)
10. Holzer, M., Kutrib, M.: Descriptional complexity — an introductory survey. In: Martín-Vide, C. (ed.) Scientific Applications of Language Methods, pp. 1–58. Imperial College Press (2010)
11. Hopcroft, J.E., Motwani, R., Ullman, J.D.: Introduction to Automata Theory, Languages, and Computation. Addison-Wesley, Reading (2001)
12. Hromkovič, J.: Algorithmics for Hard Problems, 2nd edn. Springer (2003)
13. Kapoutsis, C.A.: Size Complexity of Two-Way Finite Automata. In: Diekert, V., Nowotka, D. (eds.) DLT 2009. LNCS, vol. 5583, pp. 47–66. Springer, Heidelberg (2009)
14. Mereghetti, C., Pighizzini, G.: Optimal simulations between unary automata. SIAM J. Comput. 30, 1976–1992 (2001)
15. Meyer, A.R., Fischer, M.J.: Economy of description by automata, grammars and formal systems. In: IEEE 12th Symp. Switching and Automata Theory, pp. 188–191 (1971)
16. Nielsen, M.A., Chuang, I.L.: Quantum Computation and Quantum Information, 10th edn. Cambridge University Press (2010)
17. Rabin, M., Scott, D.: Finite automata and their decision problems. IBM J. Res. Develop. 3, 114–125 (1959)
18. Shepherdson, J.C.: The reduction of two-way automata to one-way automata. IBM J. Res. Develop. 3, 198–200 (1959)

# On Inverse Operations
# and Their Descriptional Complexity[*]

Maria Paola Bianchi[1], Markus Holzer[2],
Sebastian Jakobi[2], and Giovanni Pighizzini[1]

[1] Dipartimento di Informatica, Università degli Studi di Milano,
Via Comelico 39, 20135 Milano, Italy
{maria.bianchi,giovanni.pighizzini}@unimi.it
[2] Institut für Informatik, Universität Giessen,
Arndtstr. 2, 35392 Giessen, Germany
{holzer,jakobi}@informatik.uni-giessen.de

**Abstract.** We investigate the descriptional complexity of some inverse language operations applied to languages accepted by finite automata. For instance, the *inverse* Kleene star operation for a language $L$ asks for the smallest language $S$ such that $S^*$ is equal to $L$, if it exists [J. BRZOZOWSKI. Roots of star events. J. ACM 14, 1967]. Other inverse operations based on the chop operation or on insertion/deletion operations can be defined appropriately. We present a general framework, that allows us to give an easy characterization of inverse operations, whenever simple conditions on the originally considered language operation are fulfilled. It turns out, that in most cases we obtain exponential upper and lower bounds that are asymptotically close, for the investigated inverse language operation problems.

## 1 Introduction

The study of the descriptional complexity of language operations is a vivid area of research. After its decline in the mid 1970's, a renewal initiated by the late Sheng Yu in his influential paper [17] brought descriptional complexity issues, not only for finite automata, back to life. Since then many aspects of descriptional complexity of deterministic and nondeterministic finite automata, pushdown automata, and other language-accepting or -generating devices were studied. For a recent survey on descriptional complexity issues on finite automata we refer to [10] and [18]. In truth there is much more to regular languages, deterministic finite automata, nondeterministic finite automata, etc., than one can summarize in these surveys.

The operation problem on languages is well studied in the literature, and is defined as follows: let ○ be a fixed binary operation on languages that preserves regularity; then given an $n$-state finite automaton $A$ and an $m$-state finite automaton $B$, how many states are sufficient and necessary in the worst case (in

---

[*] This paper is partially supported by CRUI/DAAD under the project "Programma Vigoni: Descriptional Complexity of Non-Classical Computational Models."

M. Kutrib, N. Moreira, and R. Reis (Eds.): DCFS 2012, LNCS 7386, pp. 89–102, 2012.
© Springer-Verlag Berlin Heidelberg 2012

terms of $n$ and $m$) to accept the language $L(A) \circ L(B)$ by some automaton? Obviously, this problem generalizes to unary operations on languages like, e.g., complementation or Kleene star. Tight bounds in the exact number of states for classical language operations such as the Boolean operations union, intersection, complement, and moreover concatenation, and Kleene star are known for deterministic finite automata (DFAs) and nondeterministic finite automata (NFAs). For instance, for the Kleene star operation, the tight bound on DFAs [17] reads as $2^{n-1} + 2^{n-2}$, while for NFAs [9] it drops to $n + 1$ states. Thus, in general, the Kleene star operation is expensive for DFAs, but cheap for NFAs, but there are also other language operations such as, e.g., the complementation operation, where it is exactly the other way around. For more results on some classical language operations we refer to the already mentioned surveys. Besides these classical operations also more exotic ones were investigated. Here we only want to mention operations based on (alternative) forms of concatenations such as, e.g., the chop operation [8] or the cyclic shift [12], and insertion/deletion related operations such as, e.g., building the upward- or downward-closure of a language [5,6,14]. In most cases tight bounds in the exact number of states, except for some asymptotic bounds, were obtained.

Now the question arises, whether certain language operations, in particular unary operations, can be inverted. It is clear, that this cannot always be done, but one can find some examples in the literature where this problem was already considered—see, e.g., [2,3,15]. For instance, in [2] the inverse Kleene star was investigated. There it was shown that every Kleene star closed language $L$, that is, $L = L^*$, gives rise to an inclusion minimal set $S_{\min}$ such that $S_{\min}^* = L$—cf. Equation (1). Moreover, an elegant characterization of this set was obtained, which implies that the inverse Kleene star is a regularity preserving operation. The descriptional complexity of the inverse Kleene star lacks investigation. In this paper, we first identify conditions on unary operations $\circ$, which are recursively defined on a language operation $\bullet$, that allow the operation $\circ$ to be inverted. Here the inversion is meant as in the case of the inverse Kleene star, giving an inclusion minimal solution $S$ satisfying $S^\circ = L$, for a $\circ$-closed language $L$. Roughly speaking, this minimal solution is described easily by means of removing the elements from $L$ that can be constructed with the help of the $\bullet$ operation. Then we apply our findings to the following $\circ$-operations—the basic operation $\bullet$ the $\circ$-operation is build on, is listed in the corresponding bracket: Kleene star (with concatenation), iterated chop (with chop), upward-closure UP (with insertion of letters), and downward-closure DOWN (with deletion of letters). We also discuss some limitations of our inversion theorem. Moreover, we investigate the descriptional complexity of these inverse language operations, whenever the language to be inverted is given as a finite automaton. In most cases we obtain exponential upper and lower bounds, which are asymptotically close. For instance, for the inverse Kleene star we show an upper bound of $O(n \cdot 2^n)$ states and a lower bound of $\Omega(2^n)$ states.

## 2   Definitions

We recall some definitions on finite automata as contained in [11]. A *nondeterministic finite automaton* (NFA) is a quintuple $A = (Q, \Sigma, \delta, q_0, F)$, where $Q$ is the finite set of *states*, $\Sigma$ is the finite set of *input symbols*, $q_0 \in Q$ is the *initial state*, $F \subseteq Q$ is the set of *accepting states*, and $\delta : Q \times \Sigma \to 2^Q$ is the *transition function*. The *language accepted* by the finite automaton $A$ is defined as $L(A) = \{ w \in \Sigma^* \mid \delta(q_0, w) \cap F \neq \emptyset \}$, where the transition function is recursively extended to $\delta : Q \times \Sigma^* \to 2^Q$. A finite automaton is *deterministic* (DFA) if and only if $|\delta(q, a)| = 1$, for all states $q \in Q$ and letters $a \in \Sigma$. In this case we simply write $\delta(q, a) = p$, for $\delta(q, a) = \{p\}$, assuming that the transition function is a mapping $\delta : Q \times \Sigma \to Q$. So, any DFA is complete, that is, the transition function is total, whereas for NFAs it is possible that $\delta$ maps to the empty set.

In the remainder of this section we recall the definition of the inverse Kleene star operation, which was introduced in [2] to study the roots of star closed languages. Here a language $L$ is said to be *star closed* if and only if $L = L^*$. Then the *inverse star operation* on a star closed language $L$ is given by

$$L^{-*} = \bigcap_{S^* = L} S, \tag{1}$$

that is, the smallest set, such that the Kleene star of this set is equal to $L$. In [2] it is shown that the following properties hold, if $L$ is a star closed language:

1. $(L^{-*})^* = L$.
2. $L^{-*} = L_\lambda \setminus L_\lambda^2$, where $L_\lambda = L \setminus \{\lambda\}$.
3. If $L$ is regular, then $L^{-*}$ is regular, too.

Recently some aspects of inverse Kleene star applied to (star closed) context-free languages were studied in [16]. This gives rise to the following definition.

**Definition 1.** *Let* $\circ$ *be an arbitrary unary operation on languages. For a* $\circ$-*closed language* $L$, *i.e., the language* $L$ *satisfies* $L^\circ = L$, *we define the* inverse $\circ$-*operation by*

$$L^{-\circ} = \bigcap_{S^\circ = L} S.$$

In order to clarify our notation we give two examples of language operations, which are not invertible in this way. Both examples show certain subtle pitfalls that may occur, when constructing the inverse of an operation $\circ$ according to the above given definition.

*Example 2.* Let $\Sigma$ be an arbitrary alphabet. Then define the *rotation operation* $\hookleftarrow : \Sigma^* \to 2^{\Sigma^*}$ by $\hookleftarrow (\lambda) = \{\lambda\}$ and $\hookleftarrow (ua) = \{au\}$, for $a \in \Sigma$ and $u \in \Sigma^*$. Extending this language operation to sets $L$ in the natural way by $\hookleftarrow (L) = \bigcup_{u \in L} \hookleftarrow (u)$ and iterating the operation by $\circlearrowright^i (L) = \hookleftarrow (\circlearrowright^{i-1} (L))$, for $i \geq 1$, and $\circlearrowright^0 (L) = L$. Finally, the *iterated rotation* operation applied to a language $L$ is referred to $L^\circlearrowright$ and defined by $L^\circlearrowright = \bigcup_{i \geq 0} \circlearrowright^i (L)$. Alternatively one can define

$L^{\circlearrowleft} = \{\, vu \mid uv \in L \text{ with } u, v \in \Sigma^* \,\}$, which is also known under the name *cyclic shift* operation [12] in the literature.

Now consider the cyclic shift closed language $L = \{abb, bab, bba\}$. It is easy to see that any non-empty subset $S$ of $L$ satisfies $S^{\circlearrowleft} = L$. Thus, the language $L^{-\circlearrowleft}$ constructed according to Definition 1 can be written as

$$L^{-\circlearrowleft} = \bigcap_{S^{\circlearrowleft}=L} S = \bigcap_{\emptyset \neq S \subseteq L} S = \{abb\} \cap \{bab\} \cap \{bba\} \cap$$

$$\{abb, bab\} \cap \{abb, bba\} \cap \{bab, bba\} \cap \{abb, bab, bba\} = \emptyset,$$

since the three different singleton sets $\{abb\}$, $\{bab\}$, and $\{bba\}$ appear as solutions in the intersection. Therefore, the equality $(L^{-\circlearrowleft})^{\circlearrowleft} = L$ does not hold.    □

The problem in the previous example is that the language has disjoint sets of generators. Since we are interested in minimal generators, any of the three singleton languages $\{abb\}$, $\{bab\}$, and $\{bba\}$ could be seen as an appropriate inverse of $L$, because they all generate $L$, and they are minimal (with respect to set inclusion). But it can be even worse, as it may be that there is no minimal generator at all. This is demonstrated by the following example.

*Example 3.* As in the previous example, let $\Sigma$ be an alphabet. Then define the *deletion* operation $\frown : \Sigma^* \to 2^{\Sigma^*}$ by $\frown(\lambda) = \emptyset$ and for a word $u \in \Sigma^+$ let $\frown(u) = \{\, u_1 u_2 \mid u = u_1 a u_2, \text{ for } u_1, u_2 \in \Sigma^* \text{ and } a \in \Sigma \,\}$. As in the previous example this naturally extends to sets $L$ by $\frown(L) = \bigcup_{u \in L} \frown(u)$. Moreover, we define the *down* operation by iterating the deletion operation namely $L^{\text{DOWN}} = \bigcup_{i \geq 0} \text{DOWN}^i(L)$, where $\text{DOWN}^i(L) = \frown(\text{DOWN}^{i-1}(L))$, for $i \geq 1$, and the termination condition is $\text{DOWN}^0(L) = L$. Consider the DOWN closed language $L = a^*$. With a similar reasoning as in the previous example we find that $L^{-\text{DOWN}} = \emptyset$, because, for instance, the following two disjoint sets $L_{even} = (a^2)^*$ and $L_{odd} = a(a^2)^*$ both satisfy that their down-closure is equal to the language $L$. Further there cannot be an inclusion minimal language $S_{\min}$ satisfying $S_{\min}^{\text{DOWN}} = L$, which is seen as follows. Let $S_0^{\text{DOWN}} = L$ for some language $S_0 \subseteq a^*$, and let $a^i$ be the shortest word in $S_0$. Since $a^{i+1} \in L$, there must be also some longer word $a^j$ in $S_0$ with $j > i$, otherwise $a^{i+1}$ could not be generated by $S_0$. But then also $S_1 = S_0 \setminus \{a^i\}$ satisfies $S_1^{\text{DOWN}} = L$. This can be continued indefinitely, so there as an infinite descending strict inclusion chain $S_0 \supset S_1 \supset S_2 \supset \cdots$, where for each $i \geq 0$, we have $S_i^{\text{DOWN}} = a^*$. This shows the stated claim on the non-existence of an inclusion minimal generator for the language $L$ w.r.t. the down operation.    □

It turns out that the problems occurring in the above examples can be avoided by disallowing the possibility to generate a word in the given language in infinitely many ways. Now several questions on the inverse ○-operation apply: (i) are there any natural operations other than the Kleene star, for which properties similar to the above-mentioned properties of the Kleene star hold, and (ii) what can be said about the descriptional complexity of the inverse ○-operation, if the language $L$ is given by a DFA or an NFA. We answer some of these questions in the affirmative. Due to space constraints, most proofs are omitted.

# 3 Inversion Operations

In this section we generalize the inversion technique from [2]. We provide a framework of sufficient conditions, under which a unary operation on languages (e.g., Kleene star), that can be seen as an iterated version of some underlying operation (e.g., concatenation), can be inverted when applying the construction given in Definition 1. Before we come to this, we also require some reasonable properties for the basic operation, which underlies the iterated version that is to be inverted. Since most operations in formal language theory are binary or unary operations, we only consider these two cases.

First we discuss some reasonable and useful properties of operations. (i) Let $\bullet : \Sigma^* \times \Sigma^* \to 2^{\Sigma^*}$ be a *binary operation* on words, mapping to sets, that naturally extends to languages $U$ and $V$ over $\Sigma^*$ by $U \bullet V = \bigcup_{u \in U, v \in V} u \bullet v$ and which is associative on languages, i.e., $U \bullet (V \bullet W) = (U \bullet V) \bullet W$, for all languages $U, V, W \subseteq \Sigma^*$. In the given characterization of an inverse operation we will use so called pseudo-neutral elements. We call an element $e \in \Sigma^*$ *pseudo-neutral*[1] if $e \bullet v \subseteq \{v\}$ and $v \bullet e \subseteq \{v\}$, for all $v \in \Sigma^*$. Then define the *set of pseudo-neutral elements* $E_\bullet = \{ e \in \Sigma^* \mid e \text{ is pseudo-neutral} \}$. The next step is to iterate the $\bullet$-operation in a suitable way. We say that a unary operation $\circ : 2^{\Sigma^*} \to 2^{\Sigma^*}$ on languages is a *well behaved iteration operation* based on the $\bullet$-operation, if the recursive definition is written as $L^\circ = \bigcup_{i \geq 0} \circ^i(L)$, where $\circ^0(L) = E_\bullet$ and $\circ^i(L) = L \bullet (\circ^{i-1}(L))$, for $i \geq 1$. Note that if $E_\bullet = \emptyset$, then this iteration yields $L^\circ = \emptyset$ for any language $L$. But for the herein studied operations, the basic binary operations $\bullet$ will satisfy $E_\bullet \neq \emptyset$. (ii) Second, for a *unary operation* $\bullet : \Sigma^* \to 2^{\Sigma^*}$ we can do similar as above, by naturally extending it to $\bullet : 2^{\Sigma^*} \to 2^{\Sigma^*}$ acting on sets of words over the alphabet $\Sigma$. The set of pseudo-neutral elements $E_\bullet$ is then defined by $E_\bullet = \{ e \in \Sigma^* \mid \bullet(e) \subseteq \{e\} \}$ and the recursive definition of the $\circ$-operation in $L^\circ$ must be altered to $\circ^0(L) = L$ and $\circ^i(L) = \bullet(\circ^{i-1}(L))$, for $i \geq 1$, in order to be called a *well behaved iteration operation*. For unary $\bullet$, the pseudo-neutral elements are not important for the iteration, but they will play a role in the characterization of the inverse operation. The next lemma gives useful properties for well behaved iteration operations.

**Lemma 4.** *Let $\circ$ be a well behaved iteration operation on languages over the alphabet $\Sigma$ based on a binary operation $\bullet$. Then the following inclusion relations hold for all languages $L, U, U', V, V' \subseteq \Sigma^*$:*

1. *If $U \subseteq U'$ and $V \subseteq V'$, then $U \bullet V \subseteq U' \bullet V'$.*
2. *If $U, V \subseteq L^\circ$, then $U \bullet V \subseteq L^\circ$.*

*Corresponding inclusion relations are valid in case the $\circ$-operation is a well behaved iteration operation based on a unary operation $\bullet$, namely $\bullet(U) \subseteq \bullet(U')$, if $U \subseteq U'$, and $\bullet(U) \subseteq L^\circ$, if $U \subseteq L^\circ$.*

---

[1] One could also differentiate between left- and right-(pseudo-)neutrals, but assuming there are only (pseudo-)neutral elements that are both left- and right-(pseudo-)neutral simplifies our notation and some proofs, and in fact all operations that will be studied later fulfill this condition.

*Proof.* We only give the proof in case that the operation $\bullet$ is a binary operation on languages. The results for the unary case can be shown by similar arguments as given next.

The first statement is seen as follows. Let $U \subseteq U'$ and $V \subseteq V'$, then

$$U \bullet V = \bigcup_{u \in U, v \in V} u \bullet v \subseteq \bigcup_{u' \in U', v' \in V'} u' \bullet v' = U' \bullet V'.$$

For the second statement let us prove first by induction that for every $i, j \geq 0$, we have $(\circ^i(L)) \bullet (\circ^j(L)) \subseteq \circ^{i+j}(L)$, from which the second statement will then be concluded. For $i = 0$ we have $(\circ^0(L)) \bullet (\circ^j(L)) \subseteq \circ^j(L)$. Now let $i > 0$ and assume by induction hypothesis that $(\circ^k(L)) \bullet (\circ^j(L)) \subseteq \circ^{k+j}(L)$, for all $k < i$. Then

$$(\circ^i(L)) \bullet (\circ^j(L)) = (L \bullet (\circ^{i-1}(L))) \bullet (\circ^j(L))$$
$$= L \bullet ((\circ^{i-1}(L)) \bullet (\circ^j(L)))$$
$$\subseteq L \bullet (\circ^{i-1+j}(L))$$
$$= \circ^{i+j}(L).$$

Now let $U, V \subseteq L^\circ$. Since for all words $u, v \in L^\circ$ there are integers $i$ and $j$, with $i, j \geq 0$, such that $u \in \circ^i(L)$ and $v \in \circ^j(L)$, we obtain

$$u \bullet v \subseteq (\circ^i(L)) \bullet (\circ^j(L)) \subseteq \circ^{i+j}(L) \subseteq L^\circ.$$

Thus, $U \bullet V = \bigcup_{u \in U, v \in V} u \bullet v \subseteq L^\circ$ holds. □

Before we can state the main theorem on the characterization of inverse operations, which are based on iteration, we need the definition of a relation, which tells us that a "word $u$ can be generated by $v$." To this end we define for a binary operation $\bullet$ acting on words over an alphabet $\Sigma$ the relation $>_\bullet \subseteq \Sigma^* \times \Sigma^*$ as follows: for two words $u, v \in \Sigma^*$ let $u >_\bullet v$ if and only if there is a word $v' \in \Sigma^* \setminus E_\bullet$ such that $u \in v \bullet v'$ or $u \in v' \bullet v$. If $\bullet$ is a unary operation, the definition of the relation $>_\bullet$ simplifies to $u >_\bullet v$ if and only if $u \in \bullet(v)$ and $v \in \Sigma^* \setminus E_\bullet$. Then we say that the language operation $\bullet$ is *noetherian on a language* $L$ if and only if the relation $>_\bullet$ restricted to $(L \setminus E_\bullet) \times (L \setminus E_\bullet)$ is noetherian, which means, that any descending chain $v_1 >_\bullet v_2 >_\bullet v_3 >_\bullet \ldots$, with $v_i \in L \setminus E_\bullet$, for $i \geq 1$, is finite. Now we are ready for the theorem that characterizes inverse operations.

**Theorem 5.** *Let $\circ$ be a well behaved iteration operation based on a binary operation $\bullet$. Moreover, let $L \subseteq \Sigma^*$ be a $\circ$-closed language and assume that $\bullet$ is noetherian on $L$. Then (i) $(L^{-\circ})^\circ = L$ and (ii) $L^{-\circ} = L_e \setminus (L_e \bullet L_e)$, where $L_e = L \setminus E_\bullet$. A similar statement is valid in case $\bullet$ is a unary operation; then $L^{-\circ}$ must read as $L \setminus \bullet(L_e)$ in statement (ii).*

*Proof.* For proving the statement of the theorem, we discuss both cases of $\bullet$ being unary or binary in parallel. Let $M = L_e \setminus (L_e \bullet L_e)$ for the binary case and $M = L \setminus \bullet(L_e)$ in the unary case. We first show that $M \subseteq L^{-\circ}$ holds, and then we prove $M^\circ = L$, from which $M \supseteq L^{-\circ}$, and finally statements $(i)$ and $(ii)$ can be concluded.

For proving $M \subseteq L^{-\circ}$, let $v \in M$, and assume $v \notin L^{-\circ} = \bigcap_{S^\circ = L} S$. This means that $v \in S^\circ$ and $v \notin S$ holds for some $S \subseteq \Sigma^*$ that satisfies $S^\circ = L$. So there must be some integer $j \geq 1$ (even $j \geq 2$ in the binary case), such that $v \in \circ^j(S)$ but $v \notin \circ^i(S)$, for $0 \leq i < j$. We distinguish between the binary and the unary case. In the binary case we have $v \in v_1 \bullet v_2$ for some words $v_1 \in S$ and $v_2 \in \circ^{j-1}(S)$. Note that $v_1, v_2 \in L_e$ would contradict $v \in L_e \setminus (L_e \bullet L_e)$, so at least one of the words $v_1$ and $v_2$ cannot belong to $L_e$. Then at least one of these two words belongs to $E_\bullet$, since $S \subseteq L$. But if $v_1 \in E_\bullet$, then $v = v_2 \in \circ^{j-1}(S)$, and if $v_2 \in E_\bullet$, then $v = v_1 \in S$—in both cases we obtain a contradiction. In the unary case we have $v \in \bullet(u)$ for some word $u \in \circ^{j-1}(S)$, and since $v \in L \setminus (L_e)$, it must be $u \notin L_e$. But since $u \in S \subseteq L$, we obtain $u \in E_\bullet$, and so $u = v$—a contradiction to $v \notin \circ^{j-1}$. Thus the assumption $v \notin L^{-\circ}$ cannot hold, which proves $M \subseteq L^{-\circ}$.

We now show that $M^\circ = L$. Since $M \subseteq L$, by applying Lemma 4 we obtain the inclusion $M^\circ \subseteq L^\circ = L$. For the other inclusion, $L \subseteq M^\circ$, let $v \in L$. If $v \in M$, then also $v \in M^\circ$. For the case $v \notin M$ we distinguish between the binary and the unary case again.

1. If $\bullet$ is unary, for $v \notin M$, it must be $v \in \bullet(v_1)$ for some word $v_1 \in L_e$. If $v_1 \in M^\circ$, then also $v \in M^\circ$ by Lemma 4. The other case, $v_1 \notin M^\circ$ will lead to a contradiction in the following. Assume $v_1 \notin M^\circ$, then certainly $v_1 \notin M$. But since $v_1 \in L_e$ it must be $v_1 \in \bullet(L_e)$, so there must be a word $v_2 \in L_e$ with $v_1 >_\bullet v_2$, such that $v_1 \in \bullet(v_2)$. If $v_2 \in M^\circ$, then also $v_1 \in M^\circ$—a contradiction. So it must be $v_2 \notin M^\circ$, and by continuing this argumentation indefinitely, we obtain an infinite descending chain $v_1 >_\bullet v_2 >_\bullet v_3 >_\bullet \ldots$, but this is a contradiction to $\bullet$ being noetherian. Thus, the case $v_1 \notin M^\circ$ cannot appear, which implies that $v \in M^\circ$.

2. Consider now the case $v \notin M$, where $\bullet$ is binary. If $v \in E_\bullet$, then also $v \in M^\circ$, so we also assume $v \notin E_\bullet$ here. Then $v$ belongs to $L_e \bullet L_e$, because otherwise $v \in L$ would also belong to $M$—recall $M = L_e \setminus (L_e \bullet L_e)$. This means that there are words $v_1, v_2 \in L_e$, satisfying $v \in v_1 \bullet v_2$, and thus $v >_\bullet v_1$ and $v >_\bullet v_2$. If both words $v_1$ and $v_2$ belong to $M^\circ$, then by Lemma 4 also $v \in M^\circ$. Again, we show in the following, that the other case, $v_1 \notin M^\circ$ or $v_2 \notin M^\circ$, cannot appear. Assume $v^{(1)} \notin M^\circ$, where $v^{(1)} = v_1$ or $v^{(1)} = v_2$. Then we have $v^{(1)} \in L_e$, and $v^{(1)} \notin M$, and we can conclude $v^{(1)} \in \circ^2(L_e)$, as above for the word $v$. So $v^{(1)} \in v_1^{(1)} \bullet v_2^{(1)}$ for words $v_1^{(1)}, v_2^{(1)} \in L_e$, with $v^{(1)} >_\bullet v_1^{(1)}$ and $v^{(1)} >_\bullet v_2^{(1)}$. If both words $v_1^{(1)}$ and $v_2^{(1)}$ would belong to $M^\circ$, then we obtain $v^{(1)} \in M^\circ$, which is a contradiction. Then, again, there must be a word $v^{(2)} \in \{v_1^{(1)}, v_2^{(1)}\}$ that does not belong to $M^\circ$. By continuing this argumentation indefinitely again, we obtain the descending chain $v >_\bullet v^{(1)} >_\bullet v^{(2)} >_\bullet \ldots$ that is infinite—this contradicts $\bullet$ being noetherian, which implies $v \in M^\circ$.

Thus, also the inclusion $L \subseteq M^\circ$ holds, and we have shown $M^\circ = L$. This implies $L^{-\circ} = \bigcap_{S^\circ = L} S \subseteq M$, and together with the inclusion $M \subseteq L^{-\circ}$ from above, we obtain $L^{-\circ} = M$, which proves both statements $(i)$ and $(ii)$. $\square$

Note that there is a certain asymmetry in the second statement for binary and unary operations $\bullet$, which is induced by the terminating conditions of the recursion schemes that are used for the definition of the well behaved iteration operation $\circ$.

So far we have seen, that if the operation $\circ$ is the iterated version of an operation $\bullet$ with some reasonable properties, then we can construct $L^{-\circ}$ from the language $L$ by combining set difference and a single application of $\bullet$. It is immediate, that if $\bullet$ is a regularity preserving operation and $L$ is a regular language with $L^\circ = L$, then also $L^{-\circ}$ is a regular language. In fact, this is the case for all operations that will be studied in the following, namely, Kleene star, chop-star, UP, and DOWN. In the following subsections, we apply Theorem 5 to these operations, and study the descriptional complexity of the corresponding inverse operations.

## 3.1   Inverse Kleene Star

The following result on the inverse star $L^{-*}$ of a star closed language $L$, which was presented in [2], can now also be verified by using Theorem 5. To this end we have to slightly alter the standard definition of the concatenation operation from the literature to map to a singleton set, i.e., let $\cdot : \Sigma^* \times \Sigma^* \to 2^{\Sigma^*}$ be defined by $u \cdot v = \{uv\}$, for $u, v \in \Sigma^*$. This naturally extends to languages by $L_1 \cdot L_2 = \bigcup_{u \in L_1, v \in L_2} u \cdot v$ and to the Kleene star iteration by

$$L^* = \bigcup_{i \geq 0} *^i(L), \text{ where } *^i(L) = L \cdot (*^{i-1}(L)), \text{ for } i \geq 1, \text{ and } *^0 = \{\lambda\}.$$

It easy is to see that $E. = \{\lambda\}$, which induces that the Kleene star operation is a well behaved iterated operation in our terminology. Since $\cdot$ is noetherian on $\Sigma^+$ because $u >. v$ implies $|u| > |v|$, for all words $u$ and $v$ in $\Sigma^+$, we can apply Theorem 5, by choosing $\cdot$ for $\bullet$ and $*$ for $\circ$, which leads us to the next result that already appeared in [2].

**Theorem 6.** *Let $L$ be a Kleene star closed language. Then $(i)$ $(L^{-*})^* = L$, and $(ii)$ $L^{-*} = L_\lambda \setminus (L_\lambda \cdot L_\lambda)$, where $L_\lambda = L \setminus \{\lambda\}$.* $\square$

Using this characterization we get an upper bound for the state complexity of the inverse Kleene star of a regular language $L$ by constructing automata accepting $L_\lambda \setminus (L_\lambda \cdot L_\lambda)$. Since the construction will not rely on $L$ being star closed, the bound holds for regular languages in general.

**Theorem 7.** *Let $L$ be a language accepted by some $n$-state DFA. Then $n \cdot 2^n + 1$ states are sufficient for a DFA to accept $L_\lambda \setminus (L_\lambda \cdot L_\lambda)$. If $L$ is Kleene star closed, this upper bound also holds for automata accepting $L^{-*}$.* $\square$

Next we show that this bound is asymptotically close already for a binary alphabet, by proving an exponential lower bound on the state complexity of the inverse Kleene star. Note that the following lower bound even holds for NFAs.

**Theorem 8.** *For any integer $n \geq 4$ there exists a Kleene star closed language $L_n$ over a binary alphabet accepted by an $n$-state DFA, such that any NFA accepting $L_n^{-*}$ needs at least $2^{n-4}$ states.*

*Proof (Sketch).* The star closed language $L = a \cdot \{a,b\}^{n-4} \cdot b \cdot \{a,b\}^* \cup \{\lambda\}$ can be accepted by an $n$-state DFA. Further, $L^{-*} = \{ avbw \mid v \in \{a,b\}^{n-4}$, and $w$ has no infix in $a \cdot \{a,b\}^{n-4} \cdot b \}$, and $S = \{ (ab^{n-4}bw, bw) \mid w \in \{a,b\}^{n-4} \}$ is an *extended fooling set*[2] [1,4] of size $2^{n-4}$ for $L^{-*}$.    □

### 3.2  Inverse Chop-Star

Recently the chop operation and its iterated variant were used to describe regular languages by so called chop expressions [8]. The *chop*[3] or *fusion* of two words is similar to their concatenation, but it is only defined if the touching letters of the words coincide, and if so, these letters get merged. Formally $u \odot v = \{ u'av' \mid u = u'a \text{ and } v = av', \text{ for } u', v' \in \Sigma^* \text{ and } a \in \Sigma \}$, for $u, v \in \Sigma^*$. It is easy to see that the set of pseudo-neutral elements is $E_\odot = \Sigma$. Again the chop operation generalizes to languages in a similar vein as for concatenation. Then the *iterated chop* or *chop-star* of a language $L$ is defined as

$$L^\otimes = \bigcup_{i \geq 0} \otimes^i(L), \text{ where } \otimes^i(L) = L \odot (\otimes^{i-1}(L)), \text{ for } i \geq 1, \text{ and } \otimes^0(L) = \Sigma.$$

Utilizing Theorem 5, by taking $\odot$ for $\bullet$ and $\otimes$ for $\circ$, we obtain the following characterization for $L^{-\otimes}$, since all necessary preconditions, in particular, that the relation $>_\odot$ is noetherian on $\Sigma^+$, are satisfied.

**Theorem 9.** *Let $L$ be a chop-star closed language over the alphabet $\Sigma$. Then (i) $(L^{-\otimes})^\otimes = L$, and (ii) $L^{-\otimes} = L_\Sigma \setminus (L_\Sigma \odot L_\Sigma)$, where $L_\Sigma = L \setminus \Sigma$.*    □

For the descriptional complexity of the inverse chop-star, similar results as in the case of the inverse Kleene star are obtained. Using the characterization of Theorem 9, we obtain the following upper bound for the state complexity of the inverse chop-star.

**Theorem 10.** *Let $L$ be a language over alphabet $\Sigma$ accepted by an $n$-state DFA. Then $((n-1)^2 + n) \cdot 2^n + n + 1$ states are sufficient for a DFA to accept the language $L_\Sigma \setminus (L_\Sigma \odot L_\Sigma)$, where $L_\Sigma = L \setminus \Sigma$. If $L$ is chop-star closed, this upper bound also holds for automata accepting $L^{-\otimes}$.*    □

---

[2] An *extended fooling set* $S$ for a language $L$ is a set of pairs $(x_i, y_i)$, for $1 \leq i \leq n$, such that (i) $x_i y_i \in L$, and (ii) $x_i y_j \notin L$ or $x_j y_i \notin L$, for $1 \leq i, j \leq n$ and $i \neq j$. In this case, any NFA accepting $L$ needs at least $|S| = n$ states.

[3] We like to point out that this operation differs from the *latin product* defined in [13] only if the words have no overlap. In that case, the latin product is just the concatenation of both words.

This upper bound is asymptotically close to the lower bound, which can be shown with the same technique as in the proof of Theorem 8 for the inverse Kleene star.

**Theorem 11.** *For any integer $n \geq 5$ there exists a chop-star closed language $L_n$ over a binary alphabet accepted by an $n$-state DFA, such that any NFA accepting the language $L_n^{-\circledast}$ needs at least $2^{n-5}$ states.* □

### 3.3 Inverse Up and Down

In this section we consider the upward and downward closure of languages, which are operations based on the *insertion* and *deletion* of letters. The insertion operation $\curvearrowright : \Sigma^* \rightarrow 2^{\Sigma^*}$ is defined for all words $u \in \Sigma^*$ as follows: $\curvearrowright(u) = \{ u_1 a u_2 \mid u_1, u_2 \in \Sigma^*, a \in \Sigma, u_1 u_2 = u \}$, and similarly the deletion operation $\curvearrowleft : \Sigma^* \rightarrow 2^{\Sigma^*}$ is defined for all $u \in \Sigma^*$ as $\curvearrowleft(u) = \{ u_1 u_2 \mid u_1, u_2 \in \Sigma^*, a \in \Sigma, u_1 a u_2 = u \}$. Note that $\curvearrowleft(\lambda) = \emptyset$. These operations naturally generalize to languages by setting $\curvearrowright(L) = \bigcup_{v \in L} \curvearrowright(v)$, and $\curvearrowleft(L) = \bigcup_{v \in L} \curvearrowleft(v)$, for all languages $L \subseteq \Sigma^*$. Then, for a language $L \subseteq \Sigma^*$, the *upward closure* $L^{\text{UP}}$ is

$$L^{\text{UP}} = \bigcup_{i \geq 0} \text{UP}^i(L), \text{ where } \text{UP}^i(L) = \curvearrowright(\text{UP}^{i-1}(L)) \text{ for } i \geq 1, \text{ and } \text{UP}^0(L) = L,$$

and the *downward closure* $L^{\text{DOWN}}$ of $L$ is

$$L^{\text{DOWN}} = \bigcup_{i \geq 0} \text{DOWN}^i(L), \text{ where } \text{DOWN}^i(L) = \curvearrowleft(\text{DOWN}^{i-1}(L)), \text{ for } i \geq 1,$$

and $\text{DOWN}^0(L) = L$. Note that the languages $L^{\text{UP}}$ and $L^{\text{DOWN}}$ are also called Higman-Haines sets of $L$ in [5] and [6]. The upward closure $L^{\text{UP}}$ of a language $L$ over the alphabet $\Sigma$ can also be described as the *shuffle* of $L$ with $\Sigma^*$, i.e.,

$$L^{\text{UP}} = L \shuffle \Sigma^* = \bigcup_{a_1 a_2 \ldots a_n \in L} \Sigma^* a_1 \Sigma^* a_2 \Sigma^* \ldots \Sigma^* a_n \Sigma^*.$$

We will use Theorem 5 again, to characterize the inverse languages $L^{-\text{UP}}$ and $L^{-\text{DOWN}}$. For $L^{-\text{UP}}$, which is based on $\curvearrowright$, note that there are no words $e \in \Sigma^*$ with $\curvearrowright(e) \subseteq \{e\}$, i.e., there are no pseudo-neutral elements. Further the operation $\curvearrowright$ is noetherian on $\Sigma^*$, because $u \in \curvearrowright(v)$ implies $|u| > |v|$, for all words $u$ and $v$. Thus we obtain the following.

**Theorem 12.** *Let $L$ be an UP closed language over $\Sigma$. Then (i) $(L^{-\text{UP}})^{\text{UP}} = L$ and (ii) $L^{-\text{UP}} = L \setminus \curvearrowright(L)$.* □

What can be said about the state complexity of $L^{-\text{UP}}$? Using a generalized cross product construction with a power set construction in the second component, an upper bound[4] of $O(n \cdot 2^n)$ for the state complexity of $L^{-\mathrm{UP}}$ can be obtained. In fact, a tight bound of $(n-2) \cdot 2^{n-2} + 3$ for the state complexity of $L \setminus (L \sqcup \Sigma^+)$, for some (not necessarily UP closed) $n$-state DFA language $L$ is obtained in [15]. Whether such an exponential blow-up also appears for UP closed languages has to be left open for now.

We now turn to the inverse DOWN, where we want to apply Theorem 5 in the obvious way by choosing $\curvearrowleft$ for $\bullet$, and DOWN for $\circ$. But we have to be more careful about the condition of $\bullet$ being noetherian on the input language $L$, because this time the basic operation $\curvearrowleft$ is not noetherian on $\Sigma^*$. This problem already showed up in Example 3. If we consider the DOWN closed language $L = a^*$, then we have $a^i \in \curvearrowleft(a^{i+1})$, for all $i \geq 1$, so there is an infinite descending chain $a >_{\curvearrowleft} a^2 >_{\curvearrowleft} a^3 >_{\curvearrowleft} \ldots$, which shows that $\curvearrowleft$ is *not* noetherian on $L$. Thus, Theorem 5 does not apply in this case. In fact, we can show that whenever $L$ is an infinite DOWN closed language—note that any DOWN closed language is regular [7], then $L$ has no minimal regular generator, i.e., there is no regular language $S$ satisfying $S^{\mathrm{DOWN}} = L$, such that $S$ is minimal with respect to set inclusion.

**Theorem 13.** *Let $L \subseteq \Sigma^*$ be an infinite DOWN closed language and $S \subseteq \Sigma^*$ be a regular language satisfying $S^{\mathrm{DOWN}} = L$. Then there is a proper subset $S' \subsetneq S$, satisfying $S'^{\mathrm{DOWN}} = L$.* $\qquad\square$

So, whenever $L = L^{\mathrm{DOWN}}$ is infinite, then there is no minimal generator. But on the other hand, if $L$ is a *finite* and DOWN closed language, then there is such a generator again, because then $\curvearrowleft$ is easily seen to be noetherian on $L$, since $u \in \curvearrowleft(v)$ implies $|u| < |v|$. Now our result on the inverse DOWN operation for finite languages reads as follows—note that $E_{\curvearrowleft} = \{\lambda\}$.

**Theorem 14.** *Let $L$ be a finite DOWN closed language over $\Sigma$. Then we have (i) $(L^{-\mathrm{DOWN}})^{\mathrm{DOWN}} = L$ and (ii) $L^{-\mathrm{DOWN}} = L \setminus \curvearrowleft(L_\lambda)$, where $L_\lambda = L \setminus \{\lambda\}$.* $\qquad\square$

This characterization can be used to obtain an upper bound for the state complexity of $L^{-\mathrm{DOWN}}$ by constructing an automaton that accepts $L \setminus \curvearrowleft(L_\lambda)$.

**Theorem 15.** *Let $L$ be a language accepted by an $n$-state DFA. Then $n \cdot 2^n$ states are sufficient for a DFA to accept $L \setminus \curvearrowleft(L_\lambda)$, where $L_\lambda = L \setminus \{\lambda\}$. If $L$ is finite and DOWN closed, this upper bound also holds for a DFA accepting $L^{-\mathrm{DOWN}}$.* $\qquad\square$

---

[4] An upward closed language $L$ is also called an all-sided ideal in [3]. There it is said that for an all-sided ideal with quotient complexity $n$, the quotient complexity of its minimal generator is at most $n + 1$, and this bound is tight. Since the quotient complexity of a language is the same as the deterministic state complexity of the language, and $L^{-\mathrm{UP}}$ is the minimal generator for $L^{\mathrm{UP}}$, this result would imply a tight bound of $n + 1$ states for the state complexity of $L^{-\mathrm{UP}}$. We give a counter example to the above mentioned result. Consider the minimal generator language $S = \{aa, ab, ac, ba, bbb, bbc\}$, and its upward closure $L = S^{\mathrm{UP}}$. The minimal DFA for $L$ has $n = 4$ states, while the minimal DFA for $S$ has $n + 2 = 6$ states.

In the remaining part of this section we will also prove an exponential lower bound for the state complexity of $L^{-\text{DOWN}}$. To this end, we inductively define languages $G_n$ and $G'_n$ over the alphabet $\Sigma_n = \{\, a_i, b_i, c_i, d_i, e_i \mid 1 \leq i \leq n \,\}$ as follows: Let[5]

$$
\begin{aligned}
G_n = {} & d_n e_n G_{n-1} b_n && G'_n = {} && e_n G_{n-1} b_n \\
& + a_n (G_{n-1} + G'_{n-1})(b_n + c_n) && && + d_n e_n G_{n-1} c_n \\
& + e_n G_{n-1} c_n && && + d_n e_n G'_{n-1}(b_n + c_n). \\
& + e_n G'_{n-1}(b_n + c_n),
\end{aligned}
\tag{2}
$$

for $n \geq 1$, and set $G_0 = \{\lambda\}$ and $G'_0 = \emptyset$.

**Lemma 16.** *The minimal DFA for the language $G_n$ requires $\Theta(2^n)$ states.*

*Proof. (Sketch)* We inductively construct the minimal DFA $A_n$ for $G_n$ as shown in Figure 1. We omit, for brevity, the description of the base case $n = 1$: the reader can easily check that $A_1$ has the same structure as the innermost part of $D_3$. We let $A_{n-1} = (\{s_1, \ldots, s_m, q_T\}, \Sigma_{n-1}, \delta_{n-1}, s_1, \{s_m\})$ be the minimal DFA for the language $G_{n-1}$, and $A_+ = (\{p_1, \ldots, p_\ell, q_T\}, \Sigma_{n-1}, \delta_+, p_1, \{p_\ell\})$ be the minimal DFA for the set $G_{n-1} + G'_{n-1} = \left(\prod_{i=0}^{n-1}(d_{n-i}e_{n-i} + a_{n-i} + e_{n-i})\right)$ $(\prod_{i=1}^{n}(b_i + c_i))$, where, in both cases, $q_T$ indicates the trap state. One can easily check that $A_+$ has $3n + 2$ states, and only one of them is final, while we assume $A_{n-1}$ has only one accepting state by induction. In Figure 1, the states $Q^{(1)} = \{q_1^{(1)}, \ldots, q_\ell^{(1)}\}$ in $D_1$ are non-accepting copies of $p_1, \ldots, p_\ell$, while the states $Q^{(2)} = \{q_1^{(2)}, \ldots, q_m^{(2)}\}$ in $D_2$ and $Q^{(3)} = \{q_1^{(3)}, \ldots, q_m^{(3)}\}$ in $D_3$ are non-accepting copies of $s_1, \ldots, s_m$. Moreover, the function $\delta_n$ describes the transitions shown in Figure 1 involving $q_{in}, q_0$ and $q_{fin}$, plus the following ones:

$$
\delta_n(q_j^{(1)}, \sigma) = q_k^{(1)}
$$

for every $\sigma \in \Sigma_{n-1}$, $j, k \geq 1$, if $\delta_+(p_j, \sigma) = p_k$, i.e., the transitions in $A_+$ are copied in $D_1$,

$$
\delta_n(q_j^{(2)}, \sigma) = q_k^{(2)} \quad \text{and} \quad \delta_n(q_j^{(3)}, \sigma) = q_k^{(3)}
$$

for every $\sigma \in \Sigma_{n-1}$, $j, k \geq 1$, if $\delta_{n-1}(s_j, \sigma) = s_k$, i.e., the transitions in $A_{n-1}$ are copied in $D_2, D_3$,

$$
\delta_n(\delta_n(q_1^{(3)}, v_j e_{n-j} w_j), b_{n-j}) = \delta_n(\delta_n(q_1^{(3)}, v_j d_{n-j} e_{n-j} w_j), c_{n-j}) = q_{\ell-j+1}^{(1)}, \tag{3}
$$

where, for $1 \leq j \leq n-1$, $v_j \in \prod_{k=1}^{j-1}(d_{n-k}e_{n-k})$, $w_j \in G_{n-1-j}$, and $q_{\ell-j+1}^{(1)} = \delta_n(q_1^{(1)}, v_j e_{n-j} w_j b_{n-j})$. These transitions are the ones from $D_3$ to $D_1$ shown in bold in Figure 1. All the undefined transitions of $\delta_n$ go to the trap state $q_T$.

---

[5] In abuse of notation, to keep the presentation simple, we write $+$ to denote the union and $\prod$ as a short hand notation for the concatenation of elements from left to right according to the running index.

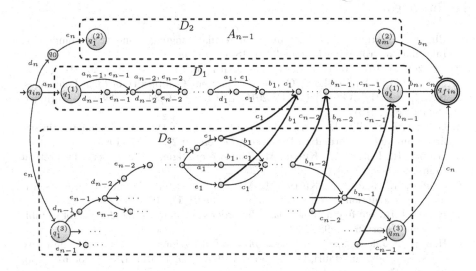

**Fig. 1.** Structure of the DFA $A_n$. The edges in bold represent the transitions from states in $D_3$ to states in $D_1$ defined in Equation (3). For sake of readability, the trap state is omitted in the figure.

It can be easily shown that $A_n$ is the minimal DFA for $G_n$: intuitively, words whose computation path goes through the whole automaton $D_1$ ($D_2$ and $D_3$, respectively) are the ones of the form $a_n(G_{n-1} + G'_{n-1})(b_n + c_n)$ ($d_n e_n G_{n-1} b_n$ and $e_n G_{n-1} c_n$, respectively), while the words whose computation goes through the edges described by Equation (3), are of the form $e_n G'_{n-1}(b_n + c_n)$. The set of states of $A_n$ is $Q_n = \{q_{in}, q_0, q_{fin}, q_T\} \cup Q^{(1)} \cup Q^{(2)} \cup Q^{(3)}$, thus we have $|Q_n| = 3n + 2|Q_{n-1}|$, with $|Q_1| = 6$, which is of order $\Theta(2^n)$. □

Since $e_n G_{n-1} b_n \in G_n^{\mathrm{DOWN}}$, when applying the down operation to $G_n$, the part $D_3$ in Figure 1 collapses into $D_2$ at each level, leading to the following bound:

**Lemma 17.** *The minimal DFA for the language $G_n^{\mathrm{DOWN}}$ requires $O(n^2)$ states.*

Since language $G_n$ is scattered subword free, it is the smallest generator set for $G_n^{\mathrm{DOWN}}$, therefore, Lemmata 16 and 17 directly imply the following result.

**Theorem 18.** *For any integer $n \geq 1$ there exists a finite DOWN closed language $L_n$ over an alphabet of size $O(\sqrt{n})$ accepted by an $n$-state DFA, such that any DFA accepting the language $L_n^{-\mathrm{DOWN}}$ needs at least $\Omega(2^{\sqrt{n}})$ states.* □

**Acknowledgments.** We want to thank the anonymous referees for their carefully reading and for providing us with helpful comments.

# References

1. Birget, J.C.: Intersection and union of regular languages and state complexity. Information Processing Letters 43(4), 185–190 (1992)
2. Brzozowski, J.A.: Roots of star events. Journal of the ACM 14(3), 466–477 (1967)
3. Brzozowski, J.A., Jiráskova, G., Li, B.: Quotient Complexity of Ideal Languages. In: López-Ortiz, A. (ed.) LATIN 2010. LNCS, vol. 6034, pp. 208–221. Springer, Heidelberg (2010)
4. Glaister, I., Shallit, J.: A lower bound technique for the size of nondeterministic finite automata. Information Processing Letters 59(2), 75–77 (1996)
5. Gruber, H., Holzer, M., Kutrib, M.: The size of Higman-Haines sets. Theoretical Computer Science 387(2), 167–176 (2007)
6. Gruber, H., Holzer, M., Kutrib, M.: More on the size of Higman-Haines sets: Effective construction. Fundamenta Informaticae 91(1), 105–121 (2009)
7. Haines, L.H.: On free monoids partially ordered by embedding. Journal of Combinatorial Theory 6, 94–98 (1969)
8. Holzer, M., Jakobi, S.: Chop Operations and Expressions: Descriptional Complexity Considerations. In: Mauri, G., Leporati, A. (eds.) DLT 2011. LNCS, vol. 6795, pp. 264–275. Springer, Heidelberg (2011)
9. Holzer, M., Kutrib, M.: Nondeterministic descriptional complexity of regular languages. International Journal of Foundations of Computer Science 14(6), 1087–1102 (2003)
10. Holzer, M., Kutrib, M.: Descriptional and Computational Complexity of Finite Automata. In: Dediu, A.H., Ionescu, A.M., Martín-Vide, C. (eds.) LATA 2009. LNCS, vol. 5457, pp. 23–42. Springer, Heidelberg (2009)
11. Hopcroft, J.E., Ullman, J.D.: Introduction to Automata Theory, Languages and Computation. Addison-Wesley (1979)
12. Jiráskova, G., Okhotin, A.: State complexity of cyclic shift. RAIRO–Informatique théorique et Applications/Theoretical Informatics and Applications 42(2), 335–360 (2008)
13. Mateescu, A., Salomaa, A.: Parallel composition of words with re-entrant symbols. Analele Universității București Matematică-Informatică 45, 71–80 (1996)
14. Okhotin, A.: On the state complexity of scattered substrings and superstrings. Fundamenta Informaticae 99(3), 325–338 (2010)
15. Pribavkina, E.V., Rodaro, E.: State complexity of code operators. International Journal of Foundations of Computer Science 22(7), 1669–1681 (2011)
16. Rampersad, N., Shallit, J., Wang, M.W.: Inverse star, border, and palstars. Information Processing Letters 111(9), 420–422 (2011)
17. Yu, S.: Regular languages. In: Rozenberg, G., Salomaa, A. (eds.) Handbook of Formal Languages, vol. 1, pp. 41–110. Springer (1997)
18. Yu, S.: State complexity of regular languages. Journal of Automata, Languages and Combinatorics 6, 221–234 (2001)
19. Yu, S., Zhuang, Q., Salomaa, K.: The state complexities of some basic operations on regular languages. Theoretical Computer Science 125, 315–328 (1994)

# Deciding Representability
# of Sets of Words of Equal Length[*]

Francine Blanchet-Sadri[1] and Sean Simmons[2]

[1] Department of Computer Science, University of North Carolina,
P.O. Box 26170, Greensboro, NC 27402–6170, USA
blanchet@uncg.edu
[2] Department of Mathematics, Massachusetts Institute of Technology,
77 Massachusetts Avenue, Cambridge, MA 02139–4307, USA
seanken@mit.edu

**Abstract.** Partial words are sequences over a finite alphabet that may
have holes that match, or are compatible with, all letters in the alphabet;
partial words without holes are simply words. Given a partial word $w$,
we denote by $\mathrm{sub}_w(n)$ the set of subwords of $w$ of length $n$, i.e., words
over the alphabet that are compatible with factors of $w$ of length $n$. We
call a set $S$ of words $h$-representable if $S = \mathrm{sub}_w(n)$ for some integer $n$
and partial word $w$ with $h$ holes. Using a graph theoretical approach,
we show that the problem of whether a given set is $h$-representable can
be decided in polynomial time. We also investigate other computational
problems related to this concept of representability.

## 1   Introduction

In the past several years, algorithms and combinatorics on words, or sequences
of letters over a finite alphabet, have been developing and many important applications in several areas including emergent areas, such as Bioinformatics and
DNA computing, have been found (see, for instance, [6,10]). In 1999, being motivated by molecular biology of nucleic acids, Berstel and Boasson [2] used the
terminoloy of *partial words* for sequences that may have undefined positions,
called don't-care symbols or holes, that match any letter in the alphabet (sequences with don't-cares were actually introduced by Fischer and Paterson [7] in
1974). Partial words are a special case of so-called generalized or indeterminate
or degenerate sequences, first discussed in 1987 by Abrahamson [1] and studied
since 2003. Algorithms and combinatorics on partial words have been recently
the subject of much investigation (see, for instance, [3]).

   In this paper, we introduce a few computational problems on partial words
related to subwords. Subwords have been studied in relation to combinatorics
on words (see, for instance, [9]). In particular, we define REP, or the problem of
deciding whether a set $S$ of words of length $n$ can be represented by a partial

[*] This material is based upon work supported by the National Science Foundation
under Grant No. DMS–1060775.

M. Kutrib, N. Moreira, and R. Reis (Eds.): DCFS 2012, LNCS 7386, pp. 103–116, 2012.
© Springer-Verlag Berlin Heidelberg 2012

word $w$, i.e., whether $S = \mathrm{sub}_w(n)$. If $h$ is a non-negative integer, we also define $h$-REP, or the problem of deciding whether $S$ can be represented by a partial word with exactly $h$ holes. Recently, Blanchet-Sadri et al. [4] started the study of representing languages by infinite partial words. Here, we deal with finite representing partial words rather than infinite ones. One of our motivations for studying representability of sets of words of equal length is the construction of compressed de Bruijn sequences, which are partial words of minimal length representing $A^n$ for some alphabet $A$ and integer $n$ [5].

It is known that 0-REP is in $\mathcal{P}$. Indeed, set $\mathrm{sub}_S(m) = \{x \mid |x| = m$ and $x$ is a subword of some $s \in S\}$ and let $G_S = (V, E)$ be the digraph where $V = \mathrm{sub}_S(n-1)$ and $E = S$, with $s \in S$ being directed from $s[0..n-1)$ to $s[1..n)$. Finding a word $w$ such that $\mathrm{sub}_w(n) = S$ is the same as finding a path in $G_S$ that includes every edge at least once. However, showing the membership of $h$-REP in $\mathcal{P}$ is not that simple.

The contents of our paper is as follows: In Section 2, we prove the membership of REP and $h$-REP in $\mathcal{NP}$. In Section 3, for any fixed non-negative integer $h$, we describe an algorithm that runs in polynomial time which, given a set $S$ of words of length $n$, decides if there is a partial word $w$ with $h$ holes such that $S = \mathrm{sub}_w(n)$ (our algorithm actually constructs $w$), showing the membership of $h$-REP in $\mathcal{P}$. In Section 4, we prove that some natural subproblem of REP is in $\mathcal{P}$. Finally in Section 5, we conclude with some remarks.

We need some background material on partial words (for more information, we refer the reader to [3]). An *alphabet* $A$ is a non-empty finite set of letters. A *(full) word* $w = a_0 \cdots a_{n-1}$ over $A$ is a finite concatenation of letters $a_i \in A$. The *length* of $w$, denoted by $|w|$, is the number of letters in $w$. The *empty word* $\varepsilon$ is the unique word of length zero. A *partial word* $w$ over $A$ is a sequence of symbols over the extended alphabet $A \cup \{\diamond\}$, where $\diamond \notin A$ plays the role of a hole symbol. The symbol at position $i$ is denoted by $w[i]$. The *set of defined positions* of $w$, denoted by $D(w)$, consists of the $i$'s with $w[i] \in A$ and the *set of holes* of $w$, denoted by $H(w)$, consists of the $i$'s with $w[i] = \diamond$. If $H(w) = \emptyset$, then $w$ is a (full) word.

For two partial words $w$ and $w'$ of equal length, we denote by $w \subset w'$ the *containment* of $w$ in $w'$, i.e., $w[i] = w'[i]$ for all $i \in D(w)$; we denote by $w \uparrow w'$ the *compatibility* of $w$ with $w'$, i.e., $w[i] = w'[i]$ for all $i \in D(w) \cap D(w')$. A *completion* $\hat{w}$ is a full word compatible with a given partial word $w$. For example, $ab\diamond\diamond b \subset ab\diamond ab$, $ab\diamond\diamond b \uparrow a\diamond a\diamond\diamond$, and $abab b$ is one of the four completions of $ab\diamond\diamond b$ over the binary alphabet $\{a, b\}$.

If $w$ is a partial word over $A$, then a *factor* of $w$ is a block of consecutive symbols of $w$ and a *subword* of $w$ is a full word over $A$ compatible with a factor of $w$. For instance, $ab\diamond\diamond b$ is a factor of $aaab\diamond\diamond ba\diamond$, while $abaab, ababb, abbab, abbbb$ are the subwords compatible with that factor. The factor $w[i]w[i+1] \cdots w[j-1]$ will be abbreviated by $w[i..j)$, the discrete interval $[i..j)$ being the set $\{i, i+1, \ldots j-1\}$. Then $\mathrm{sub}(w)$ is the set of all subwords of $w$; similarly, $\mathrm{sub}_w(n)$ is the set of all subwords of $w$ of length $n$. Letting $h$ be a non-negative integer, we call a set $S$ of words $h$-*representable* if $S = \mathrm{sub}_w(n)$ for some integer $n$ and partial word $w$ with $h$ holes; we call $S$ *representable* if it is $h$-representable for some $h$.

We also need some background material on graph theory. For instance, recall that a digraph $G$ is *strongly connected* if, for every pair of vertices $u$ and $v$, there exists a path from $u$ to $v$. For other concepts not defined here, we refer the reader to [8].

## 2   Membership of REP and $h$-REP in $\mathcal{NP}$

In this section, we show that REP and $h$-REP are both in $\mathcal{NP}$. To do this we need the following lemmas.

**Lemma 1.** *Let $S$ be a set of words of length $n$. If $S$ is representable, then there exists a partial word $w$ with $|w| \leq n(2|S| - 1) + \frac{|S|(|S|-1)}{2}$ such that $S = sub_w(n)$.*

*Proof.* Assume that $w$ is the shortest partial word such that $S = \mathrm{sub}_w(n)$. Set $S = \{s_0, \ldots, s_{|S|-1}\}$. Let $i_j$ be the smallest integer such that $s_j \uparrow w[i_j..i_j + n)$. Without loss of generality, we can assume that $0 = i_0 \leq i_1 \leq i_2 \leq \cdots \leq i_{|S|-1}$. Clearly, the partial word $w[0..i_{|S|-1} + n)$ contains every word in $S$ as a subword, so since $w$ is minimal it must be the case that $w = w[0..i_{|S|-1} + n)$, which implies

$$|w| = i_{|S|-1} + n = n + \sum_{j=1}^{|S|-1} (i_j - i_{j-1}) \tag{1}$$

Now, assume towards a contradiction that $i_j - i_{j-1} > j + 2n$ for some $j$, where $1 \leq j \leq |S|-1$. By definition of $i_j$, this implies that if $i_{j-1} \leq l < i_j$ then $w[l..l+n)$ is compatible with one of $s_0, \ldots, s_{j-1}$. However, since $i_j - i_{j-1} > j + 2n$ there must be at least $j + 1$ integers in the discrete interval $[i_{j-1} + n..i_j - n)$. By the pigeonhole principle, this implies that we can find $j'$, $l_1$, and $l_2$ such that $0 \leq j' \leq j-1$, $i_{j-1}+n \leq l_1 < l_2 < i_j - n$, $w[l_1..l_1+n) \uparrow s_{j'}$, and $w[l_2..l_2+n) \uparrow s_{j'}$. Since $s_{j'}$ is a full word, we have both containments $w[l_1..l_1 + n) \subset s_{j'}$ and $w[l_2..l_2 + n) \subset s_{j'}$.

Thus consider the partial word $w' = w[0..l_1)s_{j'}w[l_2+n..|w|)$. We want to prove that $\mathrm{sub}_{w'}(n) = S$. First, consider $s_l \in S$. If $l \leq j - 1$ we get $i_l + n \leq l_1$, thus $w[i_l..i_l + n)$ is a factor of $w[0..l_1)$, which by definition of $i_l$ means $s_l$ is a subword of $w[0..l_1)$, and thus is a subword of $w'$. A similar argument works when $l \geq j$, so $S \subseteq \mathrm{sub}_{w'}(n)$. Next, consider $s \in \mathrm{sub}_{w'}(n)$. Then $s$ is a subword of either $w[0..l_1)s_{j'}$ or $s_{j'}w[l_2 + n..|w|)$. Without loss of generality, assume it is a subword of $w[0..l_1)s_{j'}$. Since $w[l_1..l_1 + n) \subset s_{j'}$, we have $w[0..l_1 + n) \subset w[0..l_1)s_{j'}$. This implies that $s$ is a subword of $w$, and thus must be in $S$. Therefore, $S = \mathrm{sub}_{w'}(n)$.

Note, however, that $w'$ is strictly shorter than $w$, which contradicts the minimality of $w$. Therefore, $i_j - i_{j-1} \leq j + 2n$ for all $j \in [1..|S|)$. So we get

$$|w| = n + \sum_{j=1}^{|S|-1} (i_j - i_{j-1}) \leq n + \sum_{j=1}^{|S|-1} (j + 2n) = n(2|S| - 1) + \frac{|S|(|S| - 1)}{2}$$

$\square$

**Lemma 2.** *Let $S$ be a set of words of length $n$. If $S$ is $h$-representable, then there exists a partial word $w$ with $h$ holes such that $|w| \leq n + (|S| + n + 1)(|S| + h - 1)$ and such that $S = \text{sub}_w(n)$.*

*Proof.* The proof is similar to the one of Lemma 1.     □

**Proposition 1.** REP *and* $h$-REP *are in* $\mathcal{NP}$.

*Proof.* This is an immediate consequence of Lemma 1 and Lemma 2.     □

The question arises as to whether the problems REP and $h$-REP are in $\mathcal{P}$.

## 3     Membership of $h$-REP in $\mathcal{P}$

As mentioned before, 0-REP is in $\mathcal{P}$. In this section, we show that $h$-REP is also in $\mathcal{P}$ for any fixed non-negative integer $h$. We describe a polynomial time algorithm, Algorithm 3, that given a set $S$ of words of length $n$, decides if there is a partial word $w$ with $h$ holes such that $S = \text{sub}_w(n)$. If so, this algorithm constructs one such $w$.

The following definition partitions the set of vertices of a digraph into disjoint sets.

**Definition 1.** *Let $G = (V, E)$ be a digraph. If $u, v \in V$ then we write $u \rightharpoonup v$ if there exists a path in $G$ from $u$ to $v$. Then $V = \cup_{i=0}^{r} V_i$, where*

$$V_0 = \{v \in V \mid \text{if } u \in V \text{ and } u \rightharpoonup v, \text{ then } v \rightharpoonup u\}$$

*and for $i > 0$,*

$$V_i = \{v \in V - \bigcup_{j=0}^{i-1} V_j \mid \text{if } u \notin \bigcup_{j=0}^{i-1} V_j \text{ and } u \rightharpoonup v, \text{ then } v \rightharpoonup u \}$$

*Note that the $V_i$'s form a partition of $V$ into disjoint sets. Letting $G_i = (V_i, E_i)$ be the subgraph of $G$ spanned by $V_i$, we say that $V_0, \ldots, V_r$ is the decomposition of $V$ with respect to $\rightharpoonup$.*

In some sense, we can consider $V_0$ to consist of all minimal elements in $V$ with respect to $\rightharpoonup$, $V_1$ to consist of all minimal elements in $V - V_0$, and so on. This comes naturally from thinking of $\rightharpoonup$ as a preorder.

*Example 1.* Consider the set $S$ consisting of the following 30 words of length six:

aaaaaa aabbaa abbbaa baabbb bbabab bbbabb
aaaaab aabbba abbbab bababb bbabbb bbbbaa
aaaabb aabbbb abbbba babbba bbbaaa bbbbab
aaabba ababbb abbbbb babbbb bbbaab bbbbba
aaabbb abbaab baabba bbaabb bbbaba bbbbbb

Now consider the digraph $G_S = (V, E)$ where $E = S$ and $V = \text{sub}_S(5)$ is the set consisting of 20 words of length five. Then the decomposition of $V$ with respect to $\rightharpoonup$ consists of the sets: $V_0 = \{aaaaa\}$, $V_1 = \{aaaab\}$, $V_2 = \{aaabb\}$, $V_4 = \{bbaaa\}$, and $V_3 = V - (V_0 \cup V_1 \cup V_2 \cup V_4)$.

The following lemma gives useful properties of the decomposition of Definition 1.

**Lemma 3.** *Let $G = (V, E)$ be a digraph and let $V_0, \ldots, V_r$ be the decomposition of $V$ with respect to $\rightharpoonup$. If $i < j$, $u \in V_j$ and $v \in V_i$, then $u \not\rightharpoonup v$. Moreover, if $v \in V_{i+1}$ then there exists $u \in V_i$ such that $u \rightharpoonup v$. Finally for $i < r$, there exist vertices $u \in V_i$ and $v \in V_{i+1}$ such that $(u, v) \in E$.*

*Proof.* First, consider $i < j$. Assume $u \in V_j$ and $v \in V_i$ are such that $u \rightharpoonup v$. Since $u \notin \bigcup_{l=0}^{i-1} V_l$, it follows by the definition of $V_i$ that $v \rightharpoonup u$. Thus if $w \notin \bigcup_{l=0}^{i-1} V_l$ and $w \rightharpoonup u$, the assumption that $u \rightharpoonup v$ implies $w \rightharpoonup v$. Since $v \in V_i$ this implies $v \rightharpoonup w$, so since $u \rightharpoonup v$ it follows that $u \rightharpoonup w$. We get $u \in V_i$, which is impossible.

Next, consider $v \in V_{i+1}$. Assume there is no $u \in V_i$ such that $u \rightharpoonup v$. Since $v \in V_{i+1}$, if $w \notin \bigcup_{j=0}^{i} V_j$ and $w \rightharpoonup v$, then $v \rightharpoonup w$. Furthermore, if $w \notin \bigcup_{j=0}^{i-1} V_j$ and $w \rightharpoonup v$, then $v \rightharpoonup w$. This, however, implies by definition that $v \in V_i$, a contradiction.

Finally, consider $i \in [0..r)$ and let $v \in V_{i+1}$. By the above, there exists $u \in V_i$ such that $u \rightharpoonup v$. Let $u = u_0, u_1, \ldots, u_l = v$ be a path from $u$ to $v$. Note that since there is no path from any vertex in $V_{r'}$ to any vertex in $V_{i+1}$ for $r' > i+1$, it follows, since $u_l \in V_{i+1}$, that if $u_j \in V_{r'}$ then $r' \leq i+1$. By a similar argument, $r' \geq i$. Then let $l'$ be the smallest integer such that $u_{l'} \in V_{i+1}$. The above tells us that $u_{l'-1} \in V_i$, so $(u_{l'-1}, u_{l'})$ is the desired edge.                               □

The following definition introduces our set $S_h$, given a set $S$ of words of length $n$. This set is crucial in the description of our algorithm. We then show, in a lemma, that if $w$ is a partial word with $h$ holes whose set of subwords of length $n$ is a non-empty subset of $S$, then $w$ can somehow be built from a $h$-holed sequence in $S_h$.

**Definition 2.** *Given a set $S$ of words of length $n$, we define the set $S_h$ such that $(s_0, \ldots, s_{l-1}) \in S_h$ if $l > 0$ and the following conditions hold:*

1. *Each $s_i$ is a partial word with $|s_i| \geq n - 1$;*
2. *The partial word $s_0 \cdots s_{l-1}$ has exactly $h$ holes;*
3. *Each $s_i$, except possibly $s_0$ and $s_{l-1}$, has at least one hole;*
4. *If $x$ is a full word and a factor of some $s_i$, then $|x| < 2n$;*
5. *If $s_i[j] = \diamond$, then for $i > 0$ we have that $j \geq n - 1$, and for $i < l - 1$ we have that $j < |s_i| - n + 1$;*
6. *For each $i$ and for every $m \leq n$, $\text{sub}_{s_i}(m) \subseteq \text{sub}_S(m)$.*

**Lemma 4.** *Let $S$ be a set of words of length $n$ and $w$ be a partial word with $h$ holes. If $\text{sub}_w(n) \subseteq S$ and $\text{sub}_w(n) \neq \emptyset$, then there exists $(s_0, \ldots, s_{l-1}) \in S_h$ such that $w = s_0 w_0 s_1 w_1 \cdots w_{l-2} s_{l-1}$, where each $w_i$ is a full word.*

*Proof.* We proceed by induction on $|w|$. This holds trivially if $|w| = n$ by letting $s_0 = w$ and $l = 1$. Therefore assume that the claim holds for all $w'$ with $|w'| < |w|$. If $w$ does not contain any full word of length greater than or equal to $2n$ as a factor, letting $l = 1$ and $s_0 = w$, gives us what we want. Therefore, assume that $w$ contains a factor $y$ that is a full word of length at least $2n$. Furthermore, assume that $|y|$ is maximal. There exists $i$ such that $w[i..i + |y|) = y$. Furthermore, the maximality of $y$ implies that either $i + |y| = |w|$, $i = 0$, or $w[i-1] = w[i+|y|] = \diamond$.

Consider the case $w[i-1] = w[i+|y|] = \diamond$ (the other cases are similar). Then $w = x \diamond y \diamond z = x \diamond w[i..i + n - 1)y'w[i + |y| - n + 1..i + |y|) \diamond z$ for some $y'$. Assume $x_0 = x \diamond w[i..i + n - 1)$ has $h_0$ holes and $z_0 = w[i + |y| - n + 1..i + |y|) \diamond z$ has $h_1$ holes. Then by the inductive hypothesis, there exist $(t_0, \ldots, t_{l_0 - 1}) \in S_{h_0}$ and full words $w_0, \ldots, w_{l_0 - 2}$ such that $x_0 = t_0 w_0 \cdots w_{l_0 - 2} t_{l_0 - 1}$. Similarly, there exist $(t'_0, \ldots, t'_{l_1 - 1}) \in S_{h_1}$ and full words $w'_0, \ldots, w'_{l_1 - 2}$ such that $z_0 = t'_0 w'_0 \cdots w'_{l_1 - 2} t'_{l_1 - 1}$. We can let $(s_0, \ldots, s_{l-1}) = (t_0, \ldots, t_{l_0-1}, t'_0, \ldots, t'_{l_1-1}) \in S_h$ when both $t_{l_0 - 1}$ and $t'_0$ have holes; otherwise, in the case of $t_{l_0-1}$ having a hole and $t'_0$ having no hole for instance, we can let $(s_0, \ldots, s_{l-1}) = (t_0, \ldots, t_{l_0-1}, t'_1, \ldots, t'_{l_1-1})$. $\square$

*Example 2.* Returning to Example 1, let $n = 6$ and $h = 5$. Consider

$$w = aaaaaaaaaaaaaaaabb \diamond abbbbbababbbba \diamond bbbb \diamond \diamond bbbaa \diamond$$

Here, $\text{sub}_w(6) = S - \{baabba\}$. Using the proof of Lemma 4, we can factorize $w$ as follows:

$$\underbrace{aaaaa\ aaaaa\ aaaaabb \diamond abbbb}_{s_0}\ \underbrace{baba}_{s_1}\ \underbrace{bbbba \diamond bbbb \diamond \diamond bbbaa \diamond}_{s_2}$$

By Definition 2, $(s_0, s_1, s_2) \in S_5$.

Our next step is to prove that Algorithm 1, given below, generates $S_h$ in polynomial time. The idea behind the algorithm is simple. Basically if $(s_0, \ldots, s_{l-1}) \in S_h$, then $l \leq h+2$. Furthermore, there exists a constant $c$ such that $|s_i| < cn$, and each $s_i$ can be created by concatenating subwords of elements of $S$. Using this, it is easy to produce $S_h$ by enumerating all such $(s_0, \ldots, s_{l-1})$'s. Algorithm 1 works as follows:

- Creates $T_0$, the set of all $t_0 t_1 \cdots t_{2h+1}$, where each $t_j \in \text{sub}(S)$ ($\text{sub}(S)$ denotes the set of subwords of elements of $S$);
- For $h' = 1, \ldots, h$, creates $T_{h'}$ by inserting $h'$ holes into the elements of $T_0$ (i.e., by replacing $h'$ positions by $\diamond$'s);
- Creates $T = T_0 \cup T_1 \cup \cdots \cup T_h$;
- Creates $S' = T \cup T^2 \cup \cdots \cup T^{h+2}$;
- Removes from $S'$ any sequence $(s_0, \ldots, s_{l-1})$ that does not satisfy one of the conditions 1–6 of Definition 2;
- Returns $S_h = S'$.

The size of the set $\text{sub}(S)^{2h+2}$ is bounded by a polynomial in the size of the input.

---

**Algorithm 1.** Generating $S_h$, where $S$ is a set of words of length $n$

---

1: Let $T_0' = \emptyset$
2: **for** $(t_0, \ldots, t_{2h+1}) \in \mathrm{sub}(S)^{2h+2}$ **do**
3:    $T_0' = T_0' \cup \{t_0 \cdots t_{2h+1}\}$
4: Let $T_0 = T_0'$
5: **for** $h' = 1$ to $h$ **do**
6:    Let $T_{h'} = \emptyset$
7:    **for** $t \in T_{h'-1}$ **do**
8:      **for** $j = 0$ to $|t| - 1$ **do**
9:        **if** $t[j] \neq \diamond$ **then**
10:          Letting $t' = t$, replace $t'[j]$ by $\diamond$ and add $t'$ to $T_{h'}$
11: Let $T = \displaystyle\bigcup_{h'=0}^{h} T_{h'}$
12: Let $S' = \displaystyle\bigcup_{l=1}^{h+2} T^l$
13: **for** $s = (s_0, \ldots, s_{l-1}) \in S'$ **do**
14:    **for** $i = 0$ to $l - 1$ **do**
15:      **if** $s_i$ is a full word and $i \notin \{0, l-1\}$, or $s_i$ contains a $\diamond$ in its prefix of length
         $n-1$ and $i \neq 0$, or $s_i$ contains a $\diamond$ in its suffix of length $n-1$ and $i \neq l-1$, or
         $|s_i| < n - 1$, or $s_i$ contains a full word $t$ of length at least $2n$ as a factor **then**
16:        remove $s$ from $S'$
17:      **for** $m = 1$ to $n$ **do**
18:        **if** $\mathrm{sub}_{s_i}(m) \not\subseteq \mathrm{sub}_S(m)$ **then**
19:          remove $s$ from $S'$
20:    **if** $s_0 \cdots s_{l-1}$ does not contain exactly $h$ holes **then**
21:      remove $s$ from $S'$
22: **return** $S_h = S'$

---

**Lemma 5.** *For any fixed non-negative integer $h$, Algorithm 1 generates $S_h$ in polynomial time given a set $S$ of words of length $n$.*

*Proof.* Let $T_0'$, $T_h$, $T$, etc. be as in the algorithm. First we want to show that if $(s_0, \ldots, s_{l-1}) \in S_h$, then $s_i \in T$. To see this, let $\hat{s}_i$ be any completion of $s_i$. Then the facts that $s_i$ contains at most $h$ holes and no full word of length greater than or equal to $2n$ as a factor imply that $|\hat{s}_i| = |s_i| \leq 2n - 1 + h(2n) = 2(h+1)n - 1$. This means that $|\hat{s}_i| = qn + q'$ for some integers $q$ and $q'$, where $0 \leq q' < n$ and $q < 2h + 2$. Thus we can write $\hat{s}_i = t_0 t_1 \cdots t_{2h+1}$ where $t_j$ is of length $n$ for $j < q$, $t_q$ is of length $q'$, and $t_j = \varepsilon$ for all other $j$. Note for each $j$, since $|t_j| \leq n$, we have by definition of $S_h$ that $t_j \in \mathrm{sub}_{\hat{s}_i}(|t_j|) \subseteq \mathrm{sub}_{s_i}(|t_j|) \subseteq \mathrm{sub}_S(|t_j|)$. Therefore $(t_0, \ldots, t_{2h+1}) \in \mathrm{sub}(S)^{2h+2}$, where $\mathrm{sub}(S)$ is the set of all subwords of $S$, so $\hat{s}_i = t_0 t_1 \cdots t_{2h+1} \in T_0' = T_0$ by Lines 3–4.

Then by a simple induction argument, if $s'$ is formed from $\hat{s}_i$ by inserting $h' \leq h$ holes then $s' \in T_{h'} \subseteq T$ (see Lines 5–11). In particular, $s_i \in T$. Since this is true for all $i$, it follows that $(s_0, \ldots, s_{l-1}) \in T^l$. Note that $l \leq h + 2$ since $s_0 \cdots s_{l-1}$ contains $h$ holes, and for $i \in [1..l-1)$, we know that $s_i$ must contain at least one of the holes. Thus, $(s_0, \ldots, s_{l-1}) \in T^l \subseteq S'$ (see Line 12).

We have now reached the for loop on Line 13 of the algorithm. Assume that $s = (s_0, \ldots, s_{l-1}) \in S'$. Then, by looking at the interior of this for loop (Lines 14–21), $s$ is not removed from $S'$ if and only if the conditions 1–6 of Definition 2 hold. Furthermore, by construction $l > 0$. Therefore $s$ is removed from $S'$ if and only if $s \notin S_h$. Since $S_h \subseteq S'$ at the beginning of the loop, it follows that at the end of the loop $S_h = S'$. The algorithm then returns $S_h = S'$ on Line 22. We know that $|\mathrm{sub}(S)| \leq |S|n^2 + 1$ (since each element of $S$ contains at most $n$ non-empty subwords beginning at each of its $n$ positions). Thus $|\mathrm{sub}(S)^{2h+2}| \leq (|S|n^2 + 1)^{2h+2}$, a polynomial in the input. $\qquad\square$

Our next step is to prove that Algorithm 2 constructs, in polynomial time, a partial word $w$ with $h$ holes such that $\mathrm{sub}_w(n) = S$ from a given $h$-holed sequence $(s_0, \ldots, s_{l-1})$ in $S_h$ if such partial word exists. Algorithm 2 uses the decomposition of the vertex set $V$ of $G = G_S = (V, E)$ with respect to $\rightharpoonup$, i.e., $V_0, \ldots, V_r$. The partial word $w$ has the form

$$s_0[0..|s_0| - n + 1)w_0 s_1[n - 1..|s_1| - n + 1)w_1 s_2[n - 1..|s_2| - n + 1)$$
$$\cdots w_{l-2} s_{l-1}[n - 1..|s_{l-1}|)$$

where each $w_j$ is a path from $s_j[|s_j| - n + 1..|s_j|)$ to $s_{j+1}[0..n - 1)$ satisfying some conditions related to the spanned subgraphs $G_0, \ldots, G_r$.

**Lemma 6.** *Let $S$ be a set of words of length $n$ and $s = (s_0, \ldots, s_{l-1}) \in S_h$. If there exists a partial word $w'$ with $h$ holes such that $\mathrm{sub}_{w'}(n) = S$ and $w' = s_0 x_0 s_1 x_1 \cdots x_{l-2} s_{l-1}$ for some full words $x_j$, then Algorithm 2 returns a partial word $w$ with $h$ holes such that $\mathrm{sub}_w(n) = S$ and $w = s_0 y_0 s_1 y_1 \cdots y_{l-2} s_{l-1}$ for some full words $y_j$. Otherwise, it returns null. Furthermore, the algorithm runs in polynomial time.*

*Proof.* Assume the algorithm returns null (the other case is simple). Suppose towards a contradiction that there exists $w'$ with $h$ holes such that $\mathrm{sub}_{w'}(n) = S$ and $w' = s_0 x_0 s_1 x_1 \cdots x_{l-2} s_{l-1}$ for some full words $x_j$. We will check each return statement one by one to see which returned null. Let $w'_i = s_i[|s_i| - n + 1..|s_i|)x_i s_{i+1}[0..n - 1)$, then note that each $w'_i$ is a full word with

$$w' = s_0[0..|s_0| - n + 1)w'_0 s_1[n - 1..|s_1| - n + 1)w'_1 s_2[n - 1..|s_2| - n + 1) \cdots$$
$$w'_{l-2} s_{l-1}[n - 1..|s_{l-1}|)$$

Consider the return statement on Line 36 (the ones on Line 6, Line 19, Line 17, and Line 22 are simpler). This implies, if $w$ is as in the algorithm, that $\mathrm{sub}_w(n) \neq S$. Note that if $x \in \mathrm{sub}_w(n)$, then either $x \in \mathrm{sub}_{s_i}(n) \subseteq S$ for some $i$ or $x \in \mathrm{sub}_{w_i}(n) \subseteq S$ for some $i$; in either case, $\mathrm{sub}_w(n) \subseteq S$. Thus, there exists $e \in S$ such that $e \notin \mathrm{sub}_w(n)$. Since $E = S$, $e$ is an edge in the edge set $E$ of $G$.

We can show that there exist $i \neq i'$ such that $e$ is an edge from $u \in V_i$ to $v \in V_{i'}$ (the case where $e \in E_i$ for some $i$ leads to a contradiction). By Lemma 3, $i < i'$. Note that $e$ is not a subword of $s_j$ for any $j$, since otherwise it would be a subword of $w$. Thus, $e$ is a subword of some $w'_j$. Lemma 3 implies that $i_{1,j} \leq i < i' \leq i_{0,j+1}$.

---

**Algorithm 2.** Checking words for $s = (s_0, \ldots, s_{l-1}) \in S_h$, where $S$ is a set of words of length $n$

---

1: Let $G = G_S = (V, E)$
2: **if** $l = 1$ **then**
3:    **if** $\mathrm{sub}_{s_0}(n) = S$ **then**
4:       **return** $s_0$
5:    **else**
6:       **return** null
7: Decompose $V$ into $V_0, \ldots, V_r$ with respect to $\rightharpoonup$
8: **for** $j = 0$ to $l - 1$ **do**
9:    **if** $j > 0$ **then**
10:       Let $s_{0,j} = s_j[0..n-1)$
11:       Let $i_{0,j}$ be the index with $s_{0,j} \in V_{i_{0,j}}$
12:    **if** $j < l - 1$ **then**
13:       Let $s_{1,j} = s_j[|s_j| - n + 1..|s_j|)$
14:       Let $i_{1,j}$ be the index with $s_{1,j} \in V_{i_{1,j}}$
15: **for** $j = 0$ to $l - 2$ **do**
16:    **if** $i_{1,j} > i_{0,j+1}$ **then**
17:       **return** null
18:    **if** $j \neq 0$ and $i_{0,j} > i_{1,j}$ **then**
19:       **return** null
20: **for** $i = 0$ to $r$ **do**
21:    **if** $i_{1,j} \leq i \leq i_{0,j+1}$ for some $j$, and $G_i$ is not strongly connected **then**
22:       **return** null
23: **for** $i = 0$ to $r - 1$ **do**
24:    Choose $u_i \in V_i$ and $v_{i+1} \in V_{i+1}$ such that $(u_i, v_{i+1}) \in E$ (this can be done by Lemma 3)
25: **for** $j = 0$ to $l - 2$ **do**
26:    Choose a path $p_{i_{1,j}}$ from $s_{1,j}$ to $u_{i_{1,j}}$ that includes every edge in $E_{i_{1,j}}$ (this can be done since $G_{i_{1,j}}$ is strongly connected)
27:    **for** $i = i_{1,j} + 1$ to $i_{0,j+1} - 1$ **do**
28:       Choose a path $p_i$ from $v_i$ to $u_i$ that includes every edge in $E_i$ (this can be done since $G_i$ is strongly connected)
29:    If $i_{1,j} \neq i_{0,j+1}$, choose a path $p_{i_{0,j+1}}$ from $v_{i_{0,j+1}}$ to $s_{0,j+1}$ that includes every edge in $E_{i_{0,j+1}}$; else choose a path $p_{i_{0,j+1}}$ from $u_{i_{0,j+1}} = u_{i_{1,j}}$ to $s_{0,j+1}$ that includes every edge in $E_{i_{0,j+1}}$ (this can be done since $G_{i_{0,j+1}}$ is strongly connected)
30:    Let $P_j$ be the path in $G$ produced by first taking $p_{i_{1,j}}$, then the edge from $u_{i_{1,j}}$ to $v_{i_{1,j}+1}$, then $p_{i_{1,j}+1}$, then the edge from $u_{i_{1,j}+1}$ to $v_{i_{1,j}+2}$, and continuing until you reach $s_{0,j+1}$
31:    Let $w_j$ be the word associated with the path $P_j$
32: Let $w = s_0[0..|s_0| - n + 1)w_0 s_1[n - 1..|s_1| - n + 1)w_1 s_2[n - 1..|s_2| - n + 1) \cdots w_{l-2} s_{l-1}[n - 1..|s_{l-1}|)$
33: **if** $\mathrm{sub}_w(n) = S$ **then**
34:    **return** $w$
35: **else**
36:    **return** null

---

Assume that $i' > i + 1$. Set $w'_j = yez$ for some $y, z$. Every subword of $w'_j$ of length $n - 1$ is a subword of either $ye[0..n-1) = yu$ or $e[1..n)z = vz$. Since $V_{i+1} \neq \emptyset$, consider any $x \in V_{i+1}$. Then $x$ cannot be a subword of $yu$ since otherwise $x \rightharpoonup u$, contradicting Lemma 3. Similarly, it cannot be a subword of $vz$. By construction, however, $x$ is a subword of $w'_j$, a contradiction.

Now, assume that $i' = i + 1$. By construction of $P_j$, there must exist some $u' \in V_i$ and $v' \in V_{i+1}$ such that $f = (u', v')$ is an edge in $P_j$. Thus $f$ is a subword of $w$. Since $e$ is not a subword of $w$, we have $f \neq e$. However, both $e$ and $f$ must occur as subwords of $w'$. This implies that there exists a completion $\hat{w}'$ of $w'$ with $f$ as a subword. Note, however, that since $w'_j$ is full and $w'_j$ is a factor of $w'$, it must be a factor of $\hat{w}'$, so $e$ is also a subword of $\hat{w}'$. Without loss of generality, we can assume that $e$ occurs before $f$ in $\hat{w}'$. This implies that $v$ occurs before $u'$ in $\hat{w}'$, so $v \rightharpoonup u'$ (since $\hat{w}'$ corresponds to a path in $G$). The latter along with $v \in V_{i+1}$ and $u' \in V_i$ contradict Lemma 3.                                    □

*Example 3.* Returning to Examples 1 and 2, given as input $(s_0, s_1, s_2) \in S_5$, Algorithm 2 computes the following values:

| $j$ | $s_{1,j}$ | $i_{1,j}$ | $s_{0,j}$ | $i_{0,j}$ |
|---|---|---|---|---|
| 0 | $aaaaa$ | 0 | | |
| 1 | $abbbb$ | 3 | $aaaaa$ | 0 |
| 2 | | | $bbbba$ | 3 |

Then Algorithm 2 may output the following word $w$ to represent the set $S$:

$$\underbrace{aaaaa \; w'_0 \; aaaaabb\diamond abbbb}_{s_0} \; \underbrace{w'_1}_{s_1} \; \underbrace{bbbba\diamond bbbb\diamond\diamond bbbaa\diamond}_{s_2}$$

where $w'_0 = \varepsilon$ and $w'_1 = bbababbbbabbbabbbbaabbaabbbaa$. Note that

$$w_0 = s_0[|s_0| - n + 1..|s_0|)w'_0 s_1[0..n-1) = aaaaaw'_0 aaaaa$$

is a path from $aaaaa$ to $aaaaa$ visiting every edge in $G_0$ and

$$w_1 = s_1[|s_1| - n + 1..|s_1|)w'_1 s_2[0..n-1) = abbbbw'_1 bbbba$$

is a path from $abbbb$ to $bbbba$ visiting every edge in $G_3$.

Our next step is to prove that Algorithm 3 determines whether or not a given set of words of equal length is $h$-representable.

**Theorem 1.** *If a given input set $S$ of words of length $n$ is not $h$-representable, then Algorithm 3 returns null. Otherwise, it returns a partial word $w$ with $h$ holes such that $sub_w(n) = S$. Furthermore, it runs in polynomial time.*

*Proof.* It is not difficult to show that Algorithm 3 works. It also runs in polynomial time. This follows easily from the fact that Lemma 5 implies as a corollary that given any fixed non-negative integer $h$, there exists a polynomial $f_h(x, y)$ such that $|S_h| \leq f_h(|S|, n)$ (thus the for loop only iterates a polynomial number of times in the input size $|S|$), the fact that generating $S_h$ using Algorithm 1 takes polynomial time, and the fact that Algorithm 2 runs in polynomial time.                                    □

**Corollary 1.** $h$-REP *is in* $\mathcal{P}$ *for any fixed non-negative integer* $h$.

---

**Algorithm 3.** Deciding the $h$-representability of a set $S$ of words of equal length

---

1: **if** $S = \emptyset$ **then**
2:    **return** $\varepsilon$
3: Generate $S_h$ using Algorithm 1
4: **for** $s \in S_h$ **do**
5:    Let $w$ be the partial word produced by Algorithm 2
6:    **if** $w \neq$ null **then**
7:        **return** $w$
8: **return** null

---

## 4 Membership of a Subproblem of REP in $\mathcal{P}$

In this section, we give a subproblem of REP that is in $\mathcal{P}$. To prove this membership, we first need some terminology.

**Definition 3.** *Let $S$ be a set of words of length $n$ over some alphabet $A$, $|A| = k > 1$, and let $G = G_S = (V, E)$. A partial word path is a sequence $A_0, \ldots, A_m$ of non-empty subsets of $V = sub_S(n - 1)$ such that the following conditions 1–3 hold:*

1. *There exists a partial word $u_0$ satisfying $|u_0| = n - 1$ and $sub_{u_0}(n - 1) = A_0$;*
2. *For each $i$, either*

$$A_i = \{va \mid a \in A \text{ and } bv \in A_{i-1} \text{ for some } b \in A\} \tag{2}$$

*or there exists an $a \in A$ such that*

$$A_i = \{va \mid bv \in A_{i-1} \text{ for some } b \in A\}; \tag{3}$$

3. *If $bv \in A_{i-1}$ and $va \in A_i$ for some $a, b \in A$ and full word $v$, then $bva \in E$.*

*Let $h'$ be the number of $i$'s such that Eq. (2) holds. We say that the partial word path $A_0, \ldots, A_m$ has $h$ holes if $h = \log_k |A_0| + h'$ (note that $\log_k |A_0|$ is the number of holes in $u_0$, defined in Statement 1, because each hole in $u_0$ can be filled by one of $k$ letters).*

*We say that a partial word path contains an edge $e = (x, y)$ if there exists an $i$ such that $x \in A_i$ and $y \in A_{i+1}$.*

*Finally, defining $u_i$ recursively by $u_i \doteq u_{i-1}\diamond$ if $A_i$ satisfies Eq. (2) and $u_i = u_{i-1}a$ if $A_i$ satisfies Eq. (3) for some $a \in A$, we say that $u_m$ is a partial word associated with the partial word path $A_0, \ldots, A_m$.*

In the zero-hole case, the following remark tells us that $S = sub_w(n)$ for a full word $w$ if and only if there is a path in $G_S$ including every edge at least once. This is decidable in polynomial time, as we knew already. Note, however, that the remark also gives a polynomial time algorithm that works in the one-hole case.

*Remark 1.* Let $S$ be a set of words of length $n$. Then there exists a partial word $w$ with $h$ holes such that $S = \mathrm{sub}_w(n)$ if and only if there exists a partial word path with $h$ holes that includes every edge of $G_S$ at least once.

To see this, assuming that such a $w$ exists, let $A_i = \mathrm{sub}_{w[i..i+n-1)}(n-1)$. Then $A_0, \ldots, A_{|w|-n+1}$ is the partial word path we want. On the other hand, assuming that such a path $A_0, \ldots, A_m$ exists, the partial word $w = u_m$ associated with the partial word path $A_0, \ldots, A_m$, as constructed in Definition 3, has $h$ holes and satisfies $\mathrm{sub}_w(n) = S$.

We now have the terminolgy needed to prove the following lemma.

**Lemma 7.** *Let $S$ be a set of words of length $n$ and let $G = G_S = (V, E)$, where $V_0, \ldots, V_r$ is the decomposition of $V$ with respect to $\rightharpoonup$. Then there exists a partial word $w$ such that $S = \mathrm{sub}_w(n)$ and such that every subword of $w$ of length $n-1$ is compatible with exactly one factor of $w$ if and only if $V_0, \ldots, V_r$ is a partial word path including every edge.*

*Proof.* To show the backward implication, if $w$ is the partial word associated with our partial word path, every subword of $w$ of length $n-1$ occurs exactly once in $w$ and $\mathrm{sub}_w(n) = S$. To show the forward direction, assume there is a partial word $w$ such that each subword of $w$ of length $n-1$ occurs exactly once, and $\mathrm{sub}_w(n) = S$. Let $A_0, \ldots, A_r$ be the partial word path associated with $w$. We want to prove that $A_i = V_i$. By construction, $A_i = \mathrm{sub}_{w[i..i+n-1)}(n-1)$.

Suppose towards a contradiction that this is not the case, and let $j$ be the smallest index such that $A_j \neq V_j$. Then let $w' = w[j..|w|)$ and let $S' = \mathrm{sub}_{w'}(n)$. Let $G' = G_{S'} = (V', E')$. Then each word in $\mathrm{sub}_{w'}(n-1)$ occurs in $w'$ exactly once. Since each word in $\mathrm{sub}_w(n-1)$ occurs in $w$ exactly once, it follows that

$$\mathrm{sub}_{w'}(n-1) = \mathrm{sub}_w(n-1) - \bigcup_{i=0}^{j-1} A_i = \mathrm{sub}_w(n-1) - \bigcup_{i=0}^{j-1} V_i$$

Let $V'_0, \ldots, V'_s$ be the decomposition of $V' = V - \bigcup_{i=0}^{j-1} V_i$ with respect to $\rightharpoonup$. By definition of decomposition, however, it is easy to see that $V'_i = V_{i+j}$. Furthermore, $A_j, \ldots, A_r$ is a partial word path in $G'$.

If $v \in A_j$ then $v$ has no incoming edges in $G'$, since if it has an incoming edge $e$ then $A_j, \ldots, A_r$ must contain $e$. This implies $v$ must occur in $A_i$ for some $i > j$, contradicting the fact that each length $n-1$ subword of $w'$ occurs exactly once in $w'$. Since no $v \in A_j$ has incoming edges, $A_j \subseteq V'_0 = V_j$. On the other hand, assume $v \in V'_0$, $v \in A_i$ for some $i > j$. This implies there is a path from some $u \in A_j$ to $v$. By definition of $V'_0$, this implies there is a path from $v$ to $u$, contradicting the fact that $u$ has no incoming edges. Therefore it must be that $V_j = V'_0 = A_j$. This is a contradiction, so our claim follows.  □

Lemma 7 gives the following problem a membership in $\mathcal{P}$.

**Proposition 2.** *The problem of deciding whether a set $S$ of words of length $n$ can be represented by a partial word $w$, such that every subword of $w$ of length $n-1$ occurs exactly once in $w$ (in other words, every element in $\mathrm{sub}_S(n-1)$ is compatible with exactly one factor of $w$), is in $\mathcal{P}$.*

*Proof.* The proof reduces to checking that the graph $G_S$ has the properties listed in Lemma 7. This check can clearly be done in polynomial time. □

## 5  Conclusion

We provided a polynomial time algorithm to solve $h$-REP, that is, given a set $S$ of words of length $n$, our algorithm decides, in polynomial time with respect to the input size $n|S|$, whether there exists a partial word with $h$ holes that represents $S$. Our algorithm also computes such a representing partial word. To find a more tractable algorithm is an open problem.

Whether or not REP is in $\mathcal{P}$ is also an open problem. We have some hope that the following proposition might be useful in understanding REP. Letting $S$ be a set of words of length $n$, set

$$\text{Comp}(S) = \{u \mid u \text{ is a partial word and every completion of } u \text{ is in } S\}$$

The set $\text{Comp}(S)$ is important because if $\text{sub}_w(n) = S$, then every factor of length $n$ of $w$ is an element of $\text{Comp}(S)$.

**Proposition 3.** *Assume $|A| > 1$. If $S$ is a set of words of length $n$, then $|\text{Comp}(S)| \leq |S|^2$. Furthermore, $\text{Comp}(S)$ can be computed in $O(n|S|^4)$ time.*

*Proof.* Assume that $u \in \text{Comp}(S)$. Choose $a, b \in A$, $a \neq b$. Let $\hat{u}_a$ (resp., $\hat{u}_b$) be the word we get by replacing all the ◇'s in $u$ with $a$ (resp., $b$). Then $\hat{u}_a, \hat{u}_b \in S$, by definition of $\text{Comp}(S)$. Furthermore, $u$ is the partial word with the least number of holes such that $u \subset \hat{u}_a$ and $u \subset \hat{u}_b$, in other words, $u$ is the greatest lower bound of $\hat{u}_a$ and $\hat{u}_b$. Therefore,

$$\text{Comp}(S) \subseteq \{u \mid u \text{ is the greatest lower bound of } (u_1, u_2) \in S^2\}$$

However, the latter set has cardinality at most $|S^2| = |S|^2$, so $|\text{Comp}(S)| \leq |S|^2$. Therefore, all we need to do in order to compute $\text{Comp}(S)$ is to iterate through $(u_1, u_2) \in S^2$ (which takes $|S|^2$ iterations). In each iteration we calculate $u$, the greatest lower bound of $u_1$ and $u_2$. We then iterate through all completions of $u$ until either we have checked them all (in which case, we add $u$ to $\text{Comp}(S)$), or until we find one that is not in $S$ (in which case, $u$ is not in $\text{Comp}(S)$). This produces $\text{Comp}(S)$. Furthermore, each iteration takes $O(n|S|^2)$ time, so the algorithm takes $O(n|S|^4)$ time. □

A World Wide Web server interface has been established at

http://www.uncg.edu/cmp/research/subwordcomplexity6

for automated use of a program that when given as input a set $S$ of words, decides if there exists a word $w$ such that $\text{sub}_w(n) = S$ for some $n$.

# References

1. Abrahamson, K.: Generalized string matching. SIAM Journal on Computing 16(6), 1039–1051 (1987)
2. Berstel, J., Boasson, L.: Partial words and a theorem of Fine and Wilf. Theoretical Computer Science 218, 135–141 (1999)
3. Blanchet-Sadri, F.: Algorithmic Combinatorics on Partial Words. Chapman & Hall/CRC Press, Boca Raton (2008)
4. Blanchet-Sadri, F., Chen, B., Manuelli, L., Munteanu, S., Schwartz, J., Stich, S.: Representing languages by infinite partial words (2011) (preprint )
5. Blanchet-Sadri, F., Schwartz, J., Stich, S., Wyatt, B.J.: Binary De Bruijn Partial Words with One Hole. In: Kratochvíl, J., Li, A., Fiala, J., Kolman, P. (eds.) TAMC 2010. LNCS, vol. 6108, pp. 128–138. Springer, Heidelberg (2010)
6. Crochemore, M., Hancart, C., Lecroq, T.: Algorithms on Strings. Cambridge University Press (2007)
7. Fischer, M., Paterson, M.: String matching and other products. In: Karp, R. (ed.) 7th SIAM-AMS Complexity of Computation, pp. 113–125 (1974)
8. Gross, J.L., Yellen, J.: Handbook of Graph Theory. CRC Press (2004)
9. Lothaire, M.: Combinatorics on Words. Cambridge University Press, Cambridge (1997)
10. Lothaire, M.: Applied Combinatorics on Words. Cambridge University Press (2005)

# Syntactic Complexities of Some Classes of Star-Free Languages[*]

Janusz Brzozowski and Baiyu Li

David R. Cheriton School of Computer Science,
University of Waterloo, Waterloo, ON, Canada N2L 3G1
{brzozo,b5li}@uwaterloo.ca

**Abstract.** The syntactic complexity of a regular language is the cardinality of its syntactic semigroup. The syntactic complexity of a subclass of regular languages is the maximal syntactic complexity of languages in that subclass, taken as a function of the state complexity $n$ of these languages. We study the syntactic complexity of three subclasses of star-free languages. We find tight upper bounds for languages accepted by monotonic, partially monotonic and "nearly monotonic" automata; all three of these classes are star-free. We conjecture that the bound for nearly monotonic languages is also a tight upper bound for star-free languages.

**Keywords:** finite automaton, monotonic, nearly monotonic, partially monotonic, star-free language, syntactic complexity, syntactic semigroup.

## 1 Introduction

*Star-free* languages are the smallest class containing the finite languages and closed under boolean operations and concatenation. In 1965, Schützenberger proved [19] that a language is star-free if and only if its syntactic monoid is *group-free*, that is, has only trivial subgroups. An equivalent condition is that the minimal deterministic automaton of a star-free language is *permutation-free*, that is, has only trivial permutations (cycles of length 1). Such automata are called *aperiodic,* and this is the term we use. Star-free languages were studied in detail in 1971 by McNaughton and Papert [15].

The *state complexity of a regular language* is the number of states in the minimal deterministic finite automaton (DFA) recognizing that language. State complexity of operations on languages has been studied quite extensively; for a survey of this topic and a list of references see [21]. An equivalent notion is that of *quotient complexity* [2], which is the number of left quotients of the language.

Quotient complexity is closely related to the Nerode equivalence [17]. Another well-known equivalence relation, the Myhill equivalence [16], defines the syntactic semigroup of a language and its *syntactic complexity*, which is the cardinality of the syntactic semigroup. It was pointed out in [5] that syntactic complexity can be very different for languages with the same quotient complexity.

---

[*] This work was supported by the Natural Sciences and Engineering Research Council of Canada under grant No. OGP0000871.

M. Kutrib, N. Moreira, and R. Reis (Eds.): DCFS 2012, LNCS 7386, pp. 117–129, 2012.

In contrast to state complexity, syntactic complexity has not received much attention. Suppose $L$ is a regular language and has quotient complexity $n$. In 1970 Maslov [14] noted that $n^n$ is a tight upper bound on the syntactic complexity of $L$. In 2003–2004 Holzer and König [9], and Krawetz, Lawrence and Shallit [12] studied the syntactic complexity of unary and binary languages. In 2010 Brzozowski and Ye [5] showed that, if $L$ is any right ideal, then $n^{n-1}$ is a tight upper bound on its syntactic complexity. They also proved that $n^{n-1} + (n-1)$ (respectively, $n^{n-2} + (n-2)2^{n-2} + 1$) is a lower bound if $L$ a left (respectively, two-sided) ideal. In 2012 Brzozowski, Li and Ye [3] showed that $n^{n-2}$ is a tight upper bound for prefix-free languages and that $(n-1)^{n-2} + (n-2)$ (respectively, $(n-1)^{n-3} + (n-2)^{n-3} + (n-3)2^{n-3}$ or $(n-1)^{n-3} + (n-3)2^{n-3} + 1$) is a lower bound for suffix-free (respectively, bifix-free or factor-free) languages.

Here we deal with star-free languages. It has been shown in 2011 by Brzozowski and Liu [4] that boolean operations, concatenation, star, and reversal in the class of star-free languages meet all the quotient complexity bounds of regular languages, with very few exceptions. Also, Kutrib, Holzer, and Meckel [10] proved in 2012 that in most cases exactly the same tight state complexity bounds are reached by operations on aperiodic nondeterministic finite automata (NFA's) as on general NFA's. In sharp contrast to this, the syntactic complexity of star-free languages appears to be much smaller than the $n^n$ bound for regular languages. We derive tight upper bounds for three subclasses of star-free languages, the monotonic, partially monotonic, and nearly monotonic languages. We conjecture that the bound for star-free languages is the same as that for nearly monotonic languages.

The remainder of the paper is structured as follows. Our terminology and some basic facts are stated in Section 2. Aperiodic transformations are examined in Section 3. In Section 4, we study monotonic, partially monotonic, and nearly monotonic automata and languages. Section 5 concludes the paper.

## 2    Preliminaries

We assume the reader is familiar with basic theory of formal languages as in [18], for example. Let $\Sigma$ be a non-empty finite alphabet and $\Sigma^*$, the free monoid generated by $\Sigma$. A *word* is any element of $\Sigma^*$, and the empty word is $\varepsilon$. The length of a word $w \in \Sigma^*$ is $|w|$. A *language* over $\Sigma$ is any subset of $\Sigma^*$. For any languages $K$ and $L$ over $\Sigma$, we use the *boolean operations*: complement ($\overline{L}$) and union ($K \cup L$). The *product*, or *(con)catenation*, of $K$ and $L$ is $KL = \{w \in \Sigma^* \mid w = uv, u \in K, v \in L\}$; the *star* of $L$ is $L^* = \bigcup_{i \geqslant 0} L^i$, and the *positive closure* of $L$ is $L^+ = \bigcup_{i \geqslant 1} L^i$.

We call languages $\emptyset$, $\{\varepsilon\}$, and $\{a\}$ for any $a \in \Sigma$ the *basic* languages. *Regular* languages are the smallest class of languages constructed from the basic languages using boolean operations, product, and star. *Star-free* languages are the smallest class of languages constructed from the basic languages using only boolean operations and product.

A *deterministic finite automaton* (DFA) is a quintuple $\mathcal{A} = (Q, \Sigma, \delta, q_1, F)$, where $Q$ is a finite, non-empty set of *states*, $\Sigma$ is a finite non-empty *alphabet*,

$\delta : Q \times \Sigma \to Q$ is the *transition function*, $q_1 \in Q$ is the *initial state*, and $F \subseteq Q$ is the set of *final states*. We extend $\delta$ to $Q \times \Sigma^*$ in the usual way. The DFA $\mathcal{A}$ accepts a word $w \in \Sigma^*$ if $\delta(q_1, w) \in F$. The set of all words *accepted* by $\mathcal{A}$ is $L(\mathcal{A})$. Regular languages are exactly the languages accepted by DFA's. By the *language of a state* $q$ of $\mathcal{A}$ we mean the language $L_q$ accepted by the DFA $(Q, \Sigma, \delta, q, F)$. A state is *empty* if its language is empty.

An *incomplete deterministic finite automaton (IDFA)* is a quintuple $\mathcal{I} = (Q, \Sigma, \delta, q_1, F)$, where $Q$, $\Sigma$, $q_1$ and $F$ are as in a DFA, and $\delta$ is a partial function. Every DFA is also an IDFA.

The *left quotient*, or simply *quotient*, of a language $L$ by a word $w$ is the language $w^{-1}L = \{x \in \Sigma^* \mid wx \in L\}$. The *Nerode equivalence* $\sim_L$ of any language $L$ over $\Sigma$ is defined as follows [17]: For all $x, y \in \Sigma^*$,

$$x \sim_L y \text{ if and only if } xv \in L \Leftrightarrow yv \in L, \text{ for all } v \in \Sigma^*.$$

Clearly, $x^{-1}L = y^{-1}L$ if and only if $x \sim_L y$. Thus each equivalence class of the Nerode equivalence corresponds to a distinct quotient of $L$.

Let $L$ be a regular language. The *quotient DFA* of $L$ is $\mathcal{A} = (Q, \Sigma, \delta, q_1, F)$, where $Q = \{w^{-1}L \mid w \in \Sigma^*\}$, $\delta(w^{-1}L, a) = (wa)^{-1}L$, $q_1 = \varepsilon^{-1}L = L$, and $F = \{w^{-1}L \mid \varepsilon \in w^{-1}L\}$. State $w^{-1}L$ of a quotient DFA is reachable from the initial state $L$ by the word $w$. Also, the language of every state is distinct, since only distinct quotients are used as states. Thus every quotient DFA is minimal. The *quotient IDFA* of $L$ is the quotient DFA of $L$ after the empty state, if present, and all transitions incident to it are removed. The quotient IDFA is also minimal. If a regular language $L$ has quotient IDFA $\mathcal{I}$, then the DFA $\mathcal{A}$ obtained by adding the empty state to $\mathcal{I}$, if necessary, is the quotient DFA of $L$. The two automata $\mathcal{A}$ and $\mathcal{I}$ accept the same language.

The number $\kappa(L)$ of distinct quotients of $L$ is the *quotient complexity* of $L$. Since the quotient DFA of $L$ is minimal, quotient complexity is the same as state complexity. The quotient viewpoint is often useful for deriving upper bounds, while the state approach may be more convenient for proving lower bounds.

The *Myhill equivalence* $\approx_L$ of $L$ is defined as follows [16]: For all $x, y \in \Sigma^*$,

$$x \approx_L y \text{ if and only if } uxv \in L \Leftrightarrow uyv \in L \text{ for all } u, v \in \Sigma^*.$$

This equivalence is also known as the *syntactic congruence* of $L$. The quotient set $\Sigma^+ / \approx_L$ of equivalence classes of the relation $\approx_L$ is a semigroup called the *syntactic semigroup* of $L$ (which we denote by $S_L$), and $\Sigma^* / \approx_L$ is the *syntactic monoid* of $L$. The *syntactic complexity* $\sigma(L)$ of $L$ is the cardinality of its syntactic semigroup. The *monoid complexity* $\mu(L)$ of $L$ is the cardinality of its syntactic monoid. If the equivalence class containing $\varepsilon$ is a singleton in the syntactic monoid, then $\sigma(L) = \mu(L) - 1$; otherwise, $\sigma(L) = \mu(L)$.

A *partial transformation* of a set $Q$ is a partial mapping of $Q$ into itself; we consider partial transformations of finite sets only, and we assume without loss of generality that $Q = \{1, 2, \ldots, n\}$. Let $t$ be a partial transformation of $Q$. If $t$ is defined for $i \in Q$, then $it$ is the image of $i$ under $t$; otherwise it is undefined and we write $it = \square$. For convenience, we let $\square t = \square$. If $X$ is a subset of $Q$, then

$Xt = \{it \mid i \in X\}$. The *composition* of two partial transformations $t_1$ and $t_2$ of $Q$ is a partial transformation $t_1 \circ t_2$ such that $i(t_1 \circ t_2) = (it_1)t_2$ for all $i \in Q$. We usually drop the composition operator "$\circ$" and write $t_1 t_2$ for short.

An arbitrary partial transformation can be written in the form

$$t = \begin{pmatrix} 1 & 2 & \cdots & n-1 & n \\ i_1 & i_2 & \cdots & i_{n-1} & i_n \end{pmatrix},$$

where $i_k = kt$ and $i_k \in Q \cup \{\Box\}$, for $k \in Q$. The *domain* of $t$ is the set $\mathrm{dom}(t) = \{k \in Q \mid kt \neq \Box\}$. The *range* of $t$ is the set $\mathrm{rng}(t) = \mathrm{dom}(t)t = \{kt \mid k \in Q \text{ and } kt \neq \Box\}$. When the domain is clear, we also write $t = [i_1, \ldots, i_n]$.

A *(full) transformation* $t$ of a set $Q$ is a partial transformation such that $\mathrm{dom}(t) = Q$. The *identity* transformation maps each element to itself, that is, $it = i$ for $i = 1, \ldots, n$. A transformation $t$ is a *cycle* of length $k \geqslant 2$ if there exist pairwise distinct elements $i_1, \ldots, i_k$ such that $i_1 t = i_2, i_2 t = i_3, \ldots, i_{k-1}t = i_k$, $i_k t = i_1$, and $jt = j$ for all $j \notin \{i_1, \ldots, i_k\}$. Such a cycle is denoted by $(i_1, i_2, \ldots, i_k)$. For $i < j$, a *transposition* is the cycle $(i, j)$. A *singular* transformation, denoted by $\binom{i}{j}$, has $it = j$ and $ht = h$ for all $h \neq i$. A *constant* transformation, denoted by $\binom{Q}{j}$, has $it = j$ for all $i$. Let $\mathcal{T}_Q$ be the set of all transformations of $Q$, which is a semigroup under composition.

Let $\mathcal{A} = (Q, \Sigma, \delta, q_1, F)$ be a DFA. For each word $w \in \Sigma^+$, the transition function defines a transformation $t_w$ of $Q$: for all $i \in Q$, $it_w \overset{\text{def}}{=} \delta(i, w)$. The set $T_{\mathcal{A}}$ of all such transformations by non-empty words forms a subsemigroup of $\mathcal{T}_Q$, called the *transition semigroup* of $\mathcal{A}$ [18]. Conversely, we can use a set $\{t_a \mid a \in \Sigma\}$ of transformations to define $\delta$, and so the DFA $\mathcal{A}$. When the context is clear we simply write $a = t$, where $t$ is a transformation of $Q$, to mean that the transformation performed by $a \in \Sigma$ is $t$. If $\mathcal{A}$ is the quotient DFA of $L$, then $T_{\mathcal{A}}$ is isomorphic to the syntactic semigroup $S_L$ of $L$ [15], and we represent elements of $S_L$ by transformations in $T_{\mathcal{A}}$.

For any IDFA $\mathcal{I}$, each word $w \in \Sigma^*$ performs a partial transformation of $Q$. The set of all such partial transformations is the *transition semigroup* of $\mathcal{I}$. If $\mathcal{I}$ is the quotient IDFA of a language $L$, this semigroup is isomorphic to the transition semigroup of the quotient DFA of $L$, and hence also to the syntactic semigroup of $L$.

## 3    Aperiodic Transformations

A transformation is *aperiodic* if it contains no cycles of length greater than 1. A semigroup $T$ of transformations is *aperiodic* if and only if it contains only aperiodic transformations. Thus a language $L$ with quotient DFA $\mathcal{A}$ is star-free if and only if every transformation in $T_{\mathcal{A}}$ is aperiodic.

Let $A_n$ be the set of all aperiodic transformations of $Q$. Each aperiodic transformation can be characterized by a forest of labeled rooted trees as follows. Consider, for example, the forest of Fig. 1 (a), where the roots are at the bottom. Convert this forest into a directed graph by adding a direction from each child

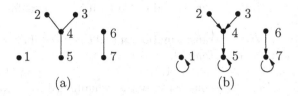

**Fig. 1.** Forests and transformations

to its parent and a self-loop to each root, as shown in Fig. 1 (b). This directed graph defines the transformation $[1, 4, 4, 5, 5, 7, 7]$ and such a transformation is aperiodic since the directed graph has no cycles of length greater than one. Thus there is a one-to-one correspondence between aperiodic transformations of a set of $n$ elements and forests with $n$ nodes.

**Proposition 1.** *There are $(n+1)^{n-1}$ aperiodic transformations of a set of $n \geqslant 1$ elements.*

*Proof.* By Cayley's theorem [6,20], there are $(n + 1)^{n-1}$ labeled unrooted trees with $n+1$ nodes. If we fix one node, say node $n + 1$, in each of these trees to be the root, then we have $(n + 1)^{n-1}$ labeled trees rooted at $n + 1$. Let $T$ be any one of these trees, and let $v_1, \ldots, v_m$ be the parents of $n + 1$ in $T$. By removing the root $n + 1$ from each such rooted tree, we get a labeled forest $F$ with $n$ nodes formed by $m$ rooted trees, where $v_1, \ldots, v_m$ are the roots. The forest $F$ is unique since $T$ is a unique tree rooted at $n + 1$. Then we get a unique aperiodic transformation of $\{1, \ldots, n\}$ by adding self-loops on $v_1, \ldots, v_m$.

All labeled directed forests with $n$ nodes can be obtained uniquely from some rooted tree with $n + 1$ nodes by deleting the root. Hence there are $(n + 1)^{n-1}$ labeled forests with $n$ nodes, and that many aperiodic transformations of $Q$.   □

Since the quotient DFA of a star-free language can perform only aperiodic transformations, we have

**Corollary 2.** *For $n \geqslant 1$, the syntactic complexity $\sigma(L)$ of a star-free language $L$ with $n$ quotients satisfies $\sigma(L) \leqslant (n + 1)^{n-1}$.*

The bound of Corollary 2 is our first upper bound on the syntactic complexity of a star-free language with $n$ quotients, but this bound is not tight in general because the set $A_n$ *is not a semigroup* for $n \geqslant 3$. For example, if $a = [1, 3, 1]$ and $b = [2, 2, 1]$, then $ab = [2, 1, 2]$, which contains the cycle $(1, 2)$. Hence our task is to find the size of the largest semigroup contained in $A_n$.

First, let us consider small values of $n$:

1. If $n = 1$, the only two languages, $\emptyset$ and $\Sigma^*$, are both star-free, since $\Sigma^* = \overline{\emptyset}$. Here $\sigma(L) = 1$, for both languages, the bound $2^0 = 1$ of Corollary 2 holds and it is tight.
2. If $n = 2$, $|A_2| = 3$. The only unary languages are $\varepsilon$ and $\bar{\varepsilon} = aa^*$, and $\sigma(L) = 1$ for both. For $\Sigma = \{a, b\}$, one verifies that $\sigma(L) \leqslant 2$, and $\Sigma^* a \Sigma^*$ meets this bound. If $\Sigma = \{a, b, c\}$, then $L = \Sigma^* a \overline{\Sigma^* b \Sigma^*}$ has $\sigma(L) = 3$.

In summary, for $n = 1$ and 2, the bound of Corollary 2 is tight for $|\Sigma| = 1$ and $|\Sigma| = 3$, respectively.

We say that two aperiodic transformations $a$ and $b$ *conflict* if $ab$ or $ba$ contains a cycle; then $(a, b)$ is called a *conflicting pair*. When $n = 3$, $|A_3| = 4^2 = 16$. The transformations $a_0 = [1, 2, 3]$, $a_1 = [1, 1, 1]$, $a_2 = [2, 2, 2]$, $a_3 = [3, 3, 3]$ cannot create any conflict. Hence we consider only the remaining 12 transformations.

Let $b_1 = [1, 1, 3]$, $b_2 = [1, 2, 1]$, $b_3 = [1, 2, 2]$, $b_4 = [1, 3, 3]$, $b_5 = [2, 2, 3]$, and $b_6 = [3, 2, 3]$. Each of them has only one conflict. There are also two *conflicting triples* $(b_1, b_3, b_6)$ and $(b_2, b_4, b_5)$, since $b_1 b_3 b_6$ and $b_2 b_4 b_5$ both contains a cycle. Figure 2 shows the conflict graph of these 12 transformations, where normal lines indicate conflicting pairs, and dotted lines indicate conflicting triples. To save space we use three digits to represent each transformation, for example, 112 stands for the transformation $[1, 1, 2]$, and $(112)(113) = 111$. We can choose at most two inputs from each triple and at most one from each conflicting pair. So there are at most 6 conflict-free transformations from the 12, for example, $b_1$, $b_3$, $b_4$, $b_5$, $c_1 = [1, 1, 2]$, $c_2 = [2, 3, 3]$. Adding $a_0, a_1, a_2$ and $a_3$, we get a total of at most 10. The inputs $a_0, b_4, b_5, c_1$ are conflict-free and generate precisely these 10 transformations. Hence $\sigma(L) \leqslant 10$ for any star-free language $L$ with $\kappa(L) = n = 3$, and this bound is tight.

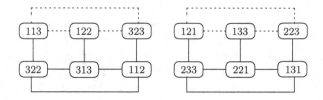

**Fig. 2.** Conflict graph for $n = 3$

# 4    Monotonicity in Transformations, Automata and Languages

We now study syntactic semigroups of languages accepted by monotonic and related automata. We denote by $C_k^n$ the binomial coefficient "$n$ choose $k$".

## 4.1    Monotonic Transformations, DFA's and Languages

We have shown that the tight upper bound for $n = 3$ is 10, and it turns out that this bound is met by a monotonic language (defined below). This provides one reason to study monotonic automata and languages. A second reason is the fact that all the tight upper bounds on the quotient complexity of operations on star-free languages are met by monotonic languages [4].

A transformation $t$ of $Q$ is *monotonic* if there exists a total order $\leqslant$ on $Q$ such that, for all $p, q \in Q$, $p \leqslant q$ implies $pt \leqslant qt$. From now on we assume that $\leqslant$ is the usual order on integers, and that $p < q$ means that $p \leqslant q$ and $p \neq q$.

Let $M_Q$ be the set of all monotonic transformations of $Q$. In the following, we restate slightly the result of Gomes and Howie [8,11] for our purposes, since the work in [8] does not consider the identity transformation to be monotonic.

**Theorem 3 (Gomes and Howie).** *When $n \geqslant 1$, the set $M_Q$ is an aperiodic semigroup of cardinality*

$$|M_Q| = f(n) = \sum_{k=1}^{n} C_{k-1}^{n-1} C_k^n = C_n^{2n-1},$$

*and it is generated by the set $H = \{a, b_1, \ldots, b_{n-1}, c\}$, where, for $1 \leqslant i \leqslant n - 1$,*
1. *$1a = 1$, $ja = j - 1$ for $2 \leqslant j \leqslant n$;*
2. *$ib_i = i + 1$, and $jb_i = j$ for all $j \neq i$;*
3. *$c$ is the identity transformation.*

*Moreover, for $n = 1$, $a$ and $c$ coincide and the cardinality of the generating set cannot be reduced for $n \geqslant 2$.*

*Remark 4.* By Stirling's approximation, $f(n) = |M_Q|$ grows asymptotically like $4^n / \sqrt{\pi n}$ as $n \to \infty$.

Now we turn to DFA's whose inputs perform monotonic transformations. A DFA is *monotonic* [1] if all transformations in its transition semigroup are monotonic with respect to some fixed total order. Every monotonic DFA is aperiodic because monotonic transformations are aperiodic. A regular language is *monotonic* if its quotient DFA is monotonic.

Let us now define a DFA having as inputs the generators of $M_Q$:

**Definition 5.** *For $n \geqslant 1$, let $\mathcal{A}_n = (Q, \Sigma, \delta, 1, \{1\})$ be the DFA in which $Q = \{1, \ldots, n\}$, $\Sigma = \{a, b_1, \ldots, b_{n-1}, c\}$, and each letter in $\Sigma$ performs the transformation defined in Theorem 3.*

DFA $\mathcal{A}_n$ is minimal, since state 1 is the only accepting state, and for $2 \leqslant i \leqslant n$ only state $i$ accepts $a^{i-1}$. From Theorem 3 we have

**Corollary 6.** *For $n \geqslant 1$, the syntactic complexity $\sigma(L)$ of any monotonic language $L$ with $n$ quotients satisfies $\sigma(L) \leqslant f(n) = C_n^{2n-1}$. Moreover, this bound is met by the language $L(\mathcal{A}_n)$ of Definition 5, and, when $n \geqslant 2$, it cannot be met by any monotonic language over an alphabet having fewer than $n + 1$ letters.*

## 4.2 Monotonic Partial Transformations and IDFA's

As we shall see, for $n \geqslant 4$ the maximal syntactic complexity cannot be reached by monotonic languages; hence we continue our search for larger semigroups of aperiodic transformations. In this subsection, we extend the concept of monotonicity from full transformations to partial transformations, and hence define a new subclass of star-free languages. The upper bound of syntactic complexity of languages in this subclass is above that of monotonic languages for $n \geqslant 4$.

A partial transformation $t$ of $Q$ is *monotonic* if there exists a total order $\leqslant$ on $Q$ such that, for all $p, q \in \mathrm{dom}(t)$, $p \leqslant q$ implies $pt \leqslant qt$. As before, we assume that the total order on $Q$ is the usual order on integers. Let $PM_Q$ be the set of all monotonic partial transformations of $Q$ with respect to such an order. Gomes and Howie [8] showed the following result, again restated slightly:

**Theorem 7 (Gomes and Howie).** *When $n \geqslant 1$, the set $PM_Q$ is an aperiodic semigroup of cardinality*

$$|PM_Q| = g(n) = \sum_{k=0}^{n} C_k^n C_k^{n+k-1},$$

*and it is generated by the set $I = \{a, b_1, \ldots, b_{n-1}, c_1, \ldots, c_{n-1}, d\}$, where, for $1 \leqslant i \leqslant n-1$,*

1. *$1a = \square$, and $ja = j - 1$ for $j = 2, \ldots, n$;*
2. *$ib_i = i + 1$, $(i+1)b_i = \square$, and $jb_i = j$ for $j = 1, \ldots, i-1, i+2, \ldots, n$;*
3. *$ic_i = i + 1$, and $jc_i = j$ for all $j \neq i$;*
4. *$d$ is the identity transformation.*

*Moreover, the cardinality of the generating set cannot be reduced.*

*Example 8.* For $n = 1$, the two monotonic partial transformations are $a = [\square]$, and $d = [1]$. For $n = 2$, the eight monotonic partial transformations are generated by $a = [\square, 1]$, $b_1 = [2, \square]$, $c_1 = [2, 2]$, and $d = [1, 2]$. For $n = 3$, the 38 monotonic partial transformations are generated by $a = [\square, 1, 2]$, $b_1 = [2, \square, 3]$, $b_2 = [1, 3, \square]$, $c_1 = [2, 2, 3]$, $c_2 = [1, 3, 3]$ and $d = [1, 2, 3]$.

Partial transformations correspond to IDFA's. For example, $a = [\square, 1]$, $b = [2, \square]$ and $c = [2, 2]$ correspond to the transitions of the IDFA of Fig. 3 (a). ∎

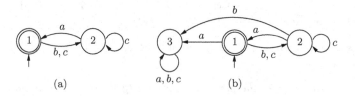

(a)    $a, b, c$    (b)

**Fig. 3.** Partially monotonic automata: (a) IDFA; (b) DFA

Laradji and Umar [13] proved the following asymptotic approximation:

*Remark 9.* For large $n$, $g(n) = |PM_Q| \sim 2^{-3/4} (\sqrt{2} + 1)^{2n+1} / \sqrt{\pi n}$.

An IDFA is *monotonic* if all partial transformations in its transition semigroup are monotonic with respect to some fixed total order. A quotient DFA is *partially monotonic* if its corresponding quotient IDFA is monotonic. A regular language is *partially monotonic* if its quotient DFA is partially monotonic. Note that monotonic languages are also partially monotonic.

*Example 10.* If we complete the transformations in Fig. 3 (a) by replacing the undefined entry $\square$ by a new empty (or "sink") state 3, as usual, we obtain the DFA of Fig. 3 (b). That DFA is not monotonic, because $1 < 2$ implies $2 < 3$ under input $b$ and $3 < 2$ under $ab$. A contradiction is also obtained if we assume that $2 < 1$. However, this DFA is partially monotonic, since its corresponding IDFA, shown in Fig. 3 (a), is monotonic.

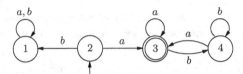

**Fig. 4.** Partially monotonic DFA that is monotonic and has an empty state

The DFA of Fig. 4 is monotonic for the order shown. It has an empty state, and is also partially monotonic for the same order.  ■

Consider any partially monotonic language $L$ with quotient complexity $n$. If its quotient DFA $\mathcal{A}$ does not have the empty quotient, then $L$ is monotonic; otherwise, its quotient IDFA $\mathcal{I}$ has $n - 1$ states, and the transition semigroup of $\mathcal{I}$ is a subset of $PM_{Q'}$, where $Q' = \{1, \ldots, n - 1\}$. Hence we consider the following semigroup $CM_Q$ of *monotonic completed transformations* of $Q$. Start with the semigroup $PM_{Q'}$. Convert all $t \in PM_{Q'}$ to full transformations by adding $n$ to $\mathrm{dom}(t)$ and letting $it = n$ for all $i \in Q \setminus \mathrm{dom}(t)$. Such a conversion provides a one-to-one correspondence between $PM_{Q'}$ and $CM_Q$. For $n \geqslant 2$, let $e(n) = g(n - 1)$. Then semigroups $CM_Q$ and $PM_{Q'}$ are isomorphic, and $e(n) = |CM_Q|$.

**Definition 11.** *For $n \geqslant 1$, let $\mathcal{B}_n = (Q, \Sigma, \delta, 1, \{1\})$ be the DFA in which $Q = \{1, \ldots, n\}$, $\Sigma = \{a, b_1, \ldots, b_{n-2}, c_1, \ldots, c_{n-2}, d\}$, and each letter in $\Sigma$ defines a transformation such that, for $1 \leqslant i \leqslant n - 2$,*
1. *$1a = na = n$, and $ja = j - 1$ for $j = 2, \ldots, n - 1$;*
2. *$ib_i = i + 1$, $(i + 1)b_i = n$, and $jb_i = j$ for $j = 1, \ldots, i - 1, i + 2, \ldots, n$;*
3. *$ic_i = i + 1$, and $jc_i = j$ for all $j \neq i$;*
4. *$d$ is the identity transformation.*

We know that monotonic languages are also partially monotonic. As shown in Table 1, $|M_Q| = f(n) > e(n) = |CM_Q|$ for $n \leqslant 3$. On the other hand, one verifies that $e(n) > f(n)$ when $n \geqslant 4$. By Corollary 6 and Theorem 7, we have

**Corollary 12.** *The syntactic complexity of a partially monotonic language $L$ with $n$ quotients satisfies $\sigma(L) \leqslant f(n)$ for $n \leqslant 3$, and $\sigma(L) \leqslant e(n)$ for $n \geqslant 4$. Moreover, when $n \geqslant 4$, this bound is met by $L(\mathcal{B}_n)$ of Definition 11, and it cannot be met by any partially monotonic language over an alphabet having fewer than $2n - 2$ letters.*

Table 1 contains these upper bounds for small values of $n$. By Remark 9, the upper bound $e(n)$ is asymptotically $2^{-3/4}(\sqrt{2} + 1)^{2n-1}/\sqrt{\pi(n - 1)}$.

## 4.3  Nearly Monotonic Transformations and DFA's

In this section we develop an even larger aperiodic semigroup based on partially monotonic languages.

Let $K_Q$ be the set of all constant transformations of $Q$, and let $NM_Q = CM_Q \cup K_Q$. We shall call the transformations in $NM_Q$ *nearly monotonic* with respect to the usual order on integers.

**Theorem 13.** *When $n \geqslant 2$, the set $NM_Q$ of all nearly monotonic transformations of a set $Q$ of $n$ elements is an aperiodic semigroup of cardinality*

$$|NM_Q| = h(n) = e(n) + (n-1) = \sum_{k=0}^{n-1} C_k^{n-1} C_k^{n+k-2} + (n-1),$$

*and it is generated by the set $J = \{a, b_1, \ldots, b_{n-2}, c_1, \ldots, c_{n-2}, d, e\}$ of $2n-1$ transformations of $Q$, where $e$ is the constant transformation $\binom{Q}{1}$, and all other transformations are as in Definition 11. Moreover, the cardinality of the generating set cannot be reduced.*

*Proof.* Pick any $t_1, t_2 \in NM_Q$. If $t_1, t_2 \in CM_Q$, then $t_1 t_2, t_2 t_1 \in CM_Q$. Otherwise $t_1 \in K_Q$ or $t_2 \in K_Q$, and both $t_1 t_2, t_2 t_1$ are constant transformations. Hence $t_1 t_2, t_2 t_1 \in NM_Q$ and $NM_Q$ is a semigroup. Since constant transformations are aperiodic and $CM_Q$ is aperiodic, $NM_Q$ is also aperiodic.

If $X$ is a set of transformations, let $\langle X \rangle$ denote the semigroup generated by $X$. Since $J \subseteq NM_Q$, $\langle J \rangle \subseteq NM_Q$. Let $I' = J \setminus \{e\}$, and $Q' = Q \setminus \{n\}$. Then $PM_{Q'} \simeq CM_Q = \langle I' \rangle$. For any $t = \binom{Q}{j} \in K_Q$, where $j \in Q$, since $s_j = \binom{Q}{j}\binom{n}{n} \in CM_Q \subseteq \langle J \rangle$, we have that $t = e s_j \in \langle J \rangle$. So $NM_Q = \langle J \rangle$. Note that $\binom{Q}{i} \in CM_Q$ if and only if $i = n$. Thus $h(n) = |NM_Q| = |PM_{Q'}| + (n-1) = e(n) + (n-1)$.

Since the cardinality of $I'$ cannot be reduced, and $e \notin \langle I' \rangle$, also the cardinality of $J$ cannot be reduced. $\square$

An input $a \in \Sigma$ is *constant* if it performs a constant transformation of $Q$. Let $\mathcal{A}$ be a DFA with alphabet $\Sigma$; then $\mathcal{A}$ is *nearly monotonic* if, after removing constant inputs, the resulting DFA $\mathcal{A}'$ is partially monotonic. A regular language is *nearly monotonic* if its quotient DFA is nearly monotonic.

**Definition 14.** *For $n \geqslant 2$, let $\mathcal{C}_n = (Q, \Sigma, \delta, 1, \{1\})$ be a DFA, where $Q = \{1, \ldots, n\}$, $\Sigma = \{a, b_1, \ldots, b_{n-2}, c_1, \ldots, c_{n-2}, d, e\}$, and each letter in $\Sigma$ performs the transformation defined in Theorem 13 and Definition 11.*

Theorem 13 now leads us to the following result:

**Theorem 15.** *For $n \geqslant 2$, if $L$ is a nearly monotonic language $L$ with $n$ quotients, then $\sigma(L) \leqslant h(n) = \sum_{k=0}^{n-1} C_k^{n-1} C_k^{n+k-2} + (n-1)$. Moreover, this bound is met by the language $L(\mathcal{C}_n)$ of Definition 14, and cannot be met by any nearly monotonic language over an alphabet having fewer than $2n-1$ letters.*

*Proof.* State 1 is reached by $\varepsilon$. For $2 \leqslant i \leqslant n - 1$, state $i$ is reached by $w_i = b_1 \cdots b_{i-1}$. State $n$ is reached by $w_{n-1}b_{n-2}$. Thus all states are reachable. For $1 \leqslant i \leqslant n - 1$, the word $a^{i-1}$ is only accepted by state $i$. Also, state $n$ rejects $a^i$ for all $i \geqslant 0$. So all $n$ states are distinguishable, and $\mathcal{C}_n$ is minimal. Thus $L$ has $n$ quotients. The syntactic semigroup of $L$ is generated by $J$; so $L$ has syntactic complexity $\sigma(L) = h(n) = \sum_{k=0}^{n-1} C_k^{n-1} C_k^{n+k-2} + (n - 1)$, and it is star-free. $\square$

As shown earlier, $e(n) > f(n)$ for $n \geqslant 4$. Since $h(n) = e(n) + (n - 1)$, and $h(n) = f(n)$ for $n \in \{2, 3\}$, as shown in Table 1, we have that $h(n) \geqslant f(n)$ for $n \geqslant 2$, and the maximal syntactic complexity of nearly monotonic languages is at least that of both monotonic and partially monotonic languages.

Although we cannot prove that $NM_Q$ is the largest semigroup of aperiodic transformations, we can show that no transformation can be added to $NM_Q$.

A set $\mathbb{S} = \{T_1, T_2, \ldots, T_k\}$ of transformation semigroups is a *chain* if $T_1 \subset T_2 \subset \cdots \subset T_k$. Semigroup $T_k$ is the largest in $\mathbb{S}$, and we denote it by $\max(\mathbb{S}) = T_k$. The following result shows that the syntactic semigroup $S_{L(\mathcal{C}_n)} = T_{\mathcal{C}_n}$ of $L(\mathcal{C}_n)$ in Definition 14 is a local maximum among aperiodic subsemigroups of $\mathcal{T}_Q$.

**Proposition 16.** *Let $\mathbb{S}$ be a chain of aperiodic subsemigroups of $\mathcal{T}_Q$. If $T_{\mathcal{C}_n} \in \mathbb{S}$, then $T_{\mathcal{C}_n} = \max(\mathbb{S})$.*

*Proof.* Suppose $\max(\mathbb{S}) = T_k$ for some aperiodic subsemigroup $T_k$ of $\mathcal{T}_Q$, and $T_k \neq T_{\mathcal{C}_n}$. Then there exist $t \in T_k$ such that $t \notin T_{\mathcal{C}_n}$, and $i, j \in Q$ such that $i < j \neq n$ but $it > jt$, and $it, jt \neq n$. Let $\tau \in \mathcal{T}_Q$ be such that $(jt)\tau = i$, $(it)\tau = j$, and $h\tau = n$ for all $h \neq i, j$; then $\tau \in T_{\mathcal{C}_n}$. Let $\lambda \in \mathcal{T}_Q$ be such that $i\lambda = i$, $j\lambda = j$, and $h\lambda = n$ for all $h \neq i, j$; then also $\lambda \in T_{\mathcal{C}_n}$. Since $T_k = \max(\mathbb{S})$, $T_{\mathcal{C}_n} \subset T_k$ and $\tau, \lambda \in T_k$. Then $s = \lambda t\tau$ is also in $T_k$. However, $is = i(\lambda t\tau) = j$, $js = j(\lambda t\tau) = i$, and $hs = n$ for all $h \neq i, j$; then $s = (i, j)\binom{P}{n}$, where $P = Q \setminus \{i, j\}$, is not aperiodic, a contradiction. Therefore $T_{\mathcal{C}_n} = \max(\mathbb{S})$. $\square$

## 5    Conclusions

We conjecture that the syntactic complexity of languages accepted by the nearly monotonic DFA's of Definition 14 meets the upper bound for star-free languages:

*Conjecture 17.* The syntactic complexity of a star-free language $L$ with $\kappa(L) = n \geqslant 4$ satisfies $\sigma(L) \leqslant h(n)$.

Our results are summarized in Table 1. Let $Q = \{1, \ldots, n\}$, and $Q' = Q \setminus \{n\}$. The figures in bold type are tight bounds verified using *GAP* [7], by enumerating aperiodic subsemigroups of $\mathcal{T}_Q$. The asterisk $*$ indicates that the bound is already tight for a smaller alphabet. The last five rows show the values of $f(n) = |M_Q|$, $e(n) = |CM_Q| = g(n-1) = |PM_{Q'}|$, $h(n) = |NM_Q|$, and the weak upper bound $(n + 1)^{n-1}$.

**Table 1.** Syntactic complexity of star-free languages

| $|\Sigma|$ / $n$ | 1 | 2 | 3 | 4 | 5 | 6 |
|:---:|:---:|:---:|:---:|:---:|:---:|:---:|
| 1 | 1 | 1 | 2 | 3 | 5 | 6 |
| 2 | * | 2 | 7 | 19 | 62 | ? |
| 3 | * | 3 | 9 | 31 | ? | ? |
| 4 | * | * | 10 | 34 | ? | ? |
| 5 | * | * | * | 37 | 125 | ? |
| $\cdots$ | $\cdots$ | $\cdots$ | $\cdots$ | $\cdots$ | $\cdots$ | $\cdots$ |
| $f(n) = |M_Q|$ | 1 | 3 | 10 | 35 | 126 | 462 |
| $e(n) = |CM_Q| = g(n-1) = |PM_{Q'}|$ | – | 2 | 8 | 38 | 192 | 1,002 |
| $h(n) = |NM_Q| = e(n) + (n-1)$ | – | 3 | 10 | 41 | 196 | 1,007 |
| $(n+1)^{n-1}$ | 1 | 3 | 16 | 125 | 1,296 | 16,807 |

**Acknowledgment.** We thank Zoltan Ésik and Judit Nagy-Gyorgy for pointing out to us the relationship between aperiodic inputs and Cayley's theorem.

# References

1. Ananichev, D.S., Volkov, M.V.: Synchronizing generalized monotonic automata. Theoret. Comput. Sci. 330(1), 3–13 (2005)
2. Brzozowski, J.: Quotient complexity of regular languages. J. Autom. Lang. Comb. 15(1/2), 71–89 (2010)
3. Brzozowski, J., Li, B., Ye, Y.: Syntactic complexity of prefix-, suffix-, bifix-, and factor-free regular languages. Theoret. Comput. Sci. (in press, 2012)
4. Brzozowski, J., Liu, B.: Quotient complexity of star-free languages. In: Dömösi, P., Szabolcs, I. (eds.) 13th International Conference on Automata and Formal Languages (AFL), pp. 138–152. Institute of Mathematics and Informatics, College of Nyíregyháza (2011)
5. Brzozowski, J., Ye, Y.: Syntactic Complexity of Ideal and Closed Languages. In: Mauri, G., Leporati, A. (eds.) DLT 2011. LNCS, vol. 6795, pp. 117–128. Springer, Heidelberg (2011)
6. Caley, A.: A theorem on trees. Quart. J. Math. 23, 376–378 (1889)
7. GAP-Group: GAP - Groups, Algorithms, Programming - a System for Computational Discrete Algebra (2010), http://www.gap-system.org/
8. Gomes, G., Howie, J.: On the ranks of certain semigroups of order-preserving transformations. Semigroup Forum 45, 272–282 (1992)
9. Holzer, M., König, B.: On deterministic finite automata and syntactic monoid size. Theoret. Comput. Sci. 327(3), 319–347 (2004)
10. Holzer, M., Kutrib, M., Meckel, K.: Nondeterministic state complexity of star-free languages. Theoret. Comput. Sci. (in press, 2012)
11. Howie, J.M.: Products of idempotents in certain semigroups of transformations. Proc. Edinburgh Math. Soc. 17(2), 223–236 (1971)
12. Krawetz, B., Lawrence, J., Shallit, J.: State complexity and the monoid of transformations of a finite set (2003), http://arxiv.org/abs/math/0306416v1
13. Laradji, A., Umar, A.: Asymptotic results for semigroups of order-preserving partial transformations. Comm. Alg. 34(3), 1071–1075 (2006)

14. Maslov, A.N.: Estimates of the number of states of finite automata. Dokl. Akad. Nauk SSSR 194, 1266–1268 (1970) (Russian); english translation: Soviet Math. Dokl. 11, 1373–1375 (1970)
15. McNaughton, R., Papert, S.A.: Counter-Free Automata. M.I.T. research monograph, vol. 65. The MIT Press (1971)
16. Myhill, J.: Finite automata and the representation of events. Wright Air Development Center Technical Report 57–624 (1957)
17. Nerode, A.: Linear automaton transformations. Proc. Amer. Math. Soc. 9, 541–544 (1958)
18. Rozenberg, G., Salomaa, A. (eds.): Handbook of Formal Languages, vol. 1: Word, Language, Grammar. Springer, New York (1997)
19. Schützenberger, M.P.: On finite monoids having only trivial subgroups. Inform. and Control 8, 190–194 (1965)
20. Shor, P.W.: A new proof of Cayley's formula for counting labeled trees. J. Combin. Theory Ser. A 71(1), 154–158 (1995)
21. Yu, S.: State complexity of regular languages. J. Autom. Lang. Comb. 6, 221–234 (2001)

# Randomness Behaviour
# in Blum Universal Static Complexity Spaces

Cezar Câmpeanu

Department of Computer Science and Information Technology,
The University of Prince Edward Island
ccampeanu@upei.ca

**Abstract.** In this paper we prove that plain complexity induces the weakest form of randomness for all Blum Universal Static Complexity Spaces [11]. As a consequence, there is all infinite sequences have an infinite number of non-random prefixes with respect to any given Blum Universal Static Complexity Space. This is a generalization of the result obtained by Solovay [27] and Calude [7] for plain complexity, and also of the result obtained by Câmpeanu [10][1], and independently, later on, by Bienvenu and Downey in [1][2] for prefix-free complexity.

## 1 Introduction

The complexity of an object can be defined in terms of *minimal description length* (MDL) as the length of the shortest string describing the object. It is obvious that the complexity depends on the alphabet used for the description and the definition of a description. If we consider as an acceptable description any Turing machine, where input is included in the description of the machine, then we obtain the plain complexity. If we restrict the type of Turing machines to self delimiting programs, we obtain the prefix complexity. Beside the plain complexity [19] and prefix complexity [14, 18, 20], there are several other forms of static or descriptional complexities considered in literature, like: process complexity [23], monotone complexity [20], uniform complexity [21], Chaitin's complexity [16], or Solomonoff's universal complexity [24–26]. Several other variants were introduced and used to accommodate various needs, most notably being the effort in finding a complexity that can be used to define in an uniform way the randomness for both strings and sequences. Chaitin [13] and, to some extent, Loveland [21] were successful in this attempt.

Developing an uniform approach for complexity measures has been always a goal for researchers, but the big factor that discouraged them to use an uniform approach was the impossibility of defining randomness for infinite sequences, by using plain complexity. Burgin proposed a generalized Kolmogorov complexity, called dual complexity measure in [4], which is based on the axioms proposed by Blum in 1967 in [3]. These axioms "are all so fantastically weak that any

---

[1] The result was never published, but cited in DCFS 2007 by Helmut Jürgensen.

[2] This is obtained as a consequence of a stronger result for Solovay functions.

M. Kutrib, N. Moreira, and R. Reis (Eds.): DCFS 2012, LNCS 7386, pp. 130–140, 2012.

reasonable model of a computer and any reasonable definition of size and step satisfies them" [3].

Thus, it is natural to consider this approach, find out common properties for dual complexity measures, and study how can we define randomness for various classes of such measures. In [11], the notions of Blum Static Complexity Space (BSC) and Blum Universal Static Complexity Space (BUSC) are introduced as a generalization of computable complexity measures, including the particular cases of plain and prefix complexity. Thus, the most general framework for a complexity measure for a family of computable functions is a BSC space. In case the algorithms considered can emulate any kind of computation, the BSC space becomes automatically a BUSC space. The notion of randomness is defined with respect to a BSC for natural numbers, and several results are proved in the most general case. Many of the plain and prefix-free complexity measures properties, including some properties of random strings, become particular cases for this new approach. In the present paper we continue this effort, and prove in Section 3 that the weakest form of randomness defined in a BUSC is the randomness defined by the plain complexity measure. As a consequence, we extend in Section 4 the negative result obtained for infinite sequences for plain complexity, to any other dual complexity defined in a BUSC. In Section 5, we conclude our work by listing a set of open problems, and possible future directions to extend this approach.

## 2   Notations

We denote by $\mathbb{N} = \{0, 1, \ldots\}$ the set of natural numbers. For a set $T$, we denote by $\#T$ its cardinal. For a finite alphabet with $p$ letters, we use the set $A_p = \{0, 1, \ldots, p-1\}$. The free monoid generated by $A_p$ is $A_p^*$, and the neutral element with respect to concatenation, i.e., the word with no letters, is $\varepsilon$ .

The length of a word $w = w_1 \ldots w_n \in A_p^*, w_i \in A_p, 1 \leq i \leq n$, is $|w| = n$. The set $A_p^*$ can be ordered using the quasi-lexicographical order: $\varepsilon, 0, 1, \ldots, p-1, 00, 01, 0(p-1), 10, \ldots$. We denote by $string_p(n)$ the one to one function between $\mathbb{N}$ and $A_p^*$, representing the $n$-th string of $A_p^*$ in the quasi-lexicographical order. Thus, $string_p(0) = \varepsilon$, $string_p(1) = 0, \ldots string_p(p) = p - 1$, $string(p + 1) = 00, \ldots$.

We also use the function $b_p : \mathbb{N} \longrightarrow A_p$ defined by

$$b_p(n) = \text{the positional representation in base } p \text{ of the number } n.$$

We denote by $bin(n) = b_2(n) = $ the binary representation of $n$.

The set of strings $w \in A_p^*$ of length equal to, less than, less than or equal to, greater than, and greater than or equal to $n$ is denoted by: $A_p^n$, $A_p^{<n}$, $A_p^{\leq n}$, $A_p^{>n}$, and respectively, $A_p^{\geq n}$ .

If $f$ is a function defined on $\mathbb{N}$ and $x \in A_p^*$, when we write $f(x)$, we always understand $f(string_p^{-1}(x))$.

The set of infinite sequences $\mathbf{x} = x_1 x_2 \ldots x_n \ldots$, with $x_i \in A_p$, for all $i \in \mathbb{N}$, over the alphabet $A_p$, is denoted by $A_p^\omega$. The prefix of length $n$ of $\mathbf{x}$ is $\mathbf{x}[n] = x_1 \ldots x_n$. We will omit the index $p$ when it can be understood from the context.

Following the terminology used in [7], an algorithm for computing a partial function $f : \mathbb{N} \xrightarrow{\circ} \mathbb{N}$ is a finite set of instructions which, on any given input $x \in dom(f)$, outputs $y = f(x)$ after a finite number of steps. The algorithm must specify how to obtain each step in the computation from previous steps and from the input. In case $f$ is computed by an algorithm, we call it *partial computable function*; if $f$ is also total, then is called a *computable function* (the old terminology referred to partial recursive and recursive functions [7]).

We consider an acceptable enumeration of the set of all partial computable functions over $\mathbb{N}$, $\mathcal{F} = (\phi_i^{(n)})_{i \in \mathbb{N}}$, i.e., an enumeration satisfying the Wagner-Strong axioms [22].

A function $< \cdot, \cdot > : \mathbb{N} \times \mathbb{N} \longrightarrow \mathbb{N}$ is called a pairing function if it is injective, and its inverses $(\cdot)_1, (\cdot)_2 : \mathbb{N} \xrightarrow{\circ} \mathbb{N}$ satisfy the following properties:

1. $< (z)_1, (z)_2 > = z$;
2. $(< x, y >)_1 = x$, $(< x, y >)_2 = y$.

In case $< \cdot, \cdot >$ is bijective, the inverses $(\cdot)_1, (\cdot)_2$ become total functions.

In what follows we will use only computable pairing functions. It is a common practice to use paring functions to extend unary functions to functions having more than one argument by defining $\phi_i^{(2)}(x, y) = \phi_i^{(1)}(< x, y >)$, and to consider that indexes of algorithms are encodings of algorithms over a finite alphabet $A_p$. In case $p = 2$, the encoding is over the binary alphabet.

*Example 1.* Let us consider the alphabet $\Sigma = A_2 = \{0, 1\}$ and the corresponding string function $string = string_2$.

1. The Cantor function $J : \mathbb{N} \times \mathbb{N} \longrightarrow \mathbb{N}$ defined by

$$J(x, y) = \frac{(x + y + 1)(x + y)}{2} + x,$$

   is a pairing function.
2. The function $< \cdot, \cdot > : \mathbb{N}^2 \longrightarrow \mathbb{N}$ defined by , $< x, y > = 2^x(2y + 1) - 1$ is a pairing function.
3. The function $< \cdot, \cdot > : \mathbb{N}^2 \longrightarrow \mathbb{N}$ defined by

$$< x, y > = string^{-1}(1^{|string(x)|}0string(x)string(y)) - 1$$

   is obviously a pairing function. If $z = < x, y >$, than $string(z + 1) = 1^i 0string(x)string(y)$, where $|string(x)| = i$.
4. The function $< \cdot, \cdot > : \mathbb{N}^2 \longrightarrow \mathbb{N}$ defined by

$$< x, y > = string^{-1}(T(string(x))string(y)),$$

   where $T(z)$ is defined by $T(z_1 \ldots z_n) = z_1 z_1 \ldots z_n z_n 01$, is a pairing function having the property: $|string(< x, y >)| \leq |string(y)| + h(x)$, where $h$ is computable function.

5. The function $< \cdot, \cdot >: \mathbb{N}^2 \longrightarrow \mathbb{N}$ defined by

$$< x, y >= string^{-1}(1^{1+\log x}0string(x)string(y))$$

is also a pairing function, [3] and $|string(< x, y >)| \leq |string(y)| + 2\log x + 1$. For the last two examples we can see that any encoding of $< x, y >$ is just injective.

We refer the reader to [8, 17] for more on computability, computable functions, and recursive function theory.

We consider an acceptable enumeration of the set of all partial computable functions over $\mathbb{N}$, $\mathcal{F} = (\phi_i^{(n)})_{i \in \mathbb{N}}$, i.e., an enumeration satisfying the Wagner-Strong axioms [22].

In [4, 5], the definitions of direct and dual complexity measures are stated in a formalism similar with what follows.

Let $\mathcal{G} \subseteq \mathcal{F}$, $\mathcal{G} = (\psi_i^{(n)})_{i \in I}$ be a class of algorithms. A function $m : I \longrightarrow \mathbb{N}$ is called a (direct) complexity measure [3, 5] if satisfies:

1. (Computational axiom) $m$ is computable;
2. (Re-computational Axiom) the set $\{j \mid m(j) = n\}$ is computable;
3. (Cofinitness Axiom) $\#\{j \mid m(j) = n\} < \infty$.

In [5], additional axioms are considered, for defining axiomatic complexity measures:

4. (Re-constructibility Axiom) For any number $n$, it is possible to build all algorithms $A$ from $\mathcal{G}$ for which $m(A) = n$, or, using our notations, the set $\{j \mid m(j) = n\}$ is computable.
5. (Compositional Axiom) If $A \subseteq B$, then $m(A) \leq m(B)$.

Since the semantics of the relation " $\subseteq$ " between algorithms is usually defined depending on some encoding of the algorithm, in this paper we will only consider axioms 1–4.

**Definition 1.** [11] A space $(\mathcal{G}, m)$ satisfying axioms 1–4 is called Blum static complexity space.

**Definition 2.** [4, 5] Let $d : \mathbb{N} \longrightarrow \mathbb{N}$ be a function. An algorithm $U : \mathbb{N} \times \mathbb{N} \stackrel{\circ}{\longrightarrow} \mathbb{N}$ is called d-universal for the set $\mathcal{G} = (\psi_i)_{i \in I}$, if $\psi_i(n) = U(d(i), n)$, for all $i \in I$ and $n \in \mathbb{N}$.

If $U$ is a two argument universal algorithm for the algorithms with one argument, i.e., $U(i, x) = \psi_i(x)$, then $U$ is $1_{\mathbb{N}}$-universal for $\mathcal{G}$.

Given a complexity measure $m : I \longrightarrow \mathbb{N}$ and $\psi \in \mathcal{G}$, the dual to $m$ with respect to $\psi$ is[4]

$$m_\psi^0(x) = \min\{m(y) \mid y \in I, \psi(y) = x\}.^{[5]}$$

---

[3] We make the convention that $\log 0 = -1$, without this convention we cannot use $x = 0$.

[4] $min\emptyset = \infty$.

[5] We can consider that $I$ is embedded in $\mathbb{N}$.

In what follows, we reiterate the convention that a function $f : \mathbb{N}^k \longrightarrow \mathbb{N}$, when applied to a string $w \in A_p^*$, is in fact the function $f$ applied to $string_p^{-1}(w)$, and when the result is in $A_p^*$, we apply the function $string_p$ to the result of $f$. Thus, we do not distinguish between a number $n \in \mathbb{N}$ and its representation $string_p(n) \in A_p^*$.

If $I$ is the encoding of algorithms over $A_p$, then $m(I)$ is usually the length of the encoding; in this case, $m_\psi^0$ is called dual to length complexity of $x$, with respect to the algorithm $\psi$.

Throughout the rest of the paper we consider that $m$ is the dual to length complexity measure, and we denote complexity by $C_\psi^{\mathcal{G}} = m_\psi^0$.

When the space $\mathcal{G}$ is understood, we may omit the superscript $\mathcal{G}$.

If there exists $i_0$ such that for all $i \in I$, there is a $c \in \mathbb{N}$ satisfying the inequality:

$$C_{\psi_{i_0}}(x) \leq C_{\psi_i}(x) + c \tag{1}$$

for all $x \in \mathbb{N}$, then the algorithm $\psi_{i_0}$ is an universal algorithm for the family $\mathcal{G}$.[6]

Since the measure $m$ satisfies the Cofinitness Axiom 3, we can define the maximum complexity of objects having a certain measure as:

$$\Sigma_\phi^{\mathcal{G}}(n) = \max\{m_\phi^0(x) \mid m(x) = n\}.$$

Using the notation $C_\phi^{\mathcal{G}} = m_\phi^0$, for dual to length complexity measures, we get:

$$\Sigma_\phi^{\mathcal{G}}(n) = \max\{C^{\mathcal{G}}(x) \mid |x| = n\}.$$

In many papers some properties are proved for plain or prefix free complexity, and is stated without any proof that the property should hold true for the other type of complexity, just because it would be a matter of encoding. However, the technical difficulties for translating the proof used for one complexity to the other one may be so big, that is simply better to write a completely new proof. In other cases, such a translation is not even possible, because that property is specific to that particular representation. Thus, it is natural to ask ourselves what would be some simple properties of encodings of natural numbers that would allow us to talk about a general type of complexity, and distinguish, using the properties of the encodings, between several complexity classes having common properties.

In [11] we propose such a set of properties for the encoding, and for keeping the paper self-contained, we include them here:

**Definition 3.** *([11]) Let e and E be two computable functions satisfying the following properties:*

1. *$E$ is injective and is a length increasing function in the second argument, i.e., there exists $c_e$, such that if $|x| \leq |y|$, then $|E(i, x)| \leq |E(i, y)| + c_e$.*
2. *$|E(i, x)| \leq |E(i', x)| + \eta(i, i')$, for some function $\eta : \mathbb{N}^2 \longrightarrow \mathbb{N}$.*

*Then we say that the pair $(e, E)$ is an encoding.[7]*

---

[6] The constant $c$ depends on $i$ and $i_0$, but does not depend on $x$.

[7] Please note that the constant $c_e$ depends on the function $e$, but does not depend on $i$ or $y$.

**Definition 4.** *([11]) We say that the family $\mathcal{G} = (\psi_j)_{j \in J}$ is an $(e, E)$-encoding of the family $\mathcal{H} = (\mu_i)_{i \in I}$, if for every $i \in I$ and all $x \in \mathbb{N}$, we have that:*

1. *$\mu_i(x) = \psi_{e(i)}(E(i, x))$, for all $i \in I$ and $x \in \mathbb{N}$,*
2. *if $\psi_j(z) = x$, then $e(i) = j$ and $E(i, y) = z$, for some $i \in I$ and $y \in \mathbb{N}$.*

**Theorem 1.** *[11] If $\mathcal{H}$ has an universal algorithm in $\mathcal{H}$, and $\mathcal{G}$ is an encoding of $\mathcal{H}$, then $\mathcal{G}$ has an universal algorithm in $\mathcal{G}$.*

In case $\mathcal{G}$ encodes $\mathcal{F}$, then $\mathcal{G}$ is called Blum universal static complexity space (BUSC). One can check that (Prefix-free) Turing Machines, together with their sizes, form a BUSC space, more details being presented in [4, 11]. Thus, it is natural to check if common properties of plain and prefix-free versions of Kolmogorov-Chaitin complexity can be proved in the general context of Blum universal static complexity.

If $\mathcal{G}$ is a Blum Universal Static Complexity space, with the universal function $\psi_{i_0}$, then the canonical program of $x$ is $x^* = \min\{y \in \mathbb{N} \mid \psi_{i_0}(y) = x\}$. Since we work with complexities that are dual to length measures, and because $x < y$ implies $|string(x)| \le |string(y)|$, it follows that we can also write $x < y$ implies $|x| \le |y|$. Thus, if $\mathcal{G}$ is an $(e, E)$-encoding of $\mathcal{F}$, then:

$$\text{if } x < y \text{ it follows that } |E(i, x)| \le |E(i, y)| + c_e. \tag{2}$$

We say that a number $x$ is $t$-compressible in $\mathcal{G}$, if $C^{\mathcal{G}}(x) < \Sigma^{\mathcal{G}}(|x|) - t$, and that is $t$-incompressible, if $C^{\mathcal{G}}(x) \ge \Sigma^{\mathcal{G}}(|x|) - t$. A $t$-incompressible element is also called random in $\mathcal{G}$, and the set of all these elements is denoted by $RAND_t^{\mathcal{G}}$. We denote by $non - RAND_t^{\mathcal{G}} = \mathbb{N} \setminus RAND_t^{\mathcal{G}}$.

The following results have already been proved in [11] for a BUSC:

1. The set of canonical programs is immune.
2. The function $f(x) = x^*$ is not computable.
3. The function $C^{\mathcal{G}}$ is not computable.
4. The set $RAND_t^{\mathcal{G}}$ is immune.

## 3   Relations between Universal Complexities

Let us set the universal algorithm $\phi_{i_0}$ for $\mathcal{F}$. Then $\mathcal{G}$ has the induced universal algorithm [11], $\psi_{e(i_0)}$.

We first prove the following technical lemma:

**Lemma 1.** *Let $\mathcal{G}$ be a BUSC space. The set*

$$non - RAND_t^{\mathcal{G}} = \{x \mid C^G(x) \le \Sigma^{\mathcal{G}}(n) - t\}$$

*is computable enumerable.*

*Proof.* We use the following algorithm:

1. Put $k = 1$, $x_k = 0$.
2. Run $\psi_{e(i_0)}(x_1), \ldots, \psi_{e(i_0)}(x_k)$, for the first $k$ steps.
3. Let $i_1, \ldots, i_n$ $n < k$ be all such values that $\psi_{e(i_0)}(x_{i_1}), \ldots, \psi_{e(i_0)}(x_{i_n})$ stop in at most $k$ steps.
   Then for $j = 1, \ldots, n$ take $y_j = \psi_{e(i_0)}(x_{i_j})$, $1 \le j \le n$, and set

$$C^{\mathcal{G},k}(y_j) = \min\{|x_{i_l}|) \mid \psi_{e(i_0)}(x_{i_l}) = y_j, 1 \le l \le n\}.$$

4. For $j = 1$ to $n$ perform:
   (a) Compute $\Sigma^{\mathcal{G},k}(|y_j|) = \max\{C^{\mathcal{G},k}(y_l) \mid |y_j| = |y_l|, 1 \le l \le n\}$.
   (b) If $C^{\mathcal{G},k}(y_j) < \Sigma^k(|y_j|) - t$, then output $y_j$.
5. Set $k = k + 1$, generate $x_k = k - 1$, and go to step 2.

We can see the following facts:

1. If $C^{\mathcal{G}}(y) = |x|$, $\psi_{e(i_0)}(x) = y$, and this computation finishes after $k$ steps. Then $C^{\mathcal{G},\max\{k,x\}}(y) = |x|$;
2. $C^{\mathcal{G}}(y) \le C^{\mathcal{G},\max\{k,x\}}(y)$.
3. $\Sigma^{\mathcal{G},k}(|y_j|) \le \Sigma^{\mathcal{G},k+1}(|y_j|) \le \Sigma^{\mathcal{G}}(|y_j|)$
4. If $y_j$ is produced, then $C^{\mathcal{G},k}(y_j) < \Sigma^{\mathcal{G},k}(|y_j|) - t$, which means that the computation

$$C^{\mathcal{G}}(y_j) < \Sigma^{\mathcal{G}}(|y_j|) - t.$$

Now let $y$ be such that $C^{\mathcal{G}}(y) < \Sigma^{\mathcal{G}}(|y|) - t$. This means that $\psi_{e(i_0)}(x) = y$ terminates in $k$ steps and $|x| < \Sigma^{\mathcal{G}}(|y|) - t$.

But $\{z \mid |z| < |y|\}$ is finite, therefore there is $m \in \mathbb{N}$ such that $C^{\mathcal{G},m}(z) = C^{\mathcal{G}}(z)$ for all $z \in \{z \mid |z| < |y|\}$. Hence, $\Sigma^{\mathcal{G},m} = \Sigma^{\mathcal{G}}$ and for $\max\{k,m\}$ we have that:

$$C^{\mathcal{G},\max\{k,m\}}(y) < \Sigma^{\mathcal{G},\max\{k,m\}}(|y|) - t.$$

We conclude that this algorithm enumerates exactly the set $non - RAND_t^{\mathcal{G}}$.

**Comment 1.** *The existence of $k, m$ in the proof of the previous Lemma is non effective.*

We enhance the condition for the encoding $(e, E)$, making it slightly stronger:

**Definition 5.** *We say that the encoding is a normal encoding if for any $T \in \mathbb{N}$, there exists $t \in N$ such that, if $|x| \le |y| - t$, then $|E(i, x)| \le |E(i, y)| - T$.*

We can see that for $T = 0$ there exists a $t \in \mathbb{N}$ such that $|x| \le |y| - t$ implies $|E(i, x)| \le |E(i, y)|$. However, $|x| \le |y| - t$ implies $|x| \le |y|$, thus $|E(i, x)| \le |E(i, y)| + O(1)$. This makes condition stated in Definition 5 somehow stronger than the original condition stated in Definition 3.

In case of a normal encoding $|E(i, x)| + T \le |E(i, y)|$, whenever $|x| + t \le |y|$. Thus, the increase of the length of the encoding can be controlled, even if we do not require any kind of effectiveness condition for the existence of $t$.

The choice of $t$ should not depend on the particular computer $i$, but to simplify things, we can ask that the normality property holds only for the universal computer.

In what follows, we will consider only BUSC spaces $\mathcal{G}$ that are normal encodings of $\mathcal{F}$, for the universal computer, i.e., for which Definition 5 is satisfied for $i = i_0$.

**Theorem 2.** *Let $\mathcal{G}$ be a normal encoding of $\mathcal{F}$. Then for every $m \in \mathbb{N}$, there is a $t \in \mathbb{N}$ such that for each $x \in \mathbb{N}$ $C^{\mathcal{F}}(x) < \Sigma^{\mathcal{F}}(|x|) - t$, implies $C^{\mathcal{G}}(x) < \Sigma^{\mathcal{G}}(|x|) - m$.*

*Proof.* Let $T \in \mathbb{N}$. Because $\mathcal{G}$ is a normal encoding of $\mathcal{F}$, there exits $t \in N$ such that:
$$|x| + t < |y| \text{ implies } |E(i,x)| + T < |E(i,y)|.$$

We choose $x \in non - RAND_t^{\mathcal{F}}$, such that $z$ is the canonical program of $x$ in $\mathcal{F}$.

Therefore, we have that: $|z| < \Sigma^{\mathcal{F}}(|x|) - t$, and $\phi_{i_0}(z) = x$, thus $\psi_{e(i_0)}(E(i_0, z)) = x$. It follows that the complexity of $x$ in $\mathcal{G}$ cannot exceed $|E(i_0, z)|$.

Let $z'$ be such that $E(i_0, z')$ is the canonical program of $x$ in $\mathcal{G}$. Then we have $\psi_{e(i_0)}(E(i_0, z')) = x$ and $C^{\mathcal{G}}(x) = |E(i_0, z')| \leq |E(i_0, z)|$.

Since $\phi_{i_0}(z') = x$, and $z$ is canonical program for $x$ in $\mathcal{F}$, we have that $z \leq z'$, therefore $|E(i_0, z)| \leq |E(i_0, z')| + c_e$. Hence, $C^{\mathcal{G}}(x) + c_e \geq |E(i_0, z)|$.

It follows that $\Sigma^{\mathcal{G}}(|x|) + c_e \geq |E(i_0, v)|$, where $v$ is such that $|v| = C^{\mathcal{F}}(y) = \Sigma^{\mathcal{F}}(|x|)$ and $|y| = |x|$.

Now, using that $|z| < |v| - t$ and the fact that the encoding is normal, we deduct $|E(i_0, z)| \leq |E(i_0, v)| - T$, which implies that $C^{\mathcal{G}}(x) \leq |E(i_0, v)| - T \leq \Sigma^{\mathcal{G}}(|x|) + c_e - T$.

Let $m \in N$ be an arbitrary number. We take $T = c_e + m + 1$ thus, for $x \in non-RAND_t^{\mathcal{F}}$, we have that $C^{\mathcal{G}}(x) \leq \Sigma^{\mathcal{G}}(|x|) + c_e - c_e - m - 1 < \Sigma^{\mathcal{G}}(|x|) - m$, which is the conclusion of the theorem.

Therefore, we just proved the following as a consequence:

**Corollary 1.** *Randomness with respect to prefix-free complexity is stronger than randomness with respect to plain complexity.*

*Proof.* We just need to observe that the BUSC for prefix-free complexity is a normal encoding of $\mathcal{F}$, because $E(i, z)$ is a prefix free encoding of $z$.

Since any BUSC $\mathcal{G}$ is an $(e, E)$-encoding of $\mathcal{F}$, it follows that the weakest form of randomness is represented by the plain complexity.

## 4   Infinite Sequences and Randomness

In this section we prove that all infinite sequences have an infinite number of non-random prefixes, regardless of the universal complexity space selected. We prove the statement for the general case of a BUSC $\mathcal{G}$, that has a normal encoding of $\mathcal{F}$.

In [7], the following theorem is proved:

**Theorem 3.** *Let* $\mathbf{x} \in A_p^\omega$. *Then for every* $t \in \mathbb{N}$, *there exists infinitely many values of* $n$, *such that*

$$C^{\mathcal{F}}(\mathbf{x}(n)) \leq n - t.$$

We prove now the same result, but this time for the more general case of a BUSC space.

**Theorem 4.** *Let* $\mathbf{x} \in A_p^\omega$. *Then for every* $T \in \mathbb{N}$, *there exists infinitely many values of* $n$, *such that*

$$C^{\mathcal{G}}(\mathbf{x}(n)) \leq \Sigma^{\mathcal{G}}(n) - T.$$

*Proof.* Let $\mathbf{x} \in A_p^\omega$, $t \geq 0$ and $T$ as in Theorem 2.

Because $C^{\mathcal{F}}(\mathbf{x}(n)) < \Sigma^{\mathcal{F}}(n) - t$ for an infinity of $n$, it follows that for the exact same $n$'s, we also have: $C^{\mathcal{G}}(\mathbf{x}(n)) < \Sigma^{\mathcal{G}}(n) - T$.

It is clear that in case $\mathcal{G} = \mathcal{F}$, we obtain the result of Calude [7], and in case $\mathcal{G}$ is the set of prefix-free computers, we obtained the result in [10], which also appears in [1].

## 5    Conclusions

In this paper we proved the following results for the general case of BUSC spaces:

1. The set of non random strings is computable enumerable.
2. If BUSC space $\mathcal{G}$ is a normal encoding of $\mathcal{F}$, then the definition of randomness in $\mathcal{G}$ is always stronger than randomness in $\mathcal{F}$.

   One can verify that this result can be extended to an arbitrary normal encoding of a BUSC space $\mathcal{G}$ of a BUSC space $\mathcal{H}$, since we did not use any particularity of the BUSC $\mathcal{F}$.
3. We proved that all infinite sequences have an infinite number of non-random prefixes, regardless of what ever complexity measure[8] we consider, and not only for the plain and prefix free complexity.

Since we have done the proofs just for BUSC spaces, it is natural to ask what happens for BSC spaces, i.e., the ones that are not universal. Will a theorem like Theorem 2 hold true?

If we consider the BSC of finite transducers [9, 11], can we conclude that any infinite string has a limited number of prefixes of maximal complexity? If not, how would such an infinite sequence look like? Can we relax the condition for the encoding? What would be the weakest reasonable condition that we could consider for the encoding?

We may also examine the following condition:

$$|z| \leq |E(i_0, z)| + O(1). \tag{3}$$

In this case, we say that $\mathcal{G}$ is a non-compressing encoding of $\mathcal{F}$.

---

[8] That can be expressed as a dual complexity measure.

How would this condition, or the opposite condition, influence the results proved in this paper? What are other properties of BSC spaces with this extra condition?

# References

1. Bienvenu, L., Downey, R.: Kolmogorov Complexity and Solovay Functions. In: Symposium on Theoretical Aspects of Computer Science, Freiburg, pp. 147–158 (2009)
2. Blum, M.: A machine-independent theory of the complexity of recursive functions. Journal of the ACM 14(2), 322–336 (1967)
3. Blum, M.: On the size of machines. Information and Control 11, 257–265 (1967)
4. Burgin, M.: Generalized Kolmogorov complexity and other dual complexity measures. Translated from Kibernetica 4, 21–29 (1990); Original article submitted June 19 (1986)
5. Burgin, M.: Algorithmic complexity of recursive and inductive algorithms. Theoretical Computer Science 317, 31–60 (2004)
6. Burgin, M.: Algorithmic complexity as a criterion of unsolvability. Theoretical Computer Science 383, 244–259 (2007)
7. Calude, C.: Information and Randomness - An Algorithmic Perspective. Springer, Berlin (1994)
8. Calude, C.: Theories of Computational Complexity. North-Holland, Amsterdam (1988)
9. Calude, C., Salomaa, K., Roblot, T.K.: Finite State Complexity and Randomness. Technical Report CDMTCS 374 (December 2009) (revised June 2010)
10. Câmpeanu, C.: Private Communication to Helmut Jurgensen and Cristian Calude at first edition of DCAGRS (1999)
11. Câmpeanu, C.: A Note on Blum Static Complexity Measures. In: Dinneen, M.J., Khoussainov, B., Nies, A. (eds.) Computation, Physics and Beyond. LNCS, vol. 7160, pp. 71–80. Springer, Heidelberg (2012)
12. Chaitin, G.J.: On the Length of Programs for Computing Finite Binary Sequences. J. ACM 13(4), 547–569 (1966)
13. Chaitin, G.J.: On the Length of Programs for Computing Finite Binary Sequences: statistical considerations. J. ACM 16(1), 145–159 (1969)
14. Chaitin, G.J.: A Theory of Program Size Formally Identical to Information Theory. J. ACM 22(3), 329–340 (1975)
15. Chaitin, G.J.: A Theory of Program Size Formally Identical to Information Theory. J. ACM 22(3), 329–340 (1975)
16. Chaitin, G.J.: Algorithmic Information Theory. Cambridge Tracts in Theoretical Computer Science, vol. I. Cambridge University Press (1987)
17. Davis, M., Sigal, R., Weyuker, E.: Computability, Complexity, and Languages, 1st edn. Academic Press, New York (1994)
18. Gacs, P.: On the symmetry of algorithmic information. Soviet Mathematics Doklady 15, 1477–1480 (1974)
19. Kolmogorov, A.N.: Problems Inform. Transmission 1, 1–7 (1965)
20. Levin, L.A.: Laws of information conservation (non-growth) and aspects of the foundation of probability theory. Problems of Information Transmission 10(3), 206–210 (1974)

21. Loveland, D.A.: On Minimal-Program Complexity Measures. In: STOC, pp. 61–65 (1969)
22. Papadimitriou, C.H., Lewis, H.: Elements of the theory of computation. Prentice-Hall, Englewood Cliffs (1982); 2nd edn. (September 1997)
23. Schnorr, C.-P.: Process complexity and effective random tests. Journal of Computer and System Sciences 7(4), 376–388 (1973)
24. Solomonoff, R.J.: A Formal Theory of Inductive Inference, Part I. Information and Control 7(1), 1–22 (1964)
25. Solomonoff, R.J.: A Formal Theory of Inductive Inference, Part II. Information and Control 7(2), 224–254 (1964)
26. Solomonoff, R.J.: Complexity-Based Induction Systems: Comparisons and Convergence Theorems. IEEE Trans. on Information Theory IT-24(4), 422–432 (1978)
27. Solovay, R.M.: Draft of paper (or series of papers) on Chaitin's work. Unpublished notes, pp. 1–215 (May 1975)

# Production Complexity of Some Operations on Context-Free Languages

Jürgen Dassow and Ronny Harbich

Fakultät für Informatik, Otto-von-Guericke-Universität Magdeburg,
PSF 4120, 39016 Magdeburg, Germany
dassow@iws.cs.uni-magdeburg.de,
ronny@raubvogel.net

**Abstract.** We investigate context-free languages with respect to the measure Prod of descriptional complexity, which gives the minimal number of productions necessary to generate the language. In particular, we consider the behaviour of this measure with respect to operations. For given natural numbers $c_1, c_2, \ldots, c_n$ and an $n$-ary operation $\tau$ on languages, we discuss the set $g_\tau(c_1, c_2, \ldots, c_n)$ which is the range of $\mathrm{Prod}(\tau(L_1, L_2, \ldots, L_n))$ where, for $1 \leq i \leq n$, $L_i$ is a context-free language with $\mathrm{Prod}(L_i) = c_i$. The operations under discussion are union, concatenation, reversal, and Kleene closure.

## 1 Introduction

One interesting question which has been investigated very intensively over the last 20 years concerns the behaviour of descriptional complexity under operations. More precisely, for a language family $\mathcal{L}$, a measure $K$ of descriptional complexity, an $n$-ary operation $\tau$ on languages under which $\mathcal{L}$ is closed, and natural numbers $m_1, m_2, \ldots, m_n$, one tries to determine the set $g_{\tau,K}(m_1, m_2, \ldots, m_n)$ of all values $K(\tau(L_1, L_2, \ldots, L_n))$, where $L_i$ is a language of $\mathcal{L}$ with $K(L_i) = m_i$ for $1 \leq i \leq n$, and the number $f_{\tau,K}(m_1, m_2, \ldots, m_n)$ which is given by the maximal number in $g_{\tau,K}(m_1, m_2, \ldots, m_n)$.

There are many papers devoted to the study of $f_{\tau,sc}$ where $sc$ is the state complexity of regular languages (i. e., $sc(L)$ is given by the number of states of a minimal deterministic automaton accepting $L$) and $\tau$ is an operation under which the family of regular languages is closed. For example, for union and concatenation, one has $f_{\cup,sc}(m,n) = mn$ and $f_{\cdot,sc}(m,n) = (2m-1)2^{n-1}$. For further results, we refer to [1,17,12,11] and the summarizing articles [15,16].

For some operations, the number $f_{\tau,nsc}$ where $nsc$ is the state complexity with respect to nondeterministic automata is studied in [4] and [10], and research on $f_{\tau,tr}$ where $tr$ is the complexity measure given by the number of transitions is done in [3].

There is only a small number of papers investigating the range $g_{\tau,K}$. For complementation $C$, $g_{C,nsc}(n)$ is partially determined in [11].

With respect to context-free languages and the nonterminal complexity Var ($\mathrm{Var}(L)$ gives the number of nonterminals which are required for the generation

M. Kutrib, N. Moreira, and R. Reis (Eds.): DCFS 2012, LNCS 7386, pp. 141–154, 2012.
© Springer-Verlag Berlin Heidelberg 2012

of $L$ by context-free grammars), an early result can be found in [13]. A systematic study was presented in [2], where the sets $g_{\tau,\mathrm{Var}}(m_1, m_2)$ and $g_{\tau,\mathrm{Var}}(m_1)$ were extensively determined for the unary and binary AFL operations. Besides concatenation, the presented results are complete.

In this paper we consider context-free grammars and their production complexity Prod introduced by J. GRUSKA (see [5], [6], [7], [8]). Formally, for a context-free grammar $G = (N, T, P, S)$ (with the sets $N$, $T$ and $P$ of nonterminals, terminals and productions, respectively, and the axiom $S$), we define $\mathrm{Prod}(G)$ as the cardinality of $P$. For a context-free language $L$, we set

$$\mathrm{Prod}(L) = \min\{\mathrm{Prod}(G) \mid G \text{ is a context-free grammar and } L(G) = L\}.$$

Moreover, for an $r$-ary operation $\tau$ under which the family of context-free languages is closed and natural numbers $n_1, n_2, \ldots, n_r$, we define $g_\tau(n_1, n_2, \ldots, n_r)$ as the set of all natural numbers $k$ such that there are context-free languages $L_i$, $1 \leq i \leq r$, such that $\mathrm{Prod}(L_i) = n_i$ for $1 \leq i \leq r$ and $\mathrm{Prod}(\tau(L_1, \ldots, L_r)) = k$.

In this paper we discuss $g_\tau$ for the unary operations of reversal and Kleene closure and the binary operations of union and concatenation, i.e., we study $g_R(n)$, $g_*(n)$, $g_\cup(n, m)$, and $g.(n, m)$. For the unary operations, we determine the sets completely; for union, the results are almost complete; for concatenation, we only present a partial solution.

## 2   Production Complexity of Some Languages

We assume that the reader is familiar with the basic concepts of the theory of formal languages (see [14]). For the sake of completeness, we start with some notation. For an alphabet $V$, i.e, $V$ is a finite non-empty set, the set of all words and all non-empty words over $V$ are denoted by $V^*$ and $V^+$, respectively. The empty word is denoted by $\lambda$. Throughout the paper, we assume that a language over $V$, i.e., a subset of $V^*$, is a non-empty set. For a language $L$, let $\mathrm{alph}(L)$ be the minimal set $V$ such that $L \subseteq V^*$. For a word $w \in V^*$ and a subset $C$ of $V$, the number of occurrences of letters of $C$ in $w$ is denoted by $\#_C(w)$. If $C$ only consists of the letter $a$, we write $\#_a(w)$ instead of $\#_{\{a\}}(w)$.

In order to simplify the formulations we introduce the following concept.

**Definition 1.** *A context-free language $L$ is called a language with initial loops if, for any context-free grammar $G = (N, T, P, S)$ with $L(G) = L$ and $\mathrm{Prod}(G) = \mathrm{Prod}(L)$, there is a derivation $S \Longrightarrow^* xSy$ with $x, y \in T^*$ and $xy \neq \lambda$.*

Obviously, no finite languages is a language with initial loops.

We now determine the production complexity of some languages which will be used later.

**Lemma 1.** *i) For a context-free language $L$, we have $\mathrm{Prod}(L) = 1$ if and only if $L$ is a singleton.*

*ii) For a finite language $L$, we have $\mathrm{Prod}(L) = 2$ if and only if $L$ consists of exactly two words.*

*iii)* For any two natural numbers $r$ and $s$ with $0 \leq r$ and $r+2 \leq s$, the relation $\mathrm{Prod}(\{a^i \mid r \leq i \leq s\}) = 3$ holds.

*iv)* For any natural number $r \geq 1$, we have $\mathrm{Prod}(\{a^i \mid i \geq r\}) = 2$.     □

**Lemma 2.** Let $n$ and $m$ be natural numbers with $n \geq 1$ and $m \geq 1$, $C = \{c_1, c_2, \ldots, c_n\}$ and $D = \{d_1, d_2, \ldots, d_m\}$ disjoints alphabets consisting of $n$ and $m$ letters, respectively, and $a$ and $b$ two additional letters not contained in $C \cup D$. Let $R_1(n) = \{a^t x b^t \mid t \geq 0, x \in C\}$. Then

*i)* $\mathrm{Prod}(R_1(n)) = n + 1$,

*ii)* $\mathrm{Prod}(R_1(n)^*) = n + 3$, and

*iii)* $\mathrm{Prod}(R_1(n)D) = n + m + 1$.

*Proof.* i) Let $G = (N, T, P, S)$ be a context-free grammar with $L(G) = R_1(n)$ and $\mathrm{Prod}(G) = \mathrm{Prod}(R_1(n))$. Since no word of $R_1(n)$ contains two letters of $C$, for any $i$, $1 \leq i \leq n$, we need a rule $A_i \to x_{1,i} c_i x_{2,i}$ with $A_i \in N$ and $x_{1,i}, x_{2,i} \in (N \cup \{a, b\})^*$. Moreover, $R_1(n)$ is infinite, and therefore we need a derivation $A \Longrightarrow^* uAv$ with $u, v \in T^*$ and $uv \neq \lambda$ and have a derivation

$$S \Longrightarrow^* u'Av' \Longrightarrow^* u'uAvv' \Longrightarrow^* u'u^2Av^2v' \Longrightarrow^* u'u^2wv^2v' \in T^*$$

for certain words $u', v', w \in T^*$. Hence $u$ and $v$ cannot contain any letter of $C$. Thus we also have a rule $A \to z$ where $z$ contains no letter of $C$. Thus we obtain $n + 1 \leq \mathrm{Prod}(G) = \mathrm{Prod}(R_1(n))$.

On the other hand, the grammar

$$G' = (\{S\}, C \cup \{a, b\}, \{S \to aSb\} \cup \{S \to c_i \mid 1 \leq i \leq n\}, S)$$

generates $R_1(n)$ with $n+1$ rules which implies $\mathrm{Prod}(R_1(n)) \leq \mathrm{Prod}(G') = n+1$.

The combination of the derived inequalities gives the first statement of the lemma.

ii) Let $G^* = (N, T, P, S)$ be a context-free grammar with $L(G^*) = R_1(n)^*$ and $\mathrm{Prod}(G^*) = \mathrm{Prod}(R_1(n)^*)$. Since $R_1(n) \subset R_1(n)^*$, by the same arguments as in i) we have rules $A_i \to x_{1,i} c_i x_{2,i}$ with $A_i \in N$ and $x_{1,i}, x_{2,i} \in (N \cup \{a, b\})^*$ and a derivation $A \Longrightarrow^* uAv$ with $u, v \in \{a, b\}^*$ and can derive the words $u'v^r wv^r v' \in R_1(n)$ with some $u', v', w \in T^*$. Since any word in $R_1(n)$ contains the same number of occurrences of $a$ and $b$, it is easy to prove that $u = a^s$, $v = b^s$ for some $s \geq 1$, $u' \in \{a\}^*$, and $v' \in \{b\}^*$.

Let us assume that there is a word $z$ with $A \Longrightarrow^* z \in T^*$ and $\#_C(z) \geq 2$. Then we have the derivations $S \Longrightarrow^* u'uzvv'$ and $S \Longrightarrow^* u'u^2zv^2v'$ in $G^*$ and hence $u'u^2zv^2v'$ and $u'uzvv'$ in $L(G^*)$. But only one of these words can be in $R_1(n)^*$ since we only change the numbers of occurrences of $a$ and $b$ before and after $z$, respectively. This contradiction shows that any such letter $A$ can derive at most one occurrence of a letter of $C$. The same holds for the nonterminals $A_i$ given above since $A_i$ has such a loop derivation or it derives only a finite set of words.

Since the axiom derives words with at least two occurrences of letters of $C$, $S$ has no loop derivation like those considered above. If there are two rules for $S$

we have at least $n+3$ rules. If there is only one rule for $S$, then its right-hand side cannot contain $S$ since we cannot terminate the derivation otherwise. If the right-hand side only contains the nonterminals $A_i$ and those with a loop derivation as above, we can only produce words with a limited number of occurrences of $C$. This implies $L(G^*) \neq R_1(n)^*$ in contrast to our choice. Therefore the right-hand side contains a further nonterminal for which we have an additional rule. Thus we get $n+3 \geq \text{Prod}(G^*) = \text{Prod}(R_1(n)^*)$.

On the other hand, the language $R_1(n)^*$ is generated by the context-free grammar with the rules $S \to AS$, $S \to \lambda$, $A \to aAb$ and, $A \to x$ with $x \in C$, i.e., $\text{Prod}(R_1(n)^*) \leq n+3$.

iii) Let $G = (N, T, P, S)$ be a grammar with $L(G) = R_1(n)D$ and $\text{Prod}(G) = \text{Prod}(R_1(n)D)$. Obviously, $T = \{a, b\} \cup C \cup D$.

For $1 \leq i \leq n$ and sufficiently large $r$, we consider the word $w = a^r c_i b^r d_1$ of $R_1(n)D$. As above we get the existence of a derivation

$$S \Longrightarrow^* u'Av' \Longrightarrow^* u'uAvv' \Longrightarrow^* u'uzvv' = w$$

with $uv \neq \lambda$, which implies the existence of derivations

$$S \Longrightarrow^* u'Av' \Longrightarrow^* u'uAvv' \Longrightarrow^* u'u^2Av^2v'$$
$$\Longrightarrow^* u'u^sAv^sv' \Longrightarrow^* u'u^szv^sv' = w_s \text{ for } s \geq 0.$$

Since $w_s \in R_1(n)D$, we obtain

- that $u$ and $v$ cannot contain $c_i$ or $d_1$ (otherwise, we can produce words in $R_1(n)D$ with at least two occurrences of $c_i$ or $d_1$, respectively), i.e., $u, v$ are in $\{a, b\}^*$,
- that $u$ and $v$ cannot contain occurrences of $a$ as well as $b$ (otherwise, we can produce words where $b$ occurs before $a$), i.e., $u$ and $v$ are contained in $\{a\}^*$ or $\{b\}^*$,
- that $\#_a(w_s) - \#_a(w) = \#_b(w_s) - \#_a(w)$,
  $\#_a(w_s) - \#_a(w) = \#_a(u^{s-1}v^{s-1})$,
  $\#_b(w_s) - \#_a(w) = \#_b(u^{s-1}v^{s-1})$,
  which implies $\#_a(u^{s-1}v^{s-1}) = \#_b(u^{s-1}v^{s-1}) > 0$ and $\#_a(uv) = \#_b(uv) > 0$.

Combining these facts and taking into consideration the order of the letters we have

$$u' \in \{a\}^*, \ u \in \{a\}^+, \ z \in \{a\}^*\{c_i\}\{b\}^*, \ v \in \{b\}^+, \ v' \in \{b\}^*\{d_1\}.$$

Moreover, by changing the order of the application of rules, the derivation $A_i \Longrightarrow^* z_i$ can be written as

$$A \Longrightarrow^* xA_ix' \Longrightarrow xyc_iy'x' \Longrightarrow^* xqc_iq'x'$$

with $x, q \in \{a\}^*$, $x', q' \in \{b\}^*$, $A_i \to yc_iy' \in P$, $y \in (N \cup \{a\})^*$, and $y' \in (N \cup \{b\})^*$. Because $1 \leq i \leq n$, this gives the existence of $n-1$ rules. (We note that the nonterminals $A_i$ and $A_j$ can be equal, but the rules $A_i \to yc_iy' \in P$ and $A_j \to y''c_jy''' \in P$ are different.)

Furthermore, $A \Longrightarrow^* uAv$ can be written as

$$A \Longrightarrow^* hCh' \Longrightarrow hgh' \Longrightarrow^* hg'h' = uAv$$

where $C \to g \in P$, $g \in (\{a, b\} \cup N)^*$ and $\#_{\{a,b\}}(g) \geq 1$. Thus we get a further rule.

Moreover, for any $1 \leq j \leq m$, we need at least one rule $p_j$ whose right-hand side contains $d_j$. Since the right-hand side of $p_j$ cannot contain two symbol of $D$, we obtain $m$ additional rules.

Thus $\mathrm{Prod}(R_1(n)D) \geq n + 1 + m$.

Since

$$H = (\{S, A\}, \{a, b\} \cup C \cup D, \{S \to Ad \mid d \in D\} \cup \{A \to aAb\} \cup \{A \to c \mid c \in C\}, S)$$

generates $R_1(n)D$, we also have $\mathrm{Prod}(R_1(n)D) \leq n + 1 + m$, which implies the statement. □

**Lemma 3.** *Let $R_2(n) = \{a_1, a_2, \ldots, a_n\}$ where $a_i$, $1 \leq i \leq n$, are pairwise different letters of some alphabet. Then $\mathrm{Prod}(R_2(n)) = n$, $\mathrm{Prod}(R_2(n)^*) = n+1$, and $\mathrm{Prod}(R_2(n)^+) = n + 1$. Moreover $R_2(n)^*$ and $R_2(n)^+$ are languages with initial loops.* □

**Lemma 4.** *For any numbers $n$ and $m$ with $0 \leq m < n$, let*

$$R(m, n) = \{a^{2^i} \mid m \leq i \leq n\} \text{ and } R'(m, n) = \{a^{2^i - 1} \mid m \leq i \leq n\}.$$

*Then $\mathrm{Prod}(R(m, n)) = \mathrm{Prod}(R'(m, n)) = n - m + 1$.*

*Proof.* The statement for $R(m, n)$ follows by slight modifications of the proof for $R(1, n)$ in [5].

Using the rules $S \to a^{2^i - 1}$ for $n \leq i \leq m$, we get $\mathrm{Prod}(R'(m, n)) \leq n - m + 1$.

Assume that $\mathrm{Prod}(R'(m, n)) < n - m + 1$. Let $G = (N, T, P, S)$ be a grammar with $L(G) = R'(m, n)$ and $\mathrm{Prod}(G) = \mathrm{Prod}(R'(m, n))$. Obviously, there is no rule $S \to xSy \in P$. (If $xy = \lambda$, the cancellation of the rule does not change the generated language, and hence $P$ is not a minimal production set in contrast to the choice of $G$; if $xy \neq \lambda$, then we can generate an infinite language, because any nonterminal occurring in $xy$ has a derivation to a non-empty word.) Now we construct $G' = (N, T, P', S)$ where $P'$ is obtained from $P$ by replacing $S \to w \in P$ by $S \to wa$. Then $\mathrm{Prod}(G') < n - m + 1$. It is easy to see that $L(G') = R(m, n)$. This implies $\mathrm{Prod}(R(m, n)) < n - m + 1$. This assertion contradicts our shown statement for $R(m, n)$. □

**Lemma 5.** *Let $R_3 = \{a\} \cup \{a^i \mid i \geq 3\}$ and $R_4 = \{a, a^2, a^3\} \cup \{a^i \mid i \geq 5\}$. Then $\mathrm{Prod}(R_3) = 3$ and $\mathrm{Prod}(R_4) = 4$. Moreover, $R_3$ and $R_4$ are languages with initial loops.* □

# 3    Behaviour under Operations

We start with the reversal (or mirror image) $R$ (which is defined by $\lambda^R = \lambda$, $a^R = a$ for letters $a$, $(uv)^R = v^R u^R$ for words $u, v$, $L^R = \{w^r \mid w \in L\}$ for languages $L$), where the situation is very easy.

**Theorem 1.** For any $n \geq 1$, we have $g_R(n) = \{n\}$.

*Proof.* Let $L$ be a context-free language, and let $G = (N, T, P, S)$ be a context-free grammar with $L = L(G)$ and $\mathrm{Prod}(L) = \mathrm{Prod}(G)$. Since the grammar $G' = (N, T, \{A \to w^R \mid A \to w \in P\}, S)$ generates $L^R$, we have $\mathrm{Prod}(L^R) \leq \mathrm{Prod}(L)$. Analogously, we get $\mathrm{Prod}(L) = \mathrm{Prod}((L^R)^R) \leq \mathrm{Prod}(L^R)$. Therefore, $\mathrm{Prod}(L^R) = \mathrm{Prod}(L)$. The statement follows immediately.    □

We now discuss the binary operations union and concatenation. Our first result shows that both corresponding functions $g_\tau(m, n)$ are symmetric in the arguments. Thus in the sequel we can restrict to the case where $m \leq n$.

**Lemma 6.** For any positive natural numbers $n$ and $m$, the equalities $g_\cup(m, n) = g_\cup(n, m)$ and $g_.(m, n) = g_.(n, m)$ hold.

*Proof.* Let $k \in g_\cup(m, n)$. Then there are context-free languages $L_1$ and $L_2$ such that $\mathrm{Prod}(L_1) = m$, $\mathrm{Prod}(L_2) = n$, and $\mathrm{Prod}(L_1 \cup L_2) = k$. Since we have $L_1 \cup L_2 = L_2 \cup L_1$, we get immediately $k \in g_\cup(n, m)$. Thus $g_\cup(m, n) \subseteq g_\cup(n, m)$. The converse inclusion can be shown analogously.

Let $k \in g_.(m, n)$. Then there are languages context-free $L_1$ and $L_2$ such that $\mathrm{Prod}(L_1) = m$, $\mathrm{Prod}(L_2) = n$, and $\mathrm{Prod}(L_1 \cdot L_2) = k$. Then we have

$$k = \mathrm{Prod}(L_1 \cdot L_2) = \mathrm{Prod}((L_1 \cdot L_2)^R) = \mathrm{Prod}(L_2^R \cdot L_1^R).$$

Since $\mathrm{Prod}(L_1^R) = \mathrm{Prod}(L_1) = m$ and $\mathrm{Prod}(L_2^R) = \mathrm{Prod}(L_2) = n$, we get immediately $k \in g_.(n, m)$. Therefore $g_.(m, n) \subseteq g_.(n, m)$. The converse inclusion can be proved analogously.    □

We now give a lemma which gives the production complexity of the union in the case that the languages are defined over disjoint alphabets.

**Lemma 7.** If $L_1$ and $L_2$ are context-free languages with $\mathrm{alph}(L_1) \cap \mathrm{alph}(L_2) = \emptyset$, $\lambda \notin L_1$, and $\lambda \notin L_2$, then the following assertions hold:

*i)* If $L_1$ as well as $L_2$ are languages with initial loops, then $\mathrm{Prod}(L_1 \cup L_2) = \mathrm{Prod}(L_1) + \mathrm{Prod}(L_2) + 2$.

*ii)* If $L_1$ is a language with initial loops and $L_2$ is not a language with initial loops, then $\mathrm{Prod}(L_1 \cup L_2) = \mathrm{Prod}(L_1) + \mathrm{Prod}(L_2) + 1$.

*iii)* If neither $L_1$ nor $L_2$ is language with initial loops, then the equality $\mathrm{Prod}(L_1 \cup L_2) = \mathrm{Prod}(L_1) + \mathrm{Prod}(L_2)$ holds.

*iv)* The language $L_1 \cup L_2$ is not a language with initial loops.    □

We are now in the position to determine the sets $g_\cup(m, n)$ for most values $m$ and $n$.

**Theorem 2.** *Let* $2 \leq m \leq n$.

 i) *The number 1 and all numbers* $k$ *with* $k > n + m + 2$ *are not in* $g_\cup(n, m)$.

 ii) *If* $m \geq 7$, *then* $\{k \mid 6 \leq k \leq n + m + 2\} \subseteq g_\cup(m, n)$.

 iii) *If* $m \in \{5, 6\}$, *then* $\{k \mid 4 \leq k \leq n + m + 2\} \subseteq g_\cup(m, n)$.

 iv) *If* $m = 4$, *then* $\{2\} \cup \{k \mid 4 \leq k \leq n + m + 2\} \subseteq g_\cup(m, n)$.

 v) *If* $m \in \{2, 3\}$, *then* $\{k \mid 2 \leq k \leq n + m + 2\} = g_\cup(m, n)$.

*Proof.* i) By the standard construction for the closure of context-free grammars under union, one gets immediately that $\mathrm{Prod}(L_1 \cup L_2) \leq \mathrm{Prod}(L_1) + \mathrm{Prod}(L_2) + 2$. Hence $g_\cup(m, n)$ cannot contain numbers which are strictly larger than $m + n + 2$. Since $m \geq 2$ and $n \geq 2$, the languages $L_1$ and $L_2$ with $\mathrm{Prod}(L_1) = m$ and $\mathrm{Prod}(L_2) = n$ have at least two words. Hence the union also contains at least two words. Thus $\mathrm{Prod}(L_1 \cup L_2) \geq 2$, too, i.e., we have $1 \notin g_\cup(m, n)$.

 ii) We distinguish the following cases.

$k = n + m + 2$. Let $L_1 = \{a_1, a_2, \ldots, a_{m-1}\}^+$ and $L_2 = \{b_1, b_2, \ldots, b_{n-1}\}^+$ where $a_1, a_2, \ldots, a_{m-1}, b_1, b_2, \ldots, b_{n-1}$ are pairwise different letters. By Lemmas 3 and 7, we get $\mathrm{Prod}(L_1) = m$, $\mathrm{Prod}(L_2) = n$, and $\mathrm{Prod}(L_1 \cup L_2) = m + n + 2$.

$k = n + m + 1$. Let $L_1 = \{a_1, a_2, \ldots, a_{m-1}\}^+$ and $L_2 = \{a^{2^i} \mid 1 \leq i \leq n\}$ where $a_1, a_2, \ldots, a_{m-1}, a$ are pairwise different letters. By Lemmas 3, 4, and 7, we get $\mathrm{Prod}(L_1) = m$, $\mathrm{Prod}(L_2) = n$, and $\mathrm{Prod}(L_1 \cup L_2) = m + n + 1$.

$k$ with $n \leq k \leq n + m$. Let $L_1 = R(1, m)$ and $L_2 = R(k - n + 1, k)$. By Lemma 4, we get $\mathrm{Prod}(L_1) = m$, $\mathrm{Prod}(L_2) = n$, and $\mathrm{Prod}(L_1 \cup L_2) = \mathrm{Prod}(R(1, k)) = k$.

$k$ with $6 \leq k \leq n$. Let $a, b, c$ be three pairwise different letters and

$$L_1 = \{c^{2^r} \mid 1 \leq r \leq m - 3\} \cup \{b\}^+ \quad \text{and}$$
$$L_2 = \{a^{2^i} \mid 1 \leq i \leq k - 6\} \cup \{b^{2^j} \mid 1 \leq j \leq n - k + 3\} \cup \{c\}^+.$$

Then we obtain by Lemmas 3, 4, and 7,

$$\mathrm{Prod}(L_1) = (m - 3) + 2 + 1 = m,$$
$$\mathrm{Prod}(L_2) = ((k - 6) + (n - k + 3)) + 2 + 1 = n,$$
$$\mathrm{Prod}(L_1 \cup L_2) = \mathrm{Prod}(\{a^{2^i} \mid 1 \leq i \leq k - 6\} \cup \{b\}^+ \cup \{c\}^+)$$
$$= (k - 6) + (2 + 2 + 2) = k.$$

 iii) The cases $k$ with $6 \leq k \leq n + m + 2$ can be taken from the constructions given in ii).

$m = 6$ and $k = 5$. We consider the languages $L_1 = R_3 \cup \{b, c\}$ and $L_2 = R(1, n)$. By Lemmas 1, 4, 5, and 7, we get

$$\mathrm{Prod}(L_1) = 3 + 2 + 1 = 6, \ \mathrm{Prod}(L_2) = n, \ \text{and}$$
$$\mathrm{Prod}(L_1 \cup L_2) = \mathrm{Prod}(\{a\}^* \cup \{b, c\}) = 2 + 2 + 1 = 5.$$

$m = 6$ and $k = 4$. Using $L_1 = R_4 \cup \{b\}$ and $L_2 = R(1, n)$, we get as above

$$\mathrm{Prod}(L_1) = 4 + 1 + 1 = 6, \ \mathrm{Prod}(L_2) = n, \ \text{and}$$
$$\mathrm{Prod}(L_1 \cup L_2) = \mathrm{Prod}(\{a\}^* \cup \{b\}) = 2 + 1 + 1 = 4.$$

$m = 5$ and $k = 5$. We give the proof for the more general situation $3 \le m \le k$. Let $a$ and $b$ be different letters and

$$L_1 = \{a^{2^i} \mid 1 \le i \le m - 3\} \cup \{b^r \mid 1 \le r \le 2^{n-k+3}\} \quad \text{and}$$
$$L_2 = \{a^{2^i} \mid 1 \le i \le k - 3\} \cup \{b^{2^j} \mid 1 \le j \le n - k + 3\}.$$

Then we obtain by Lemmas 1, 3, 4, and 7,

$$\mathrm{Prod}(L_1) = (m - 3) + 3 = m,$$
$$\mathrm{Prod}(L_2) = (k - 3) + (n - k + 3) = n,$$
$$\mathrm{Prod}(L_1 \cup L_2) = \mathrm{Prod}(\{a^{2^i} \mid 1 \le i \le k - 3\} \cup \{b^r \mid 1 \le r \le 2^{n-k+3}\}$$
$$= (k - 3) + 3 = k.$$

$m = 5$ and $k = 4$. We repeat the proof for $m = 6$ and $k = 5$ with $L_1 = R_3 \cup \{b\}$.

iv) The cases $k$ with $4 \le k \le m + n + 2$ can be shown analogously to the above proofs. It remains to show that $2 \in g_\cup(4, n)$.

By Lemmas 1, 4, and 5, we have $\mathrm{Prod}(R_4) = 4$, $\mathrm{Prod}(R(1,n)) = n$, and $\mathrm{Prod}(R_4 \cup R(1,n)) = Prod(\{a\}^+) = 2$.

v) Let $m = 3$. The cases $k$ with $3 \le k \le m + n + 2$ can be shown analogously to the above proofs. Because we have $\mathrm{Prod}(R_3) = 3$, $\mathrm{Prod}(R(1,n)) = n$, and $\mathrm{Prod}(R_3 \cup R(1,n)) = Prod(\{a\}^+) = 2$, we also have $2 \in g_\cup(3, n)$.

Now let $m = 2$. For $k \ge n$, we take the constructions as above.
For $k$ with $4 \le k \le n$, we take

$$L_1 = \{b\}^+ \text{ and } L_2 = \{a^{2^i} \mid 1 \le i \le k - 3\} \cup \{b^{2^j} \mid 1 \le j \le n - k + 3\},$$

which satisfy $\mathrm{Prod}(L_1) = 2$ by Lemma 3, $\mathrm{Prod}(L_2) = n$ by Lemmas 4 and 7, and $\mathrm{Prod}(L_1 \cup L_2) = \mathrm{Prod}(\{b\}^* \cup \{a^{2^i} \mid 1 \le i \le k - 3\}) = k$ by Lemma 7.

For $k = 3$, we take $L_1 = \{a^i \mid i \ge 4\}$ and $L_2 = R'(1, n)$. Then $\mathrm{Prod}(L_1) = 2$ and $\mathrm{Prod}(L_2) = n$ by Lemmas 1 and 4. Moreover, $L_1 \cup L_2 = R_3$ and thus $\mathrm{Prod}(L_1 \cup L_2) = 3$ by Lemma 5.

For $k = 2$, let $L_1 = \{a\}^+$ and $L_2 = R(1, n)$. Then we have $\mathrm{Prod}(L_1) = 2$, $\mathrm{Prod}(L_2) = n$, and $\mathrm{Prod}(L_1 \cup L_2) = 2$ by Lemmas 3 and 4.    $\square$

**Theorem 3.** *i) For all numbers $n$ with $n \ge 2$, the number 1 and all numbers $k$ with $k > n + 2$ are not in $g_\cup(1, n)$.*

*ii) For $n \ge 2$, we have $\{k \mid n \le k \le n + 2\} \subseteq g_\cup(1, n)$. For $n \ge 5$ and $n \ge 6$, the relations $n - 1 \in g_\cup(1, n)$ and $n - 2 \in g_\cup(1, n)$ hold, respectively. Moreover, we have $g_\cup(1, 1) = \{1, 2\}$.*    $\square$

We now turn to concatenation.

**Theorem 4.** *i) For any natural numbers $m$ and $n$ with $1 \le m \le n$, all numbers $k$ with $k > n + m + 1$ are not contained in $g.(m, n)$. If $n \ge 2$, then $1 \notin g.(m, n)$.*

*ii) For any natural numbers $m \ge 1$ and $n \ge 2$, we have $n + m + 1 \in g.(m, n)$.*

*iii) For any natural numbers $m \geq 2$ and $n \geq 3$, we have $n + m \in g.(m, n)$.*

*iv) For any natural numbers $m \geq 3$ and $n \geq 3$, we have $n + m - 1 \in g.(m, n)$.*

*v) For any natural numbers $m \geq 5$ and $n \geq 5$, the relation $\{k \mid n + 2 \leq k \leq m + n - 2\} \subseteq g.(m, n)$ holds.*

*vi) Let $m \in \{2, 3, 4\}$. Then $2 \in g.(m, n)$. If, in addition, $n \geq 7$, then we have $\{4, 5, \ldots, n - 3\} \subseteq g.(m, n)$.*

*Proof.* i) can be shown as statement i) of Theorem 2. We only give the proof for ii), iii), and v).

ii) If $n = 1$, we take $L_1 = \{d\}$ and $L_2 = R_1(m-1)$. Then we get $\mathrm{Prod}(L_1 \cdot L_2) = \mathrm{Prod}((L_1 \cdot L_2)^R) = 1 + m + 1$ by Lemma 2.

If $n \geq 2$, we set

$$L_1 = R_1(m - 1) \text{ and } L_2 = \{d^r y e^r \mid r \geq 0, y \in \{f_1, f_2, \ldots, f_{n-1}\}\}.$$

Obviously, $L_2$ can be obtained from $R_1(m - 1)$ by renaming of the letters. By Lemma 2, we get $\mathrm{Prod}(L_1) = m$ and $\mathrm{Prod}(L_2) = n$.

We now prove that $\mathrm{Prod}(L_1 \cdot L_2) = n + m + 1$. Let $G = (N, T, P, S)$ be a grammar with $L(G) = L_1 \cdot L_2$ and $\mathrm{Prod}(G) = \mathrm{Prod}(L_1 \cdot L_2)$. Obviously, $T = \{a, b, d, e, c_1, c_2, \ldots, c_{m-1}, f_1, f_2, \ldots, f_{n-1}\}$.

We consider the words $w = a^r c_i b^r f_1$ and $w' = c_1 d^r f_j e^r$ of $L_1 \cdot L_2$ for a sufficiently large number $r$, $1 \leq i \leq m - 1$ and $1 \leq j \leq n - 1$. As in the proof of Lemma 2 iii), we can show that there are rules

- $A_i \to y c_i y' \in P$ with $y \in (N \cup \{a\})^*$ and $y' \in (N \cup \{b\})^*$ and
- $C \to g \in P$, $g \in (\{a, b\} \cup N)^*$ and $\#_{\{a,b\}}(g) \geq 1$,
- $D_j \to p_j f_j p'_j$ with $p_j \in (\{d\} \cup N)^*$ and $p'_j \in (\{e\} \cup N)^*$,
- $E \to k \in (\{d, e\} \cup N)^*$ with $\#_{\{d,e\}}(k) \geq 1$.

The letter $S$ is different from all the letters $A_i, C, D_j, E$, $1 \leq i \leq n - 1$, $1 \leq j \leq m - 1$. We only give the proof for $A_i$, for the other letters the statement follows analogously. If $S = A_i$, we have a derivation (see proof of Lemma 2 iii))

$$S \Longrightarrow^* u'u^s A v^s v' \Longrightarrow^* u'u^s x A_i x' v^s v' = u'u^s x S x' v^s v' \Longrightarrow^* u'u^s x c_1 f_1 x' v^s v'$$

because $S \Longrightarrow^* c_1 f_1$ is a valid derivation in $G$. However, because $u \in \{a\}^+$ and $v \in \{b\}^+$, the generated word does not belong to $L_1 \cdot L_2$ in contrast to $L(G) = L_1 \cdot L_2$.

Thus we require an additional rule for $S$. Altogether, we have at least $m + n + 1$ rules in $G$, which results in $\mathrm{Prod}(L_1 \cdot L_2) \geq n + m + 1$.

On the other hand, the grammar with axiom $S$ and the rules

$$S \to AB, \ A \to aAb, \ B \to dBe, \ A \to c_i, 1 \leq i \leq m - 1, \ B \to f_j, 1 \leq j \leq n - 1$$

generates $L_1 \cup L_2$, which implies $\mathrm{Prod}(L_1 \cup L_2) \leq m + n + 1$.

Combining the relations, we have $\mathrm{Prod}(L_1 \cup L_2) = m + n + 1$.

iii) We take

$$L_1 = R_1(m - 2)\{c\} \text{ and } L_2 = \{d^n x e^n \mid n \geq 0, x \in \{f_1, f_2, \ldots, f_{n-1}\}\}.$$

Then $\mathrm{Prod}(L_1) = m$ and $\mathrm{Prod}(L_2) = n$ by Lemma 2.

Let $G$ be a grammar such that $L(G) = L_1 \cdot L_2$ and $\mathrm{Prod}(G) = \mathrm{Prod}(L_1 \cdot L_2)$. As in i) we can show that, for the generation of $L_1 \cdot L_2$, we need rules

- $A_i \to y c_i y' \in P$, $y \in (N \cup \{a\})^*$ and $y' \in (N \cup \{b\})^*$, $1 \le i \le m-2$,
- $C \to g \in P$, $g \in (\{a,b\} \cup N)^*$ and $\#_{\{a,b\}}(g) \ge 1$,
- $D_j \to p_j f_j p'_j$ with $p_j \in (\{d\} \cup N)^*$ and $p'_j \in (\{e\} \cup N)^*$, $1 \le j \le n-1$,
- $E \to k \in (\{d,e\} \cup N)\}^*$ with $\#_{\{d,e\}}(k) \ge 1$,
- and an additional rule for the axiom $S$.

Hence we need at least $(m-2)+1+(n-1)+1+1 = m+n$ rules. On the other hand, the grammar with axiom $S$ and the rules

$$S \to AcB, \ A \to aAb, \ B \to dBe, \ A \to c_i, 1 \le i \le m-2, \ B \to f_j, 1 \le j \le n-1$$

generates $L_1 \cdot L_2$ and thus $m+n$ rules are sufficient, too.

iv) We take

$$L_1 = R_1(m-2)\{c\} \text{ and } L_2 = \{d^r x e^r \mid r \ge 0, x \in \{f_1, f_2, \ldots, f_{n-2}\}\}\{f\}.$$

By Lemma 2, $\mathrm{Prod}(L_1) = m$ and $\mathrm{Prod}(L_2) = n$.

Let $G$ be a grammar such that $L(G) = L_1 \cdot L_2$ and $\mathrm{Prod}(G) = \mathrm{Prod}(L_1 \cdot L_2)$. Again, we need $m-2$ rules for the generation of the $c_i$, $1 \le i \le m-2$, one rule for the generation of words containing an arbitrary number of $a$s or $b$s, $n-2$ rules for the generation of the $f_j$, $1 \le j \le n-2$, one rule for the generation of words containing an arbitrary number of $d$s or $e$s, and a rule for the axiom. Hence $\mathrm{Prod}(L_1 \cdot L_2) \ge m+n-1$.

The grammar with axiom $S$ and the rules

$$S \to AcBf, \ A \to aAb, \ B \to dBe, \ A \to c_i, 1 \le i \le m-2, \ B \to f_j, 1 \le j \le n-2$$

generates $L_1 \cdot L_2$. Therefore $\mathrm{Prod}(L_1 \cdot L_2) \le m+n-1$.

v) Let $5 \le m \le n$. We choose a number $x$ such that $2 \le x \le m-3$. Let

$$a, b, d, e, p, q, c_1, c_2, \ldots, c_{m-x-2}, f_1, f_2, \ldots f_{n-x-2}, g_1, g_2 \ldots, g_{x-1}$$

be pairwise different letters. Then we set

$$\begin{aligned} Q &= \{p^r g_k q^r \mid r \ge 0, 1 \le k \le x-1\}, \\ L_1 &= R_1(m-x-2)Q, \text{ and} \\ L_2 &= \{d^r f_j e^r \mid r \ge 0, 1 \le j \le n-x-2\}Q. \end{aligned}$$

By part i), we get

$$\mathrm{Prod}(L_1) = (m-x-1)+x+1 = m \text{ and } \mathrm{Prod}(L_2) = (n-x-1)+x+1 = n.$$

Let $G$ be a grammar such that $L(G) = L_1 \cdot L_2$ and $\mathrm{Prod}(G) = \mathrm{Prod}(L_1 \cdot L_2)$. As in the proof of Lemma 2 iii), we can show that we need $m-x-1$ rules for the generation of words with $c_i$, $1 \le i \le m-x-2$, one rule for the generation of words containing arbitrarily many letters $a$ or $b$, $n - x - 2$ rules for the generation of words with $f_j$, one rule for the generation of words containing arbitrarily many letters $d$ or $e$, and $x - 1$ rules for the generation of words with $g_k$, $1 \leq k \leq x - 1$, one rule for the generation of words containing arbitrarily many letters $p$ or $q$, and an additional rule for the axiom. Thus $\text{Prod}(L_1 \cdot L_2) \geq (m - x - 2) + 1 + (n - x - 2) + 1 + x - 1 + 1 + 1 = m + n - x - 1$.

Since the grammar with the rules

$$S \to ACBC, \ A \to aAb, \ B \to dBe, \ C \to pCq, A \to c_i, 1 \leq i \leq m - x - 1,$$
$$B \to f_j, 1 \leq j \leq n - x - 1, \ C \to g_k, 1 \leq k \leq x - 1$$

generates $L_1 \cdot L_2$, we obtain $\text{Prod}(L_1 \cdot L_2) \leq 4 + (m - x - 2) + (n - x - 2) + (x - 1) = m + n - x - 1$.

By our choice of $x$, $2 \leq x \leq m - 2$, we can cover all the values given in the statement.

vi) Let $m = 2$ and $m \leq n$. We consider $L_1 = \{c\}^+$ and $L_2 = \{c^j \mid 0 \leq j \leq n - 1\}$. Then $L_1 \cdot L_2 = \{c^i \mid i \geq 2\}$. By Lemmas 1, 4, and 5, we obtain $\text{Prod}(L_1) = 2$, $\text{Prod}(L_2) = n$, and $\text{Prod}(L_1 \cdot L_2) = 2$

Let $m = 2$, $4 \leq k$ and $k + 3 \leq n$. We consider

$$L_1 = \{c\}^+ \text{ and } L_2 = \{c^i \mid 0 \leq i \leq n - k - 3\} R_1(k - 3).$$

Obviously, $L_1 \cdot L_2 = \{c^i \mid i \geq 2\} R_1(k - 2)$.

By Lemma 1, $\text{Prod}(L_1) = 2$.

We now prove that $\text{Prod}(L_2) = n$. Let $G = (N, T, P, S)$ be a context-free grammar with $L(G) = L_2$ and $\text{Prod}(G) = \text{Prod}(L_2)$. As in the preceding proofs, we get the existence of rules $A_i \to y_i$ with $y_i \in (N \cup \{c_i, a, b\})^+$ and $\#_{c_i}(y_i) = 1$, $1 \leq i \leq k - 3$ and a rule $B \to x$ with $x \in (N \cup \{a, b\})^+$. Moreover, $B$ occurs in the derivation $A \Longrightarrow^* a^s Ab^s$ for some $s > 0$ and the nonterminals $A_i$ occur in derivations $A \Longrightarrow^* a^{r_i} c_i b^{s_i}$ with $r_i, s_i \geq 0$. Thus there are no derivation starting in $B$ or $A_i$ which produce a word containing $c$ (otherwise, for $B$, we would have derivations $S \Longrightarrow^* cuAv \Longrightarrow^* cuA^{st} Ab^{st} v \Longrightarrow cxBy \Longrightarrow^* cxzy$ with $\#_a(x) \geq 1$, $\#_b(y) \geq 1$, and $\#_c(z) \geq 1$ which is impossible for words in $L_2$).

We construct the grammar $G'$ as follows: we cancel all rules for $B$ and $A_i$, $1 \leq i \leq k - 3$. In the remaining rules we replace all occurrences of $a, b, B, c_i$ and $A_i$, $1 \leq i \leq k - 3$, in right hand sides by $\lambda$. Obviously, $L(G') = \{c^i \mid 0 \leq i \leq n - k - 3\}$. Hence $G'$ has at least $n - k - 2$ rules. Consequently, $G$ has at least $(n - k - 2) + (k - 2) = n$ rules. Therefore $\text{Prod}(L_2) \geq n$.

The grammar

$$(\{S, A\}, \{a, b, c\} \cup \{c_i \mid 1 \leq i \leq k - 3\}, Q, S)$$

with

$$Q = \{S \to c^j A \mid 0 \leq j \leq n - k - 3\} \cup \{A \to aAb\} \cup \{A \to c_i \mid 1 \leq i \leq k - 3\}$$

generates $L_2$ with $n$ rules. Hence $\text{Prod}(L_2) = n$.

Analogously we can prove that the generation of $\{c^i \mid c \geq 2\}R_1(k-2)$ requires at least $2 + (k - 2)$ (the first summand 2, because we need two rules for the generation of $\{c^i \mid c \geq 2\}$ by the grammar $G'$, and $k - 2$ rules for $cR_1(k-3)$, and it can be generated by

$$(\{S, A\}, \{a, b, c\} \cup \{c_i \mid 1 \leq i \leq k - 3\}, Q', S)$$

with

$$Q' = \{S \to cS, S \to c^2A, A \to aAb\} \cup \{A \to c_i \mid 1 \leq i \leq k - 3\}.$$

Thus $\mathrm{Prod}(L_1 \cdot L_2) = k$.

The proof for $m = 3$ and $m = 4$ can be given analogously using

$$L_1 = \{c\} \cup \{c^j \mid j \geq 3\} \text{ and } L_1 = \{c, c^2, c^3\} \cup \{c^j \mid j \geq 5\},$$

respectively, instead of $L_1 = \{c\}^+$.  □

Finally, we discuss the behaviour under Kleene closure.

**Theorem 5.** *i) For any $n \geq 2$, we have $g_*(n) = \{k \mid 2 \leq k \leq n + 2\}$.*
*ii) The equality $g_*(1) = \{1, 2\}$ holds.*

*Proof.* i) By the standard construction for the closure of context-free grammars under Kleene closure, one gets immediately that $\mathrm{Prod}(L^*) \leq \mathrm{Prod}(L) + 2$. Hence $g_*(n)$ cannot contain numbers which are strictly larger than $n + 2$. Since $n \geq 2$, any language $L$ with $\mathrm{Prod}(L) = n$ has at least two words. Hence its Kleene closure $L^*$ also contains at least two words (more precisely, $L^*$ is infinite). Thus, by Lemma 1 i), $\mathrm{Prod}(L^*) \geq 2$, too, i.e., $1 \notin g_*(n)$.

We now prove that the remaining cases can occur.

$k = n + 2$. The assertion follows from Lemma 2 by consideration of $R_1(n-1)$.

$k$ with $3 \leq k \leq n + 1$. Let $L = R_2(k-2) \cup R(0, n-k+1)$. Since $R_2(k-2)$ and $R(0, n-k+1)$ are finite, they are languages without initial loops. Therefore, by Lemmas 3, 4, and 7, we obtain $\mathrm{Prod}(L) = (k - 2) + (n - k + 2) = n$. Because $L^* = \{a, a_1, a_2, \ldots, a_{k-2}\}^*$, we get $\mathrm{Prod}(L^*) = k$ by Lemma 3.

$k = 2$. By Lemma 4, we have $\mathrm{Prod}(R(1, n)) = n$. Moreover, $\mathrm{Prod}(R(1, n)^*) = \mathrm{Prod}(\{a\}^*) = 2$ by Lemma 3.

ii) If $L$ is a language with $\mathrm{Prod}(L) = 1$, then $L = \{w\}$ for some $w$. If $w = \lambda$, then $L^* = \{\lambda\}$ and $\mathrm{Prod}(L^*) = 1$. If $w \neq \lambda$, then $L^* = \{\lambda, w, w^2, w^3, \ldots\}$, and $L^*$ is generated by the grammar with the two rules $S \to wS$ and $S \to \lambda$.  □

## 4  Conclusion

In this paper we have studied the sets $g_\tau(m_1, m_2, \ldots, m_n)$ for union, concatenation, Kleene closure and reversal. With respect to reversal and Kleene closure the results are complete, i.e., we have determined the sets $g_R(n)$ and $g_*(n)$ for all numbers $n \geq 1$. Concerning union, we have determined the sets

$g_\cup(2,n)$ and $g_\cup(3,n)$ for all values $n$. For $m \geq 4$, we know that all numbers $k$ with $6 \leq k \leq n+m+2$ are in $g_\cup(m,n)$, but we do not know whether some small numbers are in $g_\cup(m,n)$. More precisely, it is open whether $3 \in g_\cup(4,n)$, $2,3 \in g_\cup(m,n)$ for $m \in \{5,6\}$, and $2,3,4,5 \in g_\cup(m,n)$ for $m \geq 7$. Moreover, we do not know whether $k \in g_\cup(1,n)$ for $k \in \{2,3,\ldots,n-3\}$. With respect to the concatenation, we have presented an almost complete result for $m \in \{2,3,4\}$ and $n \geq 7$ (we only left open whether $3, n-2, n-1, n, n+1 \in g.(m,n)$); for other values of $m$, only numbers larger than the maximal argument are obtained. This corresponds to the situation for the nonterminal complexity.

In order to obtain the results, in most cases, we have used languages over alphabets which have a cardinality depending on $m$ and $n$. It remains to investigate whether all results hold over alphabets with bounded cardinality.

As we already mentioned in the Introduction, most result on regular language and state complexity, nondeterministic state complexity and transition complexity concern only the maximal value which can be obtained by application of operations to languages with a given complexity. Thus it is of interest, for an $n$-ary operation $\tau$ under which the family of context-free languages is closed, to study the function $f_\tau : \mathbb{N}^n \to \mathbb{N}$ defined by

$$f_\tau(m_1, m_2, \ldots, m_n) = \max g_\tau(m_1, m_2, \ldots, m_n).$$

From the constructions/proofs of the preceding section, we get immediately the following result.

**Theorem 6.** *i) If $m \geq 2$ and $n \geq 2$, then $f_\cup(m,n) = m+n+2$. If $n \geq 2$, then $f_\cup(1,n) = f_\cup(n,1) = n+2$. Furthermore, we have $f_\cup(1,1) = 2$.*

*ii) If $m \geq 2$ and $n \geq 2$, then $f.(m,n) = m+n+1$. If $n \geq 2$, then $f.(1,n) = f.(n,1) = n+1$. Furthermore, we have $f.(1,1) = 1$.*

*iii) If $n \geq 2$, then $f_*(n) = n+2$. Furthermore, we have $f_*(1) = 2$.*

*iv) For $n \geq 1$, the equality $f_R(n) = n$ holds.* $\qquad \square$

Again, it remains open whether the statements of Theorem 6 are valid for languages over alphabets with bounded size.

Besides the nonterminal complexity (where the behaviour under operations is studied in [2]) and the production complexity, the total number of symbols is a further well investigated measure of descriptional complexity for context-free grammars and languages. In the dissertation [9], the behaviour under operations with respect to the total number of symbols is also investigated.

# References

1. Câmpeanu, C., Culik, K., Salomaa, K., Yu, S.: State Complexity of Basic Operations on Finite Languages. In: Boldt, O., Jürgensen, H. (eds.) WIA 1999. LNCS, vol. 2214, pp. 60–70. Springer, Heidelberg (2001)
2. Dassow, J., Stiebe, R.: Nonterminal Complexity of Some Operations on Context-Free Languages. Fundamenta Informaticae 83, 35–49 (2008)

3. Domaratzki, M., Salomaa, K.: Transition complexity of language operations. In: Proc. Intern. Workshop Descriptional Complexity of Formal Systems 2006, New Mexico State Univ. Las Cruces, pp. 141–152 (2006)
4. Ellul, K.: Descriptional complexity measures of regular languages. Master Thesis, University of Waterloo (2002)
5. Gruska, J.: Some classifications of context-free languages. Information and Control 14, 152–179 (1969)
6. Gruska, J.: Generation and approximation of finite and infinite languages. In: Internat. Symp. Summer School Math. Found. Comp. Sci., Warsaw, pp. 1–7 (1972)
7. Gruska, J.: On the size of context-free grammars. Kybernetika 8, 213–218 (1972)
8. Gruska, J.: Descriptional complexity of context-free languages. In: Proc. Math. Found. Comp. Sci., Strebske Pleso, pp. 71–83 (1973)
9. Harbich, R.: Beschreibungskomplexität kontextfreier Sprachen bezüglich der AFL-Operationen. Dissertation, Otto-von-Guericke-Universität Magdeburg, Fakultät für Informatik (2012)
10. Holzer, M., Kutrib, M.: Nondeterministic descriptional complexity of regular languages. Intern. J. Found. Comp. Sci. 14, 1087–1102 (2003)
11. Jirásek, J., Jirásková, G., Szabari, A.: State Complexity of Concatenation and Complementation of Regular Languages. In: Domaratzki, M., Okhotin, A., Salomaa, K., Yu, S. (eds.) CIAA 2004. LNCS, vol. 3317, pp. 178–189. Springer, Heidelberg (2005)
12. Jiraskova, G., Okhotin, A.: State Complexity of cyclic shift. In: Proc. Descriptional Complexity of Formal Systems, Univ. Milano, pp. 182–193 (2005)
13. Păun, G.: On the smallest number of nonterminals required to generate a context-free language. Mathematica 18, 203–208 (1976)
14. Rozenberg, G., Salomaa, A. (eds.): Handbook of Formal Languages, vol. I–III. Springer (1997)
15. Yu, S.: State complexity of regular languages. J. Automata, Languages and Combinatorics 6, 221–234 (2001)
16. Yu, S.: State complexity of finite and infinite regular languages. Bulletin of the EATCS 76, 142–152 (2002)
17. Yu, S., Zhuang, Q., Salomaa, K.: The state complexity of some basic operations on regular languages. Theor. Comp. Sci. 125, 315–328 (1994)

# State Complexity of Star and Square of Union of $k$ Regular Languages*

Yuan Gao and Lila Kari

Department of Computer Science, The University of Western Ontario,
London, Ontario, Canada N6A 5B7
{ygao72,lila}@csd.uwo.ca

**Abstract.** In this paper, we study the state complexities of $(\bigcup_{i=1}^{k} L_i)^*$ and $(\bigcup_{i=1}^{k} L_i)^2$, where $L_i$, $1 \leq i \leq k$, $k \geq 2$ are regular languages. We obtain exact bounds for both of these multiple combined operations and show that they are much lower than the mathematical compositions of the state complexities of their basic individual component operations, but have similar forms with the state complexities of some participating combined operations.

*In Memory of Dr. Sheng Yu*

## 1 Introduction

State complexity is a fundamental topic in automata theory and its study dates back to the 1950's [16]. State complexity is a type of descriptional complexity for regular languages based on the number of states in their minimal finite automata. The state complexity of a language operation gives an upper bound for both the time and space complexity of the operation [20]. The study of state complexity is motivated by the use of automata of very large sizes in multiple areas, e.g. programming languages, natural language and speech processing, and so on.

Many papers on state complexity appeared in the literature, see, e.g., [4–6, 10, 12, 14, 15, 20, 21]. The state complexities of almost all the individual standard regular language operations, e.g., union, intersection, catenation, star, reversal, shuffle, orthogonal catenation, proportional removal, and cyclic shift, etc., have been obtained.

In practice, not only a single operation, but also a sequence of operations can be applied in some specific order. For example, primer extension, which is a basic biological operation, can be formalized as a combination of catenation and antimorphic involution [1]. Therefore, in the mid of 2000s, the study of state complexity of combined operations was initiated [18, 22]. Following that, many results on this topic were obtained, e.g., [2, 3, 7–9, 13].

---

* This research was supported by Natural Science and Engineering Council of Canada Discovery Grant R2824A01, Canada Research Chair Award to L. K.

M. Kutrib, N. Moreira, and R. Reis (Eds.): DCFS 2012, LNCS 7386, pp. 155–168, 2012.

A theoretical reason for studying the state complexity of combined operations is that, given an arbitrary combined operation, we cannot use the mathematical composition of the state complexities of its individual component operations as its state complexity. The state complexity of a combined operation can be much lower than the aforementioned composition, because the resulting languages of one individual operation may not be among the worst case inputs of the next operation [13, 18]. An often used example for this phenomenon is $(L_1 \cup L_2)^*$, where $L_1$ and $L_2$ are regular languages accepted by $n_1$- and $n_2$-state DFAs, respectively. In [18], the state complexity of the combined operation $(L_1 \cup L_2)^*$ was proved to be $2^{n_1+n_2-1} - 2^{n_1-1} - 2^{n_1-1} + 1$, whereas the mathematical composition of the state complexities of union and star is $\frac{3}{4}2^{n_1n_2}$.

It has been proved that there does not exist a general algorithm that, for an arbitrarily given combined operation and a class of regular languages, computes the state complexity of the operation on this class of languages [19]. It seems that every combined operation must be investigated separately. However, the number of combined operations is obviously unlimited, and it is impossible to investigate all of them. Thus, the combined operations with arbitrarily many individual operations should be the emphasis of theoretical studies because they are more general than the basic combined operations which are composed of only a limited number of individual operations. The latter can indeed be viewed as the special cases of the former.

In this paper, we study such two general combined operations: $(\bigcup_{i=1}^{k} L_i)^*$ and $(\bigcup_{i=1}^{k} L_i)^2$, where $L_i$, $1 \leq i \leq k$, $k \geq 2$ are regular languages. Clearly, the combined operation $(L_1 \cup L_2)^*$ is an instance of $(\bigcup_{i=1}^{k} L_i)^*$. We show that the state complexity of star of union on $k$ regular languages is not only much lower than the mathematical composition of the state complexities of union and star, but also in a similar form with the state complexity of $(L_1 \cup L_2)^*$.

We obtain tight bounds for $(\bigcup_{i=1}^{k} L_i)^2$ as well. One interesting thing is, when we investigated this combined operation, we found that it could be considered as a combination of (1) union and square, or (2) union-catenation $((L_1 \cup L_2)L_3)$ and union, or (3) union and catenation-union $(L_1(L_2 \cup L_3))$. Finally, the tight upper bound was obtained with the last combination which has a similar form with the state complexity of $L_1(L_2 \cup L_3)$. It seems that decomposing a combined operation into its participating combined operations can give better upper bounds than the mathematical composition of the state complexities of its individual component operations.

In the next section, we introduce the basic notation and definitions used in this paper. In Sections 3 and 4, we investigate the state complexities of $(\bigcup_{i=1}^{k} L_i)^*$ and $(\bigcup_{i=1}^{k} L_i)^2$, respectively.

## 2    Preliminaries

A DFA is denoted by a 5-tuple $A = (Q, \Sigma, \delta, s, F)$, where $Q$ is the finite set of states, $\Sigma$ is the finite input alphabet, $\delta : Q \times \Sigma \to Q$ is the state transition function, $s \in Q$ is the initial state, and $F \subseteq Q$ is the set of final states. A DFA is said to be complete if $\delta(q, a)$ is defined for all $q \in Q$ and $a \in \Sigma$. All the DFAs we mention in this paper are assumed to be complete. We extend $\delta$ to $Q \times \Sigma^* \to Q$ in the usual way.

In this paper, the state transition function $\delta$ of a DFA is often extended to $\hat{\delta} : 2^Q \times \Sigma \to 2^Q$. The function $\hat{\delta}$ is defined by $\hat{\delta}(R, a) = \{\delta(r, a) \mid r \in R\}$, for $R \subseteq Q$ and $a \in \Sigma$. We just write $\delta$ instead of $\hat{\delta}$ if there is no confusion.

A string $w \in \Sigma^*$ is accepted by a DFA if $\delta(s, w) \in F$. Two states in a DFA $A$ are said to be *equivalent* if and only if for every string $w \in \Sigma^*$, if $A$ is started in either state with $w$ as input, it either accepts in both cases or rejects in both cases. A language accepted by a DFA is said to be *regular*. The language accepted by a DFA $A$ is denoted by $L(A)$. The reader may refer to [11] for more details about regular languages and finite automata.

The *state complexity* of a regular language $L$, denoted by $sc(L)$, is the number of states of the minimal complete DFA that accepts $L$. The state complexity of a class $S$ of regular languages, denoted by $sc(S)$, is the supremum among all $sc(L)$, $L \in S$. The state complexity of an operation on regular languages is the state complexity of the resulting languages from the operation as a function of the state complexity of the operand languages. Thus, in a certain sense, the state complexity of an operation is a worst-case complexity.

## 3    State Complexity of $(\bigcup\limits_{i=1}^{k} L_i)^*$

We first consider the state complexity of $(\bigcup\limits_{i=1}^{k} L_i)^*$, where $L_i$, $1 \le i \le k$, $k \ge 2$ are regular languages accepted by $n_i$-state DFAs. It has been proved that the state complexity of $L_i^*$ is $\frac{3}{4}2^{n_i}$ and the state complexity of $L_i \cup L_j$ is $n_i n_j$ [14, 21].

Their mathematical composition for the combined operation $(\bigcup\limits_{i=1}^{k} L_i)^*$ is $\frac{3}{4}2^{\prod\limits_{i=1}^{k} n_i}$.

As we mentioned in Section 1, this upper bound is too high to be reached even when $k = 2$, that is, $(L_1 \cup L_2)^*$ [18]. The combined operation $(L_1 \cup L_2)^*$ can be viewed as not only a base case of $(\bigcup\limits_{i=1}^{k} L_i)^*$ when $k = 2$, but also its participating combined operation.

In the following, we show that the state complexity of $(\bigcup\limits_{i=1}^{k} L_i)^*$ has a similar form with that of $(L_1 \cup L_2)^*$. Note that although these two state complexities look similar, the proofs for the general case $k \ge 2$ is very different from those for $k = 2$, especially the proof for the highest lower bound. This is because, when $k$

is arbitrarily many, a lot more questions need to be considered which are easy to solve or do not exist for the case with only two operand languages, e.g., how to update the $i$th component of a state of the resulting DFA without interfering with the other $k-1$ components, and so on.

**Theorem 1.** *Let* $L_i$, $1 \leq i \leq k$, $k \geq 2$ *be regular languages accepted by* $n_i$-*state DFAs. Then* $(\bigcup\limits_{i=1}^{k} L_i)^*$ *is accepted by a DFA of no more than*

$$\prod_{i=1}^{k}(2^{n_i-1}-1) + 2^{\sum\limits_{j=1}^{k} n_j - k}$$

*states.*

*Proof.* For $1 \leq i \leq k$, let $L_i = L(A_i)$ and $A_i = (Q_i, \Sigma, \delta_i, s_i, F_i)$ be a DFA of $n_i$ states. Without loss of generality, we assume that the state sets of $A_1$, $A_2$, ..., $A_k$ are disjoint. We construct a DFA $A = (Q, \Sigma, \delta, s, F)$ to accept the language $(\bigcup\limits_{i=1}^{k} L_i)^*$ similarly with [18]. We define $Q$ to be $Q = \{s\} \cup P \cup R$ where

$$P = \{\langle P_1, P_2, \ldots, P_k \rangle \mid P_i \subseteq Q_i - F_i, P_i \neq \emptyset, 1 \leq i \leq k\},$$

$$R = \{\langle R_1, R_2, \ldots, R_k \rangle \mid (\bigcup_{j=1}^{k} R_j) \cap (\bigcup_{h=1}^{k} F_h) \neq \emptyset, s_i \in R_i \subseteq Q_i, 1 \leq i \leq k\}.$$

If $s_i \notin F_i$ for every DFA $A_i$, $1 \leq i \leq k$, the initial state $s$ of the DFA $A$ is then a new symbol, because the empty word is not in the language $\bigcup\limits_{i=1}^{k} L_i$. If there exists an $i$ such that $s_i \in F_i$, we choose $s = \langle s_1, s_2, \ldots, s_k \rangle$ to be the initial state of $A$. In this case, $s$ is clearly contained in the set $R$. Note that the sets $P$ and $R$ are always disjoint.

We define the set of final states $F$ to be $R \cup \{s\}$. The transition function $\delta$ of the DFA $A$ is defined as follows.

For each letter $a \in \Sigma$,

$$\delta(s, a) = \begin{cases} \langle \{\delta_1(s_1, a)\}, \ldots, \{\delta_k(s_k, a)\} \rangle, & \text{if } \delta_i(s_i, a) \notin F_i \text{ for all } 1 \leq i \leq k; \\ \langle \{\delta_1(s_1, a)\} \cup \{s_1\}, \ldots, \{\delta_k(s_k, a)\} \cup \{s_k\} \rangle, & \text{otherwise,} \end{cases}$$

and for each state $p = \langle P_1, P_2, \ldots, P_k \rangle \in Q - \{s\}$,

$$\delta(p, a) = \begin{cases} \langle \delta_1(P_1, a), \ldots, \delta_k(P_k, a) \rangle, & \text{if } \delta_i(P_i, a) \cap F_i = \emptyset \text{ for all } 1 \leq i \leq k; \\ \langle \delta_1(P_1, a) \cup \{s_1\}, \ldots, \delta_k(P_k, a) \cup \{s_k\} \rangle, & \text{otherwise.} \end{cases}$$

The DFA $A$ can simulate the computation of the DFAs $A_1$, $A_2$, ..., $A_k$ and when one of them enter a final state, the initial states $s_1$, $s_2$, ..., $s_k$ are added. It is easy to see that $L(A) = (\bigcup\limits_{i=1}^{k} L(A_i))^*$.

Now let us count the number of states of $A$ which is an upper bound of the state complexity of the combined operation $(\bigcup_{i=1}^{k} L_i)^*$.

For the DFAs $A_1$, $A_2$, ..., $A_k$, denote $|F_i|$ by $t_i$. The resulting language

$$(\bigcup_{i=1}^{k} L_i)^* = \begin{cases} \Sigma^*, & \text{if } t_i = n_i; \\ (L_1 \cup L_2 \cup \ldots \cup L_{i-1} \cup L_{i+1} \ldots \cup L_k)^*, & \text{if } t_i = 0. \end{cases}$$

Both of the above cases are trivial. Therefore, we only need to consider the case when $0 < t_i < n_i$. There are $\prod_{i=1}^{k} (2^{n_i-t_i} - 1)$ states in the set $P$. The cardinality of the set $R$ is

$$|R| = \begin{cases} 2^{\sum_{j=1}^{k} n_j - k}, & \text{if } \exists p(s_p \in F_p), 1 \leq p \leq k; \\ 2^{\sum_{j=1}^{k} n_j - k} - 2^{\sum_{j=1}^{k} n_j - \sum_{r=1}^{k} t_r - k}, & \text{otherwise.} \end{cases}$$

There are $2^{\sum_{j=1}^{k} n_j - k}$ states $\langle R_1, R_2, \ldots, R_k \rangle$ in $A$ such that $s_i \in R_i$ for all $1 \leq i \leq k$. When $s_p \notin F_p$ for all $1 \leq p \leq k$, the number of states $\langle R'_1, R'_2, \ldots, R'_k \rangle$ such that $s_p \in R_p$ and $F_p \cap R_p = \emptyset$ is $2^{\sum_{j=1}^{k} n_j - \sum_{r=1}^{k} t_r - k}$. In this case, these states are contained in the set $P$ rather than $R$ according to the definition.

Since $Q = \{s\} \cup P \cup R$, the size of the state set $Q$ is

$$|Q| = \begin{cases} \prod_{i=1}^{k} (2^{n_i-t_i} - 1) + 2^{\sum_{j=1}^{k} n_j - k}, & \text{if } \exists p(s_p \in F_p), 1 \leq p \leq k; \\ \prod_{i=1}^{k} (2^{n_i-t_i} - 1) + 2^{\sum_{j=1}^{k} n_j - k} - 2^{\sum_{j=1}^{k} n_j - \sum_{r=1}^{k} t_r - k} + 1, & \text{otherwise.} \end{cases}$$

As we mentioned before, a new symbol is needed to be the initial state only when $s_i \notin F_i$ for all $1 \leq i \leq k$. Thus, the upper bound of the number of states in $A$ reaches the worst case when $A_i$ has only one final state ($t_i = 1$) for all $1 \leq i \leq k$ and at least one of the initial states of these DFAs is final. $\quad \square$

Next, we show that this upper bound is reachable.

**Theorem 2.** *For any integer $n_i \geq 3$, $1 \leq i \leq k$, there exist a DFA $A_i$ of $n_i$ states such that any DFA accepting $(\bigcup_{i=1}^{k} L(A_i))^*$ needs at least*

$$\prod_{i=1}^{k} (2^{n_i-1} - 1) + 2^{\sum_{j=1}^{k} n_j - k}$$

*states.*

*Proof.* For $1 \leq i \leq k$, let $A_i = (Q_i, \Sigma, \delta_i, 0, \{0\})$ be a DFA, where $Q_1 = \{0, 1, \ldots, n_i - 1\}$, $\Sigma = \{a_i \mid 1 \leq i \leq k\} \cup \{b_j \mid 1 \leq j \leq k\} \cup \{c\}$ and the transitions of $A_i$ are

$$\delta_i(q, a_i) = q + 1 \bmod n_i, \, q = 0, 1, \ldots, n_i - 1,$$
$$\delta_i(q, a_j) = q, \, j \neq i, \, q = 0, 1, \ldots, n_i - 1,$$
$$\delta_i(q, b_i) = 0, \, q = 0, 1, \ldots, n_i - 1,$$
$$\delta_i(q, b_j) = q, \, j \neq i, \, q = 0, 1, \ldots, n_i - 1,$$
$$\delta_i(0, c) = 1, \, \delta_i(q, c) = q, \, q = 1, \ldots, n_i - 1.$$

The transition diagram of $A_i$ is shown in Figure 1.

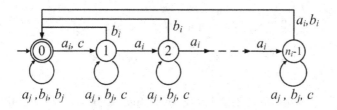

**Fig. 1.** Witness DFA $A_i$ for Theorems 2

Then we construct the DFA $A = (Q, \Sigma, \delta, s, F)$ exactly as described in the proof of Theorem 1, where

$$Q = P \cup R,$$
$$P = \{\langle P_1, P_2, \ldots, P_k \rangle \mid P_i \subseteq Q_i - \{0\}, P_i \neq \emptyset, 1 \leq i \leq k\},$$
$$R = \{\langle R_1, R_2, \ldots, R_k \rangle \mid 0 \in R_i \subseteq Q_i, 1 \leq i \leq k\},$$
$$s = \langle \{0\}, \{0\}, \ldots, \{0\} \rangle,$$
$$F = \{\langle \{0\}, \{0\}, \ldots, \{0\} \rangle\},$$

and for each state $p = \langle P_1, P_2, \ldots, P_k \rangle \in Q$,

$$\delta(p, a) = \begin{cases} \langle \delta_1(P_1, a), \delta_2(P_2, a), \ldots, \delta_k(P_k, a) \rangle, & \text{if } 0 \notin \delta_i(P_i, a) \text{ for all } 1 \leq i \leq k; \\ \langle \delta_1(P_1, a) \cup \{0\}, \delta_2(P_2, a) \cup \{0\}, \ldots, \delta_k(P_k, a) \cup \{0\} \rangle, & \text{otherwise.} \end{cases}$$

It is easy to see that $A$ accepts $(\bigcup_{i=1}^{k} L(A_i))^*$ and it has $\prod_{i=1}^{k} (2^{n_i-1} - 1) + 2^{\sum_{j=1}^{k} n_j - k}$ states. Now we need to show that $A$ is a minimal DFA.

(I) We first show that every state $p = \langle P_1, P_2, \ldots, P_k \rangle \in Q$ is reachable from the initial state $s = \langle \{0\}, \{0\}, \ldots, \{0\} \rangle$.

 1. $|P_1| \geq 1$, $|P_2| = |P_3| = \ldots = |P_k| = 1$. According to the nature of the combined operation of star of union, the order of $|P_1|, |P_2|, \ldots, |P_k|$ does not matter. Thus, in this case, we just let $|P_1| \geq 1$ and $|P_2|, \ldots, |P_k|$ be

1 without loss of generality. Let us use induction on the cardinality of $P_1$ to prove this.

**Base:** We show that, when $|P_1| = |P_2| = |P_3| = \ldots = |P_k| = 1$, the state $p$ is reachable from the initial state. Assume that $P_i = \{q_i\} \subseteq Q_i$, $1 \le i \le k$. Then

$$\langle P_1, P_2, \ldots, P_k \rangle = \begin{cases} s, & \text{if } q_1 = 0; \\ \delta(s, ca_1^{q_1-1} a_2^{q_2-1} \cdots a_k^{q_k-1}), & \text{if } q_1 > 0. \end{cases}$$

Note that when $q_1 = 0$, $q_2, \ldots, q_k$ must also be 0 according to the construction of the DFA $A$. Similarly, when $q_1 > 0$, all of $q_2, \ldots, q_k$ must be greater than 0.

**Induction Step:** Assume that all states in $A$ such that $|P_1| = m_1 \ge 1$, $|P_2| = |P_3| = \ldots = |P_k| = 1$ are reachable from $s$. Then we prove any state $p$ such that $|P_1| = m_1 + 1$, $|P_2| = |P_3| = \ldots = |P_k| = 1$ is also reachable.

Assume $P_1 = \{q_{11}, q_{12}, \ldots, q_{1m_1}, q_{1(m_1+1)}\} \subseteq Q_1$, $q_{11} < q_{12} < \ldots < q_{1m_1} < q_{1(m_1+1)}$, $P_j = \{q_{j1}\} \subseteq Q_j$, $2 \le j \le k$. Then

$$p = \begin{cases} \delta(p', b_2 b_3 \cdots b_k), & \text{if } q_{11} = 0; \\ \delta(p'', ca_1^{q_{11}-1} a_2^{q_2-1} a_3^{q_3-1} \cdots a_k^{q_k-1}), & \text{if } q_{11} > 0, \end{cases}$$

where

$$p' = \langle \{q_{12}, q_{13}, q_{14}, \ldots, q_{1(m_1+1)}\}, \{1\}, \ldots, \{1\} \rangle,$$
$$p'' = \langle \{0, q_{12} - q_{11} + 1, \ldots, q_{1(m_1+1)} - q_{11} + 1\}, \{0\}, \ldots, \{0\} \rangle.$$

Since the state $p'$ is reachable according to the induction hypothesis and $p''$ has been proved to be reachable in the case when $q_{11} = 0$, the state $p$ can also be reached.

2. $|P_1| \ge 1, |P_2| \ge 1, \ldots, |P_t| \ge 1, |P_{t+1}| = |P_{t+2}| \ldots = |P_k| = 1, 2 \le t \le k$. We use induction on $t$ to prove that $p$ is reachable in this case. Case 1 can be used as the base of the induction.

**Induction Step:** Assume all states in $A$ such that $|P_1| = m_1 \ge 1$, $|P_2| = m_2 \ge 1, \ldots, |P_{t-1}| = m_{t-1} \ge 1, |P_t| = |P_{t+1}| \ldots = |P_k| = 1$, $2 \le t \le k$, can be reached from the initial state $s$. Let us prove any state $p$ such that $|P_1| = m_1 \ge 1, |P_2| = m_2 \ge 1, \ldots, |P_t| = m_t \ge 1$, $|P_{t+1}| = |P_{t+2}| \ldots = |P_k| = 1$ can also be reached.

Assume $P_i = \{q_{i1}, q_{i2}, \ldots, q_{im_i}\} \subseteq Q_i$, $q_{i1} < q_{i2} < \ldots < q_{im_i}$, $2 \le m_i \le n_i$ $P_j = \{q_{j1}\} \subseteq Q_j$, $1 \le i \le t, t+1 \le j \le k$. In the following, let us first consider the case when $q_{11} > 0$ this time.

(2.1) $q_{11} > 0$. If $q_{11} > 0$, then $q_{21} > 0$, $q_{31} > 0$, $\ldots$, $q_{k1} > 0$ and $P_i \ne Q_i$ for all $1 \le i \le t$. According to the induction hypothesis, the state

$$p' = \langle P_1, P_2, \ldots, P_{t-1}, \{1\}, \{1\}, \ldots, \{1\} \rangle$$

is reachable from $s$. We begin the computation from $p'$ by reading $q_{tm_t} - q_{t(m_t-1)} - 1$ symbols $a_t$.

$$\delta(p', a_t^{q_{tm_t} - q_{t(m_t-1)} - 1}) = \langle P_1, \ldots, P_{t-1}, \{q_{tm_t} - q_{t(m_t-1)}\}, \{1\}, \ldots, \{1\} \rangle.$$

Denote the resulting state by $r$. Next, we apply $n_1 - q_{1m_1}$ symbols $a_1$ and the DFA $A$ reaches the state

$$r' = \langle P_1', P_2 \cup \{0\}, \ldots, P_{t-1} \cup \{0\}, \{0, q_{tm_t} - q_{t(m_t-1)}\}, \{0, 1\}, \ldots, \{0, 1\}\rangle$$

where

$$P_1' = \{0, q_{11} + n_1 - q_{1m_1}, q_{12} + n_1 - q_{1m_1}, \ldots, q_{1(m_1-1)} + n_1 - q_{1m_1}\}.$$

Now we apply an $a_t$-transition and the resulting state $r''$ is

$$\langle P_1', P_2 \cup \{0\}, \ldots, P_{t-1} \cup \{0\}, \{0, 1, q_{tm_t} - q_{t(m_t-1)} + 1\}, \{0, 1\}, \ldots, \{0, 1\}\rangle.$$

We cycle using $a_1$-transitions as long as elements of $P_1'$ are consecutively passing by 0. The last $a_1$-transition increases the cardinality of $P_1'$ by 1 and after that we apply a $c$-transition which removes the 0 in every component of the state. We continue to apply $a_1$-transitions until a sequence of consecutive elements of $P_1'$ passed by 0 and the cardinality of $P_1'$ is increased by 1. Then a $c$-transition is applied to eliminate 0. Clearly, we can cyclicly shift the set $P_1'$ back into $P_1$ by repeating these two steps. Now the DFA $A$ reaches the state

$$p'' = \langle P_1, P_2, \ldots, P_{t-1}, \{1, q_{tm_t} - q_{t(m_t-1)} + 1\}, \{1\}, \ldots, \{1\}\rangle.$$

The state $p''$ is the same as $p$ except that $q_{tm_t} - q_{t(m_t-1)} + 1$ is added into the $t$th set. Therefore, we can continue in the same way to add more elements to it. After the next loop, the state reached will be

$$\langle P_1, \ldots, P_{t-1}, \{1, q_{t(m_t-1)} - q_{t(m_t-2)} + 1, q_{tm_t} - q_{t(m_t-2)} + 1\}, \{1\}, \ldots, \{1\}\rangle.$$

In this way, we add all the $m_t$ elements of $P_t$ but keep them in a position that is shifted backwards $q_{t1} - 1$ steps so that $q_{t1}$ is in the position 1, $q_{t2}$ is in the position $q_{t2} - q_{t1} + 1$, and so on. Now we use an input word $a_t^{q_{t1}-1}$ to shift all the elements of $P_t$ into correct positions, which does not change the other elements of the state, and the state is

$$p''' = \langle P_1, P_2, \ldots, P_{t-1}, P_t, \{1\}, \ldots, \{1\}\rangle.$$

Finally, by reading a word $a_{t+1}^{q_{(t+1)1}-1} a_{t+2}^{q_{(t+2)1}-1} \cdots a_k^{q_{k1}-1}$, the DFA $A$ reaches the state $p = \langle P_1, P_2, \ldots, P_k\rangle$.

(2.2) $q_{11} = 0$. When $q_{11} = 0$, we know that $q_{21} = q_{31} = \ldots = q_{k1} = 0$. Then the state $p$ is

$$\langle \{0, q_{12}, \ldots, q_{1m_1}\}, \ldots, \{0, q_{t2}, \ldots, q_{tm_t}\}, \{0\}, \ldots, \{0\}\rangle.$$

To prove $p$ is reachable, we start from a state

$$p' = \langle \{q_{12}, \ldots, q_{1m_1}\}, \ldots, \{q_{t2}, \ldots, q_{tm_t}\}, \{1\}, \ldots, \{1\}\rangle.$$

The state $p'$ has been proved to be reachable in the case (2.1). It is easy to see that $\delta(p', b_{t+1} b_{t+2} \cdots b_k) = p$. Thus, the state $p$ can be reached from the initial state $s$ when $q_{11} = 0$.

Now we have proved that all the states in $A$ are reachable.

(II) Any two different states $p_1$ and $p_2$ in $Q$ are distinguishable.

Let $p_1$ and $p_2$ be $\langle P_1, P_2, \ldots, P_k \rangle$ and $\langle P_1', P_2', \ldots, P_k' \rangle$, respectively. Since $p_1$ and $p_2$ are different, without loss of generality we can assume that there exists an integer $1 \le t \le k$ such that $P_t \ne P_t'$ and $x \in P_t - P_t'$.

1. $x = 0$. If $x = 0$, then $0 \in P_i$ for all $1 \le i \le k$ and the state $p_1$ is a final state of $A$. Oppositely, since $x \notin P_t'$, none of $P_i'$ contains 0, which makes the state $p_2$ a nonfinal state. Therefore, $p_1$ and $p_2$ are distinguishable.

2. $x > 0$. For this case, we claim that $\delta(p_1, a_t^{m_t-1-x}ca) \in F$. In the DFA $A_t$, the transition function $\delta_t$ on the input word $a_t^{m_t-1-x}$ takes the state $x$ to $m_t - 1$. The input letter $c$ does not change the state $m_t - 1$ and the letter $a$ takes from $m_t - 1$ to 0. The last $a$-transition also adds 0 into the other components in $p_1$ according to the definition of $A$. Thus, the resulting state is final.

   Next, we show that $\delta(p_2, a_t^{m_t-1-x}ca) \notin F$. Since $x \notin P_t'$, it is easy to see that $m_t - 1 \notin \delta(P_t', a_t^{m_t-1-x})$. Note that 0 may be added into the other components in $p_2$ if the state 0 in $A_t$ is passed by when processing the input word $a_t^{m_t-1-x}$. However, since $x > 0$, it is impossible for a computation from the newly added 0's to reach $m_t - 1$ on $a_t^{m_t-1-x}$. Then the input letter $c$ removes the 0 in $P_i'$ for all $1 \le i \le k$. The last input letter $a$ shifts the states in $\delta(P_t', a_t^{m_t-1-x}c)$ by 1 but none of its elements can reach 0 because it does not contain $m_t - 1$. The $a$-transition does not change the other elements in $P_2$. Clearly, the resulting state is nonfinal. Thus, the states $p_1$ and $p_2$ are distinguishable.

Since all states in $A$ are reachable and distinguishable, $A$ is a minimal DFA.  □

This lower bound coincides with the upper bound in Theorem 1. Thus, it is the state complexity of $(\bigcup_{i=1}^{k} L(A_i))^*$.

# 4    State Complexity of $(\bigcup_{i=1}^{k} L_i)^2$

In this section, we consider the state complexity of $(\bigcup_{i=1}^{k} L_i)^2$, where $L_i$, $1 \le i \le k$, $k \ge 2$ are regular languages accepted by $n_i$-state DFAs. As we mentioned in Section 1, this combined operation can be viewed as a combination of (1) union and square, or (2) union-catenation $((L_1 \cup L_2)L_3)$ and union, or (3) union and catenation-union $(L_1(L_2 \cup L_3))$. It was shown that the state complexity of $L_1^2$ is $n_1 2^{n_1} - 2^{n_1-1}$ [17] and the state complexity of $L_1 \cup L_2$ is $n_1 n_2$ [14, 21]. Thus, for combination (1), we can get an upper bound through mathematical composition

$$\prod_{h=1}^{k} n_h \cdot 2^{\prod_{i=1}^{k} n_i} - 2^{\prod_{j=1}^{k} n_j - 1}$$

Next, we consider $(\bigcup_{i=1}^{k} L_i)^2$ as the second combination. The state complexity of $(L_1 \cup L_2)L_3$ was proved to be $n_1 n_2 2^{n_3} - (n_1 + n_2 - 1)2^{n_3 - 1}$ in [2]. Then its naive mathematical composition with the state complexity of union is

$$\prod_{h=1}^{k} n_h \cdot 2^{\prod_{i=1}^{k} n_i} - (n_1 + \prod_{j=2}^{k} n_j - 1)2^{\prod_{l=1}^{k} n_l - 1}$$

which is better than the first upper bound.

Now, let us consider the last combination. In [3], the state complexity of $L_1(L_2 \cup L_3)$ is shown to be

$$(n_1 - 1)[(2^{n_2} - 1)(2^{n_3} - 1) + 1] + 2^{n_2 + n_3 - 2}$$

and its naive mathematical composition with the state complexity of union is

$$\prod_{h=1}^{k} (n_h - 1)[(2^{n_2} - 1)(2^{n_1 \prod_{i=3}^{k} n_i} - 1) + 1] + 2^{\sum_{j=1}^{k} n_j - 2}$$

which is the best among the three upper bounds.

In the following, we will show that the state complexity of $(\bigcup_{i=1}^{k} L_i)^2$ has a similar form with the third bound. Again, although the two state complexities look similar, the proofs vary a lot because one is a general combined operation for $k \geq 2$ and the other is a specific combined operation. Besides, the base case of the combined operation when $k = 2$, that is, $(L_1 \cup L_2)^2$, has never been studied. Its state complexity is obtained in this paper as a case of the general operation.

**Theorem 3.** *Let $L_i$, $1 \leq i \leq k$, $k \geq 2$ be regular languages accepted by DFAs of $n_i$ states and $f_i$ final states. Then $(\bigcup_{i=1}^{k} L_i)^2$ is accepted by a DFA of no more than*

$$\prod_{h=1}^{k} (n_h - f_h)[\prod_{i=1}^{k} (2^{n_i} - 1) + 1] + [\prod_{j=1}^{k} n_j - \prod_{l=1}^{k} (n_l - f_l)]2^{\sum_{m=1}^{k} n_m - k}.$$

*states.*

*Proof.* For $1 \leq i \leq k$, let $L_i = L(A_i)$ and $A_i = (Q_i, \Sigma, \delta_i, s_i, F_i)$ be a DFA of $n_i$ states and $f_i$ final states. We construct a DFA $A = (Q, \Sigma, \delta, s, F)$ to accept the language $(\bigcup_{i=1}^{k} L_i)^2$. We define the state set $Q$ to be $Q = P \cup R \cup T$, where

$$P = \{\langle p_1, p_2, \ldots, p_k, P_1, P_2, \ldots, P_k \rangle \mid p_i \in Q_i - F_i, P_i \in 2^{Q_i} - \{\emptyset\}, 1 \leq i \leq k\},$$
$$R = \{\langle p_1, p_2, \ldots, p_k, \emptyset, \ldots, \emptyset \rangle \mid p_i \in Q_i - F_i, 1 \leq i \leq k\},$$
$$T = \{\langle p_1, p_2, \ldots, p_k, \{s_1\} \cup P_1, \ldots, \{s_k\} \cup P_k \rangle \mid p_i \in F_i, P_i \in 2^{Q_i - \{s_i\}}, 1 \leq i \leq k\}.$$

The initial state $s$ is

$$s = \begin{cases} \langle s_1, s_2, \ldots, s_k, \emptyset, \emptyset, \ldots, \emptyset \rangle, \text{ if } s_i \notin F_i, 1 \leq i \leq k; \\ \langle s_1, s_2, \ldots, s_k, \{s_1\}, \{s_2\}, \ldots, \{s_k\} \rangle, \text{ otherwise.} \end{cases}$$

We define the set of final states $F$ to be

$$F = \{\langle p_1, p_2, \ldots, p_k, P_1, P_2, \ldots, P_k \rangle \in Q \mid \exists i (P_i \cap F_i \neq \emptyset), 1 \leq i \leq k\}.$$

For any $p \in Q$ and $a \in \Sigma$, the transition function $\delta$ is defined as:

$$\delta(p, a) = \begin{cases} \langle p_1', p_2', \ldots, p_k', P_1', P_2' \ldots, P_k' \rangle, \text{ if } p_i' \cap F_i = \emptyset \text{ for all } 1 \leq i \leq k; \\ \langle p_1', p_2', \ldots, p_k', P_1' \cup \{s_1\}, P_2' \cup \{s_2\}, \ldots, P_k' \cup \{s_k\} \rangle, \text{ otherwise,} \end{cases}$$

where $p_i' = \delta_i(p_i, a)$ and $P_i' = \delta_i(P_i, a)$, $1 \leq i \leq k$.

An arbitrary state in $A$ is a $2k$-tuple whose first $k$ components can be viewed as a state in the DFA accepting $\bigcup_{i=1}^{k} L_i$ constructed through cross-product and last $k$ components components are subsets of $Q_1$, $Q_2$, ..., $Q_k$, respectively.

If the first $k$ components of a state are non-final states in $A_1$, $A_2$, ..., $A_k$, respectively, then the last $k$ components are either all empty sets or all nonempty sets, because the last $k$ components always change from the empty set to a non-empty set at the same time. This is why $P$ and $R$ are subsets of $Q$.

Also, we notice that if at least one of the first $k$ components of a state in $A$ is final in the corresponding DFA, then the last $k$ components of the state must contain the initial states of $A_1$, $A_2$, ..., $A_k$, respectively. Such states are contained in the set $T$.

It is easy to see that $A$ accepts $(\bigcup_{i=1}^{k} L_i)^2$. Now let us count the number of states in $A$. The cardinalities of $P$, $R$ and $T$ are respectively

$$|P| = \prod_{h=1}^{k} (n_h - f_h)[\prod_{i=1}^{k} (2^{n_i} - 1)], \qquad |R| = \prod_{h=1}^{k} (n_h - f_h),$$

$$|T| = [\prod_{j=1}^{k} n_j - \prod_{l=1}^{k} (n_l - f_l)]2^{\sum_{m=1}^{k} n_m - k}.$$

Thus, the total number of states in $A$ is $|P| + |R| + |T|$ which is the same as the upper bound shown in Theorem 3. $\qquad\square$

Next, we show this upper bound can be reached.

**Theorem 4.** *For any integer $n_i \geq 3$, $1 \leq i \leq k$, there exist a DFA $A_i$ of $n_i$ states such that any DFA accepting $(\bigcup_{i=1}^{k} L(A_i))^2$ needs at least*

$$\prod_{h=1}^{k} (n_h - 1)[\prod_{i=1}^{k} (2^{n_i} - 1) + 1] + [\prod_{j=1}^{k} n_j - \prod_{l=1}^{k} (n_l - 1)]2^{\sum_{m=1}^{k} n_m - k}$$

*states.*

*Proof.* For $1 \leq i \leq k$, let $A_i = (Q_i, \Sigma, \delta_i, 0, \{n_i - 1\})$ be a DFA, where $Q_1 = \{0, 1, \ldots, n_i - 1\}$, $\Sigma = \{a_i \mid 1 \leq i \leq k\} \cup \{b_j \mid 1 \leq j \leq k\} \cup \{c\}$ and the transitions of $A_i$ are

$$\delta_i(q, a_i) = q + 1 \bmod n_i, \; q = 0, 1, \ldots, n_i - 1,$$
$$\delta_i(q, a_j) = q, \; j \neq i, \; q = 0, 1, \ldots, n_i - 1,$$
$$\delta_i(1, b_i) = 0, \; \delta_i(q, b_i) = q, \; q = 0, 2, 3 \ldots, n_i - 1,$$
$$\delta_i(q, b_j) = q, \; j \neq i, \; q = 0, 1, \ldots, n_i - 1,$$
$$\delta_i(q, c) = q + 1 \bmod n_i, \; q = 0, 1, \ldots, n_i - 1.$$

The transition diagram of $A_i$ is shown in Figure 2.

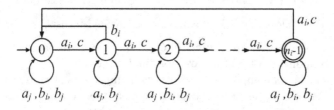

**Fig. 2.** Witness DFA $A_i$ for Theorems 4

Now we construct the DFA $A = (Q, \Sigma, \delta, s, F)$ accepting $(\bigcup_{i=1}^{k} L(A_i))^2$ exactly as described in the proof of Theorem 3. The number of states in $A$ is clearly

$$\prod_{h=1}^{k}(n_h - 1)[\prod_{i=1}^{k}(2^{n_i} - 1) + 1] + [\prod_{j=1}^{k} n_j - \prod_{l=1}^{k}(n_l - 1)]2^{\sum_{m=1}^{k} n_m - k}.$$

Next, we will prove that $A$ is a minimal DFA.

(I) We first need to show that every state

$$p = \langle p_1, p_2, \ldots, p_k, P_1, P_2, \ldots, P_k \rangle \in Q$$

is reachable from the initial state $s = \langle 0, 0, \ldots, 0, \emptyset, \emptyset, \ldots, \emptyset \rangle$. The reachability of $p$ can be proved by considering the following three cases.
1. $p_i \notin F_i, P_i = \emptyset, 1 \leq i \leq k$.
2. $|P_1| \geq 1, |P_2| = |P_3| = \ldots = |P_k| = 1$.
3. $|P_1| \geq 1, |P_2| \geq 1, \ldots, |P_t| \geq 1, |P_{t+1}| = \ldots = |P_k| = 1, 2 \leq t \leq k$.
Due to the page limitation, we omit the proof for the three cases above.
(II) Any two different states $p$ and $p'$ in $Q$ are distinguishable.
    Assume that

$$p = \langle p_1, p_2, \ldots, p_k, P_1, P_2, \ldots, P_k \rangle,$$
$$p' = \langle p_1', p_2', \ldots, p_k', P_1', P_2', \ldots, P_k' \rangle.$$

1. $\exists t(P_t \neq P'_t), 1 \leq t \leq k$.

   Let $x \in P_t - P'_t$ without loss of generality. Then there exists a word $w$ such that

   $$\delta(p, w) = \langle 0, \ldots, 0, r_t, 0, \ldots, 0, \{0\}, \ldots, \{0\}, R_t, \{0\}, \ldots, \{0\}\rangle \in F,$$
   $$\delta(p', w) = \langle 0, \ldots, 0, r'_t, 0, \ldots, 0, \{0\}, \ldots, \{0\}, R'_t, \{0\}, \ldots, \{0\}\rangle \notin F,$$

   where

   $$w = a^{n_t - 1 - x} w_1 w_2 \cdots w_{t-1} w_{t+1} w_{t+2} \cdots w_k,$$
   $$w_j = (a_j b_j)^{n_j}, 1 \leq j \leq k, j \neq t.$$

   It is easy see that $R_t \cap F_t \neq \emptyset$ whereas $R'_t \cap F_t = \emptyset$.

2. $\exists t(p_t \neq p'_t), 1 \leq t \leq k$ and $P_i = P'_i$ for all $1 \leq i \leq k$.

   For this case, there exists a word $w'$ such that

   $$\delta(p, w') = \langle 0, \ldots, 0, R_1, \{0\}, \ldots, \{0\}\rangle \in F,$$
   $$\delta(p', w') = \langle 0, \ldots, 0, R'_1, \{0\}, \ldots, \{0\}\rangle \notin F,$$

   where

   $$w' = w_1 w_2 \cdots w_{t-1} w_{t+1} w_{t+2} \cdots w_k w_t,$$
   $$w_j = (a_j b_j)^{n_j}, 1 \leq j \leq k, j \neq t,$$
   $$w_t = a_t^{n_t + 1 - p_t} (a_t b_t)^{n_t - 2} a_1^{n_1} a_t b_t.$$

   We can see that $R_1 \cap F_1 \neq \emptyset$ whereas $R'_1 \cap F_1 = \emptyset$.

Since all the states in $A$ are reachable and pairwise distinguishable, $A$ is a minimal DFA. Therefore, any DFA that accepts $(\bigcup\limits_{i=1}^{k} L(A_i))^2$ needs at least

$$\prod_{h=1}^{k} (n_h - 1)[\prod_{i=1}^{k} (2^{n_i} - 1) + 1] + [\prod_{j=1}^{k} n_j - \prod_{l=1}^{k} (n_l - 1)]2^{\sum\limits_{m=1}^{k} n_m - k}$$

states.                                                                          □

Since this lower bound coincides with the upper bound in Theorem 3, it is the state complexity of the combined operation $(\bigcup\limits_{i=1}^{k} L_i)^2$.

# References

1. Cui, B., Gao, Y., Kari, L., Yu, S.: State complexity of two combined operations: catenation-star and catenation-reversal. International Journal of Foundations of Computer Science 23(1), 51–56 (2012)

2. Cui, B., Gao, Y., Kari, L., Yu, S.: State complexity of combined operations with two basic operations. Theoretical Computer Science (2011) (accepted)
3. Cui, B., Gao, Y., Kari, L., Yu, S.: State complexity of two combined operations: catenation-union and catenation-intersection. International Journal of Foundations of Computer Science 22(8), 1797–1812 (2011)
4. Câmpeanu, C., Culik, K., Salomaa, K., Yu, S.: State Complexity of Basic Operations on Finite Languages. In: Boldt, O., Jürgensen, H. (eds.) WIA 1999. LNCS, vol. 2214, pp. 60–70. Springer, Heidelberg (2001)
5. Campeanu, C., Salomaa, K., Yu, S.: Tight lower bound for the state complexity of shuffle of regular languages. Journal of Automata, Languages and Combinatorics 7(3), 303–310 (2002)
6. Daley, M., Domaratzki, M., Salomaa, K.: State complexity of orthogonal catenation. In: Proceedings of DCFS 2008, Charlottetown, pp. 134–144 (2008)
7. Domaratzki, M., Okhotin, A.: State complexity of power. Theoretical Computer Science 410(24-25), 2377–2392 (2009)
8. Ésik, Z., Gao, Y., Liu, G., Yu, S.: Estimation of State Complexity of Combined Operations. Theoretical Computer Science 410(35), 3272–3280 (2008)
9. Gao, Y., Salomaa, K., Yu, S.: The state complexity of two combined operations: star of catenation and star of Reversal. Fundamenta Informaticae 83(1-2), 75–89 (2008)
10. Holzer, M., Kutrib, M.: State Complexity of Basic Operations on Nondeterministic Finite Automata. In: Champarnaud, J.-M., Maurel, D. (eds.) CIAA 2002. LNCS, vol. 2608, pp. 148–157. Springer, Heidelberg (2003)
11. Hopcroft, J.E., Motwani, R., Ullman, J.D.: Introduction to Automata Theory, Languages, and Computation, 2nd edn. Addison-Wesley (2001)
12. Jirásek, J., Jirásková, G., Szabari, A.: State complexity of concatenation and complementation of regular languages. International Journal of Foundations of Computer Science 16, 511–529 (2005)
13. Jirásková, G., Okhotin, A.: On the state complexity of star of union and star of intersection, TUCS Technical Report No. 825 (2007)
14. Maslov, A.N.: Estimates of the number of states of finite automata. Soviet Mathematics Doklady 11, 1373–1375 (1970)
15. Pighizzini, G., Shallit, J.O.: Unary language operations, state complexity and Jacobsthal's function. IJFCS 13, 145–159 (2002)
16. Rabin, M., Scott, D.: Finite automata and their decision problems. IBM Journal of Research and Development 3(2), 114–125 (1959)
17. Rampersad, N.: The state complexity of $L^2$ and $L^k$. Information Processing Letters 98, 231–234 (2006)
18. Salomaa, A., Salomaa, K., Yu, S.: State complexity of combined operations. Theoretical Computer Science 383, 140–152 (2007)
19. Salomaa, A., Salomaa, K., Yu, S.: Undecidability of the State Complexity of Composed Regular Operations. In: Dediu, A.-H., Inenaga, S., Martín-Vide, C. (eds.) LATA 2011. LNCS, vol. 6638, pp. 489–498. Springer, Heidelberg (2011)
20. Yu, S.: State complexity of regular languages. Journal of Automata, Languages and Combinatorics 6(2), 221–234 (2001)
21. Yu, S., Zhuang, Q., Salomaa, K.: The state complexity of some basic operations on regular languages. Theoretical Computer Science 125, 315–328 (1994)
22. Yu, S.: On the State Complexity of Combined Operations. In: Ibarra, O.H., Yen, H.-C. (eds.) CIAA 2006. LNCS, vol. 4094, pp. 11–22. Springer, Heidelberg (2006)

# State Complexity of Chop Operations
# on Unary and Finite Languages

Markus Holzer and Sebastian Jakobi

Institut für Informatik, Universität Giessen,
Arndtstr. 2, 35392 Giessen, Germany
{holzer,jakobi}@informatik.uni-giessen.de

**Abstract.** We continue our research on the descriptional complexity of chop operations. Informally, the chop of two words is like their concatenation with the touching letters merged if they are equal, otherwise their chop is undefined. The iterated variants chop-star and chop-plus are defined similar as the classical operations Kleene star and plus. We investigate the state complexity of chop operations on unary and/or finite languages, and obtain similar bounds as for the classical operations.

## 1  Introduction

An interesting field of descriptional complexity of formal languages is the state complexity of regular languages. Given a regular language $L$, its state complexity is the minimum number of states that are sufficient and necessary for a finite automaton to accept $L$. This can be adopted to operations on languages. Given a (regularity preserving) $k$-nary operation $\circ$ and regular languages $L_1, L_2, \ldots, L_k$, the state complexity of $\circ$ is the minimum number of states that are sufficient and necessary for a finite automaton to accept $\circ(L_1, L_2, \ldots, L_k)$, as a function depending on the state complexities of the input languages. First results on the state complexity of operations on regular languages were obtained about more than three decades ago in [11] and [12]. Later in [15], besides some other operations, the state complexity of concatenation and Kleene star, which are basic operations for describing regular languages, was studied. Also the special case of unary input languages was investigated there, for which significantly different bounds than in the general case were obtained. Similarly, research on these operation problems on finite languages was done in [3]. All these results concentrated on deterministic finite automata, but one can study the same problems on nondeterministic finite automata. Research on the nondeterministic state complexity of concatenation, Kleene star and Kleene plus was done in [9], where it turned out that, unlike in the deterministic case, the bounds for general regular input languages and those for unary or finite input languages do not differ much.

Recently in [1], the chop operation and its iterated variant were introduced as alternatives for concatenation and Kleene star. Substituting these operations, so called chop expressions, which are defined similarly to regular expressions, can be used to describe exactly the family of ($\lambda$-free) regular languages—here $\lambda$ is the

M. Kutrib, N. Moreira, and R. Reis (Eds.): DCFS 2012, LNCS 7386, pp. 169–182, 2012.
© Springer-Verlag Berlin Heidelberg 2012

empty word. Various other operations that are more or less closely related to the herein studied chop operations can be found in, e.g., [4,5,8,10,13]. Descriptional complexity of chop expressions and chop operations on regular expressions and finite automata, as introduced in [1], was studied in [7]. There, tight bounds of $m+n$, $n+1$, and $n+2$ for the nondeterministic state complexity of, respectively, chop, chop-plus, and chop-star were obtained. This should be compared to the results for the classical operations concatenation, Kleene plus, and Kleene star, which yield the tight bounds $m+n$, $n$, and $n+1$, respectively, on the number of states. When considering the deterministic state complexity instead, the bounds for (iterated) chop differ from those for (iterated) concatenation, since the size of the alphabet appears as a parameter.

The deterministic state complexity of (iterated) concatenation was also investigated for the special cases of finite languages [3], and unary languages [15], where notably different bounds than in the general case could be found. On the other hand, as shown in [9], the bounds for the nondeterministic state complexity of (iterated) concatenation on unary and/or finite languages are nearly the same as for general regular languages. Following these results for (iterated) concatenation on specific language families, we investigate the corresponding operation problems for chop, chop-star, and chop-plus on deterministic and nondeterministic finite automata accepting unary and/or finite languages. The situation will be quite similar to concatenation, which perhaps may be expected—but in the light of [7], where it was shown that chop expressions can be exponentially more succinct than regular expressions, this is also a bit surprising.

Results on the deterministic state complexity of chop operations compared to the corresponding classical operations can be found in Table 1, and the corresponding results for the nondeterministic state complexity are presented in Table 2. The next section provides basic definitions concerning finite automata and chop operations. After that, we first discuss the nondeterministic state complexity, and Section 4 will deal with the deterministic case.

## 2    Definitions

We investigate the descriptional complexity of the chop operation, which was recently introduced in [1], and its iterated variants. The *chop* or *fusion* of two words $u$ and $w$ in $\Sigma^*$ is defined as

$$u \odot v = \begin{cases} u'av' & \text{if } u = u'a \text{ and } v = av', \text{ for } u',v' \in \Sigma^* \text{ and } a \in \Sigma \\ \text{undefined} & \text{otherwise,} \end{cases}$$

which is extended to languages as $L_1 \odot L_2 = \{ u \odot v \mid u \in L_1 \text{ and } v \in L_2 \}$. Note that in the case of a unary alphabet, the chop of two non-empty words is always defined, in particular, $a^m \odot a^n = a^{m+n-1}$, for all $m, n \geq 1$. For the chop iteration, we set $L^{\otimes_0} = \Sigma$ and $L^{\otimes_i} = L \odot L^{\otimes_{i-1}}$, for $i \geq 1$, and the *iterated chop* or *chop-star* of a language $L$ is defined as $L^{\otimes} = \bigcup_{i \geq 0} L^{\otimes_i}$. Moreover the *chop-plus* is denoted by $L^{\oplus} = \bigcup_{i \geq 1} L^{\otimes_i}$. It is easy to see that the chop

**Table 1.** Deterministic state complexities of chop $\odot$, chop-star $\otimes$, and chop-plus $\oplus$, compared to their classical counterparts concatenation $\cdot$, Kleene star $*$, and Kleene plus $+$ on different language families. Here $m$ and $n$ are the number of states of the input automata (where $m$ corresponds to the "left" automaton in the case of $\cdot$ and $\odot$), $k$ is the alphabet size, and $t$ is the number of accepting states (of the "left" automaton).

| | Deterministic state complexity | | | |
|---|---|---|---|---|
| | Language family | | | |
| | Regular | Unary | Finite unary | Finite |
| $\cdot$ | $m \cdot 2^n - t \cdot 2^{n-1}$ | $m \cdot n$ | $m + n - 2$ | $(m - n + 3)2^{n-2} - 1$ |
| $\odot$ | $m \cdot 2^n - t \cdot 2^{n-\min(k,n)} + 1$ | $m \cdot n + 1$ | $m + n - 3$ | $(m - n + 2)2^{n-2} - 1$ |
| $*$ | $2^{n-1} + 2^{n-2}$ | $(n-1)^2 + 1$ | $n^2 - 7n + 13$ | $2^{n-3} + 2^{n-4}$ |
| $\otimes$ | $2^n - 1 + \min(k,n)$ | $(n-1)^2 + 2$ | $n^2 - 9n + 22$ | $2^{n-3} + 2^{n-3-t} + 2$ |
| $+$ | $2^{n-1} + 2^{n-2} + 1$ | $(n-1)^2 + 1$ | $n^2 - 7n + 13$ | $2^{n-3} + 2^{n-4} + 1$ |
| $\oplus$ | $2^n$ | $(n-1)^2 + 2$ | $n^2 - 9n + 22$ | $2^{n-3} + 2^{n-3-t} + 1$ |

operation $\odot$ is associative and by definition the set $\Sigma$ acts as the neutral element on all languages $L$ from $\Sigma^+$. This is compatible with the definition of chop-star, because $\emptyset^\otimes = \Sigma$. In general, an application of the chop operation with $\Sigma$ will cancel $\lambda$ from the language $L$. Therefore, we have $\Sigma \odot L = L \odot \Sigma = L \setminus \{\lambda\}$, for every $L \subseteq \Sigma^*$.

A *nondeterministic finite automaton* (NFA) is a quintuple $A = (Q, \Sigma, \delta, q_0, F)$, where $Q$ is the finite set of *states*, $\Sigma$ is the finite set of *input symbols*, $q_0 \in Q$ is the *initial state*, $F \subseteq Q$ is the set of *accepting states*, and $\delta : Q \times \Sigma \to 2^Q$ is the *transition function*. If $p \in \delta(q, a)$ for $p, q \in Q$ and $a \in \Sigma$, then we say that $(q, a, p)$ is a *transition* of $A$. As usual the transition function is extended to $\delta : Q \times \Sigma^* \to 2^Q$, reflecting sequences of inputs: $\delta(q, \lambda) = \{q\}$ and $\delta(q, aw) = \bigcup_{p \in \delta(q,a)} \delta(p, w)$, for $q \in Q$, $a \in \Sigma$, and $w \in \Sigma^*$. Automaton $A$ *accepts* the word $w \in \Sigma^*$ if $\delta(q_0, w) \cap F \neq \emptyset$. The *language accepted* by $A$ is $L(A) = \{w \in \Sigma^* \mid w \text{ is accepted by } A\}$. A finite automaton is *deterministic* (DFA) if and only if $|\delta(q, a)| = 1$, for all states $q \in Q$ and symbols $a \in \Sigma$. In this case we simply write $\delta(q, a) = p$ for $\delta(q, a) = \{p\}$ assuming that the transition function is a mapping $\delta : Q \times \Sigma \to Q$. Note that the transition function of a DFA is required to be total, while in an NFA, the transition function may map to the empty set.

## 3   Nondeterministic State Complexity

In this section we investigate the nondeterministic state complexity of chop operations applied to unary and/or finite languages. For the convenience of the reader we restate the constructions from [7] of nondeterministic finite automata for the operations under consideration on arbitrary regular languages.

**Table 2.** Nondeterministic state complexities of chop $\odot$, chop-star $\otimes$, and chop-plus $\oplus$, compared to their classical counterparts concatenation $\cdot$, Kleene star $*$, and Kleene plus $+$ on different language families. Again, $m$ and $n$ are the number of states of the input automata. Concerning the nondeterministic state complexity of the concatenation of (infinite) unary languages, an $m + n$ upper bound an $m + n - 1$ lower bound was shown in [9]. Whether the upper bound can be lowered or not is still open.

| | | Nondeterministic state complexity | | |
|---|---|---|---|---|
| | | Language family | | |
| | Regular | Unary | Finite unary | Finite |
| $\cdot$ | $m + n$ | $m + n - 1 \leq \cdot \leq m + n$ | $m + n - 1$ | $m + n - 1$ |
| $\odot$ | $m + n$ | $m + n$ | $m + n - 2$ | $m + n - 2$ |
| $*$ | $n + 1$ | $n + 1$ | $n - 1$ | $n - 1$ |
| $\otimes$ | $n + 2$ | $n + 2$ | $n - 1$ | $n$ |
| $+$ | $n$ | $n$ | $n$ | $n$ |
| $\oplus$ | $n + 1$ | $n + 1$ | $n$ | $n$ |

**Theorem 1.** Let $A_i = (Q_i, \Sigma, \delta_i, s_i, F_i)$, for $i = 1, 2$, be two nondeterministic finite automata with $|Q_1| = m$ and $|Q_2| = n$. Then the following holds:

1. Let $A^{\odot} = (Q_1 \cup Q_2, \Sigma, \delta, s_1, F_2)$ such that for all states $p, q \in Q_1 \cup Q_2$ and $a \in \Sigma$ we have $p \in \delta(q, a)$ if either $p, q \in Q_i$ and $p \in \delta_i(q, a)$, for $i \in \{1, 2\}$, or if $q \in Q_1$ and $p \in Q_2$, such that $\delta_1(q, a) \cap F_1 \neq \emptyset$ and $p \in \delta_2(s_2, a)$. Then $L(A^{\odot}) = L(A_1) \odot L(A_2)$.
2. Let $A^{\oplus} = (Q_1 \cup \{s\}, \Sigma, \delta^{\oplus}, s, F_1)$ such that for all $a \in \Sigma$ we have $\delta^{\oplus}(s, a) = \delta_1(s_1, a)$, and for all states $p, q \in Q_1$ we have $p \in \delta^{\oplus}(q, a)$ if $p \in \delta_1(q, a)$, or if $\delta_1(q, a) \cap F_1 \neq \emptyset$ and $p \in \delta_1(s_1, a)$. Then $L(A^{\oplus}) = L(A_1)^{\oplus}$.
3. Let $A^{\otimes} = (Q_1 \cup \{s, f\}, \Sigma, \delta^{\otimes}, s, F_1 \cup \{f\})$ such that for all $a \in \Sigma$ we have $f \in \delta^{\otimes}(s, a)$ if $\delta_1(s_1, a) \cap F_1 = \emptyset$, and further, for all states $p \in Q_1$ and $q \in Q_1 \cup \{s\}$ we have $p \in \delta^{\otimes}(q, a)$ if $p \in \delta^{\oplus}(q, a)$. Then $L(A^{\otimes}) = L(A_1)^{\otimes}$.

As for the corresponding operations based on concatenation, the bounds for the general case are tight already for unary languages. We start with the chop of two languages.

**Theorem 2.** Let $A$ be an $m$-state and $B$ be an $n$-state nondeterministic finite automaton for any integers $m, n \geq 1$. Then $f(m, n)$ states are sufficient and necessary in the worst case for any nondeterministic finite automaton to accept the language $L(A) \odot L(B)$, where $f(m, n) = m + n$ if $L(A)$ and $L(B)$ are unary, and $f(m, n) = m + n - 2$ if $L(A)$ and $L(B)$ are finite, or finite and unary.

*Proof.* Let $L_i = L(A_i)$ for some NFAs $A_i = (Q_i, \Sigma, \delta_i, s_i, F_i)$, for $i = 1, 2$, and $A^{\odot}$ be the NFA constructed as described in Theorem 1 such that $L(A^{\odot}) = L(A_1) \odot L(A_2)$. We begin with the unary case. The upper bound is trivial and for the lower bound consider the languages $(a^m)^*$ and $(a^n)^*$, that can be accepted by minimal $m$-state and $n$-state NFAs, respectively. Since $a^{m+n-1}$ is the shortest word in the language $L = L_1 \odot L_2$, any NFA accepting $L$ needs at least $m + n$ states.

We now turn to finite languages. Here the state graphs of $A_1$ and $A_2$ are acyclic, from which immediately follows that $s_2$ is not reachable in $A^\odot$. Further, since we may assume $A_1$ to be minimal and $L_1$ not to be empty, there must be some state $f \in F_1$, such that $\delta_1(f, a) = \emptyset$ for all $a \in \Sigma$. This state is not useful in $A^\odot$ and may be eliminated. So $A^\odot$ needs at most $m + n - 2$ states. The lower bound for finite unary languages is easily verified with the languages $\{a^{m-1}\}$ and $\{a^{n-1}\}$.                                                                 □

Next we investigate the chop-star operation, where we get slightly different bounds for all three language families.

**Theorem 3.** *Let $A$ be an $n$-state nondeterministic finite automaton for $n \geq 4$. Then $f(n)$ states are sufficient and necessary in the worst case for any non-deterministic finite automaton to accept the language $L^\otimes$, where $f(n) = n + 2$ if $L(A)$ is unary, $f(n) = n$ if $L(A)$ is finite, and $f(n) = n - 1$ if $L(A)$ is finite and unary.*

*Proof.* Theorem 1 provides the upper bound for the unary case. For the lower bound consider the language $L = (a^n)^*$ for some $n \geq 4$. We will show that

$$S = \{(\lambda, a), (a, \lambda), (a^{n-1}, a^{n+1}), (a^{n+1}, a^{n-1}), (a^n, a^n)\}$$
$$\cup \{ (a^i, a^{n-i}) \mid 2 \leq i \leq n - 2 \}$$

is an extended fooling set[1] [2,6] for $L^\otimes$, so any NFA needs at least $n + 2$ states to accept $L^\otimes$. Notice that $(u, v) \in S$ implies $(v, u) \in S$. The words represented by these pairs of words are $a$, $a^n$ and $a^{2n}$, which all belong to $L^\otimes$. We now consider the possible combinations of different pairs from $S$. The pair $(\lambda, a)$ cannot be combined with $(a^n, a^n)$, for this results in the word $a^n a = a^{n+1} \notin L^\otimes$ for $n > 2$, and it cannot be combined with any other pair $(u, v) \in S$ because $\lambda v \notin L^\otimes$ for all possible $v$. Combinations with the pair $(a, \lambda)$ behave symmetrically. The combination $(a^{n-1}, a^{n+1})$ with its symmetric counterpart results in $a^{2n-2}$, and the combination with $(a^n, a^n)$ gives $a^n a^{n+1} = a^{2n+1}$. Further, $(a^{n-1}, a^{n+1})$ and $(a^i, a^{n-i})$ produces words $a^{n+1}, \ldots, a^{2n-3} \notin L^\otimes$, for $n > 3$. Again, we can argue symmetrically for $(a^{n+1}, a^{n-1})$. Pairs $(a^n, a^n)$ and $(a^i, a^{n-i})$ result in $a^{n+i} \notin L^\otimes$, since $n < n + i < 2n - 1$. Finally, let $2 \leq i < j \leq n - 2$ and consider two pairs from the second subset of $S$. Then we have the word $a^i a^{n-j} = a^{n+i-j} \notin L^\otimes$, because $n + i - j \leq n - 1$. So $S$ is a fooling set.

Now let $L = L(A)$ for some NFA $A$ be finite. The construction from Theorem 1 provides two additional states $s$ and $f$. As in the previous proof we argue, that

---

[1] An *extended fooling set* $S$ for a language $L$ is a set of pairs $(x_i, y_i)$, for $1 \leq i \leq n$, such that (i) $x_i y_i \in L$, and (ii) $x_i y_j \notin L$ or $x_j y_i \notin L$, for $1 \leq i, j \leq n$ and $i \neq j$. In this case, any NFA accepting $L$ needs at least $|S| = n$ states.

the initial state of $A$ is not reachable in the NFA for the chop-star language, so this state can be eliminated. And further, the additional accepting state $f$ can be eliminated as well, since there must be some accepting state in $A$ with no outgoing transitions. This gives an upper bound of $n$ states. For the lower bound consider the language $\{a^{n-2}b\}$, which is accepted by a minimal $n$-state NFA. The corresponding chop-star language is $\{a, b, a^{n-2}b\}$, which also needs any NFA to have at least $n$ states.

It remains to consider the case of $L$ being both, finite and unary. Here, the minimal NFA can be assumed to be a string of $n$ states, where the first state is the initial state and the last state is an accepting state. From this, an NFA for the chop-star language can be constructed by making the second state in the string an accepting state and rerouting the ingoing transition of the last state onto the second state (and possibly adding some additional transitions as required). This allows us to eliminate this last state, yielding an upper bound of $n - 1$ states. The lower bound is easily verified with the language $\{a^{n-1}\}$.     □

Finally we turn to chop-plus. Here the upper bound of $n + 1$ from Theorem 1 is easily seen to be optimal for unary languages *via* the $n$-state witness language $L = (a^n)^*$—the length of the shortest word in $L^\oplus$ is $n$. And for finite languages note again, that no new initial state is needed. This gives a bound of $n$ states, which is necessary for the language $\{a^{n-1}\}$. Thus we can state the following.

**Theorem 4.** *Let $A$ be an $n$-state nondeterministic finite automaton for $n \geq 1$. Then $f(n)$ states are sufficient and necessary in the worst case for any nondeterministic finite automaton to accept $L(A)^\oplus$, where $f(n) = n + 1$ if $L(A)$ is unary, and $f(n) = n$ if $L(A)$ is finite, or finite and unary.*     □

## 4   Deterministic State Complexity

Now we study the deterministic state complexity of chop operations, beginning with unary languages. In this case, there obviously cannot be any dependency on the size of the alphabet, so the corresponding bounds and proofs are almost the same as in [15]. But also for finite languages, where the alphabet size could play an important role, there is hardly a difference between the bounds for chop operations and the bounds for the corresponding classical operations based on concatenation, as studied in [3]. This contrasts the situation for general regular languages, where the size of the alphabet matters for chop operations [7], but is mostly irrelevant for concatenation and related operations. We first recall a lemma from [15], that is useful for unary languages.

**Lemma 5 ([15]).** *Let $m$ and $n$ be relatively prime. Then the largest integer that cannot be presented as $i \cdot m + j \cdot n$, for any integers $i, j \geq 0$, is $m \cdot n - m - n$.*

The proofs of the following statements on unary languages utilize this lemma and use similar proof strategies as for the corresponding statements for (iterated) concatenation from [15]. Note that deterministic finite automata that accept unary languages have a very simple structure: an initial tail, possibly of length zero, attached to a cycle of size at least one. For any unary $n$-state DFA $A = (Q, \{a\}, \delta, q_0, F)$ we assume $Q = \{0, 1, \ldots, n-1\}$ with $q_0 = 0$ and $\delta(0, a^i) = i$, for $0 \leq i \leq n-1$.

We now come to the state complexity of the chop of two unary languages.

**Theorem 6.** *Let $A$ be an $m$-state and $B$ be an $n$-state unary deterministic finite automaton for $m, n \geq 1$. Then $m \cdot n + 1$ states are sufficient and, if $m$ and $n$ are relatively prime, also necessary in the worst case for any deterministic finite automaton to accept $L(A) \odot L(B)$.*

*Proof.* We first prove sufficiency. Let $A$ be an $m$-state DFA with transition function $\delta_1$, state set $Q_1$, final states $F_1$, and let $B$ be an $n$-state DFA with transition function $\delta_2$, states $Q_2$, and final states $F_2$. Let $C$ be the DFA for $L(A) \odot L(B)$, with transition function $\delta$, such that for all states $q \in Q_1$ and sets $P \subseteq Q_2$:

$$\delta(\langle q, P \rangle, a) = \begin{cases} \langle \delta_1(q,a), \bigcup_{p \in P} \{\delta_2(p,a)\} \rangle & \text{if } \delta_1(q,a) \notin F_1, \\ \langle \delta_1(q,a), \bigcup_{p \in P} \{\delta_2(p,a)\} \cup \{\delta_2(0,a)\} \rangle & \text{if } \delta_1(q,a) \in F_1. \end{cases}$$

Accepting states are pairs $\langle q, P \rangle$ where $P \cap F_2 \neq \emptyset$ and the initial state is $\langle 0, \emptyset \rangle$.

We differentiate between $L(A)$ being finite and $L(A)$ being infinite: first, assume $L(A)$ to be finite. Then state $m - 2$ from $A$ is accepting and $m - 1$ is a non-accepting sink state. Consider the states $C$ traverses, while reading $a^{m+n-1}$, starting in the initial state $\langle 0, \emptyset \rangle$: after reading $m - 1$ letters, $C$ is in the state $\langle m-1, M_0 \rangle$ for some nonempty set $M_0 \subseteq \{0, 1, \ldots, n-1\}$ of states from $B$. From there on, only the second component changes: $\delta(\langle m-1, M_0 \rangle, a^i) = \langle m-1, M_i \rangle$. If we look at what happens to the smallest element $q$ of $M_0$ when reading $a^n$, we see that there must be integers $j$ and $k$ with $0 \leq j < k \leq n$ such that $\delta_2(q, a^j) = \delta_2(q, a^k)$. Thus, $q$ enters the loop of $B$. Since $q$ also "pushes" all larger elements into the loop, we can conclude $M_j = M_k$. So there are no more than $n - 1$ states of the form $\langle m-1, M_i \rangle$, which together with the first $m$ states are obviously less than $m \cdot n + 1$ states.

Now let $|L(A)| = \infty$, let $t$ be the first accepting state in the loop of $A$, and $\ell$ be the length of that loop. In the case $t = 0$, which means that $A$ is a loop of length $m$, we define $t = m$ instead, so we have $1 \leq \ell, t \leq m$. We count all reachable states. From the initial state $\langle 0, \emptyset \rangle$, reading $a^t$, automaton $C$ reaches $\langle t, \{1\} \cup S_0 \rangle$ for some (possibly empty) set $S_0$ of states from $B$. By reading $a^{i \cdot \ell}$, for $i \geq 1$, we always reach a state $\langle t, P_i \rangle$ for some set $P_i \subseteq \{0, 1, \ldots, n-1\}$. We investigate these sets in more detail now. Let $t, t + r_1, t + r_2, \ldots, t + r_s$ for some $s < \ell - 2$ be the accepting states in the loop of $A$. Then we have $P_1 = M_1 \cup S_1$ with $M_1 = \bigcup_{i=1}^s \delta_2(1, a^{\ell - r_i}) \cup \{1\}$ and $S_1 = \bigcup_{q \in S_0} \delta_2(q, a^\ell) \setminus M_1$. Further, for $i > 1$, let $M_i = \bigcup_{q \in M_{i-1}} \delta_2(q, a^\ell) \cup M_1$ and $S_i = \bigcup_{q \in S_{i-1}} \delta_2(q, a^\ell) \setminus M_i$, then we have $P_i = M_i \cup S_i$. Note that $M_{i-1} \subseteq M_i$ for $i \geq 2$, and so there must be some $i \leq n$ such that $M_{i-1} = M_i$. If this occurs not until $i = n$, then $M_{i-1} = \{0, 1, \ldots, n-1\}$ and then from $\langle t, P_{i-1} \rangle$ on, every state is accepting, so this is an accepting sink state in the minimal DFA. Then $C$ needs at most $1 + t + (n-1) \cdot \ell \leq m \cdot n + 1$ states, since $a^{t+(n-1)\cdot \ell}$ leads to the accepting sink.

Finally let $M_{i-1} = M_i$ for some integer $i \leq n-1$. If $S_j = \emptyset$ for some integer $j$ with $i - 1 \leq j \leq n - 1$, then $\langle t, P_j \rangle$ is an accepting sink again, and $C$ needs at most $1 + t + j \cdot \ell \leq m \cdot n + 1$ states. Otherwise there is a subset $S \subseteq S_i$ such that $\delta_2(q, a^{h \cdot \ell}) \notin M_{i-1}$ for all $q \in S$ and $h \geq 0$. Since at most $n - i$ states are not in $M_{i-1}$, there are integers $j$ and $k$ with $0 \leq j < k \leq n - i$ such that $\delta_2(q, a^{j \cdot \ell}) = \delta_2(q, a^{k \cdot \ell})$ for all $q \in S$, which results in $\langle t, P_{i-1+j} \rangle = \langle t, P_{i-1+k} \rangle$. Then $C$ has at most $1 + t + (i - 1 + k) \cdot \ell \leq m \cdot n + 1$ states.

Utilizing Lemma 5, this bound is easy to prove optimal. Let $m$ and $n$ be relatively prime and consider the languages $L_1 = (a^m)^*$ and $L_2 = (a^n)^*$. Then $L_1 \odot L_2 = \{a^{m+n-1+i \cdot m + j \cdot n} \mid i, j \geq 0\}$ and corresponding to Lemma 5, word $a^{m \cdot n - 1}$ is the longest word that is not in $L_1 \odot L_2$. So any DFA accepting the language $L_1 \odot L_2$ needs at least $m \cdot n + 1$ states.    □

The bounds for iterated chop can be proven in a similar manner, resulting in a quadratic blow-up of states. We give a detailed proof for chop-star only, since the only possible difference to chop-plus is $L^\otimes \setminus L^\oplus = \{a\}$. It will turn out that the initial tail of the corresponding DFAs is long enough, so the successor of the initial state can freely be chosen to be accepting or non-accepting.

**Theorem 7.** *Let $A$ be an $n$-state unary deterministic finite automaton for $n \geq 3$. Then $(n-1)^2 + 2$ states are sufficient and necessary in the worst case for any deterministic finite automaton to accept $L(A)^\otimes$ or $L(A)^\oplus$.*

*Proof.* Let $L = L(A)$ for some minimal $n$-state DFA $A$ with transition function $\delta$. Recall that we assumed the state set to be ordered such that $\delta(0, a^i) = i$ for $0 \leq i \leq n - 1$. If $\delta(0, aa)$ is accepting, then $L^\otimes = a^+$ and $L^\oplus \supseteq aa^+$, and both languages can be accepted with 2 or 3 states. Further, if 1 is the only accepting state, the accepted language must be $L = a(a^n)^*$, or $L = a(a^{n-1})^*$, or $L = \{a\}$, but then $L^\otimes = L^\oplus = L$, so $n$ states are sufficient. Therefore let $t$ with $3 \leq t \leq n$ be the smallest integer such that $\delta(0, a^t)$ is an accepting state. An NFA for the language $L^\otimes$ can be constructed by adding a new initial state $s$, an additional final state $f$, and the transitions $(s, a, f)$, $(s, a, 1)$, and $(q, a, 1)$ for all states $q$ for which $\delta(q, a)$ is accepting. In particular we get the transition $(t - 1, a, 1)$.

Let $A'$ be the corresponding powerset automaton with transition function $\delta'$, and let $S_i = \delta'(\{s\}, a^{1+i(t-1)})$, for all $i \geq 1$. Then $S_i \subseteq S_{i+1}$, because every set $S_i$ contains the state $1 = \delta(0, a)$. Since $|S_i| \leq n$, either $S_{n-1} = \{0, 1, \ldots, n-1\}$ or there must be some integer $i \leq n - 2$ such that $S_i = S_{i+1}$. In the first case, $S_{n-1}$ is an accepting sink state and $A'$ needs at most $2 + (n-1)(t-1) \leq (n-1)^2 + 2$ states. If $S_i = S_{i+1}$, for $i \leq n - 2$, there are at most $(i+1)(t-1) \leq (n-1)^2$ states.

To construct an automaton for $L^\oplus$, if $a \notin L$, we simply omit state $f$ and associated transitions, obtaining the same upper bound. For the lower bound we use the language $L = (a^n)^*$, for $n \geq 3$. Then $L^\oplus = \{a^{n+i \cdot n + j \cdot (n-1)} \mid i, j \geq 0\}$ and according to Lemma 5, the longest word that does not belong to $L^\otimes$ is $a^{n+n \cdot (n-1) - n - (n-1)} = a^{(n-1)^2}$. Naturally, $n$ and $n - 1$ are relatively prime. So any DFA accepting $L^\otimes$ needs at least $(n-1)^2 + 2$ states. The same lower bound holds for $L^\oplus$, since $L^\otimes = L^\oplus \cup \{a\}$.    □

We briefly discuss the case of finite unary languages. Given two $m$-state and $n$-state DFAs, accepting finite unary languages, the longest word in the corresponding chop-language has length $m + n - 5$, so we immediately get the following.

**Theorem 8.** *Let $A$ be an $m$-state and $B$ be an $n$-state deterministic finite automaton for $m, n \geq 3$, such that $L(A)$ and $L(B)$ are finite unary languages. Then $m + n - 3$ states are sufficient and necessary in the worst case for any deterministic finite automaton to accept $L(A) \odot L(B)$.*  □

For the iterated chop of finite unary languages, again, Lemma 5 gives a bound for the length of the longest word that is not accepted.

**Theorem 9.** *Let $A$ be an $n$-state deterministic finite automaton for $n \geq 4$, such that $L(A)$ is a finite unary language. Then $n^2 - 9n + 22$ states are sufficient and necessary in the worst case for any deterministic finite automaton to accept the language $L(A)^{\otimes}$ or $L(A)^{\oplus}$.*

*Proof.* Let $L = L(A)$ be a finite unary language of some minimal $n$-state DFA $A$ with transition function $\delta$. State $n - 1$ must be a non-accepting sink state, and $n - 2$ must be an accepting state. If this is the only accepting state, then $L^{\oplus} = a^{n-2}(a^{n-3})^*$ and $L^{\otimes} = L^{\oplus} \cup \{a\}$ can be accepted by $(n - 1)$-state and, respectively, $(n - 2)$-state DFAs. Therefore let $k \leq n - 3$ be another accepting state. Then $L^{\otimes}$ contains all words $\{ a^{1+i \cdot (n-3) + j \cdot (k-1)} \mid i, j \geq 0 \}$. According to Lemma 5 we have $a^j \in L^{\otimes}$, for all $j \geq 2 + (n-3)(k-1) - (n-3) - (k-1)$, so that a DFA needs at most 1 plus this number of states to accept $L^{\otimes}$. Since $k \leq n - 3$, we get an upper bound of $3 + (n-3)(n-4) - (n-3) - (n-4) = n^2 - 9n + 22$ for the state complexity. This bound is reachable if $n - 3$ and $n - 2$ are the only accepting states of $A$. Note that the DFA for $L^{\otimes}$ differs from the one for $L^{\oplus}$ only in the acceptance value of the successor of the initial state. So we obtain the same bounds for $L^{\oplus}$.  □

Finally we turn to finite languages over arbitrary alphabets. For all three chop operations, an exponential blow-up on the number of states can be observed, again similar to the results on concatenation and iteration.

**Theorem 10.** *Let $A$ be an $m$-state and $B$ be an $n$-state deterministic finite automaton with $m, n \geq 3$ over an alphabet $\Sigma$ of size $k$, such that $L(A)$ and $L(B)$ are finite languages. Let $F_1$ be the accepting states of $A$ and $\bar{q} = \min(q, |F_1|)$. Then*

$$\sum_{q=0}^{m-2} \min \left( \sum_{i=0}^{\bar{q}} \binom{n-2}{i}, k^q \right)$$

*states are sufficient for any deterministic finite automaton to accept $L(A) \odot L(B)$. For $|\Sigma| = 2$ and $m > n \geq 3$, these are $(m - n + 2) \cdot 2^{n-2} - 1$ states and this number of states is necessary in the worst case.*

*Proof.* This proof is indeed a reformulation of the corresponding proof for concatenation of finite languages given in [3]. Let $L_1$ and $L_2$ be two finite languages. Assume without loss of generality that they are accepted by minimal DFA $A_1$ and $A_2$ with topologically ordered state sets $Q_1 = \{0, 1, \ldots, m-1\}$ and $Q_2 = \{0, 1, \ldots, n-1\}$. So in both automata 0 is the initial state, $m-1$ and $n-1$ are the non-accepting sink states, and $m-2$ and $n-2$ are accepting states that lead to the sink states on every input symbol. Note that the latter states must exist, since $A_1$ and $A_2$ are assumed to be minimal. Let $A$ be the DFA accepting $L_1 \odot L_2$ constructed by combining the construction of Theorem 1 and the powerset construction [14] with state set $Q_1 \times 2^{Q_2}$ and transition function $\delta$, such that for all $q \in Q_1$, $P \subseteq Q_2$, and $a \in \Sigma$ we have:

$$\delta(\langle q, P \rangle, a) = \begin{cases} \langle \delta_1(q,a), \bigcup_{p \in P}\{\delta_2(p,a)\} \rangle & \text{if } \delta_1(q,a) \notin F_1, \\ \langle \delta_1(q,a), \bigcup_{p \in P}\{\delta_2(p,a)\} \cup \{\delta_2(0,a)\} \rangle & \text{if } \delta_1(q,a) \in F_1. \end{cases}$$

The accepting states are the pairs $\langle q, P \rangle$ where $P \cap F_2 \neq \emptyset$ and the initial state is $\langle 0, \emptyset \rangle$. We will now show that the number of reachable and distinguishable states in this DFA does not exceed the stated bound. First note that no state $\langle q, P \rangle$ with $0 \in P$ is reachable and that all states $\langle q, P \rangle$ are equivalent to $\langle q, P \setminus \{n-1\} \rangle$. Also, since the state $m-2$ of $A_1$ is irrelevant for acceptance in $A$, all states $\langle m-2, P \rangle$ are equivalent to $\langle m-1, P \rangle$. To further restrict the number of states $\langle q, P \rangle$, we now take a more detailed look on the size of $P$ depending on $q$. From the topological ordering of $Q_1$ we know that the length of the longest word leading from 0 to $q$ in $A_1$ is at most $q$. Then on any path from 0 to $q$, there are at most $\bar{q} = \min(|F_1|, q)$ accepting states, and so $P$ has at most $\bar{q}$ elements from the set $Q_2 \setminus \{0, n-1\}$. Then for any $q \in Q_1 \setminus \{m-1\}$ there are at most $\sum_{i=0}^{\bar{q}} \binom{n-2}{i}$ states of the form $\langle q, P \rangle$. Additionally, the number of different states of that form is trivially bounded by the number of words of length $q$. Note that we need not consider words of length $i < q$, because if $q$ could be reached from 0 in $A_1$ by some word $v$ shorter than $q$, then no word $w$ that has $v$ as a prefix may lead to $q$ (or else $L_1$ could not be finite), and then we get even less possible states. So there are at most

$$\sum_{q=0}^{m-2} \min\left(\sum_{i=0}^{\bar{q}} \binom{n-2}{i}, k^q\right)$$

states of the form $\langle q, P \rangle$ where $0 \leq q \leq m-2$ and $P \subseteq \{1, 2, \ldots, n-2\}$. Note that the first argument of the min-function can never exceed $2^{n-2}$, since this is the maximum number of possible sets $P$. For $m > n$ and $k = 2$, we get

$$\sum_{q=0}^{n-3} 2^q + \sum_{q=n-2}^{m-2} 2^{n-2} = (m-n+2) \cdot 2^{n-2} - 1$$

as an upper bound for the number of states in $A$.

We now prove this bound to be reachable, with the same automata as in [3]. Let $A_i = (Q_i, \{a, b\}, \delta_i, 0, F_i)$, for $i \in \{1, 2\}$, with state sets $Q_1 = \{0, 1, \ldots, m-1\}$,

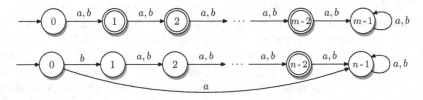

**Fig. 1.** DFAs $A_1$ (top) and $A_2$ (bottom) proving the lower bound for $L(A_1) \odot L(A_2)$

$Q_2 = \{0, 1, \ldots, n-1\}$, and final states $F_1 = \{1, 2, \ldots, m - 2\}$, and $F_2 = \{n - 2\}$. The transition function of $A_1$ is defined as $\delta_1(q, a) = \delta_1(q, b) = q+1$ for $0 \leq q \leq m - 2$ and $\delta_1(m-1, a) = \delta_1(m-1, b) = m-1$, and the transition function of $A_2$ is $\delta_2(q, a) = \delta_2(q, b) = q + 1$ for $1 \leq q \leq n - 2$, and $\delta_2(0, b) = 1$, and $\delta_2(0, a) = \delta_2(n - 1, a) = \delta_2(n - 1, b) = n - 1$—see Figure 1.

Let $A$ be the DFA for $L(A_1) \odot L(A_2)$ constructed as above. We show that there are at least $(m - n + 2) \cdot 2^{n-2} - 1$ reachable and distinguishable states. First note that states $\langle q, P \rangle$ and $\langle q', P' \rangle$ with $q < q'$ can be distinguished by reading $b^{m+n-5-q}$, since this word is accepted from the first but not from the latter state. If $q = q'$, then there must be some $p \in P \triangle P'$ and the states can be distinguished by reading $b^{n-2-p}$—here $\triangle$ refers to the symmetric difference of two sets. So all reachable states are pairwise inequivalent. To count the number of reachable states $\langle q, P \rangle$, note that different words $v$ and $w$ with $|v|, |w| \leq n - 2$ produce different sets in the second component since every input symbol shifts the set towards $n - 1$, while only the symbol $b$ produces the new element 1 in $P$. Since there are $2^{n-1} - 1$ different words with length of at most $n - 2$, this is also the number of reachable states $\langle q, P \rangle$ with $0 \leq q \leq n - 2$. In particular, any subset $P \subseteq \{1, 2, \ldots, n-2\}$ is reachable and this also holds for states $\langle q, P \rangle$ with $n - 1 \leq q \leq m - 2$. Note that we do not count states $\langle m - 1, P \rangle$ since these are equivalent to $\langle m - 2, P \rangle$. Summing up, we get $2^{n-1} - 1 + 2^{n-2} \cdot (m - 2 - n + 2) = (m - n + 2) \cdot 2^{n-2} - 1$ reachable states. $\qquad \square$

For the iterated chop of finite languages, the results depend on whether the DFA has exactly one or at least two final states. In the latter case we get an exponential blow-up, similar to iterated concatenation. But in the other case, the size of the alphabet appears as a parameter in the bounds for chop-plus and chop-star, whereas for iterated concatenation, no additional states are needed [3].

**Theorem 11.** *Let $A$ be an $n$-state deterministic finite automaton with one final state and $n \geq 4$, such that $L(A) \subseteq \Sigma^*$ is finite. Then $n - 2 + \min(|\Sigma|, n - 2)$ states are sufficient and necessary in the worst case for any deterministic finite automaton to accept $L(A)^{\otimes}$. A similar statement also holds for $L(A)^{\oplus}$, where the corresponding bound is $n - 1 + \min(|\Sigma|, n - 2)$.*

*Proof.* We begin with the chop-star operation. Let $A = (Q, \Sigma, \delta, q_0, \{q_f\})$ be a DFA accepting a finite language. Then there is a non-accepting sink state $q_s \in Q$ such that $\delta(q_s, a) = \delta(q_f, a) = q_s$, for all $a \in \Sigma$. Further there must be some state $q_1 \in Q \setminus \{q_f, q_s\}$ that is only reachable with words of length one. For constructing the NFA $A^{\otimes}$, there is no need of adding new states $s$ and $f$, since these can be identified with $q_0$ and $q_f$: the initial state $q_0$ has no ingoing transitions and $q_f$ only leads to the sink state. So we have an NFA $A^{\otimes} = (Q, \Sigma, \delta^{\otimes}, q_0, \{q_f\})$ such that for all $p, q \in Q$ and $a \in \Sigma$ we have $p \in \delta^{\otimes}(q, a)$ if $p = \delta(q, a)$, and additionally, $q_f \in \delta^{\otimes}(q_0, a)$ if $\delta(q_0, a) \neq q_f$, and $\delta(q_0, a) \in \delta^{\otimes}(q, a)$ if $\delta(q, a) = q_f$.

In the corresponding powerset automaton, only singleton sets and sets of the form $\{q, q_f\}$ for some $q \in Q \setminus \{q_f\}$ are reachable (note that all states $P \neq \{n-1\}$ are equivalent to $P \setminus \{n-1\}$). In particular, the states $\{q, q_f\}$ are actually of the form $\{\delta(q_0, a), q_f\}$ for some $a \in \Sigma$. For the singleton sets note that $\{q_1\}$ is not reachable, since states containing $q_1$ must also contain $q_f$. Further, the number of states $P$ with $q_f \in P$ is bounded by $\min(|\Sigma|, n-2)$, which can be seen as follows. If $\{q_f\}$ is reachable, then there must be some $a \in \Sigma$ with $\delta(q_0, a) = q_f$. Then there are at most $|\Sigma \setminus \{a\}|$ other states of the form $\{q, q_f\}$. Otherwise, if $\{q_f\}$ is not reachable, there are at most $|\Sigma|$ many states $\{q, q_f\}$. But even for large alphabets we cannot reach more than $n-2$ states of size two: the set $\{0, q_f\}$ is not reachable, and $\{q_s, q_f\}$ is equivalent to $\{q_s\}$. So we get the stated upper bound of $n - 2 + \min(|\Sigma|, n-2)$ states.

It suffices to prove this bound to be optimal for $\Sigma = \{a_1, a_2, \ldots, a_k\}$ with $2 \leq k \leq n-2$. Let $A = (Q, \Sigma, \delta, 0, \{n-2\})$ for $Q = \{0, 1, \ldots, n-1\}$, and

$$\delta(0, a_i) = \begin{cases} i & \text{for } i < k, \\ n-2 & \text{for } i = k, \end{cases} \qquad \delta(n-3, a_i) = \begin{cases} n-2 & \text{for } i < k, \\ n-1 & \text{for } i = k, \end{cases}$$

$$\delta(q, a_i) = q+1 \text{ for } 1 \leq q \leq n-4, \qquad \delta(n-2, a_i) = \delta(n-1, a_i) = n-1.$$

The construction of the NFA $A^{\otimes}$ as described above gives rise to the additional transitions $(0, a_i, n-2)$ and $(n-3, a_i, i)$ for $1 \leq i \leq k-1$. In the powerset automaton, the singletons $\{q\}$, for $2 \leq q \leq n-3$, are reachable from $\{0\}$ by reading the word $a_1 a_k^{q-1}$, the state $\{n-2\}$ by reading $a_k$, and the sink state $\{n-1\}$ by reading $a_1 a_k^{n-3}$. Further, the sets $\{p, n-2\}$, for $1 \leq p \leq k-1$, are reachable from $\{n-3\}$ by reading $a_p$ and no other states can be reached.

The inequivalence of distinct states $P$ and $P'$ is easy to see: it suffices to proof that singletons $\{p\}$ and $\{q\}$ with $0 \leq p < q \leq n-2$ are inequivalent, because this generalizes to the states $\{q, n-2\}$, and obviously $\{n-1\}$ cannot be equivalent to any other state. So let $p < q$. The states $\{0\}$ and $\{n-3\}$ are distinguished by $a_k$ and if $p \neq 0$ or $q \neq n-3$, then the word $a_1^{n-2-q}$ is accepted from $\{q\}$ but not from $\{p\}$.

The bounds for chop-plus can be proven with nearly the same argumentation as above. The only difference is that no additional transitions get defined for the initial state, and so $\{q_1\}$ and, respectively, $\{1\}$ are reachable in the resulting automata, so we need one more state.                                                    □

We now show that if the DFA accepting a finite language has at least two final states, we get an exponential blow-up of states in the DFA for the iterated chop language.

**Theorem 12.** *Let $A$ be an $n$-state deterministic finite automaton with $t$ final states, $2 \leq t \leq n-3$, and $n \geq 5$, such that $L(A)$ is a finite language. Then*

$2^{n-3} + 2^{n-3-t} + 2$ states are sufficient and necessary in the worst case for any deterministic finite automaton to accept $L(A)^{\oplus}$. A similar statement also holds for $L(A)^{\otimes}$, where the corresponding bound is $2^{n-3} + 2^{n-3-t} + 1$.

*Proof.* We first provide the upper bound. Let $A = (Q, \Sigma, \delta, q_0, F)$ be a minimal DFA with $n$ states from which $t$ are accepting, such that $L(A)$ is finite. Then $A$ has a sink state $q_s$ and an accepting state $q_f$ such that $\delta(q_f, a) = \delta(q_s, a) = q_s$ for all $a \in \Sigma$. Further, there must be some state $q_1 \notin \{q_f, q_s\}$ that is only reachable with words of length 1. Thus, when constructing an NFA $B$ for the language $L(A)^{\oplus}$, there is no need for an additional accepting state, and since $A$ is non-returning, i.e., no transition goes to the initial state, no new initial state is needed. We obtain the transition function $\delta_B$ from $\delta$ by adding transitions $(q, a, p)$, if $\delta(q, a) \in F$ and $p = \delta(q_0, a)$. Applying the powerset construction [14] on $B$, we obtain a DFA $A^{\oplus}$ with state set $Q' \subseteq 2^Q$. We will see that there are at most $2^{n-3} + 2^{n-3-t} + 2$ reachable and inequivalent states in $Q'$. First note that the only state containing $q_0$ is $\{q_0\}$, and if any state $P \subseteq Q$ contains the sink state $q_s$, then $P$ is equivalent to $P \setminus \{q_s\}$. Further, besides for $\{q_1\}$, for all sets $P$ containing $q_1$ it must be $P \cap F \neq \emptyset$, since the only way to reach $q_1$ is either directly from $q_0$, or by simultaneously entering an accepting state. Then there are at most $2^{n-3-t} + 2$ pairwise inequivalent non-accepting states $P$, because $P \subseteq (Q \setminus \{q_0, q_s, q_1\}) \setminus F$, or $P = \{q_0\}$, or $P = \{q_1\}$. For an accepting state $P$, note that $P$ is equivalent to $P \cup \{q_f\}$ and so we may assume that every accepting state has the form $P = P' \cup \{q_f\}$ for some $P' \subseteq (Q \setminus \{q_0, q_s, q_f\})$. These are at most $2^{n-3}$ states, which proves the upper bound for $L(A)^{\oplus}$.

For the lower bound for let $A = (Q, \{a, b, c\}, \delta, 0, F)$ with $Q = \{0, \ldots, n-1\}$, $F = \{2, \ldots, t, n-2\}$, and transition function

$$\delta(q, a) = \begin{cases} q+1 & \text{for } 0 \leq q < n-1, \\ n-1 & \text{for } q = n-1, \end{cases} \qquad \delta(q, b) = \begin{cases} q+1 & \text{for } 1 \leq q < n-1, \\ n-1 & \text{for } q \in \{0, n-1\}, \end{cases}$$

$\delta(n-3, c) = n-2$, and $\delta(q, c) = n-1$ for $q \neq n-3$. We construct an NFA $B$ for the chop-plus language by adding transitions $(q, a, 1)$, for $1 \leq q \leq t-1$ and for $q = n-3$. No other transitions need to be added, since $a$ is the only useful transition of $q_0$. Let $A^{\oplus}$ be the corresponding powerset automaton of $B$, where we associate the sink state $\{n-1\}$ with $\emptyset$. We first count reachable states, beginning with the accepting states. From the initial state $\{1\}$, by reading enough $a$ symbols, $A^{\oplus}$ reaches the state $\{1, 2, \ldots, n-2\}$ and from there, any other state $P \cup \{n-2\}$ for $P \subseteq \{1, 2, \ldots, n-3\}$ is reachable by a word $w$ of length $n-3$ where the $i$th position of $w$ is the letter $a$ if $n-2-i \in P$, otherwise it is the letter $b$. Note that all states $P$ that contain an accepting element from $\{2, 3, \ldots, k\}$ are equivalent to $P \cup \{n-2\}$, so we do not count these states. For the non-accepting states, note that $\{0\}$, $\{1\}$ and $\emptyset$ (or $\{n-1\}$) are reachable from $\{0\}$ by, respectively, $\lambda$, $a$, and $b$. The other non-accepting states are the nonempty subsets $P = \{p_1, p_2, \ldots, p_i\} \subseteq \{t+1, t+2, \ldots, n-3\}$, which are reachable from $\{p_1 - 1, p_2 - 1 \ldots, p_i - 1, n-2\}$ by reading $b$. So we have $2^{n-3}$ accepting and $2^{n-3-t} + 2$ non-accepting reachable and presumably inequivalent states. Finally we prove these states to be pairwise inequivalent. Since we did not count accepting states that do not contain the state $n - 2$, it suffices to prove that any two states $P$ and $P'$ with $q = \min(P \bigtriangleup P')$ and $1 \le q \le n - 3$ are inequivalent. Since $n - 3$ is the only state accepting the input $c$, the inequivalence is easily verified with the word $b^{n-3-q}c$.

When considering $L(A)^{\otimes}$, we need to add $\Sigma$ to the language. The argumentation for the upper bound is the same as for $L(A)^{\oplus}$, with the only difference that now $\{q_1\}$ is not reachable anymore. This also holds for the lower bound example: the non-accepting state $\{1\}$ is not reachable. So we get a tight bound for $L(A)^{\otimes}$ of $2^{n-3} + 2^{n-3-t} + 1$ states.    $\square$

# References

1. Babu, S.A., Pandya, P.K.: Chop expressions and discrete duration calculus. In: Modern Applications of Automata Theory. IISc research Monographs Series, vol. 2. World Scientific (2010)
2. Birget, J.C.: Intersection and union of regular languages and state complexity. Inform. Process. Lett. 43, 185–190 (1992)
3. Câmpeanu, C., Culik II, K., Salomaa, K., Yu, S.: State Complexity of Basic Operations on Finite Languages. In: Boldt, O., Jürgensen, H. (eds.) WIA 1999. LNCS, vol. 2214, pp. 60–70. Springer, Heidelberg (2001)
4. Cărăuşu, A., Păun, G.: String intersection and short concatenation. Rev. Roumaine Math. Pures Appl. 26, 713–726 (1981)
5. Domaratzki, M.: Minimality in Template-Guided Recombination. Inform. Comput. 270, 1209–1220 (2009)
6. Glaister, I., Shallit, J.: A lower bound technique for the size of nondeterministic finite automata. Inform. Process. Lett. 59, 75–77 (1996)
7. Holzer, M., Jakobi, S.: Chop Operations and Expressions: Descriptional Complexity Considerations. In: Mauri, G., Leporati, A. (eds.) DLT 2011. LNCS, vol. 6795, pp. 264–275. Springer, Heidelberg (2011)
8. Holzer, M., Jakobi, S., Kutrib, M.: The chop of languages. In: Automata and Formal Languages (AFL), Debrecen, Hungary, pp. 197–210 (2011)
9. Holzer, M., Kutrib, M.: Nondeterministic descriptional complexity of regular languages. Internat. J. Found. Comput. Sci. 14(6), 1087–1102 (2003)
10. Ito, M., Lischke, G.: Generalized periodicity and primitivity. Math. Logic Q. 53, 91–106 (2007)
11. Leiss, E.: Succinct representation of regular languages by Boolean automata. Theoret. Comput. Sci. 13, 323–330 (1981)
12. Maslov, A.N.: Estimates of the number of states of finite automata. Soviet Math. Dokl. 11, 1373–1375 (1970)
13. Mateescu, A., Salomaa, A.: Parallel composition of words with re-entrant symbols. Analele Universităţii Bucureşti Matematică-Informatică 45, 71–80 (1996)
14. Rabin, M.O., Scott, D.: Finite automata and their decision problems. IBM J. Res. Dev. 3, 114–125 (1959)
15. Yu, S., Zhuang, Q., Salomaa, K.: The state complexity of some basic operations on regular languages. Theoret. Comput. Sci. 125, 315–328 (1994)

# On the Number of Nonterminal Symbols in Unambiguous Conjunctive Grammars

Artur Jeż[1,*] and Alexander Okhotin[2]

[1] Institute of Computer Science, University of Wrocław, Poland
aje@cs.uni.wroc.pl
[2] Department of Mathematics, University of Turku, Finland
alexander.okhotin@utu.fi

**Abstract.** It is demonstrated that the family of languages generated by unambiguous conjunctive grammars with 1 nonterminal symbol is strictly included in the languages generated by 2-nonterminal grammars, which is in turn a proper subset of the family generated using 3 or more nonterminal symbols. This hierarchy is established by considering grammars over a one-letter alphabet, for which it is shown that 1-nonterminal grammars generate only regular languages, 2-nonterminal grammars generate some non-regular languages, but all of them have upper density zero, while 3-nonterminal grammars may generate some non-regular languages of non-zero density. It is also shown that the equivalence problem for 2-nonterminal grammars is undecidable.

## 1 Introduction

Conjunctive grammars, introduced by Okhotin [11], extend the standard context-free grammars by allowing a conjunction operation in any rules. These grammars maintain the main principle behind the context-free grammars—that of inductive definition of the membership of strings in the language—and thus augment the expressive power of the context-free grammars in a meaningful way. At the same time, conjunctive grammars inherit the context-free parsing techniques and subcubic time complexity [15].

As far as the basic language-theoretical properties are concerned, the study of conjunctive grammars is still in its infancy. Most importantly, there is no known method for proving that a given language is not generated by any conjunctive grammar. In the absence of such methods, not much is known about the descriptional complexity of the model. For the subclass of *linear conjunctive grammars* [12], it was proved that every such grammar can be transformed to an equivalent grammar with two nonterminal symbols [13]. Another known result is that one-nonterminal conjunctive grammars are strictly weaker in power than two-nonterminal grammars [17].

The limitations of conjunctive grammars with one nonterminal symbol were established by analyzing grammars over a one-letter alphabet $\Sigma = \{a\}$. The

* Supported by MNiSW grant N206 492638 2010–2012.

general non-triviality of this kind of grammars was discovered by Jeż [6], who constructed a grammar for the language $\{a^{4^n} \mid n \geqslant 0\}$. It was subsequently shown that these grammars have high expressive power, a number of undecidable properties [7] and complexity-theoretic lower bounds [8]. All these results were established using grammars with numerous nonterminal symbols, which left open the question of whether one-nonterminal conjunctive grammars can generate any non-regular unary language [6]. This question was answered by Okhotin and Rondogiannis [17], who produced a one-nonterminal grammar for a variant of the set of powers of four, as well as proved that no unary language containing almost all strings (a *dense language* [17]) can be represented by such grammars. A subsequent paper by the authors [9] extended the complexity lower bounds and the undecidability results to the one-nonterminal case.

This paper continues the study of the nonterminal complexity of conjunctive grammars over a unary alphabet by investigating the subclass of *unambiguous conjunctive grammars* [14]. Their known properties include a parsing algorithm with $|G| \cdot O(n^2)$ running time, where $n$ is the length of the input [14], and another parsing algorithm for the unary alphabet working in time $|G| \cdot n(\log n)^2 \cdot 2^{O(\log^* n)}$ developed by Okhotin and Reitwießner [16]. The authors [10] have recently constructed the first example of an unambiguous conjunctive grammar generating a non-regular unary language, as well as developed a general method for constructing such grammars, leading to undecidability results.

The investigation undertaken in this paper begins with a simple observation that unambiguous grammars with a *single nonterminal symbol* are powerless, that is, generate only regular unary languages. However, *two-nonterminal* grammars are (potentially) nontrivial, and Section 4 develops a method for encoding a grammar with an arbitrary number of nonterminals into a grammar with two nonterminal symbols, which generates a related language. For the resulting grammar to be unambiguous, this method requires the original grammar to be not only unambiguous, but to satisfy an additional condition, that of having "bi-partite unambiguous concatenation" (to be defined). As none of the known examples of unambiguous grammars [10] meet this condition, Section 5 proceeds with constructing grammars of a suitable form encoding the operation of a cellular automaton. These grammars are used in the next Section 6 to determine the undecidability of the equivalence problem for two-nonterminal grammars. At the same time, the emptiness problem—and, more generally, testing the equivalence of a grammar to a regular unary language—is shown to be decidable.

Finally, Section 7 demonstrates the limitations of two-nonterminal unambiguous conjunctive grammars, showing that all non-regular languages generated by such grammars must be sparse. This leads to a hierarchy of languages representable using 1, 2, and 3 or more nonterminal symbols.

## 2    Conjunctive Grammars and Ambiguity

Conjunctive grammars generalize context-free grammars by allowing an explicit conjunction operation in the rules.

**Definition 1 (Okhotin [11]).** *A conjunctive grammar is a quadruple $G = (\Sigma, N, P, S)$, in which $\Sigma$ and $N$ are disjoint finite non-empty sets of terminal and nonterminal symbols respectively; $P$ is a finite set of grammar rules, each of the form*

$$A \to \alpha_1 \& \ldots \& \alpha_n \quad (\text{with } A \in N,\, n \geqslant 1 \text{ and } \alpha_1, \ldots, \alpha_n \in (\Sigma \cup N)^*), \qquad (*)$$

*while $S \in N$ is a nonterminal designated as the start symbol.*

*A grammar is called **linear**, if $\alpha_i \in \Sigma^* N \Sigma^* \cup \Sigma^*$ in each rule (*).*

A rule (*) informally means that every string generated by each *conjunct* $\alpha_i$ is therefore generated by $A$. This understanding may be formalized either by term rewriting [11], or, equivalently, by a system of language equations. According to the definition by language equations, conjunction is interpreted as intersection of languages as follows.

**Definition 2.** *Let $G = (\Sigma, N, P, S)$ be a conjunctive grammar. The corresponding system of language equations is the following system in variables $N$:*

$$A = \bigcup_{A \to \alpha_1 \& \ldots \& \alpha_n \in P} \bigcap_{i=1}^{n} \alpha_i \quad (\text{for all } A \in N),$$

*where each $\alpha_i$ in the equation is a concatenation of variables and constant languages $\{a\}$ representing terminal symbols (or constant $\{\varepsilon\}$ if $\alpha_i$ is the empty string). Let $(\ldots, L_A, \ldots)$ be its least solution (that is, such a solution that every other solution $(\ldots, L'_A, \ldots)$ has $L_A \subseteq L'_A$ for all $A \in N$) and denote $L_G(A) := L_A$ for each $A \in N$. Define $L(G) := L_G(S)$.*

Such a system always has a least solution, because the operations in its right-hand side (union, intersection and concatenation) are monotone and continuous with respect to the partial ordering of vectors of languages by inclusion.

An equivalent definition of conjunctive grammars is given via *term rewriting*, which generalizes the string rewriting used by Chomsky to define context-free grammars.

**Definition 3 ([11]).** *Given a conjunctive grammar $G = (\Sigma, N, P, S)$, consider terms over concatenation and conjunction, with symbols from $\Sigma \cup N$ as atomic terms. The relation $\Longrightarrow$ of immediate derivability on the set of terms is defined as follows:*

- *Using a rule $A \to \alpha_1 \& \ldots \& \alpha_n$, a subterm $A \in N$ of any term $\varphi(A)$ can be rewritten as $\varphi(A) \Longrightarrow \varphi(\alpha_1 \& \ldots \& \alpha_n)$.*
- *A conjunction of several identical strings can be rewritten by one such string: $\varphi(w \& \ldots \& w) \Longrightarrow \varphi(w)$, for every $w \in \Sigma^*$.*

*The language generated by a term $\varphi$ is $L_G(\varphi) = \{w \mid w \in \Sigma^*,\, \varphi \Longrightarrow^* w\}$. The language generated by the grammar is $L(G) = L_G(S) = \{w \mid w \in \Sigma^*,\, S \Longrightarrow^* w\}$.*

Examples of conjunctive grammars for such non-context-free languages as $\{a^n b^n c^n \mid n \geqslant 0\}$ and $\{wcw \mid w \in \{a, b\}^*\}$ can be found in the literature [11].

This paper concentrates on a subclass of conjunctive grammars defined by analogy with unambiguous context-free grammars. Let a concatenation $L_1 \cdot \ldots \cdot L_k$ be called *unambiguous* if every string $w \in L_1 \cdot \ldots \cdot L_k$ has a unique factorization $w = u_1 \ldots u_k$ with $u_i \in L_i$.

**Definition 4 ([14]).** *Let $G$ be a conjunctive grammar. Then,*

   I. *the choice of a rule in $G$ is said to be unambiguous, if different rules for every single nonterminal generate disjoint languages;*
   II. *concatenation in $G$ is said to be unambiguous, if for every conjunct $\alpha = s_1 \ldots s_\ell$, the concatenation $L_G(s_1) \cdot \ldots \cdot L_G(s_\ell)$ is unambiguous.*

*If both conditions are satisfied, the grammar is called* unambiguous.

Every conjunctive grammar that does not generate $\varepsilon$ can be transformed to a conjunctive grammar in the *binary normal form* [11], with all rules of the form $A \to B_1 C_1 \& \ldots \& B_n C_n$ with $n \geqslant 1$ and $B_i, C_i \in N$ (referred as *non-terminating rules*), or of the form $A \to a$ with $a \in \Sigma$ (*terminating rules*). Furthermore, if the original grammar was unambiguous, then so is the resulting grammar [14]. The system of language equations corresponding to a grammar in binary normal form is known to have a unique solution in $\varepsilon$-free languages [7].

In this paper, the conditions of binary normal form are relaxed to allow terminating rules of the form $A \to w$ with $w \in \Sigma^+$.

## 3    Grammars over a One-Letter Alphabet

At the first glance, one could expect conjunctive grammars over a unary alphabet $\Sigma = \{a\}$ to generate only regular languages, similarly to standard context-free grammars. However, no proof of that conjecture could be found for some years, until a counterexample was presented by the first author [6]: that was a conjunctive grammar generating the language $\{a^{4^n} \mid n \geqslant 0\}$.

Further research, conducted by both authors, turned this single example into a general representation theorem for a large class of formal languages. This class is defined in terms of positional notations of numbers: a string $a^n$ is identified with a number $n$, which is in turn represented in base-$k$ positional notation. Let $\Sigma_k = \{0, 1, \ldots, k - 1\}$ be the alphabet of $k$-ary digits; for every $w \in \Sigma_k^*$, let $(w)_k$ be the number defined by this string of digits. For a language $L \subseteq \Sigma_k^*$ of positional notations, define $a^{(L)_k} = \{a^{(w)_k} \mid w \in L\}$. In this notation, the language $\{a^{4^n} \mid n \geqslant 0\}$ is represented as $a^{(10^*)_4}$.

**Theorem A (Jeż, Okhotin [7, Thm. 3]).** *For every $k \geqslant 2$ and for every linear conjunctive grammar $G$ over $\Sigma_k$ satisfying $L(G) \cap 0\Sigma_k^* = \varnothing$, there exists and can be effectively constructed a conjunctive grammar over $\{a\}$ generating the language $a^{(L(G))_k}$.*

This result does not extend to unambiguous grammars, as virtually all grammars given in the construction from Theorem A are ambiguous. In fact, already the first grammar for the language $\{a^{4^n} \mid n \geqslant 0\}$ [6] is ambiguous. Only recently, this example was re-created by the authors using an unambiguous grammar.

*Example 1 ([10]).* The conjunctive grammar

$$
\begin{aligned}
A_1 &\rightarrow A_1 A_3 \,\&\, A_7 A_9 \mid a \mid a^4 & A_7 &\rightarrow A_1 A_3 \,\&\, A_1 A_6 \\
A_2 &\rightarrow A_1 A_7 \,\&\, A_2 A_6 \mid a^2 & A_9 &\rightarrow A_1 A_2 \,\&\, A_2 A_7 \\
A_3 &\rightarrow A_1 A_2 \,\&\, A_3 A_9 \mid a^3 & A_{15} &\rightarrow A_6 A_9 \,\&\, A_2 A_7 \\
A_6 &\rightarrow A_1 A_2 \,\&\, A_9 A_{15} \mid a^6
\end{aligned}
$$

is unambiguous and generates the language $\{a^{4^n} \mid n \geqslant 0\} = a^{(10^*)_4}$. Each non-terminal $A_i$ generates the language $\{a^{i \cdot 4^n} \mid n \geqslant 0\}$.

In the corresponding system of language equations, the equation for $A_1$ is

$$
A_1 = (A_1 A_3 \cap A_7 A_9) \cup \{a, a^4\},
$$

etc. Substituting the intended solution into the intersection yields

$$
a^{(10^*)_4} a^{(30^*)_4} \cap a^{(130^*)_4} a^{(210^*)_4} = \left( a^{(10^+)_4} \cup a^{(10^*30^*)_4} \cup a^{(30^*10^*)_4} \right) \cap
$$
$$
\cap \left( a^{(10^{\geqslant 2})_4} \cup a^{(2110^*)_4} \cup a^{(2230^*)_4} \cup a^{(130^*210^*)_4} \cup a^{(210^*130^*)_4} \right) = a^{(10^{\geqslant 2})_4}.
$$

That is, both concatenations contain some garbage, yet the garbage in the concatenations is disjoint, and is filtered out by the intersection. The final union with $\{a, a^4\}$ yields the language $\{a^{4^n} \mid n \geqslant 0\}$, and thus the first equation turns into an equality. The rest of the equations are verified similarly, and hence the given septuple of languages forms a solution. Since the solution in $\varepsilon$-free languages is unique, this is therefore the least solution of the system. The form of both concatenations is simple enough to see that they are unambiguous.

As in the case of unrestricted conjunctive grammars over $\{a\}$, the technique used in this example can be generalised to a representation theorem, which is obtained by a careful step-by-step reimplementation of the proof of Theorem A.

**Theorem B ([10]).** *Let $L$ be any linear conjunctive language over a $d$-letter input alphabet $\Omega$, let $c \geqslant d + 2$ and assume that $\Omega = \{c, \ldots, c + d - 1\}$. Then, for every base $k \geqslant 2c + 2d - 3$, there exists an unambiguous conjunctive grammar generating the language $\{a^n \mid \text{the base-}k \text{ notation of } n \text{ is } 1w1 \text{ and } w \in L\}$.*

While positional notations used in both Theorem A and Theorem B are defined in terms of linear conjunctive grammars, the proofs are by simulating an equivalent automaton model [12]: *one-way real-time cellular automata*, also known as *trellis automata*.

A trellis automaton [3,4,12], defined as a quintuple $(\Sigma, Q, I, \delta, F)$, processes an input string of length $n \geqslant 1$ using a uniform array of $\frac{n(n+1)}{2}$ nodes, as presented in the figure below. Each node computes a value from a fixed finite set $Q$. The nodes in the bottom row obtain their values directly from the input symbols using a function $I : \Sigma \to Q$. The rest of the nodes compute the function $\delta : Q \times Q \to Q$ of the values in their predecessors. The string is accepted if and only if the value computed by the topmost node belongs to the set of accepting states $F \subseteq Q$.

**Definition 5.** *A trellis automaton is a quintuple $M = (\Sigma, Q, I, \delta, F)$, in which:*
- *$\Sigma$ is the input alphabet,*
- *$Q$ is a finite non-empty set of states,*
- *$I : \Sigma \to Q$ is a function that sets the initial states,*
- *$\delta : Q \times Q \to Q$ is the transition function, and*
- *$F \subseteq Q$ is the set of final states.*

*Extend $\delta$ to a function $\delta : Q^+ \to Q$ by $\delta(q) = q$ and*

$$\delta(q_1, \ldots, q_n) = \delta(\delta(q_1, \ldots, q_{n-1}), \delta(q_2, \ldots, q_n)),$$

*while $I$ is extended to a homomorphism $I : \Sigma^* \to Q^*$.*
*Let $L_M(q) = \{w \mid \delta(I(w)) = q\}$ and define $L(M) = \bigcup_{q \in F} L_M(q)$.*

The proof of Theorem B simulates a trellis automaton by a conjunctive grammar, whose nonterminals $C_q^{s,s'}$ with $s, s' \in \{1, 2\}$ and $q \in Q$ generate the languages $L_G(C_q^{s,s'}) = \{a^{(sws'0^*)_k} \mid \delta(w) = q\}$. The grammar encodes a recursive dependence of these languages on each other.

## 4   Encoding into Two Nonterminals

The first example of a conjunctive grammar generating a non-regular language [6] used four nonterminal symbols. Soon thereafter, a derivative example using a single nonterminal was constructed by Okhotin and Rondogiannis [17]. The latter grammar *encodes* the languages of all nonterminals of the original grammar [6] in a single language. This *ad hoc* encoding was then extended to the following general method of encoding any unary conjunctive language in a one-nonterminal conjunctive grammar:

**Theorem C (Jeż, Okhotin [9]).** *Let $G = (\{a\}, \{A_1, \ldots, A_m\}, P, A_1)$ be a conjunctive grammar in binary normal form. Assume that for every rule, each nonterminal $A$ appears at most once in its right-hand side. Furthermore, assume that each non-terminating rule is a conjunction of at least two conjuncts. Then there exist integers $p, d_1, \ldots, d_m$ with $0 < d_1 < \ldots < d_m < p$ and a conjunctive grammar $G' = (\{a\}, \{S\}, P', S)$ generating the language $L(G') = \{a^{np-d_i} \mid 1 \leqslant i \leqslant m, a^n \in L_G(A_i)\}$.*

Every conjunctive language $L \subseteq a^+$ has a grammar of the form required by Theorem C [10, Lem. 1], and hence this result is ultimately applicable to every conjunctive grammar.

For every number $t \in \{1, \ldots, p\}$, the set of strings of length $-t$ modulo $p$ is called *track* $t$. According to Theorem C, each language $L_G(A_i)$ is *encoded* on the $d_i$-th track of the language $L(G')$, in the sense that $a^n \in L_G(A_i)$ if and only if $a^{np-d_i} \in L(G')$. The values of $p$ and $d_i$ are chosen in the way that each conjunction in any rule of $G'$ *extracts* the contents of one particular track, and each rule of $G'$ simulates the corresponding rule of $G$.

For unambiguous grammars, Theorem C clearly cannot hold: the concatenation $SS$ is bound to be ambiguous, as long as $S$ generates at least two different strings. Hence, an unambiguous one-nonterminal grammar cannot use concatenations employing two or more instances of $S$. However, for one-nonterminal grammars, concatenating their initial symbol $S$ with itself is the only chance of generating anything non-regular. Indeed, if every conjunct is of the form $a^k S a^\ell$ or $a^m$, then the former can be equivalently written as $a^{k+\ell} S$, and the concatenation in the grammar becomes one-sided; and language equations with one-sided concatenation are well-known to have regular least solutions [2]. Since, conversely, all regular unary languages are generated by such grammars [17], this observation leads to the following small result.

**Lemma 1.** *One-nonterminal unambiguous conjunctive grammars over a unary alphabet generate exactly the regular languages.*

The possibility of concatenating nonterminal symbols to each other begins with two nonterminals: if $N = \{S, T\}$, then the concatenation $L_G(S)L_G(T)$ may be unambiguous. This turns out to be already sufficient to express the same idea as in Theorem C. Instead of fitting the encodings of all nonterminals of the original grammar into a single set, the same encodings shall be distributed among the two available nonterminals $S, T$ of the constructed grammar. However, this leads to certain complications.

Assume a partition of the nonterminals $A_1, \ldots, A_m$ into two classes, so that the nonterminals from the first class are encoded in $S$, and those in the second class are encoded in $T$. The concatenation $ST$ in the constructed grammar therefore reflects all possible concatenations of nonterminals from the first class with nonterminals from the second class. The simulation will work similarly to Theorem C, as long as no one ever needs to concatenate nonterminals belonging to the same class, because such concatenations are reflected nowhere. For the concatenation $ST$ to be unambiguous, the original grammar should have unambiguous concatenations *of all pairs of nonterminals* belonging to different classes, including the concatenations not used in that grammar.

These conditions of applicability are defined below, for a more general case of $k$ classes.

**Definition 6.** *A conjunctive grammar $G = (\Sigma, N, P, S)$ in binary normal form (with possible rules $A \to a^\ell$) is said to have $k$-partite unambiguous concatenation, if there is such a partition of its nonterminals $N = N_1 \cup \cdots \cup N_k$, that (i) for every conjunct $BC$ occurring in any rule, the nonterminals $B$ and $C$ belong to two different classes of $N$, and (ii) for every pair of nonterminals $B, C$ belonging* *to two different classes, the concatenation $L_G(B)L_G(C)$ is unambiguous. If the choice of a rule in $G$ is unambiguous as well, $G$ is $k$-partite unambiguous.*

Theorem C generalizes to a grammar satisfying these conditions as follows.

**Theorem 1.** *Let $G = (\{a\}, \{A_1, \ldots, A_m\}, P, A_1)$ be a $k$-partite unambiguous conjunctive grammar. Assume, that for every rule, each nonterminal $A$ appears at most once in its right-hand side; and furthermore, that every non-terminating rule is a conjunction of at least two conjuncts. Let $N_1 \cup \ldots \cup N_k$ be the partition of $N = \{A_1, \ldots, A_m\}$. Then there exist numbers $0 < d_1 < \ldots < d_m < p$ depending only on $m$, and an unambiguous $k$-nonterminal conjunctive grammar $G' = (\{a\}, \{B_1, \ldots, B_k\}, P', B_1)$, in which every nonterminal $B_j$ generates the language $L_{G'}(B_j) = \{a^{np-d_i} \mid A_i \in N_j, a^n \in L_G(A_i)\}$.*

Let $p = 4^{m+2}$ and $d_i = \frac{p}{4} + 4^i$ for each $A_i \in N$. For each $A_i \in N$, denote by $[i] \in \{1, \ldots, k\}$ the unique number with $A_i \in N_{[i]}$. Then, for each rule $A_i \to a^s$ in $G$, the new grammar $G'$ contains the rule $B_{[i]} \to a^{sp-d_i}$ and for each rule $A_i \to A_{j_1}A_{r_1} \& \ldots \& A_{j_\ell}A_{r_\ell}$ in $G$, the grammar $G'$ has the rule

$$B_{[i]} \to a^{d_{j_1}+d_{r_1}-d_i}B_{[j_1]}B_{[r_1]} \& \ldots \& a^{d_{j_\ell}+d_{r_\ell}-d_i}B_{[j_\ell]}B_{[r_\ell]}.$$

The assumptions of Theorem 1 are quite restrictive, and none of the previously known conjunctive grammars are bi-partite unambiguous. The grammar in Example 1 is tri-partite unambiguous, but not bi-partite, and hence can be encoded only in three nonterminals. A family of unambiguous conjunctive grammars meeting the conditions of the theorem for $k = 2$ is given in the next section.

## 5   Construction of Bi-partite Grammars

The goal is now to develop a variant of Theorems A and B, which would produce bi-partite unambiguous conjunctive grammars defining similar languages.

The grammars used to prove Theorem B are constructed in two stages. First, for $k \geqslant 9$, a grammar $G$ with nonterminals $A_{i,j}$ for $i, j \in \Sigma_k, i > 0$ is constructed, such that $L_G(A_{i,j}) = a^{(ij0^*)_k}$ for each nonterminal $A_{i,j}$. The grammar elaborates the ideas of Example 1 and contains the following rules:

$$A_{1,j} \to A_{k-1,0}A_{j+1,0} \& A_{k-2,0}A_{j+2,0} \mid a^{(1j)_k}, \qquad \text{for } j < \tfrac{k}{3} + 2;$$
$$A_{i,j} \to A_{i-1,k-1}A_{j+1,0} \& A_{i-1,k-2}A_{j+2,0} \mid a^{(ij)_k}, \qquad \text{for } i \geqslant 2, j < \tfrac{k}{3} + 2;$$
$$A_{i,j} \to A_{i,j-1}A_{1,0} \& A_{i,j-2}A_{2,0} \mid a^{(ij)_k}, \qquad \text{for } i \geqslant 1, j \geqslant \tfrac{k}{3} + 2.$$

Unfortunately, $G$ *is not bi-partite unambiguous*, it was not designed to be such. The following new bi-partite unambiguous grammar generates the same languages using a more elaborate collection of rules. Some generality is lost in the process, though: as the conditions imposed on the grammar are much more restrictive, the construction is given for a fixed $k = 11$:

$$A_{1,j} \to A_{k-4+j,k-1}A_{3,1} \;\&\; A_{k-4+j,9}A_{3,2} \mid a^{(1j)_k} \qquad \text{for } j \leqslant 3$$
$$A_{2,j} \to A_{j-3,0}A_{2,3} \;\&\; A_{j-4,0}A_{2,4} \mid a^{(2j)_k} \qquad \text{for } j \geqslant 6$$
$$A_{3,j} \to A_{3,1}A_{j-1,0} \;\&\; A_{2,2}A_{1,j-2} \qquad \text{for } 6 \leqslant j \leqslant 8$$
$$A_{i,j} \to A_{i-2,k+j-3}A_{1,3} \;\&\; A_{i-2,k+j-4}A_{1,4} \qquad \text{for } i \geqslant 2,\ j \leqslant 2$$
$$A_{i,j} \to A_{i-2,k+j-5}A_{1,5} \;\&\; A_{i-2,k+j-6}A_{1,6} \qquad \text{for } 2 \leqslant i \leqslant 6,\ 3 \leqslant j \leqslant 4$$
$$A_{i,5} \to A_{i-1,0}A_{1,5} \;\&\; A_{i-2,k-1}A_{1,6} \qquad \text{for } 2 \leqslant i \leqslant 6$$
$$A_{i,j} \to A_{i-1,j-2}A_{1,2} \;\&\; A_{i-1,j-3}A_{1,3} \qquad \text{in other cases}$$

Its correctness can be proved by the same type of arguments, as in Example 1; for each $i$, $j$, the nonterminal $A_{i,j}$ generates the language $a^{(ij0^*)_k}$. The authors had those arguments automatically sketched and verified by a computer program.

The second step of the construction in Theorem B is a simulation of a trellis automaton over the alphabet $\Omega = \{5, 6\}$. The constructed grammar has a nonterminal $C_q^{s,s'}$ for each $s, s' \in \{1, 2\}$ and $q \in Q$, which generates the language $\{a^{(sws'0^*)_k} \mid \delta(w) = q\}$. The rules for $C_q^{s,s'}$ are

$$C_q^{s,s'} \to C_{q''}^{1,s'} A_{s,i-1} \;\&\; C_{q''}^{2,s'} A_{s,i-2} \;\&\; C_{q'}^{s,1} A_{j-1,s'} \;\&\; C_{q'}^{s,2} A_{j-2,s'},$$
$$\text{for } i, j \in \Omega \text{ and } q', q'' \in Q \text{ with } \delta(q', q'') = q,$$
$$C_q^{s,s'} \to A_{1,s'}A_{s,b-1} \;\&\; A_{2,0}A_{s,b-2}, \qquad \text{for all } b \in \Omega \text{ with } I(b) = q.$$

It was proved that this grammar is unambiguous and generates the intended language [10].

The resulting grammar is comprised of the given new rules for $A_{i,j}$, the given old rules for $C_q^{s,s'}$ and the following rules for a new initial symbol $S$:

$$S \to \mathscr{A} \qquad \text{(there is a rule } C_q^{1,1} \to \mathscr{A} \text{ for some } q \in F)$$

The grammar accordingly generates $a^{(1L(M)10^*)_{11}}$.

It is left to show that the defined grammar is bi-partite unambiguous. The partition is defined as follows:

$$N_1 = \{A_{1,j}\}_{j=2}^6 \cup \{A_{j,1}\}_{j=2}^6 \cup \{A_{2,j}\}_{j=3}^5 \cup \{A_{j,2}\}_{j=3}^5$$

and $N_2$ contains the rest of the nonterminals. For every concatenation used in the grammar, one of the nonterminals comes from $N_1$ and the other from $N_2$. The choice of a rule for each $A_{i,j}$ is clearly unambiguous, for $C_q^{s,s'}$ the unambiguity of choice was proved earlier [10], and the same argument extends to $S$.

To see that each concatenation $XY$ with $X \in N_1$ and $Y \in N_2$ is unambiguous, consider the following two possibilities. If $X = A_{i,j}$ and $Y = A_{i',j'}$, this case is covered by the following known result.

**Lemma D ([10])** *Let $k \geqslant 2$, and consider any two different languages of the form $K = a^{(ij0^*)_k}$ and $L = a^{(i'j'0^*)_k}$, with $i, i' \in \Sigma_k \setminus \{0\}$ and $j, j' \in \Sigma_k$, except for those with $i = j = i'$ and $j' = 0$, or vice versa. Then the concatenation $KL$ is unambiguous.*

If $X = A_{i,j}$ and $Y = C_q^{s,s'}$ or $Y = S$, this follows from the below lemma:

**Lemma 2.** *Consider $i, s, s' \in \{1, 2\}$ and $j \in \{2, 3, 4, 5, 6\}$, where $i \neq j$. Let $L \subseteq a^{(s\Omega^+ s'0^*)_k}$. Then both concatenations $A_{i,j}L$ and $A_{j,i}L$ are unambiguous.*

The proof further develops the methods in the unambiguity argument for Theorem B [10], and the combinatorial details have been verified by a computer program. This leads to the following bi-partite version of Theorem B.

**Theorem 2.** *Let $L \subseteq \{5, 6\}^*$ be any linear conjunctive language. Then there exists a bi-partite unambiguous conjunctive grammar generating the language $a^{(1L10^*)_{11}}$.*

## 6   Decision Problems for Two-Nonterminal Grammars

For conjunctive grammars, most properties of a language are known to be undecidable. In particular, there is no algorithm to test equality to any fixed language.

**Theorem E ([7,10]).** *For every alphabet $\Sigma$ and for every conjunctive (unambiguous conjunctive) language $L_0 \subseteq \Sigma^*$, it is undecidable whether a given conjunctive grammar (unambiguous conjunctive grammar, respectively) generates $L_0$.*

For one-nonterminal conjunctive grammars over a unary alphabet, many properties, such as finiteness of the language generated by a given grammar, or equivalence of two given grammars, remain undecidable. On the other hand, for any given regular language $R \subseteq \Sigma_k^*$, testing whether such a grammar generates $a^{(R)_k}$—a so-called *automatic set* [1]—becomes decidable [9]. A similar, but weaker decidability result holds for two-nonterminal unambiguous grammars.

**Theorem 3.** *It is decidable whether a given two-nonterminal unambiguous conjunctive grammar generates a given regular language over a unary alphabet.*

In order to show some undecidable properties of two-nonterminal unambiguous grammars, it is necessary to recall the main undecidability method for unary conjunctive grammars. For a Turing machine $T$ over an input alphabet $\Gamma$, consider some representation of its computation histories as strings over an auxiliary alphabet $\Omega$. For every $w \in L(T)$, let $C_T(w) \in \Omega^*$ denote this history. For a certain simple encoding $C_T : \Gamma^* \to \Omega^*$, the language of all such histories

$$\text{VALC}(T) = \{C_T(w) \mid w \in \Gamma^* \text{ and } C_T(w) \text{ is an accepting computation}\}$$

is known to be an intersection of two linear context-free languages, and hence recognized by a trellis automaton [12]. Now consider the symbols in $\Omega$ as digits in a certain base-$k$ notation, for a suitable $k$. Then $\mathrm{VALC}(T) \subseteq \Sigma_k^*$, and its unary version $a^{(\mathrm{VALC}(T))_k}$ is representable by a conjunctive grammar [7]. This can be used to establish undecidability of various decision problems [7,9].

Restricting $\Omega$ to be a two-letter alphabet and regarding its elements as base-11 digits 5 and 6, one can use Theorem 2 together with Theorem 1 to obtain undecidability results for two-nonterminal grammars.

**Theorem 4.** *It is undecidable whether two given 2-nonterminal unambiguous conjunctive grammars over a one-letter alphabet generate the same language.*

**Theorem 5.** *It is undecidable to determine whether a given 2-nonterminal conjunctive grammar over a one-letter alphabet is unambiguous.*

The proofs of both theorems begin by representing the emptiness problem for a Turing machine $T$ as the emptiness of the language $L = a^{(\mathrm{VALC}(T))_{11}}$, with $\mathrm{VALC}(T) \subseteq \{4,5\}^*$, and then constructing a 2-nonterminal unambiguous grammar $G$ with $a^{np-d_1} \in L(G)$ if and only if $a^n \in L$, according to Theorems 1 and 2. The proof of Theorem 4 then proceeds by constructing a modified grammar $G'$ by omitting some of the rules of $G$, so that $L(G) = L(G')$ if and only if $L = \varnothing$. In the proof of Theorem 5, the rules generating $a^{np-d_1}$ are modified, so that if any of these strings are generated, they will be generated ambiguously.

# 7  Limitations of Two Nonterminals

It is known that one-nonterminal conjunctive grammars are strictly less expressive than those with multiple nonterminals [17]. This can be seen by analyzing the density of the generated languages. A language $L \subseteq a^*$ is said to have *density* $d(L) = \lim_{n \to \infty} \frac{|L \cap \{\varepsilon,\ldots,a^{n-1}\}|}{n}$, as long as the limit is defined. If a language has density 1, it is called *dense*, and one of the limitations of one-nonterminal grammars is that they cannot generate any dense non-regular languages.

**Theorem F (Okhotin, Rondogiannis [17]).** *Let $L \subseteq a^*$ be a non-regular language with $d(L) = 1$. Then there is no one-nonterminal conjunctive grammar generating $L$.*

A stronger result on unambiguous grammars given in this paper employs a more general notion of upper density: for every unary language $L \subseteq a^*$, its *upper density* is $\overline{d}(L) = \limsup_{n \to \infty} \frac{|L \cap \{\varepsilon,\ldots,a^{n-1}\}|}{n}$. It is shown that if a language $L \subseteq a^*$ is generated by an unambiguous conjunctive grammar with two nonterminals, then $L$ is regular or $\overline{d}(L) = 0$.

The proof is based upon the observation that a concatenation of a language of non-zero upper density with a language containing a large number of strings is always ambiguous.

**Lemma 3.** *Let a language $L \subseteq a^*$ satisfy $\overline{d}(L) > \frac{1}{c}$, and let $K \subseteq a^*$ be either a finite language with $|K| \geqslant c$, or any infinite language. Then the concatenation $KL$ is ambiguous.*

The lemma follows by estimating the size of $KL \cap \{\varepsilon, \ldots, a^{n-1}\}$ in two ways: as a subset of $\{\varepsilon, \ldots, a^{n-1}\}$, and as $c$ disjoint copies of $L \cap \{\varepsilon, \ldots, a^{n-1}\}$. These two estimations imply a bound on $|L \cap \{\varepsilon, \ldots, a^{n-1}\}|$, and the limit of these bounds contradicts the assumption that $\overline{d}(L) > \frac{1}{c}$.

With Lemma 3 established, the non-representability theorem easily follows.

**Theorem 6.** *If a non-regular language $L \subseteq a^*$ is representable by a two-nonterminal unambiguous conjunctive grammar, then $\overline{d}(L) = 0$.*

Theorem 6 is proved by considering the languages $K, L \subseteq a^*$ generated by the two nonterminals of such a grammar. The concatenation $KL$ cannot be used in the grammar due to Lemma 3, while the concatenations $KK$ and $LL$ are always ambiguous, as long as $K$ and $L$ define infinite languages. Hence, the grammar has to use only one-sided concatenation, and thus defines a regular language [2].

Three-nonterminal grammars are not subject to this restriction, and turn out to be more powerful than two-nonterminal grammars.

**Lemma 4.** *There exists a 3-nonterminal unambiguous conjunctive grammar generating a non-regular language $L \subseteq a^*$ of density $\frac{1}{2}$.*

This establishes a hierarchy of unambiguous conjunctive grammars with respect to the number of nonterminal symbols. Grammars with one, two and three non-terminals are separated according to their expressive power over a one-letter alphabet, for which 1-nonterminal grammars generate only regular languages (Lemma 1), 2-nonterminal grammars may generate some non-regular languages of upper density 0 (Theorems 1 and 2), but no non-regular languages of higher density (Theorem 6), while 3-nonterminal grammars can generate some non-regular languages of non-zero density (Lemma 4).

## 8    Open Problems

It remains unknown whether the hierarchy of unambiguous conjunctive languages with respect to the number of nonterminals continues further (like the hierarchy of $n$-nonterminal context-free languages [5]), or whether every unambiguous conjunctive language can be represented using 3 nonterminals (similarly to linear conjunctive grammars, in which 2 nonterminals are sufficient [13]). The same question stands open for conjunctive grammars of the general form, where it is not even known whether any language requires more than 2 nonterminal symbols [9].

Other suggested future work includes constructing a bi-partite unambiguous conjunctive grammar grammar for some unary language with EXPTIME-complete positional notation [8], which would allow extending the complexity lower bounds to two-nonterminal unambiguous conjunctive grammars. Furthermore, one can try establishing undecidability of some additional decision problems for two-nonterminal grammars, such as finiteness and regularity: this worked for (ambiguous) one-nonterminal conjunctive grammars [9], perhaps it could work in this case as well.

Finally, there are still no known examples of any *inherently ambiguous* conjunctive languages, which would have only ambiguous grammars [14]. Finding such a language is a worthy problem for future research.

# References

1. Allouche, J.-P., Shallit, J.: Automatic Sequences: Theory, Applications, Generalizations. Cambridge University Press (2003)
2. Baader, F., Okhotin, A.: Complexity of language equations with one-sided concatenation and all Boolean operations. In: 20th International Workshop on Unification, UNIF 2006, Seattle, USA, August 11, pp. 59–73 (2006)
3. Culik II, K., Gruska, J., Salomaa, A.: Systolic trellis automata, I and II. International Journal of Computer Mathematics 15, 195–212; 16, 3–22 (1984)
4. Dyer, C.: One-way bounded cellular automata. Information and Control 44, 261–281 (1980)
5. Gruska, J.: Descriptional complexity of context-free languages. In: Mathematical Foundations of Computer Science, MFCS 1973, Strbské Pleso, High Tatras, Czechoslovakia, September 3-8, pp. 71–83 (1973)
6. Jeż, A.: Conjunctive grammars can generate non-regular unary languages. International Journal of Foundations of Computer Science 19(3), 597–615 (2008)
7. Jeż, A., Okhotin, A.: Conjunctive grammars over a unary alphabet: undecidability and unbounded growth. Theory of Computing Systems 46(1), 27–58 (2010)
8. Jeż, A., Okhotin, A.: Complexity of equations over sets of natural numbers. Theory of Computing Systems 48(2), 319–342 (2011)
9. Jeż, A., Okhotin, A.: One-nonterminal conjunctive grammars over a unary alphabet. Theory of Computing Systems 49(2), 319–342 (2011)
10. Jeż, A., Okhotin, A.: Unambiguous conjunctive grammars over a one-letter alphabet. TUCS Technical Report 1043, Turku Centre for Computer Science (submitted for publication, April 2012)
11. Okhotin, A.: Conjunctive grammars. Journal of Automata, Languages and Combinatorics 6(4), 519–535 (2001)
12. Okhotin, A.: On the equivalence of linear conjunctive grammars to trellis automata. Informatique Théorique et Applications 38(1), 69–88 (2004)
13. Okhotin, A.: On the number of nonterminals in linear conjunctive grammars. Theoretical Computer Science 320(2-3), 419–448 (2004)
14. Okhotin, A.: Unambiguous Boolean grammars. Information and Computation 206, 1234–1247 (2008)
15. Okhotin, A.: Fast Parsing for Boolean Grammars: A Generalization of Valiant's Algorithm. In: Gao, Y., Lu, H., Seki, S., Yu, S. (eds.) DLT 2010. LNCS, vol. 6224, pp. 340–351. Springer, Heidelberg (2010)
16. Okhotin, A., Reitwießner, C.: Parsing unary Boolean grammars using online convolution. In: Advances and Applications of Automata on Words and Trees (Dagstuhl seminar 10501), December 12-17 (2010)
17. Okhotin, A., Rondogiannis, P.: On the expressive power of univariate equations over sets of natural numbers. Information and Computation 212, 1–14 (2012)

# Descriptional Complexity of Biautomata

Galina Jirásková[1,*] and Ondřej Klíma[2,**]

[1] Mathematical Institute, Slovak Academy of Sciences,
Grešákova 6, 040 01 Košice, Slovak Republic
jiraskov@saske.sk
[2] Department of Mathematics and Statistics, Masaryk University,
Kotlářská 2, 611 37 Brno, Czech Republic
klima@math.muni.cz

**Abstract.** A biautomaton is a finite automaton which arbitrarily alternates between reading the input word from the left and from the right. Some compatibility assumptions in the formal definition of a biautomaton ensure that the acceptance of an input does not depend on the way how the input is read. The paper studies the constructions of biautomata from the descriptional point of view. It proves that the tight bounds on the size of a biautomaton recognizing a regular language represented by a deterministic or nondeterministic automaton of $n$ states, or by a syntactic monoid of size $n$, are $n \cdot 2^n - 2(n-1)$, $2^{2n} - 2(2^n - 1)$, and $n^2$, respectively.

## 1 Introduction

A biautomaton is a device consisting of a finite control which reads symbols from a read-only input tape using a pair of input heads. The heads read the symbols in a sequential manner, the first head from left to right, and the second one from right to left. Initially, the first head is scanning the leftmost symbol, and the second head the rightmost symbol of an input word. The heads read symbols alternately, not depending on the current state of the finite control or on the symbol read from the tape; thus the choice of which one of the two heads will read the next symbol is completely nondeterministic. A computation ends when the heads finish the reading of the input word and meet somewhere inside the tape. Moreover, the acceptance of a word depends neither on the position, in which the heads meet, nor on the sequence of states the final control goes through while reading the input. In other words, if an input is accepted by a computation, then it must be accepted by any other computation. From this point of view, a biautomaton is a deterministic device rather than a nondeterministic one.

* Research supported by the Slovak Research and Development Agency under contract APVV-0035-10 "Algorithms, Automata, and Discrete Data Structures", and by VEGA grant 2/0183/11.
** Supported by the research center Institute for Theoretical Computer Science (ITI), project No. P202/12/G061 of the Grant Agency of the Czech Republic.

M. Kutrib, N. Moreira, and R. Reis (Eds.): DCFS 2012, LNCS 7386, pp. 196–208, 2012.

The determinism is guaranteed by the following two simple conditions. First, the heads read input symbols independently, that is, if one head reads one symbol and the other reads another, the resulting state does not depend on the order in which the heads read these single symbols. Second, if in a state of the finite control one head accepts a symbol, then this symbol is accepted in this state by the other head as well.

Biautomata have been recently introduced by Polák and Klíma [5], and recognize exactly the class of regular languages. The paper [5] shows that some useful constructions from the theory of automata work for biautomata as well. In particular, every regular language has a unique, up to isomorphism, minimal biautomaton. The main idea of the proof relies on the construction of the so-called canonical biautomaton based on quotients, and the construction is analogous to Brzozowski's construction of the minimal complete deterministic automaton for a given regular language [1].

In algebraic theory of regular languages, certain natural classes of languages are characterized by properties of their syntactic monoids or some other, more sophisticated, syntactic structures. Optimally, such a characterization gives an effective algorithm for membership problem for a considered class of languages. The most cited examples of such effective characterizations are Simon's result [13] stating that a regular language is piecewise testable if and only if its syntactic monoid is $\mathcal{J}$-trivial, and Schützenberger's result [10] stating that a regular language is star-free if and only if its syntactic monoid is aperiodic.

The authors of [5] believe that biautomata can be successfully used for a similar characterization of some classes of languages. They do not expect to get new characterizations of classes, for which the membership problem is not solved yet, but rather to get alternative biautomatas characterizations of classes, for which the membership problem is already solved. One example in [5] gives a characterization of prefix-suffix testable languages, and another one gives an alternative characterization of piecewise testable languages: A language is piecewise testable if and only if the canonical biautomaton for the language is acyclic.

As a continuation of the results in [5], the same authors in [6] point out a relationship between the complexity of piecewise testable languages and a characteristic of a graph of their biautomata, called the depth of biautomaton, and defined as the length of a longest cycle-free path in the biautomaton. Since the canonical biautomaton of a regular language contains, as a substructure, the minimal deterministic automaton for the language, many characterizations given by properties of the minimal automaton can be translated to conditions for biautomata. For practical applications it is important to know whether such characteristics can be computed efficiently.

This paper studies constructions of biautomata from the descriptional point of view. As a descriptional complexity measure, we only consider the size of a biautomaton, that is, its number of states. We represent a given regular language by a deterministic or nondeterministic automaton, or by a syntactic monoid, respectively, and ask how many states are sufficient and necessary in the worst case for a biautomaton to recognize the given language.

In all three cases, we obtain tight bounds. To prove upper bounds, we use the constructions described in [5]. To get lower bounds, we use Šebej's binary automata meeting the upper bound for reversal [12] in the deterministic case, and a modification of witness automata for left quotient from [15] in the non-deterministic case. In case languages are given by syntactic monoids, we prove the tightness of the bound in infinitely many cases using the $k$-th dihedral group $\mathbb{D}_k$, that is, the group of symmetries of a regular polygon with $k$ sides.

## 2   Biautomata

In this section we recall the necessary basis of the notion of biautomata recently developed in [5]. We refer to this paper, as well as to [11,14], for all missing information and details. For an arbitrary finite non-empty alphabet $A$, the set of all words over $A$ is denoted by $A^*$, and $\lambda$ denotes the empty word.

**Definition 1.** *A biautomaton is a sixtuple* $\mathcal{B} = (Q, A, \cdot, \circ, i, T)$ *where*

*(1) $Q$ is a non-empty finite set of states,*
*(2) $A$ is an alphabet,*
*(3) $\cdot : Q \times A \to Q$ is a left action,*
*(4) $\circ : Q \times A \to Q$ is a right action,*
*(5) $i \in Q$ is the initial state,*
*(6) $T \subseteq Q$ is the set of terminal states,*
*(7) $(q \cdot a) \circ b = (q \circ b) \cdot a$ for each $q \in Q$ and $a, b \in A$,*
*(8) $q \cdot a \in T$ if and only if $q \circ a \in T$ for each $q \in Q$ and $a \in A$.*

The left and right actions are naturally extended to the domain $Q \times A^*$ by $q \cdot \lambda = q$, $q \cdot (ua) = (q \cdot u) \cdot a$, and by $q \circ \lambda = q$, $q \circ (av) = (q \circ v) \circ a$, respectively, where $q \in Q$, $u, v \in A^*$, $a \in A$. A state $q \in Q$ *accepts* a word $u \in A^*$ if $q \cdot u \in T$, and the language of all words accepted by $q$ is denoted by $L_{\mathcal{B}}(q)$. The language *recognized* by $\mathcal{B}$ is $L_{\mathcal{B}} = L_{\mathcal{B}}(i)$. Conditions (7) and (8) stay true when words $u, v$ in $A^*$ are considered instead of letters $a, b$ in $A$ as shown in [5, Lemma 2.2].

In the definition of acceptance of a word $u$ by a biautomaton, $i \cdot u \in T$, the biautomaton reads $u$ from the left-hand side letter by letter and moves among states according to the left action. In the equivalent condition, $i \circ u \in T$, it reads $u$ from the right-hand side and moves among states according to right action. But the biautomaton can read the word $u$ in many other ways. We can divide $u = u_1 \cdots u_k v_k \cdots v_1$ arbitrarily, where $u_1, \ldots, u_k, v_k, \ldots, v_1 \in A^*$, and read $u_1$ from left first and move to the state $i \cdot u_1$, then read $v_1$ from right and move to $(i \cdot u_1) \circ v_1$, then read $u_2$ from left, and so on. In this way, the biautomaton moves from the initial state $i$ to the state

$$q = ((\cdots(((i \cdot u_1) \circ v_1) \cdot u_2) \circ v_2) \cdots) \cdot u_k) \circ v_k .$$

The basic observation in [5, Lemma 2.3] says that $q \in T$ if and only if $i \cdot u \in T$. Therefore, the acceptance of the word $u$ does not depend on the way how the biautomaton reads this word.

The proof that $q \in T$ uses the generalization of property (7) in Definition 1, and expresses $q$ as $(i \cdot (u_1 \cdots u_k)) \circ (v_k \cdots v_1)$. This basic observation leads us to the following natural definition. A state $q$ in $Q$ of biautomaton $\mathcal{B}$ is *reachable* if there exist words $u, v$ in $A^*$ such that $q = (i \cdot u) \circ v$.

The minimalization procedure for biautomata is similar to that for deterministic automata, that is, it is based on the notion of factorization. If $\mathcal{B} = (Q, A, \cdot, \circ, i, T)$ is a biautomaton and $\sim$ is an equivalence relation on the set $Q$ such that for each pair of states $p, q$ in state set $Q$ with $p \sim q$ we have

(i) $p \cdot a \sim q \cdot a$ and $p \circ a \sim q \circ a$ for each $a$ in $A$, and (ii) $p \in T$ implies $q \in T$,

then $\sim$ is called a congruence relation on $\mathcal{B}$. The class in the partition $Q/\sim$ containing a state $q$ is denoted by $[q]$. For a congruence $\sim$ on $\mathcal{B}$, we define the factor structure $\mathcal{B}/\sim = (Q/\sim, A, \cdot_\sim, \circ_\sim, [i], T/\sim)$ where $[q] \cdot_\sim a = [q \cdot a]$ and $[q] \circ_\sim a = [q \circ a]$. This structure is again a biautomaton which recognizes the same language as $\mathcal{B}$. Notice that $L_\mathcal{B}(p) = L_\mathcal{B}(q)$ whenever $p \sim q$. In other words, the congruence $\approx_\mathcal{B}$ on $\mathcal{B}$, given by the rule $p \approx_\mathcal{B} q$ if and only if $L_\mathcal{B}(p) = L_\mathcal{B}(q)$, is the maximal congruence on $\mathcal{B}$. Moreover, if we assume that all states in $\mathcal{B}$ are reachable, then the biautomaton $\mathcal{B}/\approx_\mathcal{B}$ is minimal among all biautomata recognizing language $L_\mathcal{B}$ [5, Sections 2.3 and 2.4].

In fact, it was proved that there is, up to isomorphism, a unique minimal biautomaton of a given language $L$, which is called a canonical biautomaton in [5]. Therefore, to prove that a biautomaton $\mathcal{B}$ is minimal, it is enough to show that all the states in $\mathcal{B}$ are reachable, and that $\approx_\mathcal{B}$ is the diagonal relation on $Q$. The second condition is equivalent to the fact that for each pair of states $p, q$ in $Q$ we have $L_\mathcal{B}(p) \neq L_\mathcal{B}(q)$, that is, there is a word $u$ such that $|\{p \cdot u, q \cdot u\} \cap T| = 1$.

## 3    From Deterministic Automata to Biautomata

The next construction, taken from [5], converts a deterministic automaton into a biautomaton recognizing the same language. The construction is not surprising since it is similar to the classical construction of a deterministic automaton for the reverse of a given language.

Given a complete deterministic automaton $\mathcal{A} = (Q, A, \cdot, i, T)$, we define the structure $\mathcal{A}^\mathsf{B} = (Q^\mathsf{B}, A, \cdot^\mathsf{B}, \circ^\mathsf{B}, i^\mathsf{B}, T^\mathsf{B})$ with

$$Q^\mathsf{B} = \{(q, P) \mid q \in Q, P \subseteq Q\},$$
$$i^\mathsf{B} = (i, T),$$
$$(q, P) \cdot^\mathsf{B} a = (q \cdot a, P),$$
$$(q, P) \circ^\mathsf{B} a = (q, \{p \in Q \mid p \cdot a \in P\}),$$
$$(q, P) \in T^\mathsf{B} \text{ if and only if } q \in P,$$

where $q \in Q$, $P \subseteq Q$, $a \in A$.

**Lemma 1 ([5], Lemma 2.4).** *For every complete deterministic automaton $\mathcal{A}$, the structure $\mathcal{A}^\mathsf{B}$ is a biautomaton recognizing the language $L(\mathcal{A})$.* $\qquad\square$

Since the action $\circ^B$ in $\mathcal{A}^B$ is applied only to the second component of the states in $Q^B$, we will use the symbol $\circ$ also for the corresponding operation on subsets of $Q$. More formally, for a subset $P$ of $Q$ and a word $u$ in $A^*$, we write $P \circ u = \{q \in Q \mid q \cdot u \in P\}$. Therefore, for each state $q$ in $Q$, each subset $P$ of $Q$, and each word $u$ in $A^*$, we have $(q, P) \cdot^B u = (q \cdot u, P)$ and $(q, P) \circ^B u = (q, P \circ u)$.

To factorize the biautomaton $\mathcal{A}^B$, we define an equivalence relation $\sim$ on $Q^B$ by the following rule:

$$(p, P) \sim (r, R) \quad \text{if and only if} \quad (\, (p, P) = (r, R) \text{ or } P = R = \emptyset \text{ or } P = R = Q \,).$$

**Lemma 2.** *The relation $\sim$ is a congruence of the biautomaton $\mathcal{A}^B$, and the quotient biautomaton $\mathcal{A}^B/\!\sim$ recognizes the language $L(\mathcal{A})$.*

*Proof.* The relation $\sim$ is an equivalence relation. Only two of its classes contain more than one element, namely $\top = \{(p, Q) \mid p \in Q\}$ and $\bot = \{(p, \emptyset) \mid p \in Q\}$. All the states in $\top$ are terminal and all the states in $\bot$ are non-terminal in $\mathcal{A}^B$. Moreover, for each $\rho = (q, Q)$ in $\top$ and each $a$ in $A$, we have $\rho \cdot^B a \in \top$. Furthermore, we have $\rho \circ^B a = (q, \{p \in Q \mid p \cdot a \in Q\}) = (q, Q) = \rho$ because we consider the complete deterministic automaton $\mathcal{A}$. Hence $\rho \circ^B a \in \top$. A similar property holds for $\bot$. It follows that $\sim$ is a congruence.  □

We denote the biautomaton $\mathcal{A}^B/\!\sim$ from the previous construction by $\mathcal{A}^{B,r}$. By the proof of Lemma 2, state $\top$ is an absorbing terminal state, while state $\bot$ is an absorbing non-terminal state in $\mathcal{A}^{B,r}$. All the other states in $\mathcal{A}^{B,r}$ are singleton classes, so we denote them by their single element, that is, we write $(p, P)$ instead of $[(p, P)] = \{(p, P)\}$. Next, notice that if a language is recognized by a 1-state deterministic automaton, then the corresponding biautomaton consists of one state as well. Therefore, we assume $n \geq 2$ in what follows. The construction of the biautomaton $\mathcal{A}^{B,r}$ described above and Lemma 2 provide the following result.

**Proposition 1.** *Let $L$ be an arbitrary regular language such that its minimal deterministic automaton has $n$ states, where $n \geq 2$. Then there exists a biautomaton of size $n \cdot 2^n - 2(n - 1)$ which recognizes $L$.*  □

The aim of the remaining part of this section is to show that the bound in Proposition 1 is tight. To this aim consider the $n$-state deterministic automaton $\mathcal{A} = (Q, A, \cdot, 1, \{n\})$, where $Q = \{1, 2, \ldots, n\}$, $A = \{a, b\}$, and $\cdot$ is given by Fig. 1; if $n = 2$, then $2 \cdot a = 1$, and if $n = 3$, then $3 \cdot b = 3$. Denote by $L$ the language recognized by automaton $\mathcal{A}$. Our goal is to show that the biautomaton $\mathcal{A}^{B,r}$ described above is a minimal biautomaton recognizing $L$. As shown in [4], the minimal deterministic automaton for the reverse of $L$ has $2^n$ states. In particular, paper [4] proves the next lemma, from which the reachability of all the states in $\mathcal{A}^B$ follows.

**Lemma 3 ([4], Theorem 5).** *For each subset $P$ of $Q$, there is a word $v$ such that $\{q \in Q \mid q \cdot v = n\} = P$, that is, $\{n\} \circ v = P$.*  □

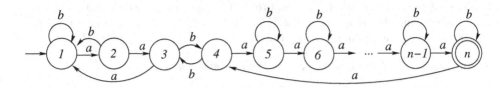

**Fig. 1.** The binary $n$-state dfa meeting the upper bound $2^n$ for reversal

**Lemma 4.** *Each state in the biautomaton $\mathcal{A}^B$ is reachable.*

*Proof.* Let $(p, P)$ be an arbitrary state in $\mathcal{A}^B$. Recall, that the initial state in $\mathcal{A}^B$ is $i^B = (1, \{n\})$. In automaton $\mathcal{A}$, there is a word $u$ in $a^*$ or in $a^*ba^*$ such that $1 \cdot u = p$. By Lemma 3, there is a word $v$ in $A^*$ such that $\{n\} \circ v = P$. Altogether, for the initial state $i^B = (1, \{n\})$ and these words $u$ and $v$, we have $(i^B \cdot^B u) \circ^B v = (p, P)$. □

The useful property in the following lemma says that automaton $\mathcal{A}$ is so-called synchronizing. After that we state one more technical observation.

**Lemma 5.** *There is a word $w$ in $\{a, b\}^*$ and a state $q$ in $Q$ such that for each state $p$ in $Q$, we have $p \cdot w = q$.*

*Proof.* The word $w = b(ab)^{n-2}$ satisfies the lemma since $p \cdot w = 1$ for each $p$. □

**Lemma 6.** *Let $P$ be a non-empty proper subset of $Q$. Then*
*(i) there exists a word $u \in A^*$ such that $|P \circ u| = |P| - 1$;*
*(ii) there exists a word $v \in A^*$ such that $|P \circ v| = |P| + 1$.*

*Proof.* First, notice that the word $bb$ acts on a subset $P$ of $Q$ as follows. If $\{1, 2\} \subseteq P$ or $\{1, 2\} \cap P = \emptyset$, then $P \circ bb = P$. If $1 \in P$ and $2 \notin P$ then $P \circ bb = P \cup \{2\}$, and if $1 \notin P$ and $2 \in P$ then $P \circ bb = P \setminus \{2\}$. Next, the word $a$ acts as a permutation, so $|P \circ a^k| = |P|$ for every subset $P$.

Now let $P$ be an arbitrary non-empty proper subset of $Q$. To prove $(i)$, we distinguish three cases depending on the size of the set $P \cap \{1, 2, 3\}$.

1. $|P \cap \{1, 2, 3\}| \in \{1, 2\}$. Then there is a word $u_1$ in $\{\lambda, a, aa\}$ such that $2 \in P \circ u_1$, and $1 \notin P \circ u_1$. Hence $|(P \circ u_1) \circ bb| = |P| - 1$, and this case is solved. An appropriate word is $u = bbu_1$ because $P \circ bbu_1 = (P \circ u_1) \circ bb$.
2. $|P \cap \{1, 2, 3\}| = 0$. Since $P$ is non-empty, it contains a state in $\{4, \ldots, n\}$, and there is a word $u_2$ in $a^*$ such that $4 \in P \circ u_2$. Now let $P' = (P \circ u_2) \circ b$. Then $|P'| = |P|$ and $P' \cap \{1, 2, 3\} = \{3\}$. As shown in case (1), there is a word $w$ with $|P' \circ w| = |P'| - 1 = |P| - 1$. Consequently $|P \circ wbu_2| = |P| - 1$.
3. $|P \cap \{1, 2, 3\}| = 3$. Since $P$ is a proper subset of $Q$, there is a state $k$ in $\{4, \ldots, n\}$ such that $k \notin P$. Similarly as in case (2) there is a word $u_3$ in $a^*$ such that $4 \notin P \circ u_3$. Then $P \circ u_3 \circ b \cap \{1, 2, 3\} = \{1, 2\}$, and we may use case (1) of our discussion.

This concludes the proof of $(i)$. The proof of $(ii)$ proceeds in a similar way; we only interchange the roles of 1 and 2. For example, in the case (1), there is a word $v_1$ in $\{\lambda, a, aa\}$ such that $1 \in P \circ v_1$ and $2 \notin P \circ v_1$. Then $|P \circ v_1 \circ bb| = |P| + 1$.    $\square$

**Lemma 7.** *The biautomaton $\mathcal{A}^{B,r}$ is the minimal biautomaton for $L$.*

*Proof.* Every state in $\mathcal{A}^B$ is reachable by Lemma 4, and hence the same is true for $\mathcal{A}^{B,r}$. We next show that two different states $\pi, \rho$ of $\mathcal{A}^{B,r}$ can be distinguished.

If $\{\pi, \rho\} = \{\top, \bot\}$, then $\pi$ and $\rho$ are distinguished by the empty word.

Let $\pi = (p, P)$ be a state in $\mathcal{A}^B$ with $P \notin \{\emptyset, Q\}$, and let $\rho \in \{\top, \bot\}$. By Lemma 6, there exist words $u$ and $v$ in $A^*$ such that $(p, P) \circ^B u = \top$ and $(p, P) \circ^B v = \bot$. Since $\top$ and $\bot$ are absorbing states, the distinguishability follows.

Now assume that $\pi = (p, P)$ and $\rho = (r, R)$, where both $P$ and $R$ are non-empty proper subsets of $Q$. First assume $P \neq R$. Without loss of generality, there is a state $q$ with $q \in P \setminus R$. By Lemma 5, there is a word $w$ such that $p \cdot w = r \cdot w$. Next, there is word $u$ such that $p \cdot w \cdot u = r \cdot w \cdot u = q$. It follows that $((p, P) \cdot^B w) \cdot^B u$ is a terminal state, while $((r, R) \cdot^B w) \cdot^B u$ is non-terminal.

If $P = R$ then $p \neq r$. By Lemma 6, which we use repeatedly, there is a word $u$ such that $|P \circ u| = 1$; thus $P \circ u = \{q\}$ for a state $q$ of $\mathcal{A}$. We claim that there is a word $v$ such that $\{q\} \circ v = \{p\}$. Indeed, if both $p$ and $q$ are in $\{1, 2, 3\}$ or in $\{4, \ldots, n\}$ then $v$ can be taken as a power of $a$, otherwise $v$ is a word in $a^*ba^*$. Then the word $v \cdot u$ distinguishes states $(p, P)$ and $(r, P)$ since $(p, P) \circ^B (v \cdot u) = ((p, P) \circ^B u) \circ^B v = (p, \{q\}) \circ^B v = (p, \{p\})$ while $(r, P) \circ^B (v \cdot u) = (r, \{p\})$.    $\square$

Summarised, we get the following theorem.

**Theorem 1.** *Let $L$ be a regular language recognized by a deterministic automaton of $n$ states, where $n \geq 2$. Then the minimal biautomaton for $L$ has at most $n \cdot 2^n - 2(n-1)$ states. The bound is tight, and it is met by a binary language.*    $\square$

## 4    From Nondeterministic Automata to Biautomata

If a regular language $L$ is given by a nondeterministic automaton, then to construct a biautomaton for $L$, we may first convert the nondeterministic automaton into deterministic automaton, and then use the construction described in the previous section. If a given nondeterministic automaton has $n$ states, then the corresponding deterministic automaton has at most $2^n$ states, and hence the resulting biautomaton has at most $2^n 2^{2^n} - 2(2^n - 1)$ states. To get a more efficient construction, we use similar ideas as in case when a biautomaton was constructed from deterministic automaton.

Let $\mathcal{N} = (Q, A, \delta, I, T)$ be a nondeterministic automaton over an alphabet $A$ with the state set $Q$, the set of initial states $I$, the set of terminal states $T$, and the transition function $\delta$ which maps $Q \times A$ to $2^Q$. The transition function $\delta$ is extended to the domain $2^Q \times A^*$ in the natural way.

Let us construct the structure $\mathcal{N}_B = (Q_B, A, \cdot_B, \circ_B, i_B, T_B)$, where

$$Q_B = \{(P, R) \mid P \subseteq Q, R \subseteq Q\},$$
$$(P, R) \cdot_B a = (\delta(P, a), R),$$
$$(P, R) \circ_B a = (P, \{q \in Q \mid \delta(q, a) \cap R \neq \emptyset\}),$$
$$i_B = (I, T),$$
$$(P, R) \in T_B \text{ if and only if } P \cap R \neq \emptyset.$$

**Lemma 8.** *For every nondeterministic automaton $\mathcal{N}$, the structure $\mathcal{N}_B$ is a biautomaton of size $2^{2n}$ recognizing the language $L(\mathcal{N})$.*

*Proof.* To prove that $\mathcal{N}_B$ is a biautomaton, we only need to check conditions (7) and (8) in Definition 1. Since actions $\cdot_B$ and $\circ_B$ act on the first and the second component independently, these actions commute and we have (7). Now $(P, R) \cdot_B a \in T_B$ if and only if $\delta(P, a) \cap R \neq \emptyset$. The latter condition is equivalent to the existence of states $r$ in $R$ and $p$ in $P$ with $r \in \delta(p, a)$, which is equivalent to $P \cap \{q \in Q \mid \delta(q, a) \cap R \neq \emptyset\} \neq \emptyset$, and hence to $(P, R) \circ_B a \in T_B$. Therefore, the structure $\mathcal{N}_B$ is a biautomaton. A word $w$ is accepted by $\mathcal{N}_B$ if and only if $(I, T) \cdot_B w \in T_B$, hence if and only if $\delta(I, w) \cap T \neq \emptyset$, that is, iff $w$ is in $L(\mathcal{N})$. $\quad\square$

Now, the situation is similar as it was in the previous section. The biautomaton $\mathcal{N}_B$ is not minimal since no terminal state can be reached from any state with one component equal to the empty set: For every word $u$ in $A^*$, we have $(\emptyset, R) \cdot_B u = (\emptyset, R)$ and $(P, \emptyset) \circ_B u = (P, \emptyset)$. Therefore, all these states can be merged. More formally, the relation $\sim$ on $Q_B$, given by the rule

$$(P, R) \sim (P', R') \quad \text{if and only if} \quad (P, R) = (P', R') \text{ or } \emptyset \in \{P, R\} \cap \{P', R'\}$$

is a congruence of biautomaton $\mathcal{N}_B$.

**Lemma 9.** *If a nondeterministic automaton $\mathcal{N}$ has $n$ states, then the biautomaton $\mathcal{N}_B/\sim$ recognizes $L(\mathcal{N})$ and has $2^{2n} - 2(2^n - 1)$ states.*

*Proof.* All the classes of congruence $\sim$ are singleton sets, except for the class $\bot = \{(P, \emptyset) \mid P \subseteq Q\} \cup \{(\emptyset, R) \mid R \subseteq Q\}$. There are $2 \cdot 2^n - 1$ elements in $\bot$. Hence there are $2^n \cdot 2^n - (2 \cdot 2^n - 1)$ singleton sets and one big class. In total, we have $2^{2n} - 2(2^n - 1)$ states in $\mathcal{N}_B/\sim$. $\quad\square$

Our next goal is to describe a nondeterministic automaton $\mathcal{N}$, for which the above mentioned biautomaton $\mathcal{N}_B/\sim$ is a minimal biautomaton. To this aim consider the $n$-state nondeterministic automaton $\mathcal{N} = (Q, A, \delta, I, T)$, where $Q = \{1, 2, \ldots, n\}$, $A = \{a, b\}$, $I = T = Q$, and $\delta$ is given by transitions in Fig. 2.

Notice that all the transitions are deterministic, and the only nondeterminism comes from having multiple initial states. Therefore, we use operation $\cdot$ for the action by a letter instead of using $\delta$. We also point out that $1 \cdot b$ is not defined. Recall that $P \circ u = \{q \in Q \mid q \cdot u \in P\}$ for any subset $P$ of $Q$.

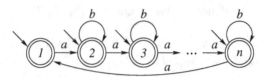

**Fig. 2.** The nondeterministic automaton meeting the bound $2^{2n} - 2(2^n - 1)$

**Lemma 10.** *Let $\mathcal{N}$ be the nondeterministic automaton depicted in Fig. 2. Then the biautomaton $\mathcal{N}_B/{\sim}$ is minimal and it has $2^{2n} - 2(2^n - 1)$ states.*

*Proof.* Consider the word $u_k = a^{n+1-k}ba^{k-1}$ for $k = 1, 2, \ldots, n$. We have $k \cdot u_k = 1 \cdot ba^{k-1} = \emptyset$. On the other hand, we have $i \cdot u_k = i$ for every state $i$ different from $k$. It follows that $P \cdot u_k = P \setminus \{k\}$ for every subset $P$ of $Q$. The same argument proves $P \circ u_k = P \setminus \{k\}$. Using this idea repeatedly, we get that for an arbitrary non-empty subset $P$ of $Q$ and an arbitrary state $p$ in $P$, there exist words $u, v$ such that $P \cdot u = P \circ v = \{p\}$. For an arbitrary state $(P, R)$ in $\mathcal{N}_B$, there exist words $u, v$ in $A^*$ such that $((Q, Q) \cdot_B u) \circ_B v = (P, R)$. Hence each state in $\mathcal{N}_B$ is reachable. Consequently, each state in $\mathcal{N}_B/{\sim}$ is reachable.

First, let us show that at least one word is accepted from any state $(P, R)$ with $P \neq \emptyset$ and $R \neq \emptyset$. Let $p \in P$ and $r \in R$. Take as $u$ the product of all the $u_k$'s, except for $u_p$. Then $P \cdot u = \{p\}$. Next, there is a word $v$ in $a^*$ such that $\{p\} \cdot v = \{r\}$. It follows that the word $uv$ is accepted from state $(P, R)$ since we have $((P, R) \cdot_B u) \cdot_B v = (\{p\}, R) \cdot_B v = (\{r\}, R)$. Hence state $\perp$ is the only state in biautomaton $\mathcal{N}_B/{\sim}$, from which no word is accepted.

Now let $(P, R)$ and $(P', R')$ be two different states in $\mathcal{N}_B/{\sim}$, both different from state $\perp$. If $P \neq P'$, then without loss of generality, there is a state $p$ with $p \in P \setminus P'$. Take as $u$ the product of all the $u_k$'s, except for $u_p$. Then $P \cdot u = \{p\}$ and $P' \cdot u = \emptyset$. Therefore, we have $(P, R) \cdot_B u = (\{p\}, R)$ and $(P', R') \cdot_B u = (\emptyset, R')$. Since no word is accepted from $(\emptyset, R')$, while at least one word is accepted from $(\{p\}, R)$, states $(P, R)$ and $(P', R')$ are distinguishable. If $P = P'$, then $R \neq R'$. To distinguish $(P, R)$ and $(P, R')$, we can construct a word $v$ for action $\circ_B$ in a similar way as we construct $u$ in the previous case.    $\square$

As a corollary of the three lemmas above, we get the following result.

**Theorem 2.** *Let $L$ be a regular language recognized by a nondeterministic automaton of $n$ states. Then the minimal biautomaton for the language $L$ has at most $2^{2n} - 2(2^n - 1)$ states. The bound is tight, and it is met by a binary nondeterministic automaton with multiple initial states.*    $\square$

If we insist on having just one initial state, then we can modify our worst-case example by adding a new letter $c$ which only acts on state 1 as $\delta(1, c) = \{1, 2, \ldots, n\}$. Theorem 2 still holds, and, moreover, the upper bound can be met by a ternary nondeterministic automaton with a single initial state.

# 5    From Syntactic Monoids to Biautomata

Let $L$ be a regular language over an alphabet $A$. The syntactic relation $\equiv_L$ of language $L$ is an equivalence relation on $A^*$ defined by $u \equiv_L v$ if and only if for every $x, y$ in $A^*$, we have $xuy \in L$ if and only if $xvy \in L$. It is known that the relation $\equiv_L$ is a congruence on the monoid $A^*$, and it has a finite index. Then the finite quotient $A^*/_{\equiv_L}$ is called *syntactic monoid* and it is denoted by $M_L$. The natural mapping $\eta_L : A^* \to M_L$ given by $\eta_L(u) = [u]_{\equiv_L}$ is called *syntactic morphism*. For simplicity, we write $\eta$, $M$, and $[u]$ instead of $\eta_L$, $M_L$, and $[u]_{\equiv_L}$, respectively. The language $L$ is a union of certain classes of $M$. If we denote by $F$ the set of these classes, that is, $F = \eta(L)$, then $L = \{u \in A^* \mid [u] \in F\}$. See [9] for other information on the notion of syntactic monoids.

For each pair $m, n$ in $M$, let $C(m, n) = \{s \in M \mid msn \in F\}$. Consider the structure $\mathcal{B}_L = (B_L, A, \cdot, \circ, i, T)$, where

$$B_L = \{C(m, n) \mid m, n \in M\},$$
$$C(m, n) \cdot a = C([a]m, n),$$
$$C(m, n) \circ a = C(m, n[a]),$$
$$i = C(1, 1) = F,$$
$$C(m, n) \in T \text{ if and only if } 1 \in C(m, n), \text{ that is, if } mn \in F.$$

We use the following result from [5] to get an upper bound on the size of the biautomaton for a language given by its syntactic monoid.

**Lemma 11 ([5], Proposition 2.9).** *Let $L$ be a regular language. Then the structure $\mathcal{B}_L$ described above is a minimal biautomaton for $L$.*    $\square$

**Proposition 2.** *Let $L$ be a regular language given by a syntactic monoid of size $n$. Then the minimal biautomaton for $L$ has at most $n^2$ states.*    $\square$

In what follows, we prove that there are languages with syntactic monoids of size $n$, for which the minimal biautomaton has $n^2$ states. To construct a worst-case example, we consider monoids which are groups. Then every subset $C(m, n)$ can be written as $\{m^{-1}fn^{-1} \mid f \in F\}$, where $x^{-1}$ denotes an inverse element of $x$ in group $M$. Next, we have $B_L = \{sFt \mid s, t \in M\}$, where $sFt = \{sft \mid f \in F\}$. Our goal is to describe a group such that state $sFt$ of $B_L$ are pairwise distinct.

We do not provide a group for every $n$, but only for even numbers $2k$ with an odd $k$. For an odd natural number $k$, we consider the $k$-th dihedral group $\mathbb{D}_k$, that is, $\mathbb{D}_k$ is a group of symmetries of a regular polygon with $k$ sides. For more precise description of these groups we refer to [3]. The group $\mathbb{D}_k$ has $2k$ elements which are of two kinds, namely rotations and reflections. We prefer to work with the usual presentation $\mathbb{D}_k = \langle \alpha, \beta \mid \alpha^k = 1, \beta^2 = 1, \beta\alpha = \alpha^{k-1}\beta \rangle$. Here $\alpha$ corresponds to a rotation through an angle of $\frac{2\pi}{k}$, and $\beta$ corresponds to a reflection across a line. The relation $\beta\alpha = \alpha^{k-1}\beta$ means, in fact, that $\alpha\beta\alpha = \beta$.

If we use relations as rewriting rules $\beta\alpha \mapsto \alpha^{k-1}\beta$, $\alpha^k \mapsto \lambda$, $\beta^2 \mapsto \lambda$, then every word over the alphabet $\{\alpha, \beta\}$ can be rewritten to the unique normal form

$\alpha^i \beta^j$ with $i \in \{0, 1, \ldots, k-1\}$ and $j \in \{0, 1\}$. We represent every element of $\mathbb{D}_k$ in this unique way. We write $\alpha^i$ for elements with $j = 0$, and denote the neutral element in $\mathbb{D}_k$ by 1 as usually. Let the parity $p(s)$ of an element $s = \alpha^i \beta^j$ be defined by $p(s) = (-1)^j$. Then $p : \mathbb{D}_k \to \{1, -1\}$ is a morphism of groups.

**Lemma 12.** *Let $k$ be an odd number with $k \geq 7$. Let $A = \{a, b\}$. Consider the subset $F = \{1, \alpha^2, \alpha^3, \beta\}$ of $\mathbb{D}_k$. Let $\eta : A^* \to \mathbb{D}_k$ be given by $\eta(a) = \alpha, \eta(b) = \beta$, and let $L = \eta^{-1}(F)$. Then the minimal biautomaton $\mathcal{B}_L$ for $L$ has $4k^2$ states.*

*Proof.* First we show that $\mathbb{D}_k$ is isomorphic to syntactic monoid $M$ of language $L$. Since $\mathbb{D}_k$ recognizes $L$, there is a monoid morphism $\psi$ from $\mathbb{D}_k$ onto $M$. Since $\mathbb{D}_k$ is a group, there is a normal subgroup $H$ of $\mathbb{D}_k$, the kernel of $\psi$, such that $F$ is a union of some classes in the partition $\mathbb{D}_k/H$. Next $H \subseteq F$ since $1 \in F$. However, only one subset of $F$, namely $\{1\}$, forms a normal subgroup of $\mathbb{D}_k$: Indeed, for a normal subgroup $H$, we see that $\alpha^2 \in H$ implies $\alpha^{k-2} \in H$, $\alpha^3 \in H$ implies $\alpha^{k-3} \in H$, and $\beta \in H$ implies $\alpha^{-1}\beta\alpha = \alpha^{k-2}\beta \in H$. Therefore, the kernel of $\psi$ is the trivial subgroup and $\psi$ is an isomorphism.

Now our goal is to prove that states $sFt$ with $s, t \in \mathbb{D}_k$ are pairwise distinct in biautomaton $\mathcal{B}_L$. For each $i$ in $\{0, 1, \ldots, k-1\}$, set

$$F_i^+ = \alpha^{k-i} F \alpha^i = \{1, \alpha^2, \alpha^3, \alpha^{k-i}\beta\alpha^i\}.$$

Since $\alpha\beta\alpha = \beta$, we can deduce $\alpha^i\beta\alpha^i = \beta$. Hence $\alpha^{k-i}\beta\alpha^i = \alpha^{2k-2i}\beta$, and we have $F_i^+ = \{1, \alpha^2, \alpha^3, \alpha^{2k-2i}\beta\}$. Let us show that $\alpha^{2k-2i}\beta \neq \alpha^{2k-2j}\beta$ whenever $i \neq j$. Recall that $k$ is odd. For each $i$ with $0 \leq 2i < k$, we have $\alpha^{2k-2i} = \alpha^{k-2i}$, where the exponent $k - 2i$ is odd. For each $i$ with $k < 2i < 2k$, that is, with $0 < 2k - 2i < k$, we have $\alpha^{2k-2i}$ with an even exponent in the set $\{0, \ldots, k-1\}$. So, states $F_0^+, F_1^+, \ldots, F_{k-1}^+$ are pairwise distinct in biautomaton $\mathcal{B}_L$. Now let

$$F_i^- = \beta F_i^+ \beta = \{1, \beta\alpha^2\beta, \beta\alpha^3\beta, \beta\alpha^{2k-2i}\},$$

where $\beta\alpha^2\beta = \alpha^{-2}$, $\beta\alpha^3\beta = \alpha^{-3}$ and $\beta\alpha^{2k-2i} = \alpha^{2i}\beta$.

Therefore we have $F_i^- = \{1, \alpha^{-2}, \alpha^{-3}, \alpha^{2i}\beta\}$. States $F_i^-$ are different from states $F_i^+$ because they contain $\alpha^{k-2}$. Furthermore, states $F_i^-$ are pairwise distinct because the equality $\beta F_i^+ \beta = \beta F_j^+ \beta$ for some $i$ and $j$ implies $F_i^+ = F_j^+$.

Next for every $j$ in $\{0, 1, \ldots, k-1\}$, consider states $\alpha^j F_i^+$ and $\alpha^j F_i^-$. Thus in total, we have $2k^2$ states, and we need to show that they are pairwise distinct. Let $G$ be one of these states, thus $G$ is a four-element subset of $\mathbb{D}_k$. We are going to show that it is possible to reconstruct $i$ and $j$ and sign $+$ or $-$ from $G$. The set $G$ consists of three elements of parity 1, and of one element of parity $-1$.

The three elements of parity 1 are powers of $\alpha$ with some exponents. Two of these exponents are consecutive numbers under the assumption that we count modulo $k$, that is, the numbers $k - 1$ and 0 are understood to be consecutive. Denote the third exponent by $\ell$. This exponent is isolated, formally $\alpha^\ell \in G$, $\alpha^{\ell-1} \notin G$, and $\alpha^{\ell+1} \notin G$. Now if $\alpha^{\ell+2} \in G$, then $G = \alpha^\ell F_i^+$ for some $i$, and if $\alpha^{\ell+2} \notin G$, then $\alpha^{\ell-2} \in G$ and $G = \alpha^\ell F_i^-$ for some $i$.

The element of parity $-1$ is of the form $\alpha^m \beta$. In case $G = \alpha^\ell F_i^+$, the exponent $m$ is congruent with $\ell - 2i$ modulo $k$. Hence $\ell - m$ is congruent modulo $k$

with $2i$. This describes $i$ uniquely because $k$ is relatively prime to 2. If $G = \alpha^\ell F_i^-$, then we have $m$ congruent with $2i$ which describes $i$ in $\{0, 1, \ldots, k-1\}$ uniquely.

Let $\mathcal{F}$ be the family of the above $2k^2$ sets. We define the second family by $\mathcal{F}' = \{G\beta \mid G \in \mathcal{F}\}$. The sets in $\mathcal{F}'$ consist of three elements of parity $-1$, and of one element of parity 1. This observation implies that the sets in $\mathcal{F}'$ are different from the sets in $\mathcal{F}$. Moreover, if two sets $G\beta$ and $H\beta$ in $\mathcal{F}'$ are equal, then after multiplying by $\beta$, we get that two sets $G$ and $H$ in $\mathcal{F}$ are equal. This is not possible. Altogether, we have $4k^2$ pairwise distinct sets of the form $sFt$, which concludes the proof.    □

Hence the upper bound $n^2$ can be met in infinitely many cases. The next theorem summarizes the above results.

**Theorem 3.** *Let $L$ be a regular language with the syntactic monoid of size $n$. Then the minimal biautomaton for $L$ has at most $n^2$ states. The bound can be met for every $n$ with $n = 2k$, where $k$ is an odd number with $k \geq 7$, by a binary language $L$ given in Lemma 12.*    □

## 6    Final Remarks

There are several natural questions that are not considered in this paper. First, we could discuss in more detail the case of a unary alphabet. This is not so interesting because both actions are identical in the minimal biautomaton for a unary language. Consequently, the minimal biautomaton is exactly of the same size as minimal deterministic automaton. For example, for the language $(a^n)^*$, the minimal deterministic automaton, the minimal nondeterministic automaton, as well as the minimal biautomaton, all have $n$ states. If a unary language is represented by a nondeterministic automaton, then the corresponding biautomaton is of size $e^{\Theta(\sqrt{n \ln n})}$ since this function provides a trade-off for the conversion of unary nondeterministic automata into deterministic automata [2,8].

Next, we could solve the missing cases in Section 5. We also could discuss in more detail the transformations in the opposite direction. More precisely, if a biautomaton is given, then how large can the other structures be? Or, equivalently, having some classical structure, like deterministic automaton, nondeterministic automaton, or syntactic monoid for a given language, how small can the biautomaton be? By the results in [5], a minimal deterministic automaton is a part of a minimal biautomaton, and this lower bound for a biautomaton is tight, as the example in the previous paragraph shows. For nondeterministic automata and syntactic monoids, we only have some asymptotic estimations.

Last but not least, there are natural questions concerning descriptional complexity of language operations. If $\mathcal{B}$ is a biautomaton for a language $L$, then a biautomaton for the reverse of $L$ can be obtained from $\mathcal{B}$ by interchanging the roles of the right and left actions. Similarly, we get a biautomaton for the complement of $L$ from $\mathcal{B}$ by interchanging the terminal and non-terminal states. The operations of union and intersection lead to classical product constructions, and it is possible to prove that the product of the sizes of the given biautomata provides

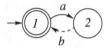

**Fig. 3.** A nondeterministic biautomaton accepting the language $\{a^n b^n \mid n \geq 0\}$; the right action is drawn by the dashed arrow

the tight bound for the resulting biautomaton. Concatenation and Kleene star could also be considered, but we only expect some asymptotic bounds here.

To conclude the paper, let us remark that allowing nondeterministic, or even undefined transitions like in Fig. 3, results in nondeterministic biautomata that recognize the class of linear context-free languages [7].

# References

1. Brzozowski, J.: Derivatives of regular expressions. J. ACM 11, 481–494 (1964)
2. Chrobak, M.: Finite automata and unary languages. Theoret. Comput. Sci. 47, 149–158 (1986); Erratum: Theoret. Comput. Sci. 302, 497–498 (2003)
3. Hall Jr., M.: Theory of Groups. Macmillan (1959)
4. Jirásková, G., Šebej, J.: Note on reversal of binary regular languages. In: Holzer, M., Kutrib, M., Pighizzini, G. (eds.) DCFS 2011. LNCS, vol. 6808, pp. 212–221. Springer, Heidelberg (2011)
5. Klíma, O., Polák, L.: On biautomata. To appear in RAIRO, http://math.muni.cz/~klima/Math/publications.html (previous version: Non-Classical Models for Automata and Applications, NCMA 2011, pp. 153–164)
6. Klíma, O., Polák, L.: Biautomata for k-Piecewise Testable Languages. Accepted at DLT (2012), preprint available at, http://math.muni.cz/~klima/Math/publications.html
7. Loukanova, R.: Linear Context Free Languages. In: Jones, C.B., Liu, Z., Woodcock, J. (eds.) ICTAC 2007. LNCS, vol. 4711, pp. 351–365. Springer, Heidelberg (2007)
8. Lyubich, Y.I.: Estimates for optimal determinization of nondeterministic autonomous automata. Sib. Mat. Zh. 5, 337–355 (1964)
9. Pin, J.-E.: Chapter 10: Syntactic semigroups. In: Rozenberg, G., Salomaa, A. (eds.) Handbook of Formal Languages, vol. I, pp. 679–746. Springer, Heidelberg (1997)
10. Schützenberger, M.P.: On finite monoids having only trivial subgroups. Information and Control 8, 190–194 (1965)
11. Sipser, M.: Introduction to the theory of computation. PWS Publishing Company, Boston (1997)
12. Šebej, J.: Reversal of regular languages and state complexity. In: Pardubská, D. (ed.) Proc. 10th ITAT, Šafárik University, Košice, pp. 47–54 (2010)
13. Simon, I.: Piecewise Testable Events. In: GI-Fachtagung 1975. LNCS, vol. 33, pp. 214–222. Springer, Heidelberg (1975)
14. Yu, S.: Chapter 2: Regular languages. In: Rozenberg, G., Salomaa, A. (eds.) Handbook of Formal Languages, vol. I, pp. 41–110. Springer, Heidelberg (1997)
15. Yu, S., Zhuang, Q., Salomaa, K.: The state complexity of some basic operations on regular languages. Theoret. Comput. Sci. 125, 315–328 (1994)

# Descriptional Complexity
# of Pushdown Store Languages[*]

Andreas Malcher[1], Katja Meckel[1], Carlo Mereghetti[2], and Beatrice Palano[2]

[1] Institut für Informatik, Universität Giessen,
Arndtstr. 2, 35392 Giessen, Germany
{malcher,meckel}@informatik.uni-giessen.de
[2] Dipartimento di Informatica, Università degli Studi di Milano,
via Comelico 39, 20135 Milano, Italy
{carlo.mereghetti,beatrice.palano}@unimi.it

**Abstract.** It is well known that the *pushdown store language* $P(M)$
of a pushdown automaton (PDA) $M$ — i.e., the language consisting of
words occurring on the pushdown along accepting computations of $M$
— is a regular language. Here, we design *succinct nondeterministic finite
automata (NFA)* accepting $P(M)$. In detail, an upper bound on the size
of an NFA for $P(M)$ is obtained, which is quadratic in the number of
states and linear in the number of pushdown symbols of $M$. Moreover,
this upper bound is shown to be asymptotically optimal. Then, several
restricted variants of PDA are considered, leading to improved constructions. In all cases, we prove the asymptotical optimality of the size of
the resulting NFA. Finally, we apply our results to decidability questions
related to PDA, and obtain solutions in deterministic polynomial time.

**Keywords:** pushdown automata, pushdown store languages, descriptional complexity, decidability questions.

## 1   Introduction

Beside the formal definition of the accepted or generated language, the introduction of an accepting or generating device always brings the attention to several
"auxiliary" formal structures related to the device itself. Such structures, which
can be either crucial part of or derived from the device definition, are not only
interesting *per se*, but their investigation has often other relevant motivations.
For instance, we can act on these structures to tune device computational capabilities. Or, they can directly imply certain device properties. Yet, they can also
be used as a theoretical tool to get results in different contexts.

Only to cite some examples, in the realm of Turing machines, the well known
language of valid computations is introduced in [11]. The study of this language
has been widely used to point out undecidability of several problems and non-
recursiveness of certain descriptional trade-offs (see, e.g., [7,14]). In quantum

[*] Partially supported by CRUI/DAAD under the project "Programma Vigoni: Descriptional Complexity of Non-Classical Computational Models."

M. Kutrib, N. Moreira, and R. Reis (Eds.): DCFS 2012, LNCS 7386, pp. 209–221, 2012.
© Springer-Verlag Berlin Heidelberg 2012

automata theory, a basic part of the definition of several variants of quantum automata is the so-called control language which, very roughly speaking, describes computational dynamics which are admissible in a given model [19]. By modifying the control language, we obtain several quantum devices with different computational power. In [3], particular families of so-called selection languages are considered to tune the generative power of contextual grammars.

In this paper, we focus on *pushdown store languages* for pushdown automata (PDA). Given a PDA $M$, its pushdown store language $P(M)$ consists of all words occurring on the pushdown store along *accepting* computations of $M$. (It should be remarked that similar sets for stack automata have been investigated in [6].) It is known from [8] that, surprisingly enough, $P(M)$ is regular for any PDA. More recently, an alternative proof of this fact has been given in [1]. Here, we tackle the study of pushdown store languages from a descriptional complexity point of view, and design *succinct nondeterministic finite automata (NFA)* for their acceptance. In Section 3, a first general construction of an NFA for $P(M)$ inspired by [1] is presented. We subsequently improve this construction and obtain an upper bound to the size (i.e., number of states) of the NFA, which is quadratic in the number of states and linear in the number of pushdown symbols of the PDA $M$. Then, we show that this bound cannot be improved in general by proving its asymptotical optimality. In Section 4, we will be dealing with restricted versions of PDA, namely: PDA which cannot pop, stateless PDA, and counter machines, i.e., PDA whose pushdown store languages are subsets of $Z^*Z_0$, for a bottom-of-pushdown symbol $Z_0$ and a different pushdown symbol $Z$. For any of these restrictions, we present NFA for pushdown store languages which are strictly smaller than the NFA given for the general case. Moreover, in all cases, we prove the optimality of our constructions.

Finally, in Section 5, we apply our results on the descriptional complexity of pushdown store languages to the analysis of the hardness of some decision problems related to PDA. We show that the questions of whether $P(M)$ of a given PDA $M$ is a finite set or is a finite set of words having at most length $k$, for a given $k \geq 1$, can be answered in deterministic polynomial time. Moreover, we also prove the P-completeness of these questions. As an application, we obtain that it is P-complete to decide whether a given unambiguous PDA is a constant height PDA or is a PDA of constant height $k$, for a given $k \geq 1$ [2,5]. As another application, we show the same complexity evaluation for the question of whether $P(M)$ is a subset of $Z^*Z_0$. This is equivalent to asking whether a given PDA is essentially a counter machine. In what follows, some proofs are omitted owing to space restrictions.

## 2    Preliminaries and Definitions

We assume that the reader is familiar with basic notions in formal language theory (see, e.g., [10,15]). The set of natural numbers, with 0, is denoted by $\mathbb{N}$. The set of all words (including the empty word $\lambda$) over a finite alphabet $\Sigma$ is denoted by $\Sigma^*$, and we let $\Sigma^+ = \Sigma^* \setminus \{\lambda\}$. The length of a word $w \in \Sigma^*$ is denoted by $|w|$, and by $\Sigma^{\leq k}$ and $\Sigma^{>k}$ we denote, respectively, the set of all words of length less than or equal to $k$ and larger than $k$. Given a language $L \subseteq \Sigma^*$, then $suf(L) = \{y \in \Sigma^* \mid \exists x \in \Sigma^*: xy \in L\}$ is the set of all suffixes of words in $L$. The reversal of a word $w$ is denoted by $w^R$, and of a language $L$ by $L^R$.

A *pushdown automaton* (PDA, see e.g. [10,15]) is formally defined to be a 7-tuple $M = \langle Q, \Sigma, \Gamma, \delta, q_0, Z_0, F \rangle$, where $Q$ is a finite set of states, $\Sigma$ is a finite input alphabet, $\Gamma$ is a finite pushdown alphabet, $\delta$ is the transition function mapping $Q \times (\Sigma \cup \{\lambda\}) \times \Gamma$ to finite subsets of $Q \times \Gamma^*$, $q_0 \in Q$ is the initial state, $Z_0 \in \Gamma$ is a particular pushdown symbol, called the bottom-of-pushdown symbol, which initially appears on the pushdown store, and $F \subseteq Q$ is a set of accepting (or final) states. Roughly speaking, a *nondeterministic finite automaton* (NFA) can be viewed as a PDA where the pushdown store is never used.

A *configuration* of a PDA is a triple $(q, w, \gamma)$, where $q$ is the current state, $w$ the unread part of the input, and $\gamma$ the current content of the pushdown store, the *leftmost* symbol of $\gamma$ being the *top* symbol. For $p, q \in Q$, $a \in \Sigma \cup \{\lambda\}$, $w \in \Sigma^*$, $\gamma, \beta \in \Gamma^*$, and $Z \in \Gamma$, we write $(q, aw, Z\gamma) \vdash (p, w, \beta\gamma)$ whenever $(p, \beta) \in \delta(q, a, Z)$. As usual, the reflexive transitive closure of $\vdash$ is denoted by $\vdash^*$. The language accepted by $M$ by *accepting states* is the set

$$L(M) = \{w \in \Sigma^* \mid (q_0, w, Z_0) \vdash^* (f, \lambda, \gamma), \text{ for some } f \in F \text{ and } \gamma \in \Gamma^*\}.$$

Throughout the paper, unless otherwise stated, we will always be considering acceptance by accepting states. We measure the *size* of a PDA $M$ by the product of the number of states, the number of pushdown symbols, the number of input symbols, and the maximum length $\mu(M)$ of strings of pushdown symbols appearing in the transition rules, i.e., $|Q| \cdot |\Gamma| \cdot |\Sigma| \cdot \mu(M)$. We also refer to [14] for a the discussion on PDA size measuring.

We consider PDA to be in *normal* form, i.e., with $\mu(M) \leq 2$. In this case, the pushdown height grows at most by 1 at each move. By introducing new states for every transition of a given PDA, it can be shown similarly to [14] that every PDA of size $n$ can be converted to an equivalent normal form PDA of size $O(n)$. *For the rest of the paper, we assume that all PDA are in normal form.*

The *pushdown store language* of a PDA $M$ (see, e.g., [1,8]) is defined as the set $P(M)$ of all words occurring on the pushdown store along accepting computations of $M$. Formally:

$$P(M) = \{u \in \Gamma^* \mid \exists x, y \in \Sigma^*, q \in Q, f \in F:$$
$$(q_0, xy, Z_0) \vdash^* (q, y, u) \vdash^* (f, \lambda, \gamma), \text{ for some } \gamma \in \Gamma^*\}.$$

To clarify the notion of pushdown store language, we continue with an example.

*Example 1.* The language $\{a^n b^n \mid n \geq 1\}$ is accepted by the following (deterministic) PDA $M = \langle \{q_0, q_1, q_2\}, \{a, b\}, \{Z, Z_0\}, \delta, q_0, Z_0, \{q_2\} \rangle$ such that

$$\delta(q_0, a, Z_0) = \{(q_0, ZZ_0)\}, \ \delta(q_0, a, Z) = \{(q_0, ZZ)\},$$
$$\delta(q_0, b, Z) = \{(q_1, \lambda)\}, \ \delta(q_1, b, Z) = \{(q_1, \lambda)\}, \ \delta(q_1, \lambda, Z_0) = \{(q_2, Z_0)\}.$$

It is easy to see that the pushdown store language is $P(M) = Z^* Z_0$. □

## 3  Pushdown Store Languages: The General Case

Already in [8], it is proved that the pushdown store language $P(M)$ of a PDA $M$ is regular. However, here we quickly review the proof given in [1], whose constructions enable us to obtain better bounds on the size of NFA accepting $P(M)$. In what follows, for $x \in \Sigma^*$, we use the short-hand notation

$$(p, w) \vdash^x (p', w') \quad \text{if and only if} \quad (p, x, w) \vdash^* (p', \lambda, w').$$

**Theorem 2 ([1]).** *The pushdown store language of any PDA is regular.*

*Proof.* The construction given in [1] can be summarized as follows. Let $M = \langle Q, \Sigma, \Gamma, \delta, q_0, Z_0, F \rangle$ be a PDA. For every $q \in Q$, the following sets are defined:

$$Acc(q) = \{u \in \Gamma^* \mid \exists x, y \in \Sigma^* : (q_0, xy, Z_0) \vdash^* (q, y, u)\},$$
$$Co\text{-}Acc(q) = \{u \in \Gamma^* \mid \exists y \in \Sigma^*,\ f \in F,\ u' \in \Gamma^* : (q, y, u) \vdash^* (f, \lambda, u')\}.$$

Then, the pushdown store language is easily seen to be

$$P(M) = \bigcup_{q \in Q} Acc(q) \cap Co\text{-}Acc(q).$$

Now, for every $q \in Q$, we construct a left-linear grammar $G_{Acc(q)}$ for $Acc(q)$ and a right-linear grammar $G_{Co\text{-}Acc(q)}$ for $Co\text{-}Acc(q)$, thus showing that $P(M)$ is regular. Informally speaking, $G_{Acc(q)}$ simulates the behavior of $M$ from an initial configuration until the state $q$ is entered, while generating $u$ on the pushdown store. Formally, $G_{Acc(q)}$ has terminal alphabet $\Gamma$, nonterminal alphabet $Q \times \Gamma$, start symbol $(q_0, Z_0)$, and the following rules:

(1) $(p, Z) \longrightarrow (p', Z')$, if there exists $x \in \Sigma^*$ such that $(p, Z) \vdash^x (p', Z')$
(2) $(p, Z) \longrightarrow (p', Z')t$, if there exists $a \in \Sigma \cup \{\lambda\}$ with $(p', Z't) \in \delta(p, a, Z)$
(3) $(p, Z) \longrightarrow \lambda$,     if there exists $x \in \Sigma^*$ such that $(p, Z) \vdash^x (q, \lambda)$
(4) $(q, Z) \longrightarrow Z$.

It is shown in [1] that $G_{Acc(q)}$ generates $Acc(q)$. On the other hand, $G_{Co\text{-}Acc(q)}$ simulates the behavior of $M$ from configurations having $q$ as state, $u$ as pushdown content, and reaching an accepting state. Formally, $G_{Co\text{-}Acc(q)}$ has terminal alphabet $\Gamma$, nonterminal alphabet $Q \cup \{s\}$, start symbol $q$, and the following rules:

(5) $p \longrightarrow Zp'$,   if there exists $x \in \Sigma^*$ such that $(p, Z) \vdash^x (p', \lambda)$
(6) $p \longrightarrow Zs$,   if there exists $x \in \Sigma^*, p' \in F, u' \in \Gamma^+ : (p, Z) \vdash^x (p', u')$
(7) $s \longrightarrow Zs \mid \lambda$, for all $Z \in \Gamma$
(8) $p \longrightarrow \lambda$,    if $p \in F$.

Again in [1], it is shown that $G_{Co\text{-}Acc(q)}$ generates $Co\text{-}Acc(q)$. Finally, it is important to stress that grammars $G_{Acc(q)}$ and $G_{Co\text{-}Acc(q)}$ can be effectively constructed. In particular, for establishing rules (1), (3), (5), and (6), the decidability of the emptiness problem for context-free languages is used (see, e.g., [15]).    $\square$

To clarify the meaning and construction of grammars $G_{Acc(q)}$ and $G_{Co\text{-}Acc(q)}$ given in the previous theorem, in the following example we provide such grammars for the PDA $M$ in Example 1 accepting the language $\{a^n b^n \mid n \geq 1\}$.

*Example 3.* For the sake of brevity, we provide grammars only for $Acc(q_0)$ and $Co\text{-}Acc(q_0)$. However, the reader may easily verify that $P(M)$ consists of only $Acc(q_0) \cap Co\text{-}Acc(q_0)$. The grammar $G_{Acc(q_0)}$ (resp., $G_{Co\text{-}Acc(q_0)}$) has start symbol $(q_0, Z_0)$ (resp., $q_0$), and the following rules:

| $G_{Acc(q_0)}$ | $G_{Co\text{-}Acc(q_0)}$ |
|---|---|
| $(q_0, Z_0) \rightarrow (q_0, Z)Z_0$ | $q_0 \rightarrow Zq_1$ |
| $(q_0, Z) \rightarrow (q_0, Z)Z \mid Z$ | $q_1 \rightarrow Zq_1 \mid Z_0 s$ |
| | $s \rightarrow Zs \mid Z_0 s \mid \lambda$ |

It is not hard to verify that $G_{Acc(q_0)}$ generates $Z^* Z_0$, while $G_{Co\text{-}Acc(q_0)}$ gives $Z^* Z_0 \{Z, Z_0\}^*$. The intersection of these languages clearly yields $Z^* Z_0$, which is $P(M)$ as pointed out in Example 1.    □

From the constructive proof of Theorem 2, we are able to provide a first upper bound on the size of NFA for pushdown store languages. From now on, for the descriptional costs of well known operations on NFA, the reader is referred to, e.g., [13,21].

**Proposition 4.** *Let $M = \langle Q, \Sigma, \Gamma, \delta, q_0, Z_0, F \rangle$ be a PDA. Then, $P(M)$ can be accepted by an NFA with $|Q|^3 |\Gamma| + |Q|^2 (|\Gamma| + 1) + |Q| + 1$ many states.*

*Proof.* By Theorem 2, we have that $P(M) = \bigcup_{q \in Q} Acc(q) \cap Co\text{-}Acc(q)$. So, we begin by constructing, for any $q \in Q$, NFA accepting $Acc(q)$ and $Co\text{-}Acc(q)$. For $Acc(q)$, we start from the left-linear grammar $G_{Acc(q)}$ and construct a right-linear grammar generating the reversal $Acc(q)^R$ by simply interchanging every type (2) rule $(p, Z) \rightarrow (p', Z')t$ with $(p, Z) \rightarrow t(p', Z')$. Second, this right-linear grammar is directly converted to an equivalent NFA of size $|Q| \cdot |\Gamma|$ plus an additional and unique accepting state due to type (3) and (4) rules. This gives an NFA $N$ of size $|Q| \cdot |\Gamma| + 1$. Now, by basically "reverting arrows" and switching the initial and final state in $N$, we get an NFA $N_{Acc(q)}$ of the same size accepting $Acc(q)$. For $Co\text{-}Acc(q)$, the right-linear grammar $G_{Co\text{-}Acc(q)}$ can be directly translated into an equivalent NFA $N_{Co\text{-}Acc(q)}$ of size $|Q| + 1$.

From NFA $N_{Acc(q)}$, $N_{Co\text{-}Acc(q)}$, and by using well known constructions on NFA, we get an NFA with $(|Q| \cdot |\Gamma| + 1)(|Q| + 1)$ states for $Acc(q) \cap Co\text{-}Acc(q)$. Finally, the union over all $q \in Q$ can be implemented by an NFA of at most $|Q|(|Q| \cdot |\Gamma| + 1)(|Q| + 1) + 1 = |Q|^3 |\Gamma| + |Q|^2 (|\Gamma| + 1) + |Q| + 1$ states.    □

We are now going to improve Proposition 4 and obtain a smaller NFA:

**Theorem 5.** *Let $M = \langle Q, \Sigma, \Gamma, \delta, q_0, Z_0, F \rangle$ be a PDA. Then, $P(M)$ is accepted by an NFA whose size is bounded by $|Q|^2 (|\Gamma| + 1) + |Q|(2|\Gamma| + 3) + 2$.*

*Proof.* The key idea is to "get rid" of the union over $q \in Q$ in the definition of $P(M)$, by defining the set $Acc(Q)$ (resp., $Co\text{-}Acc(Q)$) representing all the pushdown contents reachable from the initial configuration (resp., from which a final state can be reached). Then, we have to build only the intersection of these two sets. More precisely, we let $[Q] = \{[q] \mid q \in Q\}$ and define the following sets:

$$Acc(Q) = \{[q]u \in [Q]\Gamma^* \mid u \in Acc(q)\},$$
$$Co\text{-}Acc(Q) = \{[q]u \in [Q]\Gamma^* \mid u \in Co\text{-}Acc(q)\}.$$

A left-linear grammar for $Acc(Q)$ is built similarly as $G_{Acc(q)}$ in Theorem 2, but we enlarge the terminal alphabet by the set $[Q]$, and have the following rules:

(1) $(p, Z) \longrightarrow (p', Z')$, if there exists $x \in \Sigma^*$ such that $(p, Z) \vdash^x (p', Z')$
(2) $(p, Z) \longrightarrow (p', Z')t$, if there exists $a \in \Sigma \cup \{\lambda\}$ such that $(p', Z't) \in \delta(p, a, z)$
(3)' $(p, Z) \longrightarrow [q]$,      if there exists $x \in \Sigma^*$ such that $(p, Z) \vdash^x (q, \lambda)$
(4)' $(q, Z) \longrightarrow [q]Z$.

Similarly as in Proposition 4, from this left-linear grammar we can obtain an NFA for $Acc(Q)$ featuring $|Q| \cdot (|\Gamma| + 1) + 1$ many states.

The right-linear grammar for $Co\text{-}Acc(Q)$ is also built similarly as $G_{Co\text{-}Acc(q)}$ in Theorem 2. We enlarge again the terminal alphabet by $[Q]$, and we add a new nonterminal $S$ which will be the start symbol. Then, we have the same rules (5) to (8) and additional rules $S \longrightarrow [p]p$, for all $p \in Q$. As in Proposition 4, this right-linear grammar can be converted to an NFA having at most $|Q| + 2$ states.

From the two obtained NFA, an NFA $N$ for $Acc(Q) \cap Co\text{-}Acc(Q)$ can be constructed, featuring $(|Q| \cdot (|\Gamma| + 1) + 1)(|Q| + 2) = |Q|^2(|\Gamma| + 1) + |Q|(2|\Gamma| + 3) + 2$ many states. Now, notice that $P(M)$ can be obtained by deleting the initial symbols $[q]$ from every string in $L(N)$. Thus, by simply substituting in $N$ the initial transitions taking place on $[q]$ with $\lambda$-transitions, we get an NFA for $P(M)$ with $|Q|^2(|\Gamma| + 1) + |Q|(2|\Gamma| + 3) + 2$ states.                    □

Our construction in Theorem 5 is the best possible. In fact, we are able to show an optimal lower bound of $\Omega(|Q|^2|\Gamma|)$. To achieve this, we start by introducing a simple language with the corresponding accepting PDA, and study the lower limit to the size of NFA for the pushdown store language of the given PDA. The result is contained in the following

**Lemma 6.** *For a fixed $m \geq 2$, let the single word language $L_m = \{a^{m^2}b\}$. Then, $L_m$ can be accepted by a PDA $M_{m,1}$ of size $O(m)$ such that every NFA accepting $P(M_{m,1})$ needs at least $m^2 + 3$ states.*

This result can then be generalized to the following lemma which gives the desired lower bound of $\Omega(|Q|^2|\Gamma|)$. More precisely, PDA for the finite languages $L_{m,k} = \{(a^{m^2}b^{m^2})^{k/2}c\}$ for even $k$, and $L_{m,k} = \{(a^{m^2}b^{m^2})^{(k-1)/2}a^{m^2}c\}$ for odd $k \geq 3$, can be provided and lower limits to the size of NFA for their pushdown store languages can be shown:

**Lemma 7.** *For $m, k \geq 2$, there exist PDA $M_{m,k} = \langle Q, \Sigma, \Gamma, \delta, q_0, Z_0, F \rangle$ accepting $L_{m,k}$ such that $|Q| = 2m + 2$ and $|\Gamma| = 2k + 1$. Moreover, any NFA for $P(M_{m,k})$ needs at least $k \cdot m^2 + 3 \in \Omega(|Q|^2|\Gamma|)$ states.*

As a consequence of Lemma 7, we obtain that our construction in Theorem 5 of NFA for pushdown store languages is the best possible:

**Theorem 8.** *Let* $M = \langle Q, \Sigma, \Gamma, \delta, q_0, Z_0, F \rangle$ *be a PDA. Then, an NFA for* $P(M)$ *exists with* $O(|Q|^2|\Gamma|)$ *states. On the other hand, there exist infinitely many PDA* $M_{Q,\Gamma}$ *of size* $O(|Q| \cdot |\Gamma|)$ *such that every NFA accepting* $P(M_{Q,\Gamma})$ *needs* $\Omega(|Q|^2|\Gamma|)$ *states.*

# 4  Pushdown Store Languages for Special Cases

Here, we consider restricted models of PDA for which we are able to provide NFA for their pushdown store languages, whose size is strictly below the general upper bound given in Theorem 5.

## 4.1  PDA Which Can Never Pop

As a first restriction, we consider PDA *which never pop* a symbol from the pushdown. Thus, for such devices, once stored in the pushdown, symbols can never be modified. It is easy to see that these PDA accept exactly the regular languages. In what follows, given a PDA $M = \langle Q, \Sigma, \Gamma, \delta, q_0, Z_0, F \rangle$ of this kind, we quickly outline the construction of an NFA for $P(M)$ of size $|Q| \cdot |\Gamma| + 1$.

It is not hard to see that, in this case, we have

$$P(M) = \{ u \in \Gamma^* \mid u \in Acc(q) \text{ and } q \in F \}.$$

Moreover, the left-linear grammars for $Acc(q)$, with $q \in F$, given in Theorem 2 now drop type (1) and type (3) rules, and can be summarized in a single left-linear grammar with terminal alphabet $\Gamma$, nonterminal alphabet $Q \times \Gamma$, start symbol $(q_0, Z_0)$, and the following rules:

(1) $(p, Z) \longrightarrow (p', Z')t$, if there exists $a \in \Sigma \cup \{\lambda\}$ such that $(p', Z't) \in \delta(p, a, Z)$
(2) $(q, Z) \longrightarrow Z$,　　 if $q \in F$.

From this left-linear grammar, we can easily obtain an NFA for $P(M)$ with $|Q| \cdot |\Gamma| + 1$ states. This upper bound is also tight owing to the following

**Lemma 9.** *For* $m, k \geq 2$, *there exist PDA* $M_{m,k}$ *which can never pop having* $m$ *states and* $k$ *pushdown symbols, for which every NFA for* $P(M_{m,k})$ *needs at least* $k \cdot m + 1$ *states.*

Altogether, for PDA which can never pop, we get that $|Q| \cdot |\Gamma| + 1$ is a tight bound for the size of NFA accepting their pushdown store languages.

## 4.2  Stateless PDA

Next, we consider PDA which have *one state only*, whose acceptance policy is clearly by *empty pushdown* (i.e., they accept by completely sweeping the input and emptying the pushdown store [10,15]). Such devices are also called *stateless PDA*. It is well known that they are equivalent to PDA, while their deterministic version is strictly less powerful, characterizing the class of *simple* languages (see, e.g., [10]). Clearly, for stateless PDA the upper bound of Theorem 5 reduces to $3 \cdot |\Gamma| + 6$. However, we are now going to provide a better upper bound.

Let us apply the constructions in the proof of Theorem 2 to a stateless PDA $M = \langle \{q_0\}, \Sigma, \Gamma, \delta, q_0, Z_0, \emptyset \rangle$. For $Acc(q_0)$, we can take $\langle \Gamma \rangle = \{\langle Z \rangle \mid Z \in \Gamma\}$ as set of nonterminal symbols, and consider rules of the following form:

(1) $\langle Z \rangle \longrightarrow \langle Z' \rangle$,  if there exists $x \in \Sigma^*$ such that $(q_0, Z) \vdash^x (q_0, Z')$
(2) $\langle Z \rangle \longrightarrow \langle Z' \rangle t$, if there exists $a \in \Sigma \cup \{\lambda\}$ such that $(q_0, Z't) \in \delta(q_0, a, Z)$
(3) $\langle Z \rangle \longrightarrow \lambda$,    if there exists $x \in \Sigma^*$ such that $(q_0, Z) \vdash^x (q_0, \lambda)$
(4) $\langle Z \rangle \longrightarrow Z$.

This leads to an NFA of size at most $|\Gamma| + 1$. For the set $Co\text{-}Acc(q_0)$, we only have to consider rules of the form

(5) $q_0 \longrightarrow Z q_0$, if there exists $x \in \Sigma^*$ such that $(q_0, Z) \vdash^x (q_0, \lambda)$
(6) $q_0 \longrightarrow \lambda$.

An equivalent NFA can be trivially constructed, with exactly one state. Thus, an NFA for $P(M) = Acc(q_0) \cap Co\text{-}Acc(q_0)$ needs at most $|\Gamma| + 1$ states. The optimality of this bound can also be shown and, altogether, we get the following

**Theorem 10.** *Let $M = \langle \{q_0\}, \Sigma, \Gamma, \delta, q_0, Z_0, \emptyset \rangle$ be a stateless PDA. Then, every NFA for $P(M)$ needs at most $|\Gamma|+1$ states. Moreover, for any $k \geq 0$, there exists a stateless PDA $M_k$ having $|\Gamma_k| = k+1$ pushdown symbols, for which every NFA for $P(M_k)$ needs at least $k + 2 = |\Gamma_k| + 1$ states.*

## 4.3   Counter Machine

A *counter machine* (see, e.g., [9,15]) is defined as a traditional PDA with the restriction that the pushdown alphabet contains only two symbols, namely, the usual bottom-of-pushdown symbol $Z_0$, which can never be pushed or popped, and a distinguished symbol $Z$. So, the pushdown store language of a counter machine is a subset of $Z^* Z_0$ (see also [12]). As an example, the PDA in Example 1 is actually a counter machine.

We are going to show that the size of NFA accepting the pushdown store language of counter machines is linear in $|Q|$ and not quadratic as proved in Theorem 5 for general PDA. Moreover, we will show the optimality of such a size bound. Let us begin by observing the following easy fact:

**Lemma 11.** *Given a counter machine $M$, then $P(M)$ is either $Z^* Z_0$ or $Z^{\leq h} Z_0$ for a fixed $h \geq 0$.*

For a counter machine having pushdown store language of the form $Z^{\leq h} Z_0$, we are able to bound $h$ by the number of finite control states:

**Theorem 12.** *Given the counter machine* $M = \langle Q, \Sigma, \{Z_0, Z\}, \delta, q_0, Z_0, F \rangle$, *let* $P(M) = Z^{\leq h} Z_0$ *for a fixed* $h \geq 0$. *Then,* $h \leq |Q|$.

*Proof.* Let us assume that $h > |Q|$. We are going to prove that $P(M) = Z^* Z_0$, thus contradicting the supposed finiteness of $P(M)$. Consider an accepting computation $\Pi$ of $M$ on an input string $x \in L(M)$, along which the pushdown content $Z^h Z_0$ appears.

To deal with the "hardest" situation, we assume that $Z^h Z_0$ appears during a *branch* of $\Pi$ at the end of which the pushdown store is emptied. So, more formally, $\Pi$ has a branch of computation with the following features:

(1) it starts from a configuration with pushdown content $Z Z_0$,
(2) it reaches a configuration where the pushdown content $Z^h Z_0$ shows up,
(3) it starts from such a configuration and ends in a configuration with pushdown content $Z Z_0$,
(4) it never finds itself in a configuration where the pushdown contains $Z_0$ only.

At the end of this proof, we will fix the case in which (3) does not hold within $\Pi$. We call *ascending (resp., descending)* the sub-branch between breakpoints (1) and (2) (resp., (2) and (3)). During the ascending sub-branch, $M$ being in normal form, there must exist a sequence of configurations having the form $\{(q^{(i)}, x^{(i)}, Z^i Z_0)\}_{i=1}^{h}$. Since $h > |Q|$, there exist $1 \leq r < s \leq h$ such that $q^{(r)} = q^{(s)} = q$ and $x^{(r)} = w x^{(s)}$, for some $w \in \Sigma^*$. It is easy to see that, upon consuming the substring $w$, $M$ increases the pushdown content by the factor $Z^t$ with $0 < t = s - r$.

For the descending sub-branch, again due to the normal form, we get the existence of a sequence of configurations of the form $\{(p^{(i)}, y^{(i)}, Z^{h-i} Z_0)\}_{i=0}^{h-1}$. Since $h > |Q|$, there exist $0 \leq r' < s' \leq h - 1$ such that $p^{(r')} = p^{(s')} = p$ and $y^{(r')} = w' y^{(s')}$, for some $w' \in \Sigma^*$. Now, upon consuming $w'$, $M$ deletes the factor $Z^{t'}$ from the pushdown store, with $0 < t' = s' - r'$.

All this reasoning enables us to factorize the input string as $x = uwzw'v$, on which the accepting computation $\Pi$ presents the following breakpoints:

$$(q_0, uwzw'v, Z_0) \vdash^* (q, wzw'v, Z^r Z_0) \vdash^* (q, zw'v, Z^{r+t} Z_0) \vdash^*$$
$$\vdash^* (p, w'v, Z^{h-r'} Z_0) \vdash^* (p, v, Z^{h-r'-t'} Z_0) \vdash^* (f, \lambda, \gamma), \quad \text{with } f \in F, \ \gamma \in \Gamma^*.$$

**Fig. 1.** Breakpoints in the accepting computation $\Pi$ on $x$

For reader's ease of mind, we assume that both $w$ and $w'$ are not the empty string; however, situations in which this does not hold can be easily dealt with. Now, the idea is to construct from $x$ a family of strings in $L(M)$ by suitably pumping factors $w$ and $w'$, whose accepting computations, "originating" from $\Pi$, will display all the strings $Z^* Z_0$ as pushdown contents. By starting from the original accepting computation $\Pi$ of $M$ on $x$, we obtain accepting computations for strings $uw^{\alpha+1} z w'^{\beta+1} v$, with $\alpha = t'\gamma$, $\beta = t\gamma$, and any $\gamma > 0$, as follows (the reader may follow the birth of these accepting computations by scanning Fig. 1):

- PROCESSING $uw^{\alpha+1}$: After reading $u$, $M$ is in the state $q$ and has $Z^r Z_0$ as pushdown content. Processing the first occurrence of $w$ leaves $M$ in $q$ again with pushdown content $Z^{r+t} Z_0$. Notice that, along this processing, $Z$ is always seen on top of the pushdown due to feature (4). Clearly, we can repeat such processing $\alpha$ times upon consuming the subsequent factor $w^\alpha$, and finally reach the state $q$ with pushdown content $Z^{s+\alpha t} Z_0$.
- PROCESSING $z$: This branch of computation takes place exactly as in $\Pi$, but starting with the pushdown store at a higher level. Precisely, we start from the state $q$ with pushdown content $Z^{s+\alpha t} Z_0$, and end in $p$ with pushdown content $Z^{h-r'+\alpha t} Z_0$.
- PROCESSING $w'^{\beta+1}$: After reading the first occurrence of $w'$, $M$ is again in the state $p$ with pushdown content $Z^{h-r'+\alpha t-t'} Z_0$. We can repeat this branch of computation on the subsequent factor $w'^\beta$ provided that we always have $Z$ on top of the pushdown, which is always the case. Indeed, upon consuming $w'^\beta$, we delete a number of $Z$ symbols which is $\beta t' = t\gamma t' = \alpha t$, thus reducing the pushdown content to $Z^{h-r'-t'} Z_0 = Z^{h-s'} Z_0$. Notice that, at this point, $M$ is again in the state $p$.
- PROCESSING $v$: This branch of computation takes place exactly as in $\Pi$, starting from the configuration $(p, v, Z^{h-s'} Z_0)$ and ending in a final state.

The reader may easily verify that along the above constructed computation, the highest pushdown content is $Z^{h+t\gamma t'} Z_0$, reached at the end of the ascending sub-branch. Since this reasoning holds for any $\gamma > 0$, we get that there cannot exist any given constant bounding the pushdown height of $M$ along every accepting computation. This clearly implies that $P(M) = Z^* Z_0$.

As a final fixing, we discuss the case in which feature (3) does not hold within $\Pi$. In this case, there exists a branch of computation in $\Pi$ which: (i) starts from a configuration with $ZZ_0$ as pushdown content, (ii) reaches a configuration with $Z^h Z_0$ as pushdown content, but then (iii) never empties the pushdown. The sub-branch from (i) to (ii) again guarantees the existence of a factor $w$ in $x$ upon which $M$ starts and end in the same state $q$, adding on the pushdown a factor $Z^t$, for $t > 0$. So, we can "pump the computation" of $M$ on this factor and obtain accepting computations on strings $uw^\gamma v$ with pushdown height $h + \gamma t$. Indeed, after reading the last occurrence of $w$, $M$ is in the state $q$ and, while processing $v$, the symbol $Z$ is always seen as top of the pushdown. So, $M$ will end up in a final state, as in the original computation $\Pi$ for $x$.     □

As a consequence of Theorem 12, we are able to provide the exact size cost of accepting pushdown store languages of counter machines by NFA:

**Theorem 13.** *Let $M$ be a counter machine with state set $Q$. Then, $P(M)$ is accepted by some NFA with size bounded by $|Q| + 2$. Moreover, this size bound is optimal.*

## 5   Computational Complexity of Decidability Questions

In this section, we study the complexity of deciding some properties of $P(M)$ for a given PDA $M$, namely, finiteness and being subset of $Z^* Z_0$. These two questions can be answered by constructing the NFA $N$ for $P(M)$ and then deciding, respectively, finiteness or inclusion in $Z^*Z_0$ for $L(N)$. We show that the construction of $N$ as well as the decision of both questions can be done in deterministic polynomial time with respect to the size of $M$. On the other hand, we also prove the P-completeness of these two decision problems. As a consequence, we get the P-completeness of deciding whether a PDA is of a certain "nature". For a background on complexity theory, we refer to, e.g., [4,15].

**Lemma 14.** *Let $M = \langle Q, \Sigma, \Gamma, \delta, q_0, Z_0, F \rangle$ be a PDA. Then, an NFA for $P(M)$ can be constructed in deterministic polynomial time.*

*Proof.* We will show that the construction given in Theorem 5 can be done in polynomial time with respect to the size of $M$. Let us first take a close look at the construction of the set $Acc(Q)$. We have to consider every pair $(p, Z) \in Q \times \Gamma$ and, in particular, to test the existence of $x \in \Sigma^*$ such that $(p, Z) \vdash^x (p', Z')$ for some other pair $(p', Z') \in Q \times (\Gamma \cup \{\lambda\})$. As recalled in the proof of Theorem 2, this test is in essence an instance of the emptiness problem for context-free languages, which is known to be decidable in polynomial time. Since there are at most $|Q|^2(|\Gamma| + 1)^2$ such pairs, which is polynomial in the size of $M$, we obtain that the NFA for $Acc(Q)$ can be constructed in polynomial time. A similar reasoning holds for the NFA for $Co\text{-}Acc(Q)$. At this point, the NFA for $Acc(Q) \cap Co\text{-}Acc(Q)$ plus deleting the first symbol of every word in this intersection can be done in polynomial time as well. □

This is the first step to prove the P-completeness of the above mention decision problems on pushdown store languages:

**Theorem 15.** *Given a PDA $M$, it is P-complete to decide whether: (i) $P(M)$ is a finite set. (ii) $P(M)$ is a finite set of words having at most length $k$, for a given $k \geq 1$.*

*Proof.* We only show point (i). The problem belongs to P: by Lemma 14, an NFA $N$ for $P(M)$ can be built in polynomial time. Then, the infiniteness of $L(N)$ can be decided in NLOGSPACE [17]. Since NLOGSPACE is closed under complementation [16,20], we get that the finiteness of $L(N)$ can be decided in NLOGSPACE $\subseteq$ P as well.

To show the completeness of the problem, we log-space reduce to it the emptiness problem for context-free grammars, which is known to be P-complete [18]. Given a context-free grammar $G = \langle N, T, S, R \rangle$, let $\$ \notin T$ be a new terminal symbol, and $S', S'' \notin N$ be new nonterminals. We define the context-free grammar

$$G' = \langle N \cup \{S', S''\}, T \cup \{\$\}, S', R \cup \{S' \to SS'', S'' \to S''\$ \mid \$\}\rangle.$$

Observe that $L(G') = L(G)\$^+$. From $G'$, we construct an equivalent PDA $M'$ using the standard construction [15], where a stateless PDA is built which mimics a left derivation of $G'$. More precisely, let $M' = \langle\{q\}, T \cup \{\$\}, N \cup T \cup \{S', S'', \$\}, \delta, q, S', \emptyset\rangle$. Observe that $G'$ is not in Greibach normal form, but this is not essential for the construction in [15] since we can define $\delta$ to have the following transitions: $(q, \gamma) \in \delta(q, \lambda, A)$, if $A \to \gamma$ belongs to $G'$ for all $A \in N \cup \{S', S''\}$ and $\gamma \in (N \cup T \cup \{S', S'', \$\})^*$, and $(q, \lambda) \in \delta(q, a, a)$ for all $a \in T \cup \{\$\}$. Moreover, $M'$ can be converted to an equivalent PDA which is in normal form and accepts by accepting states. This conversion increases the size of $M'$ at most linearly. Due to the left-recursive rule $S'' \to S''\$$, we obtain that $P(M')$ is finite if and only if $L(G)$ is empty.

To conclude the proof, we have to make sure that our reduction can be done in deterministic logarithmic space. We quickly notice that the only possibly costly operation is the construction from [15] for the PDA $M'$. However, this construction gives that $M'$ has one state, $|N| + |T| + 3$ pushdown symbols, and $|R| + 3 + |T| + 1$ transitions. Thus, the size of $M'$ is the order of the size of $G$. Altogether, the reduction can be done in deterministic logarithmic space.     □

A PDA $M$ is of *constant height* whenever there exists a constant $k \geq 1$ such that, for any word in $L(M)$, there exists an accepting computation along which the pushdown store never contains more than $k$ symbols [2,5]. As a consequence of Theorem 15, we get the P-completeness of testing constant height property for *unambiguous* PDA, i.e., presenting at most one accepting computation on any input:

**Corollary 16.** *Given an unambiguous PDA $M$, it is P-complete to decide whether: (i) $M$ is a constant height PDA. (ii) $M$ is a PDA of constant height $k$, for a given $k \geq 1$.*

The next P-completeness result can be shown similarly as Theorem 15:

**Theorem 17.** *Given a PDA $M$, it is P-complete to decide whether $P(M)$ is a subset of $Z^* Z_0$.*

As a consequence, we get the P-completeness of deciding whether a PDA is *essentially* a counter machine, i.e., in all of its accepting computations the pushdown storage is used as a counter:

**Corollary 18.** *Given a PDA $M$, it is P-complete to decide whether $M$ is essentially a counter machine.*

**Acknowledgements.** The authors wish to thank the anonymous referees for useful comments and remarks.

# References

1. Autebert, J.-M., Berstel, J., Boasson, L.: Context-free languages and pushdown automata. In: Handbook of Formal Languages, vol. 1, pp. 111–174. Springer (1997)
2. Bednárová, Z., Geffert, V., Mereghetti, C., Palano, B.: The Size-Cost of Boolean Operations on Constant Height Deterministic Pushdown Automata. In: Holzer, M., Kutrib, M., Pighizzini, G. (eds.) DCFS 2011. LNCS, vol. 6808, pp. 80–92. Springer, Heidelberg (2011)

3. Dassow, J., Manea, F., Truthe, B.: On contextual grammars with subregular selection languages. In: Holzer, M., Kutrib, M., Pighizzini, G. (eds.) DCFS 2011. LNCS, vol. 6808, pp. 135–146. Springer, Heidelberg (2011)
4. Garey, M.R., Johnson, D.S.: Computers and Intractability: A Guide to the Theory of NP-Completeness. W.H. Freeman and Co., San Francisco (1979)
5. Geffert, V., Mereghetti, C., Palano, B.: More concise representation of regular languages by automata and regular expressions. Inf. Comput. 208, 385–394 (2010)
6. Ginsburg, S., Greibach, S.A., Harrison, M.A.: Stack automata and compiling. J. ACM 14, 172–201 (1967)
7. Goldstine, J., Kappes, M., Kintala, C.M.R., Leung, H., Malcher, A., Wotschke, D.: Descriptional complexity of machines with limited resources. J. UCS 8, 193–234 (2002)
8. Greibach, S.A.: A note on pushdown store automata and regular systems. Proc. Amer. Math. Soc. 18, 263–268 (1967)
9. Greibach, S.A.: An infinite hierarchy of context-free languages. J. ACM 16, 91–106 (1969)
10. Harrison, M.A.: Introduction to Formal Language Theory. Addison-Wesley, Reading (1978)
11. Hartmanis, J.: Context-free languages and Turing machines computations. In: Proc. Symposium on Applied Mathematics, vol. 19, pp. 42–51 (1967)
12. Hoogeboom, H.J., Engelfriet, J.: Pushdown automata. In: Formal Languages and Applications. STUDFUZZ, vol. 148, pp. 117–138. Springer (2004)
13. Holzer, M., Kutrib, M.: Nondeterministic finite automata—recent results on the descriptional and computational complexity. Int. J. Found. Comp. Sci. 20, 563–580 (2009)
14. Holzer, M., Kutrib, M.: Descriptional complexity—an introductory survey. In: Scientific Applications of Language Methods, pp. 1–58. Imperial College Press (2010)
15. Hopcroft, J.E., Ullman, J.D.: Introduction to Automata Theory, Languages, and Computation. Addison-Wesley, Reading (1979)
16. Immerman, N.: Nondeterministic space is closed under complementation. SIAM J. Comput. 17, 935–938 (1988)
17. Jones, N.D.: Space-bounded reducibility among combinatorial questions. J. Comput. System. Sci. 11, 68–85 (1975)
18. Jones, N.D., Laaser, W.T.: Complete problems for deterministic polynomial time
19. Mereghetti, C., Palano, B.: Quantum finite automata with control language. Theoretical Informatics and Applications 40, 315–332 (2006)
20. Szelepcsényi, R.: The method of forced enumeration for nondeterministic automata. Acta Inform. 26, 279–284 (1988)
21. Yu, S.: Regular languages. In: Handbook of Formal Languages, vol. 1, pp. 41–110. Springer (1997)

# On Internal Contextual Grammars
# with Subregular Selection Languages

Florin Manea[1,*] and Bianca Truthe[2]

[1] Christian-Albrechts-Universität zu Kiel, Institut für Informatik,
Christian-Albrechts-Platz 4, 24098 Kiel, Germany
`flm@informatik.uni-kiel.de`
[2] Otto-von-Guericke-Universität Magdeburg, Fakultät für Informatik,
PSF 4120, 39016 Magdeburg, Germany
`truthe@iws.cs.uni-magdeburg.de`

**Abstract.** In this paper, we study the power of internal contextual grammars with selection languages from subfamilies of the family of regular languages. If we consider families $\mathcal{F}_n$ which are obtained by restriction to $n$ states or nonterminals or productions or symbols to accept or to generate regular languages, we obtain four infinite hierarchies of the corresponding families of languages generated by internal contextual grammars with selection languages in $\mathcal{F}_n$.

## 1 Introduction

Contextual grammars were introduced by S. Marcus in [4] as a formal model that might be used in the generation of natural languages. The derivation steps consist in adding contexts to given well formed sentences, starting from an initial finite basis. Formally, a context is given by a pair $(u, v)$ of words and the external adding to a word $x$ gives the word $uxv$ whereas the internal adding gives all words $x_1ux_2vx_3$ when $x = x_1x_2x_3$. Obviously, by linguistic motivation, a context can only be added if the words $x$ or $x_2$ satisfy some given conditions. Thus, it is natural to define contextual grammars with selection in a certain family $\mathcal{F}$ of languages, where it is required that $x$ or $x_2$ have to belong to a language of the family $\mathcal{F}$ which is associated with the context. Mostly, the family $\mathcal{F}$ is taken from the families of the Chomsky hierarchy (see [3,6,5], and the references therein).

In [1], the study of external contextual grammars with selection in special regular sets was started. Finite, combinational, definite, nilpotent, regular suffix-closed, regular commutative languages and languages of the form $V^*$ for some alphabet $V$ were considered. In [2], the research was continued and new results on the effect of regular commutative, regular circular, definite, regular suffix-closed, ordered, combinational, nilpotent, and union-free selection languages on the generative power of external contextual grammars were obtained. Furthermore, families of regular languages which are defined by restrictions on the resources used

---

* F. Manea's work is supported by the DFG grant 582014. On leave of absence
from: *Faculty of Mathematics and Computer Science, University of Bucharest, Str.
Academiei 14, RO-010014 Bucharest, Romania* (`flmanea@fmi.unibuc.ro`).

M. Kutrib, N. Moreira, and R. Reis (Eds.): DCFS 2012, LNCS 7386, pp. 222–235, 2012.
© Springer-Verlag Berlin Heidelberg 2012

to generate or to accept them were investigated. As measures, the number of states necessary to accept the regular languages and the number of nonterminals, production rules or symbols needed to generate the regular languages have been considered. In all these cases, infinite hierarchies were obtained.

In the present paper, we continue this line of research and investigate the effect of the number of resources (states, nonterminals, production rules, and symbols) on the generative power of internal contextual grammars. This case seems more complicated than the case of external contextual grammars, as there are two important differences between the way a derivation is conducted in internal grammars and in an external one. First, in the case of internal contextual grammars, the insertion of a context in a sentential form can be done in more than one place, so the derivation becomes, in a sense, non-deterministic; in the case of external grammars, once a context was selected there is at most one way to insert it: wrapped around the sentential form, when this word was in the selection language of the context. Second, if a context can be added internally, then it can be added arbitrarily often (because the subword where the context is wrapped around does not change) which does not necessarily hold for external grammars. However, we are able to obtain infinite hierarchies with respect to the descriptional complexity measures we use, but with different proof techniques.

## 2  Definitions

Throughout the paper, we assume that the reader is familiar with the basic concepts of the theory of automata and formal languages. For details, we refer to [6]. Here we only recall some notation and the definition of contextual grammars with selection which form the central notion of the paper.

Given an alphabet $V$, we denote by $V^*$ and $V^+$ the set of all words and the set of all non-empty words over $V$, respectively. The empty word is denoted by $\lambda$. For a word $w \in V^*$ and a letter $a \in V$, by $|w|$ and $\#_a(w)$ we denote the length of $w$ and the number of occurrences of $a$ in $w$, respectively. The cardinality of a set $A$ is denoted by $\#(A)$.

Let $G = (N, T, P, S)$ be a regular grammar (specified by finite sets $N$ and $T$ of nonterminals and terminals, respectively, a finite set of productions of the form $A \to wB$ or $A \to w$ with $A, B \in N$ and $w \in T^*$ as well as $S \in N$). Further, let $A = (X, Z, z_0, F, \delta)$ be a deterministic finite automaton (specified by sets $X$ and $Z$ of input symbols and states, respectively, an initial state $z_0$, a set $F$ of accepting states, and a transition function $\delta$) and $L$ be a regular language. Then we define

$$State(A) = \#(Z),$$

$$Var(G) = \#(N), \ Prod(G) = \#(P), \ Symb(G) = \sum_{A \to w \in P} (|w| + 2),$$

$$State(L) = \min \{ \, State(A) \mid A \text{ is a det. finite automaton accepting } L \, \},$$

$$K(L) = \min \{ \, K(G) \mid G \text{ is a reg. grammar for } L \, \} \ (K \in \{ Var, Prod, Symb \}),$$

and, for $K \in \{ State, Var, Prod, Symb \}$, we set

$$REG_n^K = \{ L \mid L \text{ is a regular language with } K(L) \leq n \}.$$

**Remark.** We note that if we restricted ourselves to rules of the form $A \rightarrow aB$ and $A \rightarrow \lambda$ with $A, B \in N$ and $a \in T$, then we would have $State(L) = Var(L)$.

We now introduce the central notion of this paper.

Let $\mathcal{F}$ be a family of languages. A *contextual grammar with selection in $\mathcal{F}$* is a triple

$$G = (V, \{ (S_1, C_1), (S_2, C_2), \ldots, (S_n, C_n) \}, B)$$

where

- $V$ is an alphabet,
- for $1 \leq i \leq n$, $S_i$ is a language over $V$ in $\mathcal{F}$ and $C_i$ is a finite set of pairs $(u, v)$ with $u \in V^*$, $v \in V^*$,
- $B$ is a finite subset of $V^*$.

The set $V$ is called the basic alphabet; the languages $S_i$ and the sets $C_i$, $1 \leq i \leq n$, are called the *selection languages* and the sets of *contexts* of $G$, respectively; the elements of $B$ are called *axioms*.

We now define the internal derivation for contextual grammars with selection.

Let $G = (V, \{ (S_1, C_1), (S_2, C_2), \ldots, (S_n, C_n) \}, B)$ be a contextual grammar with selection. A direct *internal derivation step* in $G$ is defined as follows: a word $x$ derives a word $y$ (written as $x \Longrightarrow y$) if and only if there are words $x_1$, $x_2$, $x_3$ with $x_1 x_2 x_3 = x$ and there is an integer $i$, $1 \leq i \leq n$, such that $x_2 \in S_i$ and $y = x_1 u x_2 v x_3$ for some pair $(u, v) \in C_i$. Intuitively, we can only wrap a context $(u, v) \in C_i$ around a subword $x_2$ of $x$ if $x_2$ belongs to the corresponding language $S_i$. We call a word of a selection language useful, if it is a subword of a word of the generated language – if it is really selected from wrapping a context around it.

By $\Longrightarrow^*$ we denote the reflexive and transitive closure of $\Longrightarrow$. The *internal language generated by $G$* is defined as

$$L(G) = \{ z \mid x \Longrightarrow^* z \text{ for some } x \in B \}.$$

By $\mathcal{L}(IC, \mathcal{F})$ we denote the family of all internal languages generated by contextual grammars with selection in $\mathcal{F}$. When we speak about contextual grammars in this paper, we mean contextual grammars with internal derivation (also called internal contextual grammars).

*Example 1.* Let $n \geq 1$ and $V = \{a\}$ be a unary alphabet. We set

$$B_n = \{ a^i \mid 1 \leq i \leq n \}, \quad U_n = \{ a^n \}^+, \quad \text{and} \quad L_n = B_n \cup U_n.$$

The contextual grammar $G_n = (V, \{ (U_n, \{(\lambda, a^n)\}) \}, B_n)$ generates the language $L_n$. This can be seen as follows. The context $a^n$ can be added to a word $w$ if and only if $w$ contains at least $n$ letters. The only axiom to which a context can be added is $a^n$. From this, we get the unique derivation

$$a^n \Longrightarrow a^{2n} \Longrightarrow a^{3n} \Longrightarrow \cdots.$$

It is easy to see that the set $U_n$ is accepted by the automaton

$$(V, \{z_0, z_1, \ldots, z_n\}, z_0, \{z_n\}, \delta_n)$$

where the graph

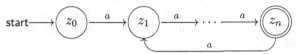

represents the transition function $\delta_n$.

Hence, we have $L_n \in \mathcal{L}(IC, REG_{n+1}^{State})$.    ◊

## 3  Selection with Bounded Resources

First we prove that we obtain an infinite hierarchy with respect to the number of states.

**Theorem 2.** *For any natural number $n \geq 1$, we have the proper inclusion*

$$\mathcal{L}(IC, REG_n^{State}) \subset \mathcal{L}(IC, REG_{n+1}^{State}).$$

*Proof.* For $n \geq 2$, let

$$B_n = \{\, a^i \mid 1 \leq i \leq n \,\}, \ U_n = \{\, a^n \,\}^+, \ \text{and} \ L_n = B_n \cup U_n$$

be the languages from Example 1, where we have shown the relation

$$L_n \in \mathcal{L}(IC, REG_{n+1}^{State}).$$

We now prove that $L_n \notin \mathcal{L}(IC, REG_n^{State})$ for $n \geq 2$.

Let $G = (V, \{\, (S_1, C_1), (S_2, C_2), \ldots, (S_m, C_m) \,\}, B)$ be a contextual grammar with $L(G) = L_n$ and where every selection language is an arbitrary regular language.

Let $k' = \max\{\, |uv| \mid (u, v) \in C_i, 1 \leq i \leq m \,\}$, $k'' = \max\{\, |z| \mid z \in B \,\}$, and $k = k' + k''$. Let us consider the word $w = a^{(k+1)n} \in L_n$. Obviously, $w \notin B$ because the length $(k + 1)n$ is greater than $k''$. Thus, the word $w$ is obtained from some word $w' = w_1' w_2' w_3' \in L_n$ by adding a context $(u, v) \in C_i$ for some index $i$ with $1 \leq i \leq m$ around the subword $w_2' \in S_i$. Then $w = w_1' u w_2' v w_3'$. For the length of the word $w'$, we obtain

$$|w'| = |w| - |uv| = (k' + k'' + 1)n - |uv| \geq k'(n - 1) + k''n + n > n.$$

The word $w'$ belongs to the language $L_n$ and has a length greater than $n$ which implies $w' \in U_n$. Hence, $w' = a^{jn}$ for some $j$ with $2 \leq j \leq k$ and $uv = a^{(k+1-j)n}$. If $S_i$ contains the empty word $\lambda$, then also the word $auv$ belongs to the language $L_n$ (since $a \in L_n$). However, the length $|auv| = 1 + (k + 1 - j)n$ is greater than $n$ but not a multiple of $n$ which is a contradiction. If $S_i$ contains a non-empty word $z$ that has a length smaller than $n$, then $z$ belongs to the language $L_n$ and also $uzv \in L_n$. But then the length $|uzv| = |z| + (k + 1 - j)n$ is greater than $n$ but not a multiple of $n$ which is again a contradiction. Hence, the set $S_i$ does not contain a word with a length smaller than $n$. Let $r = \min \{ l \mid a^l \in S_i \}$. Then $r \geq n$. We set $z_i = a^{r-i}$ for $0 \leq i \leq r$. Then we have the relations $a^i z_i \in S_i$ and $a^j z_i \notin S_i$ for $0 \leq j < i \leq r$ because $a^i z_i = a^r$ and $|a^j z_i| < r$ for $0 \leq j < i \leq r$.

Therefore the words $\lambda, a, a^2, \ldots, a^r$ are pairwise not in the Myhill-Nerode relation. Thus, the minimal deterministic finite automaton accepting $S_i$ has at least $r + 1 \geq n + 1$ states.

For $n = 1$, consider the language

$$L_1 = \{ \lambda \} \cup \{ w \mid w \in \{a, b\}^+, \ \#_b(w) = 1 \} .$$

This language can be generated by the contextual grammar

$$G_1 = (\{a, b\}, \{ (\{a, b\}^+, \{(\lambda, a), (a, \lambda)\}) \} , \{\lambda, b\}).$$

Since the language $\{a, b\}^+$ can be accepted by an automaton with two states, we have the relation

$$L_1 \in \mathcal{L}(IC, REG_2^{State}).$$

For every contextual grammar $G = (V, \{ (S_1, C_1), (S_2, C_2), \ldots, (S_m, C_m) \} , B)$ with $S_i \in REG_1^{State}$ for $1 \leq i \leq m$, we have $S_i = \emptyset$ or $S_i = V^*$ for $1 \leq i \leq m$. If all selection languages are empty, the generated language is the set $B$ of axioms and hence finite. In order to obtain the infinite language $L_1$, one set $S_i$ is equal to $V^*$. Then any context of $C_i$ can be applied to any word of the language $L_1$. If such a context consists of letters $a$ only, we obtain from the empty word a word which does not belong to the language $L_1$ (which has only letters $a$). If such a context contains a letter $b$, we obtain from a word with a $b$ another word with two letters $b$ and hence does not belong to the language $L_1$. Thus, the language $L_1$ does not belong to the family $\mathcal{L}(IC, REG_1^{State})$.     □

We now consider the measure $Var$.

**Theorem 3.** *For any natural number $n \geq 0$, we have the proper inclusion*

$$\mathcal{L}(IC, REG_n^{Var}) \subset \mathcal{L}(IC, REG_{n+1}^{Var}).$$

*Proof.* Let $V = \{a, b\}$. For each natural number $n \geq 1$, we consider a language $L_n$ which consists of words formed by $2n$ blocks of letters $a$, ended by the letter $b$ each, where the block lengths coincide in a crossed agreement manner:

$$L_n = \{ a^{p_1} b a^{p_2} b \ldots a^{p_n} b a^{p_1} b a^{p_2} b \ldots a^{p_n} b \mid p_i \geq 1, \ 1 \leq i \leq n \} .$$

A contextual grammar generating the language $L_n$ is

$$G_n = (V, \{ (S, \{ (a, a) \}) \} , \{ w \mid w = abab \ldots ab, \ |w| = 4n \})$$

with

$$S = (\{b\}\{a\}^+)^{n-1}\{b\}\{a\}.$$

The selection language $S$ can be generated by the following regular grammar

$$G = (\{\, N_1, N_2, \ldots, N_n \,\}, V, P, N_1)$$

with the rules

$$N_1 \to ba N_2,$$
$$N_k \to a N_k \mid ba N_{k+1} \text{ for } 2 \leq k \leq n - 1,$$
$$N_n \to a N_n \mid ba.$$

Hence, we obtain $L_n \in \mathcal{L}(IC, REG_n^{Var})$ for all numbers $n \geq 1$.

It remains to show that, for any $n \geq 1$, the language $L_n$ cannot be generated by a contextual grammar where, for generating the selection languages, less than $n$ nonterminal symbols are sufficient.

Let $n \geq 1$ and $G_n' = (V, \{\, (S_1, C_1), (S_2, C_2), \ldots, (S_m, C_m) \,\}, B)$ be a contextual grammar with $L(G_n') = L_n$ and where every selection language is an arbitrary regular language. Since the language $L_n$ is infinite, there are words that do not belong to the set $B$ of axioms and which are therefore generated by adding a context. Whenever a context $(u, v) \in C_i$ for some $i$ with $1 \leq i \leq m$ can be wrapped around a subword $z$ of a word $z_1 z z_2 \in L_n$, it can be added infinitely often because the subword $z$ remains unchanged. Hence, the letter $b$ cannot occur in any context because otherwise words with an unbounded number of the letter $b$ could be generated. Thus, every context $(u, v)$ of the system consists of letters $a$ only and, moreover, $u = v = a^{n_c}$ for some number $n_c$. Otherwise, a word would be generated which does not belong to the language $L_n$. Any useful word of a selection language of the system belongs to the set

$$F = \{a\}^* (\{b\} \{a\}^+)^n,$$

otherwise the application of a context would yield a word which does not belong to the language $L_n$. We consider only the useful words of the selection languages. All these words contain exactly $n$ letters $b$ and at least a letter $a$ after each $b$. The maximal word which is between two letters $b$ and consists of letters $a$ only is called an inner $a$-block.

There is a selection language $S_i$ ($1 \leq i \leq m$) where all inner $a$-blocks are unbounded. Suppose that this is not the case. Then in every selection language, at least one inner $a$-block is bounded. Let $l$ be the maximal length of bounded inner $a$-blocks over all selection languages $S_i$ ($1 \leq i \leq m$) and the set $B$ of axioms. Let $k = l + 1$. We consider the word $w = a^k ba^k b \ldots a^k b \in L_n$. By the choice of $k$, the word $w$ is not an axiom. Hence, it is derived from a word $w' \in L_n$ by wrapping a context $(a^{n_c}, a^{n_c})$ around a subword $w'' = a^{q_1} (ba^k)^{n-1} ba^{q_2}$ where $q_1 \geq 0$ and $q_2 \geq 1$. This word $w''$, however, does not belong to any selection language (because in every word of any selection language, at least one of the inner $a$-blocks has a length less than $k$). This contradiction implies that there is a selection language $S_i$ ($1 \leq i \leq m$) where all inner $a$-blocks are unbounded.

When generating such a language $S_i$, a second nonterminal must appear before the second letter $b$ is generated because otherwise the first inner $a$-block would be bounded or the number of letters $b$ would be unbounded and a word with $n + 1$ letters $b$ would be generated (because a derivation of a word $w \in S_i$ would exist with the form $A \Longrightarrow a^q b a^r A \Longrightarrow^* w \in S_i$ and hence, also the derivation $A \Longrightarrow^* a^q b a^{r+q} b a^r A \Longrightarrow^* w'$ would exist which yields a word $w'$ with $\#_b(w') = \#_b(w) + 1$). Such a word should not be in the language $S_i$ because otherwise the lengths of two $a$-blocks not corresponding to each other would be increased but not the corresponding ones. By induction, one obtains that an $n$-th nonterminal must appear before the $n$-th letter $b$ is generated.

From this follows, that $n - 1$ nonterminals are not sufficient.

As a result, we have $L_n \in \mathcal{L}(IC, REG_n^{Var}) \setminus \mathcal{L}(IC, REG_{n-1}^{Var})$ for any natural number $n \geq 1$.     $\square$

As consequences from the previous theorem, we obtain also infinite hierarchies with respect to the number of production rules and the number of symbols. However, to show that the inclusions $\mathcal{L}(IC, REG_n^K) \subseteq \mathcal{L}(IC, REG_{n+1}^K)$ with $K \in \{ Prod, Symb \}$ are proper for each number $n \geq n_0$ for some start number $n_0$, we need further investigations.

We start with the complexity measure $Prod$. Let us consider a generalization of the languages $L_n$ for $n \geq 1$ used in the proof of the previous theorem.

Let $m \geq 1$, $A_m = \{ a_1, \ldots, a_m \}$, and $V = A_m \cup \{b\}$. The languages $L_n$ consist again of words formed by $2n$ $a$-blocks ended by the letter $b$ each and where the block lengths coincide in a crossed agreement manner. However, an $a$-block now consists of letters from the set $A_m$ instead of the single letter $a$ only.

Formally, we define for $n \geq 1$ the languages

$$L_n^{(m)} = \{ \, w_1 b w_2 b \ldots w_n b w_{n+1} b w_{n+2} b \ldots w_{2n} b \mid$$
$$w_i, w_{n+i} \in A_m^+, \ |w_i| = |w_{n+i}|, \ 1 \leq i \leq n \, \}.$$

*Example 4.* Let us consider the languages $L_n^{(m)}$ for $n = 1$, $n = 2$, and $n = 3$. Then

$$L_1^{(m)} = \{ \, w_1 b w_2 b \mid \{w_1, w_2\} \subset A_m^+, \ |w_1| = |w_2| \, \},$$
$$L_2^{(m)} = \{ \, w_1 b w_2 b w_3 b w_4 b \mid \{w_1, w_2, w_3, w_4\} \subset A_m^+, |w_1| = |w_3|, |w_2| = |w_4| \, \},$$
$$L_3^{(m)} = \{ \, w_1 b w_2 b w_3 b w_4 b w_5 b w_6 b \mid \{w_i, w_{3+i}\} \subset A_m^+, |w_i| = |w_{3+i}|, 1 \leq i \leq 3 \, \}.$$

The following contextual grammar generates the language $L_1^{(m)}$:

$$G_1^{(m)} = (V, \mathcal{S}, B)$$

with

$$B = \{ \, xbyb \mid \{x, y\} \subseteq A_m \, \} \text{ and } \mathcal{S} = \{ \, (S_x, C) \mid x \in A_m \, \}$$

where

$$S_x = \{ \, bx \, \} \text{ and } C = \{ \, (x, y) \mid \{x, y\} \subseteq A_m \, \}.$$

For generating such a selection language $S_x$, only one rule is necessary. Hence, $L_1^{(m)} \in \mathcal{L}(IC, REG_1^{Prod})$ for each number $m \geq 1$.

For generating the language $L_2^{(m)}$ by a contextual grammar, we first increase the lengths of the first and third $a$-blocks and then the lengths of the remaining blocks.

The language $L_2^{(m)}$ is generated by the contextual grammar

$$G_2^{(m)} = (V, \mathcal{S}, B)$$

with

$$B = \{\, x_1 b x_2 b x_3 b x_4 b \mid x_i \in A_m, 1 \le i \le 4 \,\},$$
$$\mathcal{S} = \{\, (S_{i,j}, C) \mid 1 \le i, j \le m \,\}$$

where

$$S_{i,j} = \{\, ba_i w ba_j \mid w \in A_m^* \,\},$$
$$C = \{\, (x, y) \mid \{x, y\} \subseteq A_m \,\}.$$

Each selection language $S_{i,j}$ can be generated by $m + 2$ rules ($N_1 \to ba_i N_2$, $N_2 \to x N_2$ for any $x \in A_m$ and $N_2 \to ba_j$). Hence, $L_2^{(m)} \in \mathcal{L}(IC, REG_{m+2}^{Prod})$ for each number $m \ge 1$.

A contextual grammar for the language $L_3^{(m)}$ for an arbitrary number $m \ge 1$ is

$$G_3^{(m)} = (V, \mathcal{S}, B)$$

with

$$B = \{\, x_1 b x_2 b x_3 b x_4 b x_5 b x_6 b \mid x_i \in A_m, 1 \le i \le 6 \,\},$$
$$\mathcal{S} = \{\, (S_{i,j,k}, C) \mid 1 \le i, j, k \le m \,\}$$

where

$$S_{i,j,k} = \{\, ba_i w_1 ba_j w_2 ba_k \mid \{w_1, w_2\} \subset A_m^* \,\},$$
$$C = \{\, (x, y) \mid \{x, y\} \subseteq A_m \,\}.$$

The following picture shows where contexts can be added:

A grammar generating a selection language $S_{i,j,k}$ with $1 \le i, j, k \le m$ is $G_{i,j,k} = (\{N_1, N_2, N_3\}, V, P, N_1)$ with the rules

$$N_1 \to ba_i N_2,$$
$$N_2 \to x N_2 \mid ba_j N_3,$$
$$N_3 \to x N_3 \mid ba_k$$

for $x \in A_m$. Hence, $L_3^{(m)} \in \mathcal{L}(IC, REG_{2(m+1)+1}^{Prod})$ for each number $m \ge 1$.    $\Diamond$

If the number of rules of a regular grammar is equal to zero, the language generated is empty. Hence, the class $\mathcal{L}(IC, REG_0^{Prod})$ contains only finite languages. Since $L_1^{(m)} \in \mathcal{L}(IC, REG_1^{Prod})$ (as shown in the previous example) and $L_1^{(m)} \notin \mathcal{L}(IC, REG_0^{Prod})$ (because the language is infinite), we have the first proper inclusion.

**Corollary 5.** *The proper inclusion*

$$\mathcal{L}(IC, REG_0^{Prod}) \subset \mathcal{L}(IC, REG_1^{Prod})$$

*holds.*

Let us now have a closer look at the relation between the $L_n^{(m)}$ languages and the *Prod*-hierarchy.

For $n = 3$, we have found in the Example 4 that $(m+1)(n-1)+1$ rules is an upper bound for generating the selection languages. This bound also holds for $n = 1$ and $n = 2$, as one can see from the example.

We now investigate the languages $L_n^{(m)}$ for $n \geq 4$ and prove the tightness of the bound for $n \geq 1$.

**Lemma 6.** *Let $m \geq 1$, $n \geq 1$, and*

$$L_n^{(m)} = \{ \, w_1 b w_2 b \ldots w_n b w_{n+1} b w_{n+2} b \ldots w_{2n} b \, | $$
$$w_i, w_{n+i} \in A_m^+, \ |w_i| = |w_{n+i}|, \ 1 \leq i \leq n \, \}.$$

*Then*

$$L_n^{(m)} = \mathcal{L}(IC, REG_{(m+1)(n-1)+1}^{Prod}) \setminus \mathcal{L}(IC, REG_{(m+1)(n-1)}^{Prod})$$

*holds.*

*Proof.* A contextual grammar for the language $L_n^{(m)}$ for arbitrary numbers $m \geq 1$ and $n \geq 1$ is

$$G_n^{(m)} = (V, \mathcal{S}, B)$$

with

$$B = \{ \, x_1 b x_2 b \ldots x_{2n} b \mid x_i \in A_m, 1 \leq i \leq 2n \, \},$$
$$\mathcal{S} = \{ \, (S_{i_1, i_2, \ldots, i_n}, C) \mid 1 \leq i_j \leq m, 1 \leq j \leq n \, \}$$

where

$$S_{i_1, i_2, \ldots, i_n} = \{ \, ba_{i_1} w_1 ba_{i_2} w_2 \ldots ba_{i_{n-1}} w_{n-1} ba_{i_n} \mid w_i \in A_m^*, 1 \leq i \leq n_1 \, \},$$
$$C = \{ \, (x, y) \mid \{x, y\} \subseteq A_m \, \}.$$

A grammar generating a selection language $S_{i_1, i_2, \ldots, i_n}$ with $1 \leq i_j \leq m$ for $1 \leq j \leq n$ is $G_{i_1, i_2, \ldots, i_n} = (\{N_1, N_2, \ldots, N_n\}, V, P, N_1)$ with the rules

$$N_1 \to ba_{i_1} N_2,$$
$$N_k \to x N_k \mid ba_{i_k} N_{k+1} \text{ for } 2 \leq k \leq n-1,$$
$$N_n \to x N_n \mid ba_{i_n}$$

for $x \in A_m$. Hence, $L_n^{(m)} \in \mathcal{L}(IC, REG_{(m+1)(n-1)+1}^{Prod})$ for each number $m \geq 1$ and $n \geq 2$ and, together with the considerations in the beginning, also for $n \geq 1$.

We now show that, for any $m \geq 1$ and $n \geq 1$, the language $L_n^{(m)}$ cannot be generated by a contextual grammar where, for generating every selection language, at most $(m+1)(n-1)$ nonterminal symbols are sufficient.

Let $n \geq 1$, $m \geq 1$, and $H_n^{(m)} = (V, \{(S_1, C_1), (S_2, C_2), \ldots, (S_m, C_m)\}, B)$ be a contextual grammar with $L(H_n^{(m)}) = L_n^{(m)}$ and where every selection language is an arbitrary regular language. Since the language $L_n^{(m)}$ is infinite, there are words that do not belong to the set $B$ of axioms and which are therefore generated by adding a context. Whenever a context $(u, v) \in C_i$ for some $i$ with $1 \leq i \leq m$ can be wrapped around a subword $z$ of a word $z_1 z z_2 \in L_n^{(m)}$, it can be added infinitely often because the subword $z$ remains unchanged. Hence, the letter $b$ cannot occur in any context because otherwise words with an unbounded number of the letter $b$ could be generated. Thus, every context $(u, v)$ of the system consists of letters from the alphabet $A_m$ only and, moreover, $|u| = |v|$. Otherwise, a word would be generated which does not belong to the language $L_n^{(m)}$. Any useful word of a selection language of the system belongs to the set

$$F = A_m^*(\{b\}A_m^+)^n,$$

otherwise the application of a context would yield a word which does not belong to the language $L_n^{(m)}$. We consider only the useful words of the selection languages. All these words contain exactly $n$ letters $b$ and at least a letter of the set $A_m$ after each $b$. The maximal word which is between two letters $b$ and consists of letters from the set $A_m$ only is called an inner $a$-block.

There is a selection language $S_i$ ($1 \leq i \leq m$) where in every inner $a$-block the number of occurrences of each letter of the alphabet $A_m$ is unbounded. Suppose that this is not the case. Then for every selection language, there is a letter $a_j \in A_m$ such that at least one inner $a$-block contains a bounded number of the letter $a_j$. Let $l$ be the maximal number of each letter in an inner $a$-block (if the number of occurrences of this letter is bounded in this block) over all selection languages $S_i$ ($1 \leq i \leq m$) and the set $B$ of axioms. Let $k = l + 1$ and $w_a = a_1^k a_2^k \ldots a_m^k$. We consider the word $w = w_a b w_a b \ldots w_a b \in L_n$. By the choice of $k$, the word $w$ is not an axiom. Hence, it is derived from a word $w' \in L_n$ by wrapping a context $(u, v) \in A_m^+ \times A_m^+$ around a subword $w'' = u_a(bw_a)^{n-1}bv_a$ where $u_a$ is a suffix of the word $w_a$ and $v_a$ is a prefix of the word $w_a$. This word $w''$, however, does not belong to any selection language (because in every word of any language, at least one of the inner $a$-blocks contains less than $k$ occurrences of a certain letter of $A_m$). This contradiction implies that there is a selection language $S_i$ ($1 \leq i \leq m$) where in every inner $a$-block the number of occurrences of each letter of the alphabet $A_m$ is unbounded.

When generating such a language $S_i$, a second nonterminal must appear before the second letter $b$ is generated because otherwise the first inner $a$-block would be bounded or the number of letters $b$ would be unbounded and a word with $n + 1$ letters $b$ would be generated. Such a word should not be in the language $S_i$

because otherwise the lengths of two $a$-blocks not corresponding to each other would be increased but not the corresponding ones. By induction, one obtains that an $n$-th nonterminal must appear before the $n$-th letter $b$ is generated. Since, in every inner $a$-block, the number of each letter from $A_m$ is unbounded and the appearance is in arbitrary order, one needs a 'loop' for every letter of the set $A_m$. Hence, for each inner $a$-block, one needs a rule for generating every letter of $A_m$ and the letter $b$. Since, we have to remember in which block we are, we need those $m+1$ rules for every inner $a$-block. Furthermore, we need a rule for the first nonterminal symbol. Thus, $(n-1)(m+1)+1$ rules are necessary for at least one selection language. From this follows, that $(n-1)(m+1)$ rules are not sufficient.

Hence, $(m+1)(n-1)+1$ rules are sufficient for generating every selection language and necessary for at least one selection language in a contextual grammar generating the language $L_n^{(m)}$. $\qquad\square$

From the previous result, we obtain the strictness of the following inclusions.

**Lemma 7.** *Let* $m \geq 1$. *For* $n \geq 1$, *the proper inclusion*

$$\mathcal{L}(IC, REG^{Prod}_{(m+1)(n-1)}) \subset \mathcal{L}(IC, REG^{Prod}_{(m+1)(n-1)+1})$$

*holds.*

Let us now consider the inclusion

$$\mathcal{L}(IC, REG^{Prod}_{k-1}) \subseteq \mathcal{L}(IC, REG^{Prod}_k)$$

for some number $k \geq 1$.

For $k = 1$, we know from Corollary 5 that the inclusion is proper.

For $k \geq 3$, we obtain the strictness of the inclusion from Lemma 7 when we set $n = 2$ and $m = k - 2$.

We now prove that the inclusion is also proper for $k = 2$.

**Lemma 8.** *Let* $V = \{a, b, c, d, e\}$ *and*

$$L = \{\, w_{ab}cd^n e^m \mid m \geq 0, n \geq 0, w_{ab} \in \{a, b\}^*, \#_a(w_{ab}) = n, \#_b(w_{ab}) = m \,\}.$$

*Then* $L \in \mathcal{L}(IC, REG^{Prod}_2)$ *but* $L \notin \mathcal{L}(IC, REG^{Prod}_1)$.

*Proof.* The contextual grammar

$$G = (V, (\{ce\}, \{(b, e)\}), (\{b\}^*\{c\}, \{(a, d)\}), \{c, bce\})$$

generates the language $L$ as can be seen as follows.

Let $m \geq 0$, $n \geq 0$, and $w_{ab} \in \{a, b\}^*$ with $\#_a(w_{ab}) = n$ and $\#_b(w_{ab}) = m$. Then there exist numbers $m_1, m_2, \ldots m_{n+1}$ with $m_i \geq 0$ for $1 \leq i \leq n + 1$ and $m_1 + m_2 + \cdots + m_{n+1} = m$ such that $w_{ab} = b^{m_1}ab^{m_2}a \ldots b^{m_n}ab^{m_{n+1}}$. How is the word $w = w_{ab}cd^n e^m \in L$ generated? If $n = m = 0$, then $w = c \in B$. If $n = 0$ and $m = 1$, then $w = bce \in B$. Otherwise, the word $w$ is derived from the axiom $bce$

by first wrapping the letters $b$ and $e$ around the subword $ce$ until the word $b^m ce^m$ is obtained and then wrapping the letters $a$ and $d$ around the subwords $b^{m-m_1}c$, $b^{m-m_1-m_2}c$, and so on until $b^{m_n+1}c$. This yields the derivation

$$bce \Longrightarrow^* b^m ce^m \Longrightarrow b^{m_1} ab^{m-m_1} cde^m$$
$$\Longrightarrow b^{m_1} ab^{m_2} ab^{m-m_1-m_2} cd^2 e^m$$
$$\Longrightarrow^* b^{m_1} ab^{m_2} ab^{m-m_1-m_2} a \ldots b^{m_n} ab^{m_n+1} cd^n e^m = w.$$

Hence, every word of the language $L$ is generated by the contextual grammar $G$.

On the other hand, from a word of the language $L$, only words of the language $L$ are obtained. Let $w = w_{ab} cd^n e^m \in L$. If $n = 0$, then $w = b^m ce^m$. From the word $w$, the word $b^{m+1} ce^{m+1}$ can be obtained in one derivation step as well as any word $b^{m_1} ab^{m_2} cde^m$ with $m_1 \geq 0$, $m_2 \geq 2$, and $m_1 + m_2 = m$. These words belong to the language $L$, too; other words cannot be derived in one step. If $n > 0$, then the number of the letters $b$ and $e$ cannot be increased further. Hence, only words $w'_{ab} ab^k cd^{n+1} e^m$ with $k \geq 0$ and $w'_{ab} b^k = w_{ab}$ can be derived in one step. All these words also belong to the language $L$.

Thus, we obtain $L = L(G)$. The selection language $\{ce\}$ can be generated by a grammar with only one rule. The selection language $\{b\}^*\{c\}$ can be generated by a grammar with exactly two rules ($S \to bS$ and $S \to c$).

Hence, $L \in \mathcal{L}(IC, REG_2^{Prod})$.

We now show that the language $L$ cannot be generated by a contextual grammar where every selection language is generated by a grammar with one rule only.

Suppose, $L \in \mathcal{L}(IC, REG_1^{Prod})$. Then there is a contextual grammar

$$G' = (V, \{ (S_1, C_1), (S_2, C_2), \ldots, (S_p, C_p) \}, B')$$

with $L(G') = L$ and every language $S_i$ is a singleton set for $1 \leq i \leq p$. Let $k$ be the length of the longest word in the union of these sets and $B'$ as well as among the contexts:

$$k_1 = \max \{ |w| \mid w \in B' \},$$
$$k_2 = \max \bigcup_{i=1}^{p} \{ |w| \mid w \in S_i \},$$
$$k_3 = \max \bigcup_{i=1}^{p} \{ |w| \mid (u,w) \in C_i \text{ or } (w,u) \in C_i \},$$
$$k = \max \{ k_1, k_2, k_3 \}.$$

Let us consider the word $w = a^{2k} b^{2k} cd^{2k} e^{2k} \in L$. Due to its length, it is not an axiom of the set $B'$. Hence, it is derived from another word of the language $L$. The number of letters $a$ and $d$ as well as $b$ and $e$ must be increased by the same number in each derivation step. For any context $(u, v)$, we know that $v \in \{d\}^+$ or $v \in \{e\}^+$, otherwise also a word which does not belong to the language $L$

could be generated. Let $(u, v)$ be a context that was added to a word to obtain the word $w$. If $v \in \{d\}^+$, then the word $u$ contains an occurrence of the letter $a$ and the subword where the context is wrapped around contains at least $k + 1$ letters. If $v \in \{e\}^+$, then the word $u$ contains an occurrence of the letter $b$ and the subword also contains $k + 1$ letters. However, no such word exists in any selection language. Because of this contradiction, the assumption is not true. This yields that $L \notin \mathcal{L}(IC, REG_1^{Prod})$.                               $\square$

Together, we obtain the following result.

**Theorem 9.** *The relation*

$$\mathcal{L}(IC, REG_n^{Prod}) \subset \mathcal{L}(IC, REG_{n+1}^{Prod})$$

*holds for every natural number $n \geq 0$.*

We now consider the complexity measure *Symb*. Both the language families $\mathcal{L}(IC, REG_0^{Symb})$ and $\mathcal{L}(IC, REG_1^{Symb})$ are equal to the class of finite languages (every selection language is the empty set; the language generated coincides with the set of axioms). The class $\mathcal{L}(IC, REG_2^{Symb})$ contains infinite languages; for instance, the language $L = \{a\}^*$ is generated by the contextual grammar $G = (\{a\}, \{(\{\lambda\}, \{(\lambda, a)\})\}, \{\lambda\})$. This yields the proper inclusion

$$\mathcal{L}(IC, REG_1^{Symb}) \subset \mathcal{L}(IC, REG_2^{Symb}).$$

Also the further inclusions are proper.

**Lemma 10.** *We have $\mathcal{L}(EC, REG_n^{Symb}) \subset \mathcal{L}(EC, REG_{n+1}^{Symb})$ for $n \geq 2$.*

*Proof.* Let $n \geq 2$, $V_n = \{a, b, c_1, c_2, \ldots, c_{n-1}\}$, and

$$L_n = \{a^m c_1 c_2 \ldots c_{n-1} b^m \mid m \geq 0\}.$$

This language is generated by the contextual grammar

$$G_n = (V_n, \{(\{c_1 c_2 \ldots c_{n-1}\}, \{(a, b)\})\}, \{c_1 c_2 \ldots c_{n-1}\}).$$

Hence, $L_n \in \mathcal{L}(IC, REG_{n+1}^{Symb})$. Let $G'_n$ be a contextual grammar generating the language $L_n$. Every applicable context is of the form $(a^k, b^k)$ (with another context, a word would be generated which does not belong to the language). When such a context is inserted, the word that selects it contains the word $c_1 c_2 \ldots c_{n-1}$. Hence, any selection language contains a word which contains $n-1$ different letters. Thus, at least $n + 1$ symbols are necessary for generating each selection language. Hence, $L_n \notin \mathcal{L}(IC, REG_n^{Symb})$.                               $\square$

Together, we obtain the following result.

**Theorem 11.** *We have the relations*

$$\mathcal{L}(IC, REG_0^{Symb}) = \mathcal{L}(IC, REG_1^{Symb}) = FIN$$

*and*

$$\mathcal{L}(IC, REG_n^{Symb}) \subset \mathcal{L}(IC, REG_{n+1}^{Symb})$$

*for every natural number $n \geq 1$.*

# 4   Conclusions and Further Work

The main contribution of our paper consists in exhibiting a series of languages that highlight the difference between the power of internal contextual grammars that have the selection languages from different families of subregular languages. Here we only considered families defined by imposing restriction on the number of states, nonterminals, productions, or symbols needed to accept or generate them. It seems a natural continuation to consider in this context other families of subregular languages, defined by restrictions of combinatorial nature, like the ones considered in [1,2] for external contextual grammars.

Also, it may be interesting to show that there are languages over a constant alphabet that separate the classes on consecutive levels of every hierarchy we defined. While such a result was obtained in the case of the *State*-hierarchy, by Theorem 2, as well as in the case of the *Var*-hierarchy, by Theorem 3, showing the existence of such languages remains an open problem in the other two cases.

**Acknowledgements.** We thank Jürgen Dassow for fruitful discussions and the anonymous referees for their remarks which helped to improve the paper.

# References

1. Dassow, J.: Contextual grammars with subregular choice. Fundamenta Informaticae 64(1-4), 109–118 (2005)
2. Dassow, J., Manea, F., Truthe, B.: On Contextual Grammars with Subregular Selection Languages. In: Holzer, M., Kutrib, M., Pighizzini, g. (eds.) DCFS 2011. LNCS, vol. 6808, pp. 135–146. Springer, Heidelberg (2011)
3. Istrail, S.: Gramatici contextuale cu selectiva regulata. Stud. Cerc. Mat. 30, 287–294 (1978)
4. Marcus, S.: Contextual grammars. Revue Roum. Math. Pures Appl. 14, 1525–1534 (1969)
5. Păun, G.: Marcus Contextual Grammars. Kluwer Publ. House, Dordrecht (1998)
6. Rozenberg, G., Salomaa, A. (eds.): Handbook of Formal Languages. Springer, Berlin (1997)

# An Infinite Hierarchy of Language Families Resulting from Stateless Pushdown Automata with Limited Pushdown Alphabets

Alexander Meduna, Lukáš Vrábel, and Petr Zemek

Brno University of Technology, Faculty of Information Technology, IT4Innovations, Centre of Excellence, Božetěchova 1/2, 612 66 Brno, Czech Republic
{meduna,ivrabel,izemek}@fit.vutbr.cz

**Abstract.** As its name suggests, a stateless pushdown automaton has no states. As a result, each of its computational steps depends only on the currently scanned symbol and the current pushdown-store top. In this paper, we consider stateless pushdown automata whose size of their pushdown alphabet is limited by a positive integer. More specifically, we establish an infinite hierarchy of language families resulting from stateless pushdown automata with limited pushdown alphabets. In addition, we prove analogous results for stateless deterministic pushdown automata and stateless real-time pushdown automata. A formulation of an open problem closes the paper.

**Keywords:** stateless pushdown automata, limited pushdown alphabets, generative power, infinite hierarchy of language families.

## 1 Introduction

A *stateless pushdown automaton* (see [6,12,11,5]) is an ordinary pushdown automaton with only a single state. Consequently, the moves of a stateless pushdown automaton do not depend on internal states but solely on the symbols currently scanned by its head accessing the input tape and pushdown store. Recently, there has been a renewed interest in the investigation of various types of stateless automata. Namely, consider stateless restarting automata [8,9], stateless multihead automata [4,7], a relation of stateless automata to P systems [13], and stateless multicounter machines and Watson-Crick automata [3,1,2].

It is well known that stateless pushdown automata (accepting by empty pushdown) still characterize the family of context-free languages (see [10]), while for deterministic pushdown automata their computational power strictly increases with the number of states (see [6]). Also, recall that stateless two-way pushdown automata induce an infinite hierarchy of language families resulting from the number of their input reading heads (see [4]).

In this paper, we consider the impact of the size of pushdown alphabets to the power of stateless pushdown automata. More specifically, we establish an infinite hierarchy of language families resulting from stateless pushdown automata with

M. Kutrib, N. Moreira, and R. Reis (Eds.): DCFS 2012, LNCS 7386, pp. 236–243, 2012.

limited pushdown alphabets. For every positive integer $n$, we give a language which can only be accepted by a stateless pushdown automaton with at least $n$ pushdown symbols. This result is in contrast with the fact that in terms of ordinary pushdown automata and their deterministic variant, two pushdown symbols suffice to generate any context-free language. Indeed, one can use a binary alphabet to encode any finite number of symbols. Hence, we see that in the case of stateless pushdown automata, the absence of states do not allow us to use the encoding trick.

In addition, we prove analogous results for stateless deterministic pushdown automata and stateless real-time pushdown automata. Recall that a *deterministic pushdown automaton* has the choice of making no more than one move from any configuration, and a *real-time pushdown automaton* is a deterministic pushdown automaton that reads an input symbol during every move (see [6]).

From a theoretical viewpoint, infinite hierarchies reflect the impossibility to limit certain abilities or resources of language-defining devices. From a practical viewpoint, limited resources might result in a more efficient implementation of language processing tools. However, from the obtained results, we see that we cannot simultaneously limit the number of states to one and the size of pushdown alphabets. The achieved results can be seen as a continuation of existing studies on infinite hierarchies resulting from limited resources of various types of stateless automata (see [1,2,7,3,4]).

The paper is organized as follows. First, Section 2 gives all the necessary terminology. Then, Section 3 establishes the infinite hierarchies mentioned above. In the conclusion, Section 4 gives an observation regarding yet another variant of a stateless pushdown automaton, and states an open problem related to the achieved results.

## 2    Preliminaries and Definitions

In this paper, we assume that the reader is familiar with the theory of formal languages (see [6]). For a set $Q$, $card(Q)$ denotes the cardinality of $Q$. For an alphabet (finite nonempty set) $V$, $V^*$ represents the free monoid generated by $V$ under the operation of concatenation. The unit of $V^*$ is denoted by $\varepsilon$. Set $V^+ = V^* - \{\varepsilon\}$; algebraically, $V^+$ is thus the free semigroup generated by $V$ under the operation of concatenation. For $w \in V^*$, $|w|$ denotes the length of $w$, and $prefix(w)$ denotes the set of all proper[1] prefixes of $w$. For $w \in V^*$ and $a \in V$, $\#_a w$ denotes the number of occurrences of $a$ in $w$.

Next, we define stateless pushdown automata. Since these automata have only a single state, for brevity, we define them without any states at all.

**Definition 1 (see [11]).** A *stateless pushdown automaton* (an *SPDA* for short) is a quadruple

$$M = (\Sigma, \Gamma, R, \alpha),$$

---

[1] A prefix $p$ of $w \in V^*$ is *proper* if $p \neq \varepsilon$ and $p \neq w$.

where $\Sigma$ is an *input alphabet*, $\Gamma$ is a *pushdown alphabet*, $R \subseteq \Gamma \times (\Sigma \cup \{\varepsilon\}) \times \Gamma^*$ is a finite relation, called the set of *rules*, and $\alpha \in \Gamma^+$ is the *initial pushdown string*. Instead of $(A, a, w) \in R$, we write $Aa \to w$ throughout the paper. For $r = (Aa \to w) \in R$, $Aa$ and $w$ represent the *left-hand side* of $r$ and the *right-hand side* of $r$, respectively.

The *configuration* of $M$ is any element of $\Gamma^* \times \Sigma^*$. For a configuration $c = (\pi, w)$, $\pi$ is called the *pushdown* of $c$ and $w$ is called the *unread part of the input string* (or just *input string* for short) of $c$.

The *direct move relation* over the set of all configurations, symbolically denoted by $\vdash$, is a binary relation over the set of all configurations defined as follows: $(\pi A, au) \vdash (\pi w, u)$ in $M$ if and only if $Aa \to w \in R$, where $\pi, w \in \Gamma^*$, $A \in \Gamma$, $a \in \Sigma \cup \{\varepsilon\}$, and $u \in \Sigma^*$. Let $\vdash^k$ and $\vdash^*$ denote the $k$th power of $\vdash$, for some $k \geq 1$, and the reflexive-transitive closure of $\vdash$, respectively.

The *language accepted by* $M$ is denoted by $L(M)$ and defined as

$$L(M) = \{w \in \Sigma^* \mid (\alpha, w) \vdash^* (\varepsilon, \varepsilon)\}. \qquad \square$$

**Definition 2 (see [11]).** Let $M = (\Sigma, \Gamma, R, \alpha)$ be an SPDA. If $Aa \to w \in R$ implies that $R - \{Aa \to w\}$ contains no rule with its left-hand side equal to $Aa$ or $A$, then $M$ is a *stateless deterministic pushdown automaton* (an *SDPDA* for short). $\qquad \square$

**Definition 3 (see [6]).** Let $M = (\Sigma, \Gamma, R, \alpha)$ be an SDPDA. If $Aa \to w \in R$ implies that $a \neq \varepsilon$, then $M$ is a *stateless real-time pushdown automaton* (an *SRPDA* for short). $\qquad \square$

Next, we define SPDAs with limited pushdown alphabets, which are central to this paper.

**Definition 4.** Let $M = (\Sigma, \Gamma, R, \alpha)$ be an SPDA. $M$ is an *n-pushdown-alphabet-limited SPDA* (an *n-SPDA* for short) for $n \geq 1$ if $\mathrm{card}(\Gamma) \leq n$. $\qquad \square$

By analogy with $n$-SPDAs, we define their deterministic and real-time versions.

**Definition 5.** Let $M = (\Sigma, \Gamma, R, \alpha)$ be an SDPDA. $M$ is an *n-pushdown-alphabet-limited SDPDA* (an *n-SDPDA* for short) for $n \geq 1$ if $\mathrm{card}(\Gamma) \leq n$. $\qquad \square$

**Definition 6.** Let $M = (\Sigma, \Gamma, R, \alpha)$ be an SRPDA. $M$ is an *n-pushdown-alphabet-limited SRPDA* (an *n-SRPDA* for short) for $n \geq 1$ if $\mathrm{card}(\Gamma) \leq n$. $\qquad \square$

For every $n \geq 1$, let $_n\mathbf{SPDA}$, $_n\mathbf{SDPDA}$, and $_n\mathbf{SRPDA}$ denote the families of languages accepted by $n$-SPDAs, $n$-SDPDAs, and $n$-SRPDAs, respectively.

## 3    Results

In this section, we establish three infinite hierarchies of language families induced by $n$-SPDAs, $n$-SDPDAs, and $n$-SRPDAs, where $n \geq 1$.

For each positive integer $n$, define the language $L_n$ as

$$L_n = \bigcup_{1 \leq k \leq n} \{w \in \{a_k, b_k\}^+ \mid \#_{a_k}(w) = \#_{b_k}(w) \text{ and} \\ p \in \text{prefix}(w) \text{ implies that } \#_{a_k}(p) > \#_{b_k}(p)\}.$$

First, we show that for every positive integer $n$, $n+1$ pushdown symbols suffice to generate $L_n$.

**Lemma 1.** $L_n \in {}_{n+1}\mathbf{SPDA}$ *for each* $n \geq 1$.

*Proof.* Let $n$ be a positive integer, and consider the $(n+1)$-SPDA

$$M = (\Sigma, \Gamma, R, S),$$

where

$$\Sigma = \{a_i, b_i \mid 1 \leq i \leq n\},$$
$$\Gamma = \{S\} \cup \{A_i \mid 1 \leq i \leq n\},$$
$$R = \bigcup_{1 \leq i \leq n} \{Sa_i \to A_i, A_i a_i \to A_i A_i, A_i b_i \to \varepsilon\},$$

with $S \notin \{A_i \mid 1 \leq i \leq n\}$. Observe that $L(M) = L_n$, so the lemma holds.    □

Now, we show that any SPDA accepting $L_n$ has to have at least $n + 1$ unique pushdown symbols. To simplify the proof, we first establish three lemmas illustrating the inability of SPDAs to transfer any kind of information during steps that decrease the pushdown.

The first lemma illustrates the effect of the statelessness on the direct move relation.

**Lemma 2.** *Let* $M = (\Sigma, \Gamma, R, \alpha)$ *be an SPDA. If* $(\pi_1, u_1) \vdash^* (\pi_2, u_2)$ *for some* $\pi_1, \pi_2 \in \Gamma^*$ *and* $u_1, u_2 \in \Sigma^*$, *then* $(\pi\pi_1, u_1 u) \vdash^* (\pi\pi_2, u_2 u)$ *for all* $\pi \in \Gamma^*$ *and* $u \in \Sigma^*$.

*Proof.* This lemma follows from the fact that the definition of $\vdash$ depends only on the topmost symbol of the pushdown and on the leftmost symbol of the input string.    □

Notice that Lemma 2 implies that if $(\pi_1, u_1) \vdash^* (\varepsilon, \varepsilon)$, then $(\pi\pi_1, u_1 u) \vdash^* (\pi, u)$ for each $\pi \in \Gamma^*$ and $u \in \Sigma^*$. This implication is used extensively throughout the rest of this paper.

The next lemma shows that we can erase a part of the pushdown with some corresponding part of the input string independently of the rest of the pushdown and of the rest of the input string.

**Lemma 3.** *Let* $M = (\Sigma, \Gamma, R, \alpha)$ *be an SPDA. If* $(\pi\sigma, u) \vdash^* (\pi, v)$ *for some* $\pi \in \Gamma^*$, $\sigma \in \Gamma^+$, *and* $u, v \in \Sigma^*$, *then there is* $s \in \Sigma^*$ *such that* $s$ *is a prefix of* $u$ *and* $(\sigma, s) \vdash^* (\varepsilon, \varepsilon)$.

*Proof.* Clearly, $(\pi\sigma, u) \vdash^* (\pi, v)$ can be written as

$$(\pi\sigma_1, u_1) \vdash (\pi\sigma_2, u_2) \vdash \cdots \vdash (\pi\sigma_n, u_n) \vdash (\pi, u') \vdash^* (\pi, v)$$

where $\sigma_1, \ldots, \sigma_n \in \Gamma^+$, $u_1, \ldots, u_n \in \Sigma^*$, $\sigma_1 = \sigma$, $u_1 = u$, and $n \geq 1$. Observe that by the definition of $\vdash$, $u'$ is a suffix of each $u_j$, where $1 \leq j \leq n$. Thus, $u_1 = su'$ for some $s \in \Sigma^*$. As $|\sigma_j| > 0$, where $1 \leq j \leq n$, all the rules used in $(\pi\sigma_1, u_1) \vdash (\pi\sigma_2, u_2) \vdash \cdots \vdash (\pi\sigma_n, u_n) \vdash^* (\pi, u')$ are not working with any symbol from $\pi$ or from $u'$. Thus, their applicability depends only on $\sigma_1$ and $s$. Hence, the lemma holds. □

The next lemma shows that we can rewrite the pushdown with some corresponding part of the input string independently of the rest of the input string.

**Lemma 4.** *Let $M = (\Sigma, \Gamma, R, \alpha)$ be an SPDA. If $(\pi_1, uv) \vdash^* (\pi_2, v)$ for some $\pi_1, \pi_2 \in \Gamma^*$ and $u, v \in \Sigma^*$, then $(\pi_1, u) \vdash^* (\pi_2, \varepsilon)$.*

*Proof.* The lemma follows from the fact that the rules used in $(\pi_1, uv) \vdash^* (\pi_2, v)$ are not working with any symbols from $v$. □

Now, we use the three previously established lemmas to show that we need at least $n + 1$ pushdown symbols to accept $L_n$.

**Lemma 5.** *Let $M = (\Sigma, \Gamma, R, \alpha)$ be an SPDA such that $L(M) = L_n$, where $n \geq 1$. Then, $\mathrm{card}(\Gamma) \geq n + 1$.*

*Proof.* First, we introduce some notation to simplify the proof. Let $\Sigma_k = \{a_k, b_k\}$ for $k = 1, 2, \ldots, n$, $\Sigma_a = \{a_1, a_2, \ldots, a_n\}$, and $\Sigma_b = \{b_1, b_2, \ldots, b_n\}$. Furthermore, we suppose that there are no useless rules in $R$ and no useless symbols in $\Gamma$ (by a useless rule, we mean a rule that is not used during the acceptance of any $w \in L(M)$).

Before proving that $\mathrm{card}(\Gamma) \geq n + 1$, we prove a claim. It shows that there is a unique $A \in \Gamma$ for each $b \in \Sigma_b$. This claim together with the fact that each $b \in \Sigma_b$ has to occur in some rule implies that $\mathrm{card}(\Gamma) \geq n$. Then, we show that there has to be at least one more symbol in $\Gamma$ in order to have $L(M) = L_n$, thus proving that $\mathrm{card}(\Gamma) \geq n + 1$.

*Claim 1.* For each $b_j, b_k \in \Sigma_b$ such that $b_j \neq b_k$, there is no $A \in \Gamma$ such that $Ab_j \to \sigma_j \in R$ and $Ab_k \to \sigma_k \in R$, where $\sigma_j, \sigma_k \in \Gamma^*$.

*Proof.* By contradiction. Without any loss of generality, we use $b_1 \in \Sigma_1 \cap \Sigma_b$ and $b_2 \in \Sigma_2 \cap \Sigma_b$. For the sake of contradiction, assume that there is $A \in \Gamma$ such that $Ab_1 \to \sigma_1 \in R$ and $Ab_2 \to \sigma_2 \in R$, where $\sigma_1, \sigma_2 \in \Gamma^*$. As there are no useless rules in $R$, there is $w_1 \in L_n \cap \Sigma_1^*$ such that $Ab_1 \to \sigma_1$ is used during its acceptance. Then,

$$(\alpha, w_1) \vdash^* (\pi_1 A, b_1 w') \vdash (\pi_1 \sigma_1, w') \vdash^* (\pi_1, w'') \vdash^* (\varepsilon, \varepsilon), \tag{1}$$

where $\pi_1 \in \Gamma^*$ and $w', w'' \in \Sigma^*$. Next, we show that there is $s_1 \in \Sigma^*$ such that $s_1$ is a prefix of $w'$ and $(\sigma_1, s_1) \vdash^* (\varepsilon, \varepsilon)$. Consider two possible cases, (i) and (ii), discussed next, based on whether $\sigma_1 = \varepsilon$ or $\sigma_1 \neq \varepsilon$:

(i) $\sigma_1 = \varepsilon$. Then, $s_1 = \varepsilon$ since $(\varepsilon, \varepsilon) \vdash^* (\varepsilon, \varepsilon)$.

(ii) $\sigma_1 \neq \varepsilon$. Observe that $(\pi_1\sigma_1, w') \vdash^* (\pi_1, w'')$ in (1), so by Lemma 3, there is $s_1$ such that $(\sigma_1, s_1) \vdash^* (\varepsilon, \varepsilon)$.

Therefore, (1) can be rewritten using $w_1 = u_1 b_1 s_1 v_1$, where $u_1, v_1 \in \Sigma^*$, to

$$(\alpha, u_1 b_1 s_1 v_1) \vdash^* (\pi_1 A, b_1 s_1 v_1) \vdash (\pi_1\sigma_1, s_1 v_1) \vdash^* (\pi_1, v_1) \vdash^* (\varepsilon, \varepsilon). \qquad (2)$$

Note that by Lemma 4, $(\alpha, u_1) \vdash^* (\pi_1 A, \varepsilon)$.

Now, let $w_2 \in L_n \cap \Sigma_2^*$ be a string such that $Ab_2 \to \sigma_2$ is used during its acceptance. In the same way as with $w_1$, we can find $s_2$ such that $(\sigma_2, s_2) \vdash^* (\varepsilon, \varepsilon)$. Let $w_2 = u_2 b_2 s_2 v_2 \in L_n$, where $u_2, v_2 \in \Sigma_2^*$. Then,

$$(\alpha, u_2 b_2 s_2 v_2) \vdash^* (\pi_2 A, b_2 s_2 v_2) \vdash (\pi_2\sigma_2, s_2 v_2) \vdash^* (\pi_2, v_2) \vdash^* (\varepsilon, \varepsilon), \qquad (3)$$

where $\pi_2 \in \Gamma^*$. As $(A, b_2 s_2) \vdash (\sigma_2, s_2)$ by $Ab_2 \to \sigma_2$ and $(\sigma_2, s_2) \vdash^* (\varepsilon, \varepsilon)$, $(A, b_2 s_2) \vdash^* (\varepsilon, \varepsilon)$.

To complete the proof, let $x = u_1 b_2 s_2 v_1$. Recall that $(\alpha, u_1) \vdash^* (\pi_1 A, \varepsilon)$, so by Lemma 2,

$$(\alpha, u_1 b_2 s_2 v_1) \vdash^* (\pi_1 A, b_2 s_2 v_1).$$

Furthermore, recall that $(A, b_2 s_2) \vdash^* (\varepsilon, \varepsilon)$, so by Lemma 2,

$$(\pi_1 A, b_2 s_2 v_1) \vdash^* (\pi_1, v_1).$$

Finally, according to (2),

$$(\pi_1, v_1) \vdash^* (\varepsilon, \varepsilon).$$

Thus, $(\alpha, x) \vdash^* (\varepsilon, \varepsilon)$, so $x \in L(M)$. However, as $u_1$ is followed by $b_1$ in $w_1 \in L_n$, by the definition of $L_n$, it has to contain at least one occurrence of $a_1$. Then, since $x = u_1 b_2 s_2 v_1$ contains both $a_1$ and $b_2$, it is not in $L_n$, which is a contradiction. Thus, the claim holds. $\qquad \square$

Now, we show that $\text{card}(\Gamma) \geq n + 1$. Again, we proceed by contradiction. By Claim 1, $\text{card}(\Gamma) \geq n$. For the sake of contradiction, suppose that $\text{card}(\Gamma) = n$. Let $\alpha = \alpha' A$ for some $\alpha' \in \Gamma^*$ and $A \in \Gamma$. Furthermore, let $w = uv \in L_n$ be a string such that

$$(\alpha' A, uv) \vdash^* (\alpha', v) \vdash^* (\varepsilon, \varepsilon). \qquad (4)$$

Observe that $\text{card}(\Gamma) = \text{card}(\Sigma_b)$ and $A \in \Gamma$. By Claim 1, there is a unique pushdown symbol for each input symbol in $\Sigma_b$, so there has to be some $b \in \Sigma_b$ such that $Ab \to \sigma \in R$, where $\sigma \in \Gamma^*$. As there are no useless rules in $R$, there is also $w' \in L_n$ such that $Ab \to \sigma$ is used during its acceptance. Therefore, in the same way as with $w_1$ in Claim 1, we can find $s$ such that $(\sigma, s) \vdash^* (\varepsilon, \varepsilon)$. Let $w' = u'bsv' \in L_n$ be a string such that

$$(\alpha, u'bsv') \vdash^* (\pi A, bsv') \vdash (\pi\sigma, sv') \vdash^* (\pi, v') \vdash^* (\varepsilon, \varepsilon), \qquad (5)$$

where $\pi \in \Gamma^*$. Note that according to (5) and Lemma 3, $(A, bs) \vdash^* (\varepsilon, \varepsilon)$. To obtain a contradiction, let $x = bsv$. Then, by Lemma 2,

$$(\alpha' A, bsv) \vdash^* (\alpha', v).$$

Furthermore, according to (4),

$$(\alpha', v) \vdash^* (\varepsilon, \varepsilon).$$

Thus, $(\alpha'A, bsv) \vdash^* (\varepsilon, \varepsilon)$. As $\alpha'A = \alpha$ and $bsv = x$, $x \in L(M)$. However, $x$ begins with $b \in \Sigma_b$, which is a contradiction with the definition of $L_n$. Hence, the lemma holds.    □

The next theorem represents the main achievement of this paper.

**Theorem 1.** $_n$**SPDA** $\subset$ $_{n+1}$**SPDA** *for every* $n \geq 1$.

*Proof.* By Lemma 5, $L_n \notin$ $_n$**SPDA**. However, $L_n \in$ $_{n+1}$**SPDA** by Lemma 1. Hence, the theorem holds.    □

Observe that the SPDA constructed in the proof of Lemma 1 is, in fact, deterministic and realtime. Furthermore, the argumentation used in the proofs of Lemmas 2 through 5 holds also for SDPDAs and SRPDAs. Therefore, the following two theorems also hold.

**Theorem 2.** $_n$**SDPDA** $\subset$ $_{n+1}$**SDPDA**, *for every* $n \geq 1$.    □

**Theorem 3.** $_n$**SRPDA** $\subset$ $_{n+1}$**SRPDA**, *for every* $n \geq 1$.    □

# 4    Concluding Remarks

In this concluding section, we first discuss another version of stateless pushdown automata. Then, we propose an open problem related to the topic of this paper.

Considered a stateless version of *extended pushdown automata* (see [6]). Recall that an extended pushdown automaton may read a string from the top of its pushdown during a single step, not just a single symbol. Observe that in this case, we may convert any pushdown automaton $M$ into an equivalent stateless extended pushdown automaton $M'$ with only two pushdown symbols in the following way. We encode every pushdown symbol of $M$ into a binary string using the two pushdown symbols of $M'$. Then, in $M'$, we read and modify encoded strings rather than the original symbols. Hence, we see than in terms of stateless extended pushdown automata, a limitation of the number of pushdown symbols is possible while in terms of ordinary stateless pushdown automata, this is not possible as proved in the present paper.

We close the paper by proposing an open problem. Reconsider Definition 4. Modify it so that $M$ is an $n$-SPDA if $\text{card}(\Gamma) - \text{card}(\Sigma) \leq n$; that is, we count only the number of non-input symbols. Do the results proved in this paper hold even with this modified definition?

**Acknowledgments.** This work was supported by the following grants: FRVŠ MŠMT FR271/2012/G1, BUT FIT-S-11-2, MŠMT ED1.1.00/02.0070, and CEZ MŠMT MSM0021630528.

# References

1. Eğecioğlu, Ö., Hegedüs, L., Nagy, B.: Hierarchies of stateless multicounter 5' → 3' Watson-Crick automata languages. Fundamenta Informaticae 110(1-4), 111–123 (2011)
2. Nagy, B., Hegedüs, L., Eğecioğlu, Ö.: Hierarchy Results on Stateless Multicounter 5ʹ → 3ʹ Watson-Crick Automata. In: Cabestany, J., Rojas, I., Joya, G. (eds.) IWANN 2011, Part I. LNCS, vol. 6691, pp. 465–472. Springer, Heidelberg (2011)
3. Eğecioğlu, Ö., Ibarra, O.H.: On Stateless Multicounter Machines. In: Ambos-Spies, K., Löwe, B., Merkle, W. (eds.) CiE 2009. LNCS, vol. 5635, pp. 178–187. Springer, Heidelberg (2009)
4. Frisco, P., Ibarra, O.H.: On Stateless Multihead Finite Automata and Multi-head Pushdown Automata. In: Diekert, V., Nowotka, D. (eds.) DLT 2009. LNCS, vol. 5583, pp. 240–251. Springer, Heidelberg (2009)
5. Gallier, J.H.: DPDA's in 'atomic normal form' and applications to equivalence problems. Theoretical Computer Science 14(2), 155–186 (1981)
6. Harrison, M.: Introduction to Formal Language Theory. Addison-Wesley, Boston (1978)
7. Ibarra, O.H., Karhumäki, J., Okhotin, A.: On Stateless Multihead Automata: Hierarchies and the Emptiness Problem. In: Laber, E.S., Bornstein, C., Nogueira, L.T., Faria, L. (eds.) LATIN 2008. LNCS, vol. 4957, pp. 94–105. Springer, Heidelberg (2008)
8. Kutrib, M., Messerschmidt, H., Otto, F.: On stateless deterministic restarting automata. Acta Informatica 47(7), 391–412 (2010)
9. Kutrib, M., Messerschmidt, H., Otto, F.: On stateless two-pushdown automata and restarting automata. International Journal of Foundations of Computer Science 21(5), 781–798 (2010)
10. Meduna, A.: Elements of Compiler Design. Auerbach Publications, Boston (2007)
11. Oyamaguchi, M., Honda, N.: The decidability of equivalence for deterministic stateless pushdown automata. Information and Control 38(3), 367–376 (1978)
12. Valiant, L.G.: Decision procedures for families of deterministic pushdown automata. Research Report CS-RR-001, Department of Computer Science, University of Warwick, Coventry, UK (1973)
13. Yang, L., Dang, Z., Ibarra, O.H.: On stateless automata and P systems. International Journal of Foundations of Computer Science, 1259–1276 (2008)

# Centralized PC Systems of Pushdown Automata versus Multi-head Pushdown Automata

Friedrich Otto

Fachbereich Elektrotechnik/Informatik, Universität Kassel,
34109 Kassel, Germany
otto@theory.informatik.uni-kassel.de

**Abstract.** In returning mode centralized PC systems of pushdown automata of degree $n$ can simulate $n$-head pushdown automata (Csuhaj-Varjú et. al. 2000). At DCFS 2009, Balan claimed that also the converse holds. Here we show that Balan's proof of this claim is not correct[1]. Accordingly it is still open whether $n$-head pushdown automata and centralized PC systems of pushdown automata of degree $n$ working in returning mode accept the same class of languages.

**Keywords:** PC system of pushdown automata, centralized PC system, multi-head pushdown automaton.

## 1 Introduction

Parallel communicating grammar systems, or PC grammar systems for short, have been invented to model a certain type of cooperation: the so-called *class room model* [2]. Here a group of experts, modelled by grammars, work together in order to produce a document, that is, an output word. These experts work on their own, but synchronously, and they exchange information on request.

In the literature many different types and variants of PC grammar systems have been studied (see, e.g., [2,4]). Also the notion of PC system has been carried over to various types of automata. Here we are interested in the *PC systems of pushdown automata* as introduced in [3]. In such a system a finite number $n$ of pushdown automata, say $A_1, \ldots, A_n$, work in parallel in a synchronous way, where the number $n$ of components is called the *degree* of the PC system. If one of these pushdown automata, say $A_i$, encounters a special *communication symbol* as the topmost symbol on its pushdown store, say $K_j$, then a *communication step* takes place: the symbol $K_j$ on the top of the pushdown of $A_i$ is replaced by the complete pushdown contents of the pushdown automaton $A_j$, provided that the topmost symbol of it is not a communication symbol. The PC system is said to work in *returning mode*, if by this communication step the contents of the pushdown of $A_j$ is reset to its initial symbol $Z_j$. It is known that PC systems

---

[1] We tried to contact M. Balan by e-mail, but unfortunately this was not possible, as his e-mail address, given in [1], is not valid anymore, and we did not succeed in finding a more recent one.

M. Kutrib, N. Moreira, and R. Reis (Eds.): DCFS 2012, LNCS 7386, pp. 244–251, 2012.

of pushdown automata of degree 3 working in returning mode do already accept all recursively enumerable languages [3].

If there is only one component, called the *master* of the system, that can use communication symbols, then the PC system is called *centralized*. It is known that a centralized PC system of pushdown automata of degree $n$ that is working in returning mode can simulate an $n$-head pushdown automaton [3]. In [1] it is claimed that also conversely, centralized PC systems of pushdown automata of degree $n$ working in returning mode can be simulated by $n$-head pushdown automata. Using its first head the $n$-head pushdown automaton simulates the master of the PC system until a communication step is to be simulated, and then it uses one of its other heads to simulate the component from which the master requests the pushdown contents. The simulation turns back to simulating the master as soon as the other component has been simulated up to the time of the communication step. In order to detect this, Balan coined the notion of *known communication property*, which states that the non-master components can detect when they have been subjected to a communication step. Balan proved that each centralized PC system of pushdown automata working in returning mode is equivalent to a PC system of the same type that has this known communication property. This is proved by showing that a non-master component can detect a communication step by simply checking the contents of its pushdown. However, in the simulating $n$-head pushdown automaton, no equivalent of the communication step takes place, and accordingly, the $n$-head pushdown automaton cannot detect the exact moment when it has to stop the simulation of a non-master component. This means that it is *still open* whether or not all centralized PC systems of pushdown automata of degree $n$ working in returning mode can be simulated by $n$-head pushdown automata.

Here we present an example language $L$ that is accepted by a centralized PC system of pushdown automata of degree 2 working in returning mode, where the inherent synchronization of the two components is used in an essential way. The simulation of Balan [1] does not work for this system. In fact, we expect that the language $L$ cannot be accepted by any 2-head pushdown automaton at all.

The paper is structured as follows. In Section 2 we restate the definition of PC systems of pushdown automata from [3] in short and recall some of their properties. In the next section we recall the definition of the multi-head pushdown automaton and describe Balan's simulation of centralized PC systems of pushdown automata working in returning mode by multi-head pushdown automata from [1] in some detail. Then in Section 4 we present and discuss our example language.

## 2   PC Systems of Pushdown Automata

Here we restate the definition of the PC system of pushdown automata from [3] in short.

**Definition 1.** *A* PC system of pushdown automata *is given through a tuple*

$$\mathcal{A} = (\Sigma, \Gamma, A_1, \ldots, A_n, K),$$

*where*

- $\Sigma$ *is a finite input alphabet and* $\Gamma$ *is a finite pushdown alphabet,*
- *for each* $1 \le i \le n$, $A_i = (Q_i, \Sigma, \Gamma, \delta_i, q_i, Z_i, F_i)$ *is a nondeterministic pushdown automaton with finite set of internal states* $Q_i$, *initial state* $q_i \in Q_i$ *and set of final states* $F_i \subseteq Q_i$, *input alphabet* $\Sigma$, *pushdown alphabet* $\Gamma$, *initial pushdown symbol* $Z_i \in \Gamma$, *and transition relation* $\delta_i : Q_i \times (\Sigma \cup \{\varepsilon\}) \times \Gamma \to 2^{Q_i \times \Gamma^*}$, *where, for each triple* $(q, a, A) \in Q_i \times (\Sigma \cup \{\varepsilon\}) \times \Gamma$, $\delta_i(q, a, A)$ *is a finite subset of* $Q_i \times \Gamma^*$,
- *and* $K \subseteq \{K_1, K_2, \dots, K_n\} \subseteq \Gamma$ *is a set of* query symbols.

Here the pushdown automata $A_1, \dots, A_n$ are the *components* of the system $\mathcal{A}$, and the integer $n$ is called the *degree* of this PC system.

**Definition 1 (cont.).** *A* configuration *of* $\mathcal{A}$ *is described by a* $3n$-*tuple*

$$(s_1, x_1, \alpha_1, s_2, x_2, \alpha_2, \dots, s_n, x_n, \alpha_n),$$

*where, for* $1 \le i \le n$,

- $s_i \in Q_i$ *is the current state of component* $A_i$,
- $x_i \in \Sigma^*$ *is the remaining part of the input which has not yet been read by component* $A_i$, *and*
- $\alpha_i \in \Gamma^*$ *is the current contents of the pushdown of* $A_i$, *where the first symbol of* $\alpha_i$ *is the topmost symbol on the pushdown.*

On the set of configurations $\mathcal{A}$ induces a *computation relation* $\vdash_{\mathcal{A},r}^*$ that is the reflexive and transitive closure of the following relation $\vdash_{\mathcal{A},r}$.

**Definition 2.** *For two configurations*

$$(s_1, x_1, c_1\alpha_1, \dots, s_n, x_n, c_n\alpha_n) \text{ and } (p_1, y_2, \beta_2, \dots, p_n, y_n, \beta_n),$$

*where* $c_1, \dots, c_n \in \Gamma$,

$$(s_1, x_1, c_1\alpha_1, \dots, s_n, x_n, c_n\alpha_n) \vdash_{\mathcal{A},r} (p_1, y_1, \beta_1, \dots, p_n, y_n, \beta_n)$$

*if and only if one of the following two conditions is satisfied:*

(1) $K \cap \{c_1, \dots, c_n\} = \emptyset$, *and* $x_i = a_i y_i$ *for some* $a_i \in \Sigma \cup \{\varepsilon\}$, $(p_i, \gamma_i) \in \delta_i(s_i, a_i, c_i)$, *and* $\beta_i = \gamma_i\alpha_i$ *for all* $1 \le i \le n$, *or*
(2)     – $K \cap \{c_1, \dots, c_n\} \ne \emptyset$,
    – *for all* $i \in \{1, \dots, n\}$ *such that* $c_i = K_{j_i}$ *and* $c_{j_i} \notin K$, $\beta_i = c_{j_i}\alpha_{j_i}\alpha_i$ *and* $\beta_{j_i} = Z_{j_i}$,
    – $\beta_r = c_r\alpha_r$ *for all other values of* $r \in \{1, \dots, n\}$,
    – $y_t = x_t$ *and* $p_t = s_t$ *for all* $t \in \{1, \dots, n\}$.

The steps of form (1) are called *local steps*, as in them each component $A_i$ ($1 \leq i \leq n$) performs a local step, concurrently, but otherwise independently. The steps of form (2) are called *communication steps*, as in them the topmost symbol $K_{j_i}$ on the pushdown of component $A_i$ is replaced by the complete contents $c_{j_i}\alpha_{j_i}$ of the pushdown of component $A_{j_i}$, provided that the topmost symbol $c_{j_i}$ is itself not a query symbol. At this time also the pushdown of $A_{j_i}$ is reset to its initial symbol $Z_{j_i}$. Accordingly, it is said that $\mathcal{A}$ works in *returning mode*. If the contents of the pushdown of $A_{j_i}$ were to remain unchanged by the communication step, then $\mathcal{A}$ would work in *nonreturning mode*. Here, however, we are only interested in PC systems of pushdown automata that work in returning mode.

**Definition 3.** (a) *The language $L_r(\mathcal{A})$ that is accepted by $\mathcal{A}$ working in returning mode is defined by*

$$L_r(\mathcal{A}) = \{\, w \in \Sigma^* \mid (q_1, w, Z_1, \ldots, q_n, w, Z_n) \vdash^*_{\mathcal{A},r} (s_1, \varepsilon, \alpha_1, \ldots, s_n, \varepsilon, \alpha_n)$$
$$\text{for some } s_i \in F_i \text{ and } \alpha_i \in \Gamma^*, 1 \leq i \leq n \,\}.$$

(b) *By $\mathcal{L}_r(\mathrm{PCPDA}(n))$ we denote the class of languages that are accepted by PC systems of pushdown automata of degree $n$ working in returning mode.*

(c) *A PC system of pushdown automata $\mathcal{A} = (\Sigma, \Gamma, A_1, \ldots, A_n, K)$ is centralized if there is a single component, say $A_1$, that can use query symbols. In this case, $A_1$ is called the* master *of the system $\mathcal{A}$. By $\mathcal{L}_r(\mathrm{CPCPDA}(n))$ we denote the class of languages that are accepted by centralized PC systems of pushdown automata of degree $n$ working in returning mode.*

In [3] the following result is established on the expressive power of PC systems of pushdown automata working in returning mode.

**Theorem 1.** *The class $\mathcal{L}_r(\mathrm{PCPDA}(3))$ coincides with the class of all recursively enumerable languages.*

This result is proved by showing that a pushdown automaton with two pushdown stores can be simulated by a PC system of pushdown automata of degree 3 working in returning mode.

Let $\mathcal{A} = (\Sigma, \Gamma, A_1, \ldots, A_n, K)$ be a centralized PC system of pushdown automata, and let

$$(s_1, x_1, K_j\alpha_1, \ldots, s_j, x_j, \alpha_j, \ldots) \vdash_{\mathcal{A},r} (s_1, x_1, \alpha_j\alpha_1, \ldots, s_j, x_j, Z_j, \ldots)$$

be a communication step of $\mathcal{A}$. The component $A_1$ is actively involved in this communication step, while component $A_j$ is only passively involved in this communication step, that is, it does not really notice its involvement in this step. To remedy this situation, Balan introduced the so-called *known communication property*.

**Definition 4.** [1] *Let $\mathcal{A} = (\Sigma, \Gamma, A_1, \ldots, A_n, K)$ be a centralized PC system of pushdown automata, where, for each $1 \leq i \leq n$, $A_i = (Q'_i, \Sigma, \Gamma, \delta_i, q_i, Z_i, F_i)$*

and $Q'_i$ has the form $Q'_i = Q_i \times \{0,1\}$. Then $\mathcal{A}$ is said to have the known communication property if, whenever component $A_j$, being in state $(p_j, 0)$, has communicated the contents of its pushdown to component $A_1$, then in the next local transition $A_j$ will enter the state $(p_j, 1)$, and this is the only way in which a state of this form can be reached.

Thus, the second component 1 of a state $(q_j, 1) \in Q'_j$ indicates that component $A_j$ has just sent its pushdown contents to $A_1$ in the previous step. On the known communication property Balan derived the following result.

**Theorem 2.** [1] For every centralized PC system of pushdown automata $\mathcal{A}$, there exists a centralized PC system of pushdown automata $\mathcal{A}'$ of the same degree as $\mathcal{A}$ such that $L_r(\mathcal{A}') = L_r(\mathcal{A})$, and $\mathcal{A}'$ has the known communication property.

Essentially component $A_j$ replaces its initial pushdown symbol $Z_j$ by a new symbol $Z'_j$, and hence, when it detects in the following that $Z_j$ is the topmost symbol on its pushdown, then it realizes that it has just passively taken part in a communication step. Observe that the detection of a passive involvement in a communication step is not done internally within $A_j$'s finite-state control, but that it is done simply by observing the pushdown of $A_j$.

## 3   Multi-head Pushdown Automata

Next we repeat in short the definition of the multi-head pushdown automaton, where we follow the presentation in [3].

**Definition 5.** For $n \geq 1$, an $n$-head pushdown automaton is given through an 8-tuple $B = (n, Q, \Sigma, \Gamma, \delta, q_0, Z_0, F)$, where $Q$ is a finite set of internal states, $q_0 \in Q$ is the initial state and $F \subseteq Q$ is a set of final states, $\Sigma$ is a finite input alphabet and $\Gamma$ is a finite pushdown alphabet with initial pushdown symbol $Z_0 \in \Gamma$, and $\delta : Q \times (\Sigma \cup \{\varepsilon\})^n \times \Gamma \to 2^{Q \times \Gamma^*}$ is a transition relation. For each tuple $(q, a_1, \ldots, a_n, X) \in Q \times (\Sigma \cup \{\varepsilon\})^n \times \Gamma$, $\delta(q, a_1, \ldots, a_n, X)$ is a finite subset of $Q \times \Gamma^*$. If $(q', \alpha) \in \delta(q, a_1, \ldots, a_n, X)$, then this means that $B$, when in state $q$ with $X$ as the topmost symbol on its pushdown and reading $a_i$ with its $i$-th head $(1 \leq i \leq n)$, can change to state $q'$ and replace the symbol $X$ by the string $\alpha$ on the top of the pushdown. In addition, if $a_i \in \Sigma$, then head $i$ moves one step to the right, and if $a_i = \varepsilon$, then head $i$ remains stationary.

A configuration of $B$ is described by an $(n+2)$-tuple

$$(q, x_1, \ldots, x_n, \alpha) \in Q \times (\Sigma^*)^n \times \Gamma^*,$$

where $q$ is the current internal state, $x_i$ is the remaining part of the input still unread by head $i$ $(1 \leq i \leq n)$, and $\alpha$ is the current contents of the pushdown, where the first symbol of $\alpha$ is the topmost symbol. By $\vdash_B$ we denote the single-step computation relation that $B$ induces on its set of configurations, and $\vdash_B^*$ is its reflexive and transitive closure.

*The language $L(B)$ accepted by $B$ is now defined as*

$$L(B) = \{\, w \in \Sigma^* \mid (q_0, w, \dots, w, Z_0) \vdash^*_B (s, \varepsilon, \dots, \varepsilon, \alpha)$$
$$\text{for some } s \in F \text{ and } \alpha \in \Gamma^* \,\}.$$

In [3] the following result is shown.

**Theorem 3.** *If $L$ is accepted by some $n$-head pushdown automaton, then it is also accepted by some centralized PC system of pushdown automata of degree $n$ that is working in returning mode.*

Essentially the master of the simulating PC system simulates one of the heads and the pushdown of the $n$-head pushdown automaton, while the other $n-1$ components each simulate one of the other heads of the $n$-head pushdown automaton. Each of them guesses the next operation of the head it simulates and stores it in the topmost symbol on its pushdown, from where the master obtains it by a communication step.

In [1] Balan claims that also the converse of Theorem 3 holds:

*Claim.* If $L$ is accepted by some centralized PC system of pushdown automata of degree $n$ that is working in returning mode, then $L$ is also accepted by some $n$-head pushdown automaton.

In his proof Balan presents a simulation of a centralized PC system of pushdown automata of degree $n$ working in returning mode by an $n$-head pushdown automaton. This simulation works as follows. Each of the $n$ heads of the $n$-head pushdown automaton $B$ will simulate the input head of one of the components of the PC system $\mathcal{A}$. First, using head 1, $B$ simulates the master $A_1$ of the system $\mathcal{A}$ up to the point, where a query symbol $K_j$ occurs as the topmost symbol on the pushdown. Then using head $j$, $B$ simulates the component $A_j$ using the pushdown of $B$. Thus, at the time of the communication step, the pushdown contents of $B$ will correspond exactly to the pushdown contents of the master $A_1$ *after* execution of the communication step. Now the problem is that $B$ must recognize this moment in time, and then it must switch back to simulating the master component $A_1$. For this Balan uses the *known communication property* of the PC system $\mathcal{A}$, but as remarked above, the component $A_j$ realizes its having been subjected to a communication step only after the fact by looking at its pushdown. By a communication step, its pushdown is reset to the initial symbol, but when $B$ is simulating the component $A_j$, no actual communication takes place, that is, $B$ will not be able to recognize the exact moment in time when to abandon the simulation of $A_j$ in order to switch back to simulating the master component. Thus, the above claim must still be considered to be open!

The problem with the above simulation is the inherent synchronization of the components of a PC system of pushdown automata. While the master $A_1$ is doing some computation, the other components may also be doing some steps in synchronization with $A_1$. Below we present an example language that is accepted by a centralized PC system of pushdown automata of degree 2 working in returning mode, where this synchronous behaviour is used in an essential way.

## 4  An Example Language

Let $\Sigma = \{a, b\}$, and let $L = \{\, uvu^Rv^Ru^R \mid u, v \in \Sigma^+, |u| = |v| \,\}$, where $w^R$ denotes the *reversal* (or *mirror image*) of $w$.

**Proposition 1.** $L \in \mathcal{L}_r(\mathrm{CPCPDA}(2))$, *that is, the language $L$ is accepted by a centralized PC system of pushdown automata of degree 2 that is working in returning mode.*

*Proof.* Let $\mathcal{A} = (\Sigma, \Delta, A_1, A_2, \{K_2\})$ be the centralized PC system of pushdown automata of degree 2 that is defined as follows:

- $\Delta = \Sigma \cup \{Z_1, Z_2, K_2\}$, where $Z_i$ is the initial symbol for the pushdown of $A_i$, $i = 1, 2$,
- $A_1 = (Q_1, \Sigma, \Delta, \delta_1, q_0, Z_1, \{q_4\})$, where $Q_1 = \{q_0, q_1, q_2, q_3, q_4\}$,
- $A_2 = (Q_2, \Sigma, \Delta, \delta_2, p_0, Z_2, \{p_4\})$, where $Q_2 = \{p_0, p_1, p_2, p_3, p_4\}$, and
- the transition relations $\delta_1$ and $\delta_2$ are given through the following table, where $x \in \Sigma$:

$$
\begin{aligned}
\delta_1(q_0, a, Z_1) &= \{(q_1, aZ_1)\}, & \delta_2(p_0, \varepsilon, Z_2) &= \{(p_1, Z_2)\}, \\
\delta_1(q_0, b, Z_1) &= \{(q_1, bZ_1)\}, & \delta_2(p_1, a, Z_2) &= \{(p_2, a)\}, \\
\delta_1(q_1, a, x) &= \{(q_2, ax), (q_3, K_2ax)\}, & \delta_2(p_1, b, Z_2) &= \{(p_2, b)\}, \\
\delta_1(q_1, b, x) &= \{(q_2, bx), (q_3, K_2bx)\}, & \delta_2(p_2, \varepsilon, x) &= \{(p_3, x)\}, \\
\delta_1(q_2, a, x) &= \{(q_1, ax)\}, & \delta_2(p_2, \varepsilon, Z_2) &= \{(p_4, Z_2)\}, \\
\delta_1(q_2, b, x) &= \{(q_1, bx)\}, & \delta_2(p_3, a, x) &= \{(p_2, ax)\}, \\
\delta_1(q_3, a, a) &= \{(q_3, \varepsilon)\}, & \delta_2(p_3, b, x) &= \{(p_2, bx)\}, \\
\delta_1(q_3, b, b) &= \{(q_3, \varepsilon)\}, & \delta_2(p_4, a, Z_2) &= \{(p_4, Z_2)\}, \\
\delta_1(q_3, \varepsilon, Z_1) &= \{(q_4, Z_1)\}, & \delta_2(p_4, b, Z_2) &= \{(p_4, Z_2)\}, \\
\delta_1(q_4, \varepsilon, Z_1) &= \{(q_4, Z_1)\}, & \delta_2(p_4, \varepsilon, Z_2) &= \{(p_4, Z_2)\}.
\end{aligned}
$$

We claim that $L_r(\mathcal{A}) = L$ holds. First let $u, v \in \Sigma^+$ such that $u = a_1 a_2 \ldots a_n$ and $v = b_1 b_2 \ldots b_n$, $a_1, \ldots, a_n, b_1, \ldots, b_n \in \Sigma$ and $n \geq 1$. On input $w = uvu^Rv^Ru^R$, $\mathcal{A}$ can execute the following computation:

$$
\begin{aligned}
&(q_0, uvu^Rv^Ru^R, Z_1, p_0, uvu^Rv^Ru^R, Z_2) \\
&\vdash_{\mathcal{A},r} (q_1, a_2 \ldots a_n vu^Rv^Ru^R, a_1 Z_1, p_1, uvu^Rv^Ru^R, Z_2) \\
&\vdash_{\mathcal{A},r} (q_2, a_3 \ldots a_n vu^Rv^Ru^R, a_2a_1 Z_1, p_2, a_2 \ldots a_n vu^Rv^Ru^R, a_1) \\
&\vdash_{\mathcal{A},r}^{2n-3} (q_1, b_n u^Rv^Ru^R, b_{n-1} \ldots b_1 u^R Z_1, p_3, a_n vu^Rv^Ru^R, a_{n-1} \ldots a_1) \\
&\vdash_{\mathcal{A},r} (q_3, u^Rv^Ru^R, K_2 v^Ru^R Z_1, p_2, vu^Rv^Ru^R, u^R) \\
&\vdash_{\mathcal{A},r} (q_3, u^Rv^Ru^R, u^R v^R u^R Z_1, p_2, vu^Rv^Ru^R, Z_2) \\
&\vdash_{\mathcal{A},r}^{3n} (q_3, \varepsilon, Z_1, p_4, b_1 u^R, Z_2) \\
&\vdash_{\mathcal{A},r} (q_4, \varepsilon, Z_1, p_4, u^R, Z_2) \\
&\vdash_{\mathcal{A},r}^{n} (q_4, \varepsilon, Z_1, p_4, \varepsilon, Z_2),
\end{aligned}
$$

which shows that $L \subseteq L_r(\mathcal{A})$. On the other hand, if $w \in L_r(\mathcal{A})$, then we consider an accepting computation of $\mathcal{A}$ on input $w$:

$$
(q_0, w, Z_1, p_0, w, Z_2) \vdash_{\mathcal{A},r}^{+} (q_4, \varepsilon, Z_1, p_4, \varepsilon, \alpha)
$$

for some $\alpha \in \Delta^+$. From the form of $\delta_1$, we see that $w = w_1 w_2$ such that $(q_0, w_1 w_2, Z_1) \vdash_{A_1}^{|w_1|} (q_3, w_2, K_2 w_1^R Z_1)$ holds. In addition, we see that $|w_1|$ is even, and that $(p_0, w_1 w_2, Z_2) \vdash_{A_2}^{|w_1|} (p_2, w_{1,2} w_2, w_{1,1}^R)$, where $w_1 = w_{1,1} w_{1,2}$ and $|w_{1,1}| = |w_{1,2}|$. Now the communication step takes $\mathcal{A}$ into the configuration $(q_3, w_2, w_{1,1}^R w_1^R Z_1, p_2, w_{1,2} w_2, Z_2)$, from which the final configuration $(q_4, \varepsilon, Z_1, p_4, \varepsilon, \alpha) = (q_4, \varepsilon, Z_1, p_4, \varepsilon, Z_2)$ is reached if and only if $w_2 = w_{1,1}^R w_1^R$. This implies that $w = w_1 w_2 = w_{1,1} w_{1,2} w_{1,1}^R w_{1,2}^R w_{1,1}^R$, and since $|w_{1,1}| = |w_{1,2}|$, this shows that $w \in L$. Thus, it follows that $L_r(\mathcal{A}) = L$. $\qquad\square$

The 2-head pushdown automaton from Balan's proof cannot possibly simulate the above PC system correctly. After simulating the component $A_1$ for an even number of steps, the simulating 2-head pushdown automaton $B$ has moved its first head across a prefix $uv$ of the input, where $|u| = |v|$, pushing $v^R u^R$ onto its pushdown. Then it starts to simulate the component $A_2$ for a number of steps, using its second head. During this phase it moves its second head across a prefix $x$ of the input, pushing $x^R$ onto the pushdown. However, there is no synchronisation between these two phases, that is, $|x|$ is not related to $|uv|$. Now $B$ gets either stuck in this phase, or it switches at some nondeterministically chosen time to the third phase, during which it uses its first head to check that the remaining part of the input is of the form $x^R v^R u^R$. Thus, either $B$ does not accept any word at all, or it accepts all words of the form $uvx^R v^R u^R$, where $|u| = |v|$ and $x$ is a prefix of $uv$, or $x = uvz$ for some word $z$ satisfying $z = z^R$. In any case it follows that $L(B)$ differs from the language $L$.

Actually, we expect that the above language $L$ is not accepted by any 2-head pushdown automaton at all; however, we do not yet have a formal proof for this claim. Finally, we would like to point out that the language $L$ is accepted by a 4-head pushdown automaton.

# References

1. Balan, M.: Serializing the parallelism in parallel communicating pushdown automata systems. In: Dassow, J., Pighizzini, G., Truthe, B. (eds.) 11th International Workshop on Descriptional Complexity of Formal Systems (DCFS 2009). Electronic Proceedings in Theoretical Computer Science, vol. 3, pp. 59–68 (2009), doi:10.4204/EPTCS.3.5
2. Csuhaj-Varjú, E., Dassow, J., Kelemen, J., Păun, G.: Grammar Systems - A Grammatical Approach to Distribution and Cooperation. Gordon and Breach, London (1994)
3. Csuhaj-Varjú, E., Martin-Vide, C., Mitrana, V., Vaszil, G.: Parallel communicating pushdown automata systems. Intern. J. Found. Comput. Sci. 11, 631–650 (2000)
4. Dassow, J., Păun, G., Rozenberg, G.: Grammar Systems. In: Rozenberg, G., Salomaa, A. (eds.) Handbook of Formal Languages, Linear Modelling: Background and Applications, vol. 2, pp. 101–154. Springer, Heidelberg (1997)

# State Complexity and Limited Nondeterminism

Alexandros Palioudakis, Kai Salomaa, and Selim G. Akl

School of Computing, Queen's University,
Kingston, Ontario K7L 3N6, Canada
{alex,ksalomaa,akl}@cs.queensu.ca

**Abstract.** We consider nondeterministic finite automata having finite tree width (ftw-NFA) where the computation on any input string has a constant number of branches. We give effective characterizations of ftw-NFAs and a tight worst-case state size bound for determinizing an ftw-NFA $A$ as a function of the tree width and the number of states of $A$. We introduce a lower bound technique for ftw-NFAs and consider the operational state complexity of this model.

**Keywords:** finite automata, limited nondeterminism, state complexity, language operations.

## 1  Introduction

The descriptive complexity of finite automata has been studied for over half a century, and there has been particularly much work done over the last two decades. Various ways of quantifying the nondeterminism of finite automata have been considered since the 70's. The ambiguity of a nondeterministic finite automaton (NFA) refers to the number of accepting computations, and other nondeterminism measures count, roughly speaking, the amount of guessing in both accepting and non-accepting computations.

Schmidt [23] first established an exponential trade-off between the size of unambiguous finite automata and general NFAs, and the bound was later refined in [19,25]. The relationship between the degree of ambiguity and succinctness of finite automata was considered in [13,18,22] and the state complexity of unambiguous finite automata over a unary alphabet has been recently studied in [21].

The branching measure of an NFA is the product of the degrees of nondeterministic choices on the best accepting computation [6,17], and the guessing measure counts the minimum (or maximum) number of advice bits used on a computation on a given input [6,13]. The reader is referred to [5] for more details on the different notions of limited nondeterminism.

Here we focus on the state complexity of NFAs having finite *tree width*. By the tree width of an NFA $A$ on input $w$ we mean the total number of nondeterministic branches the computation tree of $A$ on $w$ has, and $A$ has finite tree width if the number is bounded for all inputs. The tree width of an NFA $A$ is called in [13] the *leaf size* of $A$ and in [2] it is denoted as "*computations*$(A)$". It is known that the tree width of an NFA on inputs of length $m$ is either constant (which

M. Kutrib, N. Moreira, and R. Reis (Eds.): DCFS 2012, LNCS 7386, pp. 252–265, 2012.
© Springer-Verlag Berlin Heidelberg 2012

situation will be our focus here), or in between linear and polynomial in $m$, or otherwise $2^{\Theta(m)}$ [13].

The tree width measure can be viewed to be more restrictive than the other nondeterminism measures for NFAs considered in the literature, with the exception of the $\delta$NFAs of [2] that are a special case of tree width 2 NFAs. Note that while a DFA equivalent to an $n$ state unambiguous NFA may need $2^n - 1$ states [19], the size blow-up of determinizing a constant tree width NFA is clearly polynomial. Here we give a tight upper bound for the conversion as a function of the size of an NFA and its tree width.

We show that there exist regular languages for which any $n$-state NFA needs finite tree width $2^{n-2}$. We establish that an NFA $A$ has finite tree width if and only if $A$ can be subdivided into deterministic components that are connected by the reachability relation in an acyclic way. We introduce a separator set technique that gives considerably better lower bounds for the size of finite tree width automata than the known fooling set and biclique edge-cover methods [1,4,8] for general NFAs. However, even the separator set technique is not powerful enough to handle, for example, the constructions we use to give lower bounds for the state complexity of union and intersection of finite tree width NFAs. Due to the inherent hardness of minimization of very restricted NFAs [2,9,20], it can perhaps be expected that general techniques do not give optimal lower bounds even for finite tree width NFAs.

Following the convention used by the overwhelming majority of the literature on finite automata, we use an NFA model that allows only one initial state. Some of our state complexity results could be stated in a nicer form if the NFA model were to allow multiple initial states; see Remark 4.1.

Many proofs are omitted due to the limitation on the number of pages.

## 2    Preliminaries

We assume that the reader is familiar with the basic definitions concerning finite automata [24,26] and descriptional complexity [5,11]. Here we just fix some notation needed in the following.

The set of strings over a finite alphabet $\Sigma$ is $\Sigma^*$, the length of $w \in \Sigma^*$ is $|w|$ and $\varepsilon$ is the empty string. The set of positive integers is denoted $\mathbb{N}$. The cardinality of a finite set $S$ is $\#S$.

A nondeterministic finite automaton (NFA) is a 5-tuple $A = (Q, \Sigma, \delta, q_0, F)$, where $Q$ is a finite set of states, $\Sigma$ is a finite alphabet, $\delta : Q \times \Sigma \to 2^Q$ is the transition function, $q_0 \in Q$ is the start state and $F \subseteq Q$ is the set of accepting states. The function $\delta$ is extended in the usual way as a function $Q \times \Sigma^* \to 2^Q$ and the language recognized by $A$, $L(A)$, consists of strings $w \in \Sigma^*$ such that $\delta(q_0, w) \cap F \neq \emptyset$.

If $\delta$ is as above, we denote $\mathrm{rel}(\delta) = \{(q, a, p) \mid p \in \delta(q, a), q, p \in Q, a \in \Sigma\}$. We call $\mathrm{rel}(\delta)$ as the *transition relation* of $A$. A transition of $A$ is an element $\mu = (q, a, p) \in \mathrm{rel}(\delta)$. The transition $\mu$ is nondeterministic if there exists $p' \neq p$ such that $p' \in \delta(q, a)$ and otherwise $\mu$ is deterministic. The NFA $A$ is deterministic (a DFA) if all transitions of $A$ are deterministic, this is equivalent to saying that $\#\delta(q,a) \leq 1$ for all $q \in Q$ and $a \in \Sigma$. Note that we allow DFAs to have undefined transitions. Unless otherwise mentioned, we assume that any state $q$ of an NFA $A$ is reachable from the start state and some computation originating from $q$ reaches a final state.

A *computation chain* of $A$ from state $s_1$ to $s_2$ is a sequence of transitions $(q_i, a_i, p_i)$, $1 \leq i \leq k$, where $p_{i+1} = q_i$, $i = 1, \ldots, k-1$, and $s_1 = q_1$, $s_2 = p_k$. A *cycle* of $A$ is a computation chain from state $s$ to the same state $s$.

Note that we can specify an NFA either as a tuple $(Q, \Sigma, \delta, q_0, F)$ or as $(Q, \Sigma, \mathrm{rel}(\delta), q_0, F)$. In the former notation $\delta$ is a function with domain $Q \times \Sigma$ and when we want to specify the transitions as a subset of $Q \times \Sigma \times Q$ we write $\mathrm{rel}(\delta)$. By the *size of $A$* we mean the number of states of $A$, $\mathrm{size}(A) = \#Q$.

The minimal size of a DFA or an NFA recognizing a regular language $L$ is called the (nondeterministic) state complexity of $L$ and denoted, respectively, $sc(L)$ and $nsc(L)$. Note that we allow DFAs to be incomplete and, consequently, the deterministic state complexity of $L$ may differ by one from a definition using complete DFAs. If $A = (Q, \Sigma, \delta, q_0, F)$ is an NFA (respectively, DFA), the triple $(Q, \Sigma, \delta)$ without the start state and the set of accepting states is called a semi-NFA (respectively, semi-DFA).

For $q \in Q$ and $w \in \Sigma^*$, the *$q$-computation tree of $A$ on $w$*, $T_{A,q,w}$, is a finite tree where the nodes are labeled by elements of $Q \times (\Sigma \cup \{\varepsilon, \natural\})$. We define $T_{A,q,w}$ inductively by first setting $T_{A,q,\varepsilon}$ to consist of one node labeled by $(q, \varepsilon)$. When $w = au$, $a \in \Sigma$, $u \in \Sigma^*$ and $\delta(q,a) = \emptyset$ we set $T_{A,q,w}$ to be the singleton tree where the only node is labeled by $(q, \natural)$. Then assuming $\delta(q,a) = \{p_1, \ldots, p_m\}$, $m \geq 1$, we define $T_{A,q,w}$ as the tree where the root is labeled by $(q, a)$ and the root has $m$ children where the subtree rooted at the $i$th child is $T_{A,p_i,u}$, $i = 1, \ldots, m$. For our purposes the order of children of a node is not important and we can assume that the elements of $\delta(q,a)$ are ordered by a fixed but arbitrary linear order. Note that in $T_{A,q,w}$ every path from the root to a leaf has length at most $|w|$. A path may have length less than $w$ because the corresponding computation of $A$ may become blocked at a node labeled by a pair $(p,b)$ where $\delta(p,b) = \emptyset$.

The tree $T_{A,q_0,w}$ is called the *computation tree of $A$ on $w$* and denoted simply as $T_{A,w}$. The NFA $A$ accepts $w$ if and only if $T_{A,w}$ contains a leaf labeled by an element $(q, \varepsilon)$, where $q \in F$. Note that a node label $(q, \varepsilon)$ can occur in $T_{A,w}$ only after the corresponding computation branch has consumed the entire string $w$.

*Remark 2.1.* We mostly refer to a node of a computation tree of $A$ to be labeled simply by an element $q \in Q$. This is taken to mean that the node is labeled by a pair $(q, x)$ where $x \in \Sigma \cup \{\varepsilon, \natural\}$ is arbitrary.

To conclude the preliminaries, we recall and introduce a few definitions concerning NFAs for unary languages. The below notion of *simple normal form* is from [14] and it is a special case of the Chrobak normal form [3,14]. Note that simple normal form automata do not recognize all unary regular languages.

**Definition 2.1.** *Let $\Sigma = \{a\}$ and let $(m_1, \ldots, m_k) \in \mathbb{N}^k$. An NFA $A$ over $\Sigma$ is said to be in $(m_1, \ldots, m_k)$-simple normal form if $A$ consists of an initial state*

$q_0$ and $k$ disjoint cycles $C_i$, where the length of $C_i$ is $m_i$, $1 \leq i \leq k$. The initial state $q_0$ is not part of any of the cycles and from $q_0$ there is a transition to one state of $C_i$, for each $1 \leq i \leq k$. An NFA is in $k$-simple normal form if it is in $(m_1, \ldots, m_k)$-simple normal form for some positive integers $m_1, \ldots, m_k$, and it is in simple normal form if it is in $k$-simple normal form for some $k \geq 1$.

# 3   Nondeterministic Tree Width

Various ways to measure the nondeterminism in finite automata have been considered in [6,13,17,19]. The tree width measure was used in [13] under the name of leaf size.

**Definition 3.1.** *Let* $A = (Q, \Sigma, \delta, q_0, F)$ *be an NFA and* $w \in \Sigma^*$. *The* tree width *of* $A$ *on* $w$, $\text{tw}_A(w)$, *is the number of leaves of the tree* $T_{A,w}$. *The tree width of* $A$ *is defined as* $\text{tw}(A) = \sup\{\text{tw}_A(w) \mid w \in \Sigma^*\}$. *We say that* $A$ *has* finite tree width *if* $\text{tw}(A)$ *is finite.*

Note that $\text{tw}_A(w)$ is simply the number of all (accepting and non-accepting) branches in the computation tree of $A$ on $w$. An NFA in $k$-simple normal form has tree width $k$. In the following, ftw-NFA (respectively, tw($k$)-NFA) stands for a finite tree width NFA (respectively, an NFA having tree width at most $k$, $k \in \mathbb{N}$).

We will be mainly concerned with the state complexity of NFAs of given finite tree width and for this purpose define, for a regular language $L$ and $k \in \mathbb{N} \cup \{\infty\}$,

$$\text{sctw}_k(L) = \inf\{\text{size}(A) \mid A \text{ is a tw}(k)\text{-NFA and } L(A) = L\}.$$

Above $\text{sctw}_k(L)$ is the smallest number states needed by an NFA of tree width at most $k$ to recognize the language $L$. In particular, $\text{sctw}_1(L) = \text{sc}(L)$ and $\text{sctw}_\infty(L) = \text{nsc}(L)$.

**Definition 3.2.** *We say that an NFA* $A$ *has* optimal tree width *if* $L(A)$ *is not recognized by any NFA* $B$ *where* $\text{size}(B) \leq \text{size}(A)$ *and* $\text{tw}(B) \leq \text{tw}(A)$ *where one of the inequalities is strict. We say that a regular language* $L$ *has* tree width $k$ *if* $L$ *has an optimal* tw($k$)-NFA $A$ *such that* $A$ *has a minimal number of states among all ftw-NFAs for* $L$.

When $A$ has optimal tree width, $\text{sctw}_{\text{tw}(A)}(L(A)) = \text{size}(A)$. A language $L$ having tree width $k$ means, roughly speaking, that an NFA recognizing $L$ can "make use of" limited nondeterminism of tree width $k$, that is, the tree width $k$ nondeterminism allows us to reduce the number of states, but any additional finite nondeterminism would not allow a further reduction of the number of states. If $L$ has tree width 1 this means any ftw-NFA for $L$ cannot be smaller than the minimal (incomplete) DFA.

For a given NFA $A$, the tree width of the language $L(A)$ can be determined by a brute-force algorithm that checks all NFAs of size less than the size of the minimal DFA for $L(A)$. The problem of finding the tree width of a regular language is intractable because it is known that minimizing bounded tree width NFAs is NP-hard [2,20].

**Lemma 3.1.** *A regular language $L$ has tree width $k$ $(k \geq 1)$ iff $L$ has a $\mathrm{tw}(k)$-NFA with optimal tree width and, for any $\ell > k$, $L$ does not have a $\mathrm{tw}(\ell)$-NFA with optimal tree width.*

## 3.1    Characterizations of ftw-NFAs

An immediate observation is that if some cycle of an NFA $A$ contains a nondeterministic transition, then the tree width of $A$ on words that repeat the cycle cannot be bounded.

**Lemma 3.2.** *If $A$ is an ftw-NFA, then no cycle of $A$ can contain a nondeterministic transition.*

We want to show that the condition of Lemma 3.2 is also sufficient to guarantee that an NFA has finite tree width. For this purpose we establish an upper bound for the tree width of an NFA where no cycle contains a nondeterministic transition.

**Theorem 3.1.** *If $A$ is an NFA with $n$ states and no cycle contains a nondeterministic transition, then*

$$\mathrm{tw}(A) \leq 2^{n-2}$$

From Lemma 3.2 and Theorem 3.1 we get a characterization of finite tree width NFAs.

**Corollary 3.1.** *An NFA $A$ has finite tree width iff no cycle of $A$ contains a nondeterministic transition. We can decide in polynomial time whether or not a given NFA has finite tree width.*

The upper bound of Theorem 3.1 is tight as seen in the below example which gives an $n$-state NFA having optimal tree width $2^{n-2}$.

*Example 3.1.* Let $n \geq 2$, $\Sigma = \{a, b\}$ and $A = (Q, \Sigma, \delta, 1, \{n\})$ where $Q = \{1, \ldots, n\}$ and we define for $i \in \{1, \ldots, n-1\}$, $\delta(i, a) = \{i+1, i+2, \ldots, n\}$, $\delta(i, b) = \{i+1\}$, $\delta(n, a) = \delta(n, b) = \emptyset$.

Since $L(A) \cap b^* = \{b^{n-1}\}$, in any $n$-state NFA $B = (\{1, \ldots, n\}, \Sigma, \gamma, 1, F_B)$ for the language $L(A)$ there can be only one final state. Without loss of generality, we can set $F_B = \{n\}$ and $\gamma(i, b) = \{i+1\}$, $1 \leq i \leq n-1$. Once the $b$-transitions are fixed, we observe that

$$(\forall 1 \leq i < j \leq n) : \ b^{i-1}ab^{n-j} \in L(B) \text{ iff } j \in \gamma(i, a).$$

The above means that $B$ must be an isomorphic copy of $A$ and, consequently, $A$ has optimal tree width. It is easy to calculate that $\mathrm{tw}(A) = 2^{n-2}$. Furthermore, since $A$ is a minimal NFA for $L(A)$ the tree width of the language $L(A)$ is $2^{n-2}$.

An NFA $A$ with finite tree width can be thought to consist of a finite number of deterministic "components" that are connected by the reachability relation in an acyclic way. This can be formalized as follows.

**Definition 3.3.** *Let* $A = (Q, \Sigma, \mathrm{rel}(\delta), q_0, F)$ *be an NFA. Let* $B_i = (P_i, \Sigma, \mathrm{rel}(\gamma_i))$, $P_i \subseteq Q$, $1 \le i \le k$, *be a collection of semi-DFAs. We say that the tuple* $\mathcal{D} = (B_1, \ldots, B_k)$ *is a* deterministic decomposition *of* $A$ *if the sets* $P_1, \ldots, P_k$ *form a partition of* $Q$, $\mathrm{rel}(\gamma_i)$ *is the restriction of* $\mathrm{rel}(\delta)$ *to* $P_i \times \Sigma \times P_i$, *and every transition of* $A$ *of the form* $(p_1, a, p_2) \in \mathrm{rel}(\delta)$, $p_1, p_2 \in P_i$, $a \in \Sigma$, $1 \le i \le k$ *is deterministic.*

Note that the above definition says that the transitions of $\mathrm{rel}(\gamma_i)$ have to be deterministic as transitions of the original NFA $A$, which is more restrictive than just requiring that the transition relation $\mathrm{rel}(\gamma_i)$ of each $B_i$ is deterministic.

For a decomposition $\mathcal{D} = (B_1, \ldots, B_k)$ we can order the components by setting $B_i <_{\mathcal{D}} B_j$, $i \ne j$, if some state of $B_j$ is reachable in $A$ from a state of $B_i$. We say that the decomposition $\mathcal{D} = (B_1, \ldots, B_k)$ is *acyclic* if $<_{\mathcal{D}}$ is a partial order.

An NFA $A$ where no state $q$ has a nondeterministic transition that is a self-loop on $q$ has always a trivial deterministic decomposition where each component consists of a single state. The property of having an acyclic deterministic decomposition exactly characterizes NFAs having finite tree width.

**Theorem 3.2.** *An NFA $A$ has finite tree width iff $A$ has an acyclic deterministic decomposition.*

## 3.2   Converting Finite Tree Width NFAs to DFAs

When applying the subset construction to an NFA with tree width $k$, only sets of states of size at most $k$ can be reachable. This idea, together with some refinements, yields the following upper bound:

**Lemma 3.3.** *Let $L$ be a regular language where* $\mathrm{sctw}_k(L) = n$ *for some* $k \le n - 1$. *Then* $\mathrm{sc}(L) \le 1 + \sum_{j=1}^{k} \binom{n-1}{j}$.

A $k$-entry DFA [12,16] ($k \ge 1$) has a deterministic transition function but allows $k$-initial states. The computation of a $k$-entry DFA has at most $k$ branches, however, strictly speaking a $k$-entry DFA is not a special case of an ftw-NFA because, following usual conventions, our NFA model allows only one initial state. By using a modification of the worst-case construction from [12] that converts a $k$-entry DFA to an ordinary DFA we see that the upper bound of Lemma 3.3 can be reached.

**Theorem 3.3.** *For every $1 \le k \le n - 1$ there exists an $n$-state NFA $A_{n,k}$ such that* $\mathrm{tw}(A_{n,k}) = k$ *and* $\mathrm{sc}(L(A_{n,k})) = 1 + \sum_{j=1}^{k} \binom{n-1}{j}$.

Note that, in general, the finite tree width of an $n$-state NFA is bounded only by $2^{n-2}$ (Theorem 3.1), however, in cases where the tree width is greater than the number of states, estimates for the size of an equivalent DFA analogous to Lemma 3.3 would clearly not be useful.

As a consequence of results and constructions in [6,19] we observe that there exist regular languages where the unambiguous NFA to ftw-NFA conversion causes an exponential size blow-up.

**Proposition 3.1.** *For $n \geq 4$, there exists an unambiguous NFA $A$ with $n$ states such that, for any $k \in \mathbb{N}$, $\mathrm{sctw}_k(L(A)) = 2^{n-1}$.*

*Proof.* Let $L_n^{\mathrm{Leung}}$, $n \geq 3$, be the language having an $n$-state unambiguous NFA (UFA) $A_n$ used in Theorem 1 of [19]. From there we know that any incomplete DFA for $L_n^{\mathrm{Leung}}$ needs $2^n - 1$ states.

As in Theorem 4.2 of [6] we now define $L_n = (\$L_{n-1}^{\mathrm{Leung}}\$)^*$, $n \geq 4$. The language $L_n$ has an $n$-state UFA. (It is easy to verify that the NFA constructed as in the proof of Theorem 4.2 of [6] is unambiguous.)

As in Theorem 4.2 of [6] it is seen that any NFA $B$ with *finite branching* for the language $L_n$ has at least $2^{n-1}$ states. Note that the construction of Theorem 4.2 of [6] relies only on the size of the minimal DFA for the original regular languages used to define $L_n$, and exactly the same construction works when $L_n$ is defined in terms of $L_{n-1}^{\mathrm{Leung}}$. The branching measure of an NFA $B$, $\beta_B$, is not the same as tree width, but it is immediate that any NFA with finite tree width has finite branching. (The converse does not hold in general.) $\qquad\square$

### 3.3   Lower Bounds for the Size of ftw-NFAs

Recently Björklund and Martens [2] have shown that minimization is NP-hard for any class of finite automata that contains the so called $\delta$NFAs, which are a restriction of NFAs with tree width 2. Thus, in order to establish lower bounds for the size of ftw-NFAs we need to rely on ad hoc methods inspired by the fooling set techniques used for general NFAs [1,4,8,11].

Let $S$ be a finite set. By an $(S, k)$-family of sets we mean a family $\mathcal{C} \subseteq 2^S$ such that all sets in $\mathcal{C}$ have cardinality at most $k$, and any two sets in $\mathcal{C}$ are incomparable as subsets of $S$.

**Lemma 3.4.** *Let $S$ be a finite set of cardinality $n$ and $k \leq \frac{n}{2}$. If $\mathcal{C}$ is an $(S, k)$-family, then $\#\mathcal{C} \leq \binom{n}{k}$. (Here $\#\mathcal{C}$ is the number of sets in the family $\mathcal{C}$.)*

Let $L$ be a regular language over $\Sigma$. We say that a finite set of strings $\{u_1, \ldots, u_t\}$, $u_i \in \Sigma^*$, $1 \leq i \leq t$, is a $t$-separator set for the language $L$ if

$$(\forall 1 \leq i, j \leq t, \ i \neq j)(\exists z \in \Sigma^*) \ u_i z \in L \text{ and } u_j z \notin L. \tag{1}$$

Note that the above definition treats $(i, j)$ as an ordered pair, and it is not sufficient if $z \in \Sigma^*$ satisfies the corresponding condition where $i$ and $j$ are interchanged. On the other hand, the condition (1) allows $z$ to depend on the pair $(i, j)$ and, consequently, for a given regular language we can typically find a much larger separator set than a fooling set; see Example 3.2.

**Lemma 3.5.** *Suppose that a regular language $L$ has a $t$-separator set $\{u_1, \ldots, u_t\}$, $t \geq 1$. If $L$ has a $tw(k)$-NFA $A$ with $n$ states, where $k \leq \frac{n}{2}$, then*

$$\binom{n}{k} \geq t.$$

*Proof.* Let $A = (Q, \Sigma, \delta, q_0, F)$ be an NFA with $\#Q = n$ and $\mathrm{tw}(A) = k$. Define $P_i = \delta(q_0, u_i)$, $i = 1, \ldots, t$. Since $A$ has tree width $k$, $\#P_i \leq k$. Consider $1 \leq i, j \leq t$, $i \neq j$, and suppose $P_i \subseteq P_j$. This means that, for any $z \in \Sigma^*$, $u_i z \in L$ implies $u_j z \in L$. Thus the sets $P_i$, $i = 1, \ldots, t$, have to be pairwise incomparable as subsets of $Q$ and the claim follows from Lemma 3.4. $\square$

*Example 3.2.* Consider the unary language $L_m = \{w \in a^* \mid |w| \not\equiv 0 \pmod{m}\}$, $m \geq 1$. The language $L_m$ has a separator set $\{\varepsilon, a, a^2, \ldots, a^{m-1}\}$. According to Lemma 3.5, if $L_m$ has a $\mathrm{tw}(k)$-NFA with $n$ states where $k \leq \frac{n}{2}$, we have the estimation $\binom{n}{k} \geq m$. This is exponentially better than the lower bound obtained for the size of (general) NFAs with the bipartite dimension method (Theorem 9 in [8]). Recall that the bipartite dimension method is guaranteed to give at least as good bounds as (and often better bounds than) the fooling set methods [8,11].

However, also our bound does not coincide with the real lower bound except in the case $k = 1$.

*Example 3.3.* For $\{m_1, \ldots, m_k\} \subseteq \mathbb{N}$, $k \geq 1$, we define

$$L_{\{m_1, \ldots, m_k\}} = \{w \in a^* \mid (\exists 1 \leq j \leq k) \, |w| \equiv 0 \pmod{m_j}\}. \tag{2}$$

When $m_1, \ldots, m_k$ are pairwise relatively prime, $\{a^1, a^2, \ldots, a^{\prod_{i=1}^k m_i}\}$ is a separator set and, consequently, if $L_{\{m_1, \ldots, m_k\}}$ has a $\mathrm{tw}(k)$-NFA $A$ where $k \leq \frac{\mathrm{size}(A)}{2}$, we have

$$\binom{\mathrm{size}(A)}{k} \geq \prod_{i=1}^k m_i.$$

Again this is not an optimal bound and, in the next section, we will see that under the above assumptions for any $h \geq k \geq 2$, $\mathrm{sctw}_h(L_{\{m_1, \ldots, m_k\}}) = 1 + \sum_{i=1}^k m_i$.

## 4    The State Complexity of Union and Intersection

We consider the union and intersection of languages recognized by a $\mathrm{tw}(k_1)$-NFA and a $\mathrm{tw}(k_2)$-NFA. For union (respectively, intersection) we give a state complexity upper bound in terms of a $\mathrm{tw}(k_1 + k_2)$-NFA (respectively, $\mathrm{tw}(k_1 \cdot k_2)$-NFA), and almost matching lower bounds.

**Lemma 4.1.** *For regular languages $L_i$ and $k_i \geq 1$, $i = 1, 2$,*

*(i)* $\mathrm{sctw}_{k_1+k_2}(L_1 \cup L_2) \leq \mathrm{sctw}_{k_1}(L_1) + \mathrm{sctw}_{k_2}(L_2) + 1$.
*(ii)* $\mathrm{sctw}_{k_1 \cdot k_2}(L_1 \cap L_2) \leq \mathrm{sctw}_{k_1}(L_1) \cdot \mathrm{sctw}_{k_2}(L_2)$.

*Proof.* Let $A_i = (Q_i, \Sigma, \delta_i, q_{0,i}, F_i)$ be a $\mathrm{tw}(k_i)$-NFA recognizing $L_i$, $i = 1, 2$.

(i) Without loss of generality we assume that $Q_1 \cap Q_2 = \emptyset$. We define $B = (P, \Sigma, \gamma, p_0, F_B)$ where $P = Q_1 \cup Q_2 \cup \{p_0\}$, $p_0 \notin Q_1 \cup Q_2$ is a new state,

$$F_B = \begin{cases} F_1 \cup F_2 & \text{if } q_{0,i} \notin F_i, i = 1, 2, \\ F_1 \cup F_2 \cup \{p_0\} & \text{otherwise,} \end{cases}$$

and for $b \in \Sigma$, $q \in Q_i$, we set $\gamma(q, b) = \delta_i(q, b)$, $i = 1, 2$, and $\delta(p_0, b) = \delta_1(q_{0,1}, b) \cup \delta_2(q_{0,1}, b)$.

It is sufficient to verify that $\mathrm{tw}(B) \leq k_1 + k_2$. Consider $w = bw'$, where $b \in \Sigma$, $w \in \Sigma^*$. If $\delta_i(q_{0,i}, b) = \emptyset$, $i = 1, 2$, $T_{B,w}$ and $T_{A_i,w}$, $i = 1, 2$, each are a singleton tree and we are done. (The same holds in the case when $w = \varepsilon$.)

If $\delta_1(q_{0,1}, b) \neq \emptyset$ and $\delta_2(q_{0,2}, b) = \emptyset$, the tree $T_{B,w}$ is obtained from $T_{A_1,w}$ by changing the label of the root.

Finally consider the case where $\delta_i(q_{0,i}, b) \neq \emptyset$, $i = 1, 2$. Now the sequence of immediate subtrees of the root of $T_{B,w}$ consists of the immediate subtrees of the root of $T_{A_1,w}$ and of $T_{A_2,w}$.[1] This means that the number of leaves of $T_{B,w}$ is the sum of the numbers of leaves of $T_{A_1,w}$ and of $T_{A_2,w}$, respectively.

(ii) We define $C = (Q_1 \times Q_2, \Sigma, \gamma, (q_{0,1}, q_{0,2}), F_1 \times F_2)$ where for $b \in \Sigma$, $q_i \in Q_i$, $i = 1, 2$, $\gamma((q_1, q_2), b) = \delta_1(q_1, b) \times \delta(q_2, b)$.

Again it is suffcient to verify the claimed bound for the tree width: $\mathrm{tw}(C) \leq k_1 \cdot k_2$. We denote the number of leaves of a tree $T$ as $\#\mathrm{leaves}(T)$. We claim that for all $w \in \Sigma^*$ and $q_i \in Q_i$, $i = 1, 2$,

$$\#\mathrm{leaves}(T_{C,(q_1,q_2),w}) \leq \#\mathrm{leaves}(T_{A_1,q_1,w}) \cdot \#\mathrm{leaves}(T_{A_2,q_2,w}). \qquad (3)$$

We prove the claim using induction on the length of $w$. When $w = \varepsilon$, $T_{C,(q_1,q_2),\varepsilon}$, and $T_{A_i,q_i,\varepsilon}$, $i = 1, 2$, each are a singleton tree.

Consider then $w = bw'$, where $b \in \Sigma$, $w \in \Sigma^*$. If $\delta_i(q_1, b) = \emptyset$ or $\delta_i(q_2, b) = \emptyset$, $T_{C,(q_1,q_2),w}$ is a singleton tree and we are done. Hence, without loss of generality, we can assume $\delta_i(q_i, b) \neq \emptyset$, $i = 1, 2$. Now the subtrees corresponding to the children of the root of $T_{C,(q_1,q_2),w}$ are the trees $T_{C,(p_1,p_2),w'}$, $p_i \in \delta_i(q_i, b)$, $i = 1, 2$. Thus, by the inductive assumption,

$$\#\mathrm{leaves}(T_{C,(q_1,q_2),w}) = \sum_{p_i \in \delta_i(q_i,b), i=1,2} \#\mathrm{leaves}(T_{C,(p_1,p_2),w'})$$

$$\leq \sum_{p_i \in \delta_i(q_i,b), i=1,2} \#\mathrm{leaves}(T_{A_1,p_1,w'}) \cdot \#\mathrm{leaves}(T_{A_2,p_2,w'}).$$

Since the number of leaves of $T_{A_i,q_i,w}$ is equal to $\sum_{p_i \in \delta_i(q_i,b)} \#\mathrm{leaves}$ $(T_{A_i,p_i,w'})$, $1 \leq i \leq 2$, we have verified that (3) holds for the string $w$.

□

The proof of Lemma 4.1 uses the "natural" constructions, respectively, for the union and intersection of two NFAs. Note that the cross-product of a $\mathrm{tw}(k_1)$- and a $\mathrm{tw}(k_2)$-NFA, typically, has tree width considerably less than $k_1 \cdot k_2$, however, as we will see, in the worst case the upper bound of Lemma 4.1 (ii) cannot be improved, at least not by much.

Our lower bound constructions are based on languages of the form $L_{\{m_1,\ldots,m_k\}}$ considered in Example 3.3. When the integers $m_i$, $1 \leq i \leq k$, are pairwise

---

[1] Recall that for our purposes the order of children of a node is not important and we assume that the elements of $\gamma(p_0, b)$ have an arbitrary, but fixed, order.

relatively prime, from Theorem 2.1 of [14] it follows easily that $L_{\{m_1,\ldots,m_k\}}$ has a minimal NFA in $k$-simple normal form. We will need a corresponding property also under slightly less restrictive conditions.

Before establishing lower bounds for the size of ftw-NFAs for the unary languages (2) we state the following corollary which follows from Lemma 3.2 using the observation that a unary NFA may exit a cycle only using a nondeterministic transition.

**Corollary 4.1.** *If $A$ is an ftw-NFA over a unary alphabet, then no cycle $C$ of $A$ has a transition exiting $C$ and, in particular, no two cycles of $A$ can share a state. Furthermore, if $A$ has more than one cycle, then the start state of $A$ cannot be part of any cycle.*

Below we will show that, under certain assumptions on the numbers $m_i$, the language $L_{\{m_1,\ldots,m_k\}}$ has a unique minimal ftw-NFA in $k$-simple normal form. More generally, from Corollary 4.1 it follows that any unary regular language has a (not necessarily unique) minimal ftw-NFA that is in Chrobak normal form [3,14].

We say that a set of integers $\{m_1,\ldots,m_k\}$, $m_i \geq 2$, $1 \leq i \leq k$, is *pairwise relatively prime* if, for all $i \neq j$, $m_i$ and $m_j$ do not have any common factor greater than one. A set of integers $P$ is said to be an *independent set of prime pairs* if we can write $P = \{p_1 \cdot p_2 \mid p_i \in P_i, i = 1, 2\}$, for two sets of prime numbers $P_1$ and $P_2$ where $P_1 \cap P_2 = \emptyset$. Note that the elements of an independent set of prime pairs $P$ are not pairwise relatively prime, however, no element of $P$ is a multiple of any other element.

**Lemma 4.2.** *Let $k \geq 2$ and assume that the set $\{m_1,\ldots,m_k\}$, $m_i \geq 2$, $1 \leq i \leq k$, is either a set of independent prime pairs, or a pairwise relatively prime set that is not $\{2,3\}$. Then the minimal ftw-NFA for $L_{\{m_1,\ldots,m_k\}}$ is unique (up to renaming of states) and it is in $(m_1,\ldots,m_k)$-simple form.*

**Corollary 4.2.** *Let $k \geq 2$. Assume that the set $\{m_1,\ldots,m_k\}$, $m_i \geq 2$, $1 \leq i \leq k$, is either an independent set of prime pairs or a pairwise relatively prime set. Then*

$$\mathrm{sctw}_k(L_{\{m_1,\ldots,m_k\}}) = 1 + \sum_{i=1}^{k} m_k.$$

*Furthermore, assuming we exclude the case $k = 2$, $\{m_1, m_2\} = \{2,3\}$, the language $L_{\{m_1,\ldots,m_k\}}$ has tree width $k$.*

Note that if a regular language $L$ has tree width $k$, the maximum amount of limited nondeterminism an NFA recognizing $L$ can "make use of" is precisely $k$ (see Definition 3.2). By relying on Corollary 4.2, in the following lemmas we give state complexity lower bounds for the union and intersection of ftw-NFAs.

**Lemma 4.3.** *For every $k_i, n_i \in \mathbb{N}$, $i = 1, 2$, there exist regular languages $L_i$ of tree width $k_i$ such that $\mathrm{sctw}_{k_i}(L_i) \geq n_i$ and*

$$\mathrm{sctw}_{k_1+k_2}(L_1 \cup L_2) \geq \mathrm{sctw}_{k_1}(L_1) + \mathrm{sctw}_{k_2}(L_2) - 1.$$

*Furthermore, $L_1 \cup L_2$ has tree width $k_1 + k_2$.*

*Proof.* First consider the case $k_1, k_2 \geq 2$. Choose a set of pairwise relatively prime integers $\{m_{1,i}, m_{2,j} \mid m_{1,i}, m_{2,j} \geq 2, 1 \leq i \leq k_1, 1 \leq j \leq k_2\}$, where $\sum_{i=1}^{k_h} m_{h,i} \geq n_h$, $h = 1, 2$. Define $L_h = L_{\{m_{h,1}, \ldots, m_{h,k_h}\}}$, $h = 1, 2$. Directly from the definition (2) it follows that

$$L_1 \cup L_2 = L_{\{m_{1,1}, \ldots, m_{1,k_1}, m_{2,1}, \ldots, m_{2,k_2}\}}.$$

Immediately from Corollary 4.2, we get that

$$\text{sctw}_{k_1+k_2}(L_1 \cup L_2) = \text{sctw}_{k_1}(L_1) + \text{sctw}_{k_2}(L_2) - 1, \tag{4}$$

and $L_i$ has tree width $k_i$, $i = 1, 2$, as well as, $L_1 \cup L_2$ has tree width $k_1 + k_2$.

When $k_1 \geq 2$ and $k_2 = 1$, the construction is the same but instead of (4) we get $\text{sctw}_{k_1+1}(L_1 \cup L_2) = \text{sctw}_{k_1}(L_1) + \text{sctw}_1(L_2)$.

Finally, with $k_1 = k_2 = 1$, by choosing two relatively prime numbers $m_i \geq n_i$, $\{m_1, m_2\} \neq \{2, 3\}$, $L_i = L_{\{m_i\}}$, $i = 1, 2$, we have $\text{sctw}_2(L_1 \cup L_2) = \text{sctw}_1(L_1) + \text{sctw}_1(L_2) + 1$, and the language $L_1 \cup L_2$ has tree width 2. Note that $\{m_1, m_2\} = \{2, 3\}$ is the one exception in Lemma 4.2, and the tree width of $L_{\{2,3\}}$ would be one. □

Above note that since $L_1 \cup L_2$ has tree width $k_1 + k_2$, it follows that for any $k < k_1 + k_2$, $\text{sctw}_k(L_1 \cup L_2)$ is strictly larger than $\text{sctw}_{k_1}(L_1) + \text{sctw}_{k_2}(L_2) - 1$.

**Lemma 4.4.** *For every $k_i, n_i \in \mathbb{N}$, $i = 1, 2$, there exist regular languages $L_i$ of tree width $k_i$ such that $\text{sctw}_{k_i}(L_i) \geq n_i$ and*

$$\text{sctw}_{k_1 \cdot k_2}(L_1 \cap L_2) \geq (\text{sctw}_{k_1}(L_1) - 1) \cdot (\text{sctw}_{k_2}(L_2) - 1) + 1.$$

*Furthermore, $L_1 \cap L_2$ has tree width $k_1 \cdot k_2$.*

*Proof.* We begin by considering the case $k_1, k_2 \geq 2$. Let $p_{i,j}$, $1 \leq j \leq k_i$, $1 \leq i \leq 2$, be distinct prime numbers, where $\sum_{j=1}^{k_i} p_{i,j} \geq n_i$, $i = 1, 2$.

We define $L_i = L_{\{p_{i,1}, \ldots, p_{i,k_i}\}}$, $i = 1, 2$. By Corollary 4.2 we know that

$$\text{sctw}_{k_i}(L_i) = 1 + \sum_{j=1}^{k_i} p_{i,j}, \quad 1 \leq i \leq 2, \tag{5}$$

where the tree width of $L_i$ is $k_i$. Define $P(k_1, k_2) = \{p_{1,j_1} \cdot p_{2,j_2} \mid 1 \leq j_i \leq k_i, i = 1, 2\}$. Here $P(k_1, k_2)$ is an independent set of prime pairs. Also we note that $L_1 \cap L_2 = L_{P(k_1,k_2)}$. Now, again using Corollary 4.2, the tree width of $L_1 \cap L_2$ is $\#P(k_1, k_2) = k_1 \cdot k_2$ and

$$\text{sctw}_{k_1 \cdot k_2}(L_1 \cap L_2) = 1 + \sum_{1 \leq j_1 \leq k_1, 1 \leq j_2 \leq k_2} p_{1,j_1} \cdot p_{2,j_2}.$$

Comparing this with (5) we get that the inequality in the claim of the lemma holds as an equality.

In the case where $k_1 \geq 2$ and $k_2 = 1$, instead of (5), we have $\mathrm{sctw}_1(L_2) = p_{2,1}$ and, using Corollary 4.2, we get

$$\mathrm{sctw}_{k_1}(L_1 \cap L_2) = (\mathrm{sctw}_{k_1}(L_1) - 1) \cdot \mathrm{sctw}_1(L_2) + 1.$$

Finally, when $k_1 = k_2 = 1$, the inequality in the statement of the lemma holds due to the well-known lower bound for the deterministic state complexity of intersection. $\quad\square$

According to Lemmas 4.3 and 4.4 the lower bound can, corresponding to any tree widths $k_i$, $i = 1, 2$, be reached with automata of arbitrarily large sizes. In particular, in the case of intersection, it is not clear whether the construction could be modified to always allow us to choose $\mathrm{sctw}_{k_i}(L_i)$ to be exactly $n_i$.

The lower bound for union differs only by a constant 2 from the upper bound in Lemma 4.1 and for intersection the gap is larger. We conjecture that the bounds of Lemma 4.1 are optimal for the NFA model (used here and in most of the literature) that allows only a single initial state. However, we might need to use NFAs over a nonunary alphabet to get exactly matching lower bounds.

*Remark 4.1.* For an NFA model that allows multiple initial states, the upper bound (of Lemma 4.1) for union would be changed to be $\mathrm{sctw}_{k_1}(L_1) + \mathrm{sctw}_{k_2}(L_2)$, while the upper bound for intersection would stay the same. For NFAs with multiple initial states, the lower bound constructions of the proof of Lemma 4.3 and 4.4 will exactly match the corresponding state complexity upper bounds that are modified from Lemma 4.1 as described above.

## 4.1   Other Language Operations

A general NFA recognizing the concatenation of an $n_1$ and an $n_2$ state NFA needs only $n_1 + n_2$ states [10]. For ftw-NFAs the situation is not equally simple because, with only limited nondeterminism available, the automaton is not able to guess when a string belonging to the first language ends. The following upper bound is inspired by the construction originally used for deterministic state complexity of concatenation [26,27]. Note however that, with $k = 1$, the result of Lemma 4.5 does not coincide with the deterministic state complexity of concatenation. This is because a tw(1)-NFA is an incomplete DFA, and the well-known deterministic state complexity results [26,27] are stated in terms of complete DFAs.

**Lemma 4.5.** *For regular languages $L_i$, $i = 1, 2$, and $k \geq 1$,*

$$\mathrm{sctw}_k(L_1 \cdot L_2) \leq \mathrm{sctw}_k(L_1) \cdot 2^{\mathrm{nsc}(L_2)} + 2^{\mathrm{nsc}(L_2)-1} - 1.$$

The bound of Lemma 4.5 is stated in terms of the nondeterministic state complexity of the second language $L_2$ because the construction used in the proof would result in the same bound even if $L_2$ were recognized by an ftw-NFA. We do not have a lower bound construction that would be close to the upper bound of Lemma 4.5 for general values $k \geq 2$.

Determining the worst-case state complexity of operations such as concatenation and Kleene-star for ftw-NFAs remains open. For the Kleene-star operation it seems that, in the worst-case, an ftw-NFA cannot be smaller than a DFA.

Note that using constructions inspired by [6], similar to the one used here in the proof of Proposition 3.1, it is, in fact, possible to construct regular languages $L$ such that any ftw-NFA for $L^*$ cannot be smaller than a DFA. However, the construction delimits the strings of $L$ by end-markers, which makes it seem unsuitable to be used in worst-case constructions for the state complexity of Kleene-star (or concatenation) where we, roughly speaking, need to make it hard for the NFA to detect the end of a substring belonging to $L$.

## 5  Conclusion and Open Problems

The results of the previous section have barely scratched the surface of operational state complexity of ftw-NFAs and most questions in this area remain open. Below we mention some other possible future research directions.

Hromkovič et al. [13] have given upper and lower bounds for the tree width of an NFA $A$ in terms of the ambiguity of $A$ and the number of advice bits required by $A$. (The tree width is called "leaf size" in [13].) The *guessing measure* of $A$ [6] is related to the advice measure, except that for a given input it considers the computation of $A$ using the least (as opposed to the largest) number of advice bits. Also, Goldstine et al. [7] have studied the relationships between the ambiguity of an NFA $A$ and the amount of nondeterminism used by $A$.

In the context of state complexity, similar questions could be asked for regular languages, as opposed to individual NFAs. For example, it would be interesting to know, for a given regular language $L$, how the optimal sizes of an NFA recognizing $L$, respectively, with advice measure $k$ and with tree width $k'$ relate to each other. Similar questions can be asked also for other combinations of the complexity measures. Note that from Proposition 3.1 we know that there exist regular languages for which an unambiguous NFA can be exponentially smaller than any ftw-NFA. On the other hand, the state complexity of converting an ftw-NFA to an unambiguous NFA remains, to the best of our knowledge, open.

## References

1. Birget, J.C.: Intersection and union of regular languages and state complexity, Inform. Process. Lett. 43, 185–190 (1992)
2. Björklund, H., Martens, W.: The tractability frontier for NFA minimization. J. Comput. System Sci. 78, 198–210 (2012)
3. Chrobak, M.: Finite automata and unary languages. Theoret. Comput. Sci. 47, 149–158 (1986)
4. Glaister, I., Shallit, J.: A lower bound technique for the size of nondeterministic finite automata. Inf. Proc. Lett. 59, 75–77 (1996)
5. Goldstine, J., Kappes, M., Kintala, C.M.R., Leung, H., Malcher, A., Wotschke, D.: Descriptional complexity of machines with limited resources. J. Univ. Comput. Sci. 8, 193–234 (2002)

6. Goldstine, J., Kintala, C.M.R., Wotschke, D.: On measuring nondeterminism in regular languages. Inform. Comput. 86, 179–194 (1990)
7. Goldstine, J., Leung, H., Wotschke, D.: On the relation between ambiguity and nondeterminism in finite automata. Inform. Comput. 100, 261–270 (1992)
8. Gruber, H., Holzer, M.: Finding Lower Bounds for Nondeterministic State Complexity Is Hard. In: Ibarra, O.H., Dang, Z. (eds.) DLT 2006. LNCS, vol. 4036, pp. 363–374. Springer, Heidelberg (2006)
9. Gruber, H., Holzer, M.: Inapproximability of Nondeterministic State and Transition Complexity Assuming **P** $\neq$ **NP**. In: Harju, T., Karhumäki, J., Lepistö, A. (eds.) DLT 2007. LNCS, vol. 4588, pp. 205–216. Springer, Heidelberg (2007)
10. Holzer, M., Kutrib, M.: Nondeterministic descriptional complexity of regular languages. Internat. J. Foundations of Comput. Sci. 14, 1087–1102 (2003)
11. Holzer, M., Kutrib, M.: Descriptional and computational complexity of finite automata — A survey. Inf. Comput. 209, 456–470 (2011)
12. Holzer, M., Salomaa, K., Yu, S.: On the state complexity of k-entry deterministic finite automata. J. Automata, Languages and Combinatorics 6, 453–466 (2001)
13. Hromkovič, J., Seibert, S., Karhumäki, J., Klauck, H., Schnitger, G.: Communication complexity method for measuring nondeterminism in finite automata. Inform. Comput. 172, 202–217 (2002)
14. Jiang, T., McDowell, E., Ravikumar, B.: The structure and complexity of minimal NFA's over a unary alphabet. Internat. J. Foundations Comput. Sci. 2, 163–182 (1991)
15. Jiang, T., Ravikumar, B.: Minimal NFA problems are hard. SIAM J. Comput. 22, 1117–1141 (1993)
16. Kappes, M.: Descriptional complexity of deterministic finite automata with multiple initial states. J. Automata, Languages, and Combinatorics 5, 269–278 (2000)
17. Kintala, C.M.R., Wotschke, D.: Amounts of nondeterminism in finite automata. Acta Inform. 13, 199–204 (1980)
18. Leung, H.: Separating exponentially ambiguous finite automata from polynomially ambiguous finite automata. SIAM J. Comput, 1073–1082 (1998)
19. Leung, H.: Descriptional complexity of NFA of different ambiguity. Internat. J. Foundations Comput. Sci. 16, 975–984 (2005)
20. Malcher, A.: Minimizing finite automata is computationally hard. Theoret. Comput. Sci. 327, 375–390 (2004)
21. Okhotin, A.: Unambiguous Finite Automata over a Unary Alphabet. In: Hliněný, P., Kučera, A. (eds.) MFCS 2010. LNCS, vol. 6281, pp. 556–567. Springer, Heidelberg (2010)
22. Ravikumar, B., Ibarra, O.: Relating the type of ambiguity of finite automata to the succinctness of their representation. SIAM J. Comput. 18, 1263–1282 (1989)
23. Schmidt, E.M.: Succinctness of description of context-free, regular and unambiguous languages. Ph.D. thesis, Cornell University (1978)
24. Shallit, J.: A Second Course in Formal Languages and Automata Theory. Cambridge University Press (2009)
25. Stearns, R., Hunt, H.: On the equivalence and containment problems for unambiguous regular expressions, regular grammars and finite automata. SIAM J. Comput. 14, 596–611 (1985)
26. Yu, S.: Regular languages. In: Rozenberg, G., Salomaa, A. (eds.) Handbook of Formal Languages, vol. I, pp. 41–110. Springer (1997)
27. Yu, S., Zhuang, Q., Salomaa, K.: The state complexity of some basic operations on regular languages. Theoret. Comput. Sci. 125, 315–328 (1994)

# Bounded Counter Languages*

Holger Petersen

Reinsburgstr. 75, 70197 Stuttgart, Germany

**Abstract.** We show that deterministic finite automata equipped with $k$ two-way heads are equivalent to deterministic machines with a single two-way input head and $k - 1$ linearly bounded counters if the accepted language is strictly bounded, i.e., a subset of $a_1^* a_2^* \cdots a_m^*$ for a fixed sequence of symbols $a_1, a_2, \ldots, a_m$. Then we investigate linear speed-up for counter machines. Lower and upper time bounds for concrete recognition problems are shown, implying that in general linear speed-up does not hold for counter machines. For bounded languages we develop a technique for speeding up computations by any constant factor at the expense of adding a fixed number of counters.

## 1 Introduction

The computational model investigated in the present work is the two-way counter machine as defined in [4]. Recently, the power of this model has been compared to quantum automata and probabilistic automata [14,17].

We will show that bounded counters and heads are equally powerful for finite deterministic devices, provided the languages under consideration are strictly bounded. By equally powerful we mean that up to a single head each two-way input head of a deterministic finite machine can be simulated by a counter bounded by the input length and vice versa. The condition that the input is bounded cannot be removed in general, since it is known that deterministic finite two-way two-head automata are more powerful than deterministic two-way one counter machines if the input is not bounded [2]. The special case of equivalence between deterministic one counter machines and two-head automata over a single letter alphabet has been shown with the help of a two-dimensional automata model as an intermediate step in [10], see also [11].

Adding resources to a computational model should intuitively increase its power. This is true in the case of time and space hierarchies for Turing machines, see the text book [15, Chapter 9]. The language

$$\{x_0 \# \cdots \# x_k \mid k \geq 0, x_j \in \{0,1\}^* \text{ for } 0 \leq j \leq k, \text{ for some } 1 \leq i \leq k \ x_i = x_0\}$$

from [2] cited above is easily acceptable with two counters. Notice that the language formalizes a simplified string matching problem where the possible

* Research partially supported by "Deutsche Akademie der Naturforscher Leopoldina", grant number BMBF-LPD 9901/8-1 of "Bundesministerium für Bildung und Forschung".

positions of string $x_0$ are marked. If two counters are available, then one counter can keep track of the symbols being compared while the other counter stores the number $j$ of the string $x_j$ under consideration. The input head travels back and forth between $x_0$ and $x_j$. Thus this language shows that two counters are more powerful than one. A further growing number of unbounded counters does however not increase the power of these machines due to the classical result of Minsky [8], showing that machines with two counters are universal. Thus the formally defined hierarchy of language classes accepted by machines with a growing number of counters collapses to the second level. A tight hierarchy is obtained if the counters are linearly bounded [9] or if the machines are working in real-time [4, Theorem 5.1]. In the latter case the machines are allowed to make one step per input symbol and there is obviously no difference in accepting power between one-way and two-way access to the input. If we restrict the input to be read one-way (sometimes called on-line [5]), a hierarchy in exponential time can be shown [12].

The starting point of our investigation of time hierarchies is Theorem 1.3 of [4], where the authors show that the language of marked binary palindromes has time complexity $\Theta(n^2/\log n)$ on two-way counter machines. By techniques from descriptional complexity [7] for the lower bounds we are able to separate classes of machines with different numbers of counters. A main motivation for this work is of course a fundamental interest in the way the capabilities of a computational device influence its power.

Regarding time bounded computations, we present an algorithm for the recognition of marked palindromes working with only two counters, while the upper bound outlined in the proof of [4, Theorem 1.3] requires at least three counters (one for storing $\log_2 m$ and two for encoding portions of the input). We show that counter machines lack general linear speed-up. Other models of computation with this property include Turing machines with tree storages [6] and Turing machines with a fixed alphabet and a fixed number of tapes [1]. By adapting the witness language, we disprove a claim that these machines satisfy speed-up for polynomial time bounds [5]. Finally we present a class of languages where linear speed-up can be achieved by adding a fixed number of counters.

## 2    Definitions

A language is *bounded* if it is a subset of $w_1^* w_2^* \cdots w_m^*$ for a fixed sequence of words $w_1, w_2 \ldots, w_m$ (which are not necessarily distinct). We call $w_1^* w_2^* \cdots w_m^*$ the *bound* of the language. A language is *strictly bounded* if it is a subset of $a_1^* a_2^* \cdots a_m^*$ for pairwise distinct symbols $a_1, a_2, \ldots, a_m$. A maximal sequence of symbols $a_i$ in the input will be called a *block*.[1]

---

[1] As pointed out by one of the referees, strictly bounded languages have been defined without requiring symbols from non-adjacent blocks to be distinct. Our constructions can be adapted to this more general definition by keeping the information which block is read by the input head in the finite control.

Formal definitions of variants of counter machines can be found in [4]. We only point out a few essential features of the models. The main models of computation investigated here are the *k-head automaton*, the *bounded counter machine with k counters*, and the *register machine with k bounded registers*, cf. [9]. The two former types of automata have read-only input tapes bordered by end-markers. Therefore on an input of length $n$ there are $n + 2$ different positions that can be read. The $k$-head automaton is equipped with $k$ two-way heads that may move independently on the input tape and transmit the symbols read to the finite control. Note that informally two heads of the basic model cannot see each other, i.e., the machine has no way of finding out that they happen to be reading the same input square. Heads with the capability of "seeing" each others are called sensing.

The bounded counter machine is equipped with a single two-way head and $k$ counters that can count up to the input length. The operations it can perform on the counters are increment, decrement, and zero-test. The machines start their operation with all heads next to the left end-marker (on the first input symbol if the input is not empty) and all counters set to zero. Acceptance is by final state and can occur with the input head at any position.

A register machine with $k$ registers receives an input number in its first register, all other registers are initially zero. The finite control of a register machine can increment and decrement registers or test them for being zero. Notice that in contrast to the models with one or more input heads, a register machine can erase its input.

We compare register machines with the other types of machines by identifying nonnegative integers and strings over a single letter alphabet of a corresponding length. All machines have deterministic and nondeterministic variants and accept by entering a final state.

For machines with a single input-head, the sequence of states the machine enters when the head moves across the border between two adjacent symbols, is called the *crossing sequence* at this position.

The set of *marked palindromes* over a binary alphabet is $L = \{x\$x^R \mid x \in \{0,1\}^*\}$, where $x^R$ denotes the reversal of $x$ (in [4] the notation $x^T$ is used for the reversal of $x$).

With the restriction that at least approximately half of the input is filled by zeros, we obtain

$$L' = \{x0^{|x|}\$0^{|x|}x^R \mid x \in \{0,1\}^*\}.$$

The central portion of the strings will be called the *desert* and $L'$ the language of marked palindromes with desert. A further restriction to only a logarithmic information content leads to the family

$$L_m = \{x0^{2^{|x|/m}-|x|}\$0^{2^{|x|/m}-|x|}x^R \mid x \in \{0,1\}^*\}$$

for $m \geq 1$.

The languages introduced will separate classes of languages accepted by different computational models and thus serve as witnesses for their difference in power. The family $L_m$ will allow us to disprove a claimed speed-up in linear time. This would not be possible with the more natural languages based on palin-dromes, since their optimum recognition time is between linear and quadratic.

In our proofs of lower bounds we make use of the concept of Kolmogorov Complexity [7]. The descriptional complexity of a string is measured in terms of the minimum size of programs for a universal computational model, e.g., a universal Turing machine generating the string. A key fact is that for every length, at least one incompressible string exists that cannot be generated by a program shorter than the string itself.

## 3   Equivalence of Heads and Counters for Deterministic Machines

In order to simplify the presentation we assume below without loss of generality that a multi-head automaton moves exactly one head in every step. Suppose a multi-head automaton operates on a word from a strictly bounded language. We call a step in which a head passes from one block of identical symbols to a neighboring block or an end-marker an *event*. The head moved in this step is said to *cause the event*.

**Lemma 1.** *Let the input of a deterministic multi-head automaton be strictly bounded. It is possible to determine whether a head will cause the next event (under the assumption that no other head does) by inspecting an input segment of fixed length around this head independently of the input size. If it can cause the next event it will also be determined at which boundary of the scanned block it will happen.*

*Proof.* Let the automaton have $r$ internal states. If the head moves to a square at least $r$ positions away from its initial position within the same block before the next event, then some state must have been repeated (since all other heads keep reading the same symbols) and the automaton, receiving the same information from its heads while no event occurs, will continue to work in a cycle until a head causes an event. Therefore it suffices to simulate the machine on a segment of $2r - 1$ symbols under and around the head under consideration (or less symbols if the segment exceeds the boundaries of the input tape). We assume that no other head causes the next event, therefore at most $2r^2 - r$ different partial configurations consisting of state, symbols read by the heads and the position on the segment are possible before one of the following happens:

- The head leaves the current block causing an event.
- The head leaves the segment around the initial position of the head.
- The automaton gets into a loop repeating partial configurations within the segment.

In the two former cases the boundary at which the next event is possibly caused by the head under consideration is easily determined. In the first case the event obviously occurs, since a different symbol is read by the head. In the second case a state has been repeated while the head under consideration has moved and all input symbols read have been equal (otherwise there would have been an event). Therefore the head will continue to move towards one of the boundaries until an event occurs. In the latter case the head cannot cause the next event.    □

**Theorem 1.** *Deterministic multi-head automata with $k$ two-way heads and deterministic bounded counter machines with $k - 1$ counters are equivalent over strictly bounded languages.*

*Proof.* Any bounded counter machine with $k-1$ counters can easily be simulated by a $k$-head automaton, independently of the structure of the input string. The multi-head automaton simulates the input head of the counter machine with one of its heads and encodes the values stored by the counters as the distances of the remaining head positions from the left end-marker.

For the converse direction we will describe the simulation of a deterministic multi-head automaton $M$ by a deterministic bounded counter machine $C$ and call $C$'s single input head its pointer, thus avoiding some ambiguities. The counters and the pointer of $C$ are assigned to the heads of $M$, this assignment varies during the simulation.

The counters will store distances between head positions and boundaries of blocks of the input, where distances to left or right boundaries may occur in the course of the simulation. The finite amount of information consisting of the assignment and the type of distance for each counter is stored in $C$'s finite control. Depending on the type of distance stored for a head, movements of $M$'s heads are translated into the corresponding increment and decrement operations. If a distance to a left boundary is stored, a left movement causes a decrement and a right movement an increment operation on the counter. For distances to a right boundary the operations are reversed.

We divide the computation of the multi-head automaton $M$ into intervals. Each interval starts with a configuration in which at least one head is next to a boundary (i.e., on one of the two positions left or right of the boundary between blocks), one of these heads being represented by $C$'s pointer. Notice that the initial configuration satisfies this requirement. Each interval except the last one ends when the next event occurs. After this event the machine is again in a configuration suitable for a new interval.

Counter machine $C$ always updates the symbols read by the heads of $M$ (initially the first input symbol or the right end-marker) and keeps this information in its finite control. A counter assigned to a head encodes the number of symbols within the block that are to the left resp. right of the head position. The counter machine also maintains the information which of these two numbers is stored.

We start our description of the algorithm that $C$ executes in a configuration with the property that at least one head of $M$ is next to a boundary. One of these heads is represented by the single pointer of $C$. First $C$ moves its pointer to every block that is read by some head of $M$. It can determine these blocks uniquely from the symbols stored in the finite control. It moves its pointer next to the boundary that is indicated by the type of distance stored on the counter assigned to the head under consideration. While the counter is not zero it decrements the counter and moves the pointer towards the head position. Then it determines whether this head could cause the next event, provided that no other head does, by applying Lemma 1. For this purpose the pointer reads the surrounding segment of fixed length without losing the head position. Then the test is carried out in $C$'s finite control.

Suppose the head could cause the next event at some boundary. Then $C$ updates the contents of the counter to reflect the distance of $M$'s head from that boundary. If the block has the form $a_i^{x_i}$ and the head is on position $n \geq 1$ in this block, then the counter machine moves its pointer towards the boundary where the event possibly occurs and measures the distance with the help of the counter. Thus $C$ updates the contents of the counter with either $n - 1$ or $x_i - n$, respectively, depending on whether the event can occur at the left or right boundary. If no event can be caused by the head currently considered, one of the distances is stored, say to the left boundary.

These operations are carried out for every head. Finally $C$ moves its pointer back to the initial position, which is possible since it is next to a boundary. Then it starts to simulate $M$ step by step, translating head movements into counter operations according to the distance represented by the counter contents. If $M$ gets into an accepting state, $C$ accepts. If the pointer leaves its block the next interval starts. If a counter is about to be decremented from zero this operation is not carried out. Instead the current pointer position is recorded in this counter and the roles of pointer and counter are interchanged. The symbols read by the heads that pointer and counter are now assigned to, as well as the internal state of $M$ are updated. This information can clearly be kept in $C$'s finite control. A new interval starts.

The initial configuration of $C$ has all counters set to zero with the pointer and all simulated heads reading the first input symbol. The assignment of heads to counters is arbitrary, all counters store the distance to the left boundary.    □

*Remark 1.* One of the referees asked why the equivalence is not stated for the general bounded language case. The difficulty in adapting the proof is, that the detection of borders of blocks in the general case is more difficult than suggested by the definition. If the bound is $a^*(ba)^*b^*(ab)^*$ (with $w_1 = a$, $w_2 = ba$, $w_3 = b$, and $w_4 = ab$), then strings of the form $(ab)^i$ with $i \geq 1$ can be written $(ab)^i = w_1 w_2^{i-1} w_3 = w_4^i$. In contrast $(ab)^i b = w_1 w_2^{i-1} w_3^2$ is unique and no finite look-ahead suffices for a distinction of the cases when parsing a prefix of the input.

The equivalence of heads and counters implies that the intermediate concept of simple heads — two-way heads that cannot distinguish different input symbols — also coincides in power with counters over strictly bounded languages. It is open whether the analogous equivalence holds over arbitrary input or, as conjectured in [10,11], simple heads are more powerful than counters. [2] Finding a candidate

---

[2] The $n$-bounded counters of [10,16] can count from 0 up to $n$ and can be tested for these values. They are easily seen to be equivalent to simple heads. The class of deterministic two-way machines equipped with $k$ such counters is denoted $C(k)$ in [10,16], while machines with $k$ unbounded counters are denoted by $D(k)$.

for the separation even of one simple head from a counter seems to be difficult. In recognizing their language $L_4 = \{ww \mid w \in \{0,1\}^*\}$ the full power of a simple head was used in [16], but this is not necessary. A counter machine without the the ability to compare its counter to the input length can first check that the input contains an even number of symbols. Starting with the first symbol it then stores the distance of the current symbol to the left end-marker on the counter. Sweeping its head over the entire input it increments the counter in every second step and thus computes the offset of the corresponding symbol, moves its head to this position and compares the symbols. Then it reverses the computation to return to the initial position and moves its head to the next symbol. If all corresponding symbols are equal it accepts.

Finally we compare the power of register machines and multi-head automata over a single letter alphabet. For the simulation we will identify lengths of input strings and input numbers. In Lemma 5 of [9] a simulation of $k$-head automata over a single letter alphabet by $k + 1$ register machines is given. The simulation is rather specialized, since it applies only to subsets of words that have a length which is a power of two. We will generalize this simulation to arbitrary languages over a single letter alphabet.

**Theorem 2.** *Every deterministic (nondeterministic) $k$-head automaton over a single letter alphabet can be simulated by a deterministic (nondeterministic) $k+1$ register machine. The heads of the automata being simulated may even be sensing (they can see each others).*

*Proof.* First we normalize multi-head automata that can detect heads scanning the same square such that the heads appear in a fixed left-to-right sequence on the tape (if some heads are on the same square we allow any sequence, which includes this fixed one). This is easily achieved because the automata can internally switch the roles of two heads which are about to be transposed.

The register machine simulating a $k$-head automaton with the help of $k + 1$ registers stores in its registers the distances between neighboring heads or the end-marker, where the distance is the number of steps to the right a head would have to carry out in order to reach the next head or end-marker. Register 1 represents the distance of the last head to the right end-marker. Whenever a head moves the register machine updates the two related distances. A small technical problem is the distance to the left end-marker, which formally should be $-1$ in the initial configuration. The register machine stores the information whether the left-most heads scan the left end-marker in its finite control. In this way all distances can be bounded by the input length.                               □

# 4   Time-Bounds for Counter Machines

The purpose of this section is to establish lower and upper time-bounds on counter machines for concrete recognition problems.

**Theorem 3.** *The recognition of the language $L'$ of marked palindromes with desert requires*

$$\frac{n^2 - 16n \log_2 n - dn}{8(\log_2 n + 2 \log_2 s + 1)}$$

*steps for input strings of length $n$ on 1-counter machines and*

$$\frac{n^2 - 16n \log_2 n - dn}{8(2k \log_2 n + \log_2 s)}$$

*steps on $k$-counter machines in the worst case and for $n$ sufficiently large, where $s$ and $d$ are constants depending on the specific counter machine.*

*Proof.* Let $M$ be a 1-counter machine with $s \geq 2$ states accepting $L'$ and let $x$ be an incompressible string with $|x| = m \geq 1$. Consider the accepting computation of $M$ on $x0^{|x|}\$0^{|x|}x^R$ and choose position $i$ adjacent to or within the central portion $0^{|x|}\$0^{|x|}$ with a crossing sequence $c$ having $\ell$ entries of minimum length. Notice that for 1-counter machines the counter is bounded from above by $s(n + 2) < 2sn$, since $n \geq 2m + 1$.

String $x$ can be reconstructed from the following information:

- A description of $M$ ($O(1)$ bits).
- A self-delimiting encoding of the length of $x$ ($2 \log_2 n$ bits).
- Position $i$ of $c$ ($\log_2 n$ bits).
- Length $\ell$ of $c$ ($\log_2(4s^2n)$ bits).
- Crossing sequence $c$ recording the counter contents and the state $M$ enters when crossing position $i$ ($\ell(\log_2 n + 2 \log_2 s + 1)$ bits).
- A formalized description of the reconstruction procedure outlined below ($O(1)$ bits).

For reconstructing $x$ from the above data, a simulator sets up a section of length $|x|$ followed by all symbols (0 or $) up to position $i$. Then the simulator cycles through all strings $y$ of length $|x|$ and simulates $M$ step by step. Whenever position $i$ is reached, it is checked that the current entry of the crossing sequence matches state and counter contents. If not, the current $y$ is discarded and the next string is set up. If it matches, the simulation continues from state and counter contents of the next entry of the crossing sequence. If $M$ accepts, the encoded $x$ has been found and the simulation terminates.

Since $x$ is incompressible, for some constant $d$ compensating the $O(1)$ contributions we must have:

$$|x| = (n - 1)/4 \leq \ell(\log_2 n + 2 \log_2 s + 1) + 4 \log_2 n + d/4 - 1/4$$

and thus

$$\ell \geq \frac{n - 16 \log_2 n - d}{4(\log_2 n + 2 \log_2 s + 1)}.$$

There are $(n - 1)/2 + 2 \geq n/2$ positions of crossing sequences with length at least $\ell$, thus we get

$$T(n) \geq \frac{n^2 - 16n \log_2 n - dn}{8(\log_2 n + 2 \log_2 s + 1)}.$$

For machines with $k \geq 2$ counters we bound the counter contents by the coarse upper bound $n^2$ (since the asymptotical bound grows more slowly, this bound suffices). This increases the bound on the length of the encoding of crossing sequences to $\ell(2k \log_2 n + \log_2 s)$ bits. The time bound becomes:

$$T(n) \geq \frac{n^2 - 16n \log_2 n - dn}{8(2k \log_2 n + \log_2 s)}.$$

□

Next we present an upper bound for the full language $L$ and give an algorithm that uses only two counters in comparison to at least three in [4]. We conjecture that this cannot be reduced to one counter for subquadratic algorithms.

**Theorem 4.** *Language $L$ of marked palindromes can be accepted in $O(n^2/\log n)$ steps by a two-counter machine.*

*Proof.* We describe informally the work of a machine $M$ accepting $L$ on an input of length $n \geq 1$. The idea is to encode segments of length $\log_2 n$ and iteratively compare segment by segment.

First $M$ scans the input and counts the symbols before the $\$$ (if no $\$$ is found, $M$ rejects). After the $\$$ the counter is decremented and the input is rejected, if zero is not reached on the right end-marker or a second $\$$ is encountered. The first scan takes $n$ steps if $M$ starts on the leftmost input-symbol as defined in [4].

First $M$ puts 1 on counter 1, repeatedly reads a symbol, doubles the counter contents (exchanging roles for each bit read), and adds 1 if the symbol read was 1. Notice that after such a doubling one of the counter contents is zero. Then $M$ makes excursions to the left and to the right counting up on the empty counter and down on the counter holding the encoding until the latter counter becomes empty or $\$$ resp. an end-marker is reached. The net effect is an (attempted) subtraction of $n/2$ from the encoding. If the counter becomes zero, the initial encoding was less than $n/2$. After each of the excursions, the other counter is used for returning to the initial position and the encoding is restored. If the encoding exceeds $n/2$, the process stops and the segment is compared to the corresponding portion to the right of $\$$. Using the empty counter, $M$ moves to the corresponding portion and in a symmetrical way as for the encoding decodes the segment. Since the encoding has a 1 as its most significant bit, no excursions are necessary. In order to return to the last position in the segment, $M$ repeats the encoding process. Then it continues with the next segment. The iterations stop if the marker $\$$ is reached.

For the time analysis we omit constant and linear contributions to the number of steps, these are accounted for by an appropriately chosen constant factor of the leading term. The initial scan is clearly linear. By the doubling procedure the amortized cost of encoding and decoding is linear per segment. Notice that the excusions are aborted if the counter holding the encoding is empty and thus also the excursions have linear complexity per segment. Since the number of segments is $O(n/\log n)$, the bound follows.

□

**Theorem 5.** *For $k$-counter machines with fixed $k \geq 2$ accepting $L$ in $O(n^2/\log n)$ steps there is no linear speed-up.*

*Proof.* The lower bounds for a subset of $L$ in Theorem 3 carry over to the full language, since running times on input strings from the subset are also under consideration for time bounds on $L$. These lower bounds show that the algorithm from Theorem 4 cannot be accelerated by an arbitrary factor.    $\square$

*Remark 2.* By adding counters and encoding larger segments of the input a speed-up for the recognition of $L$ is possible.

We now adapt the witness language to the bounds considered in [5, p. 273]. There speed-up results for deterministic and nondeterministic two-way machines with $r$ counters and time bounds of the form $pn^k$ with $p > 1$ and $k \geq 1$ are stated. No formal proofs are given, but the preceding section contains a reference to [4]. We note here that the speed-up results in [4, Section 5.2] are based on Theorem 1.1 and 1.2 of [4] , which appear before the definition of two-way machines and therefore applys to one-way models only.

In the special case of linear time bounds we will disprove the claimed speed-up. For at least quadratic bounds the technique does not apply, since the type of languages considered can be accepted in quadratic time comparing bit by bit and constant speed-up by forming blocks of constant size can clearly be achieved. Whether a general linear speed-up is possible is open, since there seems to be no efficient way to compress the contents of the input tape.

**Theorem 6.** *The recognition of the language $L_m$ requires $(m/13)n$ steps on 4-counter machines in the worst case and for $n$ sufficiently large.*

*Proof.* The proof is adapted from the one given for Theorem 3 and we only describe the differences.

We assume $|x| > m \log_2 |x|$ in the following. Since the part $x$ is now only a logarithmic portion of the input, $2 \log_2 \log_2 n$ bits suffice for encoding the length. The time bound is the linear function $pn$, therefore the crossing sequence can be described in $\ell(4(\log_2 n + \log_2 p) + \log_2 s)$ bits.

For an incompressible $x$ we obtain:

$$m \log_2 n - 2m \leq |x| = m \log_2((n-1)/2)$$
$$\leq \ell(4(\log_2 n + \log_2 p) + \log_2 s) + 2 \log_2 n + d$$
$$= \ell(6 \log_2 n) + d'$$

with constants $d, d'$ and $\ell \geq m/6 - o(1)$. Since the desert is at least $n/2$ symbols long for $|x| > m \log_2 |x|$ we get the time bound $T(n) \geq (m/12)n - o(n)$.    $\square$

We now have to show that there is a linear recognition algorithm for $L_m$.

**Theorem 7.** *The language $L_m$ can be accepted in $(2m+3)n + o(n)$ steps by a 4-counter machine.*

*Proof.* In a first left-to-right scan, an acceptor $M_m$ for $L_m$ determines the length of the part of the input before the \$, compares it to the part after \$ and at the same time counts that length again in another counter. By repeatedly dividing by two, it computes $|x|/m$ in at most $n$ steps and checks in a right-to left scan, whether the middle portion of the input contains only 0's. While doing so, $M_m$ preserves $|x|/m$ and computes $2^{|x|/m} - |x|$ for checking the left half of the input.

Then $M_m$ starts to encode blocks of $|x|/2m$ bits on two counters while using the other two counters for checking the length of the block. Since $|x| \leq m \log_2 n$, the encoding can be done in $O(\sqrt{n})$ steps. Then $M_m$ moves its input head to the other half of the input, decodes the stored information, and contiues with the next iteration. The number of $2m$ iterations of $n + o(n)$ steps each can be counted in the finite control. □

As an example take $L_{39}$, which can be accepted in $82n$ steps by Theorem 7 for sufficiently large $n$, but a linear speed-up to $2n$ is impossible by Theorem 6.

## 5    Speed-Up for Counter Machines on Bounded Input

In Section 4 we have shown that linear speed-up for certain recognition problems on counter machines can only be achieved by adding counters. If the input is compressible, the situation is different and a fixed number of counters depending on the structure of the language suffices for speeding up by any constant factor.

We will apply the classical result of Fine and Wilf on periodicity of sequences:

**Theorem 8 ([3]).** *Let $(f_n)_{n \geq 0}$ and $(g_n)_{n \geq 0}$ be two periodic sequences of period $h$ and $k$, respectively. If $f_n = g_n$ for $h + k - \gcd(h, k)$ consecutive integers, then $f_n = g_n$ for all $n$.*

**Theorem 9.** *For every $k$-counter machine accepting a bounded language with $m$ blocks and operating in time $t(n)$ there is an equivalent counter machine with $k + m$ counters operating in time $n + ct(n)$ for any constant $c > 0$.*

*Proof.* The strategy is to encode the input of a counter machine $M$ with $k$ counters on $m$ counters of a simulator $M'$ in a first stage and simulate the two-way machine $M$ with speed-up using the method suitable for one-way machines from the proofs of Theorems 1.1, 1.2, and 5.2 of [4] (the speed-up is stated in Theorem 5.2, but the compression technique is sketched in the proofs of the other results) .

For nondeterministic machines the encoding can be based on guessing the distribution of input segments on blocks. We describe in the following a method that works in the deterministiccase as well.

Let the accepted language be a subset of $w_1^* w_2^* \cdots w_m^*$. Note that in general the exponents $k_1, \ldots, k_m$ of $w_1, \ldots, w_m$ for a given input are not easily recognizable, since the borders between the factors might not be evident. We will show that an encoding of the input is nevertheless possible.

The encoding of the input will work in stages. At the end of stage $i$ the encoding covers at least the first $i$ blocks. Let $\mu = \max\{|w_j| \mid 1 \leq j \leq m\}$. At the start of stage $i$ simulator $M'$ reads $2\mu$ additional input symbols if possible (if the end of the input is reached, the suffix is recorded in the finite control). Machine $M'$ records this string $y$ in the finite control. Then for each conjugate $vu$ of $w_i = uv$ the input segment $y$ is compared to a prefix of length $2\mu$ of $(vu)^\omega$. If no match is found, the segment $y$ and its position is stored in the finite control and the next stage starts. If a match to some $vu$ is found, $M'$ assigns a counter to this $vu$, stores the number of copies of $vu$ within $y$ (including a trailing prefix of $vu$ if necessary) are recorded in the finite control, and then $M'$ continues to count the number of copies of $vu$ found in the input until the end of the input is reached or the next $|vu|$ symbols do not match $vu$. These $|vu|$ symbols are stored in the finite control. The process ends when the input is exhausted. Then $M'$ has stored an encoding of the input, which can be recovered by concatenating the segments stored in the finite control and the copies of the conjugates of the $w_i$.

We now argue that at the end of stage $i$ the encoding has reached the end of block $i$. Initially the claim holds vacuously. Suppose by induction that the claim holds for stage $i - 1$. The next $2\mu$ symbols are beyond block $i - 1$ and if they do not match a power of a conjugate, then the string is not embedded into a block. Thus it extends over the end of block $i$ and the claim holds. Otherwise a match between some $vu$ and $y$ is found. String $y$ is a factor of some $w_j^\omega$ and by the Fine and Wilf Result (Theorem 8) both are powers of the same $z$ since $2\mu \geq h + k - \gcd(h, k)$ with $h = |vu|$ and $k = |w_j|$. Therefore $M'$ is able to encode all of the copies of $w_j$ on the counter. Notice that $vu$ is not necessarily a conjugate of $w_j$. Thus the claim also holds in this case.

Since each stage requires at most one counter, the $m$ additional counters suffice.

After encoding the input, the two-way input-head of $M$ is simulated by $M'$ with the help of $m$ counters and its input-head, which is used as an initially empty counter measuring the distance to the right end-marker. Whenever the simulated head enters a block $i$, the simulator starts to decrement the corresponding counter and increment a counter available (since it has just been zero). The input head is simulated on $w_i$, where the position of the input head position modulo $|w_i|$ is kept in the finite control of $M'$. Also the assignment of counters to blocks is dynamic and stored in the finite control.

Now $M'$ is replaced by $M''$ with compressed counter contents and operating with speed-up according to the proof of Theorem 5.2 from [4]. For completeness we include a sketch here. In order to obtain a compression by a factor $c$, a counter value $m$ is split into a portion $r < 2c$ stored in the finite control and $m' = (m - r)//c$ stored on a counter. A decrement operation on the counter is applied to $r$ if $r > 0$, otherwise $m'$ is decremented and $r$ is set to $c - 1$. Similarly an increment operation is applied to $r$ if $r < 2c$, otherwise $m'$ is incremented and $r$ is set to $c$. Notice that at least another $c$ operations are carried out before the next update on $m'$. Finally $c$ consecutive operations are combined into a "macro" step. □

## 6  Discussion

The results presented have some technical consequences, that we outline in this section. Special cases of strictly bounded languages are languages over a single letter alphabet. Our simulation of heads by counters thus eliminates the need for hierarchy results separating $k+1$ bounded counters from $k$ bounded counters for deterministic devices with the help of single letter alphabet languages; the hierarchy for deterministic devices stated in Theorem 3 of [9] follows from the corresponding result for multi-head automata in Theorem 1 of [9].

In comparison with multi-head automata, counter machines appear to be affected by slight technical changes of the definition. There are, e.g., several natural ways to define counter machines with counters bounded by the input length [13]. One could simply require that the counters never overflow, with the drawback that this property is undecidable in general. Alternatively the machine could block in the case of overflow, acceptance then being based on the current state, a specific error condition could be signaled to the machine, with the counter being void, or the counter could simply remain unchanged. The latter model is clearly equivalent to the known concept of a *simple* multi-head automaton. All these variants, which seem to be slightly different in power, can easily be simulated with the help of heads and therefore coincide, at least for strictly bounded input.

**Acknowledgments.** I would like to thank Amir Ben-Amram and the anonymous referees for many helpful remarks. Thanks are due to A. C. Cem Say for a stimulating discussion about the time complexity of counter machines and bringing references [14,17] to my attention.

## References

1. Ben-Amram, A.M., Christensen, N.H., Simonsen, J.G.: Computational models with no linear speedup, Typescript (2011)
2. Ďuriš, P., Galil, Z.: Fooling a two way automaton or one pushdown store is better than one counter for two way machines. Theoretical Computer Science 21, 39–53 (1982)
3. Fine, N.J., Wilf, H.S.: Uniqueness theorems for periodic functions. Proc. Amer. Math. Soc. 16, 109–114 (1965)
4. Fischer, P.C., Meyer, A.R., Rosenberg, A.L.: Counter machines and counter languages. Mathematical Systems Theory 2, 265–283 (1968)
5. Greibach, S.A.: Remarks on the complexity of nondeterministic counter languages. Theoretical Computer Science 1, 269–288 (1976)
6. Hühne, M.: Linear speed-up does not hold on Turing machines with tree storages. Information Processing Letters 47, 313–318 (1993)
7. M. Li and P. Vitányi. An Introduction to Kolmogorov Complexity and its Applications. Springer (1993)

8. Minsky, M.L.: Recursive unsolvability of Post's problem of "tag" and other topics in theory of Turing machines. Annals of Mathematics 74, 437–455 (1961)
9. Monien, B.: Two-way multihead automata over a one-letter alphabet. R.A.I.R.O. — Informatique Théorique et Applications 14, 67–82 (1980)
10. Morita, K., Sugata, K., Umeo, H.: Computation complexity of $n$-bounded counter automaton and multidimensional rebound automaton. Systems Computers Controls 8, 80–87 (1977); Translated from Denshi Tsushin Gakkai Ronbunshi (IEICE of Japan Trans.) 60-D, 283–290 (1977) (Japanese)
11. Morita, K., Sugata, K., Umeo, H.: Computational complexity of n-bounded counter automaton and multi-dimensional rebound automaton. IEICE of Japan Trans. 60-E, 226–227 (1977); Abstract of [10]
12. Petersen, H.: Simulations by time-bounded counter machines. International Journal of Foundations of Computer Science 22, 395–409 (2011)
13. Ritchie, R.W., Springsteel, F.N.: Language recognition by marking automata. Information and Control 20, 313–330 (1972)
14. Cem Say, A.C., Yakaryilmaz, A.: Quantum counter automata (2011) (submitted for publication)
15. Sipser, M.: Introduction to the Theory of Computation, 2nd edn. Thomson (2006)
16. Sugata, K., Morita, K., Umeo, H.: The language accepted by an n-bounded multicounter automaton and its computing ability. Systems Computers Controls 8, 71–79 (1977); Translated from Denshi Tsushin Gakkai Ronbunshi (IEICE of Japan Trans.) 60-D, 275–282 (1977) (Japanese)
17. Yamasaki, T., Kobayashi, H., Imai, H.: Quantum versus deterministic counter automata. Theoretical Computer Science 334, 275–297 (2005)

# State Complexity of Projection and Quotient
# on Unranked Trees

Xiaoxue Piao and Kai Salomaa

School of Computing, Queen's University,
Kingston, Ontario K7L 3N6, Canada
{piao,ksalomaa}@cs.queensu.ca

**Abstract.** We consider projection and quotient operations on unranked
tree languages, and investigate their state complexities on deterministic
unranked tree automata. We give a tight upper bound on the number
of vertical states which is different than the known state complexity
of projection for string language. Since there are two ways to define
concatenation on trees, we define four different quotient operations on
trees and obtain tight bounds for each operation. The state complexity of
sequential bottom-quotient differs by a multiplicative factor $(n+1)$ from
the corresponding result of left-quotient on ordinary finite automata.

**Keywords:** unranked trees, deterministic tree automata, projection,
sequential (or parallel) bottom-quotient (or top-quotient), operational
state complexity.

## 1   Introduction

In recent years, a lot of work has been done on the descriptional state complexity
of finite automata and related structures [6–8, 24, 25]. While the corresponding
results for string languages are well known [24, 26], very few results have been
obtained for tree automata. Modern applications of tree automata, such as XML
processing, use unranked trees where the label of a node does not determine the
number of children [3, 12, 21]. Due to this reason, many problems turn out
to be essentially different than the corresponding problems for finite automata
operating on strings [24] or for tree automata operating on ranked trees [3, 5].
An early reference on regular unranked tree languages is [2].

Since there is no a priori restriction on the number of children of a node in unranked trees, the set of transitions of an unranked tree automaton is, in general,
infinite and the transitions are usually specified in terms of a regular language,
which is called a *horizontal language*. Thus, in addition to the finite set of *vertical states* used in the bottom-up computation, an unranked tree automaton
needs for each vertical state $q$ and input symbol $\sigma$ a finite string automaton to
recognize the horizontal language consisting of strings of states defining the transitions associated with $q$ and $\sigma$ [3]. The states of the finite string automata used
to recognize the horizontal languages are collectively called *horizontal states*.

M. Kutrib, N. Moreira, and R. Reis (Eds.): DCFS 2012, LNCS 7386, pp. 280–293, 2012.
© Springer-Verlag Berlin Heidelberg 2012

A deterministic unranked tree automaton where the horizontal languages are specified by deterministic finite automata is called a DTA(DFA), for short. It is possible that by adding redundant vertical states to a DTA(DFA) the total size of the automaton can be reduced. The above phenomenon is called a *state trade-off* and state trade-offs can be viewed as the cause for the hardness of DTA(DFA) minimization [11], and they make it hard to prove lower bounds for the total size of a DTA(DFA) recognizing a given regular tree language [15, 17]. It should be mentioned that, although the model discussed here is perhaps the commonly used definition of determinism for unranked tree automata [3], there are two alternative definitions of determinism that guarantee the uniqueness of the minimal automaton, the syntactically deterministic tree automata of [4, 19] and the step-wise tree automata considered in [3, 11]. The state complexity of transformations between different unranked tree automaton models has been studied in [11, 15].

The natural projection on strings is a mapping that erases from the string all *unobservable symbols*. The underlying alphabet $\Sigma$ is considered to be a disjoint union of observable and unobservable symbols. The natural projection could be extended to trees in (at least) two different ways. The first possibility is to delete from a given tree all subtrees where the root is labeled by an unobservable symbol. The second possible way is to delete each node $u$ labeled by an unobservable symbol and then "attach" the children of $u$ as the children of the parent of $u$ (the children will be listed after the left sibling of $u$ and before the right sibling of $u$). Note that both variants of the definition rely on the fact that we are dealing with unranked trees, i.e., the label of a node does not need to fix the number of children.

As will be illustrated later in Example 1 the latter definition of natural projection does not preserve regularity of tree languages. Hence we concentrate on the first mentioned variant of natural projection on trees. We give a tight upper bound on the number of vertical states that is different than the known state complexity $3 \cdot 2^{n-2} - 1$ of projection for string languages [9, 23]. We also give an exponential lower bound on the number of horizontal states by relying on existing bounds for the size of unambiguous finite automata [10]. Note that due to the existence of state trade-offs it is, in general, hard to prove lower bounds for the number of horizontal states and we need specialized techniques for this purpose.

As it is possible to extend the concatenation operation from strings to trees either as a sequential concatenation operation, where one occurrence of a leaf of $t_2$ with a designated label is replaced by $t_1$, or a parallel concatenation operation, where all occurrences of leaves of $t_2$ with a designated label are replaced by $t_1$ [16] (the tree concatenation considered in [3, 5] is the parallel concatenation), we can define sequential (respectively, parallel) top-quotient and sequential (respectively, parallel) bottom-quotient operations on trees. The operations correspond, respectively, to right- and left-quotient of string languages, when dealing with automata that process the input tree from the leaves to the root.

We investigate the state complexity of these four operations on deterministic unranked tree automata and obtain tight upper bounds for each operation. For a tree language $T$ recognized by an $n$ vertical state deterministic unranked tree automaton, the tight state complexity bound for the sequential bottom-quotient operation is $(n+1)2^n - 1$ which is of a different order of magnitude than the state complexity of left-quotient for automata operating on strings. Recall that the state complexity of left-quotient is $2^n - 1$ [24]. The upper bounds of the other three operations coincide with the corresponding bounds for string languages. To obtain tight upper bounds for the number of horizontal states will be a topic for future research.

## 2  Preliminaries

Here we recall some notations on unranked trees. For more information on tree automata see the electronic book by Comon et al. [3] or the handbook article by Gécseg and Steinby [5].

A *tree domain* is a prefix-closed subset $D$ of $\mathbb{N}^*$ such that always when $ui \in D$, $u \in \mathbb{N}^*$, $i \in \mathbb{N}$ and $1 \leq j < i$, then also $uj \in D$. The set of nodes of a tree $t$ is represented in the well-known way as a tree domain $\mathrm{dom}(t)$ and when the nodes are labeled by elements of alphabet $\Sigma$ the tree $t$ can be viewed as a mapping $\mathrm{dom}(t) \to \Sigma$. We consider unranked trees and hence the node label does not determine the number of children of the node. The set of unranked trees over an alphabet $\Sigma$ is $T_\Sigma$. For $t, r_1, \ldots, r_m \in T_\Sigma$ and $u_1, \ldots, u_m \in \mathrm{dom}(t)$, $m \geq 1$, $t(u_1 \leftarrow r_1, \ldots, u_m \leftarrow r_m)$ is the tree obtained from $t$ by replacing the subtree at node $u_i$ by $r_i$, $i = 1, \ldots, m$. For $L \subseteq T_\Sigma$, the Nerode-congruence of $L$ is defined by setting, for $t_1, t_2 \in T_\Sigma$,

$$t_1 \cong_L t_2 \ \text{ iff } \ [(\forall t \in T_\Sigma)(\forall u \in \mathrm{dom}(t))t(u \leftarrow t_1) \in L \Leftrightarrow t(u \leftarrow t_2) \in L].$$

We introduce the following notation for trees. For $i \geq 0$, $a \in \Sigma$ and $t \in T_\Sigma$, we denote by $a^i(t) = a(a(...a(t)...))$ a tree where on top of subtree $t$ there is a unary branch labeled by $a$'s. When $a \in \Sigma$, $w = b_1 b_2 ... b_n \in \Sigma^*$, we use $a(w)$ to denote a tree $a(b_1, b_2, ..., b_n)$. When $L$ is a set of strings, $a(L) = \{a(w) \mid w \in L\}$. The set of all $\Sigma$-trees, where exactly one leaf is labeled by a special symbol $x$ ($x \notin \Sigma$) is $T_\Sigma[x]$. For $t \in T_\Sigma[x]$ and $t' \in T_\Sigma$, $t(x \leftarrow t')$ denotes the tree obtained from $t$ by replacing the unique occurrence of variable $x$ by $t'$.

A *nondeterministic unranked tree automaton* is a tuple $A = (Q, \Sigma, \delta, F)$, where $Q$ is the finite set of states, $\Sigma$ is the alphabet labeling nodes of input trees, $F \subseteq Q$ is the set of final states, and $\delta$ is a mapping from $Q \times \Sigma$ to the subsets of $Q^*$ which satisfies the condition that, for each $q \in Q$, $\sigma \in \Sigma$, $\delta(q, \sigma)$ is a regular language. The language $\delta(q, \sigma)$ is called the *horizontal language* associated with $q$ and $\sigma$.

Intuitively, if a computation of $A$ has reached the children of a $\sigma$-labeled node $u$ in a sequence of states $q_1, q_2, \ldots, q_m$, the computation may nondeterministically assign a state $q$ to the node $u$ provided that $q_1 q_2 \cdots q_m \in \delta(q, \sigma)$. For $t \in T_\Sigma$, $t^A \subseteq Q$ denotes the set of states that in some bottom-up computation

$A$ may reach at the root of $t$. The *tree language recognized by* $A$ is defined as $L(A) = \{t \in T_\Sigma \mid t^A \cap F \neq \emptyset\}$.

For a tree automaton $A = (Q, \Sigma, \delta, F)$, we denote by $H^A_{q,\sigma}$, $q \in Q$, $\sigma \in \Sigma$, a nondeterministic finite automaton (NFA) on strings recognizing the horizontal language $\delta(q, \sigma)$. The NFA $H^A_{q,\sigma}$ is called a *horizontal NFA*, and states of different horizontal automata are called collectively *horizontal states*. We refer to the states of $Q$ that are used in the bottom-up computation as *vertical states*.

We define the *(state) size of* $A$, size($A$), as a pair of integers $[|Q|; n]$, where $n$ is the sum of the sizes of all horizontal automata $H^A_{q,\sigma}$ that recognize a nonempty language. When comparing sizes of automata, $[m_1; m_2] \geq [n_1; n_2]$ means $m_i \geq n_i$, $i = 1, 2$.

A tree automaton $A = (Q, \Sigma, \delta, F)$ is said to be *deterministic* if for $\sigma \in \Sigma$ and any two states $q_1 \neq q_2$, $\delta(q_1, \sigma) \cap \delta(q_2, \sigma) = \emptyset$. The above condition guarantees that the state assigned by $A$ to a node $u$ of an input tree is unique (but $A$ need not assign any state to $u$ if the computation becomes blocked below $u$). We use DTA(DFA) (respectively, NTA(NFA)) to denote the class of deterministic (respectively, nondeterministic) tree automata where each horizontal language is specified by a DFA (respectively, an NFA).

We denote by $t(u \leftarrow q)$ the tree over alphabet $\Sigma \cup Q$ that is obtained from $t$ by labeling the node $u$ by $q$. We say that states $q_1$ and $q_2$ of a DTA(DFA) $A$ are *equivalent* if for any $t \in T_\Sigma$ and any leaf $u$ of $t$, the computation of $A$ accepts $t(u \leftarrow q_1)$ if and only if it accepts $t(u \leftarrow q_2)$. The condition means that the states $q_1$ and $q_2$ are equivalent in terms of the vertical computation of $A$, however, the horizontal languages associated with $q_1$ and $q_2$ need not coincide.

The extension of the Nerode congruence is called the top-congruence in [2], and the corresponding definition for tree languages over ranked alphabets can be found in [5].

## 2.1  Projection on Unranked Trees

To begin with we recall the definition of the projection operation on strings as studied in [9, 23]. For an alphabet $\Sigma$, $\Sigma_P \subseteq \Sigma$, and a string $w = \sigma_0\sigma_1 \ldots \sigma_n \in \Sigma^*$, a natural projection $P_{\Sigma \to \Sigma_P}$ is defined as: $P_{\Sigma \to \Sigma_P}(w) = \sigma'_0\sigma'_1 \ldots \sigma'_n$ such that

$$\sigma'_i = \begin{cases} \sigma_i, \text{ if } \sigma_i \in \Sigma_P; \\ \epsilon, \text{ otherwise.} \end{cases}$$

Now we define projection operation on trees. For alphabets $\Sigma$ and $\Sigma_P \subseteq \Sigma$, all $\Sigma$-labeled ($\Sigma_P$-labeled respectively) trees are denoted $T_\Sigma$ ($T_{\Sigma_P}$ respectively). Symbols in $\Sigma \backslash \Sigma_P$ are called unobservable symbols. A projection on trees is a mapping $\mathcal{M}_{\Sigma \to \Sigma_P} : T_\Sigma \to T_{\Sigma_P}$. When $\Sigma$ and $\Sigma_P$ are understood from the context, we denote $\mathcal{M}_{\Sigma \to \Sigma_P}$ simply by $\mathcal{M}$. $\mathcal{M}$ is inductively defined as below.

- For a tree $\sigma \in T_\Sigma$ of height zero[1],

$$\mathcal{M}(\sigma) = \begin{cases} \sigma, & \text{if } \sigma \in \Sigma_P; \\ undefined, & \text{if } \sigma \in \Sigma \backslash \Sigma_P. \end{cases}$$

---

[1] We use the convention that the height of a leaf node is zero.

- For a tree $t = \sigma(t_1,\ldots,t_n)$, let the sequence $t_{i_1},\ldots,t_{i_k}$, $1 \leq i_1 < i_2 < \ldots < i_k \leq n$, consist of trees $t_j$, where $\mathcal{M}(t_j)$ is defined.

$$\mathcal{M}(t) = \begin{cases} \sigma(\mathcal{M}(t_{i_1}),\ldots,\mathcal{M}(t_{i_k})), & \text{if } \sigma \in \Sigma_P; \\ undefined, & \text{otherwise.} \end{cases}$$

The projection operation is extended to trees by deleting from a given tree all subtrees where the root is labeled by an unobservable symbol, and the definition relies on the fact that we are dealing with unranked trees.

We note that it is also possible to define the projection on trees in another way as follows, denoted by $\mathcal{M}'_{\Sigma \to \Sigma_P}$.

- For a tree $\sigma \in T_\Sigma$ of height zero,

$$\mathcal{M}'(\sigma) = \begin{cases} \sigma, & \text{if } \sigma \in \Sigma_P; \\ undefined, & \text{if } \sigma \in \Sigma \backslash \Sigma_P; \end{cases}$$

- For a tree $t = \sigma(t_1,\ldots,t_n)$, let the sequence $t_{i_1},\ldots,t_{i_k}$, $1 \leq i_1 < i_2 < \ldots < i_k \leq n$, consist of trees $t_j$, where $\mathcal{M}'(t_j)$ is defined,

$$\mathcal{M}'(t) = \begin{cases} \sigma(\mathcal{M}'(t_{i_1}),\ldots,\mathcal{M}'(t_{i_k})), & \text{if } \sigma \in \Sigma_P; \\ \mathcal{M}'(t_{i_1}),\ldots,\mathcal{M}'(t_{i_k}), & \text{otherwise.} \end{cases}$$

When the root node of $t$ is labeled by a symbol that is not in $\Sigma_P$, by the definition of $\mathcal{M}'_{\Sigma \to \Sigma_P}$, the root node labeled by $\sigma$ of $t$ is deleted and the children of $t$ are kept as a sequence of trees $\mathcal{M}'(t_{i_1}),\ldots,\mathcal{M}'(t_{i_k})$. This sequence of trees become the children of $t$'s parent, and are listed between the left sibling and the right sibling of $t$. However, this definition does not preserve regularity as shown in Example 1.

*Example 1.* Consider $\Sigma = \{a,b,c,d\}$, $\Sigma_P = \{a,b,d\}$, and $T = \bigcup_{i \geq 0} f_i$ is inductively defined as,

- $t_0 = c(a,c,b)$,
- for $i \geq 1$, $t_{i+1} = c(a,t_i,b)$,
- for $i \geq 0$, $f_i = d(t_i)$.

We get $\mathcal{M}'_{\Sigma \to \Sigma_P}(T) = \{d(a^i b^i) \mid i \geq 1\}$, which is not regular.

## 2.2  Quotient

We need to define concatenation for unranked trees before we can define quotient operation. Concatenation of strings can be extended to trees as a sequential operation, where one occurrence of a leaf with a given label is replaced by a tree, or as a parallel operation, where all occurrences of a leaf with a given label are replaced [14, 16]. For $\sigma \in \Sigma$ and $T_1 \subseteq T_\Sigma$, $t_2 \in T_\Sigma$, we define their *sequential $\sigma$-concatenation*

$$T_1 \cdot^s_\sigma t_2 = \{\, t_2(u \leftarrow t_1) \mid u \in \text{leaf}(t_2,\sigma), t_1 \in T_1 \,\}. \tag{1}$$

That is, $T_1 \cdot_\sigma^s t_2$ is the set of trees obtained from $t_2$ by replacing one occurrence of a leaf labeled by $\sigma$ with some tree of $T_1$. In order to get concatenation of individual trees we can choose $T_1$ as a singleton set.

The *parallel $\sigma$-concatenation* of $T_1$ and $t_2$ is

$$T_1 \cdot_\sigma^p t_2 = t_2(\text{leaf}(t_2, \sigma) \leftarrow T_1). \tag{2}$$

That is, $T_1 \cdot_\sigma^p t_2$ is the set of trees obtained from $t_2$ by replacing every occurrence of a leaf labeled by $\sigma$ with some tree of $T_1$. Note that when $T_1 = \{t_1\}$ consists of one tree, $t_1 \cdot_\sigma^p t_2$ is an individual tree while $t_1 \cdot_\sigma^s t_2$ is a set of trees. In the case where no leaf of $t_2$ is labeled by $\sigma$, $t_1 \cdot_\sigma^s t_2 = \emptyset$ and $t_1 \cdot_\sigma^p t_2 = t_2$.

Note that in both definitions $T_1 \cdot_\sigma^s t_2$ and $T_1 \cdot_\sigma^p t_2$, the resulting trees are obtained from $t_2$ by replacing a leaf node (leaf nodes) with some tree in $T_1$. This is done so to keep the correspondence with strings. A string automaton processing concatenation of $L_1 \cdot L_2$ reads a string in $L_1$ first and then a string in $L_2$. When processing a tree $t_1 \cdot_\sigma^p t_2$ (or $t_1 \cdot_\sigma^s t_2$), a bottom-up tree automaton processes first $t_1$ and then $t_2$.

Based on parallel and sequential concatenation, we define four different quotient operations on unranked trees.

**Definition 1 (Sequential $\sigma$-top-quotient).** *The sequential $\sigma$-top-quotient of a tree language $T$ with respect to a tree language $T'$ is defined as:*

$$T' \top_\sigma^s T = \{t \mid \exists t' \in T', t \cdot_\sigma^s t' \in T\}.$$

**Definition 2 (Sequential $\sigma$-bottom-quotient).** *The sequential $\sigma$-bottom-quotient of a tree language $T$ with respect to a tree language $T'$ is defined as:*

$$T \bot_\sigma^s T' = \{t \mid \exists t' \in T', t' \cdot_\sigma^s t \in T\}.$$

Before we introduce the definition of parallel $\sigma$-top-quotient, we define $tuples(t' \top_\sigma^p T)$ to consist of all $m$-tuples of trees $(r_1, \ldots, r_m)$ such that

$$t'(u_1 \leftarrow r_1, \ldots, u_m \leftarrow r_m) \in T \text{ where } leaf(t', \sigma) = \{u_1, \ldots, u_m\}.$$

The parallel $\sigma$-top-quotient of a tree language $T$ with respect to a single tree $t'$, denoted $t' \top_\sigma^p T$, is defined to consist of all trees that occur as a component in some $m$-tuple in $tuples(t' \top_\sigma^p T)$. The definition is extended to a set of trees as below:

**Definition 3 (Parallel $\sigma$-top-quotient).** *The parallel $\sigma$-top-quotient of a tree language $T$ with respect to a tree language $T'$ is defined as:*

$$T' \top_\sigma^p T = \bigcup_{t' \in T'} t' \top_\sigma^p T.$$

**Definition 4 (Parallel $\sigma$-bottom-quotient).** *The parallel $\sigma$-bottom-quotient of a tree language $T$ with respect to a tree language $T'$ is defined as:*

$$T \bot_\sigma^p T' = \{t \in T_\Sigma \mid T' \cdot_\sigma^p t \cap T \neq \emptyset\}.$$

When considering computations that process a tree in the bottom-up direction, the top-quotient can be viewed as an extension of right-quotient from strings to trees, and similarly, the bottom-quotient extends the left-quotient operation from strings to trees. When $\sigma \in \Sigma$ and the method of concatenation are understood from the context, we simply call the operations top-quotient and bottom-quotient and write $T'\top T$ (respectively $T \bot T'$) in place of $T'\top_\sigma^p T$ and $T'\top_\sigma^s T$ (respectively $T \bot_\sigma^p T'$ and $T \bot_\sigma^s T'$).

## 2.3    Auxiliary Results on String Languages

We present the following technical lemma on string languages that will be used to establish the upper bound for the state complexity of projection.

Let $A = (Q, \Sigma, \delta, s, F)$ be a DFA. We say that an NFA $B$ with $\epsilon$-transitions is an $\epsilon$-*variant of* $A$ if $B$ is obtained from $A$ by adding an $\epsilon$-transition between some pairs of states $s_i$ and $s_j$ that are connected by a real transition on input symbol $\sigma$ in $A$. The NFA $B$ retains all the transitions of the DFA $A$ and has additional $\epsilon$-transitions as described above. The set of all $\epsilon$-variants of $A$ is denoted $\mathcal{E}(A)$.

**Lemma 1.** *If a DFA $C$ has $n$ states, then any NFA in $\mathcal{E}(C)$ has an equivalent DFA with at most $\frac{3}{4}2^n - 1$ states and this upper bound is tight.*

## 2.4    Lower Bound Technique

We introduce the following technique for establishing lower bounds on the number of horizontal states in tree automata. Lower bounds for the number of horizontal states that rely on the size of unambiguous NFAs were used also in [18], however, the details of Lemma 2 below differ from the technique used in [18]. Before we start, recall that an NFA is unambiguous if it has at most one accepting computation on any string [10, 13].

Let $L$ be a regular tree language over $\Sigma$. We say that $\sigma \in \Sigma$ is a *unique height-one label for $L$* if

(i) in trees of $L$, $\sigma$ occurs only as a label of nodes of height one, and,
(ii) for any $\tau_1, \tau_2 \in \Sigma, \tau_1 \neq \tau_2$, that label leaves below a height one node $u$ labeled by $\sigma$, $\tau_1$ and $\tau_2$ are inequivalent with respect to the Nerode congruence of the tree language $L$.

**Lemma 2.** *Let $A = (Q_A, \Sigma, \delta_A, F_A)$ be a DTA(DFA) with minimal number of vertical states for tree language $L$ and let $B = (Q_B, \Sigma, \delta_B, F_B)$ be an arbitrary DTA(DFA) for $L$.*

*Suppose that $\sigma \in \Sigma$ is a unique height-one label for $L$. Then for any $q \in Q_A$,*

$$\sum_{p \in [q]_B} |H_{p,\sigma}^B|$$

*is greater or equal than the size of the smallest unambiguous NFA for $L(H_{q,\sigma}^A)$. (Following [10] we allow here an NFA to have multiple initial states.)*

*Proof.* Since $\sigma$ is a unique height-one label for $L$, both $A$ and $B$ assign a unique state to any leaf labeled by $\tau$ that in some tree of $L$ may occur below a height-one node labeled by $\sigma$. Denote by $\Omega_\sigma$ the set of symbols that in trees of $L$ may label a leaf occurring below a node labeled by $\sigma$. Let $f_\sigma$ be the bijection

$$P_{\text{states\_below\_}\sigma} =$$
$$\{s \in Q_B \mid \varepsilon \in \delta_B(s,\tau), \tau \in \Omega_\sigma\} \to \{r \in Q_A \mid \varepsilon \in \delta_A(r,\tau), \tau \in \Omega_\sigma\}$$

that for each $\tau \in \Omega_\sigma$, maps the unique $s \in Q_B$ such that $\varepsilon \in \delta_B(s,\tau)$ to the unique $r \in Q_A$ such that $\varepsilon \in \delta_A(r,\tau)$.

The DTA(DFA) of a regular tree language with a minimal number of vertical states is unique. By considering the usual equivalence relation among vertical states of $B$, as defined in Section 2, we see that the states of $B$ can be partitioned into equivalence classes, each consisting pairwise equivalent states (in terms of the vertical computation) that were used to replace one vertical state of $A$. For a state $q$ of $A$, we denote by $[q]_B$ the set of states of $B$ that correspond to $q$ in this way.

Let $q \in Q_A$ be arbitrary (such that $\delta_A(q,\sigma) \neq \emptyset$). Let $t = \sigma(\tau_1, \ldots, \tau_m)$ be a tree of height one with root labeled by $\sigma$. For any $p \in [q]_B$, if $B$ reaches the root of $t$ in state $p$ then $A$ reaches the root of $t$ in state $q$, and conversely if $A$ reaches the root of $t$ in state $q$ then $B$ reaches the root of $t$ in some of the states of $[q]_B$. This means that from the DFAs $H^B_{p,\sigma}$, $p \in [q]_B$, we can construct for the language $\delta_A(q,\sigma)$ a DFA $C$ with multiple initial states simply by taking their disjoint union and replacing each transition labeled by $s \in P_{\text{states\_below\_}\sigma}$ by $f_\sigma(s)$. Since $B$ is deterministic, the languages $L(H^B_{p_1,\sigma})$ and $L(H^B_{p_2,\sigma})$, $p_1, p_2 \in [q]_B$, $p_1 \neq p_2$, are disjoint. This means that for $w \in Q_A^*$, $C$ has at most one accepting computation on $w$ and $C$ is an unambiguous NFA (with multiple initial states). □

Here we develop a lower bound criterion that, roughly speaking, from the horizontal languages associated with an input symbol $\sigma$ and $q_1, \ldots, q_k$ constructs an unambiguous finite automaton for the horizontal language of $A$ associated with $q$ and $\sigma$. Then if $A$ is chosen to be the DTA(DFA) with the minimal number of vertical states (which is unique), we get a lower bound for the total size of horizontal DFAs associated, respectively, with $\sigma$ and $q_i$, $i = 1, \ldots, k$.

Lemma 2 gives a lower bound condition for the number horizontal states in terms of the size of a smallest unambiguous NFA for the horizontal language. A useful lower bound condition for the size of unambiguous NFAs has been given by [22], for a good presentation of this result see also [10]. We denote the *rank* of a (square) matrix $M$ as rank($M$).

**Theorem 1.** [22] *Given a regular language $L$ and strings $x_i$, $y_i$ for $i = 1, \ldots, n$, let $M$ be an $n \times n$ matrix such that $M[x_i, y_i] = 1$ if $x_i y_i \in L$, and $0$ otherwise. Then any unambiguous NFA for $L$ has at least rank($M$) states.*

## 3    State Complexity of Projection on Unranked Trees

In this section we present a lower bound for the vertical and horizontal state complexity of the projection operation on unranked tree languages. The lower bound for the number of vertical states coincides with the upper bound and is different than the known state complexity of projection of string languages [9, 23]. The lower bound for the number of horizontal states is exponential, however, it does not coincide with the known upper bound.

## 3.1    Upper Bound for Projection on Unranked Trees

Given a DTA(DFA) $A$ we construct an NTA(NFA) $C$ recognizing the language $\mathcal{M}(L(A))$ and determinizing $C$ then gives an upper bound for the state complexity of projection. For readability it is useful to give the construction in two stages. First we construct an DTA(DFA) $B$ that has two copies of each state of $A$, and after that construct $C$. Note that half of the states of $B$ can be omitted.

Given $\Sigma_P \subseteq \Sigma$ and a DTA(DFA) $A = (Q, \Sigma, \delta, F)$, where the horizontal language associated with $\sigma \in \Sigma$ and $q \in Q$ is recognized by a DFA $H_{\sigma,q}^A$ with size $m_{q,\sigma}$, we can construct an equivalent DTA(DFA) $B = (P, \Sigma_P, \gamma, E)$ as follows. As the set of state of $B$ we choose

$$P = \{q^{\Sigma \backslash \Sigma_P}, q^{\Sigma_P} \mid q \in Q\}.$$

Define a finite substitution $h \colon Q^* \to P^*$ by setting $h(q) = \{q^{\Sigma \backslash \Sigma_P}, q^{\Sigma_P}\}$. Now we define the horizontal languages of $B$ by setting, for $q \in Q$ and $\sigma \in \Sigma_P$:

- $\gamma(q^{\Sigma_P}, \sigma) = h(\delta(q, \sigma))$,
- $\gamma(q^{\Sigma \backslash \Sigma_P}, \sigma) = \emptyset$.

Similarly for $q \in Q$ and $\sigma \in \Sigma \backslash \Sigma_P$ we set

- $\gamma(q^{\Sigma \backslash \Sigma_P}, \sigma) = h(\delta(q, \sigma))$,
- $\gamma(q^{\Sigma_P}, \sigma) = \emptyset$.

States $q^{\Sigma \backslash \Sigma_P}, q^{\Sigma_P}$ are final if $q \in F$.

The DTA(DFA) $B$ is obtained from $A$ by doubling the number of states. The computation of $B$ simply simulates the computation of $A$ and "remembers" (using the superscript of the states) whether the current node is labeled by a symbol of $\Sigma_P$ or of $\Sigma \backslash \Sigma_P$.

The horizontal language in $B$ can be recognized by a DFA constructed from $H_{\sigma,q}^A$ by replacing each transition labeled with $q$ by a transition labeled by $q^{\Sigma_P}$ and $q^{\Sigma \backslash \Sigma_P}$. Thus, the size of the horizontal DFA associated with $q^{\Sigma_P}, \sigma$ is the same as the DFA associated with $q, \sigma$. That is $m_{q,\sigma}$.

Now we construct an NTA(NFA) $C$ recognizing $\mathcal{M}(L(A))$ from $B$ as follows.

Step 1 Delete all the horizontal languages associated with $q^{\Sigma \backslash \Sigma_P}$,
Step 2 Replace by $\epsilon$ each occurrence of $q^{\Sigma \backslash \Sigma_P}$ in the remaining horizontal languages.

Since all the horizontal languages associated with $q^{\Sigma \backslash \Sigma_P}$ are deleted, $C$ has $|Q|$ vertical states. Since each horizontal NFA in $C$ is an $\epsilon$-variant of a horizontal DFA in $B$, according to Lemma 1, each horizontal NFA in $C$ has an equivalent DFA with at most $\frac{3}{4} 2^{m_{\sigma,q}} - 1$ states.

To convert the NTA(NFA) $C$ to a DTA(DFA) $D$, a powerset construction is applied to the vertical states of $C$ and $\mathcal{P}(Q)$ is the set of states in $D$. As we do not require tree automata to be complete, $\emptyset$ is omitted from the set of states in $D$. For the horizontal states, the horizontal DFA in $D$ must simulate all the NFAs in $C$ to get disjoint horizontal languages. (The details of determinizing an NTA(NFA) please refer to Lemma 4.4 in [15].) The size of a horizontal DFA associated with a state in $\mathcal{P}(Q)$ and $\beta \in \Sigma_P$ in $D$ is at most $\prod_{q \in Q}(\frac{3}{4}2^{m_{\beta,q}} - 1)$. Thus, we have the following lemma.

**Lemma 3.** *Given $\Sigma_P \subseteq \Sigma$ and a DTA(DFA) $A = (Q, \Sigma, \delta, F)$, where the horizontal language associated with $\sigma \in \Sigma$ and $q \in Q$ is recognized by a DFA with size $m_{q,\sigma}$, we can construct a DTA(DFA) $D$ recognizing $\mathcal{M}(L(A))$ with size at most*

$$size(D) \leq [\, 2^{|Q|} - 1;\ 2^{|Q|} \cdot (\sum_{\beta \in \Sigma_P} \prod_{q \in Q}(\frac{3}{4}2^{m_{\beta,q}} - 1))\,]. \tag{3}$$

## 3.2   A Lower Bound Construction

We present a tree language whose projection needs exactly the claimed number of vertical states in equation (3). The lower bound for the number of horizontal states is also exponential but does not exactly match the numbers in (3).

Let $\Sigma = \{a, b, c, d, e, f, g\}$ and $\Sigma_P = \{a, b, d, e, g\}$. Consider the tree language

$$T = \{k(g(c^i f^j l)) \mid 1 \leq i \leq n,\ 1 \leq j \leq m,\ k \in K_i,\ l \in L_j\}, \tag{4}$$

where $K_i$ and $L_j$ are the string languages recognized by the DFAs $C_i$ and $M_j$ shown in Figure 1(a) and 1(b), respectively. The final states are the odd numbered states. All the $M_j$'s ($C_i$, respectively) are the same except that each $M_j$ ($C_i$, respectively) has a unique initial state $j$ ($i$, respectively). In a tree of $T$, the nodes of height one are always labeled by $g$. The sequence $k$ of labels of nodes from height two to the root forms a string in $K_i$, if the number of leading $c$'s in the sequence of leaves is $i$. The sequence of leaves of a tree of $T$ contains after the initial $c$'s some number $j$ of symbols $f$ and after that a sequence in $\{e, d\}^*$ that is accepted by the DFA $M_j$ determined by $j$.

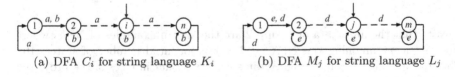

(a) DFA $C_i$ for string language $K_i$        (b) DFA $M_j$ for string language $L_j$

**Fig. 1.** DFAs $C_i$ and $M_j$ (final states not shown)

**Lemma 4.** *$T$ can be recognized by a DTA(DFA) $A$ with $size(A) = [\, n+4;\ 2m + 5n + 5\,]$.*

*Proof.* Choose the DTA(DFA) $A = (\{q_1, \ldots, q_n, q_c, q_d, q_e, q_f\}, \Sigma, \delta, F)$ where $\delta$ is defined as follows.

- $\delta(q_c, c) = \epsilon,$     $\delta(q_d, d) = \epsilon,$     $\delta(q_e, e) = \epsilon,$     $\delta(q_f, f) = \epsilon,$
- $\delta(q_i, g) = q_c^i q_f^j \phi(L_j), 1 \leq i \leq n, 1 \leq j \leq m,$
- $\delta(q_{i+1}, a) = q_i, 1 \leq i \leq n-1,$     $\delta(q_1, a) = q_n,$
- $\delta(q_i, b) = q_i, 2 \leq i \leq n,$     $\delta(q_2, b) = q_1.$

Above $\phi$ is a mapping $\phi : (d, e)^* \rightarrow (q_d, q_e)^*$ defined as $\phi(d) = q_d$ and $\phi(e) = q_e$. The set of final states contains all the odd numbered states. A DFA for the horizontal language needs $n+1$ states to count $c$'s, $m$ states to count $f$'s and $m$ states to check whether the sequences of leaf nodes belong to $L_j$. Two states are needed for each horizontal language $\{q_i\}$. Additionally $A$ needs four horizontal states to recognize the four horizontal languages each consisting only of the empty string $\epsilon$.     □

The prefixes $q_c^i$ in the horizontal languages are used to make the vertical computation deterministic. The prefixes $q_f^j$ are used to make the horizontal languages disjoint. After the projection, all nodes labeled by $c$ and $f$ are deleted, and we note that

$$\mathcal{M}(T) = \{k(g(l)) \mid k \in \bigcup_{i=1}^{n} K_i, l \in \bigcup_{j=1}^{m} L_j\}, \tag{5}$$

In trees of $\mathcal{M}(T)$, the sequence $k$ of labels of nodes from height two to the root forms a string in $\bigcup_{i=1}^{n} K_i$, and the sequence $l$ of leaf nodes forms a string in $\bigcup_{j=1}^{m} L_j$. The NFAs $C$ and $M$ recognizing $\bigcup_{i=1}^{n} K_i$ and $\bigcup_{j=1}^{m} L_j$ are shown in Figure 2(a) and 2(b), respectively. Final states are the odd numbered states.

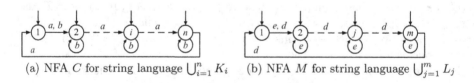

(a) NFA $C$ for string language $\bigcup_{i=1}^{n} K_i$     (b) NFA $M$ for string language $\bigcup_{j=1}^{m} L_j$

**Fig. 2.** NFAs $C$ and $M$ with multiple initial states (final states not shown)

Note that the automata of Figure 2 are the known examples of NFAs where any equivalent unambiguous NFA needs an exponential number of states [10]. The tree language $T$ was "designed" in such a way that in trees of the projected language $\mathcal{M}(T)$ both the set of strings labeling the vertical branch and the sequences of leaves defining the horizontal language have a small NFA while requiring a large unambiguous NFA.

**Lemma 5.** *For any DTA(DFA) $B$ recognizing the tree language $\mathcal{M}(T)$ we have*

$$\text{size}(B) \geq [2^n - 1; 2^m - 1].$$

*Proof.* Using Theorem 1, Leung [10] shows that any unambiguous NFA recognizing $L(M)$ ($L(C)$, respectively) has at least $2^m - 1$ ($2^n - 1$, respectively) states. This means any DFA for $L(C)$ has at least $2^n - 1$ states. Thus, $B$ has at least $2^n - 1$ vertical states. Now consider the number of horizontal states required by $B$. Since the symbol $g$ always labels a node of height one, it is obvious that $g$ is a *unique height-one label*. The leaves below $g$ spell out a word in $\bigcup_{j=1}^m L_j$. According to Lemma 2, the total size of all horizontal DFAs associated with $g$ in $B$ is greater or equal than the size of the smallest unambiguous NFA for the horizontal language $\bigcup_{j=1}^m L_j$, which is $L(C)$. This means $B$ needs at least $2^m - 1$ horizontal states.                                                                         □

From Lemma 3, 5 and 4, we have the following theorem.

**Theorem 2.** *There exist tree languages $T_{m,n}$ that can be recognized by a DTA(DFA) $A$ with* $size(A) = [\, n+4;\ 2m + 5n + 5\,]$, *and for any DTA(DFA) $B$ recognizing $\mathcal{M}(T_{m,n})$, $size(B) \geq [\, 2^n - 1;\ 2^m - 1\,]$.*

The lower bound above gives an exponential blow-up for both the number of vertical states and of horizontal states. Furthermore, the lower bound on the number of vertical states coincide with the upper bound.

Next we present another lower bound construction for the state complexity of projection that is a consequence of results from [15]. The estimates for the sums and products of the first $n$ primes can be found in [1].

**Proposition 1.** *Let $p_1, \ldots, p_n$ be prime numbers. There exist tree languages $T_n$ that can be recognized by a DTA(DFA) $A$ with*

$$size(A) = \left[\, n+2;\ (\sum_{i=1}^n p_i) + n^2 + 2n - 1\,\right],$$

*and for any DTA(DFA) $B$ recognizing $\mathcal{M}(T_n)$,*

$$size(B) \geq \left[\, 2^n - 1;\ (2^n - 1) \cdot \prod_{i=1}^n p_i\,\right].$$

Note that especially when the horizontal size of the original DFA is much larger than the number of vertical states, that is, in the statement of Theorem 2 $m >> n$, the lower bound for the number of horizontal states given by Theorem 2 is considerably better than the corresponding bound given by Proposition 1. When in the original DTA(DFA) the size of the horizontal DFA associated with each vertical state is small (compared to $n$), the lower bound from Proposition 1 is often better.

Note that due to the possibility of having state trade-offs, it is, in general, hard to prove lower bounds for the number of horizontal states in a DTA(DFA). The specialized techniques in Proposition 1 (actually Theorem 4.1 of [15]) and here in Lemma 5 were needed to establish that the number of horizontal states cannot be reduced by introducing additional vertical states.

# 4   State Complexity of Quotient Operations

In this section we establish upper bounds for the state complexity of sequential (parallel) top-quotient and sequential (parallel) bottom-quotient operations that are tight for the numbers of vertical states. The state complexity bound for sequential bottom-quotient is of a different order of magnitude than the corresponding state complexity bound for left-quotient of string languages.

We start with sequential bottom-quotient operation.

**Theorem 3.** *For any integer $n \geq 1$, $(n+1)2^n - 1$ vertical states are necessary and sufficient in the worst case for a deterministic unranked tree automaton to accept sequential bottom-quotient of the tree language recognized by an $n$ vertical states deterministic unranked tree automaton w.r.t. an arbitrary tree language $T'$.*

Note that the bound for sequential bottom-quotient differs, roughly, by a multiplicative factor $n+1$ from the corresponding result for ordinary finite automata. The precise state complexity of left-quotient for ordinary finite automata is $2^n - 1$ [26].

We present the following theorem for sequential top-quotient operation on unranked tree automata.

**Theorem 4.** *For any integer $n \geq 1$, $n$ vertical states are necessary and sufficient in the worst case for a deterministic unranked tree automaton to accept the sequential top-quotient of the tree language recognized by an $n$ vertical states deterministic unranked tree automaton $A$ with respect to an arbitrary tree language $T'$, $T' \top_\sigma L(A)$, $\sigma \in \Sigma$.*

It is easy to see that the upper bound and the lower bound in Theorem 4 also work for parallel top-quotient on trees. Here we only present a theorem for parallel bottom-quotient.

**Theorem 5.** *For any integer $n \geq 1$, $2^n - 1$ vertical states are necessary and sufficient in the worst case for a deterministic unranked tree automaton to accept parallel bottom-quotient of the tree language recognized by an $n$ vertical states deterministic unranked tree automaton w.r.t. an arbitrary tree language $T'$.*

# References

1. Bach, E., Shallit, J.: Algorithmic number theory, vol. I. MIT Press (1996)
2. Brüggemann-Klein, A., Murata, M., Wood, D.: Regular tree and regular hedge languages over unranked alphabets. HKUST Technical report (2001)
3. Comon, H., Dauchet, M., Gilleron, R., Jacquemard, F., Lugiez, D., Löding, C., Tison, S., Tommasi, M.: Tree Automata Techniques and Applications (2007), electronic book, tata.gforge.inria.fr
4. Cristau, J., Löding, C., Thomas, W.: Deterministic Automata on Unranked Trees. In: Liśkiewicz, M., Reischuk, R. (eds.) FCT 2005. LNCS, vol. 3623, pp. 68–79. Springer, Heidelberg (2005)

5. Gécseg, F., Steinby, M.: Tree languages. In: Rozenberg, G., Salomaa, A. (eds.) Handbook of Formal Languages, vol. III, pp. 1–68. Springer (1997)
6. Gruber, H., Holzer, M.: Tight Bounds on the Descriptional Complexity of Regular Expressions. In: Diekert, V., Nowotka, D. (eds.) DLT 2009. LNCS, vol. 5583, pp. 276–287. Springer, Heidelberg (2009)
7. Holzer, M., Kutrib, M.: Nondeterministic finite automata – Recent results on the descriptional and computational complexity. Internat. J. Foundations Comput. Sci. 20, 563–580 (2009)
8. Holzer, M., Kutrib, M.: Descriptional and computational complexity of finite automata — A survey. Inf. Comput. 209, 456–470 (2011)
9. Jirásková, G., Masopust, T.: State Complexity of Projected Languages. In: Holzer, M., Kutrib, M., Pighizzini, G. (eds.) DCFS 2011. LNCS, vol. 6808, pp. 198–211. Springer, Heidelberg (2011)
10. Leung, H.: Descriptional complexity of NFA of different ambiguity. International Journal of Foundations of Computer Science (16), 975–984 (2005)
11. Martens, W., Niehren, J.: On the minimization of XML schemas and tree automata for unranked trees. J. Comput. System Sci. 73, 550–583 (2007)
12. Neven, F.: Automata theory for XML researchers. SIGMOD Record (31), 39–46 (2002)
13. Okhotin, A.: Unambiguous Finite Automata over a Unary Alphabet. In: Hliněný, P., Kučera, A. (eds.) MFCS 2010. LNCS, vol. 6281, pp. 556–567. Springer, Heidelberg (2010)
14. Piao, X.: State complexity of tree automata. PhD thesis, School of Computing, Queen's University (2011)
15. Piao, X., Salomaa, K.: Transformations between different models of unranked bottom-up tree automata. Fundamenta Informaticae (109), 405–424 (2011)
16. Piao, X., Salomaa, K.: State complexity of concatenation of regular tree languages. Theoretical Computer Science (accepted for publication), doi:10.1016/j.tcs.2011.12.048
17. Piao, X., Salomaa, K.: State trade-offs in unranked tree automata. In: Holzer, M., Kutrib, M., Pighizzini, G. (eds.) DCFS 2011. LNCS, vol. 6808, pp. 261–274. Springer, Heidelberg (2011)
18. Piao, X., Salomaa, K.: Lower bounds for the size of deterministic unranked tree automata. Theoretical Computer Science, doi:10.1016/j.tcs.2012.03.043
19. Raeymaekers, S., Bruynooghe, M.: Minimization of finite unranked tree automata (2004) (manuscript)
20. Rozenberg, G., Salomaa, A.: Handbook of Formal Languages, vol. I–III. Springer (1997)
21. Schwentick, T.: Automata for XML. J. Comput. System Sci. (73), 289–315 (2007)
22. Schmidt, E.M.: Succinctness of descriptions of context-free, regular and finite languages. PhD thesis, Cornell University (1978)
23. Wong, K.: On the complexity of projections of discrete-event systems. In: Proc. of WSDES, Cagliari, Italy, pp. 201–206 (1998)
24. Yu, S.: Regular languages. In: [20], vol. I, pp. 41–110 (1997)
25. Yu, S.: State complexity: Recent results and open problems. Fundamenta Informaticae (64), 471–481 (2005)
26. Yu, S., Zhuang, Q., Salomaa, K.: The state complexity of some basic operations on regular languages. Theoretical Computer Science (125), 315–328 (1994)

# Iterating Invertible Binary Transducers

Klaus Sutner[1] and Kevin Lewi[2,*]

[1] Carnegie Mellon University,
Pittsburgh, PA 15213
sutner@cmu.edu
[2] Stanford University,
Stanford, CA 94305
klewi@cs.standford.edu

**Abstract.** We study iterated transductions defined by a class of invertible transducers over the binary alphabet. The transduction semigroups of these automata turn out to be free Abelian groups and the orbits of finite words can be described as affine subspaces in a suitable geometry defined by the generators of these groups. We show that iterated transductions are rational for a subclass of our automata.

## 1 Motivation

An *invertible transducer* is a type of Mealy automaton where all transitions are of the form $p \xrightarrow{a/\pi(a)} q$; here $\pi$ is a permutation of the alphabet depending on the source state $p$. We only consider $\mathbf{2} = \{0,1\}$ as input and output alphabet. Selecting an arbitrary state $p$ as the initial state, we obtain a transduction $\mathcal{A}(p)$ from $\mathbf{2}^*$ to $\mathbf{2}^*$. These transductions can be viewed as automorphisms of the complete binary tree $\mathbf{2}^*$ and the collection of all transductions generates a subsemigroup $\mathcal{S}(\mathcal{A})$ of the full automorphism group $\mathrm{Aut}(\mathbf{2}^*)$. Similarly one can associate a group $\mathcal{G}(\mathcal{A})$ with $\mathcal{A}$ by including the inverses of all transductions. These groups are called *automata groups* or *self-similar groups* and have been studied in great detail in group theory and symbolic dynamics, see [9,15] for extensive pointers to the literature. Automata groups have many interesting properties and have lead to elegant solutions to several outstanding problems. For example, Grigorchuk's well-known example of a group of intermediate growth has a description in terms of a 5-state invertible transducer. Automata groups should not be confused with *automatic groups* as introduced in [6] or *automatic structures*, see [11,13]. The former are characterized by the group operations being described directly by finite state machines operating on words over the generators. The latter are first-order structures whose carrier sets and relations are represented by finite state machines. A comparison of the two models can be found in [10].

We are here interested in both connections between automata theory and group theory as discussed in [1]. More precisely, we study the effect of iteration on transductions: given a transduction $f \in \mathcal{S}(\mathcal{A})$, write $f^* \subseteq \mathbf{2}^* \times \mathbf{2}^*$ for

---

\* This work was done at Carnegie Mellon University.

M. Kutrib, N. Moreira, and R. Reis (Eds.): DCFS 2012, LNCS 7386, pp. 294–306, 2012.

the binary relation obtained by iterating $f$. Note that $f^*$ is a length-preserving equivalence relation on $\mathbf{2}^*$. While the first-order structure $\langle \mathbf{2}^*, f \rangle$ is clearly automatic and thus has decidable first-order theory, it is difficult to determine when $\langle \mathbf{2}^*, f, f^* \rangle$ is automatic. We introduce a class of invertible transducers called *cycle-cum-chord (CCC)* transducers in section 2 and characterize their transduction semigroups as free Abelian groups. Moreover, for some CCC transducers the orbit relations $f^*$ turn out to be automatic for all transductions $f$ in the semigroup. Since $f^*$ is length-preserving, it follows from a result by Elgot and Mezei, [5] that this is equivalent to $f$ being rational. To show that $f^*$ is automatic we construct a canonical transition system, which turns out to be finite for some of the automata under consideration. This scenario is somewhat similar to the discussion of digital circuits computing functions on the dyadic numbers in [22]; note that we are dealing with relations rather than functions, though.

The construction of the transition system is based on a normal form for transductions proposed by Knuth [14] that allows one to show that $\mathcal{S}(\mathcal{A})$ is in fact a free Abelian group. The normal form is also useful to define a natural geometry on $\mathbf{2}^*$ that describes the orbits of words under $f$ as affine subspaces. As a consequence, it is polynomial-time decidable whether two transductions give rise to the same equivalence relation and we can in fact construct the minimal transition system for $f^*$ in the sense of Eilenberg [4]. In addition, we obtain fast algorithms to compute $x\, f^t$, to test whether two words belong to the same orbit under $f$ and the calculate coordinates in the geometry introduced below.

This paper is organized as follows. In section 2 we introduce invertible transducers and define cycle-cum-chord transducers. We also show how to construct the canonical transition system that tests orbit equivalence. In the next section, we discuss Knuth normal form, characterizes the transduction semigroups of CCC transducers and determine the rationality of orbits of some of these machines. Section 4 contains comments on related decision problems and mentions open problems.

## 2   Invertible Transducers

### 2.1   Transduction Semigroups

We consider Mealy machines of the form $\mathcal{A} = \langle Q, \mathbf{2}, \delta, \lambda \rangle$ where $Q$ is a finite set, $\mathbf{2} = \{0, 1\}$ is the input and output alphabet, $\delta : Q \times \mathbf{2} \to Q$ the transition function and $\lambda : Q \times \mathbf{2} \to \mathbf{2}$ the output function. We can think of $\mathbf{2}^*$ as acting on $Q$ via $\delta$, see [2,18,12] for background. We are here only interested in *invertible transducers* where $\lambda(p, .) : \mathbf{2} \to \mathbf{2}$ is a permutation for each state $p$. When this permutation is the transposition in the symmetric group $\mathfrak{S}_2$ on two letters, we refer to $p$ as a *toggle state* and as a *copy state*, otherwise. Fixing a state $p$ as initial state we obtain a transduction $\mathcal{A}(p) : \mathbf{2}^* \to \mathbf{2}^*$ that is easily seen to be a length-preserving permutation. If the automaton is clear from context we write $\underline{p}$ for this functions; $\mathcal{S}(\mathcal{A})$ denotes the semigroup and $\mathcal{G}(\mathcal{A})$ denotes the group generated by all these functions.

If we think of $2^*$ as an infinite, complete binary tree in the spirit of [19], we can interpret our transductions as automorphisms of this tree, see [15,20]. Clearly any automorphism $f$ of $2^*$ can be written in the form $f = (f_0, f_1)s$ where $s \in \mathfrak{S}_2$: $s$ describes the action of $f$ on $2$, and $f_0$ and $f_1$ are the automorphisms induced by $f$ on the two subtrees of the root. The automorphisms $f$ such that $f = (f_0, f_1)\sigma$ are *odd*, the others *even*. The whole automorphism group can be described in terms of wreath products thus:

$$\mathsf{Aut}(2^*) \simeq \mathsf{Aut}(2^*) \wr \mathfrak{S}_2 = (\mathsf{Aut}(2^*) \times \mathsf{Aut}(2^*)) \rtimes \mathfrak{S}_2$$

The components $f_i$ arise naturally as the *left residuals* of $f$, first introduced by Raney [17]. It was shown by Gluškov that the residuals of a sequential map are sufficient to construct a corresponding Mealy automaton, see [7] and [15]. More precisely, for any word $x$, define the function $\partial_x f$ by $(x\,f)\,(z\,\partial_x f) = (xz)\,f$ for all words $z$ (for transductions, we write function application on the right and use diagrammatic composition for consistency with relational composition). It follows that

$$\partial_{xy} f = \partial_y \partial_x f$$
$$\partial_x f g = \partial_x f\, \partial_{f(x)} g$$

The transduction semigroup $\mathcal{S}(\mathcal{A})$ is naturally closed under residuals. In fact, we can describe the behavior of all the transductions by a transition system $\mathcal{C}$, much the way $\mathcal{A}$ describes the basic transductions: the states are $\mathcal{S}(\mathcal{A})$ and the transitions are $f \xrightarrow{s/f(s)} \partial_s f$. Thus $\mathcal{C}$ contains $\mathcal{A}$ as a subautomaton. Of course, this system is infinite in general; it is referred to as the *complete automaton* in [15]. Also note that, in terms of residuals, the group operation in the wreath product has the form

$$(f_0, f_1)s\,(g_0, g_1)t = (f_0 g_{s(0)}, f_1 g_{s(1)})\,st$$

This provides a convenient notation system for invertible transducers. For example, writing $\sigma$ for the transposition in $\mathfrak{S}_2$, $\alpha = (I, \alpha)\,\sigma$ and $I = (I, I)$ specifies an automaton $\mathcal{A}$ known as the "adding machine," see [15]. The transduction semigroup generated by $\mathcal{A}$ is isomorphic to $\mathbb{N}$, and the group is isomorphic to $\mathbb{Z}$. If we think of automorphism $\alpha$ as a map on $\mathbb{Z}_2$, the ring of dyadic numbers, as in [22], we have $x\,\alpha = x + 1$ and the orbit of $0^\omega$ under $\alpha$ is dense in $\mathbb{Z}_2$.

## 2.2  Orbit Equivalence and the Orbit Automaton

Consider an automorphism $f$ in $\mathsf{Aut}(2^*)$. The iterate $f^*$ is an equivalence relation on $2^*$, the *orbit relation* of $f$, written $\equiv_f$. Two automorphism $f$ and $g$ are *star equivalent* if they have the same orbit relation. It is easy to see that any orbit $xa\,f^*$ either has the same length as $x\,f^*$, or twice that length. We will say correspondingly that $x$ *splits* or *doubles* under $f$: in the first case the orbits of $x0$ and $x1$ are distinct, in the second case they coincide (as sets). Hence, any orbit has length $2^k$ for some $k \geq 0$ and it follows that for any odd integer $r$ the maps $f$ and $f^r$ are star equivalent.

In order to show that some orbit relations are rational, it is useful to generalize the notion of orbit slightly. Given two automorphisms $f$ and $h$ and a word $u$, define the *orbit of $u$ under $f$ with translation $h$* to be $u\,f^*h = \{\,u\,f^i h \mid i \geq 0\,\}$. Correspondingly, the relation $\mathbf{R}(f, h)$ holds on $u$ and $v$ if $v \in u\,f^*h$. When $h$ is the identity then $\mathbf{R}(f, I)$ is simply the orbit relation of $f$. In general, $\mathbf{R}(f, h)$ fails to be an equivalence relation (and even to be reflexive), but, as we will show in the following lemma, orbits with translation are closed under Brzozowski [3] quotients. Here we interpret $\mathbf{R}(f, h)$ as a language over $(\mathbf{2} \times \mathbf{2})^*$.

**Lemma 1.** *Quotient Lemma*
*Let $f$ and $h$ be two automorphisms and set $b = a\,h$. For $f = (f_0, f_1)$ we have*

$$(a{:}b)^{-1}\,\mathbf{R}(f, h) = \mathbf{R}(f_a, h_a)$$

*Otherwise, for $f = (f_0, f_1)\,\sigma$, we have*

$$(a{:}b)^{-1}\,\mathbf{R}(f, h) = \mathbf{R}(f_a f_{\overline{a}}, h_a)$$
$$(a{:}\overline{b})^{-1}\,\mathbf{R}(f, h) = \mathbf{R}(f_a f_{\overline{a}}, f_a h_{\overline{a}})$$

*All other quotients are empty.*

*Proof.* In the first case we get $ax\,f^*h = b\,(x\,f_a^{\,*}h_a)$. In the second case note that $f^2 = (f_0 f_1, f_1 f_0)$. Since the first bit alternates along the orbit of $ax$ under $f$, it follows that $ax\,f^* = a\,(x\,(f_a f_{\overline{a}})^*) \cup \overline{a}\,(x\,(f_a f_{\overline{a}})^* f_a)$. Our claim follows by applying the translation $h$ to this equation. $\square$

The lemma provides a way to construct a transition system over the alphabet $\mathbf{2} \times \mathbf{2}$ that decides the orbit relation $\equiv_f$ of an automorphism $f$: starting at $(f, I)$, generate all quotients according to the lemma and record transitions $\mathbf{R}(f, h) \xrightarrow{a/b} (a{:}b)^{-1}\,\mathbf{R}(f, h)$. The initial state is $(f, I)$ and all states other than $\emptyset$ are accepting. Clearly, the system accepts the convolution $x{:}y$ of two words $x$ and $y$ of equal length if, and only if, $x \equiv_f y$. To obtain a minimal transition system $\mathcal{M}_f$ in the sense of Eilenberg [4], we have to adjust the notion of star equivalence to pairs: $(f, h)$ and $(g, h')$ are *star equivalent* if $\mathbf{R}(f, h) = \mathbf{R}(g, h')$. We write $(f, h) \approx (g, h')$ to indicate star equivalence. From the definitions we have the following sufficient condition for star equivalence.

**Proposition 1.** *Let $f$ and $h$ be automorphisms. Then for any odd $r$ and any integer $s$: $(f, h) \approx (f^r, f^s h)$.*

Of course, in general $\mathcal{M}_f$ will be infinite. For some automorphisms given by an invertible transducer, $\mathcal{M}_f$ turns out to be finite, so that the orbit relation of $f$ is rational. One well-known example are the so-called "sausage automata" $\mathrm{SA}_n$ in [15], generalizations of the adding machine from above. In wreath notation they are given by

$$\underline{1} = (0, \underline{n})\,\sigma \qquad \text{and} \qquad \underline{k} = (\underline{k-1}, \underline{k-1}), \quad 2 \leq k \leq n$$

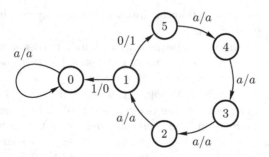

**Fig. 1.** The "sausage automaton" $\mathcal{A}_5$, an invertible transducer that generates $\mathbb{Z}^5$

where we ignore the identity $I$, as customary. Figure 1 shows $\mathcal{A}_5$.

The group generated by $\mathcal{A}_n$ is $\mathbb{Z}^n$ and the basic transductions are given by a combination of the successor function of the adding machine and a polyadic version of perfect shuffle. Let $x^i \in \mathbf{2}^r$, $1 \le i \le n$, and $1 \le k \le n$. Then

$$\underline{k}\,(\mathsf{shf}(x^1, x^2, \ldots, x^n)) = \mathsf{shf}(x^1, \ldots, x^k \alpha, \ldots, x^n)$$

Here $\alpha$ is again the successor operation defined by the adding machine from section 2.1 and $\mathsf{shf}$ is the generalization of binary perfect shuffle to a variable number of arguments of the same length:

$$\mathsf{shf}(x^1, x^2, \ldots, x^s) = x_1^1 x_1^2 \ldots x_1^s\, x_2^1 x_2^2 \ldots x_2^s\, \ldots\, x_r^1 x_r^2 \ldots x_r^s.$$

Note that automatic relations are closed under perfect shuffle. With a little bit of effort one can show that the orbit relation $\equiv_f$ is automatic for any transduction $f$ in $\mathcal{S}(\mathcal{A}_n)$.

## 2.3   Cycle-Cum-Chord Transducers

We now introduce a simple class of invertible transducers whose associated semi-groups will turn out to be free Abelian groups. Unlike with the sausage automata from above, the orbits of words under the corresponding transductions are fairly complicated. A *cycle-cum-chord (CCC)* transducer has state set $\{0, 1, \ldots, n-1\}$ and transitions

$$p \xrightarrow{a/a} p - 1, \quad p > 0 \qquad \text{and} \qquad 0 \xrightarrow{0/1} n - 1, \quad 0 \xrightarrow{1/0} m - 1$$

where $1 \le m \le n$. We will write $\mathcal{A}_m^n$ for this transducer. The diagram of $\mathcal{A}_3^5$ is shown in figure 2. The source node of the chord is the sole toggle state in these transducers. As we will see shortly, $\mathcal{S}(\mathcal{A}_m^n) = \mathcal{G}(\mathcal{A}_m^n)$.

Using wreath representations it is easy to verify algebraically that $\mathcal{S}(\mathcal{A}_m^n)$ is an Abelian group. More precisely, we can establish the following two lemmata.

**Lemma 2.** *The transduction semigroup of $\mathcal{A}_m^n$ is Abelian.*

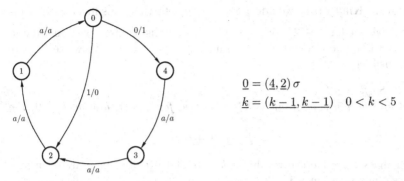

$$\underline{0} = (\underline{4}, 2)\, \sigma$$
$$\underline{k} = (\underline{k-1}, \underline{k-1}) \quad 0 < k < 5$$

**Fig. 2.** The cycle-cum-chord transducer $\mathcal{A}_3^5$, an invertible transducer on 5 states with one toggle state

*Proof.* Let $0 \leq r, s < n - 1$. Then

$$\underline{0}\,\underline{r+1} = (\underline{n-1}, \underline{m-1})\, \sigma\, (\underline{r}, \underline{r}) = (\underline{n-1}\,\underline{r}, \underline{m-1}\,\underline{r})\, \sigma$$
$$\underline{r+1}\,\underline{0} = (\underline{r}, \underline{r})\,(\underline{n-1}, \underline{m-1})\, \sigma = (\underline{r}\,\underline{n-1}, \underline{r}\,\underline{m-1})\, \sigma$$
$$\underline{r+1}\,\underline{s+1} = (\underline{r}, \underline{r})\,(\underline{s}, \underline{s}) \qquad = (\underline{r}\,\underline{s}, \underline{r}\,\underline{s})$$
$$\underline{s+1}\,\underline{r+1} = (\underline{s}, \underline{s})\,(\underline{r}, \underline{r}) \qquad = (\underline{s}\,\underline{r}, \underline{s}\,\underline{r})$$

and we are done by induction.    □

**Lemma 3.** *Cancellation Identities*

*Consider $\mathcal{A}_m^n$ where $1 \leq m \leq n$ and let $s = \gcd(n, m)$, $r = m/s$. Then the following identities hold in the transduction semigroup of $\mathcal{A}_m^n$, for $0 \leq i < s$:*

$$\underline{i}^2\,(\underline{s+i})^2 \ldots (\underline{(r-1)s+i})^2\,\underline{m+i}\,\underline{m+s+i} \ldots \underline{n-s+i} = I$$

*Proof.* For $i = 0$ we have

$$\partial_a \underline{0}^2\,(\underline{s})^2 \ldots (\underline{(r-1)s})^2\,\underline{m}\,\underline{m+s} \ldots \underline{n-s} =$$
$$\underline{s-1}^2\,(\underline{2s-1})^2 \ldots (\underline{(r-1)s-1})^2\,\underline{m+s} \ldots \underline{n-s-1}\,\underline{n-1}$$

Noting that, for $i > 0$, each term $\underline{r}$ in the equation is replaced by $\underline{r-1}$ under residuation we are done by induction.    □

## 3  Orbit Rationality

### 3.1  Knuth Normal Form

From the two lemmata it follows that $\mathcal{S}(\mathcal{A}_m^n) = \mathcal{G}(\mathcal{A}_m^n)$ is an Abelian group: by the cancellation identities the inverse of each monoid generator lies already in $\mathcal{S}(\mathcal{A}_m^n)$. Also, by the cancellation identities, the resulting group is a quotient of $\mathbb{Z}^{n-s}$. To show that the group is in fact isomorphic to $\mathbb{Z}^{n-s}$ we use a method suggested by D. Knuth [14]: we add a new state $n$ to the transducer with transitions $n \xrightarrow{a/a} n-1$ for $a \in \mathbf{2}$. By repeating this extension step, we can enlarge the state set to $\mathbb{N}$ where for all $i > 0$ we have $\underline{i} = (\underline{i-1}, \underline{i-1})$. We write $\mathcal{K}_m^n$ for the new transducer.

**Lemma 4.** *Shift Identities*
  *In the transduction semigroup of $\mathcal{K}_m^n$ we have, for $m < n$ and all $k \geq 0$, the identities*

$$\underline{k}^2 = \underline{k+m} \; \underline{k+n}$$

*Proof.* It suffices to prove the result for $k = 0$. Both $\underline{0}^2$ and $\underline{m} \; \underline{n}$ are even and we have residuals $\underline{m-1} \; \underline{n-1}$.                                                                                                              □

According to the shift identities, the transduction semigroups of $\mathcal{A}_m^n$ and $\mathcal{K}_m^n$ coincide. Likewise, the cancellation identities generalize to all transductions in $\mathcal{K}_m^n$. Since $S(\mathcal{A}_m^n) = S(\mathcal{K}_m^n)$ we have an alternative representation as $f = \underline{k_1}^{e_1} \underline{k_2}^{e_2} \ldots \underline{k_r}^{e_r}$ where $k_1 < k_2 < \ldots < k_r$ and $e_i \geq 1$. We allow $r = 0$ for the identity map. Of particular interest is the case where $e_i = 1$ for all $i$; we will refer to this flat representation $f = \underline{k_1} \, \underline{k_2} \ldots \underline{k_r}$ as the *Knuth normal form (KNF)* of $f$. To generate the KNF of $f$ we interpret the identities from lemma 4 as rewrite rules. For example, in $\mathcal{K}_2^3$ we have the shift rule $\underline{k}^2 \to \underline{k+2} \; \underline{k+3}$. Alas, application of the shift rule alone can lead to infinite loops as in $\underline{0}^2 \, \underline{1}^2 \, \underline{2} \to \underline{1}^2 \, \underline{2}^2 \, \underline{3} \to \underline{2}^2 \, \underline{3}^2 \, \underline{4} \to \ldots$ However, in this case, a single application of the cancellation identity from lemma 3 immediately terminates the process. Thus, the rewrite system is weakly terminating.

**Theorem 1.** *Knuth Normal Form*
  *Every transduction over $\mathcal{A}_m^n$ has a unique Knuth normal form.*

*Proof.* For $n = m$ the cancellation identities have the form $\underline{k}^2 = I$ and it follows immediately that every transduction can be written uniquely in the required form. So assume $m < n$. For any transduction $f$ in $S(\mathcal{A}_m^n)$ consider the standard semigroup representation

$$f = \underline{k_1}^{e_{k_1}} \underline{k_2}^{e_{k_2}} \ldots \underline{k_r}^{e_{k_r}}$$

where $e_{k_i} \geq 1$ and $0 \leq k_i < k_{i+1} < n$. If all exponents are equal 1, or if $r = 0$, we are done. Otherwise rewrite the expression as follows. First, apply cancellation according to the identities from lemma 3 in the first place possible. If none of these identities apply, use the shift rule derived from lemma 4, again in the leftmost possible position. Thus we obtain a sequence of expressions $(f_i)$ with $f_0 = f$ that all denote $f$. We claim that the sequence is finite and thus ends in the desired flat representation.

Define the *weight* of $f$ to be $\sum e_i$. Note that the shift rule preserves weight whereas a reduction reduces weight. Suppose for the sake of a contradiction that our rewrite process continues indefinitely for some initial $f$. Since weights are non-negative we may safely assume that the weight remains constant. Thus, no reductions apply and we only use shift rules. For the sake of simplicity let us assume that $s = \gcd(n, m) = 1$ so there is only a single reduction to deal with. The general argument is more tedious but entirely similar.

Observe that there must be a minimal critical index $c$ such that $e_c > 1$. Define the *essential weight* of the expression as the sum $\sum_{i \geq c} e_i$. Again we may assume that the essential weight of the expression is non-decreasing. Hence $e_c$ must always be even and the shift operation adds $e_c/2$ to $e_{c+m}$ and $e_{c+n}$. But then, after a sufficiently large number of steps, there will be a critical block of exponents $e_c, e_{c+1}, \ldots, e_{c+n-1}$ with the property that $e_i \leq 1$ for $i < c$ and $e_i = 0$ for $i \geq c + n$; $c$ increases by 1 at each step. Since $e_c$ is even we are essentially operating on an $n$-tuple of natural numbers:

$$(a_0, \ldots, a_{n-1}) \mapsto (a_1, a_2, \ldots, a_m + a_0/2, \ldots, a_{n-1}, a_0/2)$$

We may safely assume $a_0$ to be positive. Since $n$ and $m$ are coprime all entries in the vector will be positive after at most $m(n-1) + 1$ steps. But note that the leftmost $m - 1$ entries in the vector must then all be even and positive. Hence we can apply cancellation and we have the desired contradiction. Uniqueness is clear from the construction. □

We can now pin down the structure of the transductions semigroups $\mathcal{S}(\mathcal{A}_m^n)$.

**Corollary 1.** *The transduction semigroup of $\mathcal{A}_n^n$ is isomorphic to the Boolean group $\mathbf{2}^n$. For $m < n$, the transduction semigroup of $\mathcal{A}_m^n$ is isomorphic to $\mathbb{Z}^{n-\gcd(n,m)}$.*

Knuth normal form can be used to establish other properties of the group of $\mathcal{A}_m^n$. For example, the group can be shown to act transitively on all the level sets $\mathbf{2}^\ell$, $\ell \geq 0$. Here is another important property of the transduction group.

**Lemma 5.** *Let $f \neq I$ be a transduction over a CCC transducer $\mathcal{A}_m^n$ and $\underline{r}$ the first term in the KNF of $f$. Then exactly all words of length $r + m\mathbb{N}$ double for $m < n$. For $n = m$, only words of length $r$ double.*

*Proof.* For $m = n$ the orbit of a word $x$ has length 1 when $|x| \leq r$ and length 2 otherwise: letting $f = \underline{k_1}\, \underline{k_2} \ldots \underline{k_s}$ where $r = k_1$, $0 \leq k_i < k_{i+1} < n$, we can see that $f$ toggles exactly the bits in positions $k_i + m\mathbb{N}$.

Suppose $m < n$ and consider the case $r = 0$. Assume by induction that $x$ is a word of length $\ell = km$ such that the $f$-orbit of $x$ has length $2^k$. Then the first term in the KNF of $f^{2^k}$ is $\underline{km}$ so that $xa\, f^{2^k} = x\bar{a}$. Similarly $xv\, f^{2^{k+1}} = xv$ for all $v \in \mathbf{2}^m$ and our claim follows. Lastly, for $r > 0$, note that $f$ is the identity on all words up to length $r$ and, for $x = uv$ where $|u| = r$, we have $x f = u(v\, g)$ where $g = \partial_u f$ and $g$ is odd. □

**Lemma 6.** *For any CCC transducer $\mathcal{A}_m^n$ let $H$ be the group of transductions generated by $\underline{i}$, $0 \leq i < m$. Then $H$ acts transitively on the level sets $\mathbf{2}^\ell$. For $\ell = km$ the quotient group $H'$ obtained by factoring with respect to $\underline{i}^{2^k}$ acts simply transitively on $\mathbf{2}^\ell$.*

*Proof.* Since our transductions are sequential it suffices to consider only levels $\ell = km$. Consider two words $x$ and $y$ of length $\ell$. Suppose by induction that $x f = y$ for some transduction $f$ and consider arbitrary bits $a_0, \ldots, a_{m-1}$ and $b_0, \ldots, b_{m-1}$. Note that $x a_0 \, f \underline{0}^{e_0} = y b_0$ for $e_0 = 0$ or $e_0 = 2^k$. Proceeding inductively, we can find $e_i \in \{0, 2^k\}$ such that $x a_0 \ldots a_{m-1} \, f \underline{0}^{e_0} \ldots \underline{m-1}^{e_{m-1}} = y b_0 \ldots b_{m-1}$.

Since the coefficients are uniquely determined modulo $2^{k+1}$, the second claim also follows. □

## 3.2 Orbit Geometry and Rationality

One important consequence of the last lemma is that it provides a natural coordinate system for the level set $2^{km}$: for every $\ell = km$ there is a coordinate map, a bijection

$$2^\ell \to \mathbb{Z}/(2^k) \times \ldots \times \mathbb{Z}/(2^k)$$

where the product on the right has $m$ terms. We will write $\langle w \rangle_\ell \in (\mathbb{Z}/(2^k))^m$ for the coordinates of a word $w$: $\langle w \rangle_\ell = (a_0, \ldots, a_{m-1})$ if, and only if, $w = 0^\ell \underline{0}^{a_0} \underline{1}^{a_1} \ldots \underline{m-1}^{a_{m-1}}$. In terms of this coordinate system, orbits can be described as affine subspaces of $(\mathbb{Z}/(2^k))^m$:

$$\langle w f^* \rangle_\ell = \langle w \rangle_\ell + \mathbb{N} \cdot \langle f \rangle_\ell \quad (\mathrm{mod}\ 2^k)$$

In fact, all these orbits are translations of the basic linear subspace $0^\ell f^*$. But then two transductions $f$ and $g$ are star equivalent for words of length $\ell = km$ if, and only if, for some odd integer $z$ depending on $\ell$ we have $\langle f \rangle_\ell = z \cdot \langle g \rangle_\ell$ $(\mathrm{mod}\ 2^k)$. Thus, for fixed $\ell$, simple modular arithmetic suffices to determine star equivalence, given the coordinates. To deal with the general case, recall that a sequence $(a_i)$ of integers is *coherent* if $a_i = a_{i+1}$ $(\mathrm{mod}\ 2^i)$, and likewise for vectors of integers, see [8]. For any word $x$ let $x[i]$ be the prefix of $x$ of length $i$. It is easy to check that the sequence $(\langle f \rangle_\ell)$ is coherent. Thus, the local coordinates $\langle w f \rangle_{km}$ define a vector $\langle f \rangle \in \mathbb{Z}_2^m$ of $m$ dyadic numbers. For example, in $\mathcal{A}_2^3$, letting $f = \underline{0}^{-1} \underline{1}^3$ we get

$$\langle f \rangle = (0.1111\ldots, 0.11000\ldots) \in \mathbb{Z}_2^2$$

using the standard digit notation for $\mathbb{Z}_2$. Note, though, that for $\mathcal{A}_2^3$ the dimension of the coordinate system coincides with the number of generators of the transduction group; in general the situation is more complicated. Write $\nu_2(x)$ for the dyadic valuation of $x$ in $\mathbb{Z}_2$.

**Theorem 2.** *Let $\mathcal{A}$ be a cycle-cum-chord transducer and $f$ and $g$ two transductions in $\mathcal{S}(\mathcal{A})$. Then $f$ and $g$ are star equivalent if, and only if, the following two conditions hold:*

*1. $\nu_2(\langle f \rangle) = \nu_2(\langle g \rangle)$, and*
*2. $\langle f \rangle = \zeta \langle g \rangle$ for some unit $\zeta \in \mathbb{Z}_2$.*

*Likewise, $(f, h_1)$ and $(g, h_2)$ are star equivalent if, and only if, the following two conditions hold:*

1. *$f$ and $g$ are star equivalent, and*
2. *$\langle h_1^{-1} h_2 \rangle = \zeta \langle f \rangle$ for some $\zeta \in \mathbb{Z}_2$.*

There is an interesting special case where we can obtain a better description. Call a CCC transducer $\mathcal{A}_m^n$ *amenable* if the dimension of the coordinate system for words coincides with the number of free generators. In other words, the transduction group is isomorphic to $\mathbb{Z}^m$, which is equivalent $n - \gcd(n, m) = m$. It is easy to see that $\mathcal{A}_m^n$ is amenable if, and only if, $m = n - d$ where $d < n$ divides $n$.

**Corollary 2.** *For amenable cycle-cum-chord transducers, star equivalence is decidable in polynomial time.*

For any odd integer $s$ and a transduction $f$, define the fractional power $f^{1/s}$ as follows: $x\, f^{1/s} = y$ iff $x = y\, f^s$. This yields the following characterization of star equivalence for CCC transducers.

**Corollary 3.** *In any amenable cycle-cum-chord transducer, the following are equivalent for transductions $f$ and $g$:*

- *$f$ and $g$ are star equivalent,*
- *there are odd integers $r$ and $s$ such that $f^{r/s} = g$,*
- *there are odd integers $r$ and $s$ and a transduction $h$ such that $f = h^r$ and $g = h^s$.*

Call an invertible transducer $\mathcal{A}$ *orbit rational* if $f^*$ is rational for all $f$ in $\mathcal{S}(\mathcal{A})$. To simplify the discussion, consider $\mathcal{A}_m^n$ and let $s = \gcd(n, m)$ and $n' = n/s$, $m' = m/s$. We refer to $\mathcal{A}_{m'}^{n'}$ as the *reduct* of $\mathcal{A}_m^n$. The transition diagram of the reduct is $s$-partite and the orbits can be described via shuffle as follows.

**Lemma 7.** *Let $\mathcal{A}_m^n$ be a CCC transducer, $s = \gcd(n, m)$ and $\mathcal{A}_{m'}^{n'}$ its reduct; write $f = \mathcal{A}_m^n(0)$ and $g = \mathcal{A}_{m'}^{n'}(0)$. Then for words $x^i \in \mathbf{2}^k$ we have*

$$f(\mathsf{shf}(x^1, x^2, \ldots, x^s)) = \mathsf{shf}(g(x^1), x^2, \ldots, x^s)$$

As a consequence it suffices to determine orbit rationality for reducts only.

**Lemma 8.** *A transducer $\mathcal{A}_m^n$ is orbit rational if, and only if, its reduct $\mathcal{A}_{m'}^{n'}$ is orbit rational.*

### 3.3    Rational Orbit Relations

**Theorem 3.** *All transducers $\mathcal{A}_1^n$ and $\mathcal{A}_n^n$ are orbit rational, $n \geq 1$.*

*Proof.* First consider $\mathcal{A}_1^n$. We have seen that $\underline{0}$ acts transitively on all level sets, so $\equiv_{\underline{0}}$ is universal in the sense that two words are equivalent iff they have the same length. In the general case, our claim follows similarly from lemma 5: let $\underline{k}$ be the leading term of the KNF of $f$, then $x \equiv_f y$ iff $x[k] = y[k]$. Hence, $\equiv_f$ can be decided by a finite state machine of size 1 when $k = 0$, and $k + 2$ otherwise.

For transducers of the form $\mathcal{A}_n^n$ recall that every transduction in $\mathcal{S}(\mathcal{A}_n^n)$ can be written uniquely in the form $f = \underline{k_1} \underline{k_2} \ldots \underline{k_r}$ where $0 \leq k_i < k_{i+1} < n$. Thus, $f$ toggles exactly the bits in positions $k_i + n\mathbb{N}$ and the orbit of any word of length at least $k_1$ is a 2-cycle. Clearly, $\equiv_f$ can be decided by a finite state machine of size at most $n$. $\qquad\square$

**Corollary 4.** *Every transducer of the form $\mathcal{A}_m^{mt}$ is orbit rational for $m, t \geq 1$.*

By using lemma 1 and corollary 2 one can construct a minimal finite state machine on 36 states decides orbit equivalence of $\underline{0}$ for $\mathcal{A}_2^3$. The following theorem explains why this construction terminates; a similar argument also provides a plausibility argument for the state complexity of the machine.

**Theorem 4.** *Every transducer of the form $\mathcal{A}_{2t}^{3t}$ is orbit rational for $t \geq 1$.*

*Proof.* It suffices to show that the common reduct $\mathcal{A} = \mathcal{A}_2^3$ is orbit rational. As we have seen, the transduction group of $\mathcal{A}$ is isomorphic to $\mathbb{Z}^2$. Consider the set $\mathcal{Q} \subseteq \mathbb{Z}^2$ obtained by closing $(f, I)$ under quotients as in lemma 1. For the time being, let us focus on $\mathcal{Q}_0$, the projection on the first component. Note that $\mathcal{Q}_0$ is the orbit of $f$ under the map $\pi(g) = \partial_0 g$ when $g$ is even and $\pi(g) = \partial_0 g^2$ otherwise. It is not hard to see that the orbit of $f$ must contain on odd function, say, $\pi^r(f) = (a, b) \in \mathbb{Z}^2$. Then the $\pi$-orbit of $(a, b)$, modulo star equivalence, is

$$(a, b), (2b - 2a, -a), (a - 2b, a - b), (2b, 2b - a), (-a, -b) \approx (a, b)$$

Here odd and even steps alternate. At any rate, $\mathcal{Q}_0$ is finite.

To see that the second component of $\mathcal{Q}$ is also finite note that, using the group representation, we can compute residuals like so:

$$\partial_s \boldsymbol{u} = \begin{cases} A \cdot \boldsymbol{u} & \text{if } \boldsymbol{u} \text{ is even,} \\ A \cdot \boldsymbol{u} - (-1)^s \boldsymbol{a} & \text{otherwise.} \end{cases}$$

where

$$A = \begin{pmatrix} -1 & 1 \\ -1/2 & 0 \end{pmatrix} \quad \text{and} \quad \boldsymbol{a} = (1, 3/2)$$

The rational matrix $A$ has complex eigenvalues of norm $1/\sqrt{2} < 1$ and gives rise to a contraction $\mathbb{Q}^2 \to \mathbb{Q}^2$. We can over-approximate the operations required for the second components of $\mathcal{Q}$ by a map $\Phi : \mathbb{Q}^2 \to \mathfrak{P}(\mathbb{Q}^2)$ defined by

$$\Phi(\boldsymbol{u}) = \{ A \cdot \boldsymbol{u} + c\boldsymbol{a} + \boldsymbol{w} \mid c \in \{0, \pm 1\}, \boldsymbol{w} \in W \}.$$

Here $W$ is a set of residuals obtained from the transductions in $\mathcal{Q}_0$. Since $A$ is a contraction the closure of $h$ under $\Phi$ is a bounded set in $\mathbb{Q}^2$, containing only finitely many integral points. $\qquad\square$

A careful discussion of so-called 1/2-homomorphisms can be found in [16].

# 4  Summary and Open Problems

We have characterized the transduction semigroups associated with a class of invertible transducers over the binary alphabet as free Abelian groups. For a subclass of these transducers we can show that the iterates $f^*$ of any transduction is rational and hence automatic. We do not know how to decide rationality in general, and, in fact, not even for the class of amenable cycle-cum-chord transducers. As a concrete example, consider the transducers $\mathcal{A}_m^4$. It follows from our results that they are orbit rational for $m = 1, 2, 4$. In the case $m = 3$ the transducer is amenable and reduced. We are able to show that $\mathcal{A}_3^4$ indeed fails to be orbit rational, but the proof uses field theory in combination with symbolic computation and does not easily generalize to any other situation. In view of the quotient algorithm from above, it would be interesting to know whether star equivalence is decidable in general. As a special case, one can consider transduction that produce only orbits of bounded size. Again, we are currently unable to answer these questions even for non-amenable cycle-cum-chord transducers.

It is straightforward to check whether $\mathcal{S}(\mathcal{A})$ is commutative, using standard automata-theoretic methods. Similarly it is semidecidable whether $\mathcal{S}(\mathcal{A})$ is a group, though the exponential growth in the size of the corresponding automata makes it difficult to investigate even fairly small transducers. We do not know whether it is decidable whether $\mathcal{S}(\mathcal{A})$ is a group. Unsurprisingly, many other decidability questions regarding transduction semigroups or groups of invertible transducers are also open, see [9, chap. 7] for an extensive list.

Lastly, there are several computational problems that arise naturally in the context of $\mathcal{S}(\mathcal{A})$. The most basic one is the Iteration Problem: for a given transduction $f \in \mathcal{S}(\mathcal{A})$, compute $x f$ for a word $x$. For example, in the case of $\mathcal{A}_2^3$ the complete automaton mentioned in section 2.1 has 8 non-trivial strongly connected components that are all finite. As a consequence, we can compute $x f$ in time $O(|x| \log^2 w)$ where $w$ is the weight of $f$. As we have seen, for $\mathcal{A}_2^3$ the elementary decision problem of determining orbit equivalence can be handled by a finite state machine. A slightly stronger version of the decision problem is the Timestamp Problem: given two words $x, y \in \mathbf{2}^k$, find a witness $t$ such that $x f^t = y$ or determine that they are not on the same $f$-orbit. Surprisingly, for $\mathcal{A}_2^3$, there is a finite transducer that computes the minimal $t$ given input $x{:}y$. Knuth normal form is a critical tool in the corresponding correctness proofs. Lastly, in light of the description of orbits in terms of the coordinate system introduced in section 3.2, it is natural to ask how difficult it is to compute the coordinates of a given word. Again for $\mathcal{A}_2^3$, there is a finite transducer that solves the Coordinate Problem: given $x \in \mathbf{2}^{2k}$ as input, outputs the coordinates $(s, t)$ of $x$, where $0 \le s, t < 2^k$, see [21]. Note that based on the geometric description of orbits from section 3.2 the Timestamp Problem can be reduced to the Coordinate Problem. We do not know whether these problems can be solved in polynomial time in general for cycle-cum-chord transducers.

# References

1. Bartholdi, L., Silva, P.V.: Groups defined by automata. CoRR, abs/1012.1531 (2010)
2. Berstel, J.: Transductions and context-free languages (2009), http://www-igm.univ-mlv.fr/~berstel/ LivreTransductions/LivreTransductions.html
3. Brzozowski, J.A.: Derivatives of regular expressions. Journal Assoc. for Comp. Machinery 11 (1964)
4. Eilenberg, S.: Automata, Languages and Machines, vol. A. Academic Press (1974)
5. Elgot, C.C., Mezei, J.E.: On relations defined by generalized finite automata. IBM J. Res. Dev. 9, 47–68 (1965)
6. Epstein, D.B.A., Cannon, J.W., Holt, D.F., Levy, S.V.F., Patterson, M.S., Thurston, W.P.: Word Processing in Groups. Jones and Bartlett (1992)
7. Gluškov, V.M.: Abstract theory of automata. Uspehi Mat. Nauk 16(5(101)), 3–62 (1961)
8. Gouvêa, F.Q.: p-Adic Numbers: An Introduction, 2nd edn. Springer (1997)
9. Grigorchuk, R.R., Nekrashevich, V.V., Sushchanski, V.I.: Automata, dynamical systems and groups. Proc. Steklov Institute of Math. 231, 128–203 (2000)
10. Kharlampovich, O., Khoussainov, B.: A Miasnikov. From automatic structures to automatic groups. ArXiv e-prints (July 2011)
11. Khoussainov, B., Nerode, A.: Automatic Presentations of Structures. In: Leivant, D. (ed.) LCC 1994. LNCS, vol. 960, pp. 367–392. Springer, Heidelberg (1995)
12. Khoussainov, B., Nerode, A.: Automata Theory and its Applications. Birkhäuser (2001)
13. Khoussainov, B., Rubin, S.: Automatic structures: overview and future directions. J. Autom. Lang. Comb. 8(2), 287–301 (2003)
14. Knuth, D.: Private communication (2010)
15. Nekrashevych, V.: Self-Similar Groups. Math. Surveys and Monographs, vol. 117. AMS (2005)
16. Nekrashevych, V., Sidki, S.: Automorphisms of the binary tree: state-closed subgroups and dynamics of 1/2-endomorphisms. Cambridge University Press (2004)
17. Raney, G.N.: Sequential functions. J. Assoc. Comp. Mach. 5(2), 177–180 (1958)
18. Sakarovitch, J.: Elements of Automata Theory. Cambridge University Press (2009)
19. Serre, J.-P.: Arbres, Amalgames, $SL_2$. Number 46 in Astérisque. Société Mathématique de France, Paris (1977)
20. Sidki, S.: Automorphisms of one-rooted trees: Growth, circuit structure, and acyclicity. J. Math. Sciences 100(1), 1925–1943 (2000)
21. Sutner, K., Devanny, W.: Timestamps in iterated invertible transducers (in preparation, 2012)
22. Vuillemin, J.: On circuits and numbers. IEEE Transactions on Computers 43, 868–879 (1994)

# Minimal DFA for Symmetric Difference NFA*

Brink van der Merwe[1], Hellis Tamm[2], and Lynette van Zijl[1]

[1] Department of Computer Science, Stellenbosch University,
Private Bag X1, 7602 Matieland, South Africa
abvdm@cs.sun.ac.za, lvzijl@sun.ac.za
[2] Institute of Cybernetics, Tallinn University of Technology,
Akadeemia tee 21, 12618 Tallinn, Estonia
hellis@cs.ioc.ee

**Abstract.** Recently, a characterization of the class of nondeterministic finite automata (NFAs) for which determinization results in a minimal deterministic finite automaton (DFA), was given in [2]. We present a similar result for the case of symmetric difference NFAs. Also, we show that determinization of any minimal symmetric difference NFA produces a minimal DFA.

## 1   Introduction

Regular languages, and more specifically compact representations of regular languages, are important in many areas in computer science. The state minimization of deterministic finite automata (DFAs) is well-known [1,8], but the state minimization of nondeterministic finite automata (NFAs) is more complicated [9,10]. Symmetric difference NFAs ($\oplus$-NFAs) are of interest for their ability to succinctly describe regular languages [16].

In practical applications, it is often required to find the DFA equivalent to a given NFA (that is, to determinize the NFA). This is accomplished by the so-called subset construction, employing the union set operation for NFAs and the symmetric difference set operation for $\oplus$-NFAs. It is however quite possible that the equivalent DFA may have exponentially more states than the NFA or $\oplus$-NFA, and would need further minimization to reduce its number of states. It is therefore a notable advantage to be able to test in advance whether the determinization of a given NFA or $\oplus$-NFA would result in a minimal DFA. This issue was investigated by Brzozowski and Tamm [2] for the case of NFAs. They introduced so-called atoms of a regular language as non-empty intersections of uncomplemented or complemented left quotients of the language, and atomic NFAs in which the right language of every state is a union of atoms. It was shown in [2] that determinization of an NFA results in a minimal DFA if and only if the reverse of the given NFA is atomic.

* This research was supported by the National Research Foundation of South Africa, by the ERDF funded Estonian Center of Excellence in Computer Science, EXCS, by the Estonian Science Foundation grant 7520, and by the Estonian Ministry of Education and Research target-financed research theme no. 0140007s12.

M. Kutrib, N. Moreira, and R. Reis (Eds.): DCFS 2012, LNCS 7386, pp. 307–318, 2012.

In this work we show that the same characterization of when determinization leads to a minimal DFA, holds in the case of ⊕-NFAs. Also, we show that it is sufficient to require that a ⊕-NFA be minimal in order to obtain a minimal DFA by determinization.

The layout of the article is as follows. In Section 2 we define ⊕-NFAs and give some basic examples. Some properties of minimal ⊕-NFAs, that are used to obtain one of our main results, are given in Section 3. In Section 4, the notions of atomic and ⊕-atomic ⊕-NFAs are introduced. The main results, specifying conditions to obtain a minimal DFA on determinizing a ⊕-NFA, are presented in Section 5, followed by conclusions in Section 6.

## 2   Symmetric Difference NFA Definitions

⊕-NFAs are typically defined by using the symmetric difference set operation, in contrast to the union set operation as in the case of NFAs. We give this definition, in order to be consistent with previous literature, but also equivalently consider ⊕-NFAs as weighted automata over the semiring $\mathbb{Z}_2$ (the Galois field with two elements).

We begin this section by recalling the definitions for a semiring and for weighted automata.

**Definition 1.** *(from [6], [7]) A tuple $(S, \oplus, \otimes, \bar{0}, \bar{1})$ is a* semiring *if $(S, \oplus, \bar{0})$ is a commutative monoid with identity element $\bar{0}$, $(S, \otimes, \bar{1})$ is a monoid with identity element $\bar{1}$, $\otimes$ distributes over $\oplus$, and $\bar{0}$ is an annihilator for $\otimes$: for all $a \in S$, $a \otimes \bar{0} = \bar{0} \otimes a = \bar{0}$.*

*Example 1*
a) The *Boolean* semiring is the two element semiring over `true` (`true` being $\bar{1}$) and `false` (`false` being $\bar{0}$) using `and` as $\otimes$ and `or` as $\oplus$.
b) The *symmetric difference* semiring ($\mathbb{Z}_2$), is obtained by replacing `or` with `exclusive or` in the definition of the Boolean semiring.
c) The *tropical* semiring is the semiring $(\mathbb{N} \cup \{+\infty\}, min, +, +\infty, 0)$, also known as the min-plus semiring, with $min$ and $+$ extended to $\mathbb{N} \cup \{+\infty\}$ in the natural way ($\mathbb{N}$ denotes the natural numbers, including 0).

**Definition 2.** *(from [6], [7]) A* weighted automaton *(without $\varepsilon$-transitions) over a semiring $(S, \oplus, \otimes, \bar{0}, \bar{1})$ is a 5-tuple $\mathcal{A} = (Q, \Sigma, \delta, I, F)$, where $Q$ is a finite set of states, $\Sigma$ is the finite input alphabet, $\delta : \Sigma \to S^{Q \times Q}$ the transition function, $I : Q \to S$ an initial weight function and $F : Q \to S$ the final weight function.*

Note that $\delta(a)$ is a $Q \times Q$-matrix whose $(p,q)$-th entry $\delta(a)_{p,q} \in S$ indicates the weight of the transition from $p$ to $q$ on the symbol $a$.

Let $\mathcal{A}$ be a weighted automaton over the semiring $(S, \oplus, \otimes, \bar{0}, \bar{1})$. A path in $\mathcal{A}$ is an alternating sequence $P = q_0 a_1 q_1 \ldots q_{n-1} a_n q_n \in Q(\Sigma Q)^*$. Its *run weight* is the product $rw(P) = I(q_0) \otimes \delta(a_1)_{q_0, q_1} \otimes \delta(a_2)_{q_1, q_2} \otimes \ldots \otimes \delta(a_n)_{q_{n-1}, q_n} \otimes F(q_n)$. The label of path $P = q_0 a_1 q_1 \ldots q_{n-1} a_n q_n$, denoted by $label(P)$, is the word $a_1 \ldots a_n \in \Sigma^*$. The *behaviour* of a weighted automaton $\mathcal{A}$ is the function $\|\mathcal{A}\| : \Sigma^* \to S$ defined by $\|\mathcal{A}\|(w) = \oplus_{label(P)=w} rw(P)$. One can easily verify that $\|\mathcal{A}\|(a_1 \ldots a_n) = I \delta(a_1) \ldots \delta(a_n) F^{\mathrm{T}}$, with usual matrix multiplication, considering $I$ and $F$ as row vectors and denoting by $F^{\mathrm{T}}$ the column vector obtained by transposing $F$.

Note that the Boolean semiring and $\mathbb{Z}_2$ are the only semirings with two elements. In the case of two element semirings, we can interpret weights as acceptance and rejection (words with weight 1 are accepted). Also, weighted automata over the Boolean semiring and over $\mathbb{Z}_2$ accept the same class of languages, namely, the regular languages.

$\oplus$-NFAs are in fact precisely weighted automata over $\mathbb{Z}_2$, but in order to stay consistent with previous work on the topic, we next give the standard definition for $\oplus$-NFAs.

**Definition 3.** *A $\oplus$-NFA $\mathcal{N}$ is a 5-tuple $(Q, \Sigma, \delta, I, F)$, where $Q$ is the finite non-empty set of states, $\Sigma$ is the finite non-empty input alphabet, $I \subseteq Q$ is the set of initial states, $F \subseteq Q$ is the set of final states and $\delta$ is the transition function such that $\delta : Q \times \Sigma \to 2^Q$.* $\quad\square$

The transition function $\delta$ can be extended to $\delta : 2^Q \times \Sigma \to 2^Q$ by defining

$$\delta(P, a) = \bigoplus_{q \in P} \delta(q, a)$$

for any $a \in \Sigma$ and $P \in 2^Q$. We define $\delta^* : 2^Q \times \Sigma^* \to 2^Q$ by $\delta^*(P, \epsilon) = P$ and $\delta^*(P, aw) = \delta^*(\delta(P, a), w)$ for any $a \in \Sigma$, $w \in \Sigma^*$ and $P \in 2^Q$. We will denote $\delta^*$ also by $\delta$.

Let $\mathcal{N} = (Q, \Sigma, \delta, I, F)$ be a $\oplus$-NFA and let $w$ be a word in $\Sigma^*$. Then $\mathcal{N}$ accepts $w$ if and only if $|F \cap \delta(I, w)| \bmod 2 \neq 0$. In other words, a $\oplus$-NFA accepts a word $w$ by parity – if there is an odd number of accepting paths for $w$ in the execution tree, then $w$ is accepted; else it is rejected. Note that acceptance for $\oplus$-NFAs is in accordance with how acceptance is defined for weighted automata. The *language accepted* by $\mathcal{N}$, indicated by $L(\mathcal{N})$, is the set of all words accepted by $\mathcal{N}$. Given any two subsets of states $G, H \subseteq Q$ of $\mathcal{N}$, we define the *language from $G$ to $H$* as the set of words $L_{G,H}(\mathcal{N}) = \{w \in \Sigma^* \mid |H \cap \delta(G, w)| \bmod 2 \neq 0\}$. If $G = \{q\}$, we will use the notation $L_{q,H}$, and similarly if $H$ (or both $G$ and $H$) consists of a single state. Then the *left language* of a state $q$ of $\mathcal{N}$ is $L_{I,q}(\mathcal{N})$, and the *right language* of $q$ is $L_{q,F}(\mathcal{N})$. Note that $L(\mathcal{N}) = L_{I,F}(\mathcal{N})$. Two $\oplus$-NFAs are *equivalent* if they accept the same language. A $\oplus$-NFA is *minimal* if it has the minimum number of states among all equivalent $\oplus$-NFAs.

By determinizing $\mathcal{N}$, we get a complete DFA $\mathcal{N}^{\mathbb{D}}$, which is defined as follows:

**Definition 4.** *Let $\mathcal{N} = (Q, \Sigma, \delta, I, F)$ be a $\oplus$-NFA. Then the complete DFA $\mathcal{N}^{\mathbb{D}} = (Q^D, \Sigma, \delta^D, q_0, F^D)$, obtained by determinizing $\mathcal{N}$, is defined as follows:*

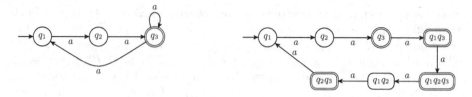

**Fig. 1.** The ⊕-NFA and corresponding DFA for Example 2

- $Q^D = \{\delta(I, w) \mid w \in \Sigma^*\}$;
- for $J \in Q^D \subseteq 2^Q$, and $a \in \Sigma$, $\delta^D(J, a) = \oplus_{q \in J}\delta(q, a)$, with $\delta^D(\emptyset, a) = \emptyset$ for all $a \in \Sigma$, if $\emptyset \in Q^D$;
- the start state $q_0$ of $\mathcal{N}^{\mathbb{D}}$ is the set $I$;
- the set of final states $F^D$ of $\mathcal{N}^{\mathbb{D}}$ is $\{K \in Q^D \mid |K \cap F| \bmod 2 \neq 0\}$.

It was shown in [15] that $\mathcal{N}^{\mathbb{D}}$ is indeed equivalent to $\mathcal{N}$.

*Example 2.* Let $\mathcal{N} = (\{q_1, q_2, q_3\}, \{a\}, \delta, \{q_1\}, \{q_3\})$ be a ⊕-NFA where $\delta$ is given by $\delta(q_1) = \{q_2\}, \delta(q_2) = \{q_3\}$, and $\delta(q_3) = \{q_1, q_3\}$.

Figure 1 shows a graphical representation of $\mathcal{N}$; note that there is no visual difference from a traditional NFA. To find the DFA $\mathcal{N}^{\mathbb{D}}$ equivalent to $\mathcal{N}$, we apply the subset construction using the symmetric difference operation instead of union. The transition function $\delta^{\mathbb{D}}$ of $\mathcal{N}^{\mathbb{D}}$ is given by

$$\{q_1\} \quad \to^{\delta^{\mathbb{D}}} \{q_2\} \quad \to^{\delta^{\mathbb{D}}} \{q_3\} \quad \to^{\delta^{\mathbb{D}}} \{q_1, q_3\} \to^{\delta^{\mathbb{D}}}$$
$$\{q_1, q_2, q_3\} \to^{\delta^{\mathbb{D}}} \{q_1, q_2\} \to^{\delta^{\mathbb{D}}} \{q_2, q_3\} \to^{\delta^{\mathbb{D}}} \{q_1\} \quad,$$

and the final states by $\{\{q_3\}, \{q_1, q_3\}, \{q_1, q_2, q_3\}, \{q_2, q_3\}\}$.

As is the case for weighted automata in general, one can encode the transition table of a unary ⊕-NFA $\mathcal{N}$ as a binary matrix $m(\delta(a))$:

$$m(\delta(a))_{ij} = \begin{cases} 1 \text{ if } q_j \in \delta(q_i, a) \\ 0 \text{ otherwise,} \end{cases}$$

and successive matrix multiplications in the Galois field $\mathbb{Z}_2$ reflect the subset construction on $\mathcal{N}$.

We call $m(\delta(a))$ the *characteristic matrix* of $\mathcal{N}$, and $c(x) = \det(m(\delta(a)) - x\mathbf{I})$, where $\mathbf{I}$ is the identity matrix of the appropriate size, is known as its characteristic polynomial.

Similarly, we can encode any set of states $B \subseteq Q$ as an $n$-entry row vector $v(B)$ by defining

$$v(B)_i = \begin{cases} 1 \text{ if } q_i \in B \\ 0 \text{ otherwise .} \end{cases}$$

We place an arbitrary but fixed order on the elements of $Q$. We refer to $v(B)$ as the *vector encoding* of $B$, and to $B$ as the *set encoding* of $v(B)$. Note that $v(B_1) + v(B_2) = v(B_1 \oplus B_2)$.

The matrix product $v(I)m(\delta(a))$ encodes the states reachable from the initial states after reading one letter, $v(I)m(\delta(a))^2$ encodes the states reachable after two letters, and in general $v(I)m(\delta(a))^k$ encodes the states reachable after $k$ letters. Standard linear algebra shows the following:

$$\mathcal{N} \text{ accepts } a^k \text{ if and only if } v(I)m(\delta(a))^k v(F)^{\mathrm{T}} = 1,$$

where $v(F)^{\mathrm{T}}$ denotes the transpose of the row vector $v(F)$. In the general case where we consider also non-unary symmetric difference automata, one can associate a matrix $m(\delta(a))$ to each symbol $a \in \Sigma$. Then a word $w = a_1 \dots a_k$, with $a_i \in \Sigma$, is accepted if and only if:

$$v(I)m(\delta(a_1)) \dots m(\delta(a_k))v(F)^{\mathrm{T}} = 1.$$

Note that if $\mathcal{N}$ is an $n$-state $\oplus$-NFA with initial vector $v(I)$, final vector $v(F)$ and transition matrices $m(\delta(a))$, and $A$ is a $n \times n$ non-singular matrix with inverse $A^{-1}$, then the $\oplus$-NFA $\mathcal{N}_A$ with initial vector $v(I)A$, final vector $A^{-1}v(F)$ and transition matrices $A^{-1}m(\delta(a))A$, accepts the same language as $\mathcal{N}$, since:

$$\begin{aligned} &v(I)m(\delta(a_1)) \dots m(\delta(a_k))v(F)^{\mathrm{T}} \\ &= v(I)AA^{-1}m(\delta(a_1))A \dots A^{-1}m(\delta(a_k))AA^{-1}v(F)^{\mathrm{T}}. \end{aligned}$$

It is shown in [17] that if $\mathcal{N}$ and $\mathcal{N}'$ are minimal $\oplus$-NFAs for the same language $L$, then we can find a non-singular matrix $A$ such that $\mathcal{N}' = \mathcal{N}_A$. We will refer to the process of changing from $\mathcal{N}$ to $\mathcal{N}_A$ as making a change of basis by using $A$.

**Definition 5.** *The* mirror image *or* reverse *of a string* $w = a_1 \dots a_n$ *is the string* $w^R = a_n \dots a_1$. *The* reverse $L^R$ *of a language* $L$ *is defined to be* $\{w^R \mid w \in L\}$.

Given a $\oplus$-NFA $\mathcal{N} = (Q, \Sigma, \delta, I, F)$, its *reverse* is $\mathcal{N}^{\mathbb{R}} = (Q, \Sigma, \delta^{\mathbb{R}}, F, I)$, where $q \in \delta^{\mathbb{R}}(p, a)$ if and only if $p \in \delta(q, a)$. In terms of vectors and matrices, the initial and final vectors are exchanged, and the transpose (that is, exchanging rows and columns) of the transition matrices of $\mathcal{N}$ is taken, in order to obtain the initial and final vectors and transition matrices of $\mathcal{N}^{\mathbb{R}}$. Note that

$$v(I)m(\delta(a_1)) \dots m(\delta(a_k))v(F)^{\mathrm{T}} = v(F)m(\delta(a_k))^{\mathrm{T}} \dots m(\delta(a_1))^{\mathrm{T}}v(I)^{\mathrm{T}}.$$

Thus $L(\mathcal{N}^{\mathbb{R}}) = (L(\mathcal{N}))^R$.

*Example 3.* Consider the $\oplus$-NFA $\mathcal{N}$ in Example 2. Its characteristic matrix is

$$m(\delta(a)) = \begin{bmatrix} 0 & 1 & 0 \\ 0 & 0 & 1 \\ 1 & 0 & 1 \end{bmatrix}$$

and its characteristic polynomial is $c(x) = x^3 + x^2 + 1$. Interested readers may note that $c(x)$ is a primitive polynomial in $\mathbb{Z}_2$. The fact that $c(x)$ is primitive implies that we obtain $2^3 - 1 = 7$ states when determinizing the given $\oplus$-NFA

$\mathcal{N}$ (see [16]). It can be shown that $\mathcal{N}$ is minimal, and that $\mathcal{N}^{\mathbb{D}}$ is a minimal DFA ([16]), which is always the case when determinizing a minimal $\oplus$-NFA, as we will show later in Theorem 4. If we encode the start state as a row vector $v(I)$, with only the first component of $v(I)$ equal to one, and compute $v(I)m(\delta(a))^k$, we end up with the $k$-th entry in the on-the-fly subset construction on $\mathcal{N}$. For example, with the start state $q_1$ encoded as $v(I) = [\,1\ 0\ 0\,]$, we see that

$$m(\delta(a))^4 = \begin{bmatrix} 1\,1\,1 \\ 1\,1\,0 \\ 0\,1\,1 \end{bmatrix},$$

and hence $v(I)m(\delta(a))^4$ is given by $[\,1\ 1\ 1\,]$. This corresponds to the state $\{q_1, q_2, q_3\}$, which is reached after four applications of the subset construction on $\mathcal{N}$. Similarly, $v(I)m(\delta(a))^6$ is given by $[\,0\ 1\ 1\,]$, which corresponds to $\{q_2, q_3\}$.

In [15] we formally showed that the state behaviour of a unary $\oplus$-NFA is the same as that of a linear feedback shift register (LFSR). The similarity is intuitively straightforward, as an LFSR is a linear machine over $\mathbb{Z}_2$, and we can encode a unary $\oplus$-NFA as a linear machine over $\mathbb{Z}_2$ as shown above. This correspondence means that we can exploit the literature on LFSRs to analyse the behaviour of unary $\oplus$-NFAs, and in particular their cyclic behaviour (see, for example, [5] or [13]). For $\oplus$-NFAs in general (whether unary or non-unary), standard techniques in linear algebra are often used. For example, to obtain a more convenient form of transition matrices, a change of basis can be performed [14].

## 3   Properties of Minimal $\oplus$-NFAs

In this section we study properties of minimal $\oplus$-NFAs, which are used to obtain one of our main results that determinization of a minimal $\oplus$-NFA leads to a minimal DFA.

**Proposition 1.** *A $\oplus$-NFA $\mathcal{N}$ is minimal if and only if $\mathcal{N}^{\mathbb{R}}$ is minimal.*

*Proof.* Suppose $\mathcal{N}$ is a minimal $\oplus$-NFA. Then $\mathcal{N}^{\mathbb{R}}$ is obtained from $\mathcal{N}$ by interchanging the initial and the final states and by taking the transpose of the transition matrices for each letter in $\Sigma$. If $\mathcal{N}^{\mathbb{R}}$ is not minimal, we can rewrite its transition matrices with fewer rows and columns to obtain $\mathcal{N}'$, where $\mathcal{N}'$ accepts the same language as $\mathcal{N}^{\mathbb{R}}$. If we now reverse $\mathcal{N}'$ by transposing its transition matrices, we obtain a $\oplus$-NFA which accepts $(L(\mathcal{N}^{\mathbb{R}}))^R$, that is, $L(\mathcal{N})$. This is a contradiction, as $\mathcal{N}$ is minimal. The converse holds by the same argument.   □

For a $\oplus$-NFA $\mathcal{N} = (Q, \Sigma, \delta, I, F)$, the *kernel* of $\mathcal{N}$ is defined as the set of subsets $I' \subseteq Q$, such that if we obtain $\mathcal{N}'$ from $\mathcal{N}$ by replacing $I$ with $I'$, then $L(\mathcal{N}') = \emptyset$.

**Definition 6.** *The* kernel $K(\mathcal{N})$ *of a $\oplus$-NFA $\mathcal{N} = (Q, \Sigma, \delta, I, F)$ is the set* $\{I' \subseteq Q \mid L_{I',F}(\mathcal{N}) = \emptyset\}$.

Note that we always have $\emptyset \in K(\mathcal{N})$.

The *range* of a $\oplus$-NFA $\mathcal{N} = (Q, \Sigma, \delta, I, F)$ is defined as the linear subspace of $2^Q$ generated by subsets of the form $\delta(I, w)$.

**Definition 7.** *The range $R(\mathcal{N})$ of a $\oplus$-NFA $\mathcal{N} = (Q, \Sigma, \delta, I, F)$ is the set of subsets of $Q$ of the form $\delta(I, w_1) \oplus \ldots \oplus \delta(I, w_k)$, with $w_1, \ldots, w_k \in \Sigma^*$, $k \geq 0$, where we assume that for $k = 0$ we obtain the empty set.*

A $\oplus$-NFA is trim if there are no states that are unreachable from start states. Instead of also removing states from which final states can not be reached, as in the case of trim (union) NFAs, we rather consider these as states that should be trimmed from $\mathcal{N}^{\mathbb{R}}$.

**Definition 8.** *A $\oplus$-NFA $\mathcal{N}$ is trim if $R(\mathcal{N}) = 2^Q$.*

Let $\mathcal{N}$ be the single state $\oplus$-NFA with no transitions, and with the single state not an initial or a final state. Then $\mathcal{N}$ is a minimal $\oplus$-NFA for $\emptyset$, but $R(\mathcal{N}) = \{\emptyset\}$. For the remainder of this paper, we either have to assume that the minimal $\oplus$-NFA for the empty language is the empty $\oplus$-NFA, or we should exclude the empty language from our discussions. To avoid technical complications, we thus do not consider the empty language in the remainder of this paper.

Next we show that $\oplus$-NFAs can be trimmed by making a change of basis.

**Proposition 2.** *Let $\mathcal{N}$ be a $\oplus$-NFA. Then there is a change of basis from $\mathcal{N}$ to $\mathcal{N}_A$, such that the $\oplus$-NFA obtained from $\mathcal{N}_A$ by removing all unreachable states from the initial states (in the usual graph theoretic sense), is trim.*

*Proof.* Assume that $\mathcal{N} = (Q, \Sigma, \delta, I, F)$. The proposition follows from the following standard fact from linear algebra. Let $V$ be a $k$-dimensional linear subspace of the $n$-dimensional vector space $\mathbb{Z}_2^n$. Then there exists a $n \times n$ non-singular matrix $A$ over $\mathbb{Z}_2$, such that $\{vA \mid v \in V\}$ is equal to $\{(v_1, \ldots, v_k, 0, \ldots, 0) \in (\mathbb{Z}_2)^n \mid v_i \in \mathbb{Z}_2\}$. Thus we can find a non-singular matrix $A$ such that the vectors $v(I)m(\delta(a_1)) \ldots m(\delta(a_l))A$, for all $w = a_1 \ldots a_l \in \Sigma^*$, which is also equal to $v(I)AA^{-1}m(\delta(a_1)) \ldots AA^{-1}m(\delta(a_l))A$, generate (by using $\oplus$) precisely all $2^k$ vectors with all components from the $(k+1)$-th component onwards being zero. Thus by removing states $q_{k+1}, \ldots, q_n$ from $\mathcal{N}_A$, we obtain a trim $\oplus$-NFA.     $\square$

**Proposition 3.** *Let $\mathcal{N} = (Q, \Sigma, \delta, I, F)$. Then $K(\mathcal{N}) = \{\emptyset\}$ if and only if $R(\mathcal{N}^{\mathbb{R}}) = 2^Q$.*

*Proof.* Assume that $K(\mathcal{N}) \neq \{\emptyset\}$ and let $\emptyset \neq J \in K(\mathcal{N})$. Then from the definition of $K(\mathcal{N})$ we have that $L_{J,F}(\mathcal{N}) = \emptyset$, and thus $L_{F,J}(\mathcal{N}^{\mathbb{R}}) = \emptyset$. But note that $L_{F,J}(\mathcal{N}^{\mathbb{R}}) = \emptyset$ implies that $R(\mathcal{N}^{\mathbb{R}}) \neq 2^Q$. The converse can be proved in a similar way.     $\square$

**Theorem 1.** *Assume that the $\oplus$-NFA $\mathcal{N} = (Q, \Sigma, \delta, I, F)$ is minimal. Then $K(\mathcal{N}) = \{\emptyset\}$, $K(\mathcal{N}^{\mathbb{R}}) = \{\emptyset\}$, $R(\mathcal{N}) = 2^Q$ and $R(\mathcal{N}^{\mathbb{R}}) = 2^Q$.*

*Proof.* Follows from Propositions 1, 2 and 3.     $\square$

*Remark 1.* It can be shown that if $K(\mathcal{N}) = \{\emptyset\}$ and $K(\mathcal{N}^{\mathbb{R}}) = \{\emptyset\}$ (or if $K(\mathcal{N}) = \{\emptyset\}$ and $R(\mathcal{N}) = 2^Q$), then $\mathcal{N}$ is minimal, but this result is not required in the remainder of this paper.

**Definition 9.** *Let $L$ be a (regular) language. The* left quotient, *or simply* quotient, *of $L$ by a word $w \in \Sigma^*$ is the language $w^{-1}L = \{x \in \Sigma^* \mid wx \in L\}$.*

Note that, if $\mathcal{D}$ is a minimal DFA accepting $L$, then the right language of every state of $\mathcal{D}$ is some quotient of $L$.

Similar to residual NFAs (as introduced in [4]), we define residual $\oplus$-NFAs. We will see in the next two sections of the paper that the more general class of automata, where the right languages of $\oplus$-NFAs are the symmetric difference of quotients, is in fact the more interesting class of $\oplus$-NFAs in our case.

**Definition 10.** *A* residual $\oplus$-NFA *($\oplus$-RFSA) is a $\oplus$-NFA $\mathcal{N} = (Q, \Sigma, \delta, I, F)$, such that for all $q \in Q$ there exists $w_q \in \Sigma^*$ with $L_{q,F}(\mathcal{N}) = w_q^{-1}L$.*

The $\oplus$-NFA given in Example 2 is a $\oplus$-RFSA, since by reading $\varepsilon$, $a$ and $aa$, each of the three states are reached respectively.

**Theorem 2.** *For any regular language $L$, there exists a minimal $\oplus$-NFA $\mathcal{N}$, which is also a $\oplus$-RFSA, with $L(\mathcal{N}) = L$.*

*Proof.* Let $\mathcal{N} = (Q, \Sigma, \delta, I, F)$ be a minimal $\oplus$-NFA accepting $L$, with $Q = \{q_1, \ldots, q_n\}$. Since $\mathcal{N}$ is minimal, it is implied by Theorem 1 that $R(\mathcal{N}) = 2^Q$. Thus we can find words $w_1, \ldots, w_n$ so that $\delta(I, w_1), \ldots, \delta(I, w_n)$ are linearly independent. We can now make a change of basis on $\mathcal{N}$ to obtain an equivalent minimal $\oplus$-NFA $\mathcal{N}' = (Q', \Sigma, \delta', I', F')$, with $Q' = \{q_1', \ldots, q_n'\}$ and $\delta'(I', w_i) = \{q_i'\}$ for $1 \leq i \leq n$. In fact, it is fairly straightforward to verify that the matrix $B$, with $B = A^{-1}$, where $A$ is a matrix with rows given by vectors $v(\delta(I, w_1)), \ldots, v(\delta(I, w_n))$, will provide the change of basis with the appropriate properties, since $v(\delta(I, w_i))B$, which is the vector of states in $\mathcal{N}'$ reached after reading $w_i$, is a vector with a 1 in the $i$th position and zeros in all other positions. Thus $\mathcal{N}'$ is residual. $\square$

*Example 4.* In Figure 2(a) we give an example of a $\oplus$-NFA $\mathcal{N}$, with the states $Q = \{q_1, q_2, q_3, q_4, q_5\}$, and the initial states $I = \{q_1, q_5\}$. Note that $\mathcal{N}^{\mathbb{D}}$, given in Figure 2(b), is not minimal. Also, $K(\mathcal{N}) = \{\emptyset, \{q_2, q_4\}\}$, and $R(\mathcal{N})$ is the symmetric difference (or union) of any subset of the set $\{\{q_1, q_5\}, \{q_2\}, \{q_3\}, \{q_4\}\}$, and therefore properly contained in $2^Q$. Thus, $\mathcal{N}$ is not minimal, and it is easy to see that $L(\mathcal{N})$ can be recognized by a three state minimal $\oplus$-NFA. If we use the $5 \times 5$ non-singular matrix $A = [a_{ij}]$ with $a_{ii} = 1$ for $i = 1, \ldots, 5$, $a_{15} = 1$, and $a_{ij} = 0$ at all other positions (i.e. $A$ has ones on the diagonal and in the fifth column of the first row, but zeros elsewhere), then we obtain the $\oplus$-NFA $\mathcal{N}_A$ in Figure 2(c), which can be trimmed by removing state $q_5$.

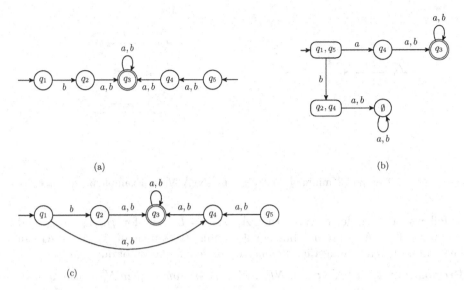

**Fig. 2.** (a) $\mathcal{N}$, (b) $\mathcal{N}^{\mathbb{D}}$, and (c) $\mathcal{N}_A$ for Example 4

## 4    Atomic and ⊕-Atomic ⊕-NFAs

Atoms of regular languages were recently introduced in [2].

**Definition 11.** *Let $L$ be a regular language and let $L_1, \ldots, L_n$ be the quotients of $L$. An* atom *of $L$ is any non-empty language of the form $\widetilde{L_1} \cap \cdots \cap \widetilde{L_n}$, where $\widetilde{L_i}$ is either $L_i$ or $\overline{L_i}$, and $\overline{L_i}$ is the complement of $L_i$ with respect to $\Sigma^*$* [1].

A language has at most $2^n$ atoms. It is easy to see from the definition of an atom that any two atoms are disjoint from each other, and every quotient is a union of atoms.

**Definition 12.** *Let $\mathcal{N} = (Q, \Sigma, \delta, I, F)$ be a ⊕-NFA. We say that $\mathcal{N}$ is* atomic *if for every state $q \in Q$, the right language $L_{q,F}(\mathcal{N})$ of $q$ is a union of some atoms (or the empty set). Similarly, $\mathcal{N}$ is* ⊕-atomic *if for every state $q \in Q$, the right language $L_{q,F}(\mathcal{N})$ of $q$ is a symmetric difference of some quotients of $L(\mathcal{N})$ (or the empty set).*

*Example 5.* In Figure 3, the minimal DFA $\mathcal{D}$ and a ⊕-NFA $\mathcal{N}$ accepting the language $L = (a+b)a^*$ are shown. The quotients of $L$ are $L_1 = (a+b)a^*$, $L_2 = a^*$, $L_3 = \emptyset$. The atoms of $L$ are $A_1 = L_1 \cap L_2 \cap \overline{L_3} = aa^*$, $A_2 = \overline{L_1} \cap L_2 \cap \overline{L_3} = \{\epsilon\}$, $A_3 = L_1 \cap \overline{L_2} \cap \overline{L_3} = ba^*$, $A_4 = \overline{L_1} \cap \overline{L_2} \cap \overline{L_3} = (a+b)^*(a+b)ba^*$. By determinization it can be verified that the right languages of the states of $\mathcal{N}$ are

---

[1] The definition in [2] does not consider $\overline{L_1} \cap \overline{L_2} \cap \cdots \cap \overline{L_n}$ to be an atom. In [3], the definition of an atom was changed to read as presented here.

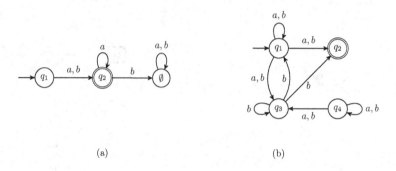

(a)                              (b)

**Fig. 3.** (a) minimal DFA $\mathcal{D}$, (b) $\oplus$-NFA $\mathcal{N}$ for Example 5

as follows: $A_1 \cup A_3$ for $q_1$ (note that $A_1 \cup A_3 = L_1$), $A_2$ for $q_2$, $A_3$ for $q_3$, and $A_4$ for $q_4$. Thus $\mathcal{N}$ is atomic, but not $\oplus$-atomic, since none of $A_2, A_3$ or $A_4$ can be expressed as a symmetric difference of any combination of quotients.

**Proposition 4.** *Let $\mathcal{N}$ be a $\oplus$-NFA. If $\mathcal{N}$ is $\oplus$-atomic, then $\mathcal{N}$ is also atomic.*

*Proof.* From the definition of an atom it follows that a quotient of a language $L$ is a (disjoint) union of atoms of $L$. It thus follows that the symmetric difference of quotients is a union of atoms. Thus if a $\oplus$-NFA is $\oplus$-atomic, it is also atomic. □

**Proposition 5.** *A minimal $\oplus$-NFA is $\oplus$-atomic.*

*Proof.* From [17] we have that if $\mathcal{N}$ and $\mathcal{N}'$ are minimal $\oplus$-NFAs with $L(\mathcal{N}) = L(\mathcal{N}')$, then we can obtain $\mathcal{N}'$ from $\mathcal{N}$ by making a change of basis. Also, by Theorem 2, there exists a minimal $\oplus$-NFA $\mathcal{N}$ for any language $L$, that is also a $\oplus$-RFSA. The result now follows from the observation that if $\mathcal{N}_A$ is obtained from $\mathcal{N}$ by a change of basis by using the non-singular matrix $A$, then the right language of a state of $\mathcal{N}_A$ is the symmetric difference of the right languages of some of the states of $\mathcal{N}$. To see this, note that from the equation

$$A^{-1}m(\delta(a_1))\ldots m(\delta(a_k))v(F)^{\mathrm{T}}$$
$$= A^{-1}m(\delta(a_1))A\ldots A^{-1}m(\delta(a_k))AA^{-1}v(F)^{\mathrm{T}},$$

it follows that if we take the symmetric difference of the right languages of states of $\mathcal{N}$ corresponding to the positions of the $i$th row of $A^{-1}$ having 1's, then we obtain the right language of the $i$th state of $\mathcal{N}_A$. □

## 5   Getting a Minimal DFA by Determinization

Let $L$ be a regular language. Let the set of atoms of the reverse language $L^R$ be $B = \{B_1, \ldots, B_r\}$. The results in [2] and [3] imply the following proposition:

**Proposition 6.** *Let $\mathcal{D} = (Q, \Sigma, \delta, q_0, F)$ be the complete minimal DFA accepting $L$. Then there is a one-to-one correspondence between the sets $Q$ and $B$, mapping a state $q \in Q$ to some atom $B_i$ so that $L_{q_0,q}(\mathcal{D}) = B_i^R$ holds.*

**Corollary 1.** Let $\mathcal{D} = (Q, \Sigma, \delta, q_0, F)$ be any DFA accepting $L$. Then for every state $q \in Q$ there is some $i \in \{1, \ldots, r\}$, such that $L_{q_0,q}(\mathcal{D}) \subseteq B_i^R$ holds.

The following theorem is similar to the result obtained in [2] for (union) NFAs. Also, the proof we present here for $\oplus$-NFAs is essentially the same as it was for NFAs in [2].

**Theorem 3.** For any $\oplus$-NFA $\mathcal{N}$, $\mathcal{N}^\mathbb{D}$ is minimal if and only if $\mathcal{N}^\mathbb{R}$ is atomic.

*Proof.* Let $\mathcal{N} = (Q, \Sigma, \delta, I, F)$ be a $\oplus$-NFA and assume that $\mathcal{N}^\mathbb{D}$ is minimal, but suppose that $\mathcal{N}^\mathbb{R}$ is not atomic. Then there is a state $q$ of $\mathcal{N}^\mathbb{R}$ that is not a union of atoms. That is, there is a word $u \in L_{q,I}(\mathcal{N}^\mathbb{R})$ such that $u \in B_i$ for some $i \in \{1, \ldots, r\}$, but for some other word $v \in B_i$, $v \notin L_{q,I}(\mathcal{N}^\mathbb{R})$. It is implied that $u^R \in L_{I,q}(\mathcal{N})$ and $v^R \notin L_{I,q}(\mathcal{N})$. Since we assumed that $\mathcal{N}^\mathbb{D}$ is a minimal DFA, by Proposition 6 there is a state $s$ of $\mathcal{N}^\mathbb{D}$ such that $L_{I,s}(\mathcal{N}^\mathbb{D}) = B_i^R$. It is implied that $u^R, v^R \in L_{I,s}(\mathcal{N}^\mathbb{D})$. Since we had $u^R \in L_{I,q}(\mathcal{N})$, we get that $q \in s$. On the other hand, because $v^R \notin L_{I,q}(\mathcal{N})$ holds, we get $q \notin s$, a contradiction.

Conversely, assume that $\mathcal{N}^\mathbb{R}$ is atomic. Then for every state $q$ of $\mathcal{N}^\mathbb{R}$, there is a set $H_q \subseteq \{1, \ldots, r\}$ such that $L_{q,I}(\mathcal{N}^\mathbb{R}) = \bigcup_{i \in H_q} B_i$. This implies $L_{I,q}(\mathcal{N}) = \bigcup_{i \in H_q} B_i^R$ for every state $q$ of $\mathcal{N}$. Consider any state $s$ of the DFA $\mathcal{N}^\mathbb{D}$. Then for any word $u$, $u \in L_{I,s}(\mathcal{N}^\mathbb{D})$ if and only if $u \in L_{I,q}(\mathcal{N})$ for every $q \in s$, and $u \notin L_{I,q'}(\mathcal{N})$ for any $q' \notin s$. That is, $L_{I,s}(\mathcal{N}^\mathbb{D}) = (\bigcap_{q \in s} \bigcup_{i \in H_q} B_i^R) \setminus (\bigcup_{q' \notin s} \bigcup_{i \in H_{q'}} B_i^R)$. On the other hand, by Corollary 1, $L_{I,s}(\mathcal{N}^\mathbb{D}) \subseteq B_k^R$ for some atom $B_k$. Since atoms are disjoint, any boolean combination of sets $B_i^R$ cannot be a proper subset of any $B_k^R$. Thus, $L_{I,s}(\mathcal{N}^\mathbb{D}) = B_k^R$. If we suppose that $\mathcal{N}^\mathbb{D}$ is not minimal, then there are some states $s'$ and $s''$ of $\mathcal{N}^\mathbb{D}$, and a state $t$ of the corresponding minimal DFA, such that $s'$, $s''$ and $t$ have the same right language. Then it is easy to see by Proposition 6 that there is some $B_i$, such that $L_{I,s'}(\mathcal{N}^\mathbb{D}) \subset B_i^R$ and $L_{I,s''}(\mathcal{N}^\mathbb{D}) \subset B_i^R$, a contradiction.    $\square$

**Theorem 4.** If $\mathcal{N}$ is a minimal $\oplus$-NFA, then $\mathcal{N}^\mathbb{D}$ is a minimal DFA.

*Proof.* The result follows from Propositions 1, 4, 5 and Theorem 3.    $\square$

## 6    Conclusions and Future Work

In this paper and in [2] the problem of when determinization of a weighted automaton leads to minimal DFA was considered, for the case where the weights are taken from the Boolean semiring and from the semiring $\mathbb{Z}_2$. We would also like to consider this problem for weighted automata over other semirings, keeping in mind that determinization is not always possible for arbitrary weighted automata (see [11], [12]).

**Acknowledgment.** We thank Jaco Geldenhuys for helpful discussions.

# References

1. Brzozowski, J.: Canonical regular expressions and minimal state graphs for definite events. In: Proceedings of the Symposium on the Mathematical Theory of Automata. MRI Symposia Series, pp. 529–561. Polytechnic Press of Polytechnic Institute of Brooklyn (1963)
2. Brzozowski, J., Tamm, H.: Theory of Átomata. In: Mauri, G., Leporati, A. (eds.) DLT 2011. LNCS, vol. 6795, pp. 105–116. Springer, Heidelberg (2011)
3. Brzozowski, J., Tamm, H.: Quotient complexities of atoms of regular languages. In: Proceedings of the 16th International Conference on Developments in Language Theory (DLT). Springer (August 2012)
4. Denis, F., Lemay, A., Terlutte, A.: Residual Finite State Automata. In: Ferreira, A., Reichel, H. (eds.) STACS 2001. LNCS, vol. 2010, pp. 144–157. Springer, Heidelberg (2001)
5. Dornhoff, L., Hohn, F.: Applied Modern Algebra. Macmillan Publishing Company (1978)
6. Droste, M., Kuich, W., Vogler, H.: Handbook of Weighted Automata, 1st edn. Springer Publishing Company, Incorporated (2009)
7. Droste, M., Rahonis, G.: Weighted Automata and Weighted Logics on Infinite Words. In: Ibarra, O.H., Dang, Z. (eds.) DLT 2006. LNCS, vol. 4036, pp. 49–58. Springer, Heidelberg (2006)
8. Hopcroft, J., Ullman, J.: Introduction to Automata Theory, Languages and Computation. Addison Wesley (1979)
9. Ilie, L., Navarro, G., Yu, S.: On NFA Reductions. In: Karhumäki, J., Maurer, H., Păun, G., Rozenberg, G. (eds.) Salomaa Festschrift. LNCS, vol. 3113, pp. 112–124. Springer, Heidelberg (2004)
10. Jiang, T., Ravikumar, B.: Minimal NFA problems are hard. SIAM Journal on Computing 22(6), 1117–1141 (1993)
11. Kirsten, D., Mäurer, I.: On the determinization of weighted automata. Journal of Automata, Languages and Combinatorics 10(2/3), 287–312 (2005)
12. Mohri, M.: Finite-state transducers in language and speech processing. Computational Linguistics 23(2), 269–311 (1997)
13. Stone, H.: Discrete Mathematical Structures. Science Research Associates (1973)
14. van der Merwe, B., van Zijl, L., Geldenhuys, J.: Ambiguity of Unary Symmetric Difference NFAs. In: Cerone, A., Pihlajasaari, P. (eds.) ICTAC 2011. LNCS, vol. 6916, pp. 256–266. Springer, Heidelberg (2011)
15. Van Zijl, L.: Generalized Nondeterminism and the Succinct Representation of Regular Languages. Ph.D. thesis, Stellenbosch University (November 1997)
16. Van Zijl, L.: On binary symmetric difference NFAs and succinct representations of regular languages. Theoretical Computer Science 328(1), 161–170 (2004)
17. Vuillemin, J., Gama, N.: Compact Normal Form for Regular Languages as Xor Automata. In: Maneth, S. (ed.) CIAA 2009. LNCS, vol. 5642, pp. 24–33. Springer, Heidelberg (2009)

# Author Index